Michael Schmidt

THE FIRST POETS

Michael Schmidt is a critic and poet and editorial and managing
director of Carcanet Press. He was born in Mexico in 1947 and
grew up there. He studied at Harvard and Oxford and is now
director of the Writing School at Manchester Metropolitan
University. His books include *Lives of the Poets*, several collections of poems, two novels, critical books, and anthologies. He
has translated Nahuatl (Aztec) poetry and essays by Mexican
writer Octavio Paz.

Also by Michael Schmidt

CRITICISM

Fifty Modern British Poets: An Introduction
Fifty English Poets 1300–1900: An Introduction
Reading Modern Poetry
Lives of the Poets
The Story of Poetry: Volume One
The Story of Poetry: Volume Two

ANTHOLOGIES

Eleven British Poets
New Poetries I, II, III
Poets on Poets (with Nick Rennison)
The Harvill Book of Twentieth-Century Poetry in English

POETRY

Choosing a Guest
The Love of Strangers
Selected Poems

FICTION

The Colonist
The Dresden Gate

TRANSLATIONS

Flower and Song: Poems of the Aztec Peoples (with Edward Kissam)
On Poets and Others, Octavio Paz

THE
FIRST
POETS

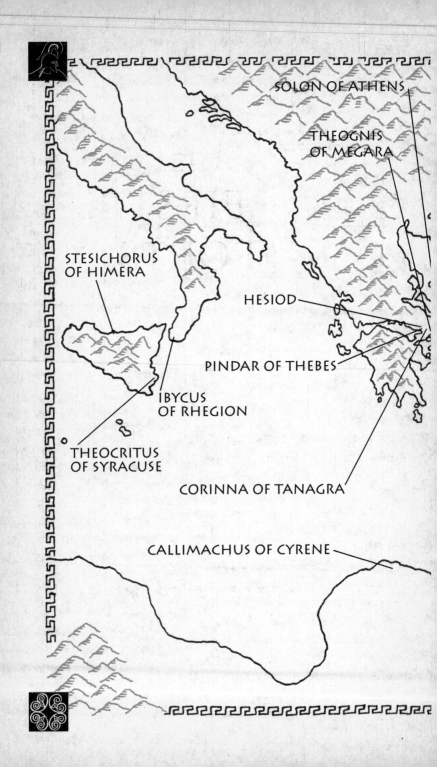

SOLON OF ATHENS

THEOGNIS
OF MEGARA

STESICHORUS
OF HIMERA

HESIOD

PINDAR OF THEBES

IBYCUS
OF RHEGION

THEOCRITUS
OF SYRACUSE

CORINNA OF TANAGRA

CALLIMACHUS OF CYRENE

ORPHEUS OF THRACE

SAPPHO OF ERESSUS
ALCAEUS OF
MYTILENE

ANACREON OF TEOS

ALCMAN OF SARDIS

MIMNERMUS OF COLOPHON

HIPPONAX OF EPHESUS

APOLLONIUS OF RHODES

BACCHYLIDES OF COS
SIMONIDES OF COS

SEMONIDES OF AMORGOS

ARCHILOCHUS OF PAROS

THE
FIRST
POETS

Lives of the
Ancient Greek Poets

MICHAEL SCHMIDT

VINTAGE BOOKS
A Division of Random House, Inc.
New York

FIRST VINTAGE BOOKS EDITION, MARCH 2005

Copyright © 2004 by Michael Schmidt

All rights reserved. Published in the United States by Vintage Books, a division of
Random House, Inc., New York. Originally published in Great Britain by Weidenfeld &
Nicolson, London, in 2004. Subsequently published in hardcover in the United States
by Alfred A. Knopf, a division of Random House, Inc., New York, in 2005.

Vintage and colophon are registered trademarks of Random House, Inc.

The Library of Congress has cataloged the Knopf edition as follows:
Schmidt, Michael, 1947–
The first poets : lives of the ancient Greek poets / Michael Schmidt.
p. cm.
Includes bibliographical references and index.
1. Poets, Greek—Biography. 2. Greek poetry—History and criticism. I. Title.
PA3064.36 2005
881'.0109—dc22
[B] 2004048840

Vintage ISBN-10: 0-375-72525-3
Vintage ISBN-13: 978-0-375-72525-8

Book design by Soonyoung Kwon

Map and motifs copyright © 2004 by Stephen Raw

www.vintagebooks.com

Printed in the United States of America
10 9 8 7 6 5 4 3 2 1

For Angel García Gómez
"fixing emblazoned zones and fiery poles"

Contents

Preface

> ... that which hath receiv'd Approbation from so many, I have chosen not to omit. Certain or uncertain, be that upon the Credit of those whom I must follow; so far as keeps aloof from impossible and absurd, attested by ancient Writers from Books more ancient, I refuse not, as the due and proper subject of Story.
>
> JOHN MILTON, *The History of Britain*

In "Mythistorema," the Greek poet George Seferis recalls waking from a dream with "this marble head in my hands." It is weighty, and he has no place to put it down. Its eyes are neither open nor closed. It is trying to speak but can say nothing. The bone of the cheeks is breaking through the skin. What was at first stone becomes flesh and bone. The poet has not asked for the burden and is not free to discard it.[1]

Things that inadvertently shape us draw upon structures, forms, legends, and myths that have their origin in ancient Mediterranean cultures. Our mother tongue may not be Greek, but—thanks to Rome's adoption of the Hellenic spirit—we, too, inherit that fragmented legacy of ideas and figures, stories and histories that can be as real to us as our own more immediate past. Even its strangest elements rise out of the darkness almost with the force of memory.

When we listen to the verse phrases and whole poems that have made the hard journey through time, space and language, phrases and poems that Shakespeare, Milton, Dickinson, Shelley, Pound, Rich and others may have heard at different times and in different ways, we are enthralled as much by what we cannot know as by what we hear. Though we are seldom certain that a text is accurate, though we cannot approach its sound, invent its musical accompaniment and ceremonial, join the general audience or the élite symposium, or affirm that something said is *literally* true, we do understand what is true in a sense, and in what sense it is true. Yet we must retain an awareness of the *otherness* of the cultures we are exploring.

This is a protestant book in a fundamental sense: it both affirms the importance of the Greek texts and believes in the possibility of English vernacular access to them. I concede that in academic terms, the scope of this book is unrealistically, perhaps improperly broad; no amateur can begin to master the accretion of two and a half millennia of patristics that by turns illuminate and obscure the core texts. The decline in the study of Greek in schools and universities has not been accompanied by a decline in critical and theoretical studies nor yet by a deliberate "opening out" of the subject. What was once a key discipline has become a series of specialisms.

The First Poets attempts an opening out. I have been beguiled by several modern scholars and wanted to follow them further than I could in an introductory book of this kind. I wanted to write a book that instructs and entertains, to suggest some of the theoretical and critical issues of the present and earlier ages, but primarily to honour ancient patterns of belief. I allow myself to err with the Alexandrians when it comes to telling about the poets' lives, because the nature of Alexandrian "error" tells us about their culture and its priorities. If I had adhered to the strictures of modern historians and theorists, who insist that because we cannot prove them we should not credit the ancient tales nor believe in the ancient gods, I would not have begun to write these lives nor wished to read these poets.

The *grands absents* are the dramatic writers of the classical period. Their omission is intended to do two things: to release the poets whom they and their Athenian shadows have obscured, and to suggest that poetry and drama are generically distinct, despite the lessons one can learn from the other.

I am indebted to many individuals for support and help with *The First Poets*. The oldest debt I owe is to the late Sir Maurice Bowra, Warden of Wadham College when I was an undergraduate, who gave me texts (his own included) and encouraged my curiosity. I also had the privilege at Harvard of attending Robert Fitzgerald's celebrated seminars on "The Epic," which, though they were intended to take us up through Perse, concentrated with passion on Homer. Evelyn Schlag commented on this informal history as it was written, providing suggestions and references, and without her I could not have completed it. Colleagues at Carcanet Press and *PN Review*, Pamela Heaton and the late Joyce Nield in particular, encouraged me. At the John Rylands University Library Stella Halkyard has always provided a reassuring presence, advised and allowed me to consult the library's astonishing holdings. To my wonderful editor at Orion, Maggie McKernan, to her indefatigable assistant, Kelly Falconer, and to Keith Egerton, proof-reader, my warmest thanks are due. Other friends and authors made suggestions which proved invaluable to me: Robert Wells, John Peck, and in particular Frederic Raphael, whose acute reading prevented some inaccuracies and many infelicities, though no responsibility for the concept or the shortcomings of this volume should attach to anyone but the author.

MICHAEL SCHMIDT

Introduction

Didymus the grammarian wrote four thousand books: I would pity him if he had merely read so many useless works. In some he investigates the birthplace of Homer, in others, the real mother of Aeneas, whether Anacreon was addicted more to lust or to liquor, whether Sappho was a prostitute, and other matters that you would forget if you ever knew them; and then people complain that life is short.

SENECA, *Letter to Lucilius*[1]

I MATERIALS

Didymus of Alexandria, who lived between 65 BC and AD 10, was nicknamed "Brass-Bowelled"[2] because of his prodigious digestion of intellectual matter. He was also called "Book-Forgetting"[3] because he contradicted himself from book to book. The Roman writer Seneca, constructed as he was on a foundation of Greek culture, developed a dislike for literature's parasites and for the secondary literature—the criticism, theorising and investigation—which men such as Didymus produced. Works of that kind interposed verbiage between a poem or play and the reader. So many of them, he tells his friend Lucilius, are simply *irrelevant*. Pedantry is a cuckoo in the nest: the poem is crowded out. Or it becomes a text, and the text a pretext for mere speculation. Such speculation—on language, prosody, historical context, audience and author—has a place, but only if the poetry is in place.

And little ancient Greek poetry *is* in place. None of the surviving bodies of work by named authors is whole or nearly whole; some writers are at best a scatter of phrases, preserved by grammarians, philologists and other Didymuses to illustrate a lexical point or for amusement, as in Athenaeus of Naucratis' rambling *Deipnosophistae* (*Scholars at Dinner* or *Learned Banquet*). This is an inadvertent parody of pedantry, the apotheosis of the sybaritic symposium, imagined as stretching over a week of evenings. It is worthy of Laurence Sterne.[4] Athenaeus quotes more than ten thousand lines of verse in it, many not preserved or attested elsewhere. *Pace* Seneca, we owe much, albeit few entire poems, to Brass-Bowelled and his nitpicking kin.

We owe a debt to the Egyptian desert as well. In the ruins of the Memphis Serapeum, near Cairo, in 1820 an earthen pot filled with papyrus scrolls was uncovered by local people. The texts, some of the earliest so far found, date from about the second century BC. The plundered scrolls and fragments were dispersed to libraries in Leyden (where important research in papyrology has been pursued), Rome, Dresden, Paris and London. In 1821 W. J. Bankes bought a roll containing Book XXIV of the *Iliad,* the first major literary papyrus that the desert yielded to scholarship. Decade by decade philological resources gathered in unprecedented quantities. The nineteenth century, a great classicist declared, belonged to epigraphy; the twentieth would see papyrology in the ascendant.[5] The discoveries at Memphis, at Fayyum in 1877, Oxyrhynchus in 1906 and elsewhere supported his contention.

Without such papyri, we would have no Greek texts at all. By the middle of the fifth century BC, "all civilised people" wrote on papyrus scrolls.[6] Papyrus was used centuries earlier than this and not only for making paper. "The papyrus, which grows in the marshes every year, the people of Egypt pull up," says Herodotus, "cut the plant in two and, keeping the top part for other uses, take the lower, about a cubit in length, and eat or sell it. Whoever wants to get the most delicious results will put it in a sealed vessel and bake it until it glows." He was fascinated with the uses of papyrus. "On alternate days the priests shave their bodies all over, so no lice or other vermin attach to them while they are dedicated to serving the gods. They dress in linen exclusively, and their footwear is made of the papyrus. No other materials are permitted." Their lives were privileged in the Egyptian heat: "They bathe two times a day and two times a night in cold water . . . " Papyrus was used to caulk the seams of Nile boats, and their sails were made of papyrus. Xerxes was not alone in employing papyrus and flax cables to suspend bridges, consulting his Phoenician and Egyptian engineers.[7]

However, had papyrus not existed, we might have had even more Greek literature to read than we actually do. Some of the earliest whispers of Greek verse are preserved on pots, for example a cup manufactured in Rhodes but excavated from a grave on Ischia, in the Bay of Naples.[8] The tablets on which the scribes of Sumeria set down their accounts, laws, legends and literature have lasted much longer and rather better than Greek texts: nine epics (including *Gilgamesh*) survive in part, the events dating from the fourth and early third millennia BC: myths of origin, not least a Paradise and a Flood story, dating from the eighteenth century BC; hymns, poems of religious and secular praise; laments and elegies for the destruction of cities such as Ur, Nippur, Agade and the land of Sumer; aphoristic statements, proverbs, fables and other didactic material. The Sumerian is the earliest hoard of written literature that we have, and it is notable for its accomplishment. We can contrast Hammurabi's Code with the Biblical articulation of Mosaic law and appreciate the subtlety of the first. The Code was inscribed on a block of black diorite well over two metres in height and set up in Babylon for all to see.[9]

> My words are well considered; there is no wisdom like mine. By the command of Shamash, the great judge of heaven and earth, let righteousness go forth in the land: by the order of Marduk, my lord, let no destruction befall my monument. In E-Sagil, which I love, let my name be ever repeated; let the oppressed, who has a case at law, come and stand before this my image as king of righteousness; let him read the inscription, and understand my precious words: the inscription will explain his case to him; he will find out what is just, and his heart will be glad . . .[10]

The period of Hammurabi (1795–1750 BC), half a millennium before the war at Troy, was a high point for Babylonian culture. Over 500,000 Babylonian and related tablets were recorded as having survived in 1953. Thousands more have been discovered since.

God made man of clay; man makes tablets of clay. In 1929 in Syria a city of 1400 BC, Ugarit, was discovered, with a library containing tablets from the fifteenth and early fourteenth centuries BC. The language of Ugarit related to Biblical Hebrew and to Phoenician; the language of Canaan, perhaps. Many of the tablets are in poetic form, and their manner is close to that of Hebrew poetry, suggesting analogies with Old Testament passages, the Psalms in particular. Elements in Hesiod and in Homer, too, originate in Mesopotamia, whence they passed, via Phoenicia or some other route, to Asia Minor, the Greek islands and subsequently to Greece itself. Certainly Greek and Hellenistic astrology and astronomy are prefigured by Babylonian. Our evidence, given the relative poverty of Greek records and sustaining archaeology, is limited to the number of parallels in narrative and detail between texts, the hidden origins of the Greek religions—Orphic, Dionysian, and others—with their parallels too, and the archaeology of the texts. But we should bear in mind that their transmission and revision down the centuries may have blurred and excised crucial elements.

In ancient Egypt, the scribe was a trained official with religious and civic duties; it is unlikely that a common man, or indeed that most uncommon men, could read. In Babylon, *all* but the lowliest and even some of them were expected to write and read. In every city, a storehouse of tablets existed. "I had my joy in reading of inscriptions on stone from the time before the Flood," said Ashurbanipal, last of the great Assyrian leaders (669–622 BC). An effective general, he was also a learned philologist; he built up a royal library in some respects as comprehensive as and more durable than the Alexandrian *mouseion*. His intellectual curiosity prompted the collecting and cataloguing of the contents. Substantial remains of his library were discovered by Hormuzd Rassam in Kuyunjik, Niniveh, in 1853.

Some twenty thousand Kuyunjik cuneiform tablets ended up in the British Museum. "Writing," proclaims one, "is the mother of eloquence and the father of artists."

The period of the Trojan War had passed when Ashurbanipal flourished; the poems of Homer and Hesiod were already being recited and codified on parchment and papyrus. Archilochus was pursuing his wars and amours. Greek oral and literary culture was not unique. It participated in traditions that went far back in time, and drew their energies from other, no less inventive, cultures. Ashurbanipal represents the climax of one such cultural line: he sent scribes all over the known world to copy and translate into the Assyrian language and script every significant text that could be found. Knowledge was power; but for Ashurbanipal knowledge was also knowledge, a reward in itself.

The easier writing materials—papyrus in particular, but also parchment—were obviously more perishable than the tablets: we learn more from Niniveh about Babylonian and Assyrian culture than we can from most Greek and Roman sources about Greek culture.[11] We cannot even chart precisely the streets of ancient Alexandria nor plot on an archaeological map the foundations of the library and its subsidiary collection. Papyrus was a great enabler; it made the act of writing easier, with the introduction of a simplified alphabet and, given the grain of papyrus, the ability to vary letter-forms. It was inevitable that a scroll-making industry should develop and the literary arts spread far and wide. But when a palace or library burned down, clay tablets were baked into stone; papyrus and parchment burned, stoking the flames. We possess substantially more textual material from the millennia before the Greeks than from the Greek periods themselves.

The Greek word for a book, that is, a papyrus scroll or roll, is *biblion,* the diminutive of *bíblos,* "the inner bark or pith of the papyrus."[12] Hence, in the plural, we get *ta biblía* or "the books," the library of scrolls which was, for the Jews, the Bible. St. Jerome referred to the Scriptures collectively as the *bibliotheca,* a collection of books, the source of the word for "library" in many languages. A *volumen,* in Latin, is a thing rolled up (from *volvere*), a volume; the Greek equivalent is *kylindros*[13] (cylinder). To unroll a *volumen* is *evolvere,* which in Latin means "to read." When the book is read, when the roll runs out, *explicatus est liber;* the things it has said to the reader are then explicit. For its part, the Latin word for book, *liber,* has a derivation similar to *biblion. Liber* described the inner bark of a tree, bast or rind, from which writing material was derived, and from *liber,* of course, we derive *library, libretto* and other words.

Such etymologies are also aetiologies, taking us back to the starting points of the material culture of writing and textual transmission. The word for anything made of wood, for example a wooden tablet, is *caudex* or *codex.*

Later it was used to refer to a wooden tablet coated with blackened wax on which a writer could draft a text, the *pugillares* (*fist*books, *hand*books, from Latin *pugillus,* handful or fist) of poets, historians, astrologers and school-children. In his *Natural History* Pliny says that these wooden tablets were used in Greece before Homer made his poems.[14] His account is based on "an unreliable source," Homer.[15] He also claims that the first writing was done on palm leaves, then on tree bark, afterwards on sheets of lead for public documents, then sheets of linen or, again, *pugillares* for private documents. In the *Metamorphoses,* Ovid brings us up close to a woman writing on one of these slates, Biblis, granddaughter of the river Maeander, ravaged by desire for her own lovely brother Caunus and at last risking a love letter to him:

> She holds in her right hand a stylus, in her left a blank
> Wax tablet. So she starts and pauses; writes and damns
> The tablet; writes then unwrites; alters, blames herself, accepts;
> Now lays the tablets by, now picks them up once more.[16]

Pugillares were used into the Renaissance because they were conveniently reusable. Greeks and Romans wrote in the fistbooks with a *graphium* or *stylus*. They were especially convenient for drafting and correcting speeches, poems, literary texts, school exercises; the completed work was then transferred onto papyrus.[17]

In Greece, and later in Rome, it was not uncommon for people to write with a *stylus* on leaves: the Sibyl made a habit of it. At Syracuse the *ostraka* for the ostracism were not the eponymous shards of pottery but olive leaves; the exile was sentenced not to ostracism but to *petalismos,* from *petalon,* leaf. We "leaf" through a book, we "take a leaf out of" another's book, we "turn over a new leaf." *Folium* is a Latin leaf, a *folio* is a book where the standard *leaf* of paper is folded once. Such modern books, however, were more than a millennium away.

From the papyrus scroll projected a label called a *sillybos* with the title of the work and perhaps a *titulus* or contents list. The full *titulus* was given, as with Spanish and French books today, at the end rather than at the start of the work; if a scroll was left un-rewound, at least the next reader would know what lay in store. And he would rewind the book on a single wooden roll rod called in Greek *omphalos,* in Latin *umbilicus,* the meanings identical. Greek scrolls usually had a single roll rod, Hebrew two, for the sacred works.

A working scribe organised his text in parallel columns. He would complete a column, roll it in with his left hand, roll out a new column space with his right, and continue thus for yards and yards. Readers handled scrolls in a similar way. The representation of a person holding a roll in the right hand denotes that the scroll is about to be read, in the left that the scroll has been finished and the reader is about to act: to speak, as an orator, for example.

No rollers survive, only portrayals of them. Longer works or multiple rolls were kept together in baskets or buckets made of leather or wood. A book of the *Iliad* or the *Odyssey* filled a single roll. But a book's length was also determined, in the case of Homer for example, by aesthetic considerations.[18]

When we arrive at the Alexandrian Library and Callimachus' *Pinakes,* the ambitious library catalogue, we shall revisit the theme of the book and the editions which that institution and that period of Greek scholarship produced.[19] Other issues relating to the manuscript tradition are discussed as they arise in the lives and times of the poets. It is important to remember that, even in Alexandria, there were no firm scribal traditions, rules or governing conventions. Greek scribes could be inaccurate, unlike the meticulous transcribers of Hebrew scripture whose work was judged, character by character, by God himself.

And no *original* Greek manuscript, in the hand of an actual author, survives. A gap of a whole millennium separates the earliest surviving manuscript of a Homeric poem from Homer himself. Where books existed in a certain order—the nine volumes of Sappho's poems, for example, or the six of Alcaeus—we do not know if they were originally assembled or sanctioned by the authors themselves, or if an editor sorted them into thematic or formal categories when the time for the definitive edition arrived. The earliest surviving manuscript is the *Persae* of Timotheus of Miletus (discovered in a tomb at Abusir, Lower Egypt, in 1902). The author lived between 447 and 357 BC and the papyrus is fourth century, the closest a text comes to the author's life.[20]

We can be confident that, by the fifth century BC, if not earlier, written literature had become a commodity. Scroll—that is book—production and the book trade were established in the larger cities. Eupolis, Aristophanes' contemporary, collaborator and eventual rival, takes it for granted that there is a book market in Athens.[21] Aristophanes himself makes it clear that books were easy to procure in specific markets: he could joke about *literary* fashion. Xenophon recalls that a wealthy youth known as Euthydemus the Handsome collected scrolls of the poets and philosophers in order to impress his contemporaries. The custom of acquiring spurious cultural *bona fides* goes back a long way. Plutarch remarks upon Alexander the Great's purchase of books—plays and poetry—in Athens. Dionysus of Halicarnassus quotes Aristotle saying that political speeches were sold by the hundred in Athens.[22] As early as 500 BC, if we credit the images on Greek pottery, Homer and other poets were being *read,* not merely performed, by individuals.[23] Schools developed where reading skills were taught. Boys benefited, but vases show women reading and singing from scrolls, too.

If there were book "shops," there was supply and some pattern of manufacture. We can conjecture that booksellers retained scribes and offered copying to order. If so, each bookseller would have had a library of template texts from which to work. Certainly by the beginning of the fourth century BC, bookselling was flourishing in various cities. In Athens the noble orator Lycurgus, who was in charge of the Athenian exchequer from 338 to 326 BC and who oversaw the reconstruction or refurbishment of Athenian cultural institutions, decreed that accurate and authoritative copies of the works of Aeschylus, Sophocles and Euripides should be kept, so as to avoid serious textual corruption when the plays were revived. The authoritative control copies were to be housed in an official records office, a kind of civic library, though one that is unlikely to have permitted popular access.

By the end of the fourth century book collecting was widespread; private libraries had developed. Euripides had one. Aristotle created a large personal collection which, Strabo declares, could "teach the kings in Egypt how to arrange a library."[24] This is precisely what tradition says it did for the Ptolemies. The dates must be stretched, but Aristotle's disciple Demetrius of Phalerum, a friend of the first Ptolemy, was perhaps a conduit for Aristotle's actual book collection, or copies of it, to be placed at the heart of the new library at Alexandria. By that time—early in the third century BC— many major cities had substantial libraries.

One problem with libraries is that they burn. In AD 1204 Constantinople was sacked and our last, richest direct textual link with the classical world was destroyed. Another problem is that, when high-cultural transactions are conducted in a different language from the vulgar tongue of the land in which it lives (Greek in Egypt, Magna Graecia, and later in the Roman world), a library both preserves and excludes. It has walls, racks, scrollbuckets, systems of control and preservation. A linguistically or ethnically separate high culture, like a colonial culture, withdraws into the handsome buildings provided, into the schools and theatres and museums, and what percolates out is careful collations of whole texts, selections, extracts, summaries, material to be used in schools to teach language and moral precept. Certain segments of certain works become canonical; other segments are either discarded or gradually degrade in the dark of their inconvenient scrolls.[25]

II HOT AND COLD CULTURES

Why did Pericles make sure that the texts of Homer's poems were written down? Was it because the oral tradition was faltering and he was afraid the poems would be lost? Or was it, on the contrary, because the oral tradition was so strong and so widespread and potentially corruptible that the poems needed to be brought under control, stabilised, fixed? A written text, too, could be corrupted. Take, for example, the famous added line in the *Iliad* (see page 52): whoever controlled the master copy controlled the poem's transmission. There is a radical distance between what are sometimes called "hot cultures" with oral traditions, the language alive on the tongue and in the ear, the absence of the first person singular narrator, and "cold cultures" which are literary, reflective, tending towards individualism. Here the poem is not a process of synthesis within family, tribe, village, town or city; it is a product to be possessed not in memory but in the home or the library. We might refer to these categories as "immediate" and "delayed" culture.

Should a poem transcribed from hot culture into the medium of the cold—into writing—be treated in the same way as a poem which was composed on *pugillares,* or papyrus, in the first place? Some argue that in terms of factuality, the poem from the oral tradition is more dependable, more responsible, than the literary poem, in part because it comes from a source deeper in language and memory than most literary works. Since before 450 BC there was almost no prose literature; our only windows on the ancient world are the poems. Aristotle and Plutarch depended on Tyrtaeus for their sense of Spartan reality and on Solon for their sense of Athens. Homer was read as history.

From the beginning, millennia before Homer, there was a human hunger for narrative, for making sense by discovering connections and making sequences of events and phenomena. Early poetry finds its stories and then finds ways of remembering them. Mnemonic patterns develop in language, music and dance which collaborate in the ceremony of transmission. The stories told begin in kinds of truth. As events recede in time, they grow not smaller but larger in language. The ancestor who fought locally becomes a hero in a battle which assumes the scale of epic: Colchis, Thebes, Troy. Such traditions are vigorous, the stories can be linked, and if a language for poetry develops which is not quite the dialect of any one place but is known to be the dialect of poetry, the stories can travel.

In oral cultures, people remember because of rhythmic, consonantal and vocalic patternings of language, formulae which convey an accepted set of meanings in received forms, with slight expressive variations. The formulae stabilise at different times and in different ways, and so the dialect of oral poetry will preserve archaic words and forms, and even elements where the meaning is quite forgotten. Orally transmitted poetry can carry memory that goes back a thousand years, even if the singer of tales is ignorant of the remote sources of his song. The scholar Gregory Nagy concentrates less on the bardic effort of memory than on the *dictation* of the oral tradition, the ways in which it makes a poem proof against the vagaries of the individual performer or rhapsode.

People who share an oral culture feel close to their stories because they carry them inside themselves; the narratives have not been downloaded. Performers recite them, but their recital is checked against memory. There is a sense of common or shared possession; the poem is a crucial constituent of community. The Homeric poems were to retain this force—in Asia Minor, the Islands, Greece, North Africa, Magna Graecia—long after writing and reading became commonplace. Because the individual "voice" is unimportant and what matters is *fidelity* to the poem, the integrity of an oral "text" is easier to preserve, proof against scribal enhancement and distortion.

Writing arrests oral culture, but we can explore a transcribed oral text as we can excavate an ancient building, and what we find is not necessarily going to be archaeologically less dependable than a potsherd or a stone inscription. It is only when transcribed oral texts begin to be played with and reworked by literary artists that distortions take them beyond historical use.

Language itself changes when it is codified and written down. When the ability to read and write spreads (as it did rapidly in a world rich in public inscriptions), the idea of culture spreads. An archaic statue might have had only the most rudimentary inscription, or none at all; the text on a classical statue would memorialise *and advertise* the nature and achievement of the object or person portrayed: memorialise for the people of the city where it was placed, or the sailors familiar with the headland they were passing; and *advertise* to visitors, enemies, slaves. By the way it is used, language becomes a means of distorting truth, limiting and pointing meaning. We should not be too sceptical of oral traditions; indeed, we might be rather less sceptical of them than of literary traditions. Archaeology is increasingly on Homer's side.

And when we come across "I" in early poetry, in Hesiod, Archilochus or Sappho or Alcman, we have to read that pronoun warily. What the "I" says belongs to the performer; it may have been factually true for the author, but we err if we invest it with a modern subjectivity or assume that it expresses an essentially lyric sensibility. The lyric may well be as conventional, as dictated and derived, as the epic. Lyric does not grow out of epic, though there is continual commerce between them. Embedded in Homer's poems there are lyric passages: "harvest song, wedding song, a paean to Apollo, a *threnos* or mourning song." "Thus," says Leslie Kurke, "epic and lyric must have co-existed throughout the entire prehistory of Greek literature. What suddenly enabled the long-term survival of the lyric . . . was, paradoxically, the same technological development that ultimately ended the living oral tradition of epic composition-in-performance"—namely, writing.[26] Lyric poetry survived thanks to writing, but it, too, began as an oral medium. "Greece down through the fifth century has aptly been described as a "song culture."[27] After that time, it was a reciting culture, moving towards the drama.

There were numerous and specific occasions when song was required;

they were embedded in a culture which was formalised and to some extent ritualised. Lyric was not a personal outpouring but a song in a determined place within the Greek day or night. It entertained, but it also had functions in religious and other terms. Kurke stresses the ways in which poetry—i.e., language—was instrumental in "constructing individuals as social objects," giving boys and girls the words, and through the words a rehearsal of the experiences, of adult life and action. "This formative process applied to both the singers and the audience of early Greek poetry, since, throughout the [pre-classical] period, the singers would have been non-professionals and members of the same community as their listeners, whether that community be the entire city or a small group of 'companions' at the symposium."[28] Modern poetry spends much of its energy deliberately deconstructing the "individual as social subject." For the ancients, poetry socialised people; for the moderns, it reflects or promotes alienation.

In the archaic period the *symposion,* or symposium, which occurred after the communal meal and in the evening, was the focal point for entertainment and instruction for the well-to-do and the well-born. The Greeks adapted from the East the reclining mode for these pastimes, which meant that only a limited number could be accommodated in the symposium room, one horizontal symposiast occupying the space of three vertical men. The word "men" is crucial: as far as we know, the symposium was generally a male occasion, except perhaps in Lesbos. Between fourteen and thirty men, two or more per couch, gathered under the guidance of a symposiarch or master of ceremonies. The symposiasts drank rather too much watered wine, wore crowns, perfumes and other embellishments, enjoyed the presence of lovely boys and hired women, and then burst out into the street, spilling their rowdiness on the neighbourhood. Sometimes poems were sung, and the occasion licensed the witty, the erotic, the light-hearted, and sometimes the elegiac, the political or philosophical. The symposium bolstered the self-identity of an élite. The audience was unlike the crowd that attended a Homeric recitation.[29]

The term *lyric poetry* applies to all the non-dramatic, non-didactic, non-epic, non-hexameter Greek verse composed up to 350 BC. A lyric poem was not always accompanied by a lyre. A sort of oboe, the *aulos,* might accompany it: a musician (*auletes*) blows into two tubes at once. Does he place his tongue between them to cross-distribute the puff? Most English translators make *aulos* mean *flute*. It doesn't, because it is a reed instrument. References to flutes in translations of ancient Greek should be adjusted. And when we imagine the *aulos* player we might bear in mind the vase on which the *auletes* is portrayed with a leather strap drawn across the cheeks for support, because very strong blowing was required to make the pipes sound. Other instruments included the more delicate-sounding harp (Sappho's *barbitos*), which Alcaeus and Anacreon also used as an alternative to the lyre.

There are three basic genres of Greek lyric poetry. Starting with the coarsest, there is the iambic. Iambic poems are not always composed in iambs: they can include trochaic or dactylic metres. Performed at popular festivals, those of Demeter and Dionysus for example, they can be playful, silly, bawdy, lewd. Sexual narrative, animal fables (with human overtones) and poems of attack come under this head. Slang is used: most of the poems were not sung but recited or spoken. They are at the root of Greek comedy and satire, and Archilochus, Hipponax and Semonides are among the leading iambolators. The chief mainland Greek practitioner was Tyrtaeus.

Elegiac poems were generally written in elegiac couplets, a dactylic hexameter followed by a dactylic pentameter. The tradition seems to be rooted in Asia Minor because there is a marked Ionic inflection to the diction. Initially the elegy was not restricted to laments. On the contrary, there was the erotic elegy (brilliantly taken up by the Latin poet Ovid in his *Amores*) and the narrative, probably intended for public recital, often hortatory in nature. Measured by the ways in which they honoured convention, Mimnermus and Theognis are among the great Greek elegists.

The third category is melic, always composed in lyric metres. Melic poems for recitation in the symposium take the form of monody, a single voice with musical and perhaps dance accompaniment. Alcaeus, Sappho and Anacreon excelled in this form, but also in the other kind of melic poetry, on a larger scale: choral, sung and danced by a group of performers to a larger audience.

Different dialects of Greek initially contributed to different genres. Ionic was spoken not only in Ionia, on the west coast of Asia Minor, but also on many of the islands that dot the sea across to mainland Hellas itself. It is here that the main ingredients of Homer's language developed. Here too the most important of epic verse forms, dactylic hexameter, seems to have taken shape, with its distinctive distribution of quantities and its shortened concluding foot:

$$—\text{uu}\ —\text{uu}\ —\text{uu}\ —\text{uu}\ —\text{uu}\ —\text{u}$$

Queen Elizabeth I in an experimental spirit composed an English hexameter which was also a diminutive essay on the movement and tone of Latin verse:

Persius a crab-staff, bawdy Martial, Ovid a fine wag.

Also from Ionia emanated early examples of iambic and elegiac poetry.

Iambic poems were composed generally in trimeter:

u-u- u-u- u-u-

a template for dialogue in dramatic verse. Other iambic poems are in a
trochaic tetrameter catalectic—

—u —u —u —u —u —u —u—

—used for comic and popular verse.[30] Archilochus first practised both
forms, and another iambic form which alternates long and short, primarily
iambic or dactylic, lines. The lyric forms of Lesbos, *i.e.,* Sapphics and Alcaics, are considered on p. 192–4; the choral forms of Sparta, to which Alcman decisively contributed, on p. 156–65. Boeotia produced Hesiod, whose
prosodic similarities to Homer are belied by his themes and forms. Later
poets could choose dialect elements which had generic or prosodic overtones. The choice of diction itself became a means of allusion.

The high classic period of Greek literature, between 480 and 400 BC, was
dominated by the dramatists Aeschylus, 525–456 BC, Sophocles, 496–406
BC, and Euripides, 484–406 BC. Writing for the speaking and chanting voice,
they combine the lessons of earlier poets, from the subtle and lucid plotting
and formal dialogue of the Homeric poems to the kinds of speech and
recitation that the lyric developed. The tragedians were less innovators than
appropriators. The success of the Athenian drama overshadows other, in
some respects more original, achievements in the wide world of Greek poetry, not least the epinicean tradition crowned by Pindar.

When Greek became a diaspora culture, poetry—that most portable of
arts—re-emerged, but under a new aspect, with different strategies and objectives from those which came to a climax in the work of Pindar. Hellenistic culture was of necessity a culture of the book. It could not count on a
popular audience: the age of the reader had arrived, and a poet was often a
man speaking to a man, not to men. Readers of Greek poetry constituted
an élite, as in the Middle Ages readers of Latin did. Poetry became more sophisticated, allusive, an insider's art, no longer for the street market. A poet
established the legitimacy of his work, validated it, as it were, through allusion, imitation, parody. An inherently conservative art became, culturally
and even politically, more so.

When Callimachus writes a Homeric hymn and continually attests to
precedent, when he revives the archaic in a deliberate, arch, knowing way,
he epitomises the new poetry at its most recondite. Straight formal imitations, for example Apollonius' attempt to write a Homeric poem, were absurd to his rival Callimachus; and to us, however beguiling the detail.
Certain kinds of poetry became no longer viable. The space in which the
imagination is free to roam is vast; its very scope hems the poet in. Greece is

now memory and fiction, and the poetry that is written writes *back* into a culture that is, to use Roberto Calasso's term, uprooted, like the gods whose powers fade as they are carted off from their landscapes and dialects and universalised.

III A SYNTHETIC LANGUAGE

For Anglophone readers, the hardest thing to come to terms with in ancient Greek poetry is the prosody, specifically what is meant when we are told that it is not accent or stress but syllable length and quantity that determine metre.

One of the first things a reader-aloud of early Greek lyric poetry will notice is how long Greek words can grow. Greek is a synthetic language, with declensions and a profusion of prefixes, suffixes, infixes. With almost weightless particles, poets sing long, light lines with great economy; the English translator must generally render this down to shorter words, lines with fewer syllables. There is no easy equivalence between the sound qualities of both languages. The apparent ease of the early Greek lyrics is the result of another quality: how richly vocalic the language can be, a modulation of vowel tones with a sparing punctuation of consonants, lines ideal for singing. And Greek itself is vowel-rich; English tends to be more consonantal.

Translators note how differently the rhythmic patterns of Greek and English move. The natural rhythms of Greek tend "downward," falling; emphases gather towards the beginnings of feet and lines. English naturally rises to points of emphasis and closure. There are elements, too, which only experts register: ancient Greek verse had an accent that does not affect the metrical pattern but does affect the sound, and the sense, of what is sung, namely pitch.[31] Michael Grant writes, "The accent on ancient Greek words was related to musical tone or pitch, but the relation between pitch and stress is obscure; the accented syllable of a word often seems to have been pitched higher than those that are unaccented. The pitch of the language was seen to relate it closely to music."[32]

The crucial difference between the prosodies is that ancient Greek verse is quantitative, English accentual. Elizabethan and later attempts to write a quantitative English verse have underlined an irreconcilable difference of sound, of the possibilities of natural melodic patterning inherent in the two languages. W. H. Auden, a great prosodist, noted this linguistic *otherness:* concentrating less on lyric than epic and dramatic verse, he drew attention to the experiments of another great prosodist, Robert Bridges, who attempted to render part of Book XXIV of the *Iliad* into English quantitative verse, de-claring, "The translation is line for line in the original metre."[33] Here is a short specimen:

> And from th' old king's seizure his own hand gently disengaged,
> And each brooded apart; Priam o'er victorious Hector
> Groan'd, low fal'n to the ground unnerved at feet of Achilles,
> Who sat mourning awhile his sire, then turn'd to bewailing
> Patroclus, while loudly the house with their sobbing outrang.

Auden chuckles at this vain experiment. "But no one can read this except as qualitative meter of an eccentric kind, and eccentricity is a very un-Homeric characteristic." But how vain is Bridges' attempt to render the otherness of the Greek in sound and in strange but strangely apposite diction? The words that stand out as odd lexically, "seizure," "unnerved," "outrang," tie this incident into the continuum of the narrative; the word order itself is in-tended to deliver the sense in the same pattern as it comes to us in the Greek. A modern bias is to make Homer sound quite colloquial, and this approach in itself yields "a very un-Homeric characteristic." Translations which purge the poem of its linguistic difference are more readable, but not more true.

The task Bridges set himself was impossible because in Greek, as an in-flected language, the word order is not so crucial as it is in English. Auden describes the difference in poetic sensibility between modern English and Homeric Greek in unsatisfactory terms: "Compared with English poetry Greek poetry is primitive, i.e. the emotions and subjects it treats are simpler and more direct than ours while, on the other hand, the *manner* of language tends to be more involved and complex." The term "primitive" is so *incor-rect* here, especially in the light of what he says about the language, as to pro-duce a senseless paradox. "Primitive poetry," he continues, "says simple things in a roundabout way where modern poetry tries to say complicated things straightforwardly." Is the *Iliad* periphrastic in expression? No: it is hard to think of any poem in which expression is more economical, direct, swift, summary or characteristic. Auden's conclusion, however, is quite cor-rect: "The continuous efforts of English poets in every generation to redis-cover 'a language really used by men' would have been incomprehensible to a Greek."[34] Less incomprehensible to them, perhaps, than the very English Renaissance attempt to create quantitative prosodies in English is to us, an attempt which persisted from the classicising age of Edmund Spenser right up to the twentieth century and Robert Bridges.

When we get to Greek drama, Auden's argument is more helpful. Dra-matic dialogue is often riddling, ornamented and ornamental, anything but natural, and in general it renders an awkward English translation. This is true of the epinicean tradition and its aftermath as well.

Greek metre is a complex business. It requires an understanding of the Greek language. In fact, as soon as we begin to consider metre we realise that there is no such thing among the early Greek poets as a standard Greek language. There is a variety of dialects, and this is one reason it was always considered important to give a poet, almost as a patronymic, his or her town of origin, and why Didymus' pedantries in seeking the actual birth-places of poets may have had some editorial and prosodic *use*. Origin carried not only ethnic, cultural and political but also dialect information in it. In the eighth century BC, certain differentiated strands existed which, in diminishing degrees, persisted right up to the fourth century. Ionian, Aeolic, Dorian, the mainland Greeks of the north-west, the Arcadian, Attic and Boeotian groups spoke and composed in different ways; different metres originate within specific dialects and answer to them. There is no single "original Greek" but a series of equal variations (isoglosses, equal versions, not the Bakhtinian diglossia, where there is a standard form against which a dialect plays).[35]

The best modern account is to be found in Martin Litchfield West's *Greek Metre* (Oxford, 1982). West is succinct and deploys the technical vocabulary with precision, establishing the origins of quantitative prosody far back in Indo-European traditions. He also provides a useful glossary of terms. But West's study is not for the beginner.

Michael Grant's summary approach to Greek metre in *The Rise of the Greeks* (1987) provides a more useful starting point. "The 'foot' is derived," he says, "from the dance with which Greek poetry was intimately connected." The foot is defined by a patterning "of long and short syllables, i.e. possessed a quantitative rhythm (in contrast to the stress accent of our own poetry, in which syllables are not long or short, but stressed or unstressed)." He emphasises the flexibility and versatility of quantitative prosodies. "The dactyl-spondee variation of the Greek hexameter means that it can contain between twelve and seventeen syllables, thus achieving a length and complexity that are unusual in the heroic verse of other literatures."[36]

When we mime iambic feet in English we say, *teTUM teTUM teTUM*. In Greek we would say *shortlooong shortlooong shortlooong*. Shortness and length, not unstress and stress, determine the quantitative base of the foot. We can think of it as *duration in time* rather than *emphasis* in relation to neighbouring syllables. The shortness and length are functions of the vowels in specific positions in terms of one another and to the consonants that make up the words. Such prosody belongs in the province of a music without percussion.

To hear the verse as it was intended to sound we should familiarise ourselves with its accompaniments, music and dance. These were already only half-remembered in Hellenistic times; our ignorance, shared with Alexandrians, is only a matter of degree. Musical notation hardly survives at all, though we know the instruments. Like the verse, the music used a range of scales and modes "which differed from one another in the sequence of their intervals and probably in the range of their tones. The Greeks invested each mode with its own distinctive emotional and moral associations."[37] The modes pertained initially to an area of origin (Phrygian, Lydian, Lesbian, Dorian, Ionian, and so on) and were related to specific prosodies. When we imagine this early music, we should not imagine harmonies.

IV OTHERNESS

"Why did the whole Greek world exult over the combat scenes in the *Iliad*?" asks Friedrich Nietzsche. We modern readers do not even begin to understand them "in a sufficiently 'Greek' manner." If we understood them in Greek, "we should shudder." Nietzsche does not mean in the Greek language but in the Greek spirit. Whoever reads the *Iliad,* Hesiod's merciless *Theogony*, Archilochus at his most vindictive, savage Hipponax and others has to come to terms with the profound "otherness" of one of the very traditions which lies at the root of ours. "When one speaks of *humanity,*" Nietzsche says,

> the idea is fundamental that this is something which separates and distinguishes man from nature. In reality, however, there is no such separation. Thus the Greeks, the most humane men of ancient times, have a trait of cruelty, a tigerish lust to annihilate—a trait that is also very distinct in that grotesquely enlarged mirror image of the Hellenes, in Alexander the Great, but that really must strike fear into our hearts throughout their whole history and mythology, if we approach them with the flabby concept of modern "humanity." When Alexander has the feet of Batis, the brave defender of Gaza, pierced, and ties him, alive, to his carriage, to drag him about while his soldiers mock, that is a revolting caricature of Achilles.[38]

Alexander re-enacted, with deliberation and conceit, what Achilles, after ten years' deprivation and struggle, had done instinctively. And in the end Alexander did not hand Batis' body back to Gaza's Priam but left it as carrion. Alexander's crude literary gesture is out of key with Homer's compelling impartiality, an impartiality determined by the ways in which the poems were composed and transmitted. Alexander is a theoretical reader: an idealist, he understands the *Iliad* as exemplary and is keen to invest himself in the narrative. An idealist can, at crucial moments, blur categories, appropriate, vulgarise.

Before we begin seriously reading Greek poetry, Nietzsche urges, we need to exercise and strengthen our concept of humanity; we have to be prepared to recognise a cultural difference so basic that we cannot assimilate it to our own ends. We seek not distance, objective detachment, but engagement that leads to illumination, a *self*-effacement that yields understanding. Nietzsche is right, but he does not make enough of the *formal* otherness of Greek poetry—its origins, its prosody, its forms—especially when it comes to Homer and Hesiod. W. H. Auden, too, insists upon the distance between Greek culture and our own, without focusing on formal issues beyond Pindar's obscure poetics.

Archaic and classical Greek poetry concentrate on male experience. Sappho is a vigorous, Corinna a frail, exception. Homer's female figures, apart from his goddesses and sorceresses, are compelling and credible but they move in restricted spaces. Hesiod introduces a strain of misogyny that marks much of the classical tradition. It is not until the Hellenistic phase, and Alexandria in particular, that female experience is given substantial imaginative space, but the poets who clear that space remain male.

Nietzsche and Jacob Burckhardt declare that at the heart of early Greek approaches to the world is the individual *agon* or contest, the desire to prevail. Competition, battle and trial, besting and revenge, keeping face, retaining divine support are compelling male motives. Both men saw the city-state and, paradoxically, the emergence of Athenian democracy as, in the end, culturally and morally destructive. Delphi was the ultimate museum of "Greek hatred for Greeks, of mutually inflicted suffering immortalised in the loftiest works of art."[39] Other critics are less comfortable with this given in Greek and other cultures. The American poet Eleanor Wilner speaks of "the historical horrors attendant on heroising male rage," and Donald Davie applies this to the two key books, the *Iliad* and the *Psalms of David*: "And the darker the deed, the brighter the fiction it has generated, the worst atrocities requiring nothing less than divine sanction."[40] It is in this spirit that Alexander marks his conquest of Gaza.

Over the *Psalms* hovers the vindictive figure of Jehovah. A whole society of gods surveys the bloody Trojan plain. Something has happened already, even at the time of Homer, to the realm of the divine. It has become infected with human motive. "Uprooted from their soil," says the Italian writer Roberto Calasso, "and exposed, in the vibration of the word, to the harsh light of day, [the gods] frequently seemed idle and impudent. Everything ends up as history of literature!"[41] His metaphor is apt: the movement from unanalytical apprehension and "worship" to spoken, liturgised and written belief, from a transcendence taken, unquestioningly, as given to a transcendence described and asserted, is a movement towards abstraction, from first to second hand. When the gods were rooted in place, in natural phenomena, they had their own specific potencies. Transported, generalised, carried about on litters, depicted in ever more sophisticated ways, they lose power; they become mere figures. The worshipper, the priest or the poet can dress and undress them, ceremonially wash them in the stream, grant them deeds, loves and losses. The narratives that surround them are adaptations of human narratives, their lusts and desires are all too human. They lose their otherness and with it their power.

The more accomplished poetry is, the more it manages to re-infuse linguistic abstraction with material presence or, rather, with a *sense* of material presence. In a poem that works, that presence is changed. It is rendered categorically. Characteristic rather than particular, it is given a general character like a template: each reader can invest it with his or her sense of the objects named.

Even in Homer's poems the gods were harder to see and appeared in their own form on earth less frequently than in more ancient texts. And if we believe the *Odyssey*, they "do not appear to everyone in all their fullness [*enargeîs*]," Calasso writes. *Enargeîs* is the technical term "for divine epiphany: a word that contains the dazzle of 'white,' *argós*, but which comes to designate a pure, unquestionable 'conspicuous-ness.'" This "conspicuousness," he adds, "will later be inherited by poetry, thus becoming perhaps the characteristic that distinguishes poetry from every other form." Achieved poetry paints with at least one colour which can be found nowhere else. Calasso has a notion of poetry as a language of presence, not unlike George Steiner's "real presence," but less charged with transcendence. The "real" in Homer is material; language and the things it names exist in a rare harmony. As classical poetry develops, the gods continue to recede: those that we meet in Apollonius are feeble and enervated beside those in the *Iliad* and *Odyssey*. When it reaches Alexandria, poetry comes in out of the sun, retires to the library, becomes one with its medium, language. And so it survives in a world where the vulgar tongue is not Greek.

THE
FIRST
POETS

Orpheus of Thrace

He left half a shoulder and half a head
To recognise him in after time.

These marbles lay weathering in the grass
When the summer was over, when the change

Of summer and of the sun, the life
Of summer and of the sun, were gone.

He said that everything possessed
The power to transform itself, or else,

And what meant more, to be transformed.

WALLACE STEVENS, "Two Illustrations
That The World Is What You Make of It," II

 "What would a man not give," declares Plato in the *Apology*, "to engage in conversation with Orpheus and Musaeus and He- siod and Homer?" Can we do something of the sort? If not to engage in conversation, then at least to glimpse them as they go about their holy and unholy business?

If I start with Orpheus, father of poetry, of music and, some say, of the art of writing itself; tamer of wilderness and wild hearts, servant of Apollo and, paradoxically, servant also of a new Dionysus; torn limb from limb as Dionysus was himself; dissuader of cannibals, maker of the ordered litur- gies that displaced the abandoned frenzy of the orgies ... If I start with Orpheus, it is to make it clear from the outset that this is a history in some- thing other than the modern sense of the word. My Muse is Clio, as she was Plutarch's and Pausanias'. My Muse is Calliope, as she was Homer's and Apollonius of Rhodes'. And Erato of the lyric, tragic Melpomene, spirited Thalia shaking with laughter at solemn, spiritual Polyhymnia, who mutters prayer and praise. Orpheus is a hero, not a god, and a hero more valuable than most of the gods, just as Prometheus was.

Modern historical scepticism must not bridle us or we will have no Or- pheus to converse with and no stories to tell. There is a wealth of stories, and they are worth telling, whether their truths are literal, as they sometimes appear to be, or indicative. Biblical scholars and theologians argue that, when a tale in the Bible is implausible, or is disproven by archaeology, it may nonetheless contain a higher truth or impart a truth of another order than the truth of fact. Without suggesting that we are dealing with holy writ or prophesy (though some see Orpheus as a purveyor of the first and an exemplar of the second), certain general truths exist within the related tales about this and other poets, and those truths emerge most vividly from the particular landscapes and timescapes which the poets may (or may not) have inhabited. Paul Cartledge reminds us that "the ancient Greek word for 'truth' meant literally 'not forgetting.'"[1]

I begin this book as a believer, then, and trust that my faith will survive the pre-Christian millennium of its journey. First, as I step beyond the threshold of my book room into a parched Aegean landscape, I know that there were once springs and trees here in what is no longer Thrace but a land divided between Greece, Bulgaria and Turkey. A man called Orpheus was born somewhere in this part of the world. We can confirm very little about him—or, for that matter, about Arion, Linos (said by some to have been Orpheus' teacher, by others his brother),[2] Musaeus (his overconfident disciple? his son?),[3] or Amphion of Thebes. We can confirm almost nothing about Homer and Hesiod, yet we have no problem, even when we should, believing in them.

Orpheus lived, and Orpheus lives. Everyone knows his name and the stories associated with it. His power was intact when in 1913, almost three millennia after his death, the French poet Apollinaire brought a band of young radical painters together under the banner of Orphism. Robert Delaunay, Fernand Léger, Francisco Picabia, Marcel Duchamp and others at that stage shared a wild fauvist colour-sense and the kinds of dislocation and surface foregrounding we associate with Cubism: a tendency towards abstraction, but always rooted in and answerable to figures in the common world.

Apollinaire's first Orpheus poem accompanies an emphatic woodcut of the First Poet by Raoul Dufy: strong lines, stiff-billowed drapery, full-frontal nakedness, a proportionate penis, a lyre in his left hand.[4] The poem says:

> Wonder at this bold vitality
> And the firm lines' nobility:
> At "Let there be light" his voice was heard,
> In *Pimander*[5] Trismegistus wrote the word.

Already magic, hermeticism, mystery—the Egyptian smoke-screen of Hermes Trismegistus,[6] high-priest of the obscure—are at hand, like three brocaded Magi at a simple manger, complicating things. They are inseparable from the first poet, and finally they swamp him. All the same, at the dawn of Modernism it was appropriate that the singer who enchanted the beasts with his lyre and charmed the trees to gather round him in attentive groves should guard the door of Apollinaire's *Bestiary*. He helps the French poet to tame his animals in epigrams that contain but do not confine them. Other poems by Apollinaire relate to Orpheus, for example "The Tortoise," whose shell—a gift from Apollo—provided the frame of his lyre. Apollo made a gift of his own name to Wilhelm-Apollinaris de Kostrowitzky (Apollinaire), because the poet's father was nowhere to be found.

What can we say for certain about Orpheus? First, that his mother was Calliope, one of the nine daughters of Zeus and Memory (Mnemosyne) and Muse of epic poetry. Who his father was is less certain: the prime suspects are an Olympian god (Apollo) and an almost-mortal Thracian (Oeagrus, possibly a river god, or a king who inherited Thrace from his father, Charops, who helped Dionysus establish himself in Greece and was his devoted follower, inheriting the original Dionysian rites). On balance, it seems probable that his father was mortal, not divine: had both his parents been Olympians, he would not have been able to die. He did die, horribly, by several different accounts and in several different ways.

The travel writer Pausanias, whose Greece visited in the second century AD is a world already bleached by time, plumps for Oeagrus. Though the traveller lived a thousand years after the poet, he was two thousand years closer to him than we are. We also doubt the place of Apollo in Orpheus' immediate family tree because the varieties of Orphic religion that grew out of his name, though hostile to the unbridled Dionysian, are certainly not Apollonian. The followers of Dionysus, keen to introduce discipline and ritual, to channel the energy and frenzy of their rites, were attracted to his interest (if it was his) in the soul's survival and residual divinity. In his person and the stories that surround it he seems to acknowledge the perennial question: How shall we come to terms with our own death? We will return to Orphism and its metamorphoses. But Orpheus the man and his songs are our quarry now. One conclusion of two leading scholars of Orphism, I. M. Linforth and the beguiling W. K. C. Guthrie, is reassuring: what we know of Orphism is less a settled philosophy or soteriology (a doctrine of salvation) than a literature.

Orpheus' hypothetical brother Linos was himself a masterful singer. His ill fortune was to be appointed tutor to the young Heracles, who brained the poet with his own lyre when he tried to discipline the unruly boy. In another story, Linos is found challenging Apollo to a singing contest, and the god slays him. More evidence for Oeagrus: Apollo is unlikely to have slain his son or step-son. Whatever the manner of Linos' death, he was thereafter mourned with the ceremonial cry of *ai Linon* (woe for Linos), a lament which may have had a place in the rituals marking the changing seasons. On the shield which Hephaestus makes for Achilles in the *Iliad* (Book XVIII),

"Youths and maidens all blithe and full of glee, carried the luscious fruit in plaited baskets; and with them there went a boy who made sweet music with his lyre, and sang the Linos-song with his clear boyish voice."[7] Orpheus, too, has a place, more prominent than his brother's, in the cycle of fertility myths.

We know beyond all but the most wilful doubt that Orpheus married, and his wife was the lovely, young and innocent Eurydice. All the accounts of their romance—and it was among the most often told and sung of stories, until Offenbach reduced it to laughter in *Orpheus in the Underworld*— agree that they were a handsome and well-matched couple. What did Offenbach find comical? Innocent romance itself, perhaps, love without ironic distance, without style if you like. He may, too, have been impatient with earlier tellings. We know how Orpheus loved Eurydice; but did she love him back? She is portrayed as the object of desire, she is ordered about and obeys, but her own character is seldom consulted. Even in Hell, when Orpheus charms the God of the Dead, he reclaims Eurydice without reference to her own will to resurrect. Jesus did the same with Lazarus, and modern painters make much of the Biblical line, spoken by Martha, that if they were to unwind the dead man from his stroud, he would stink.

Let us look a little more closely at Orpheus' wife: she may provide clues to his character, and he to hers. Some of the main sources for information about Orpheus—in particular Pausanias, whose description of the murals of Polygnotus at Delphi is such a telling reconstruction—do not mention Eurydice at all. Orpheus went to the underworld, it would seem, out of curiosity rather than love, or perhaps he was a spirit of the underworld who escaped into the upper air, and Eurydice was added by some later romancer to give the first poet a credible human motive and a credible human nature. Since I have declared myself a believer, I take Orpheus to have been an actual man with an actual harp in his hand and a voice which, if we could only hear it, would bring us a visionary calm. The vision would be of the real forms that underlie the phenomenal world we perceive, a characteristic rather than a specific world.

He did not go to Hades for fun: it was a serious and perilous undertaking, of a kind that only love motivates. Even so, it is not until we get to Virgil and Ovid that the story of Orpheus and Eurydice is fully developed—at least, those are the first *surviving* poems in which it unfolds in a familiar form; there must be many missing transitional texts. One mustn't accuse Virgil or Ovid of *originality,* of wilfully making fictions of such importance. By the time of the Roman poets, everything was done upon established authority, and what was original was the way the derived pieces were assembled.

Some poets, notably Hermesianax of Alexandria in the fourth century

BC, refer to Eurydice as Agriope ("wild-eyed" or "wild-voiced"),[8] a name suitable for a nymph or a spirit of the wood, which is what some poets thought her to be, rather than a mortal woman who might die. "Orpheus and Agriope" lacks the euphony of "Orpheus and Eurydice," and composers from Monteverdi to Offenbach would probably have given the story a wide berth had "Eurydice" not prevailed. Eurydice: her name means "wide justice," Robert Graves says, or "wide-ruling," whereas Orpheus' name is uncertain. Graves suggests that it might mean "of the river bank."

Orpheus married Eurydice on his return from the heroic journey with Jason and the Argonauts, having had sufficient adventure by then to want a quiet life. He and his bride settled in Thrace among the wild Cicones. One day, out alone "gathering flowers," as the poets say, the young bride was assaulted by Aristaeus ("the best"). Now, he *was* the son of Apollo, via a nymph, Cyrene, one of the god's successful conquests. He transported her to the area of Africa that took her name, made love to her, and there she bore him two sons,[9] the elder of whom became a crucial spirit of husbandry—hunting and bee-keeping were his special skills, and some say he learned from the Myrtle-nymphs of Cyrene how to make cheese, and brought the cultivated olive tree to men. He fathered some famous children himself, not least the hunter Actaeon, slain by his own hounds when he spied upon Artemis bathing in a spring.

Like all fertility gods, Aristaeus was sexually excitable, and finding Eurydice alone, he tried to rape her. She fled, stepped upon a serpent which bit her heel, and died. That is the story Virgil tells. Aristaeus was punished. His bees died, and he was forced to make atonements for his wickedness (which, upon his aunt Arethusa's insistence, involved snaring that most protean of gods, Proteus, in his sea cave, and securing his counsel). Proteus, according to Virgil, gave him a severe talking-to:

> "An avenging spirit pursues you, crazed by grief,
> The ghost of Orpheus, calling for his lost bride.
> If the punishment that he gives you matched the crime
> The troubles you suffer now would seem like joys.
> Remember how the doomed girl fled, you ran her down
> In the deep grass by the river, and she could not see
> The venomous viper that lay along the bank at her feet."[10]

Proteus tells the stricken Aristaeus the whole story of the descent of Orpheus in vain quest of his beloved. Then he tells him how to make atonement to the gods, because he cannot atone to man. Aristaeus follows instructions, and, after sacrifices and other penitential exercises, a new swarm of bees clouds out of one of the sacrificed carcasses and into his hives.[11] But nothing could undo the consequence of his lustful act that concerns us here, Eurydice's death.

Orpheus had lived in hope, as Proteus tells, and this is where the power of music and poetry, of love and legend, come together in the great Romantic story. A virtuous girl, a faithful wife, she was running away from Aristaeus, but after the snake struck, her legs no longer moved, she floated on the strong current of death like a figure from Chagall, out of the sunlight and into the long dark caverns leading to the kingdom of the dead. We must assume she went the same route that Orpheus was to follow in seeking her, the single route to Pluto's world, but because she was a woman and her passage was the normal one for a person dead, over the River of Forgetfulness on Charon's rickety boat, past the three-headed dog Cerberus with his three-jawed slavering and three-throated bark, none of the poets follows *her*. She, or her life, vanishes from the face of the earth, and the next time we see her is through Orpheus' eyes, when she is already dead.

Discovering her death, Orpheus wanders in sorrowful desperation. His music cannot calm him, so he decides, after a period of lament and ineffectual strumming, to seek her out in Hades and persuade the dark gods to give her back. He passes into the caverns through "the gate of Tainaron"[12] and makes his way, a mortal casting shadows in a land of shadows,[13] towards the throne of Pluto. He plays music as he goes and the spirits swarm to him as Aristaeus' bees might swarm to a flowery meadow; they go with him as far as they can. Even Cerberus' three heads stop barking and tilt, attentive, all the same way, and the Eumenides, their cheeks for the first and last time wet with tears, relax and listen, and Ixion's wheel stands still. The water rises and touches the lips of Tantalus, but he is too enchanted to drink; and the great boulder of Sisyphus becomes weightless while the music sounds. Still playing, Orpheus sings his petition to Pluto and Proserpina, Hades' seasonal queen, and it is granted: he can return to the world with Eurydice.

On condition. The condition is that he must not look back to see if she is following, not until they reach the upper air and both are in the sunlight. It is a hard command because Eurydice's sandals make no sound upon the stone, being spirit sandals, and Orpheus cannot be sure she is behind him. She is soundless as they climb slowly, the poet still making his amazing music, and Hades returning to normal as the echoes of it fade. Just as they emerge into the light, and she "felt the breeze of the world already on her face,"[14] Eurydice speaks for the first time, saying his name in a small, hoarse voice. It is her last chance to return to Hades: if she gets him to turn back, she will be released from his unnatural spell. Orpheus turns, and since she is not yet quite in the sunlight, Pluto's condition has been violated. As lightly as a feather she begins to drift back down among the dead, calling out to him a final reproach.

"Your thoughtlessness in love,
Orpheus, has wrecked us both. The current of fate
Catches me, it pulls me backward, my blurred eyes swim.
Goodbye, goodbye! I am lost in a huge darkness.
My hands have no strength, no substance, to catch at yours."
And so in Hades she remains.[15]

Philosophical Greeks and Romans, meditating on the tale, puzzled at the fact that the rescued Eurydice was substanceless; indeed, how could it be otherwise? There was nothing of this world in her to resurrect; the gods may have been playing cruel games with Orpheus. After all, he was a mere mortal: How would it have been allowed, even given the unarguable spell his music cast, for a man to break the rules of nature, of life and death, which even gods could seldom circumvent?

Plato is among those who claim that Orpheus was duped by the gods and saw the merest phantom of Eurydice. What is more, Plato, famous for wanting poets out of the commonwealth altogether because they are civically irresponsible people, is not over-fond of Orpheus. He goes so far as to question the truth and intensity of his love for Eurydice in an argument which, fortunately for poetry, did not mar the classical attitude to the poet. In the *Symposium* he makes Orpheus into a species of coward. He begins, "Love will make men dare to die for their beloved—love alone; and women as well as men." He adduces Alcestis, willing to lay down her life for her husband, "and so noble did this action of hers appear to the gods, as well as to men, that among the many who have done virtuously she is one of the very few to whom, in admiration of her noble action, they have granted the privilege of returning alive to earth; such exceeding honour is paid by the gods to the devotion and virtue of love." Contrast Orpheus, "the harper": how dismissive that epithet sounds; no reference to song, to harmony. Him the gods did not grace. He was sent away empty-handed, having been teased with a mere apparition, "because he showed no spirit; he was only a harp-player, and did not dare like Alcestis to die for love, but was contriving how he might enter Hades alive; moreover, they afterwards caused him to suffer death at the hands of women, as the punishment of his cowardliness." After a little digression on the relationship between Achilles and Patroclus (where he argues that Achilles was the younger and the beloved rather than the initiative-taking senior party) Plato says that Love, true Love, is "the eldest and noblest and mightiest of the gods; and the chiefest author and giver of virtue in life, and of happiness after death."

Plato's judgement of Love is generous and unoriginal. In Greek poetry its roots go back at least as far as Hesiod. Love sustains the world: a kind of natural magnetism, it draws together similar elements into the forms of things and beings, and then reconciles them with one another into the tense and volatile harmony which is manifest as Nature. What Plato says of Orpheus is out of keeping with his generous theory: it is dictated by a distrust of the "harper's" vocation as much as by a proper weighing of the evidence, to which he is much closer than we are. Most accounts of Orpheus present a very different, and usually a heartbreaking, picture. Eurydice died; with his subtle power as a singer and musician he went after, a living man among the dead, to retrieve her; he succeeded against all the odds, and then she died again.

From the intensity of his second grief, this time irrevocable, we can infer that he had a kind of conversion or (a more appropriate term) a metamorphosis. His own form changed. Wandering along the banks of the Strymon, plaintive and alone, he decided to leave the social world behind, he abandoned women for ever, preferring to haunt the valleys and crags playing to fauna and flora, enchanting them and eventually the men-folk of the Thracian hamlets, who left their hearths and wives and followed him. Some say that he invented, or discovered, homosexual love. Ovid evokes this charmingly.[16] When he loses Eurydice, no other woman can take her place; he lavishes affection on boys (what Victorian critics coyly refer to as "puerile love") and enjoys the "brief spring and early flowering of their youth." Ovid describes him as "the first to introduce this custom among the people of Thrace."

This is how it was: when he sat on a hill and played in the glaring sun, the trees moved close to shade him, becoming creaturely; so too he had reanimated ghosts and breathed souls into beasts, or found them there. Oaks and poplars groved about him, and the limes and beeches, the laurel that had been Daphne, the ashes and hazels and firs; there was fruit on them, and acorns; there was maple, and willow straining uphill from the river. Sycamores too, and the lotus and box and tamarisk, myrtles and the blue-black-berried viburnum. And the vines sent out long arms to the first poet; elms, mountain ash, palm trees and the pine that had been Attis and was now dear to the goddess Cybele. And the cypress, which was once a boy but whom Apollo changed to a tree: he came too. Into the trees flew birds. Orpheus sang of love: not love of the gods, but of kind, and perhaps of illicit love.

Women were strictly excluded from his concerts. Roused into an orgiastic frenzy of revenge, not only by exclusion but by their husbands' desertion, during a Dionysian festival they apprehended the poet, tore him literally to bits (Plato takes ironic pleasure in this), and threw his body into the sea. These women are variously portrayed as Maenads (mad women, votaries of Dionysus), Bacchants, Bassarids. The tearing apart was a ritual *sparagmós,* or sacrifice, of the very kind that Orphism as a religion came to oppose. What happened to the poet's body after that time is uncertain, though there are legends worth considering.

Ovid tells how the Ciconian women drowned out Orpheus' song with their cries and broke its magic charm. Then they killed him and they killed the creatures he had charmed. They seized farming implements and hacked him to bits. Vases from as early as the fifth century BC show Orpheus being set upon by women with terrible weapons: rocks and spears and what look like lethal carpet-beaters; Orpheus raises his frail lyre above his head in vain self-defence. The Hebrus swallowed his lyre and his singing head; the lyre kept playing and the dead lips sang. The head was washed up on Lesbos, near Methymna. Milton in "Lycidas" recalls the story:

> What could the Muse herself[17] that Orpheus bore,
> The Muse herself, for her enchanting son
> Whom universal nature did lament,
> When by the rout that made the hideous roar
> His gory visage down the stream was sent,
> Down the swift Hebrus to the Lesbian shore?[18]

In Lesbos the head was attacked by a snake, but Phoebus stopped the snake's assault by turning it to stone and the head was at last buried. Its presence in Lesbos made the island particularly fertile in poets and writers.

The lyre, Apollo's gift, had an interesting after-history, too. It was hung in Apollo's temple and remained there for many years. Eventually Neanthus, the unsubtle son of the tyrant Pitticus, bribed a priest and got hold of the lyre because he had heard that it drew trees and beasts together with its harmonies. Like many a later singer, he confused the instrument with the art and tried to take a short-cut. He took the lyre, leaving a forgery in its place. He knew it was risky to remain in the city with his trophy, so he fled, concealing the harp in his cloak. Once in the unpeopled countryside he began to play—badly, because he had no skill, though he delighted himself and imagined that he was Orpheus' heir. But he too was destined to be torn to pieces, by dogs whose siesta his dissonances had disturbed.[19]

The women of Thrace Dionysus cruelly and justly turned to trees; their toes took root and with desperate helplessness they watched their calves and thighs grow thick and rough with bark. No music would ever ease them back to human form.[20] So it was that Dionysus and Apollo both collaborated in making amends for the death of Orpheus, an unusual and highly significant reconciliation between opposing divinities.

There are many other versions of his death: that he committed suicide,[21] that Zeus struck him down with a thunderbolt,[22] that he was killed by people who disliked his teachings. But the women of Thrace are the most common explanation, and tradition had it that Thracian men beat their wives to continue the punishment for Orpheus' murder. But they continued to hate his teachings. Some say he was around sixty-three years old when he met his death; others calculate two hundred and seventy. Since he was a hero, the second number should not be ruled out: heroes stretch the possible and the plausible.

His body was buried by the Muses, though precisely where is uncertain. Legend favours a spot near Mount Olympus. Pausanias sets the original tomb in the town of Libethra on the side of the mountain. But a frightening story attaches to that tomb. It is from Pausanias that we learn of the curse of Orpheus' bones.[23] "The Libethrans received a message from Dionysus through an oracle in Thrace," he tells us, "that when the sun saw the bones of Orpheus the city of Libethra would be rooted up by a wild boar. They took little notice of the prophecy, thinking a wild beast could not be big and strong enough to capture the city . . ." It is unwise ever to make light of an oracle. "When the god thought fit, this is what happened to them. A shepherd was lying against Orpheus' grave during the middle of the day, and he fell asleep: in his sleep he sang the poems of Orpheus in a loud, sweet voice. Of course everyone watching their flocks close by, and even ploughmen, abandoned work and crowded to hear the shepherd singing in his sleep. They shoved and pressed to get closer to him and they overturned the pillar. The urn fell and smashed and the sun saw what was left of the bone of Orpheus. At once the very next night the god poured down water out of heaven, and the river Boar, which is one of the winter streams of Olympus, broke the walls of Libethra, overturned the sanctuaries of the gods and the houses of men, and drowned the people and every living thing in the city, all alike." Then the Macedonians of Dion took the bones of Orpheus to their country. To have famous bones in a city was a sure way of attracting religious tourists, just as the bones of a saint enriched remote towns in the Middle Ages.

Most ancient Greeks would have agreed that Orpheus was born in Thrace, though a few dissented and claimed him for the area around Mount Olympus, between Thessaly and Macedonia, where his bones ended up. He flourished in the heroic age, a generation or two before Troy. There is agreement that he travelled with the Argonauts in pursuit of the Golden Fleece. In this story he plays first and only fiddle, as it were (he is the poet in residence), though he is not the main focus of the poem. On the journey Orpheus mixes with forty-nine other great heroes including Jason and, for part of the journey, Heracles himself, against whom the poet may have borne a grudge, given the death of Linos. Also of the party, coming from Sparta, were the Dioscuri—Zeus's twin sons by Leda, Helen's brothers, Castor and Polydeuces (Pollux)—and Hermes' sons Erytos and Echion, and their brother Aithalides; and the brothers Clytios and Iphitos, "lords of Oichalia." Heroes often came in pairs. Each hero is given a geographical provenance, which, as we shall see when we reach the third century BC, was one purpose of a poem: to provide heroic ancestors for ruling families and to flatter patrons and payers.

In the third century, the librarian-poet Apollonius of Rhodes retells the tale most famously in the *Argonautica* or *The Voyage of the Argo*. He gives Orpheus pride of place, introducing him before all the other heroes.

> First in our record be Orpheus, whom famous Calliope,
> after bedding Thracian Oeagrus, bore, they tell us,
> hard by Pimpleia's high rocky lookout: Orpheus,
> who's said to have charmed unshiftable upland boulders
> and the flow of rivers with the sound of his music.
> Wild oaks still form a memorial to that singing:
> on the Thracian shore they flourish, marching in order,
> dense-packed, just as Orpheus long ago bewitched them
> with the sound of his lyre, brought them down from Pieria . . .[24]

Orpheus is the heroic chronicler of the journey: one office of poets is to keep the minutes of meetings. When, before the *Argo* sets out, Idas taunts Jason and priestly Idmon with cowardice, Orpheus steps in and sings a sort of Hesiodic theogony.[25] Orpheus, as the ship sets out on its journey, is cox, his rhythm determining the pace of the oarsmen.[26] He also plays a key role whenever loud or magical sounds are needed, or a prayer or ritual song. Such tasks also fell to poets. Thus when dawn is breaking and the *Argo* is entering the harbour of Thynias, a barren island, and the exhausted sailors tumble ashore full of grief,

> . . . there appeared before them Apollo, Leto's
> son, on his way back from Lykia to the swarming
> Hyperboreans; and golden, framing either cheek,
> the clustering curls outfloated as he strode.
> His left hand grasped a silver bow, and about his shoulders
> was slung a quiver of arrows, to hang at his back. His footsteps
> shook the whole island. Shock waves surged up the shore.

No one doubts the vision, but the crew—heroic as it is—does not know how to respond to this appearance of its great patron.

> When they saw him, helpless terror gripped them: not a single
> man dared look straight into the god's magnificent eyes,
> but they all stood staring groundward as he dwindled
> airborne into the distance, out over the sea.[27]

Orpheus restores their courage by providing a language in which to commemorate and invoke him. First they must sanctify the island, naming it after "Dawntime Apollo," since at dawn he had shown himself. They must build an altar and make sacrifice; and should the *Argo* return to Thessaly in one piece, they must promise a much greater sacrifice, with libations and this prayer: "Be gracious, O Lord, be gracious, you who were manifest to us."

The crew obeys, and when the altar is complete and the sacrifice has been offered, Orpheus accompanies their chanting on his Thracian lyre, until his voice emerges singly from the chorus, telling an ancient story:

> of how once, below Parnassus' rocky scarp, Apollo,
> while still a beardless youth, rejoicing in his tresses,
> slew with his bow the monstrous beast Delphynes . . .[28]

The mountain nymphs cheer him as he sings, calling him "healer," a word which becomes Orpheus' epithet. His words are fraught with a unique power and magic.

Orpheus sings. He sings at the ill-fated marriage of Jason and Medea; he sings to distract his shipmates from the irresistible lure of the Sirens onto the rocks; he sings to conjure water from the Hesperides.

The voyage of the *Argo* and the adventures of Jason and his crew were common knowledge to the heroes of Troy. Homer takes it for granted that his audience will know them, and alludes casually to the stories. The Argonauts were the first heroes; their adventures defined types of heroism, the mystery of journeys beyond the edges of known maps and the known world, from the Aegean to the Propontis to the Black Sea and then past coasts that even modern cartographers have not rediscovered, along the edge of Ocean, and back into the Sea of Sardinia, the Ausonian and Libyan Seas, the Ionian Gulf, until at last the ship returned to Pagasai and Iolkos, south of Mounts Olympus and Ossa, due west of Pelion.

Orpheus, whose birth, life and death were claimed by many places (he may have lived beside the Hellespont, in the land of Cicones, in western Thrace near the rivers Axius [Vardar] and Strymon [Struma]),[29] saw the whole of the known world and much of the world that remains unknown—not only the kingdom of the dead, but the East, which, pursued to its extreme, becomes the West. In his fantastic adventures, the world was very nearly round.

The *Argonautica* tells us much about the psychology of Jason and his gutsy bride, Medea; but of the other characters we gain glimpses at best, vivid but, like still photographs, we cannot splice them together into a moving image of a man in his day-to-day life or in his creative rapture—if it was rapture. Did Orpheus write his poems and commit them to memory? Or like his successor Homer, did he "write" with his voice on the white hearing of an audience? Since the only surviving Orphic poems are forgeries—are *probably* forgeries—this is a question we cannot answer. It seems unlikely that there would have been much space on the *Argo* for writing materials and parchments, however; and the maritime conditions would have been hostile to the survival of parchment and very hostile to papyrus.

Poems attributed to Orpheus were common in Greece in the sixth and fifth centuries BC. Much later, Pausanias writes: "Anyone who has already made a serious study of poetry knows the hymns of Orpheus are all extremely short, and even if they take them together not numerous. The Lykomidai know them and sing them at their mysteries. These beautiful verses are second only to the hymns of Homer, and even more honoured by the gods."[30] Pausanias' judgement of the poems is not generally corroborated. They were of dubious value because of the hermetic religious applications to which they were put. They came as close as anything in Greek literature to *scripture;* "Hieros Logos" is the title of the chief of the poems: "the sacred story." Scripture always seems to remove itself from literary evaluation, at least until belief is in retreat. Perhaps, too (we can judge only their absence, but that may tell us something), they were not very good as poetry, like the poorer hymns that congregations sing in church and are moved by because they know them by heart. Plato was familiar with them, quoting and alluding to them from time to time. Euripides slightly refers to Orpheus' writings in the *Hippolytus,* and the chorus in *Alcestis* longs for *sanides,* for remedy: "no charm of Thracian tablets which tuneful Orpheus carved out." Heracleidos of Pontus says that on Mount Haimon tablets exist with the writings of Orpheus carved on them.

This is more Orpheus as healer, mystic and magical fixer than poet. He is seen as founder of religious mysteries. Even Horace calls him *sacer interpresque deorum,* priest and interpreter of the gods, not a poet in the sense that Homer or Hesiod is. Yet when it came to the bookshop, he was there among the rest of them. Alexis,[31] the fourth-century comic poet, "describes a representative pile of books: 'Come and choose any book you like from here ... There is Orpheus, Hesiod, tragedies, Choirilos, Homer, Epicharmis' (*Athen.* 4 164)."[32]

In considering Orpheus, we cannot ignore Orphism altogether. It does flow from his real or imagined character and words. The first, most important element in all manifestations of Orphism is that it affirms the individual soul, and implicitly the individual conscience and will. Its rituals may be collective, but the consequences of them, of the purifications, the transformations, are strictly individual. Orphism evolves and changes, a reform movement, promising a defined kind of individually tailored salvation to Greeks whose experience of the city and of tradition was communal.[33] In Orphism the notion of the *person* takes shape, and it is this perception that touches Pindar in his celebration of the individual athlete and Plato in his exploration of the ways of the human mind.

There seem to have been as many forms of Orphism as there are of Islam and Christianity. Even a general account of the "beliefs" that define Orphism will be partial. In some ways the thrust of the religion is anti-Dionysian, seeking to channel ceremonial excesses into forms and rituals effective and transcendent; Orpheus preaches, or his followers do, not a new but a modified religion. His mystical interest in Apollo, and Apollo's manifest interest in him, make him a point of synthesis between opposing cults. To the Thracian, before the time of Homer, he seems to promise something eastern: the human soul as immortal and divine, and immortality to be achieved by acts of will—discipline, ritual and moral purity. He spiritualises the primitively pagan, he channels primal energies into ceremonial and creative forms.

It is hard to summarise the underlying theology of Orphism. The seemingly abstract "principle" of Time is at the origin of all things. Time formed an egg. The gods emerged from it. Zeus and Persephone conceived a son, Dionysus-Zagreus, who was torn to pieces by Titans who, in a bloody sacrament, devoured his limbs. Athena brought his heart to Zeus, and from the heart emerged the new Dionysus. With his lightning bolts Zeus incinerated the Titans. From their ashes, or the smoke that rose from their pyre, man was formed. The ashes and smoke, and therefore man himself, possess traces of soul because of Dionysus-Zagreus, consumed and digested into the Titans' physical bodies. Thus man is residually divine, though given the rest of the ash and smoke, largely an enemy of the divine, as the Titans were.

Some versions of Orphism teach transmigration of souls, retribution in future life, and the eventual release of man from his Titanic legacy if he observes strict purity in action, diet and ritual. Among the earliest surviving evidence of Orphic practice in the fifth century BC is Herodotus' reference to a prejudice against introducing wool items into temples or burials and against eating animal flesh. Human and other blood sacrifices were also proscribed.

Aspects of Orphism remind us of Christian doctrines and heresies. Sacrifice and transformation are at its heart. Manicheism, formulated in the third century AD and proposing the co-eternity of Satan with God, is uncannily Orphic in several ways. It is not surprising that it was in the early Christian era that the Orphic texts which survive were collected and, perhaps, composed, though Orphism itself probably came into its own in the sixth century BC and had become a sect and set of superstitions a century later.

Pausanias reports that there were statues and images of Orpheus all over Greece. Plutarch speaks of a *xoanon*[34] of Orpheus in Macedonia made of cypress-wood. A *xoanon* was often placed in inaccessible, even hidden, places, an idol not for worship but for the god or demi-god himself; magical in intention, it was not meant to be seen but to *do* something.

Orpheus the man, the god, giver of the Promethean gift of selfhood; and Orpheus the false god, enemy of the city, destroyer of pleasure in the here-and-now, thwarter of natural instinct, perverter of the natural order, breaker of taboos . . . How can there be such confusion, disagreement, such belief and disbelief, around one figure? It is in large part a problem of transmission. Orpheus: the name itself imparts authority because he is the hero with the harp, the brave heart who can also sing. He has seen more than any man can see and done more than any man can do. In order to legitimise a ritual, a religious instinct or deceit, appropriating his name, bending his meanings, was a clever strategy. Christ's name has similarly been taken in vain. The more Orpheus was invoked, the less clever the strategy became: the paler his poems, his meanings and his legacy. Aristotle says Orpheus never existed. Homer makes no mention of him, though he is supposed to predate the blind poet. Herodotus makes no mention of him either; unsurprisingly, Aristotle omits him altogether from the *Poetics*. The poems assigned to him were apocryphal, Aristotle believed, and Onomacritos was not only a textual adjuster or partial forger but, in his view, the author himself.

Onomacritos. At this point we must meet a villain. His villainy landed him in great trouble and blurred the name of Orpheus in aftertime. Here is how Herodotus reports his unmasking: "Onomacritos was banished from Athens by Hipparchus, the son of Pisistratus, because he foisted onto the writings of Musaeus a prophecy that the islands which lie off Lemnos would one day disappear in the sea. Lasus of Hermione caught him in the act of so doing. For this cause Hipparchus banished him, though till then they had been the closest of friends."[35] And it was not only Musaeus he is said to have tampered with, but Orpheus too, and he may even have had a hand in retouching Homer.

Who did write the Orphic poems that Plato talks about as if they were by Orpheus? Some South Italian devotee centuries later, hiding his light under the bushel of a sacred name? Pythagoras is said to have circulated his own poems under Orpheus' name.[36] But the prime suspicion falls on Ono-macritos. He was a flatterer. If a rich or powerful family wanted to legitimise itself, it could pay an editor-scribe like Onomacritos to insert matter into a poem or record which tied that family into the world of the heroes or, more materially, gave them claims on property held by others or secured illicitly from others. If a tyrant wanted to justify an action, the editor-scribe could be suborned to add a line to something as sacred as Homer. Pisistratos was not above such subterfuge. Written records proved mutable, but their authority remained more or less intact until the forger was apprehended, as Onomacritos was.[37]

The sixth-century BC poet Ibycus is the first to name Orpheus. He calls
him *Onomakluton Orfen*. Guthrie declares that, from his first mention, Orpheus was *famous*. But Ibycus may have had an ironic intent: not only *famous
Orpheus* but—by extension, Onomacritos' Orpheus, punning on the first
three syllables of Onomacritos' name. Yet Onomacritos could not erase,
through his fictions, if they were his (and if they were fictions), the durable
legacy or the fame of Orpheus.

Still, it must be confessed that we cannot point to a single line of verse or
prose that is undenibly by Orpheus. Pausanias names five major early hymn
writers: Homer, Olen,[38] Pamphos,[39] Musaeus[40] and Orpheus. We cannot
point to a single line that is uncontestably by any one of them. Eighty-seven
"hymns" to various gods survive under Orpheus' name. These are neo-
Platonist efforts, assembled and perhaps even composed early in the Christian era. They give us an opportunity to look at the hymn genre, so
important a form in the early period of Greek poetry and so crucial as a
source of allusion and resonance to later poets. The Orphic hymns are in
not very subtle hexameters (though Greek hymns are found in a variety of
metres and also in prose). A hymn is a praise poem, often with religious intent. It may have served as a first course in the feast of epic recitations, and
perhaps also as a dessert.

The most famous Greek hymns are those attributed to Homer. They
provided models for Pindar, Callimachus and others. Charles Boer, who
translates them over-fancifully in formal terms,[41] tells us in an afterword
that the word *hymn* is of eastern derivation and the Greek word *hymnos* relates to the word for *woven* or *spun*. Bacchylides in Ode V, line 8, speaks of
"weaving a hymn." Homer (*Iliad* III, line 212) "speaks of Menelaus and
Odysseus as having 'spun' (*hyphainon*) 'their words and their counsels.'"
Boer says: "in its primal sense, a hymn was thought of as what results when
you intertwine speech with rhythm and song. And it is in this sense precisely
that the word 'hymn' appears in its oldest recorded usage, in the *Odyssey*
(VIII, 429) when Alcinoos invites Odysseus to 'enjoy dinner and listen to
the spinning of a yarn' (*aoides hymnon*)."[42] Boer's "yarn" is an English rather
than a Greek figure of speech.

Is there an Orphic manner, a characteristic style? The language of the
surviving hymns makes them peculiarly rebarbative as poetry. Introducing
his translations in the late eighteenth century, Thomas Taylor declared,
"Thus most of the compound epithets of which the following Hymns
chiefly consist, though very beautiful in the Greek language, yet, when literally translated into ours, lose all their propriety and force. In their native
tongue, as in a prolific soil, they diffuse their sweets with full-blown elegance, but shrink like the sensitive plant at the touch of the verbal critic, or
the close translator. He who would preserve their philosophical beauties,

and exhibit them to others in a different language, must expand their elegance, by the supervening and enlivening rays of the philosophic fire; and, by the powerful breath of genius, scatter abroad their latent but copious sweets."[43]

There is something cloyingly Palgravian about the elaborate conceit of the translator, a manner in keeping with the baroquery of the hymns, where verbal thickness and opacity must pass for depth of thought and symbol. Certainly every detail in the poems requires symbolic reading, and since there is no dictionary of symbols to which we can refer, an excess of interpretative activity, and an excess of freedom, is allowed.[44] The poems can come to mean whatever the explainer wants them to. A person or a god is generally addressed, but not as in a prayer; his or her nature is blurred in the elaborate mirror of the forger's language. Here is an initiation hymn to Hecate, which, like the other hymns, is prefaced by a note of the appropriate incense to be burned during the recitation:

> Hecate, lady of the path, I conjure you, lovely mistress of the trivium,[45]
> Of heaven and underworld, of sea, of the saffron gown,
> Of the grave, celebrant of Dionysus' mysteries among dead souls,
> Perses' child, happy alone, rejoicing among the untamed creatures,
> At home in the midnight, lady of hounds, unconquerable queen,
> Of the beasts' cry, of the ungirded robe, of the ravishing form,
> Herder of livestock, you the guardian of the doors of all the world, lady,
> Mistress betrothed who nourish the young, who wander the ridges,
> Be present, I beg, at our sacred rites, rites of passage,
> Giving your grace, gracious lady, to the young oxherd . . .

Voluminous explanatory notes to a poem of this size deal with untranslatable phrases, the connections each epithet attempts to make with other gods, other areas of the fluid theology that follows from the very instability of myth. Thomas Taylor speaks of "philosophical mythology," as though the argument in early philosophy can be conducted solely through narrative, symbol and metaphor.

All the documents and artefacts that relate to the historical Orpheus are late and wildly out of "historical" range. Even though Aristotle insists that Orpheus never existed, tentative details can be fitted together. How close can they take us to his flickering presence? "It is no mere frivolity," says W. K. C. Guthrie, "to remind ourselves that in Orpheus we are dealing with someone who has many of the qualities of the Snark and one important point of resemblance to the Cheshire Cat."[46] Part of the problem is that the accounts we have of the poet differ so fundamentally. Orpheus' name became a kind of candle drawing the forger moths, who singed their wings there and perished; but also thinkers who wanted their ideas to be taken seriously and immolated themselves in the interests of illumination. Orpheus is a flame; or Orpheus is a tribe of writers anonymising themselves in order to grace their words with the authority of the Thracian bard.

More schematically, Orpheus is, as Marsilio Ficino suggested in the fifteenth century, the third in the six steps to theological wisdom which begin in Zoroaster, "the greatest of the Magi," and—via Hermes Trismegistus, Orpheus, Aglaophamus and Pythagoras—leads to Plato, in whose writings all wisdom is distilled.[47] For Apollinaire, he "invented all the sciences and all the arts. Rooted in magic, he inferred the future and predicted the coming of the Saviour, Christ."[48]

From our point of view, he is at least the *first* poet.

II

The Legend Poets

... O had I lived when song was great
  In days of old Amphion,
And ta'en my fiddle to the gate,
  Nor cared for seed or scion!
And had I lived when song was great,
  And legs of trees were limber,
And ta'en my fiddle to the gate,
  And fiddled in the timber!

ALFRED, LORD TENNYSON,
"Amphion"

 A first-century Roman acquired an ancient statue of the comic poet Poseidippus (c. 316–250 BC).[1] He had a local craftsman resculpt it into—or after—his own face and form, appropriating the features but not the identity of the poet. As in palimpsests, the earlier identity shows through in a shadowy way. Poseidippus being a comic poet, it is appropriate that his individual identity should be retained not in the bold nose nor in the ambiguous restraint of the expression (if we see the poet, he seems to be holding back a guffaw; if we see the Roman, he looks as if he is controlling wind), but in the retention of an unkempt emblematic detail. "The careless sculptor who reworked the poet's head into that of the Roman left a few locks of Poseidippus' hair on the nape of the neck, and those locks enabled Fittschen to recognise the true Poseidippus in a previously anonymous portrait type."[2] Fittschen, an admirable Poirot when it comes to such sculptural identity parades, is a patient man who, in discovering what appears to be an actual identity, also illuminates the ways in which identities are overlaid, obscured, but never entirely lost.

Never entirely found, either. There is not very much to go on when we come to Poseidippus, a stone shadow. In stone, shadows possess a vivid, almost human presence, displacing more or less the same volume of air that we do; but they are frustratingly mute. We read their white faces and it is hard to say for sure even what colour the skin would have been, and the hair. A tubbiness in Poseidippus' cheeks suggests—as do the chefs in his plays—that he ate well and would have been a ruddy sort, a Dionysian; his small boyish—girlish?—mouth suggests a certain delicacy, though not of constitution. Black hair, of course. Or grey? The statue is good, but for our purposes little better than a ghost, a Greek ghost carrying a Roman passenger.

We have a clearer and more complex image of some of the earliest Greek poets, four and more centuries Poseidippus' seniors, than we do of him, even though we can see the whites of his eyes. They survive as legends only, with at best a handful of attributable fragments of verse. As legends they are complicated, inconsistent, memory rather than stone palimpsests, but they tell us something of the kinds of regard in which poets were held, their relationship with the gods and the rulers of the day, their Odyssean wiliness in getting the better of their foes, and the simple power of their language to enchant, memorialise and condemn.

In the last chapter we met Linos, possibly Orpheus' brother, some say a victim of the infant Heracles, his name the refrain of a holy chant. He has had more parents, divine and human, attributed to him than almost any other poet in history. This befits the greatest musician who ever lived, whom Apollo, jealous of his divine prerogatives, could not tolerate alive. There wasn't room in Greece for both of them. Diodorus Siculus says Linos actually invented melody and rhythm. On Mount Helicon, Pausanias says, if you drew near the Grove of the Muses, you would find a little artificial cave in which Linos' likeness was carved on a wall. Sacrifices were made to him, before the worshippers proceeded into the Grove and paid their respects to the Muses themselves.

We might linger, if there were more to linger over, in the company of Sacadas of Argos. Pindar's poem about him, mentioned in Pausanias, has not survived. He is said to have composed, in the early seventh century, the first version of the Delphic tune. He was a famous Doric *aulos*-player.[3] "His Pythian tune was a bare, early version, probably for dancing, of the fight of Apollo with the dragon, the Python of Delphi," Peter Levi says. "An elaborate and fascinating later version which included trumpets and fifes and imitated the whizzing of arrows and the god's triumphal procession is described by Strabo (9, 3, 10). Sacadas' tune already had five movements, called introduction, trial, challenge, iambic and dactylic, and pipes."

Of these virtually poetryless ur-Homers, the most charmed and charming is Arion, after whom the constellation of the lyre is named. Arion, Robert Graves tells us, means "lofty native." He was lofty by birth, his father being no less a figure than the sea god Poseidon. A fragment of his hymn to Poseidon survives. We know he sang effectively to the waters and the creatures of the deep, and the sea succoured him.

His mother was a nymph called Oneaea—five vowels and one gentle consonant. Like the musical revolutionary Terpander,[4] who reinvented music and played his changes in ancient Sparta, Arion was a native of the poetry-nurturing island of Lesbos. He was born at Methymna (modern Mithimna) on the northern shore, facing to the west. It was near here that the celebrated Vine of Lesbos grew.

For the Russian poet Alexander Pushkir
storm-tossed sailor whose strength as mu
the storm. Seamus Heaney gives Pushkin th

> . . . The helmsman and the s
> Only I, still singing, washed
> Ashore by the long sea-swell,
> A mystery to my poet self,
> And safe and sound beneath a
> Have spread my wet clothes in

"The Corinth
took him up
ashore, pr
to him
ver

24

There was much more to him than that, however. The storm was moral, not meteorological, and the poet's survival a triumph of his art. For Arion, like Orpheus, knew how to talk to the creatures. His singing was on the side of nature and justice, over against the corrupted motives of men, and the swiftest way to truth was on a dolphin's back.

Herodotus tells the story. In the time of Periander, son of Cypselus, tyrant of Corinth and one of the legendary Seven Sages, "a very wonderful thing is said to have happened. The Corinthians and the Lesbians . . . relate that Arion of Methymna, who as a player on the harp was second to no man living at that time, and who was, so far as we know, the first to invent the dithyrambic measure, to give it its name, and to recite in it at Corinth, was carried to Taenarum on the back of a dolphin."

"He had lived for years in Corinth at the court of Periander when a longing came upon him to sail to Italy and Sicily." Graves says that he wanted to go "to compete in a musical festival." If so, he picked up all the prizes: "Having made rich profits in those parts, he wanted to recross the seas to Corinth. He hired a vessel, the crew of which were Corinthians, thinking that there was no people in whom he could more safely trust, and set sail from Tarentum. The sailors, however, when they reached the open sea, plotted to throw him overboard and seize his wealth. Discovering their plan, he fell on his knees, begging them to spare his life and offering them his money. But they refused and told him either to kill himself outright, if he wanted a grave on the dry land, or immediately to leap overboard into the sea."

A man waiting execution is permitted a final cigarette. Arion was allowed a final performance. He begged them "to let him climb to the quarter-deck, and there to play and sing," promising that as soon as he had finished he would jump from their treacherous ship into the waves. "Delighted at the prospect of hearing the best musician in the world, they agreed and withdrew from the stern to the middle of the vessel. Arion decked himself in the full regalia of his calling, took up his harp, and standing on the quarter-deck, chanted the Orthian. His music ended, he did as he had promised and flung himself, fully attired, headlong into the sea.

ans sailed on to Corinth. As for Arion, a dolphin, they say,
on his back and carried him to Taenarum. There he went
ceeding to Corinth in his costume, and told what had been done
Periander disbelieved the story and put Arion under arrest to pre-
t his leaving Corinth, while he anxiously awaited the mariners' return.

"As soon as they arrived, he summoned them and asked if they could give him news of Arion. They replied that he was alive and well in Italy, that they had left him at Tarentum, where he was thriving. Then Arion appeared before them, just as he was when he jumped from the vessel. The men, astonished and found out in their lie, could not deny their guilt . . . There is to this day at Taenarum an offering of Arion's at the shrine: a small figure in bronze, representing a man seated upon a dolphin."

Arion, as Herodotus says, may have invented the Dionysiac dithyramb, a vigorous answer to the univocal monody of, say, the Song of Linos, though the earliest surviving dithyrambs are attributed to Archilochus. In any event, in Corinth at the beginning of the sixth century BC, Arion perhaps brought into these musical celebrations the circular chorus, moving around an altar rather than processing. He might require the chorus to sing a prosodically regular poem, written or conceived in advance (not formulaic or aleatoric), and concentrating on a definite subject. The chorus would be accompanied by an *aulos*. Michael Grant is more categorical: Arion "converted" the dithyrambs "into swiftly moving, exciting hymns, sung and danced by a chorus of fifty boys wearing elaborate satyr-like costumes and impersonating their parts with mimetic gestures."[6] Bowra turns it the other way round: "He seems to have found in existence an improvised, ecstatic song to Dionysus and to have transformed it into a formal, choral hymn attached to definite festivals and accompanied by regular dancing."[7]

The dithyramb developed fully in Athens under Pisistratus and his sons, in connection with Dionysian festivals, and became a primary vehicle for narrative in lyric form. It was also adapted for other festivals, including—paradoxically—Apollo's. In 509 BC there was a celebrated dithyrambic contest in Athens and the successful chorus, hugely celebrated, erected a commemorative tripod. This was a forerunner of later competitions, a kind of Eurovision Dithyramb Contest.

Originally dithyramb was a form used in drunken (Dionysian) revelry. In the hands of a fine poet, form, repetition, measure and melody are drawn from drunkenness: the lyric itself is born out of dithyramb.[8] And was Arion the first to speak as well as write and sing verse? He may have invented *tragikos tropos,* the musical mode later adapted to dramatic tragedy. Sage Solon says so. Is Arion at two removes the grandfather of dramatic verse?[9] Arion's legacy is palpable in the work of all the choral poets.

What happened to the dolphin? Arion was not the last man to be saved in this way, but his dolphin was royally rewarded. It accompanied the poet to court (no one is quite clear in what form), and there eventually it died, after a life of tremendous luxury. Arion gave it a memorable funeral. No doubt one day archaeologists will find its aquarium in Corinth, and its tomb. No one is certain of the dolphin's name.

Arion at Periander's court may have studied and worked with the poet Alcman, some of whose poetry does survive, and who has a chapter of his own with more history but no less invention in it.

Amphion's name means "native of two lands."[10] Tradition has it that he re-built Cadmeia, charming the stones with his lyre (a gift of the Muses them-selves, or else of Hermes) and harmoniously drawing them together into temples and stoas and houses and paved streets. Orpheus moved animals and trees, but Amphion's music managed to find heart and motion even in the inanimate.

His father was Zeus. On one of his amorous escapades he seduced An-tiope, daughter of Nycteus or, according to Homer, Asopos. Pregnant, she fled and married the king of Sicyon; there was then a war against her people and her father was killed. Her uncle prevailed against the Sicyon king, slew him and brought her back. She gave birth to twins, Amphion and Zethus, and Uncle Lycus had the little bastards abandoned to the elements on the side of Mount Cithaeron (with its Dionysian connections). Back in Cad-meia Antiope was cruelly treated by her aunt Dirce, but finally escaped and found out the little hovel where her children, rescued by a passing shepherd and reared by him, now lived. They thought Antiope was a fleeing slave and would not give her hearth room, and then Dirce in a frenzy caught up with her and dragged her away.

The shepherd recognised her as their mother. He warned them that they would be pursued forever unless they came to her assistance, and so they followed after and eventually freed their mama, tying Dirce by the hair to the horns of a bull. She did not survive. Where her inert body was hurled down, a spring welled up. She was, after all, a servant of Dionysus.

Cadmus had built the upper city of Cadmeia. Amphion and his twin built the lower part, having expelled the bad king Laius. Zethus chided his brother for playing the lyre all the time, but while Zethus had to wrestle his stones into place, Amphion's assembled like beads on a string or birds on a branch, without any effort beyond melody. As Pound's Propertius says,

> And Citharaon shook up the rocks of Thebes
> and danced them into a bulwark at his pleasure . . .[11]

Zethus married Thebe and the city was renamed Thebes after her. Am-phion married Niobe, a spirited woman whose sharp tongue led to divine revenges and all but two of whose children, seven sons and seven daughters, were killed by the gods. She made fun of Leto, mother of only two, those two being effeminate Apollo and butch, burly Artemis, whose arrows slew Niobe's "surplus" children. No wonder her name became synonymous with tears. And Amphion, too, had a troubled later life, but this native of two lands, Sicyon and Thebes, was a mighty poet, having been able with his three-stringed lyre, at Hermes' behest, to build a city out of ceremonial song.

Peter Levi says, "Musaeus is a legendary half-divine poet." *Another* one, but again quite different. In the Renaissance he was thought to have pre-dated Homer. Now we are wiser: Homer may not have existed at all, and even so, Musaeus was at least two and perhaps four centuries his hypothetical junior. Pausanias says that "Musaeus sings in his poem, if he really *wrote* [my italics] it, how Triptolemos is the child of Ocean and the Earth, while Orpheus sings, though the poem looks spurious to me, that the father of Eubouleus and Triptolemos was called Dysaules, and Demeter granted them the sowing of crops because they brought news of her daughter."[12] As far as Pausanias was concerned, poets wrote and then sang their poems, and this went as much for the legendary and half-known poets as for those whose identities were fully attested to in history. Musaeus is described in some places as the *son* of Orpheus.

Like Homer's poems, his were tampered with. They had the kind of spurious legitimacy and authority that made them politically useful, especially in relation to the Persian incursions. Herodotus reports that the prime culprit in the act of forgery was Onomacritos. "The Pisistratidae had previously been at enmity with [Onomacritos] . . . He was banished from Athens by Hipparchus, the son of Pisistratus, because he foisted into the writings of Musaeus a prophecy that the islands which lie off Lemnos would one day disappear in the sea."[13] Musaeus was seen as a prophet, as in the following lines composed before Athens suffered at Aigospotamoi:

> A raging storm will burst over Athens:
> Bad leaders, but there will be one solace:
> The city won't lie down but get its own back.[14]

Herodotus too calls Musaeus a prophet, writing: "As soon as the sea-fight was ended, the Greeks drew together to Salamis all the wrecks that were to be found in that quarter, and prepared themselves for another engagement, supposing that the king would renew the fight with the vessels which still remained to him. Many of the wrecks had been carried away by a westerly wind to the coast of Attica, where they were thrown upon the strip of shore called Colias. Thus not only were the prophecies of Bacis and Musaeus concerning this battle fulfilled completely, but likewise, by the place to which the wrecks were drifted, the prediction of Lysistratus, an Athenian soothsayer, uttered many years before these events, and quite forgotten at the time by all the Greeks, was fully accomplished."

Musaeus was depicted in art. Pausanias, describing the paintings in the Shrine of Wingless Victory in Athens, told how, "if you pass over the boy carrying water-jars and the wrestler Timainetos painted, you come to Musaeus. I have read a poem in which Musaeus was able to fly, by the gift of the north-east wind." But Pausanias adds, "I think Onomacritos wrote it; nothing of Musaeus exists for certain except the 'Hymn to Demeter' for the Lykomidai."[15] For certain? Not even that . . . Yet the poet flying—a brilliant power, rivalling that of Amphion to move stones and Orpheus to move trees!

He moved to Athens, and his house, or what was reputed to have been his house, was a sort of monument. Pausanias recalls, "When Demetrios had freed Athens from dictatorship, immediately after the flight of Lachares he kept control of Piraeus, and later after some military success he brought a garrison into the city itself, and fortified what they call the Museum. The Museum is a small hill opposite the akropolis, inside the ancient ring-wall, where they say Musaeus used to sing and died of old age and was buried; later a memorial was erected there for a Syrian."[16]

There are also echoes of the vanished Musaeus at Delphi. We turn once more to Pausanias.[17] There were singing contests at Delphi and many powerful performers won, but "Orpheus they say gave himself such an air of grandeur over the mysteries and was so generally conceited that he and Musaeus who imitated him in everything refused to be tested by musical competition."

From Pausanias we learn more.[18] At the start of time the Delphic oracle belonged to Earth, and Earth appointed Daphne to be prophetess. She was a nymph native to the mountain. "The Greeks have a poem called *Eumolpia*, which they attribute to Musaeus son of Antiophemos, that says Poseidon and Earth shared the oracle: Earth prophesied herself, and Poseidon's servant for the prophecies was Pyrcon." These are the verses:

> Earth then spoke wise words, and the man
> Who serves the mighty, the earth-quaking god,
> Pyrcon, spoke in chorus with her.

Another doubtful, but influential, attribution. Those who could speak for the ancient poets themselves acquired power. How much more those who spoke *as* them.

The very first of the eighty-eight surviving poems doubtfully attributed to Musaeus' teacher, or father, is "Orphic Hymn I: Orpheus pros Mousaion," or "Orpheus to Musaeus."

> Attend Musaeus to my sacred song,
> And learn what rites to sacrifice belong.
> Jove I invoke, the earth, and solar light,
> The moon's pure splendour, and the stars of night;
> Thee Neptune, ruler of the sea profound,
> Dark-hair'd, whose waves begirt the solid ground;
> Ceres abundant, and of lovely mien,
> And Proserpine infernal Pluto's queen . . .

It invokes the Orphic hierarchy and takes the form of a kind of ritual cate-chism, Orpheus instructing his spiritual acolyte. In 1792 Thomas Taylor translated the hymn into rather stiff but not inappropriate couplets. The poem is principally evocation, or conjuration, mentioning all the gods; but the pseudo-Orpheus lingers on one goddess in particular, and whereas others, even the most powerful, receive at most two or three lines, this one receives quite a run of verse:

> I call Einodian Hecate, lovely dame,
> Of earthly, wat'ry, and celestial frame,
> Sepulchral, in a saffron veil array'd,
> Pleas'd with dark ghosts that wander thro' the shade;
> Persian, unconquerable huntress hail!
> The world's key-bearer never doom'd to fail;
> On the rough rock to wander thee delights,
> Leader and nurse be present to our rites;
> Propitious grant our just desires success,
> Accept our homage, and the incense bless.

Taylor comments usefully on this poem as first in the Orphic remains. The immediate introduction to Musaeus, "the son of Orpheus, is, as Gesner ob-serves, a summary of the work . . . and the reader will please to observe through the whole of these Hymns, that the Orphic method of instruction consists in signifying divine concerns by symbols alone." This tells us why there is no elaborated, as it were *prose,* theology attached to Orphism, and why the poetic bias throughout the Greek period favours symbolic expres-sion. Taylor is compelled to talk in terms of a "philosophical mythology," a wonderful term that applies not only to the Greek Orphics but to our own Romantics and their direct and oblique heirs.

"Indeed nature herself," he remarks, "fabricating the images of intelligi-ble essences, and of ideas totally destitute of matter, pursues this design by many and various ways. For by parts she imitates things destitute of all parts, eternal natures by such as are temporal, intelligibles by sensibles, simple essences by such as are mixt, things void of quantity by dimensions, and things stable by unceasing mutations: all which she endeavours to express as much as she is able, and as much as the aptitude of appearances will permit." Not only are metaphor, simile and symbol a way of speaking; they are a mode of true vision. "Now the authors of fables, having perceived this proceeding of nature, by inventing resemblances and images of divine concerns in their verses, imitated the exalted power of exemplars by contrary and most remote adumbrations: that is, by shadowing forth the excellency of the nature of the Gods by preternatural concerns: a power more divine than all reason, by such as are irrational: a beauty superior to all that is corporeal by things apparently base, and by this means placed before our eyes the excellence of divinity, which far exceeds all that can possibly be invented or said." It is the language of the late eighteenth century, but it touches a profound truth of pre-Hellenic poetry. Taylor may be a little too drawn to the occult, as so many were at the exhausted end of the eighteenth century; but his credulousness lets him see further than a sceptic could.

Herodotus is sceptical. He knows the real world has claims that run deeper than those of the ceremonial world; he can if necessary break through hierarchy and recast "respect" in a less hidebound, more necessary spirit. "As for the oracle of which Mardonius spoke, and which he referred to the Persians, it did not, I am well assured, mean them, but the Illyrians and the Enchelean host. There are, however, some verses of Bacis which did speak of this battle:

> By Thermodon's stream, and the grass-clad banks of Asopus,
> See where gather the Grecians, and hark to the foreigners' war-shout—
> There in death shall lie, ere fate or Lachesis doomed him,
> Many a bow-bearing Mede, when the day of calamity cometh.

These verses, and some others like them which Musaeus wrote, referred, I well know, to the Persians. The river Thermodon flows between Tanagra and Glisas."[19]

Thamyris was blinded and deprived of his musical and singing gift because he competed with the Muses and lost. "The men of Pylos and Arene, and Thryum where is the ford of the river Alpheus; strong Aipy, Cyparisseis, and Amphigenea; Pteleum, Helos, and Dorium, where the Muses met Thamyris, and stilled his minstrelsy for ever. He was returning from Oechalia, where Eurytus lived and reigned, and boasted that he would surpass even the Muses, daughters of aegis-bearing Jove, if they should sing against him; whereon they were angry, and maimed him. They robbed him of his divine power of song, and thenceforth he could strike the lyre no more."[20]

The legend poets, from Orpheus on, generally meet a sticky end.

III

Homer

Sleepless. Homer. Billowing sails.
I have read half way through the catalogue
Of ships, that spreading shoal, that flock of cranes
Once clouding the heavens above Hellas.

Birdlike, crossing coasts and borders to
Strange lands (the brows of kings wet with the spume
Of gods) where are you sailing to? With no bright Helen,
What would Troy mean to you, you men of Greece?

Love moves the sea, moves Homer, but to which
Ought I to listen now? Homer's voice is silence
While the black sea, orator, surf and thunder
Breaks and breaks on my pillow, like a pulse.

OSIP MANDELSTAM, "Stone 78" (1915)

 ". . . I wish you wouldn't keep appearing and vanishing so suddenly: you make one quite giddy," Alice declares.[1] "All right," says the Cheshire Cat; and this time "it vanished quite slowly, beginning with the end of the tail, and ending with the grin, which remained some time after the rest of it had gone." (The cat, we note, is an "it," not a "he.") "Well!" Alice reflects, "I've often seen a cat without a grin, but a grin without a cat! It's the most curious thing I ever saw in all my life!"

Over time Homer, "the blind poet with seven birthplaces,"[2] has appeared, multiplied identities, then vanished like the Cat. He was erased almost completely for a spell in a compelling spate of scholarship into "oral traditions" in the middle of the twentieth century. Now he, she, or it is emerging again, ghostly and attenuated and hedged around with postmodern quotation marks and disclaimers, but gaining a little in solidity with each new book and scholarly paper. The Cat seems to be materialising around the grin once more. We can almost see him as he was imagined more than two and half millennia ago, a travelling rhapsode entertaining and instructing now the powerful and wealthy, now humble men: "Sitting there in the tanner's yard, Homer recited his poetry to them, the *Expedition of Amphiaraus to Thebes* and the *Hymns to the Gods* composed by him."[3] Except that modern scholars are agreed that the Homer who—perhaps—composed the *Iliad* and—or—the *Odyssey* was the author neither of the *Expedition* nor of the *Hymns* that bear his name.

Why are readers so very eager to find out who Homer was, so reluctant to consider the possibility that the epics assigned to his name were not "composed" as other poems are? There is certainly a wonderful *adequacy* about what comes from the poems themselves. Theocritus says, "Homer is enough for everybody," but he doesn't quite mean it.[4] When we possess the poems, why have critics for millennia tried to track down the poet, a task recognised as impossible even by those who undertake it? We *know* nothing, but there is a considerable amount of nothing that we know.

Some modern scholars would sweep it all away: "There is, in my view, no point in searching for 'Homer' by the marshlight of a pocket biography of the author. Even if this were a good way of approaching literature in general, we simply do not have the material."[5] Such categorical purism—we cannot know and therefore we waste time in considering—impoverishes our reading in another sense. Each life of Homer tells us something about changing attitudes to the poet and the poems; those attitudes tell us something about the work and the poet himself. Factual veracity apart (and what biography can be precise about the *content* of any fact and its relation to the *content* of other facts?), the apocryphal lives tell us critical truths about the poems' place in cultural hierarchies as they developed, what they meant, what they did. In the fragments of the *Margites,* implausibly attributed to Homer, a poet writes: "There came to Colophon an old man and divine singer, a servant of the Muses and of far-shooting Apollo. In his dear hands he held a sweet-toned lyre." One word here is true: "dear," a true response. To say that we can know nothing of the poet's life is undeniable; but through the lives and the poems ancient readers inferred a great deal about their poet's nature and their own. Modern readers should not allow themselves to be so impoverished by a pragmatic sense of historical fact as to miss out on the construction and reconstruction of Homer's lives.

An initial search must be through the poems themselves, where we look for evidence of "the person of Homer." There is an ancient adage: *Homeron ex Homerou saphenizein:* "You ought to read Homer by his own light." In *Works and Days* Hesiod stands up, identifying himself and his situation in some detail. Not so Homer. There is an occasional shadow grin: bards appear in the poems (are they Homer? are they like Homer?). There are moments of opinion and point of view which cannot be assigned to any one of the many speakers in the poems; but can they be assigned to an author? There is nothing actually solid to get hold of, except at one point in the apocryphal "Hymn to Delian Apollo" where the "I" declares:

> And you, O Delian virgins, do me grace,
> When any stranger of our earthy race
> Whose restless life affliction hath in chase,

> Shall hither come and question you: "Who is,
> To your chaste ears, of choicest faculties
> In sacred poesie, and with most right
> Is author of your absolut'st delight?"
> Ye shall yourselves do all the right ye can
> To answer for our name: "The sightless man
> Of stony Chios. All whose poems shall
> In all last ages stand for capital."[6]

No false modesty or demurring here. This "I," in George Chapman's version, is sure of his mighty pre-eminence. He will "propagate mine own precedency" wherever there are "well-built cities" or "human conversation is held dear." The poem will thrive in an urban world, those city-states where many people live, solid communities with buildings made of wood and stone, in which there is leisure for human conversation and a sense of its value. The *polis,* or city-state, is a necessary institution for the Homeric rhapsode; within it, even if the economic base remains largely agricultural, the way of life is urban, the citizen travels out in the day to manage his slaves and work his land, and returns at evening to be a town-dweller.

In the eighth century BC communities gathered around strong lords, the *basilees*.[7] A century later and there were in various parts of Greece communities which, though not democratic, had a sense of mutual objectives which included self-preservation and the development of those common customs which would in retrospect be described as a culture. The little cities were surrounded by supporting fields and pastures. Laws were written down.

Countrymen became poli-tical, polis-beings. The focus of public, and therefore poetic, life was the *agora,* often crowded with statues of notables and memorials to legendary and mythical events. In the agora (from the verb *ageirein,* to assemble) was "the *prytaneion,* the *bouleuterion,* the court of justice and one or more temples; it was also used for public meetings and games." Burckhardt stresses how "even the Achaean camp before Troy had its agora with altars to the gods, where justice was meted out."[8] And yet, in Homer there is "no trace of the dissembling that is the consequence of social life."[9] The city is where the poems find patrons, are edited, performed, and yet it in no way compromises or attenuates the innocence of imagination that shaped them.

The Homer of the "Hymn to Delian Apollo" is unlikely to be the same man who, a couple of centuries earlier, composed or collated or recited the two epics on which our poetic tradition is itself founded. Some of the human traits the hymn evokes adhere to the popular sense of Homer: he is blind (like Demodocus,[10] the bard in the *Odyssey*), he is matchless and proud (like Odysseus himself, who sings false and true deeds in the courts and farmyards that he visits). Yet nothing here firmly connects the poet of Chios with the poet of the epics. This makes him rather an ideal poet from Aristotle's point of view: "Homer, admirable in all respects, has the special merit of being the only poet who rightly appreciates the part he should take himself. The poet should speak as little as possible in his own person, for it is not this that makes him an imitator. Other poets appear themselves upon the scene throughout, and imitate but little and rarely. Homer, after a few prefatory words, at once brings in a man, or woman, or other personage; none of them wanting in characteristic qualities, but each with a character of his own."[11] He remains in effect anonymous. Indeed, he may be worse than anonymous: conceivably an authoring, even a collating, individual we might call Homer never existed at all, though the poems and their attribution survive.

No one spoke the mixture of dialects in which "his" epics are composed; there are numerous incongruities and anachronisms within the narratives; there are as many fundamental differences as similarities between the forms and techniques of the *Iliad* and the *Odyssey*. Most scholars are now agreed that the Homeric Hymns come from a variety of periods and therefore a variety of authors: none belongs by rights to him. The Homeric apocrypha, too, seems sometimes to parody, sometimes to contradict the voice and values of the two great epics.

After examining the poems and finding limited information there, critics turn to the biographies of Homer. Here are copious pickings. The poet fell two lives short of being a cat: seven classical lives survive in part or in whole, each giving a rather different inflection to the poet, his actual name, place of birth, parentage, period. The most classical of nineteenth-century English poets, Walter Savage Landor, remarked: "Some tell us there were twenty Homers; some deny that there was ever one. It were idle and foolish to shake the contents of a vase, in order to let them settle at last. We are perpetually labouring to destroy our delights, our composure, our devotion to superior power. Of all the animals on earth we least know what is good for us. My opinion is, that what is best for us is our admiration of good. No man living venerates Homer more than I do." Landor seems to say we do better to regard what we have and shy away from unverifiable speculation. Biography, as opposed to hagiography, can diminish its subject.

If a poet called, or referred to as, Homer ever lived, we will want to know about the life because it will tell us something of the poetic intention, the formal and thematic choices made, the emphases of class and tone. Until the late eighteenth century it was a given that the same author composed the *Iliad,* the *Odyssey,* the *Hymns* and much else that survives as fragment or rumour. Thucydides adduced, without doubting its attribution, the "Hymn to Apollo." Longinus believed that the *Odyssey* was inferior to the *Iliad.* Neither man doubted Homer's existence. Indeed, no one assumed his non-existence. Antiquity believed in him; doubt is a modern, Enlighten-ment phenomenon, and total erasure was a programme that began in the twentieth century.

Confusion begins before the beginning of the story. Two ancient biogra-phers declare without a grain of doubt that Homer's father was Maeon, an-other says Meles (who is also a river: divine parentage). Other candidates are Mnesagoras, a merchant-trader called Daëmon, and Thamyras. In Egypt it was thought that a priest-scribe by the name of Menemachus begat him. The most suggestive and convenient candidate, from a narrative angle, is Odysseus' son Telemachus himself. It certainly would explain Homer's inwardness with the geography of Ithaca and the life of his . . . grandfather. The story comes to us on divine authority: when the emperor Hadrian made inquiries of the Pythian Sybil, she told him that Homer was Ithaca-born, sired by Telemachus. The sibyl calls him "the heavenly siren."

If biographers find it hard to pin paternity on a single man, maternity is equally plural. Was his mother Metis, Critheis, Themista or Eugnetho? Was she a woman of Ithaca sold into slavery by Phoenician merchants or pi-rates? (The distinction between the two vocations was no clearer then than it is now.) Given his talents, it is more probable, some argued, that his mother was the Muse Calliope. After all, Orpheus' mother was a Muse. The Pythian Sybil nominated Polycasta, a daughter of old Nestor, the once vig-orous, now wheezy, wise hero who fought at Troy in the *Iliad* and lavishly entertained Telemachus in the *Odyssey*. We must let the sibyl, directly in-spired by Apollo, have the last word.

One genealogy makes Hesiod and Homer contemporaries and first cousins. They were not the best of friends. They share a famous common legend. King Paneides at Chalcis commanded a contest between the two poets at his brother's funeral games. The form of the contest is such that Hesiod is the challenger and Homer the reigning champion. Hesiod needs only one victory; Homer cannot sustain a single defeat—an unequal playing field for Homer, though it acknowledges his superiority. Hesiod's victory is pigmyish, and the story belongs more to him than to Homer.[12]

One aspect of Homer modern readers sometimes find rebarbative, espe-cially in the *Iliad:* the poems' insistently male orientation and address. Even the wonderfully rendered material textures of objects, the ingredients and the smells of cooking, the delicate discrimination in description do not out-weigh the largely male cast of characters, the unrelieved harshness of the underlying reality of the poems, the ways in which the libidinal element it-self is made harsh. There are few lyrical moments, few moments of reflec-tive repose. Intimacy is absent, even in the defining scene when Odysseus brings Penelope at last back to the marriage bed. It is hardly surprising that Homer's translators have been, for the most part, male. In George Steiner's anthology *Homer in English*, only two women appear among the dozens of translators and adaptors. Barbara Leonie Picard's version is a scaling-down of the original so that the poetry will prove harmless for young readers—a prose version with Disney overtones. Thelma Sargent confines her efforts to the Homeric Hymns.

Was Homer's real name Meles, Melesigenes or Altes? "Homer" was a kind of—we cannot call it a *nom de plume*—nickname. Some said he was so called because men of Cyprus handed his father to the Persians as a slave and *omeros* means "hostage." Aeolians called a blind man "homer"—"he who sees not"—but scholars dispute this etymology.[13]

We do not *know* his father, his mother, or his own "real" name. We are uncertain of his birthplace, his class origins, his patrons, his audience. We start with a remarkably clean slate. We can either walk away or allow ourselves a few moments of traditional history, also known as legend, and range over the ancient world. The best-known version of the life is the one dubiously attributed to Herodotus. From that and other sources we can devise, as readers did right up to the eighteenth century, a more or less cogent story.

Aeolia in Asia Minor was the destination for immigrants from Greece, especially from Thessaly. A poor man, Menapolus, arrived there, at Cyme, the city from which Hesiod's father later departed, migrating west. Menapolus married, had a daughter called Critheis, and died. She was left in the care of Cleanax of Argos. Incautious during her adolescence, she had a son. He was born in Boeotia (Critheis was bundled off to bear him secretly there, in what would be Hesiod's landscape) and, being near the river Meles, he was named Melesigenes. Mother and child returned to Aeolia.

A teacher of literature and music called Phemius lived at Smyrna. He employed the young mother to look after his house and, since he was paid in flax for his teaching, it became her job to spin it. Soon he offered to marry her and adopted Melesigenes, who, he reckoned, would go far if he was properly brought up. Phemius' expectations were fulfilled. Indeed, the boy outstripped his master and when Phemius died he inherited the school, which he managed with skill and success. The people of Smyrna admired him and his reputation spread abroad.

An unusually engaging and persuasive traveller called Mentes came from far-off Leucadia,[14] on the other side of mainland Greece, north of Ithaca. He talked Melesigenes into taking a sabbatical from teaching. The young pedagogue deserved to see the world. They set off on what would now be called an odyssey, sailing in the general direction of Mentes' homeland and eventually—conveniently, fatefully—reached the island of Ithaca. Like many intellectuals, Melesigenes had trouble with his eyes, and they grew worse in Ithaca. Mentes left him there to the care of a man called Mentor, not an ophthalmologist but a sympathetic and wise friend. Mentor (a name familiar to readers of the *Odyssey*) told him the Ithacan legends of Odysseus. Melesigenes began to conceive his poem, walking the very hills that Odysseus knew. People of Ithaca claimed that Melesigines went blind on their island. The people of Colophon back in Lydia also claim his blindness, as though the poetic affliction conferred a special, local virtue. No matter where his eyes finally gave out, he returned in time to Asia Minor, to Smyrna, and applied himself to the study of poetry.

It was hard to re-establish himself. Poverty drove him on to Larissa, and then back to Cyme. He was not wholly forgotten, made friends there and, the author of the *Life of Homer* declares, "Even up to my time, the people who lived there would point out the very place where he sat reciting his verse." The spot was held to be sacred, as was the poplar tree that had sprung up at Melesigenes' arrival. He dazzled the elders with his power of reciting. He bargained with them: in return for a stipend he would bring fame to their city through verse.

The city assembly was inclined to honour this unusual "homer" ("blind man") but some killjoys cavilled: provide for one homer, whatever his talents, and you'll be expected to provide for all the rest. In the end the assembly voted against granting the poet a pension. He left a curse on the town: it would never produce a poet to celebrate it. He went on to Phocaea, south-west of Cyme, where a man called Thestorides, exploiting his need, gave him house room and encouraged him to write poems which the host deceitfully passed off under his own name. While he lived *chez* Thestorides (to whom he addresses an epigram), he is said to have composed the *Lesser Iliad* and the *Phocais;* though the Phocaeans say that he composed the latter among them. These may have been the works Thestorides laid claim to. Homer did not relish the role of ghost writer. Departing, he declared (more mildly than a modern poet might do), "Many things are dark to us, but nothing is more unknowable than the human heart."

Life continued to frown on him. One day merchants from Chios heard him reciting. Thestorides, they reported, was reciting virtually the same verses on their island. He went to Chios to confront his plagiarist. The journey was long. After mishaps he reached Pithys. He wandered lost until he heard goats bleating and was assaulted by guard dogs. Glaucos, a goatherd, came to his rescue and Homer told his tale. Deeply affected, the country-man provided him with bed and board. Next day he reported Homer's arrival to his master. The master interviewed him and was impressed with how Homer replied and how much he seemed to know. He induced him to stay as a tutor to the children, and expelled the scheming, capricious Thestorides from the island.

Homer set up a school in Chios. It was successful and at last the poet prospered. A guild of rhapsodes, or bards, the Homeridae, was established, legend says under his initial tutelage, and survived for several generations, a proper singing school. He married and fathered two daughters. One died a spinster, the other married a native of the island.

His fame spread; he was urged to visit Greece, where his name was already known. Being something of a businessman, he prepared by composing verses to flatter the Athenians. He set out for Samos, where he was made welcome and recited verse at major festivals and gave great delight. By this means and by finding patronage from the rich he made a living. One apocryphal Homeric poem is associated with his stay there, the *Oikalias Agosis* ("The Taking of Oechalia"). A historian tells how Creophylus of Samos had Homer for his guest and as a token of gratitude received not the dedication but the actual *attribution* of the poem. Others suggest that the author was Creophylus, and Homer lent his name in return for hospitality. Callimachus has the poem speak its origin: "I am the work of that Samian who once received divine Homer in his house. I sing of Eurytus and all his woes and of golden-haired Ioleia, and am reputed one of Homer's works. Dear Heaven! how great an honour this for Creophylus!"

Perhaps reluctantly, Homer set off in the spring for Athens. He was entertained in Athens by Medon, then the leader of the city. On a cold day he made the verse about the blessed hearth fire. Eventually he wandered on to Corinth, where he recited successfully, and then to Argos, where he performed *Iliad* II, 559–68, with two extra verses. The extra verses praise the Argives, his audience and hosts, demonstrating how a performer might adapt his text to please local audiences. The leading Argives were delighted and showered him with expensive gifts. They set up a brass statue, decreeing that sacrifice should be offered to Homer "daily, monthly, and yearly; and that another sacrifice should be sent to Chios every five years." He crossed to Delos, where, "standing on the altar of horns," he recited his "Hymn to [Delian] Apollo." It is a wonderfully impressive if wholly implausible image: Homer standing between the horns and celebrating his patron god. The Ionians made him a citizen of each one of their states, and a poem was written "on a whitened tablet" which he dedicated "in the temple of Artemis." Homer sailed to Ios afterwards "to join Creophylus." When he reached the island, as the Pythian Sibyl had predicted, he suddenly sickened and died.

He died of a kind of humiliation. Sitting on the shore one day he heard the sound of fisher lads returning from their work. "Oh young sirs, hunters of the creatures of the deep, have you caught anything?" "Everything we caught we left behind," they said, "and we bear away everything we failed to catch." Homer could not fathom the reply, so they had to explain it to him. They had caught no fish, but they had been catching their lice, and those that they caught they pinched and flicked away, leaving them behind, and those that they did not catch were still upon their bodies. Homer remembered with a sudden chill the prophesy that he was to die in Ios. He lurched to his feet and started to hurry off, but the ground was slippery and he fell upon his side. On the third day after his accident, he died and was interred in Ios. He had composed his own epitaph which—to hell with modesty— forthrightly declares: "Here earth covers the sacred head of divine Homer, the glorifier of hero-men."[15]

Pausanias, who began life as a Homeric scholar but gave up because the subject was so vexed with controversy, wrote his *Guide to Greece* with Odysseus as a kind of tutelary spirit. The index lists *Odyssey* as *passim*. The travel-writer tells how there was an oracle recorded beneath a bronze portrait of Homer which predicted that he would seek his father's country but die and be buried in his mother's. "The people of Ios point out Homer's tomb in the island, and Clymene's in a different part of it: they say she was Homer's mother." (So much for Critheis.) "But the Cypriots, who also lay claim to Homer, say that a woman of Cyprus called Themisto" (so much for Clymene) "was his mother, and that Euklous foretold the birth of Homer in these verses" (which Pausanias then quotes).[16] Pausanias refuses to offer a firm opinion on the matter. He had left such controversies behind. A modern guidebook says that at the northern tip of Ios flows the creek of Plakotós, and there in 1770 a Dutch traveller said he had found the tomb of Homer. All he did for certain was to break into some prehistoric graves.

Surely we *see* Homer in the many ancient busts and statues? A version of him, in any case: the earliest known portrait dates from 460 BC, centuries after his death. The life-size statue has vanished but copies of the head, thought to be relatively faithful, survive.[17] Homer is old, blind, head slightly tilted to the left as though listening. His face is lean, long, made to seem even longer by the downward strokes of the beard. A handsome old man, a *kalos geron,* he wears his hair carefully arranged on top, loose at sides and neck. Bald pates characterise statuary elders. The style of drawing hair forward, partly to conceal the baldness, is a common feature of archaic coiffing; viewers would have recognised this Homer as being from a time long before their own, and this added authority to his works. The truth is what has stood the test of time. There is no portrayal of the adolescent Homer. In fact, no portraits of young poets or philosophers survive. Youth and truth were never complementary.

Most of the cities which laid claim to Homer issued coins with his head on them. In the fourth century Ios issued an arresting portrait coin, assimilating the poet to the figure of Zeus. On this coin he does not appear to be blind. The eye has a pupil rather than a blank or a sealed lid. Smyrna minted coins at the beginning of the second century BC where Homer is Zeus-like, but "in place of a thunderbolt" he wields a book roll. Other versions—for instance, the coins of Chios—show him reading the *Iliad* to himself, or meditating.[18]

In these contrasting verbal and visual impressions of Homer and his story not a single detail can be verified, though the geography of each variation is plausible and scholar-critics have been known to invest lifetimes and fortunes in proving what is unprovable and warring with foes as ill-armed as themselves. Eratosthenes of Cyrene, the mathematical geographer (second half of the third century BC), also doubted Homer's geography.[19] He says, "You will find the island of Aeolus when you find the cobbler who sewed the bag for the winds."[20] Samuel Butler sides with Eratosthenes; his verdict is amusingly just: "Homeric commentators have been blind so long that nothing will do for them but Homer must be blind too. They have transferred their own blindness to the poet."[21] But then Butler's theory of the female author of the *Odyssey,* Homer in a gown, is itself not wholly without smoke, mirrors or a white stick.

Against the zealots, there have always been sceptics for whom the story seemed in certain places too specific, in others too vague, as though various islands and towns had invested in the account so as to derive some benefit even from a spurious association with Homer. Untruths and implausibilities were less a matter of deceit by local tourist boards, more the result of an impassioned respect for the poet. Aelian recalls how in Alexandria "Ptolemy Philopator erected a temple to Homer and placed within it a magnificent seated statue of the poet and, in a semicircle around him, all the cities that laid claim to him." Strabo saw another such temple in Smyrna.[22] Sculptural reliefs show Homer enthroned, laurel-crowned, while the Muses and other representative figures dance attendance. His two great poems may be portrayed as boys kneeling or squatting beside his seat, and there are sometimes mice (representing the *Batrachomyomachia,* or "The Battle of the Frogs and Mice") nibbling crumbs near his feet.

In the seventeenth century, doubts start to bleach out the Life. They begin within the story itself and have to do with the poetic intentions of the poet Homer. The despotic classicist Richard Bentley[23] categorically declares: "Homer wrote a sequel of songs and rhapsodies, to be sung by himself, for small comings and good cheer, at festivals and other days of merriment. These loose songs were not collected together, in the form of an epic poem, till about Pisistratus' time, about five hundred years after." Maybe wrong, maybe right. Sceptics who propose alternative narratives provide us in the end with accounts as suppositious as those they try to adjust or displace. Perhaps *more* suppositious, given that they are at least two millennia further away from Homer than the "biographers" were.

Be that as it may, over the last three centuries, Homer has flickered on and off, he has changed form like Proteus in the cave, and no single critic has managed to hold him still and force an "I am" from his lips. He has been fragmented by some into a committee of Pisistratean redactors; others see him as multiple. Was he two or even three original writers, or no one at all, like Odysseus in the Cyclops' cave? Others dissolve him into the solution of "an oral tradition." If there is no such poet as Homer, what do we make of the poems, what is their authority, how do we discuss a poem without an author, a poem of multiple authorship, a poem sung and finally written down after centuries, a poem whose existence, or at least its survival, is a function of tradition rather than individual literary imagination? We are a world away from the flustered old poet slipping and falling on a muddy track in Ios, and further still from the young man on his travels, stopping off at Ithaca and leaving his eyesight there.

There is something unprecedented (and unrepeated) about the way the poetry of the *Iliad* and *Odyssey* affects reader or audience, something which even a decent translation communicates to the attentive ear. This "something" has to do with how the language relates to the things it names, how the words relate to the world that they portray. It is more than a matter of using verbs, active verbs, much more frequently than most Greek poets do, in some passages more frequently than nouns; it is more than how he enacts thought, embeds it in the action through the use of such verbs, *embodies* it. It is more, too, than the extensive use of dialogue, the sometimes virtually performable disposition of the language in its sequence and characterisation. It starts in the unique nature of the language that is deployed.

Homeric diction is a composite of different dialect strands, not resolved into a standard language but retaining the oddness of different speech, as though a poet wrote in Scots, South African, Texan and Jamaican, all in a single poem, from hemistych to hemistych. The language deploys not only different dialects, but different *periods* of dialect. We meet Ionic (from the islands), the basic language of the poem, and Aeolic (from Asia Minor);[24] forms from one and the other are mixed without particular pattern. An Aeolic form may be chosen over an Ionic for metrical reasons, but when there is no metrical determinant there is no *logic* in the choice of one or the other. Then there are Attic (Athenian) forms from the time of Pisistratus, when the texts of the poems were put into something like their present form.

Though historically Ionian supplants Aeolian, in Homeric verse the elements do not appear as successive layers but are mixed. One might call it an artificial language, but it does not have the feel of conscious contrivance or the systematic qualities of a deliberate invention. It seems rather to have evolved, with chance inclusions and exclusions occurring for reasons we cannot confidently infer. The result is a melding of linguistic and cultural heritages and periods. There are more complex dialect features foreign to the likely time of composition, for example outcrops of Arcado-Cypriot, the Greek of the Myceneans five hundred years "before Homer."[25] The language mix is clearly not a late phenomenon: it is endemic in the evolving of a poem handed down in an oral tradition. We will consider the phenomenon of the oral tradition below.

Oliver Taplin makes much of the combinations, geographic and temporal variegations, that occur line by line, phrase by phrase, and then affirms a paradox which is partly true, one that we experience even at the remove of translation: ". . . this special poetic language will not have struck its hearers as artificial or outlandish, precisely because they knew it and expected it as the language of hexameter poetry. It is the language proper to the occasion that they will have assimilated from childhood."[26] Artificial the language is, outlandish it is not. Familiarity may have dulled but cannot erase the fact that, like liturgical language or sixteenth- and seventeenth-century Biblical translation, an appropriate idiom not continuous with any form of local speech has been devised and, while it is central to a culture, it is received as proper and not interrogated. An expressive distance between the Homeric idiom and the language spoken in the street or the agora was obvious and undeniable. Because the Homeric poems are not in a language that ever lived *as* a single spoken dialect, but rather in an amalgam with a special diction, formulaic phrases, repetitions and the like, it is possible to say that even the ancients heard and read Homer rather as we read Greek or Latin, or the King James Bible, as a language that is authoritative, stable, complete: the old lexicographer's dream of a language of fixed meanings. It could not be added to: it was the more living for never having quite lived, except in the poems.

For the reception of poetry, the consequences of using such a language are quite radical. Doctor Johnson makes an interesting point about the inimitable, irreducible simplicity of Homer's language. "Virgil wrote in a language of the same general fabric with that of Homer, in verses of the same measure, and in an age nearer to Homer's time by eighteen hundred years, yet he found, even then, the state of the world so much altered, and the demand for elegance so much increased, that mere nature would be endured no longer; and perhaps, in the multitude of borrowed passages, very few can be shown which he has not embellished."[27] Embellishment is what comes *after* Homer. There are certainly elaborate and elaborated passages in the poems, but little is included for purely decorative reasons, little simply to please the readerly eye. William Gell in 1807 published the first serious topographical account of Ithaca, *Geography and Antiquities of Ithaca,* "not entirely without hopes of vindicating the poem of Homer from the skepticism of those critics who imagine that the Odyssey is a mere poetical composition."[28] That word "mere" isolates the peculiar virtue of Homer's verse: it is not fanciful, poetical, artificial. For Homer a rose is a rose is a rose.

The Austrian scholar Albin Lesky says that in Greek epic poetry the language is always "conditioned by metre."[29] It is a simple point, but one worth making. In translation that specific condition is replaced by other conditions (iambic pentameter, poulter's measure, rhyme, etc.), yet the conditioning specific to the Greek, to Homer's curious version of Greek, and the relationship between the conditioning and that synthetic language, *is* precisely the poetry. It is not just prosody but diction and the whole strategy of delivery that are entailed. "In the comparison of Homer and Virgil," Dr. Johnson declares in his *Life of Dryden*, "the discriminative excellence of Homer is elevation and comprehension of thought, and that of Virgil is grace and splendour of diction. The beauties of Homer are therefore difficult to be lost, and those of Virgil difficult to be retained."[30]

Use of the Greek hexameter for epic poetry probably goes back very far in time: Homer (even in the apocryphal poems) is versatile, but his versatility is expressed wholly in hexameter, with variety but without variation, no embedded earlier or other prosodies. Variety is achieved by means of subtle substitutions within the metrical pattern, reversals and sanctioned "irregularities," but most of all by the use of extended syntax that runs on over the line ending (enjambement) and by the range of effects that can be achieved by positioning the caesura, or pause, within the line, even introducing secondary caesuras. This freedom within a framework of constraint sustains the shifting tonalities of the poem, its sudden changes of key and register.

Mikhail Bakhtin insists that the epic "was never a poem about the present, about its own time" and the discourse of epic is inevitably—in this case formulaically—remote from the "discourse of a contemporary about a contemporary addressed to contemporaries."[31] All this suggests a relationship between the language and the world it portrays that is highly artificial, staged, remote. Yet the opposite is true.

Reading Chapman's translation of Homer for the first time, John Keats wrote one of his most famous sonnets:

> Much have I travelled in the realms of gold,
>   And many goodly states and kingdoms seen;
>   Round many western islands have I been
> Which bards in fealty to Apollo hold.
> Oft of one wide expanse had I been told
>   That deep-brow'd Homer ruled as his demesne;
>   Yet did I never breathe its pure serene
> Till I heard Chapman speak out loud and bold:
> Then felt I like some watcher of the skies

> When a new planet swims into his ken;
> Or like stout Cortez when with eagle eyes
> He star'd at the Pacific—and all his men
> Look'd at each other with a wild surmise—
> Silent, upon a peak in Darien.

What affects Keats, who cannot read the Greek original, is at once the grandeur of Homer's poems and their new-minted immediacy. George Chapman remains Homer's most famous English translator, though his translations are little read nowadays. He completed the *Iliad* in 1611, the *Odyssey* in 1616, and the Homeric Hymns in 1624. "The work that I was born to do, is done," he declared.

He made a fundamental mistake at the outset: he took Homer to be "learning's sire." It was and is a common error. For him, Homer is a moral teacher: history and story are secondary to the psychological and ethical truths that they illuminate. The literal is not enough; he must seek out a deep sense in each phrase and action. He assumes that Homer, though remote in time and language from seventeenth-century England, was nonetheless not unlike himself. As many translators of Homer do, he over-interprets and interpolates in the very process of translation. Yet the original is so powerful that it overcomes the bias and ideology of the translator: Keats responds not to Chapman's moral sense of Homer but to the amazing, morally neutral new planet (*Iliad*) and new sea (*Odyssey*) that he presents.[32]

Chapman did have more than an inkling of the *difference* of Homer's poems from anything else he had read, a difference in kind from all the poetry they give rise to. Prefacing the *Iliad,* he writes, "It is the part of every knowing and judicious interpreter, not to follow the number and order of words, but [my italics] *the material things themselves,* and sentences to weigh diligently." The "interpreter"—and what more primary interpreter is there than a translator?—weighs the "sentences" (here signifying the underlying, weighty significance of the verse rather than its syntactical structures) and tries to render *the material things themselves.* W. H. Auden gets closer to Homer than most modern poets, not only in his apocalyptic "The Shield of Achilles" but in his calm appraisal of the poet: "The world of Homer is unbearably sad because it never transcends the immediate moment; one is happy, one is unhappy, one wins, one loses, finally one dies. That is all."[33] Homer's is a tragic world in a special, pre-classical sense: tragedy dwells not in the protagonists, their relationships and fates, but in the nature of existence itself. The understanding that comes from it is tautological, an understanding of itself.

This is why we accept even brutal and incomprehensibly cruel events in Homer, especially the deaths of men portrayed as generous, lively, and tangential to the main conflict. Bernard Williams calls Homer's world *pre-philosophical:* how things are is not constantly patrolled by a theoretical sense of how things *should be* in moral terms. Homer, like Thucydides in his histories and Sophocles in his plays, "represents human beings as dealing sensibly, foolishly, sometimes catastrophically, sometimes nobly, with a world that is only partially intelligible to human agency," for example, the fantastic world through which Odysseus sails, "and in itself is not necessarily well adjusted to ethical aspirations."[34] To read a poetry wholly without "ethical aspirations" and to leave ethical aspiration out of our reading provides us with an experience, a discipline, which we can get in no other poetry of comparable richness and complexity to the *Iliad* and the *Odyssey.* Jacob Burckhardt quotes a repeated line from the *Iliad,* "always to do the best and to outdo others,"[35] and comments: "this does not imply that the hero is an ideal of humanity. All his actions and his passions go to extremes; what is ideal in him lies in the beauty and freshness he embodies . . . [H]e represents the wholly unspoiled, spontaneous egoism of human nature." But, carried away in the cadence of his sentence, Burckhardt overshoots the landing-strip: "unrepentant but great-hearted and benign."[36] As soon as the word "benign" is introduced, his argument is fudged.

Homeric pathos is of a different order from that achieved by other poets or by the dramatists who are Homer's ultimate heirs. In the *Iliad,* he tells us of an awful death, and, once the warrior is disposed of, he evokes, briefly, the world out of which that warrior came to bleed and die on the windy plain of Troy. In this way, without sentimentality, a circumstantial account of a death juxtaposed with a circumstantial account, epithetical and elliptical, of a life, releases pathos. Moral judgement is withheld: we may come up with regret, sadness, a sense of futile loss, but these are our response, not the poet's. There are few poems in which we are left so free to feel and to align ourselves as we wish with one side, one god, one hero, or another. Facts as much as characters have an inviolable (or at least an unviolated) integrity. Because of this lucid neutrality in the delivery, the poems do not provoke our objection to the intense violence or the values that seem to motivate the protagonists, divine and human.

When translators render the epithet for Odysseus "wily," we should be prepared to insist that surely "wily" belongs to a later, ethically charged diction: wiliness suggests a calculation of motive, whereas what marks Homer's Odysseus is his knack, at the level of instinct, of individual survival. Odysseus functions well in council because he speaks well; but he loses all his men, all his ships, and all but the last helping of treasure, as he makes his journey home in ten years, a return which took some of his fellow-warriors a couple of weeks. Wily? Our problem with Odysseus is, in a sense, a semantic one: we misunderstand him because we are conditioned by the classical and its aftermaths. We find it hard to tune in to the pre-classical, without the continual fuzz of a later static marring our reception.

Homer's world is strange but at the same time *literal* in its feel. The name and the thing named belong together, irony (the first instrument of classic artifice) has not prised them apart. Here mere sentiment has no place. When I speak of the *literal* feel of the *Iliad* and the *Odyssey*, I mean a literal feel not only of the landscape, but of the larger geography; not only of the characters at rest, but of the characters in motion. The heroisms become credible because the smaller deeds are credible; the fantastic journeys of Odysseus are believable because the world through which Telemachus sails, and in which Odysseus fights to regain his wife, his house and his kingdom, are real.

What constitutes this reality? Byron, outraged that certain critics doubted the literal existence of Troy and the facts of the war itself, reflected in his journal in 1821, "We *do* care about 'the authenticity of the tale of Troy.' I have stood upon the plain *daily,* for more than a month, in 1810 . . . I still venerated the grand original as the truth of *history* (in the material *facts*) and of *place*. Otherwise it would have given me no delight."[37] The abundance of italics expresses enthusiasm, the over-emphasis of an imagination somewhat injured in its needed certainties.

Rhys Carpenter's *Folk Tale, Fiction and Saga in the Homeric Epics* would have driven Byron to an even earlier grave, since he sees the matter of Homer as largely fictitious. But other critics, equally scholarly and trusting more in the persuasive impact of the verse and the correlations between what the poem says and what topography and archaeology reveal, take an opposite view. They do not treat the poems as revelation, but they do approach them as a kind of rhetoricised history. Denys Page in *History and the Homeric Iliad* believes the poem reflects the conflict between Achaeans (based in Rhodes) "and the league of Assuwa, to which Troy belonged, at the time when Hittite power was waning."[38]

There are certainties in the poems. Charles Maclaren, founder of *The Scotsman* newspaper, depending in 1822 on "Homer's facts" rather than the geographer Strabo's speculations, correctly identified the site of ancient Troy with Hisarlik in Turkey. The poem, despite alluvial changes in the landscape, earthquakes and the apocalyptic work of Poseidon, provided him with a literal, lived geography that answered to the physical plotting of the poem. Troy stood on the site that the Greco-Roman New Ilion later occupied.[39] When a modern critic declares that "[i]nappropriate questions"—largely to do with factuality in the poems—"will lead to false answers,"[40] we can only reply that in the matter of fact and literal truth few questions addressed to the poem are likely to be inappropriate; and the answers received will not necessarily be false.

It is in the nature of oral traditions to be conservative. When writing is not the currency of knowledge, law, genealogy and the transmission of fact, the oral record is preserved with as much zeal and precision as a written account would be. There are forms, mnemonics, verbal formulae to facilitate the accurate preservation of facts, rules, liturgies, legends. Where verse narrative, which is a form of history and genealogy, is concerned, the same disciplines naturally apply. Growth and change, variation and decoration, are strictly regulated by a respect for the integrity of the material being carried forward. And an oral tradition is retentive, even when the man or woman who carries the record in memory is uncertain of a meaning. Forgetting meanings does not mean the language that conveys them has forgotten.

An oral tradition is, thus, first of all a *recording* tradition with developed mnemonics. What it selects, assembles and presents it does not distort or falsify. The purpose of recording is to preserve rather than to mutate or embellish. It is reassuring, though not surprising, to discover that the historical books of the Bible, for example, are vindicated time after time by archaeology; archaeology and geology are confirming the factuality of much of Homer. We now have Nestor's bathtub, discovered at Pylos, a significant curiosity that raises hopes that much else, of perhaps greater moment, will work its way back to the surface of the soil.

J. V. Luce insists on the almost absolute accuracy of Homer's descriptions of landscape, taking into account alluvial and other changes.[41] He writes "in the firm belief that 'truth to life' is Homer's paramount concern in local description." Luce believes that the Homeric rhapsode's audience would have been familiar with the topography and scenic qualities of many of the places described; the poet's accuracy when describing non-fantastic landscapes was crucial to his credibility. By the time the poems were put in something like the form in which they survive, between 750 and 700 BC, the Troad was fully colonised by Aeolian Greeks, and Ithaca "an important staging post on the route to the new Greek cities of southern Italy and Sicily."

The strong little city-states had begun some time before to send out colonists and the *apoikiai,* or colonies, were developing. They were not all colonies in a pejorative modern sense, necessarily, rather more like settlements, spreading especially to the west. Many Greeks were not only familiar with the seaways of the world into which they were expanding but also insistently conscious that wherever the currents took them, they belonged to Greece, and were not and would never be barbarians. Certain mainland events developed, the Olympic Games in the Peloponnese and other festivals elsewhere, which had the role of reconnecting ceremonially the scattered Hellenic settlements with the motherlands, mainland and island. Olympia burst into activity in the mid-eighth century BC, Delphi and Delos two or three decades later; and many other sanctuaries leave traces of substantial development around 700 BC. The Delphic Oracle was important in authorising and legitimising settler expeditions, and votive offerings were displayed there. Two great poems celebrated the various peoples and charted the scattered lands of the Greeks, the *Iliad* and the *Odyssey*. They were transmuted into cultural touchstones of the Greeks and performed at civic and religious festivals, a reminder of heroic roots and of the sources of a common culture.

Luce knows that his theory depends on some close geological analyses. "The precise position of the shoreline at the time of the Trojan War, say 3,250 years ago, has not been finally determined, but most, if not all, of the plain that now extends northwards from Troy to the Dardanelles (Hellespont) is the product of alluviation since c. 1250 BC."[42] Similarly, recent archaeology has established how much larger Troy was than earlier explorations suggested: a principal city and trading centre. Many of the older objections to Homer as geographer and historian have weakened in the light of recent explorations.

Homer is a poet, Homer is a historian. To insist on the modern separation of those two roles is to impose an anachronism on him. One could say that the phenomenon we call Homer is as much historical as poetic, and that the function of mnemonics, as etymology affirms, is memory. Memory is history set in order. As Luce points out, "Paradoxically, illiteracy was a safeguard rather than a threat to the authenticity of the tradition."[43] Homer presents us with a synthetic world, a world that never was in quite the forms proposed, a texture of vivid details, anachronisms, dictional syntheses. Yet the poems are what we "know" of the ancient Greeks, almost all that we know, tempered by archaeology. Early historians took Homer to be early history. This is the Greece we, and they, related to and visualised most comprehensively. In Book IV of the *Iliad*, for example, we encounter a theme that develops through the rest of the poem: the horror of death, especially the deaths of young men, in war, with precise descriptions of entry wounds, exit wounds, the way men bleed, how they fall, the noises that their falling makes and that they make in falling. The poem dwells on the number of brothers engaged in the action, many of them killed together, the poet each time casting a regretful glance in the direction of the bereaved.

"Homer's facts" is a reassuring phrase. But like Homer himself, the facts were first believed in,[44] then regarded as "poetical," part of a make-believe that, surely, is in the very nature of poetry. Poets make their freedom by breaking the rules of fact. Sir Philip Sidney, in *The Apology for Poetry*, summarises Renaissance critical thought and affirms this view. He does not express a universal truth: this is certainly not the case with the archaic poets.

The Greeks first appear in history in 1600–1200 BC, "the age reflected in the epics of Homer, in whose narrative the land is ruled by all-powerful monarchs holding court in impressive palaces amid the trappings of great wealth . . . For long the picture he presented was thought to be the stuff of mythology. Then, in the nineteenth century, archaeologists began to un-earth remains that revealed the sober reality behind Homer's words . . ."[45] Jacob Burckhardt marvelled at how Strabo credits Homer with factual accu-racy, preferring the poet's version to the physical evidence of ethnography.[46]

On what grounds can the facts of a poem be believed? If it comes from a genuine oral tradition, we must define (as far as we can from the unverifiable evidence at our disposal) the nature of an oral tradition and what happens to it when it is stilled in the luminous amber of writing. In a fourth-century BC account of Homer and Hesiod, Alcidamas (the probable author) de-clares: "Let us then thank [Homer] thus for his playful entertainment; and as for his origin and the rest of his poetry, let us hand them down through the gift of accurate memory for the common possession of those Hellenes who aspire to be Lovers of the Beautiful." Here the amber seems to dis-place the historian. Lesky says it is "unnatural" to record or transcribe the oral tradition: "one is compelling a flowing stream to freeze at one point." Yet the value of what is frozen, assuming the stream is not thawed and re-frozen in a different form, possesses behind the mimetic devices a very powerful charge of the reality from which it sets out.

In 1795 F. A. Wolf published the first serious case for regarding the *Iliad* and the *Odyssey* as compilations of miscellaneous poems rather than or-ganic, single-authored works in their own right. Taplin is willing to concede that this *might* be so, but in order to have his cake and eat it, he insists that the poet who did the assembling was "so much the best of the poets who contributed to them that he is The Poet."[47] George Steiner is similarly minded. "I have always believed our *Iliad* to be the product of an editorial act of genius, of a marvellously shaping recension of the voluminous oral material at the time in which new techniques of writing, and of the prepara-tion of papyrus or hides in quantities sufficient for so extensive an inscrip-tion, made this recension practicable. I take the editor of genius to have been the *author* of the *Odyssey*. In older age, perhaps, and at some ironic dis-tance."[48] He speaks of the *Iliad* as compiled, the *Odyssey* as composed (it has an ironic purchase on the actions and values of the first). If Taplin and Steiner are correct, editors can rejoice, because a good editor or recension-ist, on the authority of these critic-scholars, can be identified with and then identified *as* the poet himself.

The leading exponents of the oral composition theory, Milman Parry (who died at the age of 33, in 1936) and Albert B. Lord, author of *The Singer of Tales* (1960), effected the most radical change in Homeric scholarship since the texts were set down in authoritative form in Athens under Pisistratus. Steiner and Taplin are trying to take advantage of their findings and theories, which affect our approach to all primitive and ancient poetry, without quite abandoning the notion of an identifiable individual Homer. But for Parry and Lord the issue was less the unknowable Homer, more the knowable poems, and their take on the particulars of the verse itself made sense of the mixture of dialects, the copious anachronisms, the epithets and other forms of repetition. It also cast light on the odd pieces of the poems which seem not to fit, the occasional contradictions in the plots, the inconsistencies of character and action. "Parry's work on the mechanics of Homeric diction," writes Gregory Nagy, "has caused a serious problem of esthetics for generations of Hellenists reared on the classical approaches to the *Iliad* and *Odyssey*: how can compositions that have always seemed so deliberate and integral in their artistry result from a system of diction that is so mechanical—one might almost say automatic? For various Homeric experts the solution lies in objecting to various aspects of Parry's findings: the genius of Homer must somehow be rescued from the workings of a formulaic system. For me, however, it is easier to accept Parry's work and to proceed from there by looking for a solution in the factor of tradition itself."[49]

Until the "oral traditionalists" found their voices and, more, began the close analysis of the formulae which underlie the composition of the Homeric poems, there was one principal way of reading them: as deliberated, finished works, with identifiable unities. This approach assumes that the poems we have are substantially whole, discrete and complete. A new way of reading Homer, which takes nothing for granted, inquires into the poems' formation, and it comes up with results which unsettled classical studies and which, despite attempts at assimilation by later critics, remain an obstacle to anyone keen to return to the old days when the utter *difference* of the world in which the Homeric poems were composed and assembled need not be acknowledged, and the fact that Homer was European meant that in some curious way he was "like us."

Beyond metre, Parry and Lord set out three primary mimetic devices we can identify and appraise. The celebrated epithets, "grey-eyed Athena," "rosy-fingered Dawn," "Hector tamer of horses," are an initial clue. Then there are lines and whole passages that are repeated. When one figure commands another to take a message, the message is reported verbatim; when an action is repeated or imitated, the same language is used. Indeed, runs of lines from the *Iliad* recur in the *Odyssey*. Finally, there are the formulae which, working with and within the metre, structure certain kinds of diction, certain recurrent gestures, into similar or identical form.

Milman Parry showed how the epithets work in the dactylic hexameter. They are varied according to their position in the line, but the device is systematic, what Parry calls "extension" and "economy." The system is mimetic: not that it imitates or mimes what it is about but that it is a device for

linguistic remembering which is, at the same time, a way of creating and rewarding the auditor's expectation. Much of the Homeric poems is off the
peg, that peg being the conventions of an oral poetry which have survived
into the written-down form.

Most scholars now agree that the poems attributed to Homer either derive from or are combinations of verse narratives that existed in an oral tradition. We must remain alert to the otherness of the oral tradition. It may
have been developed originally to preserve genealogies, historical incidents,
laws, rituals and legends that went into the formation and definition of a
tribe or community. Even when written down and extended by successive
redactors, the oral elements show through and are part of the way in which
the poetry means, part of the way it touches and preserves the very world
that has vanished from under it. Among the most clear-headed and rigorous of Parry's heirs is Gregory Nagy, who makes assumptions so radical
about the nature of the Homeric texts that, if accepted, they would require
an even more thoroughgoing rethinking of them than has yet occurred.
Though the poems are in a profound way pre-determined, he insists that
the "literary intent" is present, but it "must be assigned not simply to one
poet but also to countless generations of previous poets steeped in the
same traditions." For him, "the artistry of the Homeric poems is traditional
both in diction *and* in theme" (my italics). We must seek out "not so much
the genius of Homer but the genius of the overall poetic tradition that cul-
minated in our *Iliad* and *Odyssey*." Nagy's understanding of the consequences of his argument is subtle, not least because it makes sense of the
"surprise" of Homer's sudden presence, and of the rootedness of the
Homeric in the ages before writing, or between traditions of writing. "To
my mind there is no question . . . about the poet's freedom to say accurately
what he means. What he means, however, is strictly regulated by tradition.
The poet has no intention of saying anything untraditional. In fact, the
poet's inherited conceit is that he has it in his power to recover the exact
words that tell what men did and said in the Heroic Age."[50] Thus Nagy
makes a compelling virtue of necessity.

How is oral poetry analogous to, and how does it differ from, a tradition
of written composition? Where in our considerations does *authorship* lie?
We know it is futile to look for Homer, but is it equally futile to speculate
that a "Homer" never existed at all? Lesky, attempting to reconcile the discoveries of Parry and Lord with the older tradition, suggests that despite
oral elements, the Homeric poems were written, and initially the texts were
handed down amongst rhapsodes, often guilds or even family units. "What
we hear of the Homeridae of Chios—the 'sons of Homer,' his 'school'—is
to be interpreted in this sense. Light is thrown on the activity of these men
by the tradition that Solon or Hipparchus the son of Pisistratus arranged to

have all the Homeric poems recited at the Panathenaea by relays of rhapsodes." Xenophon in his *Memorabilia* describes rhapsodists as "very precise about the exact words of Homer, but very idiotic themselves."

We can hear the voice of a famous Athenian rhapsode, though he comes on the scene a century and a half later than Solon. His name is Ion, and he turns up in Athens like a peacock with its tail fully fanned. Plato in the *Ion* re-stages his conversation with Socrates.[51] The philosopher begins, as is his wont, by disarming his interlocutor with a mixture of flattery and shrewd irony. "I often envy the profession of a rhapsode, Ion," he says. "You have really nice clothes; you have the continual company of good poets, especially Homer; and you develop understanding to an unusual degree." In fact, what Socrates establishes is how little understanding the rhapsode actually possesses as he enunciates, with stage feeling and received emphases, the greatest poem in Greek. "No man," says Socrates, "can be a rhapsode who does not understand the meaning of the poet. For the rhapsode ought to interpret the mind of the poet to his hearers, but how can he interpret him well unless he knows what he means? All this is greatly to be envied."

In what follows Ion gradually reveals his vanity and his vacuity: "neither Metrodorus of Lampsacus, nor Stesimbrotus of Thasos, nor Glaucon, nor any one else who ever was, had as good ideas about Homer as I have, or as many." He finds all poetry apart from Homer's boring and insignificant. But, "you really ought to hear how exquisitely I render Homer. I think that the Homeridae should give me a golden crown." Socrates demurs: "I shall take an opportunity of hearing your embellishments of him at some other time." "Embellishments" are precisely what a living oral tradition is proof against.

In the light of the *Ion,* we must distinguish between the rhapsode of the fifth century and the original carriers of the oral tradition through the archaic period, from whom the written texts were written down at Pisistratus' command, so that authoritative versions would exist for the festivals, and so that, the text being in written form, it might be scrutinised and (when politics required) added to, enhanced. The memorising performer in Plato's time is a diminished figure, compared with the Homeric "bard." The bard improvised on existing stories, while the rhapsode recited from texts which he had memorised or carried up his sleeve on a scroll. The rhapsode recited music, drumming out the emphases with a staff; the bard performed— perhaps—with a lyre. In time the word detached itself from music, gaining precedence over its accompaniment and then displacing it.

The writing-down of the Homeric poems was a risky process. In the life of Orpheus, we met with Onomacritos, the pious forger. Here, in the flickering life of Homer, he makes another appearance. Written texts in the age of the tyrant Solon were potent legitimisers. Solon, a poet himself, is reputed to have forged a line in the *Iliad*'s catalogue of ships to enforce

Athens' claim to Salamis.[32] If a tyrant was a noted forger, it is not surprising that, among the subjects, we will find successful emulators.

Onomacritos was a respected figure in the Athens of Pisistratus and his sons, an advisor to the tyrant, guardian of the oracles and texts of Bacis and Musaeus. One day Lasus, the son of a rival poet, apprehended him in the act of adding a line of "ancient prophesy" to one of the oracles.[33] Pisistratus' son, by then in power, had no choice but to expel his editor and counsellor from the city. After his departure, when the prophecies of Bacis and Musaeus failed to come true, people could blame the exiled interpolator. Onomacritos was probably among the first to write down, at the tyrant's command, an "official" text of Homer's poems, not for the general reader, who did not yet exist, but in order to hold and preserve the power of the poems, as it were to bring them under control, to make them ruly. After the text was established, there could be no radical deviations from the main lines of the narrative, no further interpolations. A rhapsode like Ion might embellish, but he could not otherwise distort the poems.

If Onomacritos was more than an occasional and strategic forger, it is not impossible (though given the quality of the poems, it is implausible) that he "forged" the *Iliad* and the *Odyssey* out of legendary and other materials. Ignorance, or a desire to archaise and give the text an authenticating varnish, led him to mix dialects and to the other anachronisms. Such a supposition would accommodate, too, the theory that the poems originate in an oral tradition and elements in the surviving text relate to that tradition. One or two critics advance this theory, just as some critics assign the plays of Shakespeare to Bacon or Oxford or another "properly educated" contemporary of the Swan of Avon.

When the stories that the poems of Homer tell were originally sung, Athens was nothing and the revival of what would become Greek culture was most energetic on the coast of Asia Minor and the eastern islands. In about 1200 BC, a period of Greek history ended and what most historians describe as "a dark age" (because there is so little evidence of what was going on at the time) followed. In the ninth century BC, the curtain begins to rise once more, though what existed on the other, previous side of the darkness was hard to make out. The Greeks had to re-learn how to write (there was, despite what Herodotus says, writing from the period 1600–1200, none from 1200 to 900 BC).

> The Phoenicians who accompanied Cadmus . . . introduced into Greece on their arrival a range of arts, among them that of writing, of which the Greeks until then, I believe, were ignorant. Originally they made their letters just like the Phoenicians, but in time, they altered their language, and the form of their letters . . . I myself saw Cadmeian characters engraved upon some tripods in

the temple of Apollo Ismenias in Boeotian Thebes . . . One of the tripods
has this inscription: "Amphitryon, coming from the far Teleboans, placed me
here." This would be about the age of Laius, the son of Labdacus, the son of
Polydorus, the son of Cadmus. Another of the tripods has this hexameter
legend: "I was offered by the boxer Scaeus to far-shooting[54] Apollo / When
thanks to Phoebus he won at the games." It is a lovely offering. Perhaps this is
Scaeus, Hippocoon's son; the tripod, if he dedicated it and not another with
the same name, belongs to the period of Oedipus, son of Laius.[55]

A simplified alphabet, with fewer letters and easier forms, evolved in Ionia
out of Phoenician practice. Here began the long process towards general literacy. In time a reading and writing culture emerged, without a clear moment in time when we can say that the oral tradition had been decisively
displaced by the writing habit. The demand for written material had to grow,
inevitably; the city-states had to develop; the need for numbers and accounts,
and for written laws and liturgies, made a gradual highway for literature.

Most of the surviving writing of the crucial period, where we can say a
culture found definition, emanates from Athens, either because it was written or it was recorded there. Lionel Casson believes the Homeric poems
were not set down in writing until a good two centuries after the new alphabet was current, "and then only to stabilise the text, not to serve readers."[56]
By 500 BC, however, Homer and other poets *were* probably being read, not
merely heard in performance. There is evidence to be found on the Greek
vases. Schools developed primarily for boys, but pottery paintings show
women reading and singing from scrolls, so some girls too did learn and engage in the arts of recitation.

Early in the fifth century BC, authors began to write down as well as to
perform their work (though "to publish" retained its meaning of "to make
public in performance"). This stimulated the growth of prose and prose
reading. In his plays, Aristophanes, in the late fifth and early fourth centuries BC, could make jokes that assumed quite general literacy, books and
their availability.[57]

The changes that occurred between the Trojan War, around 1200 BC, and
"Homer," four or five centuries later, were momentous. There is also a
yawning gap between "Homer's" time and the age of Pisistratus. When we
consider Homer as a poet we must bear three time-frames in mind: that
of the initial Trojan action, that of the early recitations and the formulation
of the narrative in the oral tradition, and finally that of the writing-down of
the text. These three frames correspond to different cultural phases, the
first being a Greek pre-history accessible if at all through archaeology, the
second being the period of Greek expansion and trade and the renewal of
contact between mainland Greece, the islands, and Asia Minor, and the

third being the well-recorded period of the tyranny of Pisistratus after his friend Solon's archonate. Each phase makes a different kind of contribution to the poetry and to the "poet" Homer.

More fragments of Homer survive among the Egyptian literary papyruses so far discovered than of all other literary papyruses combined.[58] What is remarkable is the closeness with which they agree, as though the stabilisation of the text actually worked, affecting the way the poems were transmitted in manuscript throughout the Greek world. Accuracy had an authority; the poems were transmitted with the rigour that we would normally associate with the transmission of scripture.

And this too tells us something of the place the poems held in the classical and then the Hellenistic period. They provided the common culture so that a man of Agatha, beyond Liguria on what is now the French coast, of Alalia in Corsica, Neapolis in Italy, Naxos in Sicily, Kyrene in North Africa, Knossos on Rhodes, Paphos on Cyprus, Ephesus, Chios, Corinth and Athens, not to mention the cities around the Black Sea, had a cultural *lingua franca* whatever the differences in their dialects. The poems were, in a sense, what kept the Greek from becoming a mere barbarian. And because it was poetry, it meant that those who practised the art of poetry were judged against the best and—if their work had merit—honoured and rewarded: a pension for Simonides of Cos; an invitation to honoured Anacreon to come to Athens.

The question of the place of writing in Homeric *composition,* as opposed to *transmission,* divides scholars. Some insist that the poems were largely taken down from dictation and were in a basic sense oral in conception; others, who concede that there is traditional material in the poems, formulae and the like, believe that the poems were written, adducing the remarkable integration of the material, especially in the *Iliad,* and suggesting that such close working would not have been possible or even desirable in an oral composition. If we contrast the poetry of Homer with that of Hesiod, as Martin West observes, we sense immediately that the poems attributed to Hesiod were written down, even though the texture is less complex—they have that literary feel; the narrator projects a more or less coherent and consistent "self"; stylistic irony and other devices reify a text. The Homeric poems lack this sense of artifice focussed in a self-aware "I." They are not *spoken,* they *speak.*

The written text became a battlefield for editors and critics: what truly belonged, what was forged, what was embellishment? Different kinds of exegesis were practised, moral, cultural and political. In the sixth and subsequent centuries, systematic approaches evolved, in particular allegorical reading, which began with Theagenes of Rhegion, one of the first critics to write extensively about Homer (his great work has perished). He claimed that the gods personified irresistible phenomena of nature, their arguments elemental conflicts. Allegorising patristics evolved through the fifth-century biographer and political writer Stesimbrotus of Thasos (who wrote in Athens), Crates of Mallos (librarian of Pergamum and leader of the Pergamene school in the second century) and persisted until the time of the poet-critic Tzetzes in the twelfth century AD.

Several scholars at the library in Alexandria devoted themselves to Homer. Zenodotus of Ephesus, Ptolemy's first librarian, early in the third century BC, was the first "scientific" editor of Homer, comparing and collating different manuscripts and making reasoned choices between alternative readings. Zenodotus also edited Hesiod's *Theogony* on the same principles. Aristophanes of Byzantium (*c.* 257–180), who was like Zenodotus head of the library (did chief librarians take credit for the work of their lieutenants, or did they in fact, in the first person, unroll and re-roll the long Homeric scrolls?), regularised the writing of Greek accents (indeed he may have invented the notation) and devised marks to indicate suspect or extraordinary passages (later additions, quotations, etc.). Aristarchus of Samothrace (217–145 BC), who was both a chief Alexandrian librarian and a thoroughgoing scientific editor, followed Zenodotus in applying rigorous comparative standards to Homer and Hesiod, and also to Alcaeus, Anacreon and Pindar, creating "standard editions" with commentaries. Fragments of his commentaries on Homer survive.

The Alexandrian editors would have had to collate scrolls from different cities and versions bearing the "names" of different owners who might themselves have added or subtracted matter, following in Solon's inventive wake. Versions from a specific city might have included interpolations celebrating that city. Aristarchus deleted lines he believed after careful consideration to be spurious; but where his doubts were not overwhelming he merely marked with "a horizontal stroke as a critical sign (*obelos*)."[59]

IV

The Homeric Apocrypha

> ... And through the tortoise's hard stony skin
> At proper distances small holes he made,
> And fastened the cut stems of reeds within,
> And with a piece of leather overlaid
> The open space and fixed the cubits in,
> Fitting the bridge to both, and stretched o'er all
> Symphonious cords to sheep-gut rhythmical.
>
> "Hymn to Hermes,"
> translated by PERCY BYSSHE SHELLEY

 A modern Aristarchus applies the *obelos* to the Homeric poems now regarded as apocryphal, spurious, falsely assigned; yet their original attribution to him tells us something about Homer's audience and his place in ancient culture. They illuminate, by imitation, parody or shadowy allusion, the *Iliad* and the *Odyssey*. The lost epic cycle which grew around those poems is dealt with in the next chapter. Here we look briefly at the celebrated *Homeric Hymns,* the almost vanished *Margites* and *Kerkopes,* the epigrams and the *Batrachomyomachia.* Most, it would appear, are assigned to Homer because of the Homeric metre used, the diction, and the relatively early date. None of them appears to be even an oblique product of the oral tradition, though each was composed within earshot of the *Iliad* and *Odyssey* and intended for individual or choral recitation. A poet might borrow the authority of Homer, pretending his work was by the master. Though he thus forfeited his claim to celebrity and copyright, he was a true poet in that he wanted, above all, his *poem* to be taken seriously.

The *Homeric Hymns,* read in the wake of the *Iliad* and *Odyssey,* are diverse and uneven. Some seem contrived and literary, others mere fragments. Did the short ones lead into longer epic narrations? Thucydides calls the "Hymn to Apollo" a *prooimion,* a prologue or overture. Were they preludes, invocations, the remains of the dithyrambs that introduced the festival occasions of Tragedy and Comedy? The most memorable are narratives in their own right, less hymns than forerunners of what would become—at a later date—the epyllion, or miniature epic.

There are thirty-three hymns, if we agree to divide the "Hymn to Apollo" in two, part dedicated to the Delian, part to the Pythian god; and there are scanty remains of a further hymn quoted in Diodorus. The poems were composed at different periods and places: it is unclear when they were brought together in their present form. "These hymns are wholly in the rhapsodic tradition, borrowing their language from Homer even to complete phrases," Lesky says.[1] They may have enabled a rhapsode, like Ion, to clear his throat before epic recitation. Even when their tone approaches lyric, the hymns are in hexameters. The use of epic strategies in non-heroic contexts yields new tonalities. In the "Hymn to Delian Apollo," we see how festivals brought people together in celebration.

When they take narrative form, the hymns concentrate upon the infancy, childhood and youth of the gods: used as preludes, they are also, appropriately, *about* beginnings. In this they presage the obsessive theme of the Alexandrian poets, the aetiologies of the *Aetia* of Callimachus, of Apollonius' and Theocritus' verse. They are also about change, sometimes the extreme change of metamorphosis, as in "Dionysus II." The Greek word *hymnos* means a song, speech or poem that celebrates gods or heroes.

The first hymn[2] is fragmentary, dedicated to Dionysus. In lines 13–15 it quotes directly from the *Iliad,* Book I, 528–30. The *Iliad* lines are so powerful—Zeus nodding acquiescence to Thetis' demands—that anyone familiar with the epic will hear the echo and wonder whether it is appropriate to plant so large and famous a gem in so modest a setting.

The second hymn, "Demeter I," tells of the rape of Persephone and, in due course, the origin of the Eleusinian Mysteries. The particularity of detail is Homeric, the close-up and unsentimental treatment of feelings and responses to extreme actions. Probably from the late seventh century BC, it is one of the earliest hymns. Pluto (unnamed because it is bad luck to name the god of the underworld) carries Persephone away in his chariot. The over-abundance of adjectives, the sense that everything is posed for meaning, the flow certainly ceremonial if not arrested make for stiffness, a sense of deliberate composition, even of composition to a critical prescription, namely to yield allegorical meanings. However, the metamorphosis of Demeter from an old crone nursing the baby to the goddess herself is dazzling (ll. 275–84).

The two poems titled "Hymn to Apollo," yoked together in the text, although generally separated out by editors, so as to celebrate separately the two manifestations of the god, are the hymns that have attracted most critical and scholarly attention and that seem to have had the profoundest effect on subsequent poetry. Hugh G. Evelyn-White suggests the Delian hymn comes from the eighth century BC; in the second hymn Delphi is all-important, Delos forgotten. It was probably composed around, and certainly not later than, 600 BC. The older part of the hymn is the one in which the blind singer identifies himself to the girls and paints a famous hypothetical portrait of Homer. The "Hymn to Pythian Apollo" juxtaposes the happy, beautiful lives of the immortals and the short, witless, helpless lives

of mortals. Apollo is always "far-shooting" (*ekatebol Apollon*). It explains
Hera's hatred for Thetis (she nursed Hephaestos when Hera threw her de-
fective offspring, the lame god, from heaven) and why in the *Iliad* Thetis is
able to ask such big favours of Hephaestos (the shield for her son Achilles,
for example). The poem provides the etymology of "Pythian": the slaying
of the dragoness, her physical decomposition hastened by Helios, the sun;
it evokes the origin (Cretan, Cnossan) of Apollo's priesthood.

The most complex and amusing hymn is "To Hermes." Shelley translated it, but it is more up Byron's street in its humour, burlesque and parodic
implausibilities. It was written some time after Terpander invented the
seven-string lyre, about 676 BC. A straightforward invocation, "Muse, sing
of Hermes," is followed by a tautological genealogy: son of Zeus and Maia,
whom Maia bore, when she was joined in love with Zeus . . . Maia is nicely
characterised as a privacy-loving goddess who lives in the recesses of her
cave. She has abundant tresses. Her amazing offspring Hermes, born at
dawn, by noon is already inventing and playing the lyre; in the evening he
steals the cattle of far-shooting (again) Apollo. What were his chief attributes and achievements? He was "wily, a thief, a rustler, an inducer of
dreams, a night owl, at the gates a thief, a child who would shortly display
amazing deeds among the immortal gods."

He is born with one instinct, it would seem: to steal Apollo's livestock.
But as he bustles, leaving his swaddling behind, from the maternal cave, he
comes upon a tortoise. "Hermes first made the tortoise sing. The animal
appeared to him at the gate of the courtyard; it was grazing on the lush
grass in front of the cavern, moving ungainly along. When Hermes, Zeus's
luck-bringing child, saw it, he chuckled: 'A sign of good luck for me so
early! I won't give it a miss. Ho there, fellow-comer to the feast, you of the
lovely form, who make music at the dance! I am happy to meet you! Where
did you get that lavishly patterned roof, that embossed shell—a tortoise,
mountain dwelling? Come with me, I'll take you in; you'll assist me and I
will honour you, but first you must bring me benefit. Home's the best place
to be: out of doors bad things can happen. Alive, you're a spell against
wicked magic; but dead, you'll make the most delicious music.'" The infant's *sang froid* is a kind of innocence. And, sure enough, he kills the tortoise brutally and transforms the shell into a lyre. A double "Homeric"
simile underlines his action: "Just as a quick thought flits through a man's
heart when he is troubled in spirit by flocking worries, just as an eye glances
up and dazzles, Hermes contrived the thought and the act in the same instant." This is how music happens, too: the thought and deed, the command and the act of playing, occur virtually together.

Having made the lyre, momentously he plays it: "At the merest touch of
his fingers it made a marvellous sound, and he played on, singing delicious

phrases here and there, not a song but like the melodious blurtings of young men at a festival. Then he sang of Cronus' son, father Zeus, and Maia with her pretty sandals, how they had talked together when making love, and he told the amazing story of his own conception." His first song touches on delicate themes: love, but the love his parents made to make him. The father of the lyre and of music, a baby, is at the same time practical, guileful, deceitful, cheerful, "innocent," close to the ground.

Soon he tires of singing. What he craves is meat. He steals fifty of Apollo's cattle. He is crafty: he "reversed the hoofprints, the front appeared behind and the hind appeared in front, while, for his own part, he walked the other way." Thus the cattle seem to have vanished into thin air, having arrived and not departed. He makes for himself sandals of brushwood and leaves to sweep away traces as he walks.

There is a witness: an old man within a vineyard sees him. The infant god promises him a fine vintage if he keeps his counsel. After the theft of Apollo's cattle and the slaughter of two, and a first meat feast, Hermes sleeps away from home, then returns unperceived, passing like an autumn breeze through a keyhole, re-wraps himself in swaddling, and is a simple baby, clutching his seven-string lyre. His mother *knows* as mothers always do, and they have the kind of heated exchange that usually occurs between teenagers and parents. Hermes intends to become the prince of robbers.

Meanwhile, back at the ranch, Apollo is troubled when he discovers that his herd has been raided by rustlers. The old vineyard-keeper discloses the truth and Apollo hurries to Maia's cave where he beards Hermes in his den, tries to intimidate the baby, then drags him off to trial by the highest judge, Zeus himself. The judge cannot contain his laughter when the baby god, holding in one hand his lyre and in the other his trailing swaddling clothes, pleads his case. He orders Hermes to take Apollo to the byre near the river Alphaeus. Apollo marvels at the baby's strength and cannot bind him. Hermes plays the lyre and Apollo loves the music and the instrument. Since the poem is a hymn, it issues in harmony. They become friends. Hermes gives Apollo the lyre and invents the pipes for himself so that they can play duets. Apollo grants his half-brother every skill except soothsaying. He can learn divination if he wishes, but not prediction and visionary prophecy. Zeus makes Hermes lord over birds of omen, lions, boars, dogs, flocks—country things. He also becomes the elected messenger between Olympus and Hades.

The first "Hymn to Aphrodite" is like the hymn that the blind poet Demodocus sings in *Odyssey* VIII, 266ff., though superior in subtlety and development. Three hearts are impervious to Aphrodite: those of Athena, Artemis and Hestia.[3] Aphrodite has affected every other god and the whole human world: none is left untouched. Zeus tricks her into love with a mortal, namely Anchises, so she will know what it is all about. Anchises was tending cattle—another cowboy—on Mount Ida. He is godlike in demeanour. Their courtship unfolds ceremonially and is beautifully rendered. After their initial love, she promises him dignity and offspring, a son who will reign and "children's children after him, springing up continually." He will not be immortal but his line will last for ever, which is second best. The name of Aeneas is uttered, possibly a later interpolation. The baby they have will be raised by nymphs, who are neither mortal nor immortal: at their birth great trees are born and when they are to perish the trees perish.[4] When the boy is five the goddess will bring him back to Anchises and instruct him. He is not to mention that he slept with her or Zeus will kill him. She vanishes like a rocket (or a bird soaring) into the windy sky. It is an amazing poem, full of illuminating congruities.

The second "Hymn to Dionysus" is hard to date: some critics attribute it to the fourth or third century BC, others to the seventh or sixth. The kinds of poise and polish which the language enjoys, and the efficiency rather than ease of movement in narrative, seem to argue for a later date. We encounter again a god in his youth, formally unstable, innocent, disarming in himself and in the metamorphoses he undergoes and provokes. Pirates spot the ostentatiously caped god standing on a promontory. They capture him to sell on as a slave and try to tie him up. As when Apollo tries to bind the infant Hermes, here too the bonds fall away, and the youth sits grinning at his captors. The helmsman urges the pirate master to put the god ashore but the master refuses to part with so fine a catch, this glowing youth in his purple robe. Wind takes the sails and suddenly the ship is awash with sweet wine; grape vines twine up and then dangle from cross-beams and rigging; ivy coils up the mast, flowers bloom, berries, "and all the thole pins' were covered with garlands." The sailors, terrified, try to land the lad; but he becomes a furious lion and creates amidships a grumbly shaggy bear "which stood up ravening." Lion in prow, bear amidships, the pirates crowd into the stern. The lion jumps on the pirate master and seizes him, and the pirate crew jumps overboard into the bright sea and is transformed—into a school of dolphins! Dionysus does not kill the master: he identifies himself as divine and bids him be cheerful. Here ends a beguiling lesson.

The "Hymn to Pan" is also striking. Pan is Hermes' son, though who the mother was, given Pan's goat's hooves and horns, is initially a moot point. The poem sets out to provide an explanation. Pan is a spirit of nature who also hunts. In the evening he plays the pipes, invented by his father in an earlier hymn. The noise he makes is sweeter even than that of a sweet-noted bird. The nymphs sing along with him, and the story he tells is often of the amorous adventures of his father. Hermes' first song was about the amorous adventures of his parents, too: this would appear to be the beginning of self-knowledge for a god. Hermes became the shepherd-servant of a man because he wanted to wed his daughter Dryops. They had a baby who was cheerful and strong but had goat's feet, horns and a full beard. The wet-nurse was so alarmed she ran away. The father, hugely proud, took the bearded baby wrapped in hare skins to Olympus and showed him to the gods. The gods were delighted, especially Bacchic Dionysus. The name Pan is a shortened form of *pantes,* says the hymn, "because he delighted *all* their hearts."

There are other memorable hymns, or passages in them. The second "Hymn to Artemis" evokes the huntress who, tiring of the chase, goes to the house of her brother Apollo and choreographs the dances of the Muses and Graces. The nymphs or priestesses in his house chant of Leto and her wonderful offspring. The "Hymn to Helios" invokes the Muse Calliope to help the singer celebrate glowing Helios. Again we get a genealogy: Helios is the son of Hyperion and Euryphaëssa, brother of rosy-armed (and rosy-fingered) Eos and of "rich-tressed Selene," the moon. The hymn is clearly a prelude, in this case seeming to promise an epic poem: "I will celebrate the race of mortal men half-divine whose deeds the Muses have showed to mankind." These are the heroes: Hesiod says they occupy the space between the human and the divine, transcendent but not immortal. Appropriately, the "Hymn to Selene," the moon, follows "Helios," beginning "And next," as if it was a sequel to the previous poem. The hymn-writer calls Selene "long-winged," which some translators take to mean "far-flying." It might be taken to indicate the wings of the crescent.

The hymns are an uneven anthology of preludes and narratives. They are so various and in places so charming that they do Homer no discredit, even though he is unlikely to have composed them. It is equally unlikely that the epigrams attributed to him are his. They are to be found in the *Life of Homer* attributed to Herodotus and repeated in the *Contest* and elsewhere.[6] Some are aphoristic commonplaces, but a few stand out. The fourteenth epigram is about the potter's art, blessing the virtuous potter and cursing the false promiser. It grows, as so much that is attributed to Homer does, out of an allegorising tradition. The fifteenth epigram, about the prosperous man, is also memorable, though also apocryphal.

Then there is *Margites:* "Once to Colophon an old man, a graced singer, the Muses' servant and far-shooting Apollo's, came. He bore in his dear hands a sweet-sounding lyre."[7] Margites is a simpleton, insofar as we can infer him from the few remaining fragments, who "would not sleep with his wife" for fear that "she might report ill of him to his mother." It is only with great difficulty that his young wife can persuade him to "discharge his marital duties."[8] We cannot reach a verdict on the poem, given the poverty of fragments, but its form is curious. The basic measure, as in all the Homeric attributions, is hexameter, with apparently random iambic lines interspersed. It dates possibly from the sixth century.

Even more completely vanished than *Margites* is *Cercopes* ("monkeyman"). *Cercopes* told of two cunning brothers, Acmon and Passalus. Their mother, Memnon's daughter, warns them to keep clear of Blackbottom (Heracles). They disobey and Zeus, angered, turns them to stone. The connection with Memnon and Ethiopia and the imagery smack of a kind of atavism bordering on racial fear and hostility.

Of all the apocryphal Homeric poems none is more fun, or more illuminating, than *Batrachomyomachia* ("The Battle of the Frogs and the Mice"), "the song which I have just composed on tablets upon my knee." It is a decidedly *literary* composition, working, as all parodies do, from and on existing texts. Early critics regarded it as a Homeric apprentice-piece, a kind of tiny maquette for the *Iliad.* This overlooks the elements, continuous throughout the poem, of intertextual comedy, the spoofing of conventional epic diction, simile, action, with specific passages in the *Iliad* quite deliberately burlesqued. It is a relatively early production, accepted as Homeric even in pre-Hellenic times. The tenth-century lexicon, the *Suda,* declares that the real author, also responsible for *Margites,* was Pigres, a Carian, brother of Artemisia, "wife of Mausolus." He is a man who distinguished himself at the Battle of Salamis. The *Suda* confuses two Artemisias, but the date, around 480 BC, might be right.

The poem consists of 303 hexameters in a rather chaotic state, including what may be Byzantine interpolations. Coming as it originally must from the period of allegorical readings of epic, the names are indicators, and finding English equivalents for them is a cheerful challenge for the translator.

Cheekpuffer, or Puff-jaw, the frog king takes Crumbsnatcher the mouse (who has just escaped a hungry ferret) across a lake, after first asking his name and provenance, promising him lavish gifts if he answers correctly, and receiving a suitably ceremonious reply. The mouse speaks of the differences in their natures, especially in what they eat, describing the human foods he most enjoys. He says he is brave, he runs on men's beds and nibbles them, and is afraid only of the hawk, the ferret and the trap. The frog remarks that the mouse concentrates rather a lot on belly-matters.

The mouse boards the frog and they begin their cruise of the lake. Soon the mouse gets frightened, steadying himself with his tail. Just before a water snake appears and scares the frog into a fatal dive, the mouse declares, "Not thus did the bull carry on his back the dear burden, when he bore Europa over the waves to Crete, as this Frog bears me over the waves to his dwelling, making his yellow back rise out of the bright water."

A mouse on shore witnesses the floundering death of the king. The race of mice plans its revenge. They arm ingeniously, armour made of bean pods and reeds and ferret skin, with bronze needles for spears and helmets of peanut shells. When the mice issue the challenge of battle, the frog king denies guilt. Lying thus, he puts himself and his kind in the wrong. The frogs use pointed rushes for spears and snail shells for helmets. The confrontation begins. Zeus, who has a finger in everything, summons a conclave of the gods. They look down on armies, opposed as if the centaurs confronted the giants. Zeus asks the gods to take sides. Athena will not back the mice: they have made a mess of her garlands and robes and reduced her to going to the money-lender, an outrage for an immortal. She also dislikes the frogs, who once kept her awake all night. She urges the gods not to commit but to watch with amusement. They concur. There are direct echoes of *Iliad* battles, notably of the stone wounding the shoulder, as happens to Hector.[9] The battle rages, the mice are winning, the frog cause almost lost when Zeus sends a thunderbolt. The mice will not desist so the gods send crabs to side with the frogs. The mice turn tail and the sun sets on the one-day war.

Alexander Pope's friend Thomas Parnell based his memorable attack on pedantic scholars on this poem.[10] Samuel Taylor Coleridge found the poem delightful and slight. Against the notion that it was Homer's apprentice-piece, he said: "to suppose a work of mere burlesque to be the primary effort of poetry in a simple age, seems to reverse that order in the development of national taste, which the history of every other people in Europe, and of many in Asia, has almost ascertained to be a law of the human mind; it is in a state of society much more refined and permanent than that described in the *Iliad,* that any popularity would attend such a ridicule of war and the gods as is contained in this poem." The genre itself suggests—even if the parodic elements did not—a later composition.

The convenience of finding early, middle and late poems by Homer eludes us, not only because texts have perished but because the grin and the cat refuse to stay together in the tree. It is unlikely, too, that we will learn much more than we already know about Homer's antecedents, the eastern sources for some of the elements in his poems, the tradition out of which they emerge. In poetry the miraculous coming-together of factors into a major poem cannot be explained by evolution. Indeed, the history of epic poetry is a denial of theories of cultural evolution. The great poets, the peaks, are suddenly there, without much benefit of foothills: Homer, Virgil, Dante, Chaucer, Shakespeare, Milton. They have antecedents and contexts but the lines that lead up to them are not straight, the selection they make not always natural. The great epics lead to or produce not greater epics but a kind of diminishment. In the aftermath of Milton growth was hard; it was not given to Italians to replicate or to contest the pre-eminent achievement of Dante. Leopardi, his worthiest successor, is worthy in his knowledge of

Dante's place. After Homer, the Greek epic poets become formal, literary, more "written," less direct. For a while the Greek lyric poets maintain the connection with the breathing world which is so palpable in Homer. The Homeric poems, in their concentration and power, exhausted the epic tradition. Ionia remained in thrall to romantic epic subject-matter. In Boeotia something new stirred: Hesiod exercised "freedom from classical form," and expressed "his grave, and yet child-like, outlook upon his world." And the lyric poets in their different modes, all of them steeped in Homer and not vying with him, were crawling out from under his towering shadow. As usual, the heir to great epic poetry is the lyric poet.

V

The Iliad *and the* Odyssey

From Homer and Polygnotus I every day learn more
clearly, that in our life here above ground we have, properly speaking, to enact hell.

GOETHE, letter to Schiller[1]

In Book VIII of the *Odyssey*, the blind bard Demodocus entertains King Alcinous and his anonymous guest, whom we know
to be Odysseus, with songs about Greek deeds during the Trojan War. In particular, he sings of the wooden horse. The
Phaeacian court is attentive; twice the guest sheds secret tears into his
rucked-up hood.

He weeps, the poem says, the way a woman weeps for her husband. It is
an arresting simile: this most masculine of men is emasculated by deep feeling. But the poem does not leave it there. Like many epic similes it works towards metamorphosis. Here is Samuel Butler's prose translation of the
passage:[2] "Odysseus was overcome as he heard him, and his cheeks were
wet with tears. He wept as a woman weeps when she throws herself on the
body of her husband who has fallen before his own city and people, fighting bravely in defence of his home and children." It is so real to him that,
helpless to affect the narrative (it is now history and cannot be touched), all
he can do is lament in the unbridled yet formal way of Mediterranean
mourning. The poem follows the woman in her grief: "She screams aloud
and flings her arms about him as he lies gasping for breath and dying, but
her enemies beat her from behind about the back and shoulders, and carry
her off into slavery, to a life of labour and sorrow, and the beauty fades
from her cheeks—even so piteously did Ulysses weep . . ." Only Alcinous
hears his stifled lamentation.

The simile is not content simply to illuminate its immediate visual and
emotional context. The woman Odysseus is likened to reminds us of all
Trojan women but especially of Hector's widow, Andromache.[3] She laments,
but her lamentations are interrupted by her captors, who herd her and her
sister into captivity and slavery. The poet fades out the simile with a simple
finality, "and the beauty fades from her cheeks." A cruder translation says,
"while with most pitiful grief her cheeks are wasted." The metaphor is conducted in the present tense.

This is the impact Demodocus' poem has on Odysseus, as it would on any man who is capable of being moved by heroism and tragedy. The experience belongs not to the victorious Greeks but to their foes, and yet after victory they can feel for and, more important, feel *with* the victims. This is also the power of the Homeric poems themselves. They are about wars and victors but the victims have a palpable and at some points an equal reality. Though the "insistently male orientation" of the *Iliad* has been noted, there is even in that poem a strong sense that, in the world that underpins the epic deeds of the main story, there exist people whose heroism, on a different scale, merits inclusion if only by way of simile. Thus in the *Iliad*, Book XII, we read, in Butler's version, "But even so the Trojans could not rout the Achaeans, who still held on; and as some honest hard-working woman weighs wool in her balance and sees that the scales be true, for she would gain some pitiful earnings for her little ones, even so was the fight balanced evenly between them till the time came when Zeus gave the greater glory to Hector son of Priam, who was first to spring towards the wall of the Achaeans." What, we may ask, once this startling image has had its incongruous impact, is this spinner—a mother with hungry children, perhaps a widow since she is sole provider, or a woman whose husband is away at war, a Penelope who weaves and unweaves—doing in the thick of battle, not only with the heroes but with Zeus himself, to whom she ultimately is the point of comparison? Is she another one of the bereaved? In Book VIII we have already seen Zeus with his golden scales. In Book XVI they are there again: Hector realises that the "scales of Zeus" are now weighted against him. In Book XXII the golden scales dip decisively, and Achilles knows the day is his.[4] Yet the most memorable scales are those of the widow spinner.

Even heroes can be even-handed in describing their foes. Standing on the battlements, Priam notes how much larger the gathering of men is than when he and his armies fought in Phrygia as allies, against the Amazons. He spots Odysseus and describes him as fleecy and ramlike, keeping his ewes in line. Antenor interposes: he recalls how Odysseus and Menelaus came to discuss Helen with Priam before war began. He recalls how well they spoke: first Menelaus, direct and rather precipitate, and then Odysseus, seeming slow-witted, but then unfolding a speech that dazzled and persuaded. In the *Iliad*, certainly, Odysseus is a rhetorician, always politic, sent on missions as a trusted emissary of Agamemnon. In the *Odyssey*, he is released from direct responsibility to a king. Whenever he comes into contact with courts or with common people and his story is required, he becomes a poet, sometimes telling the truth, sometimes inventing a fictitious life to keep himself safe.

The first evidence of his poetic talents comes just after he meets Nausicaa. Naked, holding a branch before his private parts (her maids having run off because he emerged like a lion from his bed of leaves), he addresses her. He says he has been adrift for twenty days. Dazzled by her beauty, he compares her to a lovely palm tree he saw once at Delos, near Apollo's altar. It is a pretty image, certainly, and the mention of Delos calls to mind not only the gods born there, Athena and Apollo, but the great festival and the poetic activities that it hosted.

At the Phaeacian court, after Demodocus reduces him to tears and draws his identity from him, it is his turn to sing his story to the assembled court. The king, he says, requires him to revisit an unspeakably painful subject. (One of Virgil's most famous lines, put into the mouth of Aeneas, is based on this speech: *Infandum, regina, iubes renovare dolorem*.) Odysseus wonders how to *shape* his tale ("What shall I tell first, what shall I save to tell you until later?"). His concerns are those of the narrative artist, to get it in the right order and proportion so that it will affect his audience properly.

When he is telling the Cyclops story, he reports on how he and the crew had stocked up on strong sweet wine. This is a crucial ingredient in drugging the monster. In terms of plot, it is crafty of Odysseus to put in the crucial detail well in advance of the point when the wine will be made use of. He *prepares* the story. Certainly his telling of the fantastic adventures he has undergone is fast-paced and thrifty. His visit to the underworld at Circe's command (Book XI) is a complicated weave of memory and prophecy, and the poet Odysseus handles it well. Indeed, his success is such that in the midst of his account of the dead he asks for largesse from the assembled court, and when the figurative hat is passed around he does remarkably well. He returns to Ithaca in a Phaeacian ship ballasted with Phaeacian treasure.

His creative phase is not over. Having told Alcinous' court the truth, he must make a fictional life to hide behind while he tests the ground at Ithaca. Athena turns him into a bald shrivelled old man and he visits the swineherd Eumaeus. He sits wizened and smelly under a cloak and tells his old retainer a plausible life story, developing one he first told to a handsome young shepherd (Athena, disguised), when he woke up on the unrecognised shore of his homeland that morning. Later he repeats the tale to the suitors.

The *Iliad* and *Odyssey* were intended for recitation, not by a hero but by a rhapsode. They were delivered at a certain speed and many of the effects which detain us as readers would have been at best fleetingly sensed by a member of an audience. But if they were recited regularly and people heard them again and again, and if the versions they heard were indeed, thanks to Solon and Pisistratus and even Onomacritos, the same, they would have heard *more* at each performance. Thus in time the self-subversiveness of these poems which anchor the Greek imagination, and in which Greek philosophy and drama have their origin, would have communicated itself to many. Whatever the brutality of the deeds recounted in the poems, what marks them both is their balance (to take up the image of the scales), an absence of partisanship, a reluctance to moralise. One is tempted, even in this age of relativities, to speak of the poems' *objectivity,* their insistence on telling it (even the fantasy passages in the *Odyssey,* even Xanthus, the loquacious horse in the *Iliad*) *how it was.* This involves an absence of sentimentality. What feelings are expressed belong to the characters and their situations, and the poem reports without colluding in them.

"Poets and their audience," Taplin insists, are a constant theme in the *Odyssey.* He exaggerates, but we do meet our first poet in line 150 of Book I. Phemius ("Famous") sings to the cithern harp. We ignore his song at first because we are listening to Athena, disguised as Mentes, talking to Telemachus about his father and prophesying his return. When she has departed, Telemachus realises a god has been with him. Phemius is still singing, bitter tales of the returning Achaeans. Penelope comes down the long stairway from her high room and tells the singer to desist. But Telemachus overrides her instructions. The poet should sing "what he has a mind to; bards do not make the ills they sing of; it is Zeus, not they, who makes them [. . .] Go, then, within the house and busy yourself with your daily duties, your loom, your distaff, and the ordering of your servants; for speech is man's matter, and mine above all others—for it is I who am master here." To modern eyes, certainly, Telemachus comes across as a young man with much to learn about good manners, and women.

Here the verse is *listened* to and it has an impact on Penelope and the suitors. The theme of return is itself inadvertently prophetic in this context. Phemius the bard leads a charmed life: he and Medon the herald alone are spared by Odysseus in Book XXII, when the suitors perish. He insists that he sang for the suitors unwillingly.

Those of us with a memory of school Latin may share a pro-Trojan take on the Trojan War. This is because Virgil, praising his emperor through legendary narrative in the *Aeneid,* knows that the Roman empire has its origins in the Trojan defeat, followed by the Trojan hero Aeneas' epic journey to Italy. By the time of Virgil, poets no longer aspired to the inclusive objectivity of Homer. Homer did not, as one critic claims, side with Troy because it was on his side of the Aegean: he belonged (a man of Smyrna) to the East. But his lack of bias does have the effect of seeming to commend Phoenician, or "eastern," values to Greek audiences that may have been a bit short on civility and sophistication when the poems were first recited. Ford Madox Ford makes no bones about it: the war was "an immense Affair—an immense, almost chemical reaction between a higher, more luxurious and more aesthetic civilisation from the East, attacking or attacked by a relatively lean, relatively puritanical, relatively, perhaps, better armed civilisation coming from the West."[5] The effects of Homeric even-handedness may be political, but they are not political by design, and their politics will be different in different ages.

Perhaps Homer in the *Iliad* tells the truth. Troy was a handsome, civilised city with open spaces; it is described as having broad streets and horse pastures within the walls. The Greek camp was temporary, without history, without elegance, though because nine years had passed there was some solidity to it. Achilles' hut was well built (Book IX). Defences are suddenly erected and as suddenly breached during the course of the poem. The bivouacs are mapped in Homer's mind, a kind of corniche with Ajax at one end and Achilles at the other. The camp, in which the men enjoy temporary women, is flanked by the ships, a perpetual reminder of arrival and departure. The Greeks don't belong. Unlike the later seafaring Greeks, they have come not to establish a colony but to sack a great city and then go home with the booty. They are in some respects little better, and little worse, than pirates.

The Trojans, on the other hand, whether inside the walls of their city or on the rare night when, getting the upper hand, they risk camping on the plain, belong, much as the stars belong in heaven. So at the end of Book VIII they are evoked: "Thus high in hope they sat through the livelong night by the highways of war, and many a watch fire did they kindle. As when the stars shine clear, and the moon is bright—there is not a breath of air, not a peak nor glade nor jutting headland but it stands out in the ineffable radiance that breaks from the serene of heaven; the stars can all of them be told and the heart of the shepherd is glad—even thus shone the watch fires of the Trojans before Ilium midway between the ships and the river Xanthus. A thousand camp-fires gleamed upon the plain, and in the glow of each there sat fifty men, while the horses, champing oats and corn beside their chariots, waited till dawn should come."

At some time between 750 and 650 BC, says Taplin, the two epics we associate with the name of Homer were written, or written down. He tries to reconcile the idea of a rooted "oral tradition" with the participation of an actual author. The poet we call Homer flourished on "the northern-Aegean coast of Asia Minor in the Smyrna area" and acquired his art from other bards. "I take it as axiomatic that these great works of art would not have come into existence without an audience."[6] This is not a very helpful axiom because "we have no firm external evidence of Homer's audience or circumstances of performance."[7] So Taplin tries to discover things about Homer's audience from the poems, both from what they say about poets and audiences and from the ways in which they speak. We can assume that the audience would have known the larger story and expected to see where consequences arose. Everything from Paris' abduction to the sack of Troy is contained as it were metonymically in the text.

Taplin believes the audience for Homer was unitary, with shared values and perspectives. Yet if the poems came from an oral tradition, or if there was room for variations in a scripted performance, the audiences would have elicited different versions from place to place, season to season, performance to performance; in sophisticated centres, a discriminating audience might engage critically with the rhapsode, the way Socrates does with Ion. Elsewhere, a star performer would be greeted with adulation. Audiences must have differed, too, at different periods. An oral tradition might have addressed Greeks right through the "dark age" between the Trojan War and the writing down of the poems. A ninth- and a seventh-century audience would have had little in common. Readers of written versions would again be quite different from the auditors of their day.

We know nothing for sure "about the original circumstances of production," Taplin concedes. "Production" is a curious word to use for the recital of the poem or its composition out of pre-existing songs. Modern theory is drawn to analogies between manufacture and creative work, forgetting that "production" is systematic, its processes mechanical, replicable, whereas creation is neither. He is drawn to using the word "production" because he has a sense of the determining role of "consumers" (the audience) in that "production."

Taplin identifies "internal audiences," those represented in the poems themselves, but cautions us: they "should not be treated as direct or 'literal' evidence for the world of the external" or actual "audiences—though that does not mean that there is *no* relationship between them." Critics and scholars tiptoe about, fearing to assert too much. It is worth remarking that, unlike Virgil, Dante, Langland, Camões or Milton, the poet in these poems never steps out of the fiction into a "real" world, never turns to address us as a man narrating a story. Taplin is convinced (we may not be) that both Homeric poems were created "very much for the same audiences and occasions,"[8] despite the quite marked differences in tone, structure, character and ethos between them.

Blind Demodocus' performance of a poem not unlike the *Iliad* has its effect on Odysseus. Odysseus himself sings of his own deeds, and lies about his own deeds, with eloquence and at length, to noble and rustic auditors. The *Iliad* itself contains no such accounts of performance. Odysseus, Ajax and Phoenix on their embassy to sulking Achilles, to try and persuade him to return to the warring fold (*Iliad* IX, 86–91), find him "playing on a lyre, fair, of cunning workmanship, and its cross-bar was of silver. It was part of the spoils which he had taken when he sacked the city of Eetion, and he was now diverting himself with it and singing the feats of heroes. He was alone with Patroclus, who sat opposite to him and said nothing, waiting till he should cease singing."[9] Perhaps from time to time they would exchange the song, Patroclus (who, it is well to remember, is older than Achilles) taking up the familiar story and moving it forward, then handing it back to his friend. This private scene, the accompaniment provided by a harp which is the spoils of some previous sacking, is remote from the performances of Demodocus and Odysseus in the *Odyssey*. At the end of Book VIII of the *Odyssey* King Alcinous explains human suffering in the strangest way: "The gods arranged all this, and sent them their misfortunes in order that future generations might have something to sing about." And he urges his nameless guest to come clean: "Did you lose some brave kinsman of your wife's when you were before Troy? a son-in-law or father-in-law—which are the nearest relations a man has outside his own flesh and blood? or was it some brave and kindly-natured comrade—for a good friend is as dear to a man as his own brother?"[10]

In the *Iliad* no such aesthetic malice is attributed to the gods. The "deeds of men," the feats of heroes, are what Achilles sings in his private symposium with Patroclus, suggesting a much later convention of performance. This is not a poet singing, however, but a warrior; and when he sings it is not to aggrandise himself but to pass the time, to remember, to entertain. The singer here is himself historical, part of the world of which he sings. Odysseus fulfils the same role in *Odyssey* XI, 367ff., but celebrates his own deeds, not without a degree of self-censure. He and Achilles are different in kind from Demodocus, a mere rhapsode, led in to the feast to entertain the mysterious visitor and the Phaeacian court. When he starts to sing we are near the opening lines of the *Iliad*.[11] Though blind, Demodocus makes his audience see the things and deeds that furnish the Greek and the Trojan worlds. He also fulfils a liturgical function in singing of Aphrodite, Ares and Hephaestus, using words that might well become the Homeric Hymns.[12] He is paid with food and drink.

We can assume that the audience for the Homeric poems knew the stories well, understood the conventions of the verse and accepted that its language belonged not to one dialect or city but was of a more generalised nature, combining archaic elements and dialect from different quarters around the Aegean. This syncretistic language is where the sense of "shared Hellenism" comes from: in the area of culture it overrides local patriotisms and inter-city rivalries.

Jacob Burckhardt notes that numerous people and places feature in the poems, yet none is singled out for special emphasis. We might instance the deaths in the *Iliad*, the catalogue of ships and the survey of the Trojan army, which are like lists of dramatis personae.[13] When the poems were performed in different cities, the specifics of that city or monarchy might be singled out and expanded, formulas for local courtesies deployed to increase the rhapsode's purse. The neutrality of the surviving text may be an aspect of a libretto susceptible to local and occasional improvisations and embellishments. Taplin leaves little room in his theories for the possibilities of variation in an oral text. He likes the "Delos model," where the text's neutrality is deliberate, politically balanced. "The Homeric poems are in a sense 'panhellenic.'" They universalise the gatherings and festivals at which (wherever) they are performed. If this is the case, it reflects a highly deliberated aesthetic intent and—unless the decision was taken by the priests of a universalising religion or politicians scheming for unification—might at first itself seem an anachronism.

Still, "Whatever their enmities," Taplin insists, the Greek city-states "share the gods, the athletics, the architecture, and the art. And they share poetry. It is here that the non-local amalgam of the 'dialect' of hexameter poetry becomes really important. And this is, I would claim, the context for the absence of 'localisation' in Homer: the poems do not give prestige and advantage to some participants over others."[14] Given the precise geography of the poems, the claims Taplin makes seem exaggerated. With a curiously Germanic sense of the nature of the "courts" of pre-democratic Greece, Burckhardt says the *Iliad* "reveals an intimate acquaintance with the whole district about Mount Ida; in the courts there, Homer's predecessors may have sung their songs . . ."[15] Most modern critics who are attentive to archaeological developments agree with him. New excavations show, for example, that Troy VI/VII was larger than Mycenae and very like the Troy depicted by Homer in his poems.

There *is*, however, a problem with the variety of dialect elements and archaisms included, as with the cacophony of *chronological* elements, namely the abundant cultural anachronisms. Taplin's sense of audience is geographical, arrested in time between 750 and 650 BC; the persistent historical incongruities are not so seriously considered. Anachronisms make the poems a real playground for archaeologists, though, given the sparsity of archaeological evidence, there can be no final answers or categorical statements about the incongruities. We conveniently divide the past into closed periods, but those periods are closed only if they end in a military or natural cataclysm. All the same, certain things are juxtaposed in the Homeric poems which look historically awkward together, and there are some passages which are, without much doubt, later interpolations.

Fundamental political and technological changes occurred between the time of the Trojan War, around 1200 BC, and the singers performing the poems, around the ninth century BC. There is an even deeper gulf between this time and Pisistratus' Athens, when the text may have been written down definitively. Three time-frames need to be considered: the time of the action, its formulation into song, and the stabilisation of the song as text. The phases have distinct historical contexts: first, a Cretan-dominated period; then the rise of Greek political identity in the city-states and the development of trade and colonial expansion, with renewed contact between Greece and Asia Minor; and finally the cultural maturity that continues during the tyranny of Pisistratus, after the archonate of his friend and eventual enemy Solon.

In Solon's time there may have been a decree that "at the four-yearly Pantheon the rhapsodes should recite the epics of Homer in order, one taking up where another left off."[16] Perhaps even before Pisistratus an established text of some kind existed. Without writing, each successive generation forgets some of the sense of what has come before, even though the lines continue to be mouthed because the poem is inviolable. The audience loses the meanings of words, lines and images, and either doggedly reiterates the incomprehensible, which becomes a form of mystery and magic, or substitutes new details and adjusts the poem so that it "makes sense." Once written down, the obscure image or allusion sticks to the poem like a burr. Scholars may debate its sense, but, without some clear metrical or linguistic imperfection, an inconsistency will not be adjusted or excised.

Here are some of the anachronisms encountered in the poems. Iron, widely used in the eighth and seventh centuries, was probably unknown to the Achaeans. Bronze was their common metal. In the *Iliad*, Book IV, anachronistic iron plays a key part. Pandarus, tricked by Athena, raises his famous bow of ibex horns and lets an arrow loose at red-headed Menelaus. He breaks the Trojan vow that the war should be settled by single combat between Menelaus, Helen's wronged husband, and Alexandrus (a.k.a. Paris). Robert Fitzgerald translates the scene with excessive particularity.

> Pinching the grooved butt and the string, he pulled
> evenly till the bent string reached his nipple,
> the arrowhead of iron touched the bow,
> and when the great bow under tension made
> a semi-circular arc, it sprang.

The arrow makes its way through layers and layers of Menelaean, padding and pricks the skin. He bleeds. Agamemnon declares the truce is at an end. He is afraid Menelaus is worse wounded than he is. Indeed, he thinks he may be dying.

The shields the poem portrays and the shields the Greeks and Trojans actually used are quite different. Some weapons are Mezzanine, or "archaic," some earlier, some contemporary with the age of the poems' inscription. The customs of cremation and inhumation are conflated. The scale and nature of ancient kingship are distorted and the heroes swollen out of all proportion by their identification with later notions of kingship. The structures of households and the wider sense of the material and spiritual organisation of the camps and cities involved are tenuous. The poems omit the

Dorians, who were a real presence at the time, but include the Phoenicians as traders and pirates even though they became prominent only two or three centuries after "the events." Heroes eat roast meat, not fish; yet fishing is a crucial element in the simile structure of the poem.

Two passages, one in each poem, appear on the evidence of diction and formal incongruity to be later interpolations, literary in conception and intention. In the *Iliad,* the "Doloneia" (Book X) tells of the ill-favoured, cowardly and treacherous Trojan "volunteer" Dolon, tricked into betrayal by Odysseus and Diomede. The incident is pasted in, not referred to elsewhere in the poem, not integrated into the larger structure. We would not be without it, it is a vivid and arresting vignette, but it cannot be made to *belong* to the poem. Here Odysseus and Diomede *ride* horses. At no other point in the poem are horses ridden. Tradition says that the long passage was added by Pisistratus (or on his authority) in the sixth century. The other substantial "spurious" addition occurs at the end of the *Odyssey,* the last two hundred lines of Book XXIII and Book XXIV. The editors Aristarchus and Aristophanes both think the poem should end at Book XXIII, line 296, when Odysseus and Penelope go to bed. What follows is a reprise, Penelope telling what she did, Odysseus what he did, without much addition or development, a pointless coda. In Book XXIV, where the relatives of the murdered suitors confront Odysseus, the language and technique go out of focus (apart from the quite remarkable simile at the opening of the book).

Oliver Taplin, despite his initial demurs, finds himself a Homer in the end, one who has become a whole creaturely cat, but he isn't smiling: perhaps, Taplin reflects, Homer's health was deteriorating at the time he was composing those passages. His Homer has acquired a human physiological identity; what is more, he revises his poems. Did Taplin consider the approach of another critic and translator of Homer, Samuel Butler, whose intimacy with the poem leads him to an unexpected conclusion? The *Odyssey* is not the work of an old man: "They say no woman could possibly have written the *Odyssey*. To me, on the other hand, it seems even less possible that a man could have done so. As for its being by a practised and elderly writer, nothing but youth and inexperience could produce anything so naive and so lovely."[17] Butler's reading stimulated Robert Graves to identify Nausicaa as a candidate for authorship and write his beguiling treatment *Homer's Daughter.*

On the analogy of the slow-growing mediaeval cathedral, every new phase extending, distorting and reconfiguring the work of the preceding phase, it is possible that the poem was "modernised" by interpolation; it was never demolished or remodelled. It hardly seems likely that the rhapsodes carrying the poem forward deliberately applied familiar templates to what was unfamiliar: it was more a case of shoring up the sense of actuality with detail which, the history having faded into legend, only the present could supply, whether literally or figuratively. The oral tradition is, as we noted, conservative by design and *conserving,* accurate, its function being to remember rather than to invent. It does not "make it new," and in this respect it is remote from the lyric.

A mix of elements from different histories, a mix of words and forms from different dialects and times: yet the syntheses that occur in the poems do not *feel* synthetic. We accept, if we recognise, the Peloponnesian, Aeolic, Ionic and Attic elements in the language. We are unlikely to have sufficient archaeology to disbelieve the material world portrayed. It may be a world that never was, quite. Yet it is the core of what we "know" of the ancient Greek world, what the early historians took to be early history. This is the anciency of Greece which we, and they, related to and visualised most comprehensively in later verse, in pottery, painting and sculpture.

At least five centuries of Greek tradition, much of it stylised in legend, precedes the writing down of "Homer." Orpheus, Musaeus, Linus and others stand behind him, and eastern traditions stand behind them: there is nothing *ex nihilo* about the art or the narrative of either the *Iliad* or the *Odyssey* even if time has kicked away the ladder of precedents up which they climbed. But how did a composer and indeed a later rhapsode, singing the tales, conceive of the language they were using? Did they have a sense of the individual *word*? Performers in Balkan oral traditions in the last century, asked what certain clusters of syllables (which we call words) "meant," could not understand the question they were asked, or separate out from the context of the verse discreet verbal elements for definition. They could not *analyse*. This is certainly the case with complex synthetic languages such as Nahuatl, the Aztec tongue, where the units of meaning consist not of words but of an accumulation of syllables and particles that, taken singly, mean little. It is hard for us to conceive of a literary culture without a sense of "the word." For the archaic bard it was equally hard to conceive of an analytical language that was built up from, or could be broken down into, word units.

Early Greek manuscripts run words together, leave no spaces, show no division at all. Up until the classical period scribes wrote in capital letters without spaces between words, without accents or breathings.[18] Metrical divisions might be indicated, if at all, by "a *coronis* or hook placed before the *parágraphos.*"[19] A singer who did not know what a *word* is might have been equally puzzled by the notion of a *line,* with a beginning and an end. Again, the indication of lineation in manuscripts comes rather late in the day: a composer, a bard, knew what he was doing, but without being able to externalise or analyse it. "What is time?" asks the child. "I knew until you asked me," replies the parent. What was the composer's and the performer's concept of the unit of sense, and was it congruent with their sense of the melodic unit? Or is it only later, when there is leisure literature, when there is writing, that language was teased out into its constituent parts? Taplin says, "Achilles remains swift however inactive he may be."[20] The sea is wine-dark, dawn rosy-fingered and Odysseus "wily" at the most inappropriate times. In epithets and other formulaic passages the sound values—metre in particular—can be strictly meaningless, which is not to say that they are without poetic effect.

Writers of blank verse, heroic couplets, ballad quatrains and other traditional forms accept certain limitations when they adopt a convention. Considering a poetry rooted in the oral formulaic tradition, we can begin by establishing the areas in which a singer of tales is *not expected to invent*, even *not allowed to invent*. With the epic, the plots, the names of principal and most minor characters, their provenance and fate were "historical" and non-negotiable. The story was *given*, though there might be flexibility in disposition, sequence, emphasis. Moreover, the metre, various as it can be thanks to the movable caesura, is fundamentally non-negotiable. Syntax and the rules of language are given, too. They too can prescribe diction and word order; and repeated epithets and other verbal constructs and iterations have their formal place.

For Aristotle, poetry could exercise more freedom than Homer allowed himself, but Aristotle wrote with the benefit of hindsight and was chiefly concerned with the drama. Homer's is a primary, not a secondary, intelligence: he makes with language a way through shared memory and animates that memory in his present world, and therefore in ours. His use of similes is not decorative: they bring distant facts into imaginative focus, they imply other possibilities of life than warfare, they are, as Frederic Raphael has written, "windows." Some critics, who follow Aristotle, assume that Homer felt free to invent how his characters moved in a given geography and to make up the stories of their existence. Others, supported by modern archaeology, argue that these elements were given, specifically remembered in the verse of the oral tradition. The poet provided an account of actual events set in the places where they occurred. An oral tradition keeps genealogies, sequences, catalogues in memory in proper order and proportion. The mnemonics are not to aid invention but to inhibit it, to enable memory and recitation. The singer's task is to evoke as truthfully as memory will permit "a world suitable for heroes."

The sense of closure that we impose on historic periods is itself a miasma. The dark age in the Greek world, from 1200 to 800 BC, is unlikely to have been uniformly dark, any more than that the European Dark Ages were, or the Renaissance uniformly renascent. Mezzanine elements, cultural customs and traditions, survived Mycenae. When the Homeric poems were composed, the lines were not all down between the age of Troy and the time in which the bard lived. "Time" moved then, as it does now, at different speeds in different places, even places adjacent to one another.

The *Iliad* and *Odyssey* survive from what scholars believe were comprehensive cycles of poems, their narrative beginning with the wars in heaven. Such cycles, orally transmitted, may have grown up during the dark ages, and Homer or "Homer" may have built on them.[21] They grew, says Hugh G. Evelyn-White, who edited the surviving fragments, without preconceived design into "a kind of epic history of the world, as known to the Greeks, down to the death of Odysseus, at which the heroic age, a categorical critic will tell us, came to an end." Alexandrian editors, Zenodotus in particular, shuffled these poems into a chronology order early in the third century BC. In the Byzantine age, Photius preserved an abridged synopsis of some of the poems which Proclus (second or fifth century AD) had recorded in his vast, largely vanished *Chrestomatheia*.

There are allusions to and quotations from the *Iliad* in the *Odyssey* and vice versa. Listeners and later readers would have noticed them. Throughout the *Odyssey* we are reminded, in considering Odysseus' actions in relation to his wife, of Agamemnon's disastrous return home, where he was murdered by his wife's lover. Shrewd Odysseus learned caution from the tale. Parts of the *Odyssey* are "modelled on an old poem, now lost, of the journey of the Argonauts to Aeetes, ruler of Aea. Circe's allusion to this poem (XI, 70) can then be taken as a valuable datum for literary history."[22] Odysseus' dog in Book XVII, which dies of old age and surprise when Odysseus returns, is called Argos. Other histories and legends are alluded to in the poems, so that we can assume they were familiar. Nestor brings in many elements not strictly related to Troy, from the stories of Thebes for example, another tale of confrontation between large powers, in central Greece and the Argolid. Diomede is a hero but (he is reminded) his father, Tydeus, was greater, one of the Seven Against Thebes. Diomede's companion Sthenelus' father, too, was involved in that war, and both are epigoni, enacting at Troy what their forebears failed to fulfil in their war. When Odysseus faces the terrifying trial in "the blue Symplegades," we are reminded that only the *Argo* had ever successfully navigated through. Critics looking at the anger of Achilles are inclined to ask whether it is historical, an independent legend, or based on the now almost vanished story of the wrath of Meleager.[23]

The power of the *Iliad* and *Odyssey* overshadowed the memory of prior traditions of epic history; it also "exercised a paralysing influence over the successors of Homer."[24] In the *Poetics* (XXIII) Aristotle justifies the superiority of the *Iliad* and the *Odyssey* over the other poems in the cycle. The heroic poem "should have for its subject a single action, whole and complete, with a beginning, a middle, and an end. It will thus resemble a living organism in all its unity, and produce the pleasure proper to it." These are the famous dramatic unities, stretched a little, but not too far, beyond the drama for epic. The epic poem "will differ in structure from historical compositions, which of necessity present not a single action, but a single period, and all that happened within that period to one person or to many, little connected together as the events may be. For as the sea-fight at Salamis and the battle with the Carthaginians in Sicily took place at the same time, but did not tend to any one result, so in the sequence of events, one thing sometimes follows another, and yet no single result is thereby produced. Such is the practice, we may say, of most poets." But not Homer.

His "transcendent excellence" is paradoxically manifest in his setting himself limits. When, centuries later, a lesser poet, Apollonius, revives the story of the Argonauts' expedition, he doggedly follows their itinerary. Homer does not set out to tell the whole story of Troy, though it had a beginning and an end. He chooses to pursue one part of the war, and while at every stage remembering the wider context, the larger narrative, he frames his tale in time. There are intrusions from outside the time-frame: the catalogue of ships, for example. But they are functional, adding to the context without dissipating the narrative. Other poets writing within the cycle focus on more than one hero, one period or action. For this reason the *Iliad* and the *Odyssey* each furnish the subject of one tragedy, or, at most, two. The *Cypria* supplies several plots, and the *Little Iliad* up to eight.[25]

There is another take on the epic cycles which better fits the hypothetical chronology of composition: that the *Iliad* and *Odyssey* were so central to Greek culture and identity, so important and celebrated, that other epics by lesser composers were built around them, the poets hitching their wagons to Homer's star and effacing themselves out of exalted respect.

The cycle would have begun with the *Titanomachia* ("War of the Titans"), composed perhaps by Eumelus ("sweet melody") of Corinth or Arctinus of Miletus, about whom we know nothing.[26] After the gods have settled their affairs, the human poems begin with the *Oidipodeia* ("The Story of Oedipus") "by Cinaethon in six thousand six hundred verses," which was to serve Sophocles as a source-book for his plays. In *The Contest Between Hesiod and Homer,* the *Thebaid* and the *Epigoni* are attributed to Homer and constitute a Theban cycle or sub-cycle. Then comes the *Kypria,* of which a full synopsis survives from Proclus' *Chrestomatheia.* The author may have been Hegesias (not the third-century rhetorician from Magnesia, but an earlier Hegesias) or Stasinus. Some say Homer gave it to Stasinus as a dowry, along with some cash. Here the full story of the Judgement of Paris is told succinctly. Alexandrus (Paris) chose Aphrodite not because she was the most beautiful but because she bribed him with the promise of Helen. Zeus plotted the Trojan War in part to depopulate the world: "the countless tribes of men, though wide-dispersed, oppressed the surface of the deep-bosomed earth." Among the fragments is some Stalinist wisdom: "He is a simple man who kills the father and lets the children live."[27] After the *Kypria* comes the *Iliad* itself.

Proclus' *Chrestomatheia* summarises the sequel to the *Iliad* in the cycle the *Aithiopis*. It was in five books, written by Arctinus of Miletus. It recounted the arrival at Troy of Memnon the Ethiopian, of the mighty Amazon Penthiseleia and her death at Achilles' hand, followed by the death of Achilles himself and the angry contest of Odysseus and Ajax for Achilles' armour. The sequel, the action-packed *Ilias Mikra* ("Little Iliad"), is said to have been by Lesches of Mitylene. It begins by settling the issue of Achilles' arms. Athena contrives that they go to Odysseus. Ajax, driven to madness, destroys the Achaean herd and slays himself. Philoctetes is brought back from Lemnos, cured of his festering snake-bite by Machaon, and kills Paris with an arrow from the bow of Heracles, which he happens to possess. Menelaus defiles Paris' body, but the Trojans recover and bury it. Odysseus, having given Neoptolemus his father, Achilles', arms, disguises himself and sneaks into Troy. He is recognised by Helen and they plot the city's over-throw. The Trojan Horse is built, the city falls. Neoptolemus captures Andromache and hurls her child Astyanax from a tower. Judging from the surviving summary, many of the images we have of the fall of Troy derive from this poem. It is followed by *Iliou Persis* ("The Sack of Ilium"), supposed again to have been by Arctinus of Miletus. Here more details of the Trojan Horse were given, with variations on other tales. Odysseus kills the child Astyanax, Ajax carries off Cassandra and damages Athena's statue, so that the Greeks want to stone him to death.

The Trojan War concluded, the Greeks go home and the *Nostoi* ("The Returns"), attributed to Agias of Troezen, delivers them all to their different fates. After the *Nostoi* comes the *Odyssey,* and then, to conclude things with a heartless symmetry, came the two books of the *Telegonia* by Eugammon of Cyrene. Here we find the tales of Odysseus' later life, culminating in his death at the hands of Telegonus, his son by Circe, who then marries Penelope while, in a double ceremony, Telemachus marries Circe, his father's divine ex-mistress. Odysseus may have had a second son with Penelope, called Acusilaus.

Odysseus was the last of the heroes and the cycle ends with his death. It may also have included a full account of the voyage of the Argonauts (later retold in Apollonius' *Argonautica*), the hunting of the Calydonian boar and much else. Some of that poetry was already lost by the time the great library at Alexandria was flourishing. Judging from Aristotle's *Poetics,* the vanished poetry was diverse and diffuse: the *Iliad* and *Odyssey* are marked by formal concentration and, through variety of incident, singleness of purpose.

The stories that the cycles told, whether they are contemporary in composition with the *Iliad* and *Odyssey* or were conceived as sequels and pre-
quels to them, with some (unsubtle for the most part) cross-referencing,
were widely known. One ancient potter shows, for example, Priam and
Achilles, Priam and Penthesileia the Amazon queen, and then Penthesileia
and Achilles. Clearly this artist accepted a link between the *Iliad* and the
Aethiopis. Prior to about 600 BC, not a single confirmable allusion or reference to Homer appears in any surviving work; there are references to epic
tales, epic values and narratives, but none specifically to Homer.[28] In the
other arts nothing specifically Homeric is found. In the mid–seventh century there are some Cyclops paintings which may be allusions to the *Odyssey*
but could draw on another, or a shared, source. Taplin affirms that in his
view the first "clearly Homer-inspired visual art" is a plate, probably from
Rhodes around 600 BC, which portrays *Iliad* XVII, 106ff.

There is an eastern Greek pitcher[29] from around 670–50 which shows
two enraged lions, tails up, mouths wide open, frightening a little mountain
goat. He stands between them and does his best to make an ugly face. His
horns, with their slightly wavy contour at the top, look as if he is wrinkling
them in anger. When Ajax has slain the rich-armoured Imbrios (*Iliad* XIII,
198ff.), there is a struggle for his armour; in the midst of this and other hec-
tic struggles comes the metaphor: "As two lions snatch a goat from the
hounds that have it in their fangs, and bear it through thick brushwood high
above the ground in their jaws, thus did the Ajaxes bear aloft the body of
Imbrios, and strip it of its armour." It is a handsome pitcher, tawny with
pale black painting, with decorations scattered in patterns, four rhombuses,
giving the impression of the air around the animals shivering with tension
or fear. This seems to indicate (assuming the images on the pitcher have
been properly read) that the *Iliad*, at the deep level of metaphor, was sufficiently known for so specific an allusion to make sense to the original artist
and to his ancient customer.

It always strikes me as puzzling that poems as different as the *Iliad* and the
Odyssey are spoken of in the same breath, as though they are unarguably by a
single author and are written in a single style. The critic Marghanita Laski
used to insist that Flaubert was the bourgeois Homer, and that *Madame Bo-
vary* and the *Odyssey* were for young readers, *A Sentimental Education* and the
Iliad for grown-ups. The first two are *agons,* Emma's and Odysseus', while
the others create a more complex and politically intense world. The first
two are about forms of love, the others about conflict and its consequences. In the ancient world, the *Iliad* was the more valued, if we believe
the evidence of bibliography: more than 188 manuscripts of the *Iliad* survive, less than half that many of the *Odyssey*.

Parallels and contrasts can be multiplied; a few, however, do illuminate the very different nature of the two poems and help us decide whether both poems emerge from a single stable.

The governing *fact* of the *Iliad,* what makes the action happen as it does and finally resolves the poem, is the wrath of Achilles. Odysseus' homing desire is less intense, and the time-span of the two poems is consequently very different. The poem with the longer time-span is about 12,000 lines, while the poem with the shorter time-span is considerably longer, about 15,000 lines. For recitation, the *Iliad* might have been divided at the end of Book IX, then XVIII, taking three nights or about twenty hours to perform. The *Odyssey* would have taken two nights. Despite the differences in focus and extent, the *Odyssey* seems longer. Constantine A. Trypanis quotes an early critic who compares the poet of the *Odyssey* to a setting sun "whose greatness remains without violence," whereas his earlier manifestations were noonlike, full of vigour and urgent engagement. Achilles knows who he is and why he acts. Odysseus' long home-coming, on the other hand, is a reassertion of his role and identity. Trypanis cannot believe that both poems were composed by one man (as though Shakespeare could not have written *The Comedy of Errors* and *Othello*). Butler rejects sunset arguments on artistic grounds: the Odyssey is cruder, more romantic, more diverse, evidence of a poet learning rather than relaxing his craft.

One basic difference between the two poems is the amount of liberty they give the reader to engage and to "make sense." The *Iliad,* not least because of the tight time-span and the close focus of the narrative, is a more "complete" poem, a finished artefact. It is in the nature of such works that they seek "to limit the possibilities of interpretation." There is not much we can do with the information beyond what the poem has done with it: the resonances are contained and powerful for that reason. Any ten people reading the *Iliad* closely, or hearing it recited, will have a more or less common sense of what the poem is saying and doing. The *Odyssey* is different, more "open" and susceptible to different readings, at literal, psychological, political, allegorical and other levels. It is a poem that "disrupts its own structural patterns or the conventions of its genre, thereby making room for—even requiring—more interpretative activity."[30]

This certainly does not make it a *better* poem. Plato in the *Hippias* declares that the *Iliad* excels the *Odyssey* as much as Achilles excels Odysseus.[31] This has something to do with the form the poem takes, something to do with the protagonists. Achilles is willing to die; Odysseus is willing to live, and to live at whatever cost. Achilles dies young, a hero whose fate is woven early; Odysseus is the hero who survives and suffers. Two *types* of man, then, and two models of action. Already in the *Iliad* Odysseus has his three epithets: "much-subtle," "much-enduring," "much-devising" (*polymetis, polytlas, polymechanos*).[32] To him are entrusted those missions which involve tact and politic action. Achilles is too much himself to dissemble. Odysseus is the anti-type of "fleet-footed Achilles." Thetis tells her almost-divine child that he can have long life (and obscurity) or early death (and glory). In Book XVIII, line 98, Achilles replies, "then let me die soon." In this he is less *Greek* than Odysseus.

The poems are, as a result of their subject matter and their themes, typologically distinct. The *Iliad* concentrates its action in two primary settings: Troy, the Greek camp and the Trojan plain on the one hand, and Olympus on the other. The *Odyssey* focuses largely on two men, Telemachus and his father, Odysseus. The *Iliad* builds towards death and destruction, the *Odyssey* towards the re-establishment of local harmony in the wake of the universal disruption of that war. Whereas in the *Iliad* things generally keep their shape and the world of cause and effect is brutal but credible, in the *Odyssey* we are in the realm of metamorphoses, of unstable identities. Aristotle in the *Poetics* says simplicity is the keynote of the *Iliad*'s structure, complexity of the *Odyssey*'s. "Again, Epic poetry must have as many kinds as Tragedy: it must be simple, or complex, or 'ethical,' or 'pathetic.' The parts also, with the exception of song and spectacle, are the same; for epic requires Reversals of the Situation, Recognitions, and Scenes of Suffering. Moreover, the thoughts and the diction must be artistic. In all these respects Homer is our earliest and sufficient model. Indeed each of his poems has a twofold character. The *Iliad* is at once simple and 'pathetic,' and the *Odyssey* complex (for recognition scenes run through it), and at the same time 'ethical.'"

The "unitarian" critics believe that both the *Iliad* and the *Odyssey* are "whole" conceptions, marred perhaps by later interpolations but their artistic integrity largely inviolate.[33] This is the line taken by Jacqueline de Romilly, who insists that both poems are wholes with "unity of action."[34] Albin Lesky contrasts the structures of the poems, but he does not suggest that they are unintentional in structure or incomplete.[35] The *Iliad*'s structure, centred insistently upon the wrath of Achilles, brings every element together in a species of continuous integration. The *Odyssey* is, at its weakest structurally (and narratively most compelling), a sequence of episodes, a gallery of framed stories, and, he concludes, we can be surer in the *Odyssey* than in the *Iliad* that there were earlier treatments of the same material.

Those of the analytical persuasion see the poems as assemblages of shorter "runs" of narrative, anthologies built out of prefabricated chunks of (oral) verse. They make more of the inconsistencies and discontinuities in the narrative than the unitarians do, insisting that each rough join proves that the poems were "put together." "Odysseus' request to the Phaeacians (VII, 215) to be allowed to have his dinner is very odd, since he had already had it (V, 177). Patroclus kills Palaemenes in *Iliad* V, 576 who then, Lazarus-like, revives to mourn his son in XIII, 658. Zeus predicts that Hector will attack Achilles' ship; in fact he attacks Protesilaus."[36] There are portions of detached, unfunctional plot, for instance the suggestion of Aeneas' hostility to Priam (XIII, 460), probably a fossilised piece of information, since Aeneas was ruler of the Dardanians (in Mount Ida's foothills, above Troy) and of parallel ancestry to Hector.

Is it possible that one of the poems, the *Iliad,* is "unitary" and the other a rich amalgam of stories assembled around a continually interrupted narrative core? Certainly the sense of difference in *kind* between the poems runs deep in any reader who holds both of them in mind at the same time. Indeed, the more closely they are observed the more it comes to seem that what makes them *seem* similar is in fact the way in which the Alexandrian textual critics applied the same template to both, an arbitrary act.

There are twenty-four letters in the Greek alphabet. There are twenty-four books in each of the poems, and in the oldest manuscripts each book is chapter-headed with a Greek letter. This division into books was done much later than "Homer's" day, probably as late as the Alexandrian period. Lesky tells us Zenodotus, who put the "cycles" in chronological order and edited Hesiod's *Theogony,* was responsible for dividing the poems. He may have set out to make them handle more easily in terms of book rolls, or to make commentary and cross-referencing easier. There could have been a numerological or mystical motive. The division for the most part makes a kind of sense, corresponding with breaks in the action, changes of perspective or setting. Lesky assumes the breaks may have coincided with the natural breaks in the rhapsodes' recitation, but the extents in the *Iliad* vary from 424 lines (XIX) to 909 (V), and it is unlikely that the audience would have accepted a half portion one night, or (if 424 lines is a natural attention span) a double portion another. It is the larger divisions in the action (the Telemachiad, which is the story of Telemachus' adventures in pursuit of his father; Odysseus' adventures; and the "return to Troy" in the *Odyssey,* for example) that are the organic and aesthetic "sections" of the poem, not the mechanical breaks usefully imposed by the first of Homer's "scientific" editors.

We have unitarians and analysts. We also have the so-called *chorizontes,* whom some regard as early Homeric heretics. They claim that the two poems are sufficiently different, despite shared epithets and some repeated passages, to have been composed by two different poets, that the distinctive styles, dictions, thematics and morality of each poem prove that the works are of distinct authorship, perhaps even from different periods. To believe in two poets is first to believe there might be one; or as few as two. The *chorizontes* are unitarians when it comes to each poem, but analysts of the tradition of single authorship. They started long before the "oral tradition" critics but are their remote forebears.

If we are tempted to become *chorizontes,* we might begin by examining Homeric similes and considering whether they are used differently in the *Iliad* and the *Odyssey.* Anyone who reads the *Odyssey* immediately after finishing the *Iliad* experiences a sense of poverty: after the metaphorical abundance of the *Iliad,* the *Odyssey* is relatively poor. The *Iliad* has, Taplin tells us, four times as many similes as the *Odyssey.*

The first significant extended simile in the *Odyssey* occurs in Book IV, lines 332ff. Telemachus tells Menelaus about the suitors, their threats, and the reason for his journey. In his response, the Trojan hero uses a simile that instantly transports us into the language-world of the *Iliad.* Butler translates the passage: "Menelaus on hearing this was very much shocked. 'So,' he exclaimed, 'these cowards would usurp a brave man's bed? A hind might as well lay her new born young in the lair of a lion, and then go off to feed in the forest or in some grassy dell: the lion when he comes back to his lair will make short work with the pair of them—and so will Ulysses with these suitors.'" The next major simile also occurs in Book IV. The scene cuts back to Ithaca, where Penelope is anxious about Telemachus. Butler again: "But Penelope lay in her own room upstairs," in the marriage bed Menelaus imagined, leading into his simile, "unable to eat or drink, and wondering whether her brave son would escape, or be overpowered by the wicked suitors. Like a lioness caught in the toils with huntsmen hemming her in on every side she thought and thought till she sank into a slumber, and lay on her bed bereft of thought and motion." Here is the lioness, after the lion; here is the figure of the huntress at bay. The similes work together, complementarily. The reader or listener registers them because they are emphatic and reinforce one another. Since similes are sparser here than in the *Iliad,* they tend to have a more calculated, even "literary," impact. They are not always effective, however. In Book XVI of the *Odyssey* Athena urges Odysseus to tell Telemachus who he is so that they can start planning the campaign against the suitors. She re-creates him, he ceases to be an old beggar man and speaks in his own person to his son. Odysseus has to persuade him, and when Telemachus accepts who he is, deep and complex emotions are elicited. The poem employs a curious simile: "As he spoke he sat down, and Telemachus threw his arms about his father and wept. They were both so much moved that they cried aloud like eagles or vultures with crooked talons that have been robbed of their half fledged young by peasants. Thus piteously did they weep . . ." The simile is powerful but dubiously appropriate at this stage in the poem, a point of restoration. Eagles and vultures elsewhere in the poem (like the lion in the *Iliad*) are violent, destructive or masterful.

Most Homeric similes deploy not specific but characteristic images which are "universal" in impact, that is, not specific to a certain place or time. The *Iliad*'s abundant sea and weather similes, for example, belong to the whole Mediterranean. Oliver Taplin insists that the language of Homeric similes is "notably non-formulaic and late."[37] As a device they supplement the narrative, doing what, at times, the narrative cannot do. Agamemnon, at the beginning of the *Iliad,* is an unjust, petty-minded and monstrous leader. It is hard for the poet to make him less repugnant through action because the time-scale is too tight and the story he is telling will not allow him to add incidents in order to alter the initial impression. As a result, the poem uses similes to build him up, to adjust the focus on him. The similes compare his face with Zeus', his waist with Ares', his chest with Poseidon's; in the end he is like a great bull standing among his grazing cows, a simile notable for its complex literal inappropriateness (unlike Priam's comparison of Odysseus to a ram), however appropriate the figurative sense. In the first place, does the peaceful bull stand well with the three preceding gods, remembering that when Zeus took bull form it was for libidinal purposes? Or are we to assume that the first three similes, which were meant to evoke the physical power and agility of the king, are switched off when the poem switches on the simile which contextualises this large, powerful figure? Is it appropriate to compare the leader of an invading army to a bull and a herd, which imply a settled rural culture such as the one the Greeks are violating? In making Agamemnon bullish among his herd, what are the feminising implications for the army itself? And there is no peace within the army itself. Compared with the lions in the *Odyssey,* this particular simile appears inappropriate, disconnected, perhaps super-added by an editor or scribe who felt that Agamemnon needed building up after his poor comportment in earlier passages.

Many similes come from one world ("modern") and do not relate directly to the customs or events of the literal world of the Trojan or Odyssean narrative. There is a distance between the audience's present and the present of the actions the poem recounts. The poem acknowledges and maintains that distance, yet does so without giving a sense of distancing. One key device is the simile's "presence" in the audience's world, even if it is anachronistic in relation to the things or events it is illuminating. These are not anachronisms in the way that iron, or burial customs, are anachronistically presented (a function of mis-remembering or forgetting). Nor is the poem archaising. It is making things that are remote and difficult familiar, drawing them into the realm of the imaginable and comprehensible.

When Odysseus, disguised as a beggar and bedding down in the forecourt, or *prodomon,* of his house, sees the women servants sneaking out to their amorous assignations with the suitors, two quite astonishing similes are unleashed. In the first (Butler again), "His heart growled within him, and as a bitch with puppies growls and shows her teeth when she sees a stranger, so did his heart growl with anger at the evil deeds that were being done." His heart crosses gender and is a bitch, but a bitch commanded to obey by a masterful will: "but he beat his breast and said, 'Heart, be still, you had worse than this to bear on the day when the terrible Cyclops ate your brave companions; yet you bore it in silence till your cunning got you safe out of the cave . . .'" Powerfully he recalls past events, the effect of patience, the instincts that have drawn him home and the natural protective instincts of any creature. Yet having calmed his bitch-heart, he is nonetheless restless. The simile that follows is domestic and in some curious way libidinal, a blood sausage: "but he tossed about as one who turns a paunch full of blood and fat in front of a hot fire, doing it first on one side and then on the other, that he may get it cooked as soon as possible, even so did he turn himself about from side to side, thinking all the time how, single handed as he was, he should contrive to kill so large a body of men as the wicked suitors." No wonder that Athena comes and cools him down. "My poor unhappy man," she says, "why do you lie awake in this way? This is your house: your wife is safe inside it, and so is your son who is just such a young man as any father may be proud of."

We audiences and readers live in a post-heroic age. The poem concedes that in these latter days men are otherwise than as they were. Their imagination and understanding have altered and diminished. It requires an effort to make sense and enter into the world of big deeds. "Thanks to the repeated phrases and scene-sequences," says Taplin, "we are in a familiar world where things have their known places. It is a world which is solid and known, and yet at the same time coloured by the special diction with an epic nobility."[38] We grow familiar with the world of the poems through repetitions, which are reassuring and stabilising, and we enter in by means of voices and similes. It is odd to hear the echoes, some of them prolonged, sounding within and between the poems. The *Odyssey,* Book V opens exactly as the *Iliad,* Book XI does: Dawn leaves the side of her once mortal lover, Tithonus. The first three lines are identical, the fourth a prosodic echo.

The gods who were worshipped by the Trojans and the Achaeans went by the same names and had the same characteristics as the gods worshipped in "Homer's" time. They too help to make the space of the poems familiar. We find ourselves on the terraces of Olympus, watching and hearing gods in their remarkably human-seeming confabulations. Their passions, pettinesses and partisanships are like men's; their deep parental loves, their settled hatreds, and the scheming social world of heaven itself, are reflected in—or from—the human world ("then" and "now") above which they hover. The organisation of heaven, with a king, assemblies and the like, is familiar not only from Trojan and Achaean structures but from the later world in which the poems took shape. Trojans and Achaeans pray to these gods; they still ruled Olympus when the poems were composed. Just as we get close to the gods in their exalted palaces, so they get close, intimately so, to the human protagonists of the poems, usually appearing in a plausible human disguise but in the end, by a gesture or by the ways in which they vanish, revealing their true nature. They come down to trick men into irrational acts of bravery or treachery; they come to console, to save, or when a great hero has been killed, to make certain the body is not spoiled, even when, as in the case of Hector, the corpse is defiled time after time.

The strangest scene in the *Iliad* occurs between the gods, in Book XIV. Hera sets out to seduce her husband, Zeus, on Mount Ida, in order to anaesthetise him so that the other gods can exercise their wills on the Trojan scene. Powerful, subversive eroticism is the prelude to hideous human combat. Nestor comes out of his hut (he has been bathing Machaon's wounds) to see the dreadful state of play with the Greeks. The situation is grave, the rows of ships exposed to possible arson. Agamemnon for the second time urges retreat, either to test the army or because he is a coward. Odysseus feels contempt for his king.

Meanwhile Hera dolls herself up and goes to distract Zeus with erotic exercise. She dresses remarkably (and undresses so). She begs from Aphrodite Longing and Desire (abstractions, not an *eau de toilette*) to intensify the seduction. With the promise of a golden chair and one of the youngest graces for his bride, she persuades Sleep to come along. Fitzgerald marks the effect of Hera on Zeus: "He gazed at her, and as he gazed desire / veiled his mind like mist . . ." It is like his first illicit love. He wants her more than all the earlier women he has lain with, and he lists them. The love-making is spectacular and has the desired effect. Zeus falls asleep, and Sleep himself tells Poseidon he is free to urge the Argives on, even to triumph, until Zeus wakes. The battle that resumes is horribly heightened after this powerful romantic interlude. It is as though Hector is pitted as an equal against Poseidon himself. Ajax wounds him with a stone; he is only just rescued from the fray and laid down by the Xanthus, where he recovers. There are deaths, and cries of brutal triumph, in contrast with the divine coition. In the next book Hector kills Patroclus and Troy's fate is sealed.

Critics fail too to find a religious or theological consistency in the poems. It is as though the gods occupy a parallel universe but not a morally higher or better space, and their judgements are as partisan and partial as human judgements can be. Taplin says, "the gods in Homer do not have a theological existence independent of particular poetic context."[39] It is worth remembering that Taplin is the same critic who regards an inquiry into the identity of Homer as a waste of time, and the geographical particulars in the poem to be largely irrelevant. For him it is a work of imagination, and there is a distance between the kinds of truth imagination tells and those that history or religion disclose. If his take on the absence of anything but an *aesthetic* theology in the poems is true, we will have to conclude that men exist largely in relation to one another and act extremely when those more or less formal relations are disrupted: the gods exist in the poems merely as emanations from or clarifications of the human impulses and conflicts, their existence no more real than that of the similes. Like any reading which tries to confine the poems to the aesthetic zone of the "poetic," this deprives them of their place in a real world and makes nonsense of the use to which the Greeks put the poems for centuries. It also makes a political reading of the poems (which Taplin is tempted to undertake)[40] a little fatuous, rather as though he was attempting a political reading of "The Walrus and the Carpenter." For the Greek audience and readership, the gap between the real and the poetic was not so absolutely marked, but then they had not lived through the European *fin de* nineteenth *siècle*.

An understanding of the strange role of the gods is important to an understanding of the dynamic of the poems. Man is constrained by time, by circumstance, but he is also *elevated* by the interest of the gods. They care for their own in curiously moving and sometimes helplessly human ways. They are parental, they are amorous. Heroes and mere mortals accept the situation, that gods make things happen but are in turn subject to laws. We can agree that impartial and resolving divine justice is hard to come by in the poems. In the end, there are the scales which Zeus holds up, and objective, final judgement is delivered by a power to which even the gods' wills are subject, the power of *moira* (destiny or fate). When Hector in the *Iliad* Book XXII sees Achilles and begins to flee, the poem provides an abundance of physical detail, architectural and geographical contingencies, which make the city rise up real before us one last time. The heroes run three times around the town, as if they competed in the Games. Zeus is moved and asks the other gods if Hector might be saved or must die. Athena reminds Zeus of *moira*. Not even Zeus can change its course. Hector dies, and when at last in Book XXIV his corpse is recovered, it is laid out and Andromache holds Hector's head in her lap, as Achilles had held Patroclus'. Her lament centres on their little son and his short future, subject also to *moira*. Hecuba laments, then Helen. Priam commands preparations for the funeral. The pyre is built and lighted. It burns, is extinguished, and the bones of Hector are duly gathered and placed in an urn.

The sharpest contrast between Olympus on the one hand and Troy, the battlefield, the Greek camp, Ithaca with its host of suitors, on the other, is to be found in the palaces of the gods which Hephaistus made, disposed as if on a giant Acropolis where location and scale symbolise the relative importance and power of each god; everything is beautiful, peaceful, stable; there is always a strictly limited cast of characters, each with clear relations and commitments to the human protagonists. In heaven, conflict is often intense, but motive, action and reaction are always clear.

The gods have a physical reality, they exist in physical terms, they can be seen and touched. In the first place, they have specific, geographical perspectives on the world, they look from and to specific points. They are assigned mountain-tops so that they have a place to alight on brief stopovers when they are travelling and, when human conflict is in progress, the seats with the most theatrically comprehensive views. J. V. Luce takes an interesting instance to demonstrate the virtually cartographic sense we get when a god is positioned in relation to a landscape or view. The poems know the lie of the land, they seem to enjoy aerial perspectives. In *Iliad* XIII, 3–6, Zeus is sitting atop Mount Ida and looking north. He sees the peoples in sequence, as far north as knowledge could go. In other words, he sees men in context, not an empty landscape. "The scene is accurately envisaged, but its primary function is to provide a theatre for human action."[41] When Poseidon views Troy from the island of Samothrace, most scholars point out that the islands of Imbros and Tenedos would block the view, being between the Trojan plain and Poseidon's vantage point. But Luce established by observation that the mountains on Samothrace are high enough for the plain to be visible. In any case, on a *very* clear day, the peaks of Samothrace are visible from Troy. The poem *answers* and *answers to* a geographical reality. Then there is Hera, setting off from Olympus to Ida to seduce and distract her husband, the most important seduction in the poem (*Iliad* XIV, 153–360). Between her departure and arrival are ten places where the journey "touches down."[42] These gods exist not in a parallel geography, but in the very world that men inhabit. For Priam, Zeus rules from Mount Ida, just as he, on a human scale, rules from the city of Troy.

Gods are like men, but they are *not* men: this is the important fact. They are immortal: when wounded they are promptly healed; they move in space as though there were no rules of space. They speak a subtly different language from men: for instance, they call what men call the river Scamander the river Xanthus. The river has a god and a being which, in due course, Achilles will violate with corpses and, aided by the gods, will dry back to its bed. Like the divine rivers, the gods exist in time and affect even as they are affected by its passing. Zeus expresses his will, but it is a will pre-tuned to the fact of *moira*. Much as he would like to, he cannot save Sarpedon and is resigned to the fact (*Iliad* XVI, 458). His resignation is not shared by other gods who fight against fate but are aware that they will lose in the end.

If we are still tempted to be *chorizontes,* the gods are on our side. In the *Odyssey* the gods are less volatile and more patently "just" than in the *Iliad*. They are, quite simply, better behaved. It is not due to a later date of composition. "The decisive factor seems to us," Albin Lesky suggests, "the following: while in the *Iliad* we have the reflection of a compact and exclusive noble class, the social range of the *Odyssey* is much wider. In the later work epic poetry had opened its doors to the wishes and beliefs of classes whom the *Iliad* excluded."[43] Odysseus and Telemachus meet in the devoted swineherd Eumaeus' emblematic, rough peasant dwelling. Melanthius, the ("swarthy") goatherd, mistreats Odysseus (XVII); then Melantho, a serving girl, does the same (XVIII). There is also the faithful oxherd Philoetius ("happy fate") and Arnaios, nicknamed Iros, the real beggar-man whom Odysseus displaces. In the *Odyssey* real choices appear to be made, less seems predetermined, perhaps because less hangs upon the outcome of the struggle: it is not the collision of states and ideologies but the story of a family, albeit a great hero's, re-establishing itself. Is it credible that a single poet could have composed two poems with such radically different earthly and Olympian politics?

The gods enjoy a degree of freedom. They can scheme, they can retard *moira* even if they cannot prevent or reverse it. Man, on the other hand, is helpless. How then can a narrative of his helplessness be made compelling? We know the end before we have even properly set out; the poems make no secret about Achilles' or Hector's fate, about the ultimate destiny of Troy or the eventual success of Odysseus in his return. Indeed they remind us time after time. Yet they do entertain a variety of alternative scenarios, what the critic James Morrison calls "misdirections," passages where alternative events are unfolded, or where the gods cause an action contrary to what they declare is its purpose.[44] Such a technique not only contributes to irony, reversal, surprise; it also causes us to reflect on what would have happened if, for example, Achilles had sailed for home, or Menelaus and Paris had completed their single combat. A story line is given, but the poem can play hard against it. Though, like *moira*, the known plot will triumph because the current of history cannot be dammed or turned, at least the bed through which it flows can be broadened. "Misdirection is Homer's means of testing the limits of his tradition by exploring possibilities outside the standard myth," Morrison argues. His reading suggests that the maker of both poems was an exceptionally deliberate artificer with clear aesthetic objectives underpinning the narrative, certainly not an absent or distant narrator or an "oral tradition." Like so many persuasively argued approaches, this is plausible enough to be satisfying while we consider it. It suggests a jazz analogy: "exposition, exploration [misdirection], recapitulation." But it depends on a crude sense of audience and it forgets that the effects will not work on second reading or performance.

What is admirable about the Homeric hero is not that he is allowed latitude but that, knowing his fate, he still behaves with courage and honour.

Hector in *Iliad* XX, 304, is terrifyingly human. Sometimes a god is required to tap an enemy on the shoulder in order to distract him, to deflect the fatal course of an arrow or a spear. But the heroes go into battle and seek to win glory, *areté* is proved by *kleos*. That is their nature, that is what the *Iliad* in particular is about. This human ideal is most clearly explored in the characters of kings, princes, noble warriors. The common soldiers in some way belong to and are extensions of the great warriors. What makes the killing so vivid and painful is the way the poem humanises each victim; they are often better than their victors, only they are less powerful, or less favoured by a god.

The Trojans share a collective take on the war: it started for them when the Greek ships arrived; it will end when they depart or the city is destroyed. The Greeks are more diverse in perspective, each with an individual point and motive of departure, each desiring to return for a different reason, and every one individually motivated in battle, though taking booty seems to be a common pursuit. The objective was to kill a well-heeled warrior, strip him then and there of his fine armour and have a runner carry the clobber back to the ships. Amongst the Trojans and their allies there was much rich armour to be captured, and some of the finest horses in the world, though none so fine as Achilles' Xanthus, which "white-armed Juno had endowed with human speech." He bows his head so low the mane touches the earth and foretells his master's death. "We two can fly as swiftly as Zephyrus who they say is fleetest of all winds; nevertheless it is your doom to fall by the hand of a man and of a god."

Achilles in Book IX famously speaks of his freedom to leave Troy, and more famously, in Book I, defines his particular objectives in joining the war: "I came not warring here for any ill the Trojans had done me. I have no quarrel with them. They have not raided my cattle nor my horses, nor cut down my harvests on the rich plains of Phthia; for between me and them there is a great space, both mountain and sounding sea. We have followed you, Sir Insolence [Agamemnon]! for your pleasure, not ours—to gain satisfaction from the Trojans for your shameless self and for Menelaus. You forget this, and threaten to rob me of the prize for which I have toiled, and which the sons of the Achaeans have given me." The candour in speech that we encounter in both poems is remarkable in an age of indirection and irony such as ours: it is no wonder that Odysseus is the most modern-seeming Homeric character: he is the most devious, the most ironic and calculating, and many younger readers find his poem far more comprehensible than Hector's and Achilles', which strike them as too predictable and burdened with detail.

In the world of peace, so vividly evoked in the shield which Thetis has Hephaestus make for Achilles (*Iliad* XVIII), the responsibilities and duties of men are different from those of wartime. In war or in peace, the human scenes generally have a formal, ritualised movement which should be borne in mind when appraising "characters." These protagonists cannot be read as we would read novel characters: the bourgeois world has not happened to them, their identities have not been made subjective. Like Greek dramatic figures, they wear a kind of mask before their human faces and it is the mask upon which we focus. Even when it slips, there is likely to be another mask behind it, as when Achilles is left alone with the corpse of Patroclus. Major characters are imbued with *ethos*. Lesky[45] identifies three such characters in the *Iliad:* Achilles, Hector and Patroclus. Each suffers (knowingly) a failure of *restraint,* a kind of forerunner of the tragic *hubris* Aristotle speaks of, and including tragic *anagnorisis,* or recognition.

Hospitality, like grief, can be ceremonial, a social given, rather than an expression of individual nature. Odysseus is moved on rapidly when he asks too much and violates conventions of hospitality in his protracted journey home. In Book XXII of the *Odyssey,* hospitality, after such a long violation of its rules, is inverted: the battle takes place in the very site of hospitality and the first two victims, Antinous and Eurylachus, die *into* their food, as it were, blood mingling with viands. Positive exceptions to the formalism of custom occur as well, for example when Priam addresses Helen in the *Iliad,* Book II, or in Book XXIV when Achilles and Priam meet in the most harrowing and powerful engagement in the poem, a battle without weapons where both protagonists prove their heroic stature in an act of mutual self-effacement. Achilles himself lifts the corpse of Hector onto Priam's wagon, an amazing moment and full of tears. These passages are susceptible to "modern" readings, but it is best not to inflict too much psychology on them.

As modern readers, however, we cannot help entering our own judgements on some of the characters. The most awkward in the *Iliad* is Agamemnon, the great king. From the first moment he speaks he is aggressive, assertive, shrill, unbrave; he needs to be calmed by venerable Nestor, he is a hot-head without qualities who alienates his chief warrior and puts the whole campaign, in its ninth year, in jeopardy all for the sake of a woman. Achilles makes it clear that Agamemnon is a coward and never leads his men but stays in the centre; he is a heavy drinker and has an insatiable sexual appetite. The poem tries to redeem him by comparing him with the gods. Zeus is the first point of comparison, and Agamemnon is within his army what Zeus is within his palace. Zeus the wife-beater . . . We have just seen him threatening his wife with violence and her child Hephaistus begging her to obey the brute because it hurts him to see her hurt by him. Agamemnon is beneath respect, contemptible in his appetites and lack of empathy.

Thersites attacks him, but because Thersites is such a repulsive and unpopular figure, his (true) accusations rebound upon his own head.

We get to know Agamemnon and most of the other leading characters not through description but by means of their own language. They speak, indeed they talk so much that Plato, in Book III of the *Republic,* reckons that epic poetry is halfway between narrative and the drama.[46] In an oral tradition, the medium of speech in which the rhapsode works is also the privileged medium within the narrative, through which the heroes make themselves known. Characters are differentiated by their diction, the length of their syntactical periods, their tones in relation to their peers and their inferiors. When in *Iliad* IX the three ambassadors, visiting Achilles in his tent, urge him to change his mind, they are carefully individualised; the middle one is fullest and clearest. In the rhetorical world of threes, it is the second that is always fullest (a rhetorical "fact"), Lesky reminds us.[47] In Book II of the *Odyssey* the suitors, especially Antinous, make fun of Telemachus and bait him: the sarcasm of the dialogue borders on dramatic form. Greek laughter often relates to mockery. It can be as cruel as the laughter in the Old Testament.

Especially in debate we hear voices, coloured by the prejudice or the wisdom that pertains to them. In the *Odyssey* speech gives us a sense of intimacy with the characters while, at the same time, keeping us at our distance: we hear the suitors, Telemachus, Menelaus, Helen, Nestor, Odysseus, the gods and many others. Speech is more immediate than reported speech, even when formalised and delivered in a ceremonious way.

We get closest to the characters of the *Iliad* in Book VI, when we are taken within the walls of Troy and allowed to see, by contrast with the Greek camp in all its functional and insistently male order, another world. At the high tower Andromache and Astyanax meet Hector. She begs her husband not to fight on, recalling the terrible place of Achilles in her own past. He slew her father and seven brothers. But Hector will not rest, though he knows Troy's eventual doom and what it will mean for her and their son. His helmet frightens the baby, both parents laugh, he removes the helmet and kisses the child. He prays. It is a wonderful moment of human laughter, the more powerful because it is the only point of intimate warmth in the poem, unless we regard the rather strained exchanges between Achilles and Patroclus as warm. Then Hector goes, Andromache returns among her women. Hector meets Paris and they prepare, after this interlude, to return to battle.

The *Odyssey* is warmer in this respect, with intimate exchanges between many characters. But since the world through which Telemachus moves, outside Ithaca, is at peace, and since Odysseus converses when he returns

home with people who love and respect him, the formality which is so pronounced in the *Iliad* becomes less insistent and we have a sense of actions
on a smaller scale, with a more focussed intensity and purpose.

The *Iliad,* Lesky declares, "does not merely fulfil the demands of epic poetry; it goes far beyond them to the realm of tragedy. Instead of uniform
flow and unhurried narration of events, we find an artistic scheme of inter-
connection and cross-reference, happenings sometimes briefly sketched,
sometimes elaborately worked out . . ." With Aristotle he speaks of the
poem's contrasting styles, one "flowing," the other "periodic," more focussed, holding attention on a single incident or scene. The stylistic distinction can be applied to the structure itself, an interplay between speeds and
depths of realisation, what the German writer Friedrich Schiller called the
"naive and the sentimentive."

Serious structural problems mar the *Iliad,* making interpretation hard.
For example, in a single day the Greeks build a mighty rampart between the
ships and the Trojan plain. Oddnesses and actual faults in the narrative are
seized upon by critics to support compositional theories. Analyticals and
the unitarians have predetermined responses which are as much to do with
their theories as with the poem itself. Of all the theories, the "gradual accretion" theory seems the most commonsensical, which does not mean that it
is correct. Gottfried Hermann (1772–1848) proposed it. The "lays" theory
suggests the *Iliad* is sixteen poems joined into one. The compilation theory
takes it a step further: they were not lays but epic episodes linked together
(this grew out of studies of the *Odyssey* but was eventually applied to the
Iliad as well). As an extension of the compilation theory came the accretion
theory. After the First World War there was a reversion to a sense of the
general unity of the *Iliad.* Unitarians who had defended the unity of plot
now began to defend the structure in greater detail.

Lesky argues that centuries of epic poetry came before Homer (the un-
writing dark ages). Oral elements survived in the written text, especially formulae and epithets and the verbatim repetition of commands and speeches.
If we bear in mind the legend of Homer's blindness and consider how
complex in thematic and textural conception *Paradise Lost* is, and how it was
orally delivered to Milton's long-suffering daughters, we might not think
recitation and even dictation quite so remarkable. Literary in source, original in prosody and concept, *Paradise Lost* was orally (because it could not
have been literarily) conceived, structured and recorded. Lesky is persuaded
that the Homeric poet could and did write. As evidence he mentions the
wide cross-referencing and self-quotation, at points distant from one another in the text. Lesky is also keen to insist that the poems are not all derivation; there is invention and originality, not least in the formal organisation

of the *Iliad*. "The scene in which Priam and Achilles, after all the pangs of battle, all the grief and cruelty of unmeasured vengeance, learn to understand and respect each other as men, is at once the culmination of the *Iliad* and the starting-point of the western conception of humanity."[48]

The title of the *Iliad* (*The Poem of Ilium* or *Troy*) could have been the *Achillead*, since his inaction, and then his action, are the mainsprings of the plot. The poem focuses on the few days in the decade of the Trojan War when Troy briefly got the upper hand, the point at which the scales of fate seemed as though they might tip contrary to expectation. They were not necessarily the most dramatic or the most decisive days, though the death of Hector accelerated the end of the war. Three weeks pass in the opening scenes, another three weeks in the closing scenes. Most of what occurs from Book II to Book XXIII, Taplin reminds us, takes place during four days and two nights.[49] Seven and a half books are devoted to a single day. Time is going fast in the opening books; it slows down and we focus on the intense action, and then at the end there is an acceleration. The opening books provide crucial information, the closing parts of the poem foreshadow Troy's fate. In terms of theme, the first two lines mention Achilles, the last two Hector, their epithets intact. The poem begins with the attempted ransoming of a child—Chryses and Chryseis—and ends with Priam's ransoming of his child Hector's corpse.

Achilles is a powerful man of selective commitments and affinities, far from home, Patroclus' intimate. Hector, the mainstay of his city, fights before the eyes of his family and his people. He believes it is equal combat until the end, and then (XXII, 304–5) he displays a true heroism which transcends mere strength, endurance and skill: that resignation which keeps him resolute and brave though he knows he is imminently doomed. "Immortal fame" is the wages of the kind of life he lives—and the death he must die.

The Italian writer Italo Calvino seems, in a modern spirit, to prefer the *Odyssey* to the *Iliad* on formal grounds. His essay entitled "The Odysseys within the *Odyssey*"[50] reflects on the number of odysseys the poem describes, how many ends are known before a traveller reaches home. In Book IV Menelaus recalls how he was caught in the doldrums off Egypt. The local goddess of Pharos urged him to beard Proteus in his den, wrestle with him and squeeze an explanation and a prophecy from him. Within the story, Menelaus tells a story in which he compels the sea god to tell a story.

The danger of forgetting is real all along: Odysseus might lose track of who he is, or forget the urgency of his calling home. There are the lotus eaters, Circe's drugs, the Sirens' song and much else to distract him. The danger is less that he will forget the past, more that he will forget his purpose, his identity and future. Where Odysseus has come from is clear and chronicled; he must constantly bear in mind where he is going, like Aeneas *en route* to Italy. Odysseus loses everything more than once on the way home: his booty, the gifts he is given, all his men, and almost his name when he visits the Cyclops. He finally declares his name, at King Alcinous' behest (IX, 19–28), in a powerful passage where he regathers his energy in the act of memory. Calvino makes Odysseus' trial universal, without reducing it to an allegory. His reading touches with a lively accuracy what many scholars overlook in considering the poem's themes.

In Book XXII the suitors are slain and compared to a harvest of fish, poured out by fishermen onto the sand, twitching still. When the female servants who consorted with the suitors are hanged by Telemachus, their dangling feet are seen to twitch as well. Then at the opening of Book XXIV, which some regard as apocryphal, the suitors' ghosts are led to Hades by Cyllenian Hermes with his golden, sleep-dispensing wand. Here we encounter one of the most apposite and precise similes in the *Odyssey,* a simile which makes visible the flight of souls. Butler translates it, "As bats fly squealing in the hollow of some great cave, when one of them has fallen out of the cluster in which they hang, even so did the ghosts whine and squeal as Hermes the healer of sorrow led them down into the dark abode of death." Other translators make the "cluster" into a "chain" or "cone." Be that as it may, when one bat is disturbed they all erupt and flock erratically out of the cave mouth. As a simile it corresponds at every point to the elements it helps us to visualise. It suggests, too, a certain kind of geography.

The *Odyssey,* J. V. Luce points out, has two quite different narrative tones, that of Odysseus' fantastic travels on the one hand, and that of the Telemachiad and Odysseus' return to Ithaca on the other. Luce is of course fascinated by the geography of Ithaca and prefers the rocks and paths and caves that he can visit; he likes it when the "fantastic gives way to the realistic."[31] Certainly the "realistic," as he calls it, has elements of implausibility, metamorphosis, magic, just as the fantastic has very particularised and credible details, however unbelievable the Cyclops, Circe, the Laestrygonians, the Sirens and the other challenges are.

What kinds of detail make the complex narrative of the *Odyssey* credible and deep in "orchestration," touching different strings of the story all at once and making those harmonies that affect us on each re-reading? Penelope's weaving is one such detail. She weaves not just anything, a table-cloth or antimacassar or bed-cover: she is weaving not some mystical cloth like the Lady of Shalott, but in fact a shroud for Odysseus' father, Laertes. It is a sacred charge laid upon her; hence she cannot be seriously interrupted by the suitors until the task is complete. In Book V, Hermes like a seagull makes his way from Olympus with Zeus' command to Calypso (whose name means "concealed" or "concealer"). She must release Odysseus from her spells so he can go home. What is Calypso doing? Weaving, which seems to be what women with servants do to pass the time. Certainly at Alcinous' court all the women are at it.

Odysseus has an awful journey. His foe Poseidon (Poseidon lay with a sea nymph and Polyphemus was the issue) spots him in the little craft he has made, churns up the seas and tries to drown him. The hero swims for two days, lands on rocks which tear his hands, is sucked out to sea again on the undertow, and at last is washed ashore exhausted. He hides in the woods, making a bed among the fallen leaves. Here again is a perfectly chosen simile: "so he laid himself down and heaped the leaves all round him. Then, as one who lives alone in the country, far from any neighbour, hides a brand as fire-seed in the ashes to save himself from having to get a light elsewhere, even so did Odysseus cover himself up with leaves . . ."

It takes him ten years to return from the ten-year war. His long relationship with Calypso issued in staleness and, for the hero, that *saudade* that the Portuguese navigators felt, far from home, a deep almost despairing sadness. The poem concentrates on the last leg of his journey and the restoration of his fortunes at home. The time-frame is just under six weeks, and Books XVI to XXIV take only three days. Not only does the *Odyssey* cover a lot of ground and sea, the whole Aegean and then some; it also evokes every class of person, from mendicants and beggars to kings. Odysseus himself crosses back and forth between classes, now a beggar, now a king. In conversation with Telemachus, Helen remembers how dressed in rags he entered Troy as if a slave to gather information, how she recognised him but kept his counsel and he returned, slaying Trojans as he went.

While in the *Iliad* women serve as motives for action (Helen, Chryseis, Briseis) but apart from Andromache have little presence, in the *Odyssey* women play important roles. Penelope, Helen, Calypso, Nausicaa, Arete and others of more humble origin can become involved in the central action of the poem, have motives and complex moral natures. We move away from the barbarities of mere heroism and approach the hard-earned zone of peace and stability, achieved in the end by calculation, deception and scrupulous conspiracy. Despite all the action of the *Iliad,* it is in the *Odyssey* that we find adventure.

The basic story is not uncommon: a husband returns after a very long absence to find his son grown up, his wife besieged by suitors. His task is to work his way back into the place he left, so he must test his wife's fidelity (especially after what happened to his friend Agamemnon upon his return from Troy), get to know his son, and purge his house of the pestilential suitors. To this core are added traveller's tales, which, Lesky says, "must have been many and varied in the second millennium BC while Crete was a great sea power." We can see the poem as an early novel of homecoming, a sea adventure, a saga of Troy, and a work which stimulated new Ionian thought and imagination.

We start in Ithaca, an anarchic island. Young Telemachus, whose name means "decisive battle," Graves tells us, is bullied and kept down in his own house. His father's long absence means that he and his mother are effectively held hostage by the suitors exploiting the traditions of hospitality. Penelope's name is variously etymologised. Graves says it means "with a web over her face" or—"striped duck." Paul Kretschmer derives it from *pene, penion,* "bobbin-thread, woof," and *elop* "as found in *olopto,*" "unravel." Kretschmer's explanation is the more satisfying since the name would describe (as Telemachus' ultimately does) the key trick action of the poem. Odysseus, Graves says, means "angry."

Telemachus sets off in quest of his father. If he is dead, Penelope will have to remarry and move on, unencumbering the estate. If he is alive, Telemachus needs him. The Telemachiad, the first four books of the poem, deal with the boy's coming of age and his education in more stable and less rustic societies. He brings back gifts and a kind of hope which within hours produces a flesh-and-blood father and elicits from him some of the heroic skills we would expect of the son of Odysseus. He is also capable of cruelty as coarse and pointless as that practised on the windy plain of Troy: not only the execution of the female servants, but also collusion in the death of the rebarbative goatherd Melanthius, whose nose and ears are removed, his genitals lopped off for the dogs to eat, and his hands and feet severed.

Wise, wily, scheming, crafty Odysseus: the old fathers of Ithaca, looking at the heap of their dead sons, had a point when they called for revenge. "They took the dead away, buried every man his own, and put the bodies of those who came from elsewhere on board the fishing vessels, for the fishermen to take each of them to his own place." Then in the meeting place they assembled and Eupeithes, father of the churlish Alcinous, Odysseus' first victim, recalled how many Ithacans died with Odysseus in the Trojan expedition, and how he had then come home and killed the flower of Ithaca youth all over again. "Let us be up and doing before he can get away to Pylos or to Elis where the Epeans rule, or we shall be ashamed of ourselves for ever afterwards. It will be an everlasting disgrace to us if we do not avenge the murder of our sons and brothers . . ." The poem tells us that "He wept as he spoke and every one pitied him." But there was to be no revenge on the returning king; on the contrary, Laertes, Odysseus' father, would have the pleasure of fighting alongside his son and grandson, backed by Athena in the likeness of Mentor, swooping down and killing more Ithacans, old men for the most part, starting with Eupeithes himself. Odysseus would have slain the lot had Zeus not sent down an insistent thunderbolt and Athena commanded him to desist. Then, "glad at heart," he obeyed, and the warring factions were compelled by the gods to make peace. Odysseus, one of the worst leaders of all time, having mislaid all his comrades and taken ten years to cover the distance his fellow combatants had covered in a few weeks, settled down to rule Ithaca, though legend has it that he led one further expedition—over the edge of the world.

VI

Hesiod

The Muses bore Hesiod; the Graces bore Homer.

SIMONIDES[1]

Consider the comedown, the loss of scale, of conjuring magic, the decay of dignity: from Orpheus, Arion and Amphion to Homer; and then from Homer to grumbling, litigious, horny-handed-son-of-toil Hesiod. It all started beside divine Olympus, then the windy plain of Troy where legend and history mingle. And now? Askre, in Boeotia, cut off from Thebes (due east) and from Athens (east-south-east) by mountains, from Corinth (due south) by the Gulf.

Here we seek a poet,[2] the very first who speaks—probably before 700 BC—with an individual voice and whose subject is nothing more, and nothing less, than the hard life he leads. If we could smell him, he would certainly reek of the human. He suffers from a need to make sense of his world and to reduce the troubling, floating legends of gods and goddesses, the rituals of religion and the rules of husbandry, to some kind of connected order. He needs a sense of control, or at least a sense of *shape,* in his physical, social and spiritual environments. And his tool is language.

Even today it is no easy matter getting to where Hesiod's farm used to be. Mount Helicon and the so-called Valley of the Muses involve a deal of rather uninteresting (though not difficult) climbing, and if you are looking for traces of Hesiod, you must brace yourself for disappointment. Bear in mind that you are traversing the merest skeleton of Hesiod's landscape: time and history have been particularly unkind to this part of Greece, removing most of the trees and giving it a parched, forgotten feel, changing its weather from the patterns Hesiod records. Here you do not feel history rising like a fine mist; you feel that it has evaporated quite.

The modern village of Palaiopanayía is as far as a car will take you on your quest. After that you need a guide, ideally a mule, patience and imagination. In about forty minutes you come upon an ancient tower, medieval in origin, perhaps earlier in the materials from which it is constructed. It is called, unsurprisingly, Palaiopirgos ("old tower") and is located, perhaps, in the site of Keressos. South of the tower are the shards of an old (Turkish?) village with a little church. Beyond a stream rises a hill crowned by a ruined Hellenic structure. It stood there eighteen hundred years ago when the traveller Pausanias passed that way, and, with his obsessive meticulousness (for modern readers a happy pedantry), he made a note of it.[3] It represents the only remains of the hamlet called Askre, which may mean "barren oak."[4] Hesiod called Askre a town "cursed, intolerable in winter, unendurable in summer, pleasing never," a Boeotian Lake Wobegon. As settings go, Askre's is neither grand nor amenable. Still, around Easter the traveller is sometimes surprised, when the sun is half way up the sky, by tiny gusts of exquisite scent: they come from the wild, almost leafless cyclamen, pale dots of purple. There are old olive trees clenched among the rock. And the streams where the Muses bathe, which are named in the *Theogony* as the Permessos and the Olmeios, come together not far from the remains of the village. From their bath, the Muses rose like wraiths to the summit of Helicon, and they danced and chanted the invocation to Zeus that Hesiod heard.

If you persist and climb on towards midday you reach, in a couple of hours, the Valley of the Muses with its scatter of ruins: an altar, a stoa, the theatre where the contests of the Mouseia were conducted every four years. To the musical and poetic contests in later years were added dramatic competitions as well. The upper valley of the Permessos belonged to the Muses, and therefore to Apollo. The sacred groves, deep shadows and cool springs were the landscape in which Greek builders set fine temples and a famous sanctuary, decorated with statues representing the Muses themselves and their servants, in particular—from our point of view—the epic and lyric poets.

Constantine the Great made off with the treasures of the sanctuary. Deforestation and erosion creased and aged the landscape, leaving bare rock and the exposed ruins. The Muses packed their bags, after coming here originally from the skirts of Mount Olympus, not too far away from where the gods live. Their town of origin was Pieria—watered by the bubbling Pierian spring, a traditional source of poetic inspiration. Thracian peasants paid homage to the feminine spirits of the mountains and the welling water. The Muses wandered south and founded Askre. Mount Helicon and the lyric springs of Hippocrene (a further two and a half hours on foot, on a spur of Mount Helicon) and Aganippe were dedicated to the Muses. Hippocrene, the Spring of the Horse, is so named because Pegasus, landing from the sky, caused it to flow when his hoof-beat struck the ground.

The Muses came from elsewhere before settling (for a time) into this place. So did Hesiod's father.

But already, in a hot, solid landscape, I am talking of Hesiod as a real person. The cautious modern historian warns us to doubt every word of every ancient biography. We can *know* nothing. I ought properly to write "'Hesiod's' 'father,'" making it clear, by using the tongs of quotation marks, that I am aware of my subject's problematic existence. His "mother" was said by later traditions to be the divine, or divinely fathered, Pycimede ("quietly clever"); his partner—perhaps even his wife—was assigned the name Eoie, and like his father he was said to have had two sons, Mnasiepes and Archiepes, "rememberer" and "beginner of epic verse," respectively.[5]

If I forego the tongs, it is in part because I want to spare the reader the irritation of so much *evidence* of caution, and in part because I believe—up to a point—in the Hesiod who emerges from the two substantial poems firmly attributed to him,[6] the grudging laureate of the Arts of Peace: *Works and Days* and *Theogony*. He may have been responsible, too, for the mini-epic *Shield of Heracles* and other fragments. Cycles of poetry grew out of the work of Hesiod, quite as much as out of Homer's. Of the poems fathered on Hesiod, the most interesting is *The Catalogue of Women,* evoking the dynasties established by gods mating with human beings. Because of the repeated phrase *e hoie* ("or like the woman who"), it is known as *Ehoiai* (plural). Ostensibly it follows the *Theogony,* but it grew in fits and starts on into the sixth century BC.

Especially from *Works and Days* a sense emerges of a man with a past, an immigrant father, a litigious layabout of a brother, a farm, and a farmer's seasonal woes. He is keen to make understanding out of what he knows. At heart he is a philosopher, the first of the Greek philosophers in fact, looking for stable forms, but without—because he comes so early in the history of his culture—the prose instruments of later thinkers. Historians of philosophy generally locate his contribution to the development of Greek thought in the *Theogony,* his account of the origins of the gods; deeper and more durable is his account of man and his relations with the physical world. The crucial poem, as a *poem,* is *Works and Days*.

Hesiod as philosopher does not so much think as affirm and assert; he is conservative, obedient to customs and superstitions, which he sets down unquestioningly: they seem to be pragmatically true, judging from his day-to-day experience. Though he might be a tyrant's ideal intellectual subject, he is not at one with Voltaire's Pangloss: "Whatever is is for the best in this best of all possible worlds." His is a glummer motto: "Whatever is, is." And most of what is is not the best. Hesiod expresses a timeless peasant conservatism. Even today it characterises rural communities which have not been transformed by modern technology, which can still accurately be called communities, that is, in eastern Europe for example, and Tras os Montes in Portugal, remote parts of Spain, Asia and Africa and Latin America.

His father, Hesiod tells us, was from Cyme in Asia Minor. Southern-most of the Aeolic ports, it is a little above Smyrna (Izmir), which claimed Homer for its own. If modern Askre is remote from our expectation, modern Smyrna is worse: an industrial city with a large oil refinery. The ruins of the ancient town are a little to the north, and right on the coast.

Cyme, like other towns in Asia Minor and the islands, sent its people out to colonise. Cyme's most famous settlement was Cumae, the western-most Greek colony in Italy, where the eponymous Sibyl lived in her cave, a figure Virgil evokes in the *Aeneid*. The people of Cyme spoke a mixed dialect of Ionian and Aeolic, widely used in northwest Asia Minor and on some of the islands, Lesbos among them.

Hesiod's poem gives us some details. Around the middle of the eighth century BC, the poet's father became an economic migrant.

> He was fleeing, you can be sure, from something other
> Than wealth and good things: loathsome poverty
> Zeus visits upon men.[7]

He sailed a long way, landed and then—as if repelled forever by Poseidon—walked and walked until he was out of sound and sight of the sea. (His poet son inherited his aversion to open water.) He settled and started his farm, and here the poet was born. Hesiod makes no mention of his mother. It is tempting to speculate that she was a Boeotian whom the man from Cyme married, rather than a goddess.[8]

At least two sons were born, industrious Hesiod and main-chancer Perses, a thorn in his brother's side. When their father died, the sons entered into a dispute over their inheritance, the meagre farm. Contention went on and on and we get a sense that Hesiod did not win the argument, though in terms of posterity he has had almost three millennia of last-laughing. His brother, who never replies to his advice or retorts to his taunts in the poem, is a mute villain. Hesiod's is a formidable voice to speak against. He tells in *Works and Days* of how he competed in the poetry contest at Chalcis in Euboea,[9] at the funeral of Amphidamas.

> The great man's sons had put up
> Prizes aplenty for the contests, and I'm proud to say
> I won in the songfest and took home an eared tripod.
> Dedicated it to the Heliconian Muses, on the very spot
> Where they first set me on the road to clear song.[10]

What is he referring to? We are perilously near to "intertextuality" for the poet draws attention to another of his poems. In *Theogony* he describes himself as having been unexpectedly inspired by the Muses. He is the first poet to portray himself thus, enabled to sing by some force outside himself. Truth and fiction are the Muses' initial themes. Some critics suggest mischievously that Hesiod may himself have "made" the Muses on Mount Helicon; indeed, that in the *Theogony* he first named them.[11] This seems unlikely: the poet we encounter in the poems is not inventive or "original" in this way.

Like his successors in the Muses' favour, he was out pasturing a flock (of sheep in his case) on the slopes of the sacred mountain. Down came the

Olympian Muses, offspring of Zeus "the holder of the goat skin," an epithet which has troubled scholars. It may mean a rustic Zeus, a god wandering like a shepherd himself on the slopes of Helicon. Indeed this may be a
way of alluding to a mighty human master who imparted the divine art of
song to the young shepherd, his poetic apprentice, and Hesiod translated
the man and the debt into a "higher register."

The Muses address the shepherd-about-to-become-a-poet. They warn
him that they know how to lie and deceive peasants and low-life such as he
is, but they also know how to tell the truth. They give their elected votary a
laurel staff, and then quite literally they *inspire,* that is, breathe into him,
a voice that is not his but is divine. The purpose? So that he might celebrate
things past and to come.

> . . . and they breathed in my frame a voice divine,
> and the power to tell of the past or future was mine,
> and they bade me sing of the gods who never may die,
> and ever, the first and the last, on themselves to cry—
> But why this wandering tale of a tree or stone?[12]

It is a good story, appropriate for the Mouseia. Enjoined by the Muses to
sing, the poet starts by singing about them, and then discloses, with their
aid, the structure of the divine world. The inspired poet is a vehicle, of use
to the Muses. The "I" of Hesiod survives, as it were, despite their injunctions; their higher rhetoric is hardly credible, as coming from so modest a
mouth as his. The poet on this inspirational model is like a spiritualist medium or, worse still, a creature whose mind is occupied and used by an alien
force, and then released back to itself in a state of confused exhaustion. It
doesn't quite work: Hesiod remains Hesiod. He starts the *Theogony* in the
third person but soon moves to the first; in the midst of narrative he finds it
impossible to withhold a comment. His repetitive demand is for justice,
fairness, order. There can be a hectoring petulance in his tone.

Works and Days is inspired differently than the *Theogony*. We ought perhaps to say it is occasioned, for the tone is dogged and resigned, by the
hard-working countryman's daily life and family gripes. It can be viewed either as the surviving fragments of a larger poem which, due to the uncer-
tainties of transmission, have reached us in a mutilated state, or as a
non-systematic anthology of lore, custom and poetry more or less harnessed by the voice of a single speaker. That speaker is not a continuous
presence in the poem: he establishes his existence and then rather forgets
himself, or we forget him, much of the time. Yet the poem somehow adds
up; what we take away from it is a sense of his presence, without which it
would fissure and fall apart.

If we consider the poem an anthology of bits, we can look for natural breaks, changes of tone, idiom and direction; we should not demand of it a coherence and structure which are in effect anachronistic, back-projections from later literature and theory. Not that theorists and critics have not spent two and a half millennia doing just that. If we wish to read *Works and Days* for pleasure, freed as much as possible from critical patristics, we do best not to make inordinate formal demands of it.

When the poem acquired its title—which describes only two parts of it and therefore mis-describes the "whole"—is uncertain. The first written attestation appears in the second century AD. The text of the poem was unstable even then. The methodical traveller Pausanias not only passed by Askre: he was shown by the Boeotians further along, near Helicon, the text of the poem inscribed on a sheet of lead and even then clearly of considerable antiquity, damaged by time and weather. All this occurred not far from the reedy pool where Narcissus reflected on himself.

Nietzsche was much taken by one particular observation of Pausanias. Not for nothing was Pausanias a recorder of every fact, for among the crowd of little irrelevant ones there is always the promise of a big one that makes a difference. "The Boeotians living around Helicon," he reports, "hand down a tradition that Hesiod wrote nothing but the *Works and Days;* and even from that they take away the 'Prelude to the Muses.'"[13] *Works and Days* would start at what we now consider the eleventh line; the invocation to the Muses and the evocation of Zeus would vanish. This alternative poem plunges straight in to the matter of Eris, the last-born and most ambiguous of the children of Night.

> It looks like there's not just one kind of Strife—
> That's Eris—after all, but two on earth.
> You'd praise one of them once you got to know her,
> But the other's plain blameworthy.[14]

We begin, not with the formal throat-clearing of invocation, Nietzsche says, but with an assertion, "There are *two* Eris-goddesses on earth." And from here begins the train of thought which shapes Nietzsche's radical reading of Greek poetry. "This is one of the most remarkable of Hellenic ideas," he says, "and deserves to be impressed upon newcomers right at the gate of entry to Hellenic ethics. 'One should praise the one Eris as much as blame the other, if one has any sense; because the two goddesses have quite separate dispositions.'" He continues with his prose translation: "'One promotes war and feuding, a cruel one, she is. No man likes her, but the yoke of necessity forces man to honour the heavy burden of this Eris according to the decrees of the gods. Black Night gave birth to this one as the older of the two; but Cronus' son [Zeus], who reigns above us, placed the other on the roots of the earth and amongst men as a much better one. She drives even the unskilled man to work; and if someone who lacks property sees someone else who is rich, he likewise hurries off to sow and plant and set his house in order; neighbour competes with neighbour for prosperity. This Eris is good for men. Even potters harbour grudges against potters, carpenters against carpenters, beggars envy beggars and poets envy poets.'"[15]

The duality of the figure of envious Eris, resolved into twins, the evil elder and the paradoxically benign younger, the spirit of rivalry and the spirit of competition: this is Hesiod's way of defining and distinguishing human motives and, as it were, laying the thematic groundwork for the human plot. His brother Perses serves the first Eris: vindictive, covetous, and destructive, whereas Hesiod serves the second in his zeal, grudging generosity of spirit, and good husbandry.

Homer is the father of the epic tradition. To Hesiod is attributed the paternity of another tradition. It is hard to define precisely what it is. As with Homer, there are two poems quite different in tone, matter, and manner. The modern poet-translator C. A. Trypannis uses the term "didactic epic." Is this conflation of two terms that are tangential to one another of any real use? Is there anything *epic* about *Works and Days*? In ancient times didactic verse was sometimes regarded as epic of a kind, but a kind which excluded narratives of conflict. There is a sort of heroism in the everyday, humble man's endurance of poverty and hardship, labour, and the absence of any durable rewards beyond survival. Such "heroism," not of the classical hero but of the common man, is hardly "epic," however, and there is no narrative or progression beyond the seasons. What is more, in *Works and Days* it is not unreasonable to see the conflation of three poems rather than a single poem, and in *Theogony* a mass of disparate material gathered and organised into a kind of theological anthology.

The word "didactic," on the other hand, gets us somewhere. The poems undeniably give practical advice and philosophical instruction. The *Theogony* tries to systematise legends of the gods, goddesses and their offspring and is an account of origins, the recurrent aetiologies that become the obsessive theme of the Alexandrian poets but are a continual concern in Greek verse from the beginning. *Works and Days* touches upon labour, the farmer's calendar, and justice, with an uneasy appendix on seafaring and housekeeping. It includes myth, too, and fable. Beside the relative elevation of language in the *Theogony*, *Works and Days* stays close to the ground and gives us serious advice.

> Don't piss standing up while facing the sun.
> Between sunset and sunrise, remember,

> Don't piss on the road or on the roadside,
> Or naked. The blessed gods own the night.
> A religious man squats down, if he's got any sense,
> Or he goes by the wall of an enclosed courtyard.[16]

It is the kind of practical-spiritual counselling that proves how inseparable the physical is from the metaphysical world. We are always watched, we are always "performing," and our performance—even the most fundamental—is judged:

> Don't let your privates be seen smeared with semen
> Near the hearth at home. Be careful to avoid this.[17]

The lines instruct us, and "we" are always men. In order to teach a wide band of men, the language chosen is less heightened, less deliberately rhetorical, than the language Homer uses in recounting heroic deeds or Hesiod in providing the gods with pedigrees. It may be remote from the language that a simple farmer working on the slopes of Mount Helicon might speak, but such a farmer, familiar with Homer's verse, and with the local poet's themes, would have no trouble in understanding it. This more relaxed, less decorous language allows a greater variety of specifically human, rather than Muse-dictated, tones. Rancour, pettiness, individual melancholy, Polonius-like pomposity, humour: all can be accommodated in the narrator's voice, rather than being confined to the *dramatis personae* of the narrative. Tonal variations occur close together—he condescends to give advice, then suddenly he loses his temper—since consistency is not a rule Hesiod has to obey.

> . . . But if you bear false witness
> Or lie under oath, and by damaging Justice
> Ruin yourself beyond hope of cure, your bloodline
> Will weaken and your descendants die out. But a man
> Who stands by his word leaves a long line of kinfolk.
>
> Now I'm speaking sense to you, Perses you fool.
> It's easy to get all of Wickedness you want.
> She lives just down the road a piece, and it's a smooth road too.
> But the gods put Goodness where we have to sweat
> To climb to her. It's a long, uphill pull
> And tough going at first. But once you reach the top
> She's as easy to have as she was hard at first.[18]

The ingredients of a speaking, satirical, iambic and finally comic verse (and comedy itself) are in the kernel of Hesiod's generically indeterminate poems. It is odd that Aristotle in the *Poetics* makes no mention of Hesiod or his achievement.

And the genre that Hesiod invents is the first to come, not from Ionia, but from the mainland of Greece itself. He does employ hexameters, like Homer, only they are (to use M. L. West's candid phrase) "hobnailed." Like Homer's, his diction mixes various dialect elements, though—unsurprisingly—Boeotian elements are in the ascendant. Athenians of the fifth century BC saw the language as bucolic and comic. The style is that of the oral tradition, and no doubt the poem survived in an oral tradition, too, even though it may have been written down or (though this is mere conjecture) composed in written form. When an oral tradition makes the momentous transition to the leaden sheet or the page of parchment or papyrus, the poet or scribe is writing from the ear, as it were, rather than from the silence of earlier pages. The writing exists to score what is conceived as an adjunct to musically accompanied, and dance-accompanied, recitation.

They say that at Delphi, at a poetic competition, Hesiod was disqualified because he could not play the harp. What does this tell us (assuming it is true)? That Hesiod practised a different kind of recitation, appropriate to a different genre of verse? This may be another of his virtues, and why his poetry is closer to speech than Homer's: a lack of skill in one component area of the art led to the development of greater skill in another. Or he composed in writing and found the task of lifting the poem off the page with music too difficult, or at odds with the content of the poem. Or he played another instrument.

Pausanias describes the statues of the poets at Thespiae, and he knows things about Hesiod which critics overlook.[19] Here is Hesiod as a statue in a context of poets, and the statue, Pausanias is in no doubt, misrepresents him: "There are portraits dedicated of poets and other distinguished musicians," he writes (and note how for him, in the second century AD, poets *are* musicians); "Thamyris is blind, touching at a broken harp, and Arion of Methymne is riding on a dolphin. The sculptor of the statue of Skadas of Argos, not knowing Pindar's prelude about him, has made a wind-player with a body no bigger than his instrument. Hesiod sits holding a harp on his knees, not at all a proper adjunct for Hesiod: it is perfectly clear from his verses that he sang holding a wand of laurel." Then he makes a comment with which every lover of poetry who has set critical or historical pen to paper will feel some sympathy: "I have made a deep study of the dates of Hesiod and Homer but I take no pleasure in writing about them, being familiar with the extraordinary censoriousness of pundits nowadays in the field of poetry." And after that deeply felt aside, he continues with his catalogue: "Mystery is carved standing beside Orpheus the Thracian; all around him beasts in stone and bronze are listening to his song . . ."

In the British Museum there are two heads thought to represent Hesiod, one in bronze—the younger man, lively and focussed—and one in marble, older, with a look of wise resignation, set on a pillar at eye-level so that he looks hauntingly into his interlocutor. Homer is to his right, with abundant and coiffed hair, a more elaborate wreath, sightless and listening.

The texts of Hesiod, like those of Homer, were assembled between 800 and 600 BC. Robert Lamberton suggests that both *Works and Days* and the *Theogony* may have been "appropriated" and doctored for use in the festivals.[20] It is possible, too, that the poems were composed for the festivals; Hesiod tells us he travelled to recite, and tradition insists that he performed, even in competition with blind Homer. In *Works and Days* the presence of Perses gives a dramatic frame to the didactic content. The poem is eminently suitable for a rural festival. The institution of the festival and of competition may have generated some of the formal elements and even imposed a Hesiodic identity on the reciter. Whether he was reciting his own poem or adapting a work of earlier composition we will know only if a variety of drafts can be found. The Egyptian desert is generous, but it is unlikely to yield Hesiod papyruses in quantity or in chronological order.

"Homer and Hesiod were the first to compose *Theogonies*," Herodotus says, "and give the gods their epithets, to allot them their several offices and occupations, and describe their forms; and they lived but four hundred years before my time, as I believe." Four centuries seemed short to Herodotus because memory was strict and relatively stable. This had something to do with the Muses, for memory herself is their mother.

Hesiod's *Theogony,* an early formulation of Greek religion and the evolution of the gods, is particularly important in what it preserves. It is also in parts obscure and confusing. In the beginning was Chaos, a yawning chasm, a darkness or an absence of light, morally neutral and less sinister than Milton's Chaos (Milton owes debts to Hesiod's account). The earliest figures in the *Theogony* are not anthropomorphic deities like Zeus, who wins and becomes king of the gods in a third-generation struggle against his father. They are forces, rather: Chaos, then Earth, Tartarus (in the guts of Earth) and eventually, Eros, who emerges as a power of nature which begins to sort the chaotic, scattered elements into wholes and beings. The power of Eros keeps the new forms and beings together; gradually Cosmos becomes a possibility.

Though Hesiod composed in the eighth century BC, the traditions he brings together in his poem have much earlier origins. His myth of creation and the succession of the gods has much in common with Hittite and earlier accounts, some dating back to Sumerian times. His chronological catalogues may be based in the succession myths of Mesopotamia: king lists, god lists, with origins and the occasional identifying epithet. His cosmic vision is a synthesis of received elements, though we have no way of knowing how these stories reached the farmer in Askre. He composed the poem, but his function, as he himself might have seen it, was more that of an editor than a maker, harmonising received material within a metrical construction. His function, if this was the case, would be analogous to that of Eros working on and through Chaos, making sense and shape of it. It is an apt analogy for what a poet with Hesiod's ambitions was setting out to do.

Chaos, Earth, Tartarus and Eros are entities, self-created and not in necessary relation to one another. From Chaos emerged Erebus and Night, from Night emerged Aether and Day. We are into material genealogies of the most cosmic sort in the *Theogony*. Earth first begets Uranus (Heaven), then Mountains and Pontus. After lying with her son Uranus, she brings forth six sons—Oceanus, Coeus, Hyperion, Crius, Iapetus, Cronus—and for the sake of symmetry, six daughters—Theia, Rhea, Themis, Mnemosyne, Phoebe, Tethys. These are the Titans and Titanesses.

Endlessly fecund, Earth is delivered then of the Cyclops and the Hundred-handed. Uranus conceals them in the bowels of the Earth. Annoyed at their exclusion, she stirs them up against their father. Of all the Titans, Cronus loathes Uranus most intensely and sets out to punish him. He puts his father down with cruel violence, hacking off his testicles. From the mess emerges none other than Aphrodite:

> The genitalia themselves, fresh cut with flint, were thrown
> Clear of the mainland into the restless, white-capped sea,
> Where they floated a long time. A white foam from the god-flesh
> Collected around them, and in that foam a maiden developed
> And grew. Her first approach to land was near holy Kythera,
> And from there she floated on to the island of Cyprus.
> There she came ashore, an awesome, beautiful divinity.
> Tender grass sprouted up under her slender feet.[21]

Cronus, learning that he himself is destined to die at the hands of his offspring, decides to devour them as they are born. His wife flees to Crete when the youngest, Zeus, is to be born, and Zeus survives, finally overthrowing Cronus and the Titans, liberating his swallowed siblings and himself becoming supreme.

Hesiod is not Homer, and the strange creatures and gods that fight across the heavens are not as human as heroes, but the verse dealing with the conflicts is vigorous and in a different key, as it were, from the reflective and the aphoristic passages that surround it. The destruction feels quite close and real, and despite the absence of human scale and human interest, we experience something of the horror of this not unfamiliar kind of war. Modern technology has made Hesiod's hyperboles comprehensible. And we have read of such things in Dante, Milton and Blake. And in the Apocalypse.

Zeus rules wisely and is just. He is also irrepressibly fertile, fathering gods and heroes by different mothers and means. Athena was born out of his head after he had consumed her mother, Metis; Themis bore him *Eunomia* (Order), *Dike* (Justice) and *Eirene* (Peace), the three Fates. Another mother bore him the Graces; Demeter gave him ill-fated, almost-mortal Persephone. Part of Hesiod's radicalism is in his insistence that *dike* is more important than *time* (honour) in the ordering of affairs in the age of Iron. His emphasis was to become that of the emerging civic units of Greece at large.

Zeus slept with Mnemosyne (Memory) for nine nights—he must have been in love to have stayed with her for such a long time—and set her apart from the other Immortals. She provided him with nine daughters, bearing them close to the summit of Olympus, near the houses of Grace and Desire. From our point of view, they are crucial children, the Muses: Cleio, Euterpe, Thaleia, Melpomene, Terpsichore, Erato, Polyhymnia, Urania and Calliope. The Muses inspire poets (Hesiod asks them to dictate to him: his modest ambition is to be their stenographer) but they also, Calliope in particular, legitimise the eloquence of kings.

> For she keeps the company of reverend kings
> When the daughters of great Zeus will honour a lord
> Whose lineage is divine, and look upon his birth,
> They distil a sweet dew upon his tongue,
> And from his mouth words flow like honey.[22]

Hesiod's ostensibly historical narration takes us from the beginning of creation to the very fringes of Homer's *Odyssey* and the heroic world Hesiod never quite shares with his fellow-founder of Greek poetry, a world he describes but cannot enter. In the *Theogony* Hesiod is a seeming historian, but the real model for the divergent traditions of Greek historical writing is Homer.

It is hard to see how a religious practice could be based on the *Theogony*, yet it is a kind of permanent point of religious reference and a text susceptible to multiple readings and perspectives. Because of its ambiguities and ir-resolutions, it gave rise, among its audiences and readers, to that busy and vexed form of humanity, the critic. One kind of critic is the king. In his *Life of Theseus* Plutarch quotes Hesiod's lines about Theseus deserting Ariadne— "A passionate love for Aigle burned in his breast, / Panopeus' daughter"— and reports that these lines were removed from Hesiod's poem by no less a figure than Pisistratus, to "protect his ancestor." The same tyrant inserted into Homer's description of the underworld the verse "Theseus and Peri-thous, illustrious children of the gods," in order to please the Athenians.[23]

A tyrant could change a text; and a text—Hesiod or Homer—was

regarded as important enough, politically, to merit tampering with, to cen-
sor information or flatter sentiment. Who were the audiences for Hesiod's
poems? We know they were largely male, given the nature of the poems and
of the world into which they came. As with Homer's two poems, we can
imagine different audiences for each. The *Theogony* has the feel of a piece
composed for recitation at a festival, conveying information in a beautiful
and more or less structured form, with points in the poem at which an audience or chorus might interject. We are tempted to reverse the generally accepted chronology of composition and to infer from this that it was
composed when Hesiod was already known. The way in which he depicts
himself in the poem as the shepherd surprised by the Muses is a kind of
packaging, building on the known fact of his rustic origins.

Works and Days would appear, in its cruder shape and more direct approach, to have come first. It addresses (albeit intermittently) Perses, a
single silent interlocutor. The reader can imagine this poem performed in a
smaller circle, as evening entertainment; certainly the subject-matter, the
coarseness of address, and the basic quality of some of the counsel given
suggest a humbler audience. The sense of a local audience is also conveyed
in the concern with specific-seeming issues: Perses' unjust claims are part
and parcel of the wider corruption the poem brings to light, the local lords
who behave unfairly. The physical world is alive in the lines, and the voice of
a man who has lived a hard life.

Poetry is a form of oral memory, *kleos;* in the *Theogony*[24] its function is described as conveying *klea proteron anthropon* ("the glorious achievements of
the people of old"). *Works and Days* is different, conveying the lived experience of a present time in which the poet himself is living.

Whether the audience was local or festive, it understood the nature and
language of Hesiod's verse. It was *trained,* to use Taplin's over-deliberate expression. It was second nature to a Greek man to understand, through the
curious amalgam of dialects, geographic and temporal variegations, what
the poetry was doing. "Yet this special poetic language will not have struck
its hearers as artificial or outlandish, precisely because they knew it and expected it as the language of hexameter poetry. It is the language proper to
the occasion that they will have assimilated from childhood."[25]

In all likelihood, the myths and legends the poet told were almost as familiar as the language he used: his audience was entertained and instructed
by how he sounded and by the ordering of the stories, what the poet added
to the familiar, what originality of detail or structure he brought to bear. In
the case of Hesiod, the first person singular may have been the key. When
he writes of Pandora, for example, the first written account of the myth
that we possess, his audience could have known a version of the story already; in his Pandora they would have found new connections to other

myths, and a striking vehemence in his conclusions. She makes her poetic début in *Theogony* as the first woman, a "lovely evil":

> And they were stunned,
> Immortal gods and mortal men, when they saw
> The sheer deception, irresistible to men.
> From her is the race of female women,
> The deadly race and population of women,
> A great infestation among mortal men.[26]

She makes a vivid appearance in *Works and Days,* coming among men with her jar (*pithos*), not box, of evils. Zeus was not wilful in having her sent, with a curse donated by each of the gods: Pan-dora, "all gift." Prometheus had stolen fire from heaven for men, and Pandora was sent to Epimetheus, Prometheus' brother, as divine punishment. Epimetheus, despite his fated brother's warning not to accept gifts from the gods, could not resist and took Pandora in. She is one of the earliest examples of the vilification of the female. Misogyny is a crucial ingredient in both Hesiod's poems. There are goddesses on the one hand, and there are women on the other, drones in the hive, layabouts of leisure, gluttons to boot. Woman is a curse; with her, unhappiness is inevitable; without her, there is no heir.

The religion Hesiod presents is human in terms of the ways the gods vie with one another and the ways they relate to the world. We also get a sense of natural balances, symmetries, dualities, complementarities. We considered the double nature of Eris, with whom *Works and Days* opens. In the Prometheus-versus-Pandora story, we have theft and retribution. Prometheus himself has a contrasting brother, Epimetheus. Their names relate them and at the same time place them at opposite ends of time's see-saw: forethought and afterthought, foresight and hindsight. For most evils there is a balancing good; the just act and the unjust act are rewarded appropriately, symmetrically if you like. The absence of a balancing element can lead, as in the history of the early gods, to violence, "war in heaven"; it is no wonder that imbalances on earth have similar consequences. In the little anecdote of the hawk with the nightingale clutched in its talons (the first fable of its kind in Greek literature) the nightingale may have a sweet voice and beauty on its side, but the hoarse-voiced hawk has power, and he is hungry. He declares,

> Only a fool struggles against his superiors.
> He not only gets beaten, but humiliated as well.[27]

Part of Hesiod's subject-matter is, inevitably, the generations of man, where he comes from, how he has developed. The poet speaks of five ages: Golden, Silver, Bronze, the age of the heroes, Iron. By adding the age of the heroes he disrupts a traditional eastern symmetry, for the progression does have its origins in eastern thought. He gives it a specifically Greek in-flection. But the thrust of his genealogy is conventional: it is an old story of decline and corruption. The age of Iron is our own. What can we do about it? Work hard, respect the gods and respect justice. The advice is not unlike that of Samuel Smiles, though without Smiles's optimism.

The *Theogony* is a useful place for readers to familiarise themselves with the Olympians. All the gods are there: Zeus first, then mighty, neglected and treacherous Hera, Aphrodite, Ares, Artemis with her bow and arrows, wise Athene, Demeter who brings the fields alive, unbridled Dionysus, Hephaistus the smith, Hermes the inventor of the lyre, and so on. Hesiod's catalogues are rather bare and peremptory compared with Homer's, but then they are very different. That difference was recognised and dramatised in a festival confrontation.

It was at Chalcis in Euboea, the funeral occasion already mentioned, and a sufficiently neutral ground for both Boeotian Hesiod and for floating Homer, that the legendary match between them took place. Here Hesiod won the coveted tripod. Homer, representing in his voice the heroic and aristocratic values, the pan-Greek spirit, confronts the everyman from Askre with his dirty fingernails, his daily concerns, his rancours and timidity, his peasant values,[28] which are in some respects bourgeois *avant-la-lettre* in their concern with legacies and lucre.

Homer, we remember, travelled around Greece as a celebrated per-former. He learned that Ganyctor was organising funeral games for his fa-ther, Amphidamas, the Euboean king, and invited not only athletes but poets too, with the promise of a generous purse. Homer decided to attend; Hesiod attended, too, and there a head-to-head contest was arranged. Be-fore their hosts, the chief Chalcidians and the brother of the dead king, Paneides, now king himself, Hesiod subjected Homer to a series of ques-tions. Here is a flavour of their exchanges. To begin with, Hesiod asks,

> "Homer, son of Meles, inspired with wisdom from heaven, come, tell me first what is best for mortal man?"
> "For men on earth 'tis best never to be born at all; or being born, to pass through the gates of Hades with all speed."

Homer's is a famous response. Hesiod has found a formidable rival. He de-cides to lighten the tone of the proceedings.

> "Come, tell me now this also, godlike Homer: what think you in your heart is most delightsome to men?"
> "When mirth reigns throughout the town, and feasters about the house, sitting in order, listening to a minstrel; when the tables beside them are laden with bread and meat, and a wine-bearer draws sweet drink from the mixing-bowl and fills the cups: this I think in my heart to be most delightsome."

The judges are ready to give Homer the prize, he has replied with such clarity and assurance, and in verse of course. Hesiod, irritated by his facility, rummages in his mind for a real poser: "Come, Muse; sing not to me of things that are, or that shall be, or that were of old; but think of another song." Homer, nonplussed and unable to think of an apt answer, replies, "Never shall horses with clattering hoofs break chariots, striving for victory about the tomb of Zeus."

There is a touch of surrealism about it, and certainly it follows Hesiod's injunction. Now Hesiod begins the game of consequences, reciting a line or more and requiring Homer to finish the sense and form of each passage, some being quotations from the work of one or the other poet. We can set out Hesiod's lines in roman type and Homer's in italic, to see how the consequences unfolded:

> Then they dined on the flesh of oxen and their horses' necks—
> *They unyoked dripping with sweat, when they had had enough of war.*

> And the Phrygians, who of all men are handiest at ships—
> *To filch their dinner from pirates on the beach.*

> To shoot forth arrows against the tribes of cursed giants with his hands—
> *Herakles unslung his curved bow from his shoulders.*

> This man is the son of a brave father and a weakling—
> *Mother; for war is too stern for any woman.*

And so the contest continues, with sequiturs and nonsequiturs.

> But for you, your father and lady mother lay in love—
> *When they begot you by the aid of golden Aphrodite.*

> But when she had been made subject in love,
> Artemis, who delights in arrows—
> *Slew Callisto with a shot of her silver bow.*

> When they had feasted, they gathered among the glowing ashes
> The bones of the dead Zeus—
> *Born Sarpedon, that bold and godlike man.*

> Now we have lingered thus about the plain of Simois,
> Forth from the ships let us go our way, upon our shoulders—
> *Having our hilted swords and long-helved spears.*

> Eat, my guests, and drink, and may no one of you
> Return home to his dear country—
> *Distressed; but may you all reach home again unscathed.*

Hesiod changes tactics. He asks Homer factual questions: How many people from Achaea went to Ilium? Homer answers with a mathematical exercise: "There were fifty hearths, and at each hearth were fifty spits, and on each spit were fifty carcasses, and there were thrice three hundred Achaeans to each joint." Hesiod and the audience begin working out this huge hyperbole: fifty hearths, 2500 spits, 125,000 carcasses . . .

Hesiod poses him moral questions and Homer replies with subtlety and ambiguity, like a rabbinical teacher who knows there are no right answers but only not wrong ones. "How would men best live in cities, and with what observances?" asks Hesiod. "By refusing to get unclean gain and if the good were honoured, but justice fell upon the unjust," Homer replies with wise facility.

> "What is the best thing of all for a man to ask of the gods in prayer?"
> *"That he may be always at peace with himself continually."*

> "Of what effect are righteousness and courage?"
> *"To advance the common good by private pains."*

> "What do men mean by happiness?"

Again, that appalling reply: "Death after a life of least pain and greatest pleasure." Homer gets the better of Hesiod at every turn; the people call for him to be declared victor. But King Paneides orders both of them to recite what they regard as the best lines from their own poems. Hesiod begins with a passage from *Works and Days* about the Pleiades, times for harvest, times to plough, lore lyricised. Homer comes back with a conflation of two passages from Book XIII of the *Iliad*.[29] It has to be said that Homer chooses magnificent fragments; but then he is spoiled for choice. Hesiod's verse looks functional and pale beside even a prose version such as this: "The ranks stood firm about the two Aiantes, such that not even Ares would have scorned them had he met them, nor yet Athena who saves armies. For there the chosen best awaited the charge of the Trojans and noble Hector, making a fence of spears and serried shields. Shield closed with shield, and helm with helm, and each man with his fellow, and the peaks of their head-pieces with crests of horse-hair touched as they bent their heads: so close they stood together. The murderous battle bristled with the long, flesh-rending spears they held, and the flash of bronze from polished helms and new-burnished breast-plates and gleaming shields blinded the eyes. Very hard of heart would he have been, who could then have seen that strife with joy and felt no pang."

Hesiod cannot stand up to such complete visualisation and, we imagine, Homer's riveting prosodic control and delivery. But the new king has a mind of his own. He overrules the crowd and crowns Hesiod on the grounds that the man who enjoined his fellows to pursue peace and good husbandry should be rewarded, not the man who celebrated war. Hesiod's was, therefore, not a poetic but a moral crown of laurel. He received also the tripod made of brass, which he immediately dedicated to the Muses, to whom he owed so much, appending this inscription: "Hesiod dedicated this tripod to the Muses of Helicon after he overcame divine Homer at Chalcis in a contest of song."

He went from Chalcis to Delphi to dedicate himself to Apollo. The prophetess, excited at his approach, called out a blessing to him in anticipation: ". . . surely his fame shall be as wide as the spreading light of morning."[30] She had a warning, however: "beware of the pleasant grove of Nemean Zeus; for there death is destined to overtake you." The poet avoided the Peloponnese, assuming the prophetess had *that* Nemea in mind. But coming to Oenoë in Locris, he stayed with the sons of Phegeus, unconsciously fulfilling the oracle; that area was sacred to Nemean Zeus.

He overstayed his welcome at Oenoë, until his young hosts, suspecting him of seducing their sister Ctimene, murdered him.[31] They threw his corpse into the sea. On the third day, as legend often has it, his body was rolled ashore by dolphins, during a local feast. The people hurried to the strand, recognised the body, lamented and buried it. They began to seek the assassins, who, in terror, had set to sea in a fishing boat, pointing the prow towards Crete. Halfway across, Zeus sent them to the bottom with a bolt of lightning. That is Alcidamas' version of events. Eratosthenes has a variant story, more grimly entertaining if less miraculous: Hesiod's travelling companion Demodes seduced the girl and was murdered along with Hesiod. The girl hanged herself. Hesiod's dog, Eratosthenes tells us, identified the murderers. The brothers were sacrificed to the gods of hospitality. It is the stuff of Jacobean theatre.

Hesiod, shepherd and hill farmer, elect of the Muses, first poet of the arts of peace, was murdered, then. Thucydides agrees that he was killed in Locris, by local people and—that prophesy—in a sanctuary of Nemean Zeus. Plutarch's version implies, says Peter Levi,[32] "the cult of Hesiod as a divine hero"—a demigod like Archilochus at Paros was to become? "He had a named companion . . . he was washed up by dolphins like Palaimon at the isthmus, his grave was a local secret like Dirke's at Thebes, and his relics were envied by the people of Orchomenos" (IX, 38, 3) in central Boeotia, as far from the sea as Hesiod could have wished.

Despite the misogyny of the poems, legend unanimously places a woman at the heart of the tragic affair. We turn to trusty Pausanias: "everyone agrees that the sons of Ganyctor"—who organised the games for his father, Amphidamas—"fled from Naupactos to Molykria because of Hesiod's murder, and there they paid Poseidon the penalty of sacrilege; but one story is that someone else disgraced their sister and Hesiod was wrongly blamed for it; another is that Hesiod was guilty."[33]

On this subject Pausanias allows himself to express no opinion. He does take the story a little further, establishing where the poet was finally interred. At Orchomenos, he declares, is Hesiod's tomb. This is how the men of Orchomenos got their hands on the coveted bones: "a plague had seized on men and cattle, so they sent off ambassadors to the god, who were told by the Pythian priestess to bring the bones of Hesiod from Naupactos, or otherwise there was no cure." They inquired how to find them at Naupactos: the priestess said that a crow, one of Apollo's sacred birds, would tell them. So when they landed on Naupactian ground they saw a rock quite near a road with the bird perching on it, and in a hollow in that rock they found the bones of Hesiod.

> A funeral verse was written on the tomb:
> Askre and the plough land were his country:
> The soil of the horse-whipping Minyai
> Covers his bones: his name rang loudest
> On the stone of Wisdom: Hesiod lies here.

That is another name critics have given to his kind of writing: not epic, but "wisdom literature." Given that wisdom advances more slowly than knowledge and outlives the vagaries of taste, the poetry of Hesiod, a constant resource for three millennia despite its archaisms, conventionality and prejudice, can be considered wise.

VII

Archilochus of Paros

The Parian: I was the first
to bring his iambs into Latium,
the metres and their matter: Archilochus!
But not the words he aimed to slay
Lycambes . . .

HORACE, *Epistles I*, XIX, ll. 23ff.

We hear snatches of song—a phrase ("tender horn,"[1] "lances . . . pierced their spirit"[2]), a longer run ("Paros, farewell, those figs too, that life by the sea"[3]), but nothing whole. As though in the old port of Parikia a sailor was singing and, because the winds move ceaselessly over Paros (as modern windsurfers know), we could make out only a teasing play of words and whispers. The voice can be ribald, erotic, cruel, lyrical. Looking west across a sea over which empires battled for millennia, this port gives the poet's voice political inflections.

The island of Paros, where Archilochus was born, bears on the map an uncanny resemblance to Thasos, the island he helped to colonise, engaging in battle with the mainland Thracians, and which some of his poems sourly evoke. Paros is well out at sea, one of the Cycladic flotilla that includes Naxos and, to the north, Miconos, Andros and others, all sailing towards Euboea. Thasos, part of a more scattered archipelago, seems solitary, stalled ten kilometres off the coast of eastern Greece. It is important and therefore vulnerable: it lies on a border. In the time of Archilochus the border divided ancient Macedonia and Thrace. It has been occupied and exploited by a dozen empires in its time.

Both islands appear to be remarkably *round*. And a mountain rises at the centre of each, a mountain with not inhospitable slopes where agriculture developed. Thasos is larger than the relatively treeless Paros and once boasted mature forests which maritime nations harvested for their fleets, most recently the Russians in the late eighteenth century. Both islands possess celebrated marble quarries. Those at Paros were revived after long neglect when Napoleon's tomb was being built in Paris and only proper classical materials were deemed appropriate. Thasos had legendary gold mines and was called "golden Thasos" as a result. Herodotus mentions how he visited the mines, and how in pursuit of ore generations of men had overturned a whole mountain.[4]

When Archilochus writes specifically about Thasos, he says some curious things. In one fragment, he declares (in M. L. West's translation)

> . . . while Thasos stands here like
> the spine of a donkey, wreathed with unkempt forests . . .

The American poet Guy Davenport renders the same fragment with fuller eloquence, providing it with closure it does not possess:

> This island,
>   garlanded with wild woods,
> Lies in the sea
>   like the backbone of an ass.

West's translation in this case is closer to Archilochus: it acknowledges that these words are a snatch of song, not a song in themselves. That larger song, which we can tenuously infer, includes the evocation of the island of Thasos, not as a conceit, which it becomes in Davenport's "garlands" and "backbone" and "Lies," but something quite literally visualised, the spine of a donkey, rising hard and rough under its skin, with the whirls and tufts of its coat down the lean, labour-frayed sides. It is a work-animal, standing up rather than lying in the sea. The image is political. It also suggests a literal point of view. From what perspective would the poet have such a vision of Thasos? This is how the island appears to a traveller approaching from the south . . . But the image is fraught with half-affectionate familiarity. The speaker is not any sailor coming, but a sailor returning to a known, tried and troubled shore.

Perhaps that is what the longer poem was about, the return from home to exile. Davenport carves this archaic poet and innovator out of Thasian or Parian marble. In fact he is as close to the earth as Hesiod, and closer to the sea; he is as unillusioned as that dogged husbandman, and a good deal more erotically charged. There is Paros, the home in defence of which he dies, and colonial Thasos. "All Greece's misery has flowed down to Thasos,"[5] he exclaims. No man in his right mind would die for that place.

Some modern historians say, with the satisfaction of a schoolteacher wiping the blackboard clean, that we know, as provable fact, nothing about Archilochus. We cannot even affirm that a single "he" wrote, or recited, the fragments that survive over his name. Some critics insist that the name itself denotes a rank rather than a person ("first sergeant," Davenport proposes), and that the people whom he names—Neobulé ("she who makes new plans"), Glaucos ("grey eyes")—are also types, not based on actual people. In legend Archilochus flickeringly lives, and since there is often substance, and always entertainment, in legend, it is worth recounting what we can never claim to know. A surprisingly real person fills out our ignorance.

Almost seven hundred years after his time—he lived from around 680 to 640 BC—the Roman poet Gaetulicus struck off a Greek epigram which alludes to many salient elements of the legend. Edward Lucie-Smith translates it thus:

> Here, by the seashore, there lies
> Archilochus, whose Muse was
> Dipped in viper's gall, who stained
> Mild Helicon with blood. The
> Father knows it, mourning for
> His three daughters hanged, shamed by
> Those bitter verses. Stranger,
> Tread softly, lest you rouse the
> Wasps that settle on this tomb.

Gaetulicus was perhaps paraphrasing Archilochus' epitaph. The Greek poet died in battle (we assume), a Parian fighting against a Naxian army. In the town of Paros today, in the archaeological museum, visitors will find a winged Victory and an inscription relating to the poet. Not far from Naoussa are the excavated ruins of a seventh-century church constructed on the site of the *heroön*[6] of Archilochus, the Archilocheion. It is associated with his tomb and with a gymnasium, built or else restored three centuries after his death by a man of Paros called Mnesiepes, whose name means "epic collector," and who followed the instructions of the Delphic oracle in honouring his countryman. Archilochus' patron, Delian Apollo, has a ruined temple nearby. The inscription from the *heroa,* partly preserved, includes a sort of legendary life which Mnesiepes claimed to have assembled from ancient tales. In fact he seems to have drawn it largely from Archilochus' poems, for then as now the untheorised reader tended to believe the poet who wrote "I" and reported that "I's" actions. An inscription added two hundred years later provides a bibliography and a hypothetical chronology of Archilochus' life.

He died, he became an exalted mortal, even a demigod. But when did he live? In the seventh century BC. Hearsay, centuries after his death, says his grandfather was Tellis, a man of distinction who appeared in the Delphic frescoes of the painter Polygnotos (himself from Thasos, two centuries Archilochus' junior). Pausanias reports, "All I heard about Tellis was that Archilochus the poet was his grandson." Tellis, depicted as a young man, accompanies Kleoboea: "they say that she was the first to bring the orgies of Demeter to Thasos from Paros." Those orgies are more tactfully referred to elsewhere as the Eleusinian Mysteries.[7]

Herodotus recalls how he went to Thasos, "where I found a temple of Hercules which had been built by the Phoenicians who colonised that island when they sailed in search of Europa. Even this was five generations earlier than the time when Hercules, son of Amphitryon, was born in Greece. These researches show plainly that there is an ancient god Hercules; and my own opinion is that those Greeks act most wisely who build and maintain two temples of Hercules, in the one of which the Hercules worshipped is known by the name of Olympian, and has sacrifice offered to him as an immortal, while in the other the honours paid are such as are due to a hero."[8] Herodotus mentions Archilochus only once, as the author of a poem which, glancingly, refers to Gyges, the rich and mighty king of Lydia, who reigned for three and a half decades. In that poem Archilochus takes a dim view of wealth and power, possessing neither himself.

It is no longer thought that Phoenicians colonised Thasos; people from Paros certainly did, from about 710 to 680 BC. It was the Parians who claimed to be following Hercules' orders (or the Pythian Apollo's, whose sanctuary was on the acropolis in the town of Thasos) in doing so. Archilochus' grandfather may have founded a town on the colonised island; his father, Telesicles (to whom the Delphic Oracle promised great things from his son), and Archilochus himself slalomed north through the Cyclades. But Archilochus arrived, not as a figure of authority, but—in all likelihood—as a mercenary. Although his father may have been distinguished, his mother, Enipo, was (legend confesses it) a slave. A child of such a misalliance, whatever his ancestry, enjoyed no privileges.

Why did this particular man, by all accounts a rough diamond, become a poet? For much the same reason as the first English poet, Caedmon, did, two millennia later: because the gods, or God, required it. An illiterate neatherd,[9] "specially distinguished and honoured by divine grace," the Venerable Bede tells us,[10] Caedmon composed his hymn extempore with the collusion of an angel Muse, at the monastery of the abbess Hild in Whitby, Yorkshire. From the remains of the Archilocheion inscription we learn that one day the Parian youth had a curious adventure.

He was sent into the country by his father, Telesicles, to fetch a cow for market. "He got up very early. It was dark still, the moon shone. He started to lead the cow to the market town. When he came to the place called Lissides, he seemed to see a group of women. Imagining that they were leaving work in the fields to go to market, he approached and began to chide them." In his disrespect, he was unlike Caedmon. "They greeted him with merriment and, laughing, asked, was he taking the cow to sell? *Yes,* he replied, and they declared that they would pay him a reasonable price. Then, in an instant, the women vanished, along with the cow. At his feet Archilochus found a lyre. He was frightened and shaken, but gathering his composure he reflected that it must have been the Muses who had materialised there and left him with the lyre. He took it and went on to town, and told his father what he had seen. Telesicles, when the story had been told him and he saw the lyre, was amazed. Immediately he had a search made all over Paros for the cow; but it was nowhere to be found."[11]

The Muses, like their chorus-leader Apollo, who may have been with them on Archilochus' fateful day, must be obeyed. So Archilochus learned to sing. He would have sung to entertain himself, fellow-countrymen, the sailors with whom he shipped to Thasos, his comrade mercenaries there. He would have sung, too, to his fellow Parians between engagements with the Naxians or the Abantes on the island of Euboea. Even at this early date, the symposium was taking shape, men of a certain class gathering of an evening for pleasure and performance, and Archilochus' poems might have addressed such an audience in his day, as they did in later times. To entertain he might have invented stories, even the cruelly ended romance with Neobulé, though it is doubtful whether his audience would have found a fiction as tantalising as a tale based on real people. And it seems that Lycambes and his daughters were real, as real as Archilochus himself.

He would have lamented exile, considered political issues, and most particularly touched upon sexual themes. Perhaps he sang to his special friend Glaucos, whom he addresses in several poems. Here he strikes a note of charged intimacy as we overhear him addressing his dear comrade:

> Their nurse brought them both forth, with scented hair
> And such breasts, why, even an aged man
> Would have lusted. Oh, Glaucos . . .[12]

And a Glaucos existed, too. In the agora at Thasos there was a monument of Glaucos and the inscription survives at the museum there. Glaucos took part in the Parian expedition to found trading ports on the mainland opposite Thasos.

In the first century BC, coins were issued on Paros which show the poet seated on a handsome stool, holding the fateful lyre and, in his right hand, a scroll book. Naked from the waist up, he has a soldier's strong physique. He is not performing but at rest, his left foot casually tucked behind the right.

A young man working for his father in the fields, he became a soldier or a mercenary and left home. His motives are uncertain. Perhaps he went after his greatest public humiliation, the cause of his durable poetic triumph that let him prove how poetry *can* make things happen.

Archilochus became engaged to a girl called Neobulé. The oldest surviving line of love poetry in Greek, Guy Davenport conjectures, may be "O to touch Neobulé's hand." Her father was a rich man, Lycambes. First, he consented to the union between poet and daughter. It might have freed

Archilochus from having to follow a soldier's career. Then, for some reason, Lycambes reneged on his promise. Neobulé's hand was placed forever beyond Archilochus' reach.

He took his revenge in verse: not only on Lycambes but on Neobulé herself, and on her sister or sisters. Was his heart broken ("Zeus, father of the gods, I did not have my wedding feast . . .")?[13] If so, that was hardly the point. In the surviving fragments of the Epodes he tells an animal fable, perhaps the first in Greek and a harbinger of Aesop's tales that come in the next century. It is a fable about—offspring. An eagle befriends a vixen, and when her cubs are born it carries two of them off to feed its young. The vixen prays for justice and, sure enough, the gods oblige: the eagle snatches up meat from a sacrificial fire to feed its chicks, but the meat contains a spark and nest and chicks perish in the conflagration. Mark this, Lycambes.

There are other animal fables and shards of fable in Archilochus, and animal allusions conveyed in verbs, a reptilian eroticism in lines such as "and you have taken in many a blind eel." In connection with his once-desired, to be sure, more and worse were to come. Archilochus so impugned the honour of Neobulé, and also of her sister, that both girls committed suicide. (Gaetulicus proposes a third martyr-sister and gives the story more Ciceronian proportions.) He claimed to have had his will of Neobulé *and* her sister, in the very precincts of Hera's temple. These poems were read in Paros and Thasos, and then throughout the Greek world. Lycambes' name became a by-word for broken promises.

The poet's betrayal of Neobulé has earned him, unaccountably, less opprobrium than fame. Few readers much mind the fact that Archilochus was a cad. The sins of "Father Lycambes" are visited upon his daughters and this visitation is at the heart of the poet's immortality. The fragments of tender poetry to her are far outweighed by the bitter and destructive.

There is a keenly unsentimental, functional eroticism in much of what survives, so that we might be inclined to think his expressions of affection for Neobulé were due less to love than to what he calls "paralysing desire."[14] And so we read,

> . . . she shuddered up and down
> as a kingfisher flaps its wings on a stone outcrop . . .[15]

or:

> Like a Thracian[16] or Phrygian slurping beer up through a straw
> she suckled hard, bent double . . .[17]

or an obscure fragment which West confidently sexualises as follows:

> . . . they stooped and spurted off
> all their accumulated wantonness . . .[18]

In the first fragment there is a sense of sexual urgency and pleasure almost desperate in its figuration; the bird is pleasuring herself, as it were, brilliant in her colours and desires. In the second fragment, the woman is like a barbarian, not a Greek: such people have their own exotic eroticism. Again, the woman is active, and also acted upon. The third fragment, if we follow West, may evoke an onanistic ritual. There is, in any case, frank sensual gratification but little amorous privacy here. Though he was a cad with Neobulé, this first poet of sexual engagement if not of love acknowledges the libidinal needs of women as well as men. But the spry functionality of his eroticism makes him an early, defining figure of patriarchy, a roguish dissenting son of the sunlit *Iliad*, not the dank and shadowy *Odyssey*.

The *Iliad* is behind him because one of his crucial themes is soldiering, but he removes from it all the ambiguous glory with which the Homeric poem instilled it. His poems sing not of great battles, with the gods lounging about the amphitheatre of the Trojan plain in amusement and judgement. They sing with the hoarse voice of a soldier paid to fight, keen to save his own skin and make a living. Most famous of all is the poem, imitated by Horace, in which he throws aside his shield and flees from battle. A new life is hard to come by, but you can always get a new shield. There is heroism of a sort in the quality of candour that emerges from the verse. And he is the only Greek soldier-poet we have. The vocation of being a soldier and that of making poems (it is perhaps safe to say that Archilochus *wrote* poems: he was certainly not ignorant of the art or of his predecessors in it) were not at odds. Homer's Achilles is not above (or below) chanting and strumming his lyre in the *Iliad*.[19] Later on the soldier fought and the poet sang his deeds. Here we are in a unique presence:

> I am a comrade[20] of the warrior lord,
> and of the Muses, too, at one with their fair trades.

If we bear in mind how he acquired his "trades," we will be moved by the account of his death, and how it made Apollo grieve.

The poet and the warrior die together, killed in fighting by a character called Corax, or Raven. According to the Delphic Oracle, Apollo drives Raven from the sanctuary at Delphi: "You have killed the Muses' companion; get out!" "But," says Corax in his defence, "I killed Archilochus as a soldier, not because he wrote poems." Corax pleads and pleads with the Oracle and at last is permitted to perform the appropriate rituals to pacify the soul, or *psyche,* of his victim.

Archilochus' military poems go beyond specific deeds to figurative distillations of general experience, for example in a famous epigram that has an air of tight completion.

> The fox has lots of cons,
> the hedgehog has but one, but one's enough.[21]

When Guy Davenport showed Ezra Pound his versions of this poem,[22] Pound commented that "there is a magpie in China that can turn a hedge-hog over and kill it." The poem makes a literal observation; it also contrasts forms of military strategy—the cavalry, for example, as the fox, and the tight-moving infantry as the phalanx-hedgehog. There is a political feel about the riddle: the fox is wily, elegant, apparently a higher creature; the hedgehog is unglamorous, slow but strong and determined. Archilochus is a man with a spear who rides on his own two feet. This poem goes with an-other in which the poet prefers a short, bandy-legged, brave commander, close to the ground, to a tall, trotting (horse-bound), vain and pomaded general.[23]

Gaetulicus says: "Tread softly, lest you rouse the / Wasps that settle on this tomb." Was he reporting legend or, as successful poetry does, creat-ing it? In any case, the wasps are drawn there as much in response to the sweetness of the verse as for its sting. And Apollo was right: Archilochus' verse will survive, even if only in scraps and tags, as long as humankind reads poetry.

The story of Archilochus is not over. In 1974 the manuscript of a poem attributed to him was published. It had been used in a papyrus mummy-cover housed in a Cologne museum, identified, meticulously restored and edited. The longest surviving fragment of his work, it may in fact conflate two poems, the first a savage continuation of his attack on Neobulé, the second his most erotic and sustained narrative of consummation. The girl he is seducing has resisted, mentioning his previous love. He dismisses his ex with scorn. He has a single desire and objective. Is the girl now in his power, as some critics conjecture, Neobulé's sister? Does this new fragment make Archilochus an even darker cad than the evidence we had before? He is recounting his exploit to an audience, giving himself credit for persuasion and proving his skills even as, incidentally, causing arousal in listeners. This is Davenport's inventive version:

> "She should get herself a job as a scarecrow.
> I'd as soon hump her as [kiss a goat's butt].
>
> "A source of joy I'd be to the neighbours
> With such a woman as her for a wife!
> How could I ever prefer her to you?
>
> "You, O innocent, true heart and bold.
> Each of her faces is as sharp as the other,
> Which way she's turning you never can guess.

"She'd whelp like the proverb's luckless bitch
Were I to foster get upon her, throwing
Them blind, and all on the wrongest day."

I said no more but took her hand,
Laid her down in a thousand flowers,
And put my soft wool cloak around her.

I slid my arm under her neck
To still the fear in her eyes,
For she was trembling like a fawn,

Touched her hot breasts with light fingers,
Spraddled her neatly and pressed
Against her fine, hard, bared crotch.

I caressed the beauty of all her body
And came in a sudden white spurt
While I was stroking her hair.[24]

The cruelty of the poem and its intense sexual drive are, as it were, the poles of Archilochus' verse. He always seems to be hungry, and to speak directly to us of his hungers. Revenge is one of them.

His language, compared with the formulaic heightenings of the Homeric poems and the formal rusticity of Hesiod, is comparatively coarse and to the point, the language of a peasant and a soldier, rich in metaphor and straightforward in sense. Perhaps that is why even the briefest snatches of language, by a curious metonymy, suggest the poem they came from. It is certainly why readers believe in the "I" of Archilochus despite the absence of hard evidence of his existence.

The use of a spoken, low diction characterises the kind of verse which Archilochus is credited with having invented, the iambic, though Aristotle is reluctant to deprive Homer, the father of all poetry, of this as of other honours. "A poem of the satirical kind cannot indeed be put down to any author earlier than Homer; though many such writers probably there were. But from Homer onward, instances can be cited—his own *Margites,* for example, and other similar compositions. The appropriate metre was also here introduced; hence the measure is still called the iambic or lampooning measure, being that in which people lampooned one another. Thus the older poets were distinguished as writers of heroic or of lampooning verse."[25]

Aristotle's is the simplest and clearest definition of iambic verse: "For the iambic is, of all measures, the most colloquial: we see it in the fact that conversational speech runs into iambic lines more frequently than into any other kind of verse; rarely into hexameters, and only when we drop the colloquial intonation." Poetry as a heightening of speech, but still dependent on speech. Iambic at first denotes less a metrical patterning (its later sense), more a genre: satirical, savage invective addressed to an everyday audience; a poetry in what the compilers of the English Prayer Book called "the vulgar tongue." Early iambic poetry can be in non-iambic metres; indeed, the term is used to describe trochaic tetrameters.[26] "Too iambic" can mean "too coarse."

There are three classic *iambopoioi*—writers of iambics. After Archilochus comes Semonides of Amorgos (pages 150–58) and then Hipponax of Ephesus (pages 232–38), the limping beggar whose invectives (like Archilochus' attack on Neobulé) caused his victims, who began as his persecutors, mortal ill. Hipponax invented the "limping iamb," a trimeter with a spondee or a trochee in the final foot. It may have been because of the figurative title given to this metre that the poet himself was portrayed, in retrospect, as lame. The iambic poets were the forefathers of Attic comedy, not only in their savage tones and colloquial metres but in their coarse diction. Iambic poetry was close to the idiom of the male populace and voiced, sometimes radically, its everyday concerns. Athenaeus recalls how the comic writer Diphilus made both Archilochus and Hipponax Sappho's lovers.

Where does the iambic tradition begin? There are threads of it in Homer and especially in Hesiod, of course, but there it is incidental, not the dominant voice. It may have come from Asia, with so much of the archaic tradition of art and song. It may have risen to prominence thanks to the verse contests at the Greek festivals of Dionysus and Demeter, fertility encouraged, as it were, but with explicit sexual content. Erotic verse and satire, however, do not naturally go hand in glove. The scurrilous and the scatological fall short of the erotic, especially in epigrams. Still, the evocation of orgies and escapades, the naming of familiar names and parts, the power of the word to expose and to wound, were aspects of this archaic tradition of *flyting*.

And Archilochus' poems were recited at festivals alongside those of Hesiod and Homer. Indeed, these three poets were the invariable presences at any festival where verse was performed. With their different takes on poetry and the world, all three were venerated. Pindar calls Archilochus "the insulter" or "the blamer," nourishing himself on words of hate,[27]

> For in the past I see
> Archilochus the scold in poverty,
> Fattening his leanness with hate and heavy words.[28]

Yet it is Archilochus whose poetry marked that of Horace and Catullus. They respect Pindar but love the earlier master, because of the freshness of his language and his unabashed approach to every sort of experience.

VIII

Alcman of Sardis

Would that, would that I were a cerylus
Flying with halcyons over wave-blooming waters
Stalwart and strong, bird blue like the sea.[1]

 The French king Louis XV, "well-beloved" and dangerously enlightened, was eager to develop his library. He sent two *abbés* to Constantinople to acquire books from the Sultan's collection. One of the *abbés,* Fourmont, on a supplementary quest, went around Asia Minor and Greece collecting—that is, stealing for the king—classical inscriptions as well. In Sparta his scavenging was dramatic and destructive: his nephew located inscriptions, and the *abbé* instructed that teams of men dig them up, and then that larger teams conduct deeper digging, disrupting the site, the very foundations of the ancient buildings overthrown. More than 300 inscriptions were unearthed, many damaged and some destroyed because Fourmont, a rosaried Onomacritos, to heighten the significance of his piracy enhanced what he had found with additions. He did not want to be rumbled later, so he adjusted the evidence.

Ancient Sparta (Lacadaimon) occupied a roughly triangular area between the river Eurotas (where Zeus in the guise of a swan had his will of Leda, who bore him Castor, Polydeuces and Helen; to her human spouse, Tyndareus, the king of Sparta, she bore Clytemnestra) and its tributary, the river Magoula. The area is large: when, in the third century BC, Spartans at last decided to build a city wall, the circuit ran to ten kilometres. Castor and Polydeuces (and their horses) inevitably figure large in the legends of Sparta. Not far away is the Menelaion, with inscriptions to Menelaus and Helen together. Also nearby are the remains of the tomb of Hyacinth with an archaic statue of Apollo; the site had been continuously occupied from Mycenaean times.

In the period of its early flowering and for more than two centuries afterwards, Sparta was unwalled. It was defensively well positioned, but also its soldiers were uncommonly brave, and even the most intrepid enemy would stop short of crossing the river Eurotas—its name means "fair-flowing"—to enter the city. If anyone had dared to cross and enter, he would have found a most un-citylike conurbation: even in the fourth century there were five hamlets, "five village settlements of the antique Greek type," says Thucydides, connected by orchards and cultivated ground, like a garden suburb, with an acropolis and five other not very pronounced hills. The buildings were unusual, too, for a city of Sparta's importance and influence. They were made of wood, not stone, and as Thucydides predicted, while the architecture of Athens survived, that of Sparta perished quite. The Abbé Fourmont assisted the deep erasure. In fact, there is no telling exactly where the agora was situated.

The inhabitants of Sparta were divided into three categories. Those who enjoyed full citizenship were called the Spartiates (also *Homoioi*, "by each other"), born and bred in the city or admitted to its native ranks because of special qualities. Next came the Perioeci, "dwellers in the neighbourhood," who were generally free to run the affairs of their communities and thrive on land granted to them by Sparta either in Laconia or annexed Messenia. The Perioeci would, among other services, provide military forces and supplies when required and probably they performed the manufacturing and commercial roles which were beneath the dignity of the Spartiates. Lowest of the social groups were the helots, local inhabitants of Spartan-controlled areas who were owned by Sparta and were required to work for the full citizens virtually as slaves, though they may have had limited property rights and been allowed to remain in their native areas and maintain family structures. Their labour made it possible for the Spartiates to fulfil their higher civic, military and cultural obligations.

Towards the end of the seventh century BC, when the Eurypontid king was Leotchydas I, Sparta achieved real eminence: the arts of peace and war were perfected. L. H. Jeffrey describes it as a period into which the poems of Alcman give us a "sharp glimpse of a Sparta freed from stress."[2] Alcman's poetry does not describe Sparta or the poet's place within it. His "I" does not, for the most part, refer to himself: it is a voice imparted to a chorus, most notably to a chorus of young women who performed poems as part of their educational process, a ritual of socialisation whose ultimate end was preparation for matrimony. The function of such poems is comparable to that of the poems of Sappho, intended to habituate the performer to certain important transitions in life, points of initiation and progression: coming of age, matrimony, battle.

The girls in Alcman's chorus are named, and their names indicate the class from which they came, the eminence of their clan. The names of these "girls from the high Spartiate families" tell a story, for the character of the father is visited even upon the girl-child in her name. We meet Astymeloisa ("citadel-care"), Megalostrata ("great army"), Agido ("leader"), Clesimbrota ("renown of man"), Timasimbrota ("honour of man").[3] They may be singing a chorus celebrating beauty, youth, and the womanly accomplishments that lead to mating, and they enjoy secure leisure in which to do so. Sparta had the stability to nurture and sustain a choral tradition because the men were successful warriors. But the Spartan warrior is different in many ways from the Homeric. The Spartan hero fights not for himself but for Sparta: to the city the warrior offers up his strength, his bravery, and if need be, his life.

Plutarch was fascinated by Sparta, and not least by its poetry. He quotes Alcman's line "Counterbalanced against the iron is the sweet lyre-playing."[4] In Sparta the arts of peace are secured by the art of war. The unique poetry was intended for performance by groups appropriate to the kind of chorus: maiden songs celebrated vigour, beauty and fertility, while the men participated in generational songs. A group of old soldiers chanted, "We were once courageous and full of youth"; the current cohort pitched in, "Now we are the brave ones; if you dare, put us to the test." The adolescents followed on: "But we in time shall be more brave than either of you." Gruff old voices, a baritone middle generation and tenor young carried the poem forward not in harmonies but responses.[5] When we read fragments of choral poetry we must remain alert to the possibility of voice changes. Alcman's verse is one ancestor of Greek dramatic writing. He did not invent the chorus, but he divided and characterised it and distributed the verse among its parts. He wrote in Laconian dialect, regarded by some as poor in euphony. The choral lyric retains a Doric inflection; the choruses in Attic tragedy "continued to be written in Doric." Pausanias declares that the pleasure of Alcman's poems was unspoiled even though he used a Spartan dialect "which is not in the least euphonious."[6]

Plutarch recounts how, when the armies of Thebes broke through into the Spartan-controlled territory of Laconia in the fourth century BC, the helots whom the Spartans had kept brutally under control refused to perform for their new masters the poems of Terpander, Alcman and the Spartan Spendon, on the grounds that their routed lords would not approve of them doing so. These were the same helots who were forced to drink undiluted wine so as to demonstrate to young Spartans how vile drunkenness was, and made to perform ridiculous dances and recitations to prove their coarse human inferiority. As Critias said, nothing compares with the freedom of a free man in Sparta, or with the slavery of the slave. Plutarch insists that these inhuman customs developed later in Spartan history, after earthquake and uprising; earlier, including during Alcman's life, there was a generally fair severity.

To Plutarch's example of the soldiers' chorus we can juxtapose Alcman's most famous poetic fragment. The papyrus was discovered by the French Egyptologist Auguste Mariette near the second pyramid of Sakkarah in 1855, part of what must have been a tomb library. Known by the generic term *partheneion,* or "maiden song," it is now held in the Louvre. Guy Davenport provides it with a highly descriptive title: "Hymn to Artemis of the Strict Observance." He appends a subtitle that sounds like stage directions:

"For a Chorus of Spartan Girls Dressed as Doves to Sing at Dawn on the
Feast of the Plough." This is an over-specific and, textually, not a wholly
sustainable take on the poem. Davenport, in presenting it so particularly, ar-
rogates a kind of Augustan authority to himself. He proceeds to translate
the poem in four complementary ways. First there is a literal version, which
shows what is missing and what survives: what survives fits into the absent
shape. At Ephesus restoration entails suspending on an unobtrusive concrete framework actual pieces of temples, leaving gaps between: a column
drum, a piece of cornice; the traveller is left to infer from the actual fragments a complete building, to join up the dots, as it were. This is Davenport's first version, revealing how much is erased from parts of the poem:

    [   ] Fate
    [   ] to friends
    [   ] gave gifts
    [   ]
    [   ] destroyed youth
    [   ]

It is as though Abbé Fourmont had ploughed a furrow straight across it.
Davenport's second version, in tetrameter couplets, sets out to suggest (if
not to replicate) some of the sound values of the imagined original. The
third version attempts restoration, rebuilding conjecturally out of Pausanias' account of the informing myth, and putting lavish flesh and fat on the
existing skeleton, concealing the missing knuckles, ribs and vertebrae. The
fourth version, in the sparest possible form, sets out "to show how phrase
follows phrase," wherever the sequence is sufficiently continuous. The last
effort is Modernist, the third Romantic, the second Classical, and the
first—simply literal.[7] He insists that the poem was performed by the dove-
disguised girls in competition with another chorus or choruses, a kind of
adolescent female *agon*.

   Most choral works and every epinicean ode have an underlying story, legend or myth. "Myths," Bowra says, "did for a choral song what sculpture
did for a temple. They illustrated the importance of a rite by depicting
episodes in legend which concerned the gods and their relations to men."[8]
The myth underlying the first part of the *partheneion* is local to Sparta, and
since Spartan audiences would have been familiar with it, the story is alluded to rather than told, an effect with which readers of Pindar are awk-
wardly familiar. The story is that of Hippocoön, a legendary king of Sparta
whose name, Graves tells us, means "horse stable." He exiled his brother
Tyndareus (whose name means "pounder" and who was to be father at one
remove of Castor and Polydeuces, Helen and Clytemnestra). Tyndareus,

with the help of Heracles (whose name means "glory of Hera"), returned and slew Hippocoön and his nine (or ten) sons.

Choral works also had a point of moral release, a maxim, something the audience could take away as the moral pith of the experience. By juxtaposing a tale of extreme disorder and violent action with the peaceful and gracious evocation of the choral ritual, a clear meaning is suggested; but suggestion is not enough, the moral needs to be fixed in an aphorism, a proverb, a summary line. Two memorable examples: "No man should set out to fly to heaven, or seek to wed queen Cyprian Aphrodite . . ."[9]—in other words, don't overreach, especially in love; and "who weaves devoutly to the end the web of his day unweeping finds grace." In Homer, by contrast, the moral inheres in action and incident. Homer would never paralyse a weaver like Penelope in a stock moral attitude. That is why his poetry is so powerfully itself, unparaphrasable, irreducible.

A choral work was intended for a specific chorus and thus included remarks, references, characterisation that tied it in to specifics of performance. The poet might even make voices refer to himself. "Alcman allows a greater degree of intimacy and even badinage than Pindar, but the difference is superficial."[10] The first person, the "I" who speaks, is, we must remember, dramatic, being performed, not spoken by the poet as a man. A choral "I" has a different value than the lyric "I." The choral "I," as if masked, retains a residue of divine sanction; such a poem's speech is never merely subjective.

The poetry of the Hesiod of *Works and Days,* of the lyric Sappho, and especially of Archilochus, is "monodic," articulated (sung or spoken) by a single voice or a group of voices moving together in time, generally accompanied by an appropriate instrument. By contrast, choral poetry is public, civic, its formal features tied in closely to the context of performance and relating to the individuals who are being initiated or celebrated. An analogy exists between such poetry and the moral purpose of a masque like Milton's *Comus.* It takes risks of scale which most monodic verse would avoid: the prosody is more complex and carefully assigned or distributed among performers. There is a sense of elevation, the diction at best decorous, at worst decorated. Underpinning the musical and strophic formal elements is usually an extended narrative based on myth. Such verse has a religious, even a liturgical feel, "where performed as part of a ritual (like Alcman's *partheneia*) or more loosely dedicated to a particular divinity (like dithyrambs in Athens)."[11] In the first half of Alcman's *partheneion,* the chorus sings of the attempted kidnap of the mythical daughters of Leukippos "by a band of violent young heroes." This, Leslie Kurke suggests, is offered as "a paradigm of overreaching and transgressive failed marriage," a kind of pre-emptive lesson, before the actual verse of sincere mating is offered. The second half of the poem concentrates on the present, touching upon themes from battle to girlish things, from transgression to propriety and conformity. "This latter half is remarkable for its carefully scripted but ostensibly spontaneous self-referentiality; the choreuts"—members of the chorus— "speak at length about their own ornaments and appearance and about their two leaders ... for whom they evince an erotic fascination."[12] This may be the obverse of Ibycus' *paideioi hymnoi*,[13] though here sung not in the intimacy of the sympoium but in the open, public air. The poem also, inevitably, celebrates the existing hierarchy.

Scholars have deduced that this first and longest surviving chunk of *partheneion* was performed by ten or eleven young women. A twelfth enacted rituals ("offering a cloak or a plough to Orthia at sunrise," for instance). Kurke insists that "such ritual conforms to the theory that in this instance, choral performance was part of an initiatory experience for the chorus members (or *choreuts*), perhaps making a life-transition before their marriage."[14] The girls who performed were also on show: their looks, the grace and strength of their movement, could be appraised by the onlooker, whether the lusty youth, the father seeking a partner for his son, the seedy bachelor or the over-sexed duffer. The words they spoke or sang and their choreographed movements were devised, of course, by men.[15]

It is possible to hear through the vivid and fresh fragments of the poem a performance. The recitation was accompanied by the *aulos*. The poet and chorus master directed, and there was a dialogue between the eleven girls and their (two) leaders and between the chorus and their master. They speak to and of one another, and of him. It is for this reason that Alcman is sometimes regarded as the father of love poetry: his verse admires the young women who celebrate, and they turn an affectionate gaze in his direction. Did he, as Athenaeus suggests, fall in love with the poet Megalostrata?[16] Was he, as Athenaeus also hints, rather incompetent in his non-professional relations with mature women? We cannot deduce such information from the poem.

But it is true, as Bowra says, that "Alcman gives to his maidens sentiments which are essentially meant for them and not for himself ... This delicate art has an air of detachment and impartiality."[17] One girl may be celebrated, as though the whole chorus is in love with her, or the whole chorus speaks in the first person as a collective or characteristic "I." The language is "more figurative than that of Sappho and more direct than Ibycus."

The presiding deity is Artemis. She is to a Spartan woman what Apollo is to a Spartan man, embodying strength, purity and a degree of ascetic discipline. Menander says that Alcman "summons Artemis from countless mountains and countless cities and from rivers too." Artemis, more than

Athena or Aphrodite, is the Lacadaimonian goddess, though both were worshipped there.

After an elaborate interpretative reconstruction of the Sakkarah *partheneion,* Bowra concludes that, though Alcman's art speaks always with a single voice, never breaking into descant or harmony, this voice is variously pitched and distributed; the individual girls in the chorus, with their names acknowledging family, and their variety of status, age and beauty, are allowed different points of view. Preference wavers between Hagesichora ("one leader") and Agido ("leader"), and there is even the hint of a contest between them. Bowra insists, too, that there is unity of tone, "a kind of gaiety, in which praise, badinage, self-depreciation, and a keen eye for physical things all play a part." Pindar, by contrast, has abrupt shifts of tone and mood. As Alcman's heir to the estate, he alters the mansion and the landscape completely.[18]

Men were responsible for all the verse, music and dance of Sparta. Alcman's contemporary Tyrtaeus, who at times seems a rival of the gentle poet, established another kind of civic verse from Alcman's, composing marching songs to rally the warriors; he set down too, in oracular form, a skeletal Spartan constitution, the work gathered under the title *Eunomia (Law and Order).*[19] "There is a story," says Plutarch, "that when Leonidas of ancient times was asked his impression of Tyrtaeus' quality as a poet, he replied: 'A good one for firing the spirits of the young.' For the poems filled them with such excitement that they stopped caring for themselves in battle."[20] He was clearly a figure of considerable power, though judging from the fragments that survive, that power tended to the gnomic, to sibylline ambiguities. The Spartans took him to heart. Plutarch says, "When someone was asking why they made the poet Tyrtaeus a citizen, he said: 'So that a foreigner should never be seen as our leader.'"[21]

Tyrtaeus was profoundly conservative and committed to the Spartan order. It was subtle in its devising and remarkably durable, if not responsive to change. Sparta had two hereditary rulers called kings, one from the Agiad, one from the Eurypontid line. Under the kings was a council of twenty-eight elders (sixty or more years in age), and under them a citizen's assembly that could approve or reject its rulings but could not initiate legislation. The established and the militarily tried and tested won Tyrtaeus' approval. He sang of heroes, a propagandist who believed what he was singing.

He was writing during and after the Second Messenian War (around 660–640 BC) when the Messenians, conquered by the Spartans in the war of 740–730, rebelled. Tyrtaeus' most famous line is this: "It is beautiful when a good man falls and dies fighting for his country." English schoolboys used to know Tyrtaeus' verse filtered through Horace's celebrated Latin translation,

Dulce et decorum est pro patria mori,[22] the bitter, ironic punch-line of Wilfred Owen's poem about a gas attack in the First World War.[23]

Victory in the Second Messenian War was a mixed blessing for the Spartans: they annexed fertile territory, but also so numerous a population of helots that one of the chief tasks for the victors, for centuries to come, was policing them. This necessity made Sparta, internally and externally, much more militaristic in its structures and its basic culture. Three centuries later, the adjective "Spartan" had become synonymous with "Philistine."[24] The helot problem inhibited Sparta from sending out colonies and ultimately paralysed it.

In the seventh century Sparta was famous for its music, pottery and poetry as well as for its military prowess. Not only did Tyrtaeus and Alcman work there, but Terpander of Lesbos had started his school of music. He invented the seven-stringed lyre on the banks of the Eurotas; he is even said to have set passages of Homer to music. Musical reforms during the century led to the establishment of a coherent musical scale, which legend attributed to Olympus of Phrygia. Terpander fitted the scale to the lyre, and as a result accompaniment to song could be played in any key. Poets—choral poets in particular—were enabled to compose, confident that the form they gave would be at least roughly replicated and respected. What Terpander did for the lyre, Clonas did for the *aulos*. The tunes they composed survived, and, such was their fame, later tunes were attributed to them.

Sparta may not have had a strong native culture but it imported its artists with a wise discretion. Thaletas of Gortyn in Crete, now entirely lost, made songs for the lyre which espoused civil obedience and unity, a lyrical complement to Tyrtaeus' choral work. There were Ionian and Aeolian contributions, their practice based on what may have been Asian traditions of musical composition. Polymnestus of Colophon, mentioned by Alcman, may have been his master, a figure very different from monodic Thaletas. Certainly the Sparta that Alcman lived in was a place of rich and conflicting musical composition.

The generic differences in early poetry have much to do with the relationship between language and musical accompaniment. Lyric poets originally composed their poems for lyre accompaniment. Thus they differ from dramatic poets, whose verse was spoken; from iambic and trochaic poets, whose verse was recited highly rhythmically rather than sung; and from elegiac poets, who were accompanied initially by an *aulos*. The distinctions, real to begin with, became blurred: lyrics were variously accompanied, the lyre was sometimes far away from the poet and his accompanist. The nature of the accompaniment (or lack thereof) initially determined genre, and some of the characteristic features of a genre keep faith with etymology.

Sappho, Alcaeus and Anacreon are poets whose work was devised, for the most part, to be performed before a group (a symposium or an open audience) by an individual, even the poet him- or herself. Alcman is different: he is giving voice, or voices; only occasionally can we say that he is, or may be, speaking "in his own person." Homer was aware of the existence of choral poetry. There are the four *threnoi,* or mourning songs; the paean to Apollo; the wedding hymn on the shield of Achilles, which meant so much to Keats; and finally the song accompanied by steps and dancing, Demodocus' account of Ares and Aphrodite, which seems to invite participation.[25] Alcman was less an inventor than a consummate practitioner.

The stanzas in choral verse tend to be longer than those in monodic verse. Sappho, Alcaeus and Anacreon write short, while Alcman, Pindar and Bacchylides write long. Length may have something to do with dance, providing sufficient verbal and musical space in which bodies can complete their ceremonial movements.

Once there are groups of performers, a degree of competitiveness enters in: in the seventh century Sparta was famous for holding competitions in choral and lyric poetry at its religious festivals. Only Alcman survives substantially enough for scholars to tease out the characteristic elements of the genre. The surviving sample is too small to sustain more than tentative generalisations. The opening stanzas of the *partheneion* are long, employ a variety of metres, and depend on an underlying narrative which is not foregrounded but upon which allusions hang. There are complex gnomic passages (a foretaste of Pindar and of Bacchylides) in which the performers suggest the larger meaning of their actions. The truths the performers tell can be profound and affecting, but the effect is not intimate, as it would be in monodic or lyric verse: an audience, not an individual, responds, hence the nuancing is of a different order from that of the lyric poet.

We live in a monodic culture and those who would break with it can appear austerely arcane, "élitist," expecting more of their audience than that audience can deliver. It is ironic that the modern poets who have most in common with the civic, choral tradition—Ezra Pound and T. S. Eliot, David Jones and W. H. Auden, Charles Olson and Geoffrey Hill—are often construed as "élitist," when in fact the intention of their poetry is to embrace and include the present, the past and the future, in the spirit of Whitman, and of Alcman.

Related to choral poetry is the hymn, a shared song addressed to a god rather than to a man (early hymns were often accompanied by the cithara) and a still-standing chorus; the processional song, or *prosodion,* frequently *aulos*-accompanied; the dithyramb, associated with Dionysus, less formal than the *prosodion;* and all forms of song for living beings—*encomia* rather than *elegia.* The victory odes (*epinicia*), the *skolion* and *erotikon* are forms of *encomia* and belong in this choral, civic zone of poetry.

When alternatives to epic poetry emerged, they were the result not so much of the inadequacy of the epic mode as of social changes which made the epic archaic, in the light of the evolving towns and independent cities and the civic cultures that came with them: different forms of expression were required to touch on different parts of life. Music was inseparable from this emergence of new forms, and the early history of poetry is inextricable from the history of music. Indeed we must remind ourselves over and over again that the fragments we have of ancient texts are fragments twice over: not only is the poem's larger form often absent, indeterminate; its music has vanished altogether. We must also remember that choral song, even in secular and epinicean use, retained a ceremonial, even a liturgical, formality, reflecting its origins in sacred ritual. This ceremonial dimension has vanished along with the music and the padding feet of the chorus.

Greek music lacked harmony as our modern ears hear harmony. What mattered were tune, patterning and repetition of strophes and stanzas, with expressive variation. "The main form of variation in choral poetry was to compose not in single strophes but in triads. Each triad was a whole which balanced metrically with every other triad, but inside it, while the strophe and the antistrophe were composed on one plan, the epode was composed on another."[26] This happened less in Alcman than in such works as Ibycus' poem to Polycrates; it may have been invented by Stesichorus. Another kind of variation, though no examples survive, might have been to change the metre in the second part of the poem.

Poetry was advancing gradually towards what would ultimately be emancipation from musical accompaniment and its rules, though the remaining prosodic rules derived their regularity from the initial adjustment of language to accompaniment. By the second half of the fifth century, when changes in music itself helped to relax the rules of poetic composition, more variety of movement was possible: the drama was in the ascendant.

By the time of the great dramatists, unflattering legends about Tyrtaeus' origins were in circulation. He was portrayed as a limping, scatter-brained teacher from Athens (the Athenians liked the idea that Sparta's great poet and law-giver was an Athenian outcast) or Miletus. Towards the beginning of the Second Messenian War Sparta was urged by an oracle to seek a counsellor from Athens. Athens packed off Tyrtaeus, an act of intended bad faith which backfired, since the poet rose to the occasion. His skill was in composing poems, and in general, poetry, as W. H. Auden remarks, "makes nothing happen." But Tyrtaeus' poems were different; they put fire in the Spartan belly and inspired warriors to victory. Lycurgus says the Spartan leaders compelled soldiers to listen to Tyrtaeus' recite verses before battle. Better death than exile (or retreat), the poet said. The first surviving fragment of Tyrtaeus is unsubtle and effective: "The time has come for a man to take his

stand, planting his feet and biting his lip."[27] Later critics make out that Tyrtaeus was a general; a statesman: surely, they insist, a poet with no more than
a semi-official brief could not have achieved as much as he did in Sparta.

Tyrtaeus provides the "iron" in Alcman's verse, "Counterbalanced against
the iron is the sweet lyre-playing." Alcman's is the "lyre-playing," in service
of a culture to which he may or may not have been born. Aristotle says Alcman was a Lydian from Sardis, a city due east of Smyrna in Asia Minor, and
down the centuries he has been described accordingly. It must have been
hard for a fifth- or fourth-century critic to believe that Sparta, that severest
of states, could have been the cradle of a poet so subtle and nuanced as Alcman. The *Suda* contradicts Aristotle and declares that he was from Messoa
in Laconia, in the Peloponnese, not a Lydian at all. (Alcman's language,
apart from a few specific words, contradicts Aristotle too.) His father was
called Damas, or maybe Titarus. Heraclides Ponticus claims Alcman was
the slave of a Spartan by the name of Agesidas, who freed him because of
his skills as a musician and poet.[28] In one of the Oxyrhinchus papyruses, *if*
he is speaking of himself, Alcman says that he is from Sardis. David A.
Campbell, trying to make sense of the confused genealogy, is not the first
to suggest that there may have been two Alcmans. One of the bright, inef-
fective parachutes that scholars deploy when biographical evidence is contradictory, and flying perilous, is this "maybe there were two of them": two
Alcmans, two Homers, two Hesiods, two Sapphos. Of course, maybe there
were; but the ancients themselves did not think so. Antiquity could not re-
solve the question of Alcman's origin; we are even less likely to be able to
do so. We can say that he flourished in Sparta around 630 BC, and he composed choral verse, a form appropriate to early Sparta and a particular part
of the Spartan community.

"Alcman's world was simple," Bowra says, "even small. Its literature was
limited to the old epics and its own songs. It had no science or history. Its
religion was that of local cults which were as yet little influenced by foreign
ideas or rationalistic simplification. Its landscape was that of a valley
flanked by high, majestic mountains and bounded on one side by the sea."[29]
Bowra idealises and simplifies, but we draw from the poems, which serve
privilege and power, the sense of a culture that is ordered, simple, strict.

The *Suda* tries to tell us about the man himself: "He was extremely
amorous and was the first to write songs of an erotic nature." It is possible
to mistake his general statements for individual candour: "and with desire
that turns the limbs to jelly, and she gazes [at me?] and sleep or death look
not more meltingly, and her sweetness is not wasted";[30] there is a lived, in-
tensifying breathlessness here, as in the praises he heaps upon Astymeloisa
and Hagesichora. The kind of vehemence that he achieves is unsentimental:

his bacchants have strong arms, sharp nails, and are far from squeamish: "Often among the steep mountains, when it's feast time and the torches delight the gods, you bear a golden bowl, a great *[scyphos]*, the kind that shepherds use, and emptying into it with your own two hands milk of a lionness, you made a round hardened cheese for the killer of Argus."[31] He was certainly a committed chorus master.

In antiquity, because he mentioned specific foods and wines with such relish and clearly enjoyed his mealtimes, he came to be regarded as a type for gluttony. Athenaeus comments on the number of specific wines Alcman names, and on how in Sparta at his time most wine was mulled, or "fired."[32] He also evokes "lettuce-cakes" (*thridakiskai*) and "pan-cakes" (*kribanai,* cakes shaped like breasts).[33] There is bean porridge, white frumenty (boiled wheaten grains), honey; poppy-seed loaves, linseed and sesame loaves, and *chrysocolla,* a dish made with honey and linseed.[34] We savour "Cydonian apples," which are quinces or medlars, depending on the authority you choose.[35] Spring, he says famously, is the season when things grow but a man cannot eat his fill. Athenaeus is bound to linger over Alcman's eating habits in a work entitled *Scholars at Dinner.* He puts words in Alcman's mouth: the tripod soon "will be filled with pea-soup, the sort that he, who eats everything that's set before him, enjoys piping hot after the solstice: he eats nothing special [sweet confections?] but looks for everyday food like common people."[36] A man of the people, then, so that when Athenaeus speaks of the "seven couches and an equal number of tables fully laid,"[37] we realise that this is not a symposium or the seat of privilege but one of the Spartan "messes" (in the military sense) where people ate together (though men and woman probably did not share mealtimes).

He wrote, we are told, six books: choral poetry, lyric poetry and a mysterious scroll entitled the *Diving Women.* He was the first poet to "introduce the custom of reciting poetry in metres other than the hexameter."[38] If this was the case, he was a genuine radical, breaking the tyranny of Homer's example. Arion may have been a student of his.

The choral tradition should remind us that, in certain city-states, the poet was more than a marginal figure. Indeed, he had specific functions which were regarded as necessary to be performed, functions which included exhortation to virtue and to action, putting the law into succinct and memorable form, establishing rites of initiation and public ritual, celebrating the collective in the individual. Epitaphs, elegies, victory poems, verbal rewards and rebukes, too, were not optional extras but necessary affirmations.

Alcman knew the matter of Homer's poetry and may have known the poems themselves and the earlier Homeric Hymns, which share the sense of *proemes* with a number of his fragments. If Terpander developed music to go with Homeric recitation, Alcman would have heard it. He certainly alluded to the same subjects and legends as Homer and wrote some hexameters, though the direct echoes are so few as to be possibly fortuitous. Like Hesiod, he is a servant of the Muses. Bowra believes that he had a very concrete and literal belief in their presence; they were certainly (symbolically at least) of central importance for composition. The Muses, taken together, embody the complex of gracious skills that his choir needed in terms of language, accompaniment and movement. He seems undecided whether the Muses are daughters of the primal Uranus and Gea, Heaven and Earth, and hence almost on a par with the highest gods, or the daughters of Zeus. Perhaps what determined their nature was specific context.[39] At one point he speaks of them as full of memory, but not mothered by her: *Mousai Mnamosuna*. Whether he was a believer or not, when he invokes a Muse's assistance he does not command but entices and courts her. She delivers him new-minted songs.

We cannot experience choral Alcman because the music is lost, the movements are forgotten, and time has so eroded the texts that all we have are scraps. Most of them have a lyric aspect. Alcman is in the traditional list of "the nine lyric poets," a list which survives with the same names, though in different order, in two epigrams: Alcaeus, Alcman, Anacreon, Bacchylides, Ibycus, Pindar, Sappho, Simonides and Stesichorus.[40] It is as a lyric poet that Goethe read and adapted him. Goethe's most famous single lyric is a version of Alcman ("Über allen Gipfeln . . ."),[41] the almost-perished Greek, who draws such a powerful and delicate spell in his three-millennia wake.

If we take him at his word, his magic owes much to the natural world. He claims to know the tunes of all the birds, a conceit which puts him almost orphically in touch with nature. "Alcman invented the words and the tune, by listening to the partridges' sharp cry."[42] The word Alcman uses for partridge is *kakkabides,* which we are told is the chukar partridge, whose cry transliterates as *kakkabi.* The word comes from the islands of the eastern Aegean (these partridges did not live on mainland Greece): such diction supports the view that Sparta imported Alcman from Asia Minor. The word for patridge-speak suggests rapid, rather harsh articulation. In the famous *partheneion* fragment, a girl admiring Hagesichora would like to praise her but is shy and "like an owl from a rafter, chatters emptily."[43] In another fragment a voice declares, "and I know the strains of all the birds."[44] The song of the choir is like "that of a swan on the waters of the Xanthus": it is hard not to think of Leda.

"And the peaks are asleep and the valleys, the headlands and the riverbeds, all the creeping creatures nourished by the damp black soil, the wild creatures that live on the mountains, the tribe of bees, and the large deep-dwelling creatures of the deep, turbulent sea; and the race of long-winged birds is sleeping."[45] We are so accustomed to his comparing birds and the girls of his chorus that we wonder: are these long-winged birds, asleep, not the girls? If they are, the poem moves from literal evocation into a kind of allegorical sense. Elsewhere, "The girls went their own ways when their chores were complete, like birds when the shadow of a hawk passes over."[46] The editor of the fragments refers us to Homer's Nausicaa and her companions, fluttering away when they discover naked Odysseus on the shore. The editor also calls attention to the number of allusions to horses, especially those of Sparta's Castor and Polydeuces, and Alcman has a talking horse, a relation of Xanthus, Achilles' articulate steed.[47]

He has, like Homer and Archilochus, an ability to see from above, looking down from the perspective of a circling bird or from a cliff top. Thus a mountain "blossoms" with forests;[48] the sea "blossoms" with waves: bursts of trees, the breaking waters, foreshadowing the imagism of H.D.'s most famous poem, "Oread."[49]

Alcman, if we have identified him correctly, appears to have been a benign character, and the manner of his death, recounted by Aristotle in his *History of Animals*, seems unjustly gruesome. Lice, Aristotle says, are produced from the flesh; a little pusless lump appears and if you prick it lice come out. Too much moisture in the air creates this condition. This is how Alcman perished, infested with lice. Dissolute living was seen as a contributory factor.

His tomb, Pausanias declares, was to the right of the temple of Sebrus in Sparta, close to the tombs of the slain sons of Hippocoön. It is as if he had been inserted into the first half of his most celebrated poem. Nearby was Helen's sanctuary, and not far off the sanctuary of Heracles.[50] History and legend are here interred together. Their site was plundered, ploughed over, erased. But out of the soil, out of the remote sands of Egypt, the poems are still audible and still accumulating. A Palatine Anthology epitaph survives: "Graceful Alcman, the swan, singer of wedding-hymns, a singing that did justice to the Muses, lies in this tomb; he delighted Sparta, and it was there that the Lydian, having cast his burden aside, departed to Hades."[51] The "burden" may have been slavery, from which his poetic skills released him.

IX

Mimnermus of Colophon (or Smyrna)
(c. 630 BC)

> . . . You say there is no substance here,
> One great reality above:
> Back from that void I shrink in fear,
> And child-like hide myself in love:
> Show me what angels feel. Till then
> I cling, a mere weak man, to men.

WILLIAM JOHNSON CORY (1823–1892)
"Mimnermus in Church"

The salt market of Dardania was called Stoboe or Stobi, says William Hazlitt in his *Classical Gazetteer.* It was a town of Pelagonia, in Paeonia, on the Erigonus River, near where it joins the Axius, between Gurbita and Antigonea. Despite this abundance of clues, it is still hard to find on a map. It became a Macedonian administrative centre. In the fifth century ad, a wealthy man of Stobi called John, known today (if known at all) as Johannes Stobaeus, had a son. Attentive to the boy's education, he compiled for him an anthology of extracts from poets and prose writers. It served as an *aide-mémoire,* giving the boy useful off-the-peg phrases and stanzas to enrich his conversation. It was also intended to edify him.

Stobaeus garnered the extracts for his anthology (much of the poetry is fragmentary) from earlier anthologies. For centuries anthologies had been popular. They were enhanced, revised and copied, generation after generation. Meleager of Gadara in the first century AD compiled a famous, now-lost anthology, mainly of epigrams (in the extended sense of the term). It may have been a source for the tenth-century Palatine Anthology of Constantinus Cephalas, discovered seven hundred years later in the Palatine Library at Heidelberg. It contains work by 340 authors. Most famous of all is the Greek Anthology with material drawn from seventeen centuries of Greek poetry, starting in 700 BC and consisting of verse from earlier anthologies, inscriptions and other texts. It contains over six thousand epigrams.

It is fortunate that Stobaeus' anthology of elegies, our chief textual source for certain poets, survived. It was arranged in four books: a theme was stated, then the verse extracts, followed by passages from the prose writers, were assembled to illustrate it. Fragment 25 of Archilochus, who survives in part thanks to this collection, begins with the line "I lie tortured by desire," which Stobaeus files under the heading, "Concerning the Vulgar Aphrodite Who Is the Reason for Procreation and About Desire for the Pleasures of the Flesh." Stobaeus Junior must often have turned for solace and arousal to the cautionary poems in this section. There are other chapters: "That Marrying Is Not Good," contrasted with "That Marriage is Most Fair." Good husbandry and metaphysics also feature in this book of counsel and consolation.[1] Stobaeus is the source of eight pieces of Archilochus, six of Simonides of Cos, five of Semonides of Amorgos, four of Phocylides, two each of Tyrtaeus, Solon and Sappho, one of Hipponax, Xenophanes, Callinus and Anacreon, and seven of Mimnermus.

In the Middle Ages, Stobaeus' anthology "was transmitted in two separate parts of two books each (*Eclogae* and *Florilegium*)."[2] The texts are much corrupted, copied from centuries of copying, and then recopied for centuries. The distortions are not quite so rapid as Chinese Whispers, but they may be as extreme, especially in terms of the original forms. In the absence of authoritative manuscripts, educated conjecture is the only judge. All the same, Stobaeus' book is a necropolis in which we can glimpse some very important, very faded ghosts, including that of Mimnermus of Colophon, from the second half of the seventh century BC.[3]

He was not, it is believed, a prolific poet. His entire *oeuvre* may have been accommodated on a single papyrus scroll at the great library in Alexandria. The title *Nanno* may have covered the elegies, both erotic and those intended for the soberer moments of the symposium, and the *Smyrneis* was a long, historical elegy. He was perhaps an *auletes,* or oboe-player, himself.[4]

For Callimachus, Mimnermus was an innovator, one of the first to compose love elegies. The Alexandrian poet-librarian celebrates his Ionian forebear in the prologue to *Aetia,* passages of which survive, including the mysterious broken lines which Trypanis translates, ". . . and not the Large Woman taught that Mimnermus is a delightful poet . . ." Mimnermus and the much later poet Philetas of Cos seemed to license Callimachus to concentrate upon the shorter poem, to dignify it in such a way as to make it possible for a poet not to feel compelled to embark upon the extended work, the epic or historical narrative. It may be, too, that Callimachus found in Mimnermus an instance of that allusiveness to earlier poems that appeals to settled and to colonial literary cultures; the act of reading one text is enhanced if that text is itself reading and redeploying recognisable elements from a dozen earlier texts. This seems to be the spirit in which Mimnermus is glancingly mentioned in the shards of Callimachus' Iambus 203 that survive.

He may have taken pleasure in some of the Mimnermean conceits, which are themselves rooted in myth and legend. For example, he knew that the sun travelled back in a cup of sorts from when it set in the west to when it rose again in the east, and alluded to this in fragment 12, "telling how he is borne over the water in a winged, golden vessel, made by Hephaistus, from the Hesperides to the land of the Aethiopians, where his horses and chariot await him."⁵ The conceit taken up by Stesichorus is that Heracles could travel back in the cup or on the couch when it returned empty to its starting point.

It is tempting to draw analogies between Callimachus' take on Mimnermus and Modernist practice. Pindar, too, may have found suggestions in Mimnermus' shorter narratives, and among the Latin poets Propertius declared that in love Mimnermus is of greater worth than Homer.⁶ He is one of those poets whose reputations we must take on trust because so little of his work remains in textual form, though it helped to shape the imaginations of others. Trypanis dubs him "the first hedonist in Western literature." In his verse he explored both sexual and intertextual pleasures, and like no other poet reflected on the horror of growing old, the horror consisting not in the death of sexual desire but in the end of sexual desirability:

> . . . Old age then arrives and with it
> Pain, and transformation to repulsive, foul,
> And the heart galled by malignancies:
> He takes no joy in the brightness of the sun
> Now, and boys revile him, women loathe:
> This is what God devised for long survivors.⁷

How short are the days of youth, how long the years of unfulfilment. The fruit ripens and as suddenly is rotten. There are two ends in view, a long and horrible old age, or death, and death is preferable. Yet to die poor, to die childless, to die sick . . . One is not far from the anxieties and regrets of Hesiod in some of the verse, though there is a noble elevation in Mimnermus which the callused Boeotian poet does not possess.

Much of the sensual particularity is gone from the fragments that remain, as though they have been washed and tidied. But he is not entirely bleached out: "One might object that there is a grotesqueness in the description of erotic sweat which is out of place in a reflective elegy of the seventh century."⁸ For a poet steeped in Homer, as his excellent modern editor Archibald Allen knows Mimnermus to be, this seems a censorious view to take. Lovers do sweat, it is part of the experience and even of the pleasure of love, and until poetry moves off from the body into the language of amorous conceit, it is not unwholesome that the literal smell and texture of love should find its way into the verbal celebration of the act. David Mulroy translates fragment 5,

> Sweat drenches my skin and I start to tremble
> when I see adolescence in bloom,
> pleasant and fair as it is, since I wish it were more,
> but precious youth is like
> a fleeting dream and hideous age, its destroyer,
> hovers overhead from the first;
> hateful, worthless, it stupefies the man it envelops,
> blurring his eyes and mind.[9]

There is a textual problem here. The first six lines of this poem appear as a poem in themselves in the Theognidean Anthology (poems gathered under Theognis' name as a flag of convenience for transmission). Lines four to eight are preserved in Stobaeus with Mimnermus' name attached. Editors bring the two texts together into one satisfactory poem, arguably greater than the sum of its parts and either a restoration or a suggestive fabrication.

Allen's take on Mimnermus' Eros may have something to do with Stobaeus. He preserved most of the fragments that survive,[10] and it is he, after all, who got rid of the sweat and left us lamenting harsh old age without the occasion of lovely youth. This may be why we are inclined to see Mimnermus as rather deodorised, like Shakespeare's *Antony and Cleopatra* passed through the filter of Dryden's couplets and turned into the marmoreal attitudes of *All for Love*: on a different scale, of course, but the effect may be similar. There are no remaining fragments where we see or touch the delectable *auletes* Nanno (was she delectable?), and the homosexual overtones are unspecific, unsweaty.

We must remember that Stobaeus made his selection according to certain educational and generic criteria. Our very sense of early elegy is conditioned by the works that survive, and the works that survive did so largely through anthologies with a pedagogic mission. We have a selective sense of elegy for this reason: we cannot know what the anthologists left out, where what seems a poem is actually a fragment, where what seems fragmentary is actually a poem, or where the attributions are wilful or suspect. In short, the anthology is a treacherous fossil ground because in the end the vertebrae that survive do not necessarily fit together into a credible skeleton. If all we had of the English eighteenth century was Palgrave's saccharine selection, or the sole record of Tudor verse was Tottel's amazing but narrowly based *Miscellany,* published in 1557 and the most popular book of its day, our take on our own past would be quite different and partial.

Strabo and Athenaeus preserve a few more fragments of Mimnermus, lines and phrases from what must have been complex narrative verse, quite different from the material in Stobaeus. Had the sources he drew on discarded Mimnermus the narrative poet and mythographer, or did he regard that kind of poetry as inappropriate for his son's education? Anthologies neglected occasional verse, too, whenever the occasion had vanished from view. Archilochus is said to have composed elegies on men who died at sea, but Stobaeus chiefly preserved the moralising passages. He also sometimes altered verses to make the sense more general.

What we would give to see even an ankle or wrist of Nanno, or her lips on the *aulos* accompanying the poet. She is erased. The love poems and elegies on short-lived pleasures were collected under the title, possibly an Alexandrian addition, of *Nanno*. The Hellenistic poets Hermesianax and Posidippus allude to it, but they are not dependable witnesses, being fanciful in their readings of other work. All the same, Allen plausibly declares: "It is hardly likely . . . that she is wholly fictional, a late classical or Alexandrian invention."[11] Stobaeus omitted her among other specifics and made Mimnermus' celebration of "the urgent, insurgent now" airy and abstract-feeling, merely poetic. There was a real flesh-and-blood woman, graceful and talented, at the end of his expressed desire, the Alexandrian editors insist. He had a complementary affection, as Solon did, for lads.

Apart from *Nanno,* his other book was called *Smyrneis,* a narrative about the founding of Colophon, Smyrna's mother city. There were also poems that told of the war between the people of Smyrna and the Lydians. Smyrna was built on a gulf that bore its name, at the end of a deep harbour. The Hermus River, with its long valley, ran to the north and east of Smyrna, and fifty miles east along the Hermus was the strong Lydian city of Sardis. Smyrna stood between Sardis and its nearest exit to the sea. The usurping Lydian shepherd-king Gyges attacked Smyrna around 680 BC, in the early years of his reign. His grandson Alyattes finally captured and razed it to the ground around 600 BC. Mimnermus was dead by then.

Given Mimnermus' debt to Homer, it is hard to think of him as an abstracting poet. The impact of Homer on those his work touched is, first of all, prosodic; second, it affects the way detail is perceived and recorded in language and determines elements of diction and description. Forms and phrases in Mimnermus grow out of Homer; there are echoes of a very close and direct nature.

Alexandrian tradition assigns Mimnermus to Colophon, one of the twelve cities of Ionia (the Dodecapolis), where many other poets, including Polymnestos, Phoenix, Antimachus, Hermesianax (who tells of Nanno), Nicandor and Xenophanes, the sage and poet, were born, as well as some great early musicians. It even laid claim to Homer, but then much of Ionia did. In political and social terms, early Colophon was an unusually attractive city. It was said to have been founded by Andraimon, from Pylos, the city which Neleus, son of Tyro and the sea god Poseidon, founded. Heracles killed Neleus when he refused to offer the sullied hero purification. He

killed, too, all of Neleus' sons except for Nestor. After Andraimon's time
there was a further influx of Ionian Greeks. Though the Pyleans arrived by
sea, the archaic city was built eight miles inland on a gradient, with an emphatic citadel. Colophon ruled the fertile, broad plain to the east and south-
east, embraced by a river called the Caystros. The families of Colophon
possessed wide estates where they bred horses. Aristotle declares that the
oligarchy that ruled Colophon was unusual in that the ruling class outnum-
bered the poorer folk. They were a vigorous people, more free-spirited than
their contemporaries at nearby Ephesus.

In the eighth century a number of political exiles from Colophon took
over and settled in Smyrna, an Aeolic town. M. L. West is keen to adjust the
record. He calls the poet "Mimnermus of Smyrna." "His name may commemorate the Smyrnaeans' famous resistance to . . . Gyges at the river Hermus sometime before 660 BC, which would imply his birth at that time." (It
certainly would.) Archibald Allen agrees with West that Smyrna has a claim
to the poet. It is an issue that can never be resolved.

Allen says the poet was born around 670 BC. From the evidence of fragment 9 he deduces the Smyrna connection, but the fragment can be taken
to belong to a narrative, perhaps part of a missing Jason story. Like some of
Mimnermus' poetry, this passage has a Homeric, not a confessional, ring to
it. This is West's translation:

> Aipy we left, and Neleus' city, Pylos,
> > and came by ship to Asia's lovely coast.
> We settled at fair Colophon with rude
> > aggression, bringers of harsh insolence;
> and there we crossed the river Asteïs
> > and took Aeolian Smyrna by God's will.

Mimnermus used elegy with energy and when necessary he used it instru-
mentally, writing polemic which must have been of use against the Lydian
foe. He rallies his fellow citizens by invoking the heroism of an earlier
Smyrnaean against the Lydians. A formal hymn, perhaps to Achilles, may
have preceded the poem about the battle of the Smyrnaean army against
the Lydians. If we are to believe Pausanias, the poet mentioned two generations of Muses, the first the children of Uranus and the second of Zeus, the
older arts having, as it were, older tutelary spirits, the younger ones younger.

The origin of the word "elegy" is obscure: it may have meant, Trypanis
suggests, "dirge metre," and yet it is first found in war songs, the ancient
war songs of Callinus of Ephesus (with his invocation of Smyrna) and Tyrtaeus of Aphidna, both near contemporaries of Mimnermus. Their writing
was direct and emphatic. Elegiacs diversified: in time they became associated particularly with love poetry. It is important to read Mimnermus not

only in the light of his contemporaries but also alongside the elegists he affected, Theognis, Xenophanes and Simonides, for example. His more amorous poetry, like theirs, was composed for recitation in the private symposium.[12] Unlike open-air Homer and storm-tossed Archilochus, Mimnermus writes poetry with a roof over its head.

The statesman and poet Solon of Athens, that city's first recorded author and one of the Seven Sages, valued Mimnermus as a near contemporary and a celebrator of pleasures. In one poem he took issue with him about how far old age can be tolerated, rebuking him as an editor might, and making an adjustment to an errored line. He quotes Mimnermus' line first.

> "O let death catch me up when I am sixty."
> If you take my advice, you'll scrap that line.
> Allow me this time to be wiser than you:
> Alter it, Ligyastades. Instead
> Sing, "O let death catch me up when I'm eighty."

Solon's fragment 20 belongs to a rare genre, one in which dialogue takes place between poets, places and periods. Solon virtually *names* the earlier poet when he quotes him. West says that "Ligyastades" could mean "melodious singer." He also comments that the poem appears to have been written to a living man. If so, Mimnermus was well advanced in years and Solon a little peremptory, unless he was adjusting the poem in order to allow the old poet twenty further years of life and—as Mimnermus would see it—decrepitude.

For Alcaeus, it is wine and love, for Mimnermus it is love first and foremost that we live for and praise.[13] Wine lets us briefly off the hook of old age, and while Solon urges Mimnermus to be lenient with himself, the old man has only to regard his paunch and wrinkles to know the game is up. We read Mimnermus if we read him at all, the phrases that remain, as an elegist of pleasure, celebrating and lamenting in equal degrees. But, as Bowra says, there was more to him than that: "Despite his professed cult of youth and pleasure, Mimnermus has a wide concept of human worth. It is the balance between action and relaxation, between effort and pleasure, which is central to his outlook, and this is why he is truly representative of the Ionian Greeks, who had dangerous enemies on their frontiers . . ."[14] Though we live for pleasure, being young, we fight for it as well, and we celebrate the warrior who moves in the sudden light of the sun, wielding his spear and with a heart intact, unharmed by the missiles of his foes.[15] When he has made a free space for himself and his kind, he can take pleasure there.

Semonides of Amorgos (630 BC)

Phocylides says this: *what's the use of blue blood*
In people whose talk and opinions lack all grace?[1]

 Hesiod wrote in hexameters, like Homer, but the strains that he
drew from that noble prosody were quite unlike the notes that
Homer struck. His verse has a homespun dignity; the reader
harvests good advice in digestible maxims and proverbs. So
much advice, in fact, that the poems' larger forms are lost sight of. *Works
and Days* sings, but in a gruff monody that reaches towards peasant candour. The dirt on his sandals is from fields rather than streets.

Yet those who learned from him were urban commentators and then
satirists. They are not dignified as Hesiod was or elevated like Homer, they
are men speaking to men. For Bowra, Semonides "turned the Hesiodic
maxim into neat, unpretentious satire, using not the stately hexameter but
an iambic line closer to the rhythm of actual conversation. The tone is unaf-
fectedly lowly . . ."[2] This judgement tends to aestheticise a poet with less
finish and more sourness, judging from the poems and fragments that survive, than his advocates allow. What are we to make of the curious fragment
in which he says, "and I drove through the back door," in which the "back
door" is the anus?[3] Is there also, perhaps, the occasional semantic allusion
to—farting?[4]

The Byzantine encyclopaedia the *Suda* reports that he was the first poet
to write in iambics. He is said to have composed two books of elegies in
that form. The Greek iambic is not directly equivalent to the English iamb.
If we scan the traditional hexameter like this:

$$—uu —uu —uu —uu —uu —u$$

the pentameter would look like this:

$$—uu —uu —uu —uu —$$

The flow is checked not by the counterpointing of syntax which moves the
cæsura around the line or even at times introduces two caesuras into a single
line. Its flow is broken regularly in the prosodic disposition itself, the two
long syllables in the middle of the line forcing a speech pause. It is a form
less versatile than the hexameter not only because it is not susceptible to
such a variety of variables, but also because it cannot "sing," being always
grounded in mid-line.

Semonides in his iambic verse paraphrases Hesiod. Early commentators, Clement of Alexandria, for example, and Porphyry, set passages of Hesiod parallel to ones from Semonides: there can be no doubt about the derivation. His most famous work, "Iambus on Women," at 118 lines the longest surviving non-hexameter poem[5] from before the fifth century BC,[6] is built more or less directly on the foundation of Hesiod's famous catalogue of misogyny: woman is an almost unmitigated plague which men encounter and endure as best they can.[7] Woman is an evil thing, *kakon*, in *Theogony* (lines 570 and 600) and in *Works and Days* (lines 88–89). In Semonides woman is associated with the word *kakon* no fewer than seven times.

He plays too with lines of Homer. One famous poem begins, "That man of Chios said something, something so beautiful: 'The generations of leaves are like those of men.'"[8] It repeats the *carpe diem* argument, yet the effects Semonides achieves are neither heroic nor bucolic. Hesiod's hexameters may stand behind the iambic tradition, where song cools to speech, but it is Archilochus who first defines the iambic style, and then Semonides and Hipponax who take it a little too far, towards self-parody. The energies of iambic poetry are taken over by the dramatists. One of the dramatists, Aristophanes, had rather a jaundiced view of Semonides, portraying him as a miserable old miser in his play *Peace:* "now he's old and shrivelled, he would even set sail on a wickerwork mat if there was profit in it."[9]

Bowra quotes the passage from "Iambus on Women" in which he likens one type of woman to the changing sea, and comments, "This is not very exalted, but it is lively and genuine and makes its point with derision." It lowers the tone of Hesiod, he adds. Is this right, or does it bring the rural sensibility to town, creating a new tone in the verse, a tone we do not hear in the more individuated passions and rancours of pugnacious Archilochus? Hesiod's disagreeable women were rural creatures, their animal nature expressed among animals. Animals were not absent from Amorgos, but they did not necessarily follow the poet into the house when he was finished for the day. What for Hesiod was an immediate and natural point of comparison for Semonides has become something of a conceit, or, when he comes to make his comparisons in detail, an allegorical figure. "The high Homeric laughter has turned sour," Bowra says, "and the poetry of contempt and denunciation, so manifest in Archilochus, has found a place in less unusual circles."[10] In Hesiod there is no contempt for any livestock, and his comparisons are briefer, more glancing and emblematic. "Among people there is no understanding; we abide," says Semonides, "like livestock, subject to each day's weather, not knowing how the god" (singular) "will sort and order things."[11]

Bowra speaks of Semonides having "rather a plebeian look, and [he] can hardly have had any social pretensions."[12] This is contradicted by others, who regard him as of better stock (like Hipponax, a twisted branch hacked from a noble tree). The poems themselves seem to go against Bowra's conclusions, too. The poet was not like that lowest of men, the potter, who provided the magnificent crockery but never drank from or ate off it. The symposium poet, a symposiast himself, was part of the class that the poems addressed. And with Semonides we are in the world of symposia, men reclining with wine, a performer entertaining them not with epic narrative but with lyric song, broad humour, elements of folklore, flattering them with their own prejudices tricked out in the efficient and memorable language of verse.

The surviving poems are in Ionic dialect and are indebted to popular fables; there is always a moral tone, even in the brisk narrative fragments, but the tone is not earnest or monitory: it invites complicity. A man's voice speaks, and it speaks to rather than at other men. It can be an ingratiating voice that invites assent, that provokes amusement and laughter, the poet as entertainer but not on a stage—entertaining us intimately, the way an English Augustan poet might have addressed his friends in a coffee house.

Semonides composed his poems in what must have been a new community, or a newly founded one. If we are to believe the *Suda,* he was born in Samos (his father a well-placed Samian called Crines), and led a party to Amorgos, where he founded a colony. Amorgos, the easternmost of the Cyclades, belongs to the eparchy of Naxos. It is a narrow island, eighteen kilometres long and slanting up from the south-west to the north-east. Today it is sparsely inhabited, with between 1,600 and 1,700 people. In Semonides' day it would have been a little more populous. It has three mountain peaks. One of them (Krikelas, the highest) lost its forest in the nineteenth century in a three-week fire and has never been the same since. When the poet arrived there from Samos, it was wooded. Landing on the north of the island, he would not immediately have seen the cliffs that hold down the sea along the rough south coast.

In antiquity, there were three cities to go with the three peaks, all on the northern coast. The *Suda* credits Semonides with establishing all three, but in fact it is likely that he was involved in the founding of only one, Minoa, the others having been founded by settlers from Naxos. Amorgos is best known not for Semonides or its vintage, but for the fact that in the Lamian wars the Athenian fleet was decisively trounced in its waters, a defeat from which Athens never quite recovered.

Semonides is an heir, even an echo, of Archilochus: David Mulroy calls him "a poor man's Archilochus." Despite the fact that both poets left home to help found new colonies, both were soldiers and perhaps adventurers, Semonides is on a smaller scale than his forebear, his voice higher-pitched, his angers and passions less extreme. Lesky indicates that Semonides, though he was the near contemporary of Archilochus, was neither as accomplished nor as versatile.[13] All the same, to be Archilochus' successor means something very specific. Archilochus, Bowra says, "put the self into poetry."[14] The self the poet invests is not of a kind with the first person in Renaissance and later European poetry; he is a singularly rancorous fellow, for whom art has a use beyond the didactic, the informative. It is a weapon to harm foes, to *make things happen*. Some of its consequences are fatal. Archilochus used verse so efficiently to defame his enemies that they destroyed themselves, and their destruction goes on ever after since each generation experiences the poems anew. Lucian declares Semonides, along with Archilochus and Hipponax, master of abusive verse. There is an eternity of sorts in the abuse.

As in the case of Mimnermus, Stobaeus is again a chief source for Semonides' surviving verse.[15] Why did Stobaeus, a responsible father of the fifth century AD, include a protracted piece of abuse of women in an anthology intended for the instruction of his son? Semonides' poem is not notably *funny*, its construction is not subtle, the animal types the poet deploys in degrading his subject, rooted in folklore, not original. It has to be assumed that Stobaeus took the poem seriously, as actually characterising women: aversion therapy for Stobaeus Junior. Was this the poet's own intention, was he a committed woman-hater, or was he dealing out stereotypes and commonplaces simply to amuse fellow (male) symposiasts? The attack is vivid, relentless, unforgiving. The worst recurrent sin of women seems to be *eating*. Such a theme in the feasting context of the symposium cannot wholly have lacked irony. What may seem less ironic to modern readers is the violence of male response, which is clearly indicated and, because it is not ironised in the text, is repugnant.

Yet the violence inheres in the traditional elements that Semonides builds upon. Folk-tales and folk wisdom have a place in the work: "a fragment of a poem by Semonides," says Lesky, "comes from a story of the dung beetle who punished the arrogance of the eagle."[16] Such uncertain fragments are like shards of pottery with sufficient detail left for us almost to infer the story that they illustrate. Some critics find a philosophical note in the poems. There are ideas, but grasped more with feeling than with thought. Man is portrayed as exiled or outcast, though where he is exiled from (certainly not, in Semonides' case, an idealised Samos) or why (is it just in the nature of things?) Semonides does not explore. The image of an exile without a homeland has a metaphysical feel about it. It may mean little more (or less) than that any creature alive in time will always be sailing away: away from youth, from moments of love and happiness, but also from pain and terror. The journey ends not in a happy homeland but in death. The best a man can do is to pluck and retain pleasure when it is offered. Where Archilochus says "what the hell" and gets on with it, however, Semonides does not accept, even grudgingly, what fate provides. His voice rises in pitch and volume. Those notes of it we still hear, at least: the *Suda* credits him with a *History of Samos* which, with any other elegy he wrote, has perished.

The "Iambus on Women," rooted in folklore and Hesiod, in turn was a source for Phocylides of Miletus, the sixth-century BC poet, writing in elegiacs and hexameters. He may have borrowed passages from Semonides to flesh out his precepts and moral tags. He managed to insinuate his own name into the verses that survive. "Phocylides says this" is his refrain. The "Iambos" retained readers down the ages. It began its widest English currency when Joseph Addison, writing in *The Spectator* for 30 October 1711, displayed it to his polite readership with a slightly naughty twinkle in his eye. He starts by reflecting on how early art is simple, but as it progresses, "and the more we come downward towards our own times," this simplicity becomes concealed "in artifices and refinements, polished insensibly out of her original plainness, and at length entirely lost under form and ceremony." Nowhere is this decline into refinement more clear than in "the accounts of men and women as they are given us by the most ancient writers," which, says Addison, make one think that one is "reading the history of another species." For modern readers, the language of the early eighteenth century seems to rise from the lips of another species: we are closer to Semonides (we tend to think) than to Addison. Or are we merely more at home with Semonides' coarseness?

Among the early classics, Addison, as we would expect, feels most at home with satire, and his valuation of Semonides is consequently high. So high, indeed, that he gives his readers a prose version of the "Iambus." "Semonides, a poet famous in his generation, is I think author of the oldest satire that is now extant; and, as some say, of the first that was ever written." Decorousness is a later invention: Addison is intrigued by the indecorous choice of simile in the Greek: "the ancients, provided there was a likeness in their similitudes, did not much trouble themselves about the decency of the comparison." More didactic than his original, he warns his polite readers: "The subject of this satire is Woman. He describes the sex in their several characters, which he derives to them from a fanciful supposition upon the doctrine of pre-existence. He tells us, that the gods formed the souls of women out of those seeds and principles which compose several kinds of animals and elements; and that their good or bad dispositions arise in them according as such and such seeds and principles predominate in their constitutions." Addison certainly takes the whole performance seriously, much as Stobaeus must have done. "I have translated the author very faithfully, and if not word for word (which our language would not bear) at least so as to comprehend every one of his sentiments, without adding any of my own."[17] He may be attributing rather more intention to the original than it actually had; certainly a "doctrine of pre-existence" attributes more to the philosophical background of the poem than we can reasonably infer. Indeed, such an attribution is an anachronism.

The "Iambus on Women" is less about women as such, more about women in marriage, wives, and the unrewarding lottery involved in getting and keeping one. Critics who take it as a serious poem insist that it reveals much about Greek attitudes to women. How typical, one must ask, is the (surely ironic) description, intended for a symposium on the easternmost Cycladic island, Amorgos, and composed in the seventh or sixth century BC, of Greek male views about women? The poem does suggest that nine out of ten types of women are a plague; in giving negative types, like all good satire, it suggests by contrast positive types of married women.

In Hesiod we read of the birth of Pandora, the divine retribution for Prometheus' sin in bringing fire to man. She is *kalon kakon,* "beautiful evil," like the woman Semonides compares to a mare (lines 67–68). Pandora is responsible, like Eve, for visiting evil on the world and for driving a terminal wedge between man and the gods, who, until that time, had existed in a kind of ecological balance. The story of Pandora expresses a widespread sense of the inconstancy and duplicity of women, an unreconstructed male perspective. Helen, whose unstated name obliquely closes the fragment, is another paradigm for female wiles, evil and (or because) inconsistent. Semonides does not repeat either story, or Hesiod's longer catalogue, but he shows in his language and by thrifty allusion that the same figures are there in his mind and in his poem. He translates what he has learned from Hesiod into a different metre and into the terms of animal fable.

Addison translates the first line of the "Iambus on Women" in a rather orotund way, appropriate to the Augustan eighteenth century, which clad every native brick wall it encountered with marble: "In the beginning God made the souls of woman kind out of different materials, and in a separate state from their bodies." The Biblical inflection gives his version an authority quite out of keeping with the ambiguous, even imprecise, opening which the modern Englishman M. L. West renders, "God made diverse the ways of womankind"; and the American Diane Arnson Svarlien, "From the start, the gods made women different." Is it God or gods? Are they creating types, or women? Is this something that occurred at the beginning of mankind, something unalterably given? The poet is less interested in metaphysics and process than in the product. Immediately, without apology, we pass from the peremptory introduction to woman as pig.

Addison's sow is figurative, she is still in the region of the spirit: "The souls of one kind of women were formed out of those ingredients which compose a swine. A woman of this make is a slut in her house, and a glutton at her table. She is uncleanly in her person, a slattern in her dress, and her family is no better than a dunghill." Svarlien goes the whole hog, as it were, towards vulgarity, and her rendition is effective but too coarse for the formalised diction of Semonides' original:

> One type is from a pig—a hairy sow
> whose house is like a rolling heap of filth;
> and she herself, unbathed, in unwashed clothes,
> reposes on the shit-pile, growing fat.

West makes the sow-woman neither a soul nor a type but an actual extension of the pig she resembles, and he retains a decorousness in his diction which is truer to the original than Svarlien's guttural version:

> One he created from a hairy sow;
> in her house everything's a mess of filth
> rolling about untidy on the floor,
> and she herself, unwashed, in dirty clothes,
> eats herself fat and wallows in the muck.

Addison's "family" vanishes in both the modern translations. The sow is plain and childless sow. "Filth" and "muck" seem more appropriate farmyard diction than "shit"; and West's avoidance of the language of simile is a sensible strategy: we are already in the zone of integrated metaphorical language.

The sow is followed by the wily vixen, notable for being changeable and contrary, praising evil and denigrating good. Then comes the bitch, perpetually on heat or in pup, getting her nose into everyone's business. Addison omits some importantly brutal lines. The man can't stop the bitch from barking and prying, not with threats or with violence, in anger knocking her teeth out with a stone, nor by means of gentler persuasion. The order of Semonides' unavailing correctives is odd, the way in which some human relationships work, from threat to violence to wheedling (when wheedling comes too late).

Next comes the waddling clay creature, without a sense of good or ill, possessing only appetite. And, Semonides adds, forgetting that he has given us no visual sense of this particular woman, when it is frosty she's quick to draw her chair up to the fire. So she is not animal at all, but like the rest of us made of clay. This switching off of the basic formal conceit, abandoning metaphor when there is no appropriate figure to convey the sense the poet intends, is one fault of Semonides, as of Hipponax. Their language is only conditionally figurative: if they have something to say that cannot be figuratively accommodated, they abandon the figure rather than bend what we might call the underlying prose sense. In satire there usually is an underlying sense of this kind.

Nowhere is this more evident than in the fifth comparison: woman is like the sea, changeable: one day dazzling and calm so a visitor declares her the finest wife in all the world, the next day stormy, "raging mad / like a bitch over her puppies"[18] (an intriguing but hardly appropriate back-reference within the metaphor). Semonides repeats the calm-and-storm image (this time with people sailing on the changeable waters). He affirms that some women are like this, but not—he adds—in their looks.[19] Such a quip, if that is what it is, drawing attention to the inappropriateness of the metaphor, having first teased out its thematic relevance, is undermining in the way that irony can be, the poet drawing attention to the artifice in order to withdraw a bit from it, to create a space between the saying and the sayer which helps to suggest a sense of complicity with the reader. It could be seen as a form of wry ingratiation, or as a serious poetic flaw, depending on whether we regard the poem as a symposium entertainment or a more public and thematically deliberated utterance.

Woman as an ass, grey and stolid and only slowly responsive to beating (what Addison renders, "upon the husband's exerting his authority"), trudging along and delivering the minimum energy, is next in the queue. She too is a great eater, all day, all night, all over the house, and she is sexually voracious to the extent that she will allow herself to be mounted by anyone. She is followed by the loathsome weasel (Addison makes her a cat), bad in bed but insatiable as well, a thief, and so ravenous that she eats the meat intended for holy sacrifice.

The mare is most familiar of Semonides' animal-women. She is vain, with her flowing mane; she refuses to work and wastes her time being beautiful. Again the figurative gives way to the literal here: she will not sieve, she will not deal with the chamberpots or cook or do any chores, yet because she is beautiful she makes men love her. She tends to bathe two or three times a day, she wears scent and combs and combs her lovely hair. She is suitable for a king—decorative, to be admired—but a waste of time and space in a normal household. She contrasts nicely with the rampant weasel, being sexually abstemious. Last of the negative portraits is the ape- or monkey-woman, most undesirable of all Zeus's malcreations. She is so ugly that everywhere she is laughed at. She has no neck to speak of, stiff joints, no rump, unlovable, but she knows what's what and gets her evil way (she spends her time plotting maliciously).

But blessed be he who finds himself a busy bee-woman, beyond blame: industrious, affectionate, constant, a good mother both in producing and rearing children (again the metaphorical value of the bee is forgotten, along with the sting). She is essentially good, no gossip but a proper and obedient life-companion to her husband.

It would have been a nice up-beat note to end on, even if the simile was, as before, unsustained. But no: Semonides recapitulates the negative theme: the other types are always there, lying in wait for unsuspecting grooms. "Yes," says West's Semonides, "the worst pestilence Zeus ever made / is women." Not a day passes in contentment or peace: women find a way of marring it; they break the rules of hospitality, and those that seem the best and most obedient harbour the deepest rancour. Remember: the Trojan War was fought because of a woman.

The problem with the long iambic fragment is that, though it is verse, the iambs effective and more or less regular, it is not poetry. Semonides does not have the courage of his conventions, not even to the degree that Hesiod did. It is the kernel of allegory, a beginning of systematic figuration, but only that. Its debts to folklore may be close, but it owes very little to the stable, the byre, the burrow; its ape never hung from a tree and its sea never bore a ship.

Is this the best Semonides has to offer? Probably not, though its subject guarantees the poet a certain notoriety. West's version of the first elegy is a beautiful and balanced statement about the unalloyed awfulness of life, the poet—having numbered them—declaring that, if he had his way, he would let go of such truths. Other fragments are about letting go as well: forgetting the dead, forgetting pain and evil deeds, leaving them behind, moving on, if not towards pleasure at least away from pain. There are tiny fragments of description: an eel squirmed down into the mud, another eel, caught by a buzzard, snatched away by a heron. And the poet travelled. The heron's eel in one poem was a delicacy from the river Maeander in Caria. When he is quoted by Athenaeus in *Scholars at Dinner,* we encounter a Tromilian cheese Semonides brought back from Achaea.[20] Food: food for birds and animals, food for men as well as for voracious women. Roasted pork, thigh bones, cups of wine, and in the end a ladleful of dregs.[21]

XI

Alcaeus of Mytilene

Amazing! Cerberus, lulled by those Alcaics
Pricks up the black ears on all his heads to harken
And the serpents twisted in the Harpies' tresses
Cease writhing and attend;

Prometheus, too, and Pelops' unhappy father[1]
Pause in their pointless labours, rapt a while;
Nor does Orion, all of a sudden, care
To track the lions or the shying lynxes.

HORACE, *Odes* 11.13

In 1881 Sir Lawrence Alma-Tadema painted a large neo-classical canvas entitled *Sappho and Alcaeus*. Sappho, chin on hands, hands and left forearm on a cushion, cushion on a low oak lectern, gazes enraptured at Alcaeus. Her laurel crown rests on the cushion as well, near her left elbow. Her features are borrowed from Greek statuary but her forehead is low. The hairdresser, whom she has visited quite recently, has fashioned her dark coil into a tight Victorian helmet. Beside her stands a blonde girl, probably her bright-haired daughter Cleis. Flanking them in the little amphitheatre are three more of Sappho's girls, two attentive, one gazing out to sea. Graffiti (in Greek of course) disfigure the marble surround, as though both poets, unable to contain themselves, have incontinently spilled their verses, or the names of their lovers, on every available surface. A twisting tree stands between us and a sea not wine-coloured but grey-blue like the eyes of Athena. On the horizon we can discern the Turkish coast. Then, at the right of the canvas, reclining on a comfortable chair and wearing a handsome toga, a hunting horn beneath him and an elaborate lyre on his lap, is Alcaeus, concentrating on the strings. He has beautiful feet.

This picture, portraying ancient Greece as a Mediterranean foretaste of the Victorian life to come, at least for the prosperous classes, is full of mistakes, architectural, sartorial, racial, biographical. Yet the lies it tells are of a kind that the Victorians were ready to believe: poets should be beautiful, the classical world should be familiar and prefigure their world, which revived and extended the classical. Alma-Tadema provides the technicolour equivalent of the plaster casts that decorated many a Victorian hall, avenue and summer house. And the imaginary model Alcaeus, ironically, survived the painter, coming to life again in the middle of the twentieth century when his *oeuvre* grew with the publication in 1955 of the Oxyrhynchus papyrus fragments identified as his verse.[2] The ancient Greek poets will never die entirely. The sands of Egypt guarantee that fragments will continue to surface for another millennium at least, extending and reshaping our sense of the Greek imagination.

In one respect Alma-Tadema was right: Alcaeus' name[3] is intimately linked with that of Sappho, though Alcaeus was probably rather older than she was and, Cicero and others suggest, for amorous purposes preferred the company of his own sex. Both were born on Lesbos, they were near contemporaries, each invented an eponymous prosodic form (Alcaics, Sapphics), both experienced exile. The surviving fragments of their poems, in the Aeolic dialect, use much the same diction, many of the same forms and tropes, and raise similar textual problems. Indeed, scholars dispute the attribution of certain fragments, and two or three dozen bright shards of language are attributed to a composite author, "Sappho or Alcaeus": *incertum utrius auctoris fragmenta.*[4] Alcaeus was possibly more prolific than Sappho. Almost three times as many fragments of and attestations to his work survive, some 450. When he died, it is said that he left behind, either in memory or on papyrus, a body of work sufficient to have filled four Loeb Classic volumes—five times as much as survives of Theocritus, more than twice as much as his greatest admirer, Horace.[5] In his *Epistles,* after preferring Alcaeus to Archilochus because of his better subject-matter, the Roman declares: "I, Latium's lyric singer, have introduced Alcaeus to the public: no mouth had uttered his songs here before me."[6]

Alcaeus is not a poet of love in the sense that Sappho is. There is desire and passion in his verse, and venom; debauchery is not absent from the drinking songs. He also has moments of serenity and philosophical clarity. Though not primarily a love lyricist, he knows what love is; he is, on the one hand, a good-time poet, and on the other, a survival poet, enduring exile and hardships with a definite sense of home and a fitful but compelling sense of justice. And there is a civic aspect to his work, too. As Sappho composed epithalamia and marriage poems, Alcaeus wrote hymns: to Castor and Polydeuces,[7] to Hermes and others.

Greek and Roman teachers of rhetoric and grammarians made much of his poems of invective and attack in which he levelled against tyrants. Some even present him as a radical and reformer, a champion of the people against usurping leaders. This is a falsification of the actual poet whose hostility to tyranny was, like Sappho's, less principled than self-interested. He is more an elegiac patrician, like Theognis of Megara, than a man of social vision. His political poems survive in such fragmentary form that it is hard to reconstruct the voice of protest which meant so much to his classical successors. What we can begin to reconstruct is a brilliant poet of wine, its virtues and consequences; of the symposium and its pleasures; of the passing of youth; of survival.

This Alcaeus, mature in years but always young at heart, even when the hairs upon his chest have turned grey,[8] is a vital lyric presence, less enigmatic and less *emblematic,* but no less a virtuoso, than Sappho. He is followed by the ghosts of his dear friends, Melanippus, Bacchis, Agesilaidas, Aesimidas, Menon, Dinnomenes. Anacreon's libido is more clearly revealed than Alcaeus', but however gently and circumspectly he expresses himself, the note that is struck, as more forcefully in Solon and Ibycus, Anacreon and Theognis, and then in Pindar, is homosexual.

Alcaeus' father may have been called Cicis: one of his brothers certainly bore that name, perhaps the eldest.[9] Another brother, almost as famous as Alcaeus in ancient times but in another field, was Antimenidas, the great fighter. His prowess was celebrated by Alcaeus, the man of words imbuing the man of action with immortality in verse. The poem is now almost lost. According to the historian Strabo, writing half a millennium after the events, it recalled how, fighting on the side of the Babylonians, probably under Nebuchadrezzar,[10] in the campaign against Ascalon, Antimenidas confronted in single battle a foe who was "only one palm's breadth short of five royal cubits." Like David in combat with Goliath, Antimenidas was victorious and rescued his comrades. Strabo quotes a line—the only surviving line—from the poem: "From the earth's furthest corner you've arrived, the hilt of your sword done up with gold."[11]

The second-century AD rhetorician Aelius Aristides quotes "words that Alcaeus the poet uttered long since," namely, "cities aren't stone or wood or the skill of labourers; wherever men know how to protect themselves, ramparts and cities stand."[12] Though Alcaeus' brothers knew how to defend themselves, Alcaeus, by his own account, did not. Herodotus recalls how during the struggle for Sigeum the Mytilenean Pittacus prevailed against the Athenian general by means of a clever ploy he might have learned from Hephaestus, who employed a net to ensnare his wife, Aphrodite, *in flagrante* with her lover Ares. He caught the Athenian in a net and slew him. But Alcaeus, in another encounter during the same campaign, threw away his armour and fled.[13] This image, already familiar from Archilochus, though Archilochus was a mercenary and Alcaeus was fighting for his own city, recommended itself to Horace. He takes it up in a famous ode, justifying his own similar action. You can replace armour; it is harder to get another life.

Alcaeus, possibly the youngest of the brothers, was the eloquent one. Strabo admires his assault on the Mytilenean tyrants. There was a succession of them in and just before his time. Their effect he famously compared to waves bursting against the bows of a weakened ship. The image becomes a figure, the figure represents the city-state. In one fragment, scholars conjecture that the assaulting weather represents the storms and strifes of civil war.[14]

The first tyrant against whom he may have plotted was Myrsilus. Under him he suffered his first exile, in Pyrrha.[15] Myrsilus was followed by Melanchrus, then the Cleanactids, and most especially his family's one-time ally Pittacus, against whom Sappho's people, too, hardened their hearts. Yet whatever Alcaeus has to say about the matter, Pittacus was different in kind from his predecessors. Alcaeus' family must have thought so too, at first, since both Cicis and Antimenidas fought alongside him against Melanchrus. But Pittacus, who became one of the Seven Sages and has attributed to him some famous aphorisms,[16] used his time in power not to advance the interests of those who helped him seize it; rather, he set out to weaken and defeat the contrary factions that had riven Mytilene. Sappho's and Alcaeus' families were implicated in these factions, and their defeat occasioned the poets' exiles. Alcaeus was in Egypt for a time[17] and probably knew Boeotia. "Choose the appropriate moment," said Pittacus. "Cultivate the appropriate friends."

Pittacus fought in the war against Athens when Athens seized the fortress of Sigeum at the entrance to the Hellespont. Then Pittacus killed the tyrant Myrsilus in single combat. He was elected by the Mytileneans to be *aisymnetes,* a tyrant chosen, initially, by plebiscite, a legitimate dictator, in 590 BC. He may have gone to Sardis to negotiate with Croesus, who, having annexed the coastal towns of western Asia Minor, was casting a golden eye on the islands. When Pittacus had achieved what he was elected to do, and carried through his own reforms, like Solon he withdrew to a decade of studious retirement. His city, with a restored sense of balance, got on with its business, which was at this time—business.

The people chose Pittacus, but because of Alcaeus the poet, Pittacus has had a bad press in afterlife. Aristotle says in the *Politics,* quoting the poet himself: "as tyrant of that coward bad-luck city they set up low-born Pittacus, and every one of them sang out his virtues."[18] Part of the tyrant's sin was his low birth (relative to Alcaeus'), part his treachery in having civic principles and vision. According to Diogenes Laertius,[19] Alcaeus was especially unpleasant about the tyrant's appearance, starting at ground level: he was "drag-foot" and "chap-foot" (suggesting that he was lame or splay-footed and chilblained); "mincer" because of the way he moved about; "pot-" and "big-bellied" because he was; "dusk-diner," "because he did not use a lamp"; and "well-swept," "since he was slovenly and dirty." Such puerile invective combined with sophisticated and substantial allegations and durable rhetorical strategies. Dionysius of Halicarnassus remarks: "Consider Alcaeus, how he evinces nobility, succinctness and generosity together with vigour; and where he uses metaphors how directly he communicates, except when his [Aeolic] dialect betrays him. Consider in particular the tone of the poems that deal with political themes. Without the prosody, they would be mere political rhetoric."[20] When we get to the great teacher of rhetoric, Quintilian, in the first century AD, we find Alcaeus transformed into the doughty tyrant-attacker, worthy of the golden plectrum, a contributor to moral education, even though "he declined into light-heartedness and songs made out of love, though he was destined for higher things."[21] And Horace in the *Odes* speaks of "Alcaeus' threatening songs."[22]

According to Diodorus Siculus,[23] Pittacus actually managed to capture Alcaeus. Instead of executing him, he let him go, because "forgiveness yields a better return than revenge." It was around 580 BC, after which the poet, we may assume, began to enjoy a serene and bibulous old age. Pittacus' refusal to punish Alcaeus, like his relinquishing power willingly after a decade of reforms, can be set in the balance against Alcaeus' bitter words. Whatever his birth, colour, diet or way of walking, he managed to find and occupy, with dignity, the moral high ground, and a mere poet could not compete with such a lenient exercise of temporal power. If Alcaeus managed to live on and die of old age, it was due in large part to the political changes Pittacus introduced.

Well might Pittacus have admired the sounds made by the poems of Sappho and Alcaeus, his disgruntled subjects. Alcaeus was a melic poet, like Sappho, composing personal and choral lyrics. Unlike other, earlier, forms of verse his admitted the personal and the emotional, even when his intentions were didactic and satirical. But "personal" and "emotional" should not suggest a poetry that is merely subjective or romantic in tenor. In the strophic compositions, very complex rhythms are closely integrated with music (*melos,* hence "melic"), and the words were intended to be sung or recited with accompaniment in symposia, the intimacy of the evening entertainment. The poems of exile, like the poems of wine, assume not a single reader but a small, informed and sympathetic audience. One critic suggests that in melic poetry we have a point of departure for the first-person, subjective and finally bourgeois lyric. This overlooks the context for which the poems were composed, the necessity of musical accompaniment, and the fact that the emotions and the "personal" elements were shared by the symposium participants. Though modern readers may at first find Sappho and Alcaeus familiar and approachable, the danger of appropriation and misreading is real. Yeats said that lyric poems are not "heard" but "overheard." Greek melic poetry is *heard*.

Like Sappho, Alcaeus was an inventor. He may have invented Alcaics, one of Horace's favourite measures for verse, with a movement which more or less reverses that of the Sapphic. An Alcaic stanza looks like this:

u— u— u— uu— u—
u— u— u— uu— u—
u— u— u— u— u
—uu —uu —u —u

Arthur Hugh Clough's English experiment, "Alcaics," makes the form sound like this (we read for length rather than accent or stress):

> So spake the voice: and as with a single life
> Instinct, the whole mass, fierce, irretainable,
> Down on that unsuspecting host swept;
> Down, with the fury of winds, that all night
> Upbrimming, sapping slowly the dyke, at dawn
> Fall through the breach o'er holmstead and harvest; and
> Heard roll a deluge: while the milkmaid
> Trips i' the dew, and remissly guiding
> Morn's first uneven furrow, the farmer's boy
> Dreams out his dream; so, over the multitude
> Safe-tented, uncontrolled and uncon-
> trollably sped the Avenger's fury.

The Alcaic form is more complex than the Sapphic:

—u —u —uu —u —u
—u —u —uu —u —u
—u —u —uu —u —u
—uu —u

Thomas Hardy accommodates the metre with some archness and archaism, but to unusual effect, in his "The Temporary the All."

> Change and chancefullness in my flowering youthtime,
> Set me sun by sun near to one unchosen;
> Wrought us fellowlike, and despite divergence,
> Fused us in friendship.
>
> "Cherish him can I while the true one forthcome—
> Come the rich fulfiller of my prevision;
> Life is roomy yet, and the odds unbounded."
> So self-communed I.
>
> 'Thwart my wistful way did a damsel saunter,
> Fair, albeit unformed to be all-eclipsing;
> "Maiden meet," held I, "till arise my forefelt
> Wonder of women."

Long a visioned hermitage deep desiring,
Tenements uncouth I was fain to house in:
"Let such lodging be for a breath-while," thought I,
    "Soon a more seemly.

"Then high handiwork will I make my life-deed,
Truth and Light outshow; but the ripe time pending,
Intermissive aim at the thing sufficeth."
    Thus I . . . But lo, me!

Mistress, friend, place, aims to be bettered straightway,
Bettered not has Fate or my hand's achievement;
Sole the showance those of my onward earth-track—
    Never transcended!

In Sapphics the movement is from long to short (analogous to the English movement from stress to unstress), a downward movement or diminution. In Alcaics the movement is from short to long in the first two lines, from short to short in the third, and from long to short in the fourth (reversals within the stanza and then between the lines themselves). Alcaics require a rather different kind of voice, a different music, than Sapphics.

One Alcaic ode, of which only the opening survives, appears to be addressed to Sappho; and there is a fragment of what may have been her reply. Between the two there is a kind of oblique dialogue which can feel like a friendship if we imagine their age, their dialect, the similarity between their antecedents and their responses to power.

Why should Alcaics be more complex than Sapphics? Perhaps because they stem from rather a different tradition. Alcaeus is indebted to a form called the *scolion,* invented (legend says) by Terpander (also) of Lesbos. The Greek word *scolios* (plural *scolia*) means "tortuous," and *scolion* is an early form of drinking song, performed at symposia, a growing challenge as the wine-bowl circulated. Alcaeus, Anacreon, then Pindar were noted for them.

Drink, Melanippus, with me, let's get drunk.
When once you've crossed the swirling[24] Acheron

Do you actually believe you'll see again the fair
Sun's light? No point in aiming high. The son

Of Aeolus himself, regal Sisyphus the sage
Came to think that he had bested Death; even so,

Twice, though he was smart, he crossed the swirling
River, twice because fate said he must. And Zeus

Child of Cronus, made a torture for him under ground.
Do not strive; now you are young, fit to endure

Whatever trials God throws at us . . .[25]

Thus the poet, with a mixture of wry sophistry and real philosophical resignation, urges his friend—the same friend to whom he confessed his failure in battle—to turn his time to pleasurable account. As Horace would say later, in an Alcaic mood, "Pluck the day."

Another fragment celebrates the river Hebrus (now called Maritza), flowing through Thrace, and the maidens bathing in it, laving their thighs "with gentle hands"; they touch and use "your wonderful water like an ointment."[26] The image intends to give us a sense of the texture of their skin beneath their hands: it is erotically charged. Other poems begin emphatically: "The story says," or with a vocative and then an invocation. "Pour balm over my brow, it has endured so much, and pour it over my grey chest . . ."[27] From such an altering beginning flows a story, and then a moral. Yes, Aesop was a man of Lesbos, too.

Another genre Alcaeus develops is the poem of civil war and exile, called *stasiotika*. One such poem is a prayer and invocation, spoken ostensibly by the people of Mytilene, to Zeus and Hera and to Dionysus, against pot-bellied Pittacus.[28] More subtle—hesitating, as it were, between the *scolion* and the *stasiotic* genres—are those poems which seem to belong to a rueful time when the poet would like to celebrate but history keeps calling him back to a world of dire events—rather like Sappho's wonderful poem about the marriage of Hector and Andromache, around which hovers the eventual fact (the poem does not directly mention it) of the Trojan War. One of Alcaeus' most powerful (and best preserved) poems is similar in texture.

The story tells it, Helen, how harsh woe befell
King Priam and his sons because of you, and Zeus
Afflicted sacred Ilium with fire. Such a girl
        Was not the tender virgin whom Aeacus'

Noble son,[29] inviting all the exalted gods of heaven
To witness their rites, wed, and took away
From Nereus home to Chiron, there undid
        Her virgin band, and Peleus' love found out

The best of Nereus' daughters. In a year she bore
A son, best demigod, graced charioteer, his team
Of chestnut horses. But on Helen's account
        All perished, all the Phrygians and their city . . .[30]

This may be a whole poem, starting and ending with Helen and destruction, but at the heart of it abide the happy marriage and the brave, incomparable infant.

The *stasiotic* poems borrow the Homeric authority of the Trojan War to talk about "present day" Mytilene and its problems, an indirection poets often practise, saying one thing to mean another. Thus we encounter a procession of beautiful women in the precinct of Hera, the sounds they make,[31] or Alcaeus celebrates the Hall of War in a passage which recalls the warriors' hall in *Beowulf*.[32] Another fragment[33] focuses again on Helen. Most powerfully Homeric is the fragment in which Ajax rapes one of Athena's suppliants in her very temple during the siege of Troy.[34] Are we expected to read Pittacus for Ajax, and Mytilene for the ravaged woman? In Homer (or in the later epic *The Sack of Troy*) Cassandra, the never-believed truthtelling prophetess, is the one whom Ajax violates.

The mighty fall, the exile returns home. Athenaeus says that Alcaeus "is discovered drinking all the time no matter what the circumstances: ... 'Now men must lose themselves in drink, and drink with all their might: Myrsilus's dead.'"[35] Back to the *scolion* and the drinking jar, or *skyphos*, brimming with lightly watered wine. "Don't give up your spirits at a time of sorrow, grief doesn't get you anywhere, Bycchis; the best cure is get wine and then get drunk."[36]

Even in the civic poems, the metaphorical expressions seem to draw on the culture of wine. To join battle, for example,[37] is "mingling" or "mixing Ares with each other": Does this evoke the mingling of wine and water or wine and another wine?

> Let's drink! Why wait for lights? Only the merest
> Inch of day remains. Comrade, take that big ornate cup.
>
> The child of Semele and Zeus granted men wine
> So they'd let sorrow go. Mix in one part
>
> Water, two parts wine, pour to the brim,
> Then cheers! Let's toast with our full cups . . .[38]

And so, as the companions quaff another *skyphos*, with beaded bubbles winking at the brim, the poet declares, "Zeus lets rain fall, a tempest bursts from heaven . . . Stoke the fire, mix the honeyed wine, don't stint, bind a soft band around your brow."[39] Unstinting? It can go too far. Proclus, writing on Hesiod, compares a poem by Alcaeus to a passage in Hesiod's *Works and Days* (lines 582ff.). Alcaeus writes: "Wash your lungs with wine: here comes the dog star, scorching the weather, everything thirsts in the heat, among the foliage sweetly the cicada plays its voice . . . the thistle flowers;

women are at their plaguey worst, men feeble, because Sirius bakes dry their pates and their knees . . ."[40] Is this a deliberate imitation of Hesiod? It is one of the few moments in Alcaeus when he attacks women: usually he looks towards them with an unenthusiastic but unjaundiced eye. Excess may be the cause: "and if . . . wine snares his brain, he won't need catching; bowing down his head, repeatedly blaming his very heart, regretting what he says; but that's gone for good."[41] Wine brings three things for which Alcaeus uses almost the same word, *epialtes:* stomach disorder, fever and nightmare.[42] Yet wine makes a man honest, as in the Alcaic proverb, taken up later by Theocritus, "Wine, my dear young fellow, and the truth."[43] It also makes a man visible in ways he might not wish: "for wine makes a spy-hole into a man."[44]

Such lines are aphoristic, the sort of thing we get from Ben Jonson in *Timber* or from the French epigrammatists who deliver depth-charges masked as clichés: "If you tell what you like, you may hear back what you dislike,"[45] or squibs about the importance of money[46] and the un-pardonable, almost impertinent base grievousness of poverty.[47] Clearly Alcaeus is a moralist, and clearly he is of his class. This does not preclude wisdom in his utterances, a wisdom underscored by balance and melody in expression. Plutarch, in *On Love and Wealth*,[48] remembers a passage from Alcaeus which we might expect from Stendhal's *De l'amour* or, in a different kind of context, from Proust: "For it's a comfort that when pleasure starts to fail, desires, which Alcaeus claims not man or woman ever got away from, start to fail at the same time."

Alcaeus was regarded as an undisputed classic and his poems were subjected to the scrupulous and methodical editing of one of the scholars at the great library in Alexandria around 200 BC. Aristophanes of Byzantium[49] began the task, and, forty years later, Aristarchus completed it. They divided the poems into ten books, it seems (there are no references to books after volume ten), dividing them not as Sappho's editors did, in accordance with prosodic form and genre, but rather according to subject matter.

The first poem in the first book of Sappho opens with a dedicatory invocation to Aphrodite, daughter of Zeus; Alcaeus' may have begun with an invocation to Apollo, son of Zeus. This symmetry between them is significant. It is useful to read Sappho and Alcaeus together if we wish to guard against some of the "excessive readings" of Sappho that modern critics can offer. If a genuinely radical feminist reading of Sappho is possible, for example, if there is a discernible difference in kind between Sappho's verse and that of her male contemporaries, would the confusion between fragments of her *oeuvre* and those of her contemporaries exist? The fact that Sappho's and Alcaeus' lines can effectively be interchanged in so many instances, and not only when the poems have for their occasion the civic disturbances of Mytilene, would seem to tell against a rigorous feminist reading. So too does Alcaeus' celebration of women and woman, in terms not remote from Sappho's. He also writes one poem[50] in the voice of a woman—or is the poem in fact by Sappho?

We learn indirectly, from the second-century AD prosodist Hephaistion (*On Critical Signs*), something about the manuscript tradition in which the poems of Alcaeus and the other early poets were written down on papyrus in Alexandria and elsewhere. "Among lyric poets, if a poem is monostrophic, a paragraph sign marks the end of each strophe. The *coronis* or curved flourish is at the end of the poem . . . An asterisk is generally used if the following poem is in a different metre, as in the monostrophic poems of Sappho, Anacreon and Alcaeus . . ."[51]

What matters to poetry readers is form, prosody and the moments of felt visualisation that stay in mind, whether they come to us in Greek or in English translation. The cicada, for example, "pours ceaselessly its pure singing from beneath its wings, as burning summer . . ."[52] And in the fourth century AD, the rhetorician Himerus in his *Orations* summarises a poem which must have been one of the most perfect in the melic tradition.[53] It was about Apollo, and perhaps stood first in the first book. Apollo returns in the midst of summer to Delphi. "Now summer has come, the very heart of summer, when Alcaeus brings the god home from the Hyperboreans: in the glare of summer and in Apollo's presence Alcaeus' lyre assumes a summer wantonness as he sings of the god: nightingales warble the sort of song you'd expect birds to warble in Alcaeus, and swallows and cicadas, declaring not their own circumstances but talking of Apollo in their songs. Castalia streams by in a poetic current, silver waters, Cephisos floods, rising with his waves, like Homer's Enupeus: Alcaeus, like Homer,[54] must grant even to water the sense to register the presence of the god." We are back to Homer, but more important, we are in a world in which even ostensibly inanimate things like water, which we believe has movement but no life, are imbued with sense, enough to attest to the presence of the god.

XII

Sappho of Eressus

It is Sappho whom you cover, Aeolian earth, she who among the
    immortal Muses
  Is renowned as the mortal Muse . . .
                . . . Winding the three-part thread,
Fates, on your spindles, was there a reason you did not spin
    for her a frayless thread,
  She who composed eternal offerings for the Heliconian Muses?

ANTIPATER OF SIDON, *c.* 100 BC,
Testimonium 27 in the Palatine Anthology

 Gaius Verres was a despicable public administrator. Appointed
propraetor[1] of Sicily from 73 to 71 BC, he outdid his predecessors in avarice and the injustice of his regime. The young Cicero, already an experienced advocate and familiar with Sicily,
where he had been quaestor in 75 BC, was retained by the people of the island to press charges against Verres. Keen to weaken the interests of the
corrupt old order and improve the government of the province, Cicero
could not have wished for a better illustration than Verres of the system's
unaccountability, its perviousness to human shortcomings. In a devastating
preamble, he summarised the charges he intended to level against the de-
fendant, who, rather than face the force of Cicero's onslaught, packed his
bags and went into exile.

"Packed his bags" is too modest an expression for what he did. In fact,
he took away in his caravan to long exile in Massilia "half the wealth of
Sicily," a collection of treasure so valuable that Antony himself coveted it
and had Verres' name added to the list of the proscribed. (Cicero's name, as
fate would have it, appeared on the same proscription list.) Verres, it is said,
was murdered, demonstrating how a larger consumes a smaller cupidity.

The people of Syracuse had set up in the town hall a statue of "the Tenth
Muse," as Plato called her,[2] the poet Sappho, carved by Silanion in the fourth
century BC, "so perfect, so gracious, so meticulously finished," Cicero said.
This famous piece was among the works of art that Verres carted off, though
he failed to carry off the plinth with its inscription, hence his theft was itself
monumental and is known forever. The statue has vanished altogether.

Why is the most famous poet of Lesbos, an island so far to the east that it
almost abuts Turkey, associated with Syracuse and Sicily, a sea and a half
away? Was this first, greatest Greek woman writer driven there by love,

exile, the colonial programme of her city? Did marriage, or an attempt to flee marriage, take her so far from home? Was her presence in Sicily a legend merely? And what had she to do with Epirus, on the Greek west coast, and did she plunge to her death, ballasted by a broken heart?

Verres stole the statue, but an image of Sappho survives in Munich, on a *crater,* or wine-mixing bowl, attributed to the Brygos painter, from about 470 BC.[3] It shows her contemporary Alcaeus with a harp, his bearded face concentrating on the music he is making, while Sappho looks back at him over her shoulder. She responds to what he is playing, judging from the way her body is inclined to sway into a dance, but she restrains herself. This is not the woman described in the Oxyrhynchus papyrus from around AD 200 as "despicable and very ill-favoured, of dark complexion and very short."[4] This scrawled caricature of Sappho reflects a judgement on her "base" moral character, the stunted body mirroring a perverted spirit.

Later writers[5] say that Sappho invented a type of lyre, the *pectis,* and the plectrum.[6] She and Anacreon certainly mentioned the *baromos* and the *barbitos* (Ezra Pound refers to "Sappho's barbitos" in "Hugh Selwyn Mauberley," a satire and lament for the decline in culture, Sappho being a high-water mark). Other ancient instruments included the *magadis,* the *trigonon* and the *sambuke.*[7] In fragment 214c we hear, fleetingly, "the clatter of castanets." Historians of music like to suggest that Sappho added not only to the instrumental resources but also to the development of composition. Plutarch declares: "The Mixolydian mode is full of feeling and appropriate to tragedy. Aristoxenus claims Sappho invented it, and the tragic poets learned it from her."[8]

These facts and suppositions are interesting but remote. Why read Sappho today? She is, even among the first Greek poets, an incomparable artist, innovative in her techniques, unique in sensibility. Even in translation it is possible to sense the force of her thinking, the way in which she feels a way through experience with the special language that poetry devised. She brings this language, in the strict prosodies she invented, and with a subtle sense of phrasing and the sounds words make, a quite perfect "pitch" when it comes to the modulation of vowels and the patterning of appropriate consonants, as close as a language can come to the experiences of which she writes. Even when her language draws on conventional elements—the moon, the sea, time passing—she imparts to them a sense of the contingent world, of a voice which inhabits a pulsing body, a body which is alive in time.

The mysterious first-century AD book entitled *Longinus on the Sublime,* addressed to the unknown author's friend Postumius Terentianus, is a fine anthology of quotations and penetrating criticism, possessing a directness and intimacy we miss in turgid grammarians. "Are you not amazed?" he exclaims, and we are. He preserves a substantial fragment of Sappho's most famous poem, imitated by the Roman poets and translated by many European and American writers.[9] The poem is composed in the eponymous Sapphic stanza, in which the emphases are distributed quite strictly in the pattern outlined on page 164. "Where," asks *On the Sublime,* "does Sappho best show her qualities? In her skill in choosing and combining the crucial and the unbridled accompaniments [of the madness of love]." He is interested in how she reifies the senses, so that she can freeze and burn, be irrational (even mad) and sane, at the same time: "we witness in her not singled out emotion but a confluence." His version of the poem begins, "To me he appears as blessed as the gods." There is a variation preserved elsewhere which makes the opening more forceful still: "To himself he appears more blessed than the gods."[10] Love is real, but its reality is subjective and confined. This is one of Sappho's themes. William Carlos Williams gets closest, among the moderns, both to the tenor of the poem and to the metre:

> Peer of the gods is that man, who
> face to face, sits listening
> to your sweet speech and lovely
>   laughter.
>
> It is this that rouses a tumult
> in my breast. At mere sight of you
> my voice falters, my tongue
>   is broken.
>
> Straightway, a delicate fire runs in
> my limbs; my eyes
> are blinded and my ears
>   thunder.
>
> Sweat pours out: a trembling hunts
> me down. I grow paler
> than dry grass and lack little
>   of dying.

That grass at the end can be read differently: Davenport and other translators insist that the jealous speaker is grass-green with envy. And there is the fragment of another line that Williams, like most translators, omits because it mars the lyric closure—quite effectively, in fact. Davenport renders it, "But endure, even this grief of love."

Something remarkable *happens* when Sappho says, in West's translation, "You came, and I was longing for you; you cooled my heart which was burning with desire."[11] The beloved arrives, even unasked, seeming to anticipate the lover's need. Such a use of language is enactive, bringing the subject and object into a tense and whole harmony of being. The lines survive because Julian the Apostate, the Roman emperor and cousin of Constantine who reverted to pagan Hellenism when he came to power, quotes them in a letter to the neo-Platonist Syrian philosopher Iambicus in the fourth century AD: some of Sappho's language of love can be invested in mystical and philosophical themes. There are passages, however, which belong only and potently in the realm of human desire and fulfilment. "Desire has shaken my mind, like a wind that thrashes mountain trees."[12] Those who are untouched by love, human or divine, are to be pitied, Artemis for example: "Love (that loosens the limbs) never visits her."[13]

"That loosens the limbs": the compound word *lusimeles* combines *lusi,* which in other combinations suggests relaxing, easing, even (for childbirth) dilating, bringing peace, freeing from exhaustion, and *meles,* which means limb but also comes to imply melody, tune; the phrase contains everything from the melting power of love to the movement—almost inadvertent—into dance. She uses the phrase again. Hephaistion of Alexandria in the second century AD quotes it in his *Handbook of Metres* to epitomise a particular prosody:[14] "Once more love that loosens the limbs makes me quiver all over: the irresistible one, both kind and unkind."[15] Was Hephaistion himself moved when, into his dry book of definitions, he introduced this grain of ancient, living passion?

Words of one of her poems, or a corruption of them, survive on an amphora attributed to Euphronios (around 510 BC, some forty years after the poet's death). They emerge as song from the lips of a full-featured, beardless young man who plays his harp, and the letters ascend in a curl around his face and head, a sort of faint halo-scroll. Could this be Cybisthus, or Execestides,[16] the nephew of the ruler, poet and sage Solon of Athens, Sappho's near contemporary? When the boy had sung one of Sappho's exquisite lyrics, Solon commanded that he sing it once again, "so I might take it to heart and die."[17] The youth on the vase is singing *mameokapoteo,* which may be Sappho's *maomai kai potheo,* "I suffer, I desire."[18]

The vase is a lovely evocation of the symposium, the youth entertaining the bearded men with a lyric in the literal sense of the word, a poem sung to the accompaniment of a lyre; the lyre clearly made—as tradition says the first one was—from a good, resonating tortoise-shell.[19]

We are used to Greek pot painters naming their characters so that we will not confuse the story they depict. Sometimes on pots that celebrate the pleasures of the symposium they go a step further, making words emerge quite naturally from the symposiast's mouth: he sings as part of the composition itself. The images speak to us not only as imagery but also as language.

And her own images? Are they distinct in some way from those of her male contemporaries and successors? Is it part of her sensibility as a

woman, or simply an inheritance from Homer, whose world is one of textures, scents and sounds, that she so often dwells upon the specifics of
cloth, of apparel, the things which women make and with which they make
themselves beautiful to others, to one another? The gods and goddesses are
generally well turned out when they appear: they glow in their skin and in
their accoutrements. Pollux in his *Vocabulary* says Sappho was the first poet
to use the word *clamus* in poetry, meaning "mantle" or "robe."[20] He also
quotes a line, "and dressed every inch of her in soft shag" (pieces of close-
woven linen).[21] This detail is extremely specific. She talks of hand cloths
which are used as head scarves.[22] A one-word fragment survives,[23] *beudos,* or
"shift," which Pollux says is the same as *kimberikon,* "a short diaphanous
dress"; she speaks, too, of the *gruta,* or "vanity-bag."[24]

She talks of the Graces' arms as being "rosy,"[25] which is striking and
humanising, until we find her calling Dawn—sometimes "golden-
sandalled"[26]—"rosy-armed" as well, perhaps remembering Homer's rosy-
fingered dawn, and the Moon too is rosy-fingered. Is the rosy-fingered
moon a wry reversal of the Homeric epithet? In fragment 92, the few remaining opening words reveal an autumn wardrobe: robe, saffron, purple
robe, cloak, garlands . . . purple.

A fascination with textures and elements of dress is certainly a mark of
Sappho, whose poems have a specific quality greater, in relation to the object world, than Alcaeus' and most of her contemporaries'. For her the
physical world exists, and though elements in it are emblematic and stand
for other things, they retain their primary character as well. Such features respond well to feminist criticism, and yet Homer's poetry would render the
approach an even richer yield. Where direct thematic parallels might be
thought to exist between Homer and Sappho, a difference of tone, as much
as of scale, is evident. One poem evokes a happy return to Troy, when Hector brought his beloved Andromache back from Cyprus as his bride.[27] It is a
wedding poem, like so many of Sappho's, but also a kind of anti-*Iliad* or
anti-*Odyssey.* No singer of the song would have been unaware of the later
story of which this joyful chapter was a prelude. There is no war as such in
Sappho, except a sweet engagement of hearts and bodies.

What of her own character? She does not have a "voice" or a marked personality in the way that modern poets seek to do, often fabricating an identity
through eccentricities of language. There is nothing deliberately "I am"
about Sappho, whatever we make of the feelings her poems convey. Yet
from the many tones audible in her work we can deduce a complex and lively
imagination. The first poem in the traditional sequence of her work, a modern editor surmises, is quoted by Dionysius of Halicarnassus in *On Literary
Composition.* It begins with a highly formal invocation of Aphrodite: "Sump-
tuously throned," "immortal." Soon the goddess is off her pedestal and ad-

dressing Sappho familiarly, a little impatiently, because again the poet is in-voking her not as a mere formality but to enlist her aid in winning, or win-ning back, the affections of a girl who has stopped or not started loving her.

Love gives her authority and makes her larger-spirited than others, so she can address an uncultured woman, probably rich, on the subject of her mortality and the afterlife, with an acerbity worthy of Archilochus.

> When death comes, there you'll lie, and in due course
> No memory of you, no desire: you never risked
> Plucking Pierian roses. Invisible also in the halls of hell,
> You'll wander back and forth alone among the ghosts.[28]

She can be sarcastic, too, to a daughter of the house of Polyanax.[29] And in fragment 68, the missing words and breaks cannot conceal the fact that there is considerable anger in what we overhear, as it were through the wall of time. Even here, even in the fragmentary flow that we have, the poem is not arrested on a single note of feeling; there appear to be changes in tone, which provide the poem's narrative and its occasion. It survives on a pa-pyrus with other fragments which may relate to the same theme, that of one of Sappho's girls choosing "intimacy with ladies of the house of Penthilus." It would seem that Sappho is trying to patch up a relationship between two of her girls, one of whom has let her eye wander into the enemy's camp.

What in Homer is simile in Sappho becomes a matter of metaphorical language, sometimes personification, not familiarising but humanising, making clear the intimate connection between human endeavour and natu-ral rhythms and patterns: "Hesperus, gathering everything the bright Dawn scattered, you call home the sheep, call home the goat, you call home the child to its mother."[30] The Greek use of syntactical and verbal repetitions is lovely, and its effect trails into even a literal English rendering. Byron teased out these two Greek lines to eight. Another poem evokes the apple and the apple of the eye. Dante Gabriel Rossetti renders it thus:

> Like the sweet apple which reddens on the topmost bough,
> A-top on the top-most twig,—which the pluckers forgot somehow,—
> Forgot it not, nay, but got it not, for none could get it till now.[31]

The apple may represent, detached though it appears to be, the beautiful and unattainable girl.

And how effortlessly she draws the gods into our sphere: Dawn, the Moon and Stars come into language not as things but as beings, alive in the way that human beings are. "Come here now, soft Graces and bright-tressed Muses."[32] The comic writers use hyperbole as a form of ridicule: "healthier than a pumpkin" or "balder than a cloudless sky." Sappho's use is intensive and never comical, and generally has to do with beauty and desire. The phrase "goldener than gold"[33] conveys a specific quality. The wonderful fragment "I desire neither the honey nor the bee"[34] is another kind of hyperbole, expressing the sufficiency of love.

Dionysius of Halicarnassus in *Demosthenes*[35] evokes the "elegant or spectacular" style, "favouring polish, not majesty." The choice of words is dictated by sound, their collocation by the need to create the most perfect harmonies. "It will always select the mellowest, least emphatic words, striving for euphony and melody and the sweetness that flows from them." Sappho's art is to dovetail, smooth and rub down, to avoid the over-emphatic and over-obvious emphases, to discover appropriate and answering harmonies. Among English poets Algernon Charles Swinburne in his notorious "Anactoria" goes all out for harmony, and Sappho is a protracted rage of passion, now tender, now sadistic, her love taking forms that would have puzzled Queen Victoria:

> . . . I feel thy blood against my blood: my pain
> Pains thee, and lips bruise lips, and vein stings vein.
> Let fruit be crushed on fruit, let flower on flower,
> Breast kindle breast, and either burn an hour.
> Why wilt thou follow lesser loves? are thine
> Too weak to bear these hands and lips of mine?[36]

Where was Sappho born? Where did she live? Where did she die? What was her actual name? Psappha, Psaffo, and even Pspha are all possible variants, all attested. Were there two Sapphos, the poet and the courtesan, living on Lesbos at about the same time, whose lives have been conflated? We know as little for certain about Sappho as we do about most of the early Greek poets, though many fragments of her work survive, and her influence on poetry persists. She is the one female poet among the "Lyric Nine." The critic Leslie Kurke, having forewarned us that in archaic times poems "construct" the poet (that is, we infer a poet's life from poems at our peril, because the writing may be generic, or spoken by a *persona*), accepts without demur that Sappho existed and that she was a woman.[37] Some of her poems were clearly composed for choric recitation (the nuptial fragments suggest female occasions). Most speak from an "I" and address a single interlocutor. We overhear, and we delight in the artistry of the language. Given the fragmentary nature of the texts, we overhear snatches of poetry and few, if any, poems entire.

Indeed, the textual problems are such that when we say we are "reading" Sappho we are in fact reconstructing her from the tiniest rags of language, much of it ambiguous and elusive. The poems are almost as evanescent as the life. The patristics that surround the poems are usually morally loaded as well. In fragment 70, one phrase can be read as "shrill (breezes?)" or "clear-voiced nightingales." In fragment 99, a phrase may mean "strings which welcome the plectrum"—a musical image appropriate to Sappho—or "women who use the dildo," an insult to the descendants of Polyanax, whom Sappho is assumed to have despised. What is more, the lines may belong to Alcaeus rather than Sappho. Textual problems of one sort or another affect every single line. Only one poem survives more or less entire.

Sappho has appealed to the sexual prurience or moral severity of centuries of scholars and readers. The whispers of sexual irregularity in her conduct and the curious geographical trajectory of the legend of her life mean that she has inevitably stimulated fiction, fantasy, legend. Her homosexual affections, real or (some moral critics claim) mischievously read into the work, mean that her island Lesbos is the etymological port of departure for women who love women, and her name gives rise to the term "Sapphic love." No place nor poet confers a similar romantic legitimacy on male homosexuality. They have to make do with Uranus, a planet and the son and husband of Gea, the Earth, grandfather of Zeus and (as Hesiod tells us) father of a fearful progeny.

The kinds of poetry Sappho composed were all in the lyric mode. Poetry which is inseparable from music (*melos*) is described as "melic" and includes lyrics that are either ostensibly personal, seeming to relate to occasions and incidents in one life, or choral, for ceremonial use on public or semi-public occasions. In neither case is the verse necessarily didactic or satirical. It is composed in strophic form and the complexities of diction and sound patterning are deliberately heightened, poet and performer enhancing pleasure by demonstrating their skills. Such verse is to be read *aloud,* composed not for the page but for the ear, and most often for the entertainment of guests at a symposium. It would be wrong to assume that melic poetry is always *song.* The accompaniment might be rhythmic in function, it might be dramatic; it was not necessary for the performer's voice to be accompanied in the way that a *Lieder* or a pop singer's is. The *recitative* of opera may approximate more to what the symposium lyric interludes entailed. There was certainly music without words—played on the *aulos,* or flute, for example, which later was regularly used to accompany verse (as in the time of Pindar). There was a complementary movement towards words without music.

Apart from Sappho and woman-love, Lesbos was also, legend says, the birthplace of music's inventor, Terpander, and of Arion, who first *spoke* verse, and who freed the dithyramb into full expressiveness. And here the other great melic poet Alcaeus was born. No one has adequately explained why Lesbos should have received such an abundance of grace from the Muses; certainly that grace was withdrawn in later centuries. The Persians took the island in 527 BC; by the time it was "freed" half a century later, "the nymphs are departed." The poets of Lesbos composed in the Aeolic dialect; its diction and rhythms prevail in Sappho's poems. Many fragments of her work survive because later grammarians made use of them to illustrate the finer points and proprieties of Greek usage and of her dialect.

After Crete and Euboea (which is virtually part of the Greek mainland), Lesbos is the largest of the Aegean islands, as large as a little country. The north-east coast faces the Gulf of Edremit, and the bronzes and greens of the coast of Turkey are clearly visible across the straits. Athens is over 300 kilometres away. On the east side, the rough island is rich in olive groves. On the west it is more barren. The climate is temperate, mild in winter, not too hot in summer. Earthquakes have done as much as invaders to erase the civic and religious monuments from earlier times, though around the Gulf of Kalloni, which cuts deep into the island, herds of horses range freely, harking back perhaps to the horse-breeding traditions of the Troad. The hot springs still flow, and the vintage is good, though not so renowned as in classical times.

Why does it matter whether Sappho was born in Eressus or in Mytilene? Not only because the landscapes differ so much: either she was born and raised in quite a cosmopolitan seaport facing the populous coast of Asia Minor, at a time when the town looked on one of the world's principal waterways; or she grew up in a port facing out into the Aegean and the vacant expanse of sea between it and the other islands, a blank ocean where history was only then about to start happening in earnest. Modern Eressus is a few miles above the sea. The site of the ancient town is at the village of Skála Eressoú on the coast, with a rocky acropolis overhanging a singularly unattractive long beach. Not far up the coast is a fascinating petrified forest. At ancient Eressus was born Theophrastus, the peripatetic philosopher and writer of delightful "characters," who died in 287 BC. But Sappho, who is usually referred to as Sappho of Eressus, belongs in spirit and perhaps in fact to the cosmopolitan east of the island, to its Manhattan, as it were, rather than its Mar Vista. Her face featured from the first to the third centuries AD on the coinage of Mytilene. There were also coins issued at Eressus with her image, and a now-vanished herm inscribed with her name.

Probably between 630 and 620 BC, Sappho came into the world. She was a few years younger than Alcaeus.[38] She shared with him an aristocratic background. Her father may have been called Scamander, Scamandronymus, Simon, Eumenus, Eerigyius, Ecrytus, Semus, Camon, or Etarchus. Her mother, it is agreed, was Cleis, and no dishonour to her is intended by the uncertainty of Sappho's paternity. We know the mother's name because the poet named her own daughter after her. She also recalls in a poem that her mother told her how, when she was herself young, a purple headband was a fine adornment, but if a girl had "hair brighter than a burning torch," blonde, it was preferable to bind it with wreaths of flowers.[39] Of her daughter Sappho says, in C. M. Bowra's translation:

> I have a child; so fair
> As golden flowers is she,
> My Cleïs, all my care.
> I'd not give her away
> For Lydia's wide sway
> Nor lands men long to see . . .[40]

The poem is broken off. If the hair of a child or woman was blonde or yellow, it was probably assisted by what Sappho called "Scythian wood"[41] or "fustic," used for dying wool and hair.

Sappho had three brothers, Eurygius, Charaxus and Larichus. Larichus, her favourite, was a wine-pourer in the town hall of Mytilene, an office held by sons of the best families.[42] Charaxus she chastises[43] for having dawdled in Egypt on the lewd day-bed of a courtesan, actually called Rhodopis, whom she dubs Doricha, after buying her out of servitude and sinking a fortune into her.[44] He was a merchant living in Naucratis on the Nile Delta, on the western branch of the river, not far from where Alexandria would be founded in 331 BC. We learn from another source[45] that Rhodopis, born in Thrace, was a slave of Iadmon, a Thracian merchant who lived in Mytilene (where, no doubt, Charaxus met her). Iadmon numbered among his possessions another, more famous, slave by the name of Aesop. Walter Savage Landor invented two *Imaginary Conversations* between the fable-teller and the courtesan.

It would help if we knew how Sappho was implicated in the complex politics of Lesbos (her surviving poems are not directly political, though we can deduce affiliations and hostilities from some of them): was she drawn into public affairs because of her family, or did she come to politics later, on the arm of a man perhaps? On doubtful authority, her husband is named as Cercylas of Andros, a trader from the northernmost of the Cyclades. It is probable that, like Alcaeus, she or her family had trouble with Pittacus of Mytilene, who led the "democracy" in Lesbos and whom we have already encountered as one of the Seven Sages.[46] These were men whose wisdom, recorded in aphorisms for the most part, was applied to the civic world. Lists of the seven vary, but every list includes four: Solon of Athens, who was an admirer of Sappho, Thales of Miletus, Bias of Priene and Pittacus. Sappho's poems record some hostility to and from the noble house of Penthilus, the house into which Pittacus married.[47]

She probably went into exile in Sicily, accompanied by her daughter, sometime between 604 and 596 BC. This is why her statue was later erected in Syracuse. She returned to Lesbos when the political turbulence—whatever the cause—had subsided. There she was involved in some way with other, generally younger, women. She names and addresses her poems to several, in particular Atthis, Telesippa and Megara, "and she got a bad reputation for her unwholesome friendship with them."[48]

We encounter Anactoria and Cydro and Gyrinna. There is also Damophyla, who, says Philostratus, was Sappho's successor, set up an academy and "devised love-poems and hymns, the way Sappho did."[49] One poem encourages Abanthis to pursue her passionate desire for Gongyla, and Ezra Pound made a wonderful poem out of a Gongyla fragment, echoing the sound-qualities, the inner assonances and alliterations (never crude rhymes) which are the weave of Sappho's verse:

> Spring . . . . .
> Too long . . . . .
> Gongula . . . . .[50]

Some people will say one thing is the most beautiful on earth, others will point to something else. What is actually most beautiful is "whatever a person loves." Sappho adduces Helen, and her own passion for Anactoria.[51] This provides a further, distinctive woman's perspective on Homer.

Was this involvement with girls, this passionate commitment to love, part of a cult of Aphrodite? Was Sappho a prostitute, as one detractor suggests? Is Horace, the Roman poet who loved her work more than any other except Catullus, right in referring to her not only as "the Aeolian girl" but as "boyish Sappho"?[52] And Ovid puts into Sappho's own mouth the words "Women of Lesbos, you who because of your love made me contemptible, don't huddle round me any more to hear my playing."[53] She grew old; she may (fragment 58) refer to her own old age. There is certainly something powerful in her sense of ephemerality, a note that Housman catches:

> The rainy Pleiads wester,
>   Orion plunges prone,
> The stroke of midnight ceases,
>   And I lie down alone.[54]

She has been kept alive by love. Loeb has as the conjectural closing line "love has obtained for me the brightness and beauty of the sun." An underpinning myth may be that of beautiful Tithonus, who wed the Dawn. She secured for him eternal life but not eternal youth, and his fate was cruel, a progressive, eternal wizening.

Sappho's was in all likelihood a long life, and she composed many poems. A scholar at the great library in Alexandria organised the work into nine books, the first eight in order of the metres she had chosen, the ninth to accommodate the *epithalamia,* or wedding poems. The first book had 1,320 lines, between sixty and seventy poems; later books were briefer. Not even a scrap of the elegiac verse survives. Some later verses attributed to her are only dubiously hers. Those who knew the body of her work claim that her sole subject was "Aphrodite and the Loves."[55]

She is the only Greek woman writer with a body of work, however damaged, still to be read. Strabo in his *Geography* does not understate her merits: "a unique being: in the whole of history I can think of no other woman who can even remotely match her as a poet."[56] It is remarkable that, despite its manifest quality, so much work by a woman survives, and that verses are still being added, discovered in the Sahara. In a society where the public role of women was (we assume, though we know little about the social systems of Lesbos at the time) restricted, a female poet is inevitably a wonder, so fine a poet a miracle. Poetry survived initially in an oral tradition, in performance. Was there a line of women performers at the symposia, or did male poets incorporate Sappho's poems in their repertoire? Did they impersonate women in performance? Even in Athenian society, a century and more after Sappho's death, few civic occasions were open to women. There were religious festivals, the Thesmophoria for example, but that was reserved *solely* for women. There was no evident context for the transmission of Sappho's poems, and yet they were transmitted, not only the poems intended for ritual use but more private-seeming ones as well.

Roman poets, Catullus and Horace and Ovid most notably, made use of Sappho's poems in shaping their own. Other types of writer make use of Sappho as a figure. The comic writers and dramatists make her into a figure of ridicule. Some report that she fell in love with a ferryman of Mytilene called Phaon. The story was first designed, we might think, to clear Sappho's name of the stigma of homosexuality. Unless there was historically a second Sappho, a courtesan of Mytilene who met a heartbreak end, as Aelian conjectures, this is so unlikely a story that it is ridiculous.[57] Aphrodite favoured Phaon—who is sometimes confused with Adonis—because he carried her, disguised as an old crone, across the water without charging her a fee. (Every goddess had a hero of this sort.) She restored his youth and his considerable beauty. Aelian, more than seven centuries after Sappho, declares as fact: "Phaon, the handsomest of mortal men, was laid among lettuces by the Goddess of Love."[58]

Phaon, we are told, repulsed Sappho's advances and fled to Sicily. According to this story, Sappho was not driven out of Lesbos by political pressures but left in pursuit of love. She followed Phaon, failed to gain his love, and so she travelled from Sicily to the west of Greece and threw herself off the two-thousand-foot-high rock of Leucadia on the coast of Epirus, a favourite point of adieu for lovers keen to cure themselves of desire. "To raging Seas unpity'd I'll remove, / And either cease to live, or cease to love!"

Strabo says there was a temple of Apollo on the heights, and the cliff is still called Sappho's Leap. Quite apart from the implausible geography—that she pursued him from Sicily to the east coast of Greece—judging from the poems that survive, this is unlikely. If Sappho died around 550 BC, as most scholars believe, her suicide would have taken place when she was in her seventies, by which time she might have been expected to have learned restraint. Indeed, in fragment 150, she seems to chide her daughter for lamenting her natural death, using words which Socrates employed to silence his intolerable wife, Xanthippe, loudly lamenting his impending death: "It is not right for there to be lamenting in a house where the Muses' servants dwell."

The comic poets and dramatists being the gutter journalists of their day, the truths they had to tell were not factual but what Ford Madox Ford called "truth to the impression." This story inspired Ovid, the great Roman amorist exiled from Italy for exercising his amours in the wrong circles, or failing to turn informer, to invent an epistle from Sappho to Phaon, a poem translated by an overheated nineteen-year-old Alexander Pope in 1707:

> No more the *Lesbian* Dames my Passion move,
> Once the dear Objects of my guilty Love;
> All other loves are lost in only thine,
> Ah Youth ungrateful to a Flame like mine!

The vocalic values of the third line are uncannily apposite, true to the art of Ovid and through his to Sappho's.

What we know as fact is only a little more certain than what the comic poets tell us. Was there in Lesbos a female group of *hetairai* (mistresses, unmarried women) parallel to Alcaeus' male symposium? In fragment 160, Sappho declares that she will sing to delight her female companions who are called *hetairai,* a word which for her was not burdened with moral denigration but which later came to mean "courtesans" or something worse.

There may have been competing "colleges" of women, and Andromeda and Gorgo are named by Maximus of Tyre as her rivals.[59] Did her group lounge about, drink and strum like the male symposiasts? Or was it Sappho's vocation to instruct girls leading them towards marriage? Did she run a kind of academy or finishing school teaching what one commentator calls "only the noblest girls" of Lesbos and Ionia, with perhaps other students from further off—boarders—such as Anagora of Miletus, Gongula of Colophon and Eunica of Salamis?[60] Was it her task to initiate them? Did she teach them, too, to make lyric verses?

Her poems generally touch upon a girl's life between childhood and marriage: would it be reductive to regard the poems as in some sense pedagogic—teaching not only expression but types of feeling, as well as ways of regulating feeling? Are they exercises for the voice, the hands, the dancing body and the shaping spirit of her charges? The epithalamia, composed for performance to a wider audience, were in all likelihood "put on" at actual weddings in Lesbos. Her dialogue poem, for members of the cult of Adonis,[61] was also intended for more public performance. Leslie Kurke suggests that Sappho led "a *thiasos* of young women, engaging in ritual homoeroticism to prepare them for marriage." It is not unthinkable: in a sense, such an arrangement might replicate some of the purpose and dynamic of the male symposium.

What if we take, as readers down the ages have tended to do, Sappho's first person as a genuine "I," trying at the same time to keep the "I" clear of our individualistic and bourgeois investments in first-person poetry, our hunger for disclosure, confession and individual voice? Sappho's desiring "I" is artful, aware that what she says has to be true to the form she has chosen and must be suitable for performance before an audience; whether a male or female symposium or a class of girls it is for us, and the poem, to determine. Kurke likes this approach, though it breaks the very rules she establishes for reading male lyric poets: "we might read the more intimate and personal quality of Sappho's poetry as a phenomenon of the marginalization and containment to the private sphere of women *as a group* in ancient Greek culture. Thus the poet spoke intimately to other women, with whom she shared the experiences of seclusion, disempowerment, and separation." Would Sappho have had any sense of what Kurke means? Or is Kurke, like earlier moral critics, applying familiar contemporary ideology to the unfamiliar and unknowable? Scholarly criticism and scholarly projection (which is a form of invention and distortion) are different in kind.[62]

The longing for other women or for girls taken from her to be married, or friends far away, compelled to go by marriage or by exile, not out of their own desire or on their own quests, might have given rise to Sappho's peculiarly plangent and erotic tonalities. "Because of this pattern of separation, memory played a much greater role in the texture of Sappho's poetry than that of the other lyric poets (and conjures up for us perhaps a stronger sense of the speaker's interiority)." Yet it is not the poetry of separation that makes us return to Sappho over and over again. It is the poetry of presence. The world is present, and the beloved. Even when she—or he—is far away, the beloved is evoked or conjured. In Sappho, too, poetry does make something happen. The magic in it has nothing to do with hocus-pocus, everything to do with the unaccountable force of love which has found phrases and patterns to keep it real. As Horace remarks in the *Odes,* "her fiery passions, committed to the lyre, live on."[63]

Alcaeus, since he knew her and her work, is the best contemporary witness—if we assume, that is, that the words attributed to him are actually *by* him. He called her "lilac-haired, sacred, sweet-smiling Sappho."[64] *Dulce ridentem,* as Roman Catullus would write in a translation of and a tribute to her. There was something less, and more, than sexual love between them: they are poetic complementarities, and together they provide a lyric sufficiency. A whole tradition springs from them.

XIII

Theognis of Megara

. . . it is interesting to establish that from those words and roots which mean *good* there often still glimmers the crucial nuance by which worthy men felt themselves to be of higher rank. Given that in most cases they define themselves simply by their superior power (as *the powerful, lords, leaders*) or by the most visible signs of superiority, as *the rich, owners,* . . . they also evince their superiority by a *typical trait of character:* This is what concerns us here. They refer to themselves, for example, as *the truthful;* this is particularly so of the Greek nobility, and Theognis of Megara is their voice. The root of the word coined for this, *esthlos,*[1] means: one who *is,* one who possesses reality, one who is *in fact,* one who is true. Then, by means of a subjective turn, *true* becomes *truthful:* at this stage of transformation it turns into a motto and byword of the nobility and comes wholly to mean *noble,* in contrast to the *dishonest* common man. This is what Theognis considers him and thus he describes him. Finally, when the nobility declines, the word remains to mean *nobility of soul* and has, as it were, ripened and grown sweet.

FRIEDRICH NIETZSCHE, *On the Genealogy of Morals*

 If you went north-north-west from Megara you would come eventually to Hesiod's steep landscapes. Megara itself is a town which sensible travellers bypass when they take the road from Athens in the east, via once-sacred Eleusis (nowadays where the shipyards are), to Corinth in the west. The boundary between ancient Attica and low-slung Megaris is marked by the Horns, the fractured southern limit of the Pateras Mountains. A long road across the isthmus provides clear views to Salamis, the island wrested from Megara by Athens in 600 BC, and in the other direction to the Gulf of Corinth. The Plain of Megaris sustains vines and olives, and this is the region which most abundantly flavours Greece with garlic.

Megara is a modest county town, the principal conurbation in the eparchy of Megaris, whose main claim to historical fame is that it stood between Corinth and Athens and was able from time to time to play one off against the other, except when they both ganged up against it. Megara is built on two unemphatic hills, citadels of the ancient city.

Pausanias has a great deal to say about the place. Unfortunately, only one of the buildings he describes has survived, in part: the Fountain of Theagenes, built by the eponymous tyrant in the seventh century BC as a fountain house and a tunnelled conduit for water, a construction immediately popular with the people. Theagenes was a patrician populist. Remnants of the ancient city—or rather, the ancient *cities* that have occupied the spot—turn up, incorporated into churches or civic walls, or surface in excavations for new buildings. Pausanias notes, what modern travellers see, the use of an unusual white mussel-stone in much of the construction. The shrine of Aphrodite, one of the most ancient in the city, had statues carved by Praxiteles (*Persuasion* and *Pleading*) and Skopas (*Eros, Desire* and *Sex*).[2] They were plundered or perished.

According to the poet Theognis, Agamemnon, setting off for Troy, founded a temple to the huntress Artemis, to whom he turns: "hear my prayer, keep me from harm: for you it is a small thing, goddess, but for me it is great."[3] This is the same temple that Pausanias mentions, walking centuries later in Theognis' town. He ascribes its construction not to Agamemnon but to Alkathous, the ancient leader of Megara. Though this Artemis was an important tutelary spirit of Megara, featuring on the coinage later on, Pausanias tells us little about the temple itself.

Megara had wealth from maritime trade. It exported red moulded pottery to the Greek world. It sustained a philosophical school, set up by a disciple of Socrates, the sophist Eukleides (450–380). It had important moments. Famous people and semi-divinities, many of them female, came there to die, or at any rate people of the area claimed their deaths and built them memorials. Ino, who as a sea-spirit helped Odysseus, lending him her scarf to save his life, was washed ashore here; the Amazon Hippolyta died here of grief ("the memorial stone is shaped like the Amazon's shield," according to Pausanias);[4] King Tereus, who married Procne, raped and mutilated Philomela, and is conjured by T. S. Eliot in *The Waste Land,* committed suicide here; Iphigeneia, ill-fated daughter of Agamemnon and Clytemnestra, is claimed as a local ghost, though she is more likely to have died, if she ever lived, in Crimea, or indeed she may have been transmogrified into Hecate and be still alive, a goddess; and Adrastos, the great king of Argos, returning via Megara from taking the city of Thebes, perished here.

In pre-Homeric times Megara was quite independent. Its chief prosperity was said to have been based on wool. In Theagenes, around 640 BC, it acquired a wise and popular tyrant, concerned—he made people believe—with bettering the conditions of the poor, though he was himself not of the people. Megara planted colonies, some of them substantial (legend says that Byzas from Megara founded no less a colony than Byzantium). It became by turns an ally and a prey of Athens; eventually it was reduced to mere provincial status and it has not prospered seriously in the last couple of thousand years.

Theagenes was expelled from his tyranny and from the city by oligarchs, those whose fortune was in the manufacture and export of wool. They were ill-born entrepreneurs of an aggressive and unenlightened kind, and certainly not the sort of whom the poet Theognis, Megara's most celebrated ancient citizen, could approve. Self-made, they conspired together, a new class which did not value the settled traditions of the old ruling class and despised the people, who despised them in return. Megara echoed the "democratic" tensions more momentously evident in Athens.

During the age of Theognis (his name means "descended from god"), change was certainly in the air. He was born—depending on the authority consulted—around 630, 620, 570 or between 544 and 541 BC in Megara or (a mischievous suggestion) in its Sicilian colony Megara Hyblaea. Perhaps he emigrated to Sicily in later life. He was a man of some inherited property and status, and both his wealth and his social position were vulnerable. This vulnerability is his primary political and cultural subject. Sparta cannot have been an easy ally, or Corinth, and Athens was not a comfortable neighbour. If the reforming spirit that Theagenes had released when he seized power at the expense of the rich still stalked the streets of Megara, there were foes inside the walls as well as outside, and a man of property and breeding might rest uneasy on his couch.

He might have tossed and turned for other reasons, too: many of Theognis' poems are addressed to a young man called Cyrnus, son of Polypas. Cyrnus, judging from the verses, was showered with advice (much of it civic and political) and affection. But if Theognis wanted some kind of affectionate response, Cyrnus did not comply. Theognis promises delights; Cyrnus finds delight elsewhere.

The poetry of Theognis gained wide currency in Greece, to such an extent that, like other famous makers of verse, he became an anthology. To appropriate his name provided a seal of quality for other poets: by attributing their work to him they tapped into his audience and readership. Editors, too, would attribute to him poems they felt might be more widely read if they were cut free of their original writer. This has kept scholars busy, sorting out which poems are Theognis' own and which are by his contemporaries, successors and predecessors, including notable figures such as Mimnermus, Phocylides, Solon and Tyrtaeus. Two centuries of poems, writing from after his death and possibly from before his birth, adhered to him. As with Ben Jonson and the Sons of Ben in the English seventeenth century, there is fascinating commerce between them, and the quality of the imitative work can be good enough to displace the originals. Apart from Phocylides, Theognis' other imitators and followers are omitted from the

Greek Anthology and its fourteen centuries of epigrammatic poetry. Perhaps they are a decade or two too early. It makes a certain sort of sense to see the *Theognidea*—the sons of Theognis—as a necessary adjunct to the Greek Anthology, even a first volume; and the addition of a handful of Solon's poems would hardly be out of place.

The *Theognidea* is, according to Leslie Kurke,[5] "the only archaic elegy handed down by direct manuscript transmission." They survive—some 1,388 verses contained in two books, the second centred on pederastic love[6]—not only excerpted in grammar and rhetoric primers but as a coherent set of texts that miraculously navigated the Middle Ages. The advice given, the rules and rituals of the symposium touched upon, the warnings against association with the *kakoi* and *deiloi* ("deceitful inferiors"), the need to choose the "right friends," *agathoi* and *esthloi,* and treat them in the right ways, mean, Kurke says, that "the corpus can be read as a kind of survival manual for an imperilled aristocracy." The low are base metal, corrupting, the high embody all the civic virtues, while the new entrepreneurs and oligarchs are false metal and merit scorn. The coherence of the *Theognidea* may have been what drew Nietzsche to the poet, more than the poems whose attribution is authentic.

The voice of the poems that are by Theognis leaves little doubt that it comes from lips that regard themselves as aristocratic:

> When I compose, Cyrnus, lock the poems away
> But if they are stolen, they'll still be recognised;
> No one selects the poor when there is better,
> They'll always say, "This verse Theognis made,
> The Megarian." My name's known far and wide
> Though there are critics of my statesmanship.
> Hardly surprising, son of Polypas: why, Zeus himself
> Can't please them all, if he sends shine or rain.[7]

Theognis' story, if we piece the poems together into a kind of narrative, wary at each moment of drawing too much circumstantial evidence from them, is one of having been as disappointed by his peers as by his inferiors. Now he can add to his disappointments a deep disappointment, body and soul, in Cyrnus as well.

> It's hard to put one over on your foe,
> Cyrnus, but simple for a friend to cheat his friend.[8]

To Cyrnus, through love and a skill at making verses, he brought immortality; *his* name will endure, and yet the poet has nothing, neither a touch nor a token, in return:

> ... Violet-crowned, the Muses
> Ensure your fame forever by their charm
> And everywhere, while sun and earth survive
> You will be sung of in my words, but I
> Cannot wrest from you the tiniest due:
> You cheat and lie to me, like a child to a child.[9]

Poor Theognis, we are tempted to say, unlucky in life, unlucky in love.

His property has been taken, he has experienced exile, yet he is a conscience and could become a law-giver if the city would recognise "my statesmanship" as it recognises his verses. A would-be Solon, he has no intention of marketing himself or his views, however: that would be to violate the very values by which he is sustained, whose truth he takes to be self-evident to right-thinking men. Theognis has a voice, that of a certain style and type of man; and if the world his poems evokes is not as rich in detail as we might wish it to be, aspects of it come into sharp focus. The diction is generally plain, heightened by vivid images, sometimes condensed into tight-lipped epigrams. Thus he says,

> I'm the dog who's crossed the flooding river,
> I've shaken everything off in the winter torrent.[10]

Is this the fragment of a fable, or a vivid and precise metaphor for his own reduced condition?

At first we sympathise with Theognis and through him with his kind. The end of an era always elicits elegies whose reactionary tone is beguiling and melancholy, but if we assent we lose sight of the wider society and the necessity for change. Theognis' tone of voice and the things he says draw us sharply to attention: his harsh dismissiveness of others, his self-righteousness, and his hubris in relation to Cyrnus make him a curious figure, archaic and coldly sentimental, like the German-language poet Stefan George.

> ... don't mix with scoundrels,[11]
> But seek out and abide with worthy men.[12]
> Drink with and eat, sit with and seek them,
> And their good will, the rich and influential.
> You'll learn true lessons from true men.
> Mingle with scoundrels and you'll waste
> Even what sense you have ...[13]

Cyrnus is perceived to be morally a little frail and vulnerable ("what sense you have"). And sound men are those of wealth and power: soundness resides nowhere else. Not all men of wealth are sound, of course: the oligarchs are beneath contempt.

It's still a city, Cyrnus, though it has new people who
Never before knew justice or the rule of law.
They clad their rumps in draggled goat-skins, lived
Beyond the city walls like beasts; and now
They're the élite, son of Polypas, while the élite
Of yesterday is residue. It's hard to bear:
Worthy men[14] despised, the worthless[15] walking tall.
Good lineage tries to splice itself with poor.
Men con one another, cheering rack and ruin,
Helpless when it comes to telling good from evil.[16]

This voice-portrait of a man of parts and privileges is sympathetic if at all because it is unvarnished, it wears no mask but itself. His terms and his eloquence celebrate what is passing. Readers may feel excluded from his consideration, and if they do they will get an adequate purchase on his partial and retrograde politics. We may weep for him but not with him, once he has cantankerously edged himself into perspective.

Theognis does not like women, though to Cyrnus he briefly praises that unlikely thing, a good marriage. He loves adolescents, but there is no suggestion that he ever made children of his own. His sense of perpetuating a value system is essentially pedagogic: choose beautiful youths and teach them what is good. Yet they are themselves susceptible to contrary influence, and there is nothing stable under the sun. When he gives what seems like bad advice, we realise that he is not only an earnest man but also an ironist:

Do not pray for rank, son of Polypas, or riches:
All a man needs now is good luck.[17]

The ironic tone almost endears him to us, but when he speaks of "the mindless people" and uses other terms of disaffection, our incipient warmth is checked.

Theognis writes not in his native Doric but in a deliberately Ionic dialect, Ionic being the chief poetic currency of the time. To write in an idiom that sets the poems apart from the immediate community in which he lives is an act of distancing, of aloofness, as if they are for a small élite who share a formal language. It also acknowledges that the poems are part of a wider culture, not a merely local exercise. They were composed to be recited with *aulos* accompaniment, for the entertainment of the symposium.

There is an austerity about Theognis which makes his verse fall short of the erotic in its terms, whatever his desires might have been; it falls short of the bibulous ribaldry of the symposium, too: when he got together with his friends, the evenings may have passed in a pensive spirit, more under the spell of Apollo than Dionysus. It is hard to drink deep when, on waking from the long sleep, the world one wakes to is as bleak-seeming as Theognis.' Perhaps it is kindest and most just to see him as the unsmiling symposiast, the lover whose hand rests only on the shoulder of his beloved.

> O son of Polypas, I have heard the crane's voice crying shrilly[18]
> To tell men that the time is right to plough and sow.
> It bruises my heart melancholy black, the thought
> That others now possess my flower-dotted fields
> And the mules do not for me draw the yoke of the plough
> Because . . .[19]

Though he stands at the end of a political moment, he also stands near the beginning of an epigrammatic tradition.

XIV

Solon of Athens (640–560 BC)

Some poems of Solon were recited by the boys. They had
not at that time gone out of fashion, and the recital of
them led someone to say, perhaps in compliment to
Critias, that Solon was not only the wisest of men but also
the best of poets. The old man brightened up at hearing
this, and said: "Had Solon only had the leisure which was
required to complete the famous legend which he brought
with him from Egypt he would have been as distinguished
as Homer and Hesiod."

PLATO, *Timaeus* 21C[1]

 Compared with Theognis, his sour-faced neighbour and near
contemporary, Solon of Athens could talk *and* walk. He wrote
verse, but he also was offered power and exercised it with pru-
dence. One of his laws established that at a time of civil strife a
citizen who did not take sides would lose his citizenship. Every man had an
unshirkable responsibility to choose what he regarded as the good, and to
bear the consequences of his choice. This was a non-negotiable civic expectation in an evolving democracy.

Solon's was one of the rare moments in history when a poet was an *acknowledged* legislator. Shelley, defending a nineteenth-century corner for the
*un*acknowledged poet-legislator, might have approved of Solon's kind of
leadership. What made it extraordinary was Solon's instinct for balance and
counterbalance, his understanding of the perspectives not only of his own
class but of all classes. He also had a responsible eye for the medium and
long term: expediency played only a small part in his calculations. He was a
man of self-effacing integrity.

This, at least, is the version of Solon that originates in his own writings
and that historians, including Herodotus and Plutarch, believed to be true.[2]
Solon may not have bequeathed sculpture, painting or architecture to the
city, but he helped to restore its balance and gain, or regain, contested
Salamis. Also, he reformed its written laws in a radical way. And finally, he
was the first poet of Athens.

It is not possible to separate his poetry from his political and civic activities. Solon is the Hesiod of the city-state, using poetry to address social husbandry, the ills, needs, and aspirations of his city. He reflects on power and
its effects, but also finds room in verse for the sensual man. Plutarch's *Life*

quotes the verse at large. In tone, texture and even in phrasing it recalls Hesiod's. Urban and rural values are not so profoundly at odds as they would be when, later on, city and sustaining countryside became divorced.

> I long to prosper, but to thrive by dishonest means
> I do not wish. Justice may be slow, but it's true.[3]

No cutting corners, on the farm or in Council. In Solon's Athens a citizen had fields and orchards; the city was small enough for every man who lived on a street to have crops and pastures along a lane. His *eunomia,* the order of good laws which harmonise the lives of citizens, is not unlike the *eunomia* Hesiod applies to the rural and the divine order. Hesiod personifies it: Eunomia is daughter of Themis, a Titaness, herself a daughter of Uranus and Gaia. She wedded Zeus and bore him several children and is the source of some of the key ordering principles of the universe.

A long fragment of Solon sets out, for the first time, to harmonise two quite disparate conceptions. On the one hand stands fallible and limited man, vain and paltry, ambitious and myopic; on the other is an ordered and potentially just society. The latter ought to take the former, provide him a place, a structure within which to work and achieve, and goals which dignify and extend him and those like him. We have human hubris and its unmitigated aftermath and, set against it, we have the mitigation of a just order, *eunomia* versus *dysnomia.* A wise moderation leads towards a *shared* golden mean.[4]

The *Suda* tells us that Solon's father was Execestides.[5] It was a matter of pride to Critias that his great-grandfather, grandfather or father, Dropides (there are variant versions), had been a lover of Anacreon, and was often mentioned in Anacreon's poetry. Solon and Dropides may have been brothers, their father being Execestides.[6] And Plutarch adds: "Solon's mother, says Heraclides of Pontus, was a cousin of the mother of Pisistratus," the man who was to become tyrant of Athens when Solon went abroad. Solon and Pisistratus "were great friends to begin with, in part because they were related, in part because of the youthful handsomeness of Pisistratus. According to some writers, Solon was passionately devoted to him." His is among the earliest poetic testimony of love between boys and men.[7] Solon, who was to become the great meter of judgement and lawmaker, could write:

> As soon as there's a bloom on him, one loves a boy,
> Thighs, and sweet lips, objects of desire . . .[8]

Pisistratus is said to have had a boy lover called Charmus and to have dedicated a statue to love in the academy, where runners in the sacred torch race lit their torches. Solon, similarly inclined, could not resist gazing upon good looks. He adopted his sister's son Cybisthus. Plutarch says, "The truth is that each man's soul has planted in it a desire to love; it is as much its nature to love as it is to feel, understand, and remember. It clothes itself in this desire. If it finds nothing to love at home it will fasten on some alien object." The love of a boy or a young man is the noblest form of love. There is no record of Solon having married or produced an heir. When he came to draft his famous laws, he explicitly forbade boy love to slaves, reserving and dignifying such activities for "reputable men."

Celebrating love of this kind was not at odds with the order of individual values he advocates in other poems (the erotic element in his surviving poems is slight, a trace among more serious concerns). *Olbios,* in Homer a word signifying material well-being, good fortune, in Solon comes to mean a higher blessedness, the pagan *beatus* of the Latin writers. It begins in a positive reputation, and it entails the love and honour of friends and the ability to terrify and harm foes.[9] *Olbios,* in one fragment, is a man who has beloved sons, horses, hounds and a hospitable friend elsewhere, a friend one can escape to.[10] Herodotus distinguishes *olbios* from a mere *eutuches,* one who enjoys superficial or momentary good fortune.

Before he found his political vocation, Solon wrote "with no serious end in view," simply to amuse himself when at leisure. He began to philosophise in aphoristic form, using verse also as a historical record and to set down his understanding of the world and his place in it. Poetry was asked to do work which in a later age would naturally have fallen to prose: exhortation, warning, rebuke, prayer. He may have tried to draft his laws in epic verse. One fragment, as if from such an attempt, declares:

> First let us pray to Zeus, royal son of Cronus
> To grant my laws success and wide renown.[11]

Poor in his youth, Solon travelled to make his fortune, Plutarch says. In his age a person of good family could work for gain without a stigma attaching to him. Foreign trade was regarded as mind-extending, especially at a time when colonies were being planted far and wide. Both Thales and Hippocrates the mathematician engaged in trade, and Plato paid for the expenses of his stay in Egypt by selling oil. Solon the merchant succeeded in a sufficient, if not a spectacular, way and around 612 BC went home. Athens was in a singularly unhappy state when he arrived back. Among other things, citizens were not permitted so much as to mention the name of the island of Salamis, to which Athens laid claim, but which it had been unable to wrest from the control of the Megarians. This rankling defeat was a focus for wider discontents.

The twenty-eight-year-old could not abide such enforced silence on an issue of popular concern. He composed "a hundred gracefully turned verses," of which only eight survive, committed them to memory, and then rushed into the public way, dressed for his madness "with a little cap upon his head," reciting them with eloquence. Plutarch declares that "a great crowd swarming about him," he climbed on to the Herald's Stone and recited his elegy. It began with the words:

> I come, a herald from delightful Salamis,
> On my tongue not a speech but a carcanet of words . . .[12]

I must, he says ironically, be a native of some little island, Sicinus or Pholegandros, certainly no Athenian: Athenians are Salamis-abandoners (*Salaminaphetae*). As the poem progressed, it urged fellow-Athenians to renew the war with Megara, to save the delightful island and revive Athenian honour.

Another late biographer, Diogenes Laertius, says that Solon did not recite the poem himself but hired a herald to do so, thus dissipating some of the impact of the story and the drama of madness. This second version is more in keeping with Solon's dislike of performance and fiction, but it issues in all likelihood, as Plutarch's does, from a traditional misreading of surviving texts. Mary R. Lefkowitz, describing how Aristotle used Solon as a source for his *Constitution of Athens,* shows how misreadings by biographers and critics unaware of semantic change can lead to mis-creation of past scenes. They take *agore* (speech) for *agora* (market-place) and thus create a powerful, inadvertent fiction. Did he in *fact* feign madness when he delivered his poem on Salamis? Was he in fact, later on, offered the tyrant's crown and did he refuse it? Was he as virtuous as the tenor of his verse suggests?[13]

Plutarch tells so good a story that, though we must doubt it, we might as well listen to it all the same. Solon was applauded by many, including Pisistratus. The law against mentioning Salamis was repealed and Athens went to war again with, as commander, the poet Solon himself. To defeat the Megarians he practised a subterfuge. We are given a choice of stories. The first involves cross-dressing. Solon sent an agent who posed as a deserter and persuaded the Megarians to try to kidnap the leading Athenian women who, he assured them, were observing the rites of Demeter at Colias. As the Megarians approached, Solon had young, sparsely bearded men dress in women's clothing; as the foe came ashore the Athenians killed every last one of them and used their ship to sail back and take the city. The second story is more conventional and Plutarch finds it more credible. It involves an oracle, sacrifices, and a feigned attack to draw the enemy out, and then the main body of men sneaking in behind and taking the city.

Athens won, but victory was not clear-cut. Conflict continued until Megara and Athens agreed to submit their claim to an arbitrator: Sparta. Solon based Athens' claim to Salamis on Homer (poetry conferred legitimacy). The question is, were the lines he adduced originally in Homer's poem, or were they interpolated? We are back with the forger-editor Ono-macritos and *Iliad* II, 557–58. Homer's great editor Aristarchus rejected both lines. They speak of Salamis' contribution to the Trojan War as part of the Athenian contingent. It followed that Salamis belonged within the Athenian sphere. "From Salamis," says Homer, or Onomacritos, "Ajax brought twelve ships, *and stationed them where the phalanxes of the Athenians stood.*" Never was so much historical weight placed upon (rather poor) lines of spurious verse. Another, Athenian, version says that Solon persuaded the Spartans that Ajax's sons Philaeus and Eurysaces became citizens of Athens and ceded the island to the city when they settled in Attica.

The main reason apologists have found for doubting the stories of sub-terfuge is the character of Solon himself: would he, a man of robust and emphatic self-declared integrity, take such devious routes? Would he feign madness? Would he, Athens' first poet, misquote the greatest poet in the world for political ends? Would he use cross-dressing as a mode of deceit in war? If the answer to any of these questions is "yes," Solon is diminished in their eyes.

After Salamis, Solon was famous. His fame grew when he defended Del-phi against the people of Cirrha, who threatened to "profane the oracle." As one of the Seven Sages, his maxims "Moderation in all things" and "Know thyself" were inscribed, Pausanias reports, in an antechamber of the temple of Apollo. That they were there in Pausanias' time proves how durable Solon's admittedly rudimentary wisdom was. The Sages used to meet in conclave at a wooden version of the temple that burned down in the middle of the sixth century BC.

Solon was the only poet among the Seven. The Sages were wise men who *performed* their wisdom in some way.[14] The Greek word for their brand of sagacity is *metis:* practical wisdom enhanced with more than a dash of cun-ning. Despite the Sages' generality of expression, *metis* itself is highly partic-ular, alive to the complexities of individual and social life. A man with *metis* "has a keen eye for the main chance, for what the Greeks called *kairos*—the right thing at the right time."[15] When the poet Simonides arrived in Athens, *kairos* had been translated and devalued: no poet ever evinced such an in-tensely successful form of it, and that success was wholly material.[16]

Membership of the ancient Sage club varies, according to the historian one reads, but Solon is always present on the list. From Plutarch's point of view, the only genuine sage among them was Thales of Miletus. He had originality. The others, applying morality to politics, are purveyors of rather commonplace maxims. The expression (as in some of Solon's more gener-alised verse) is humdrum. Other sages included Bias of Priene, Chilon of Sparta, Cleobulus of Lindos (on Rhodes), Pittacus of Mytilene and Periander of Corinth or Epimenides of Phaestus or Myson of Chen. The geographical spread is broad. Sages were not concentrated in one place.

In Plato's *Protagoras,* Socrates argues that "the Spartan gift for laconic and pointed comment showed that their intellectual ability was well trained, and that certain people in the past had realised 'that to frame such utterances is a mark of the highest culture.'"[17] They were echoed, for example in Plato's tag, "Prosperity leads to satisfaction, satisfaction to insolence," which may derive from Solon's "Satisfaction begets *hubris,* whenever great wealth follows men whose minds are not sound."[18]

Conflict between the old landed families, the aristocracy also known as the Eupatridae, and the various groups of common people developed, sometimes into bloody encounters. Certainly the situation in nearby cities, Megara for example, was worrying for anyone with a stake in the "old order" of Athens. Solon himself was a scion of the old order, and when in 594–93 he was appointed *archon,*[19] it was a delicate time. He was also named *diallaktes,* the mediator or reconciler, to negotiate between the powerless and powerful parties. Either at that time or twenty years later (scholars are divided) he introduced his famous constitution, intended to balance conflicting interests and to promote a harmony which was at once just and stable.

Before Solon reformed the laws, Draco was the legendary Athenian legislator. In 621–20 BC, he was given authority not so much to make up new laws as to set out the existing laws in terms which answered the needs of the city. His objective was to move beyond a tit-for-tat, vendetta-based tradition of common law and to replace it with authority at a remove, a public justice, an "objective" standard. To give such justice legitimacy and impact, the punishments he proposed needed to be—Draconian. Solon's task was more subtle and urgent. He had to unstitch laws which served the ruling interests and frame a new system in which equity rather than retribution was the governing dynamic. From Draco's system he preserved only the homicide laws.

His laws were known as "axles" (*axones:* "pivot boards"), the turning wooden blocks on which they were inscribed. They were also called *kyrbeis* after the bronze tablets where they were written down. A fifth-century visitor to Athens could have conned them right up to 461 BC on the Acropolis. At that time they were moved to the Agora, and "sections were later published on stone." Many of the laws postdate Solon, but his name remains in place to legitimise them.[20] In Aristotle's (or his philosophical *atelier*'s) *Constitution of Athens* Solon declared that his laws should stand for a hundred years. Then he went abroad, ostracising himself like the Duke in *Measure for Measure,* vowing not to return for a decade. He saw himself, after a few years in power, as the cornered quarry of a hunt: "I turned and was held at bay, like a wolf among a pack of hounds."[21]

Herodotus says he left Athens for another reason: "He was on his travels, having left Athens to be absent ten years, under the pretence of wishing to see the world, but really to avoid being forced to repeal any of the laws which, at the request of the Athenians, he had made for them. Without his sanction the Athenians could not repeal them, as they had bound themselves under a heavy curse to be governed for ten years by the laws which should be imposed on them by Solon." He did come back, unlike the Spartan Lycurgus who, having made the laws, compelled Sparta to agree not to change any of them until his return. They are still waiting.

Solon expressed greatest satisfaction with what he called *seisachtheia,* the "shaking off of the burdens." This entailed exonerating numerous citizens of debt, a cause of deep unrest given the excessive power of the landed and lending interests. Solon's legislation liberated land that was mortgaged and entailed and freed people sold as slaves or exiled because of debt so that they could return. He was also responsible for easing the dues of the *hektemoroi,* or "sixth-parters," citizens who had been reduced to a state of virtual servitude because they had, for one reason or another, to give a sixth of whatever they produced to a lord. Solon saw to it that enslavement for debt, when the borrower used *himself* as collateral, ceased. A free citizen could not be held as collateral and could not offer himself either. In verse he describes his achievement, how he

> lifted out
> The mortgage stones that everywhere were planted
> And freed the fields that were enslaved before.[22]

Solon introduced other reforms. He made immigration easier for people with craft skills. They were even made citizens. Exports of agricultural produce were restricted, apart from olive oil. Athenian farmers concentrated on olive production and this helped to develop a single-product export economy.

The social structures he proposed, under the eye of the Areopagus, the governing council, enfranchised every class of citizen, from the wealthy *pentakosioimedimnoi,* or 500-bushel men, the larger farmers, through the *hippeis,* or knights, to the *zeugitai* (yoke-men) and the *thetes,* peasants worth less than 200 measures a year. Each group had defined flexibility. Now it was a man's material substance rather than his birthright that determined his place in the order of things. He also reorganised the *boule* (senate) of 400 members and each adult Athenian was given a seat in the *ecclesia* (popular assembly). The *Heliaea* (popular tribunal) was established as a final court of appeal, and it was possible for even the poorest man to bring a legal action. Solon's reforms strengthened the peasants' position, weakened that of the aristocrats, put muscle in the courts and the judiciary, and laid a foundation for the institutions of classical Athens. It was a responsive and subtle series of checks and balances. Solon did not throw his power behind any one group. Aristotle in his *Constitution of Athens* quotes a wonderfully calm and even-handed passage of Solon's verse:

> I've given common folk sufficient rights
> Without surrendering or taking back;
> The rich who were resented, and the mighty,
> I saw to it that they were undiminished.
> I took my stand, my shield defends both sides
> And neither can come at and hurt the other.[23]

It would have made a worthy epitaph: he advanced the art of the possible, pushing forward no more than would be accepted or could be enforced. He sees himself as a man between contesting parties, insisting on compromise. Dialogue is at the heart of his most inventive poems. He imagines voices speaking against him, criticising him; or he works himself into the voices of contesting parties, speaking for them and then speaking for their opponents, translating conflict into argument. He begins by overhearing a critic: "Solon isn't a sage or counsellor." He listens to his critic and then frames a response. He reports speech and enters into semi-dramatised debate.[24]

"In great matters it's not easy to please everyone," Plutarch quotes him as saying.[25] Was he offered absolute power and did he refuse it? One account suggests as much. He shrank from tyranny because a tyrant, to achieve power, must compromise with one interest at the expense of others. Tyranny can work, he admits, but there is no easy political way back from it. As an institution it depends on individuals: a good political institution should depend upon the proper enforcement of equitable laws.

He left Athens and his travels took him, legend says, to several destinations, though the stories may tell, to use Lefkowitz's term, representative rather than factual truths, illuminating his exemplary character rather than his biography. Let us believe, with Herodotus and Plutarch, that there is something to the stories.

He went to Egypt and stayed "at the Nile's great mouth, near Canopus' shore."[26] From Egypt, either on this or on an earlier visit, he imported, says Herodotus, a momentous notion: income tax. "It is said that the reign of Amasis was the most prosperous time that Egypt ever saw, the river was more liberal to the land, and the land brought forth more abundantly for the service of man than had ever been known before; while the number of inhabited cities was not less than twenty thousand. It was this King Amasis who established the law that every Egyptian should appear once a year before the governor of his canton, and show his means of living; or, failing to do so, and to prove that he got an honest livelihood, should be put to death.

Solon the Athenian borrowed this law from the Egyptians, and imposed it
on his countrymen, who have observed it ever since. It is indeed an excellent custom."²⁷ Such self-assessment, issuing in a payment (the duty of
"liturgies" which the rich citizen "volunteered") or in death, sounds posi-
tively modern.

During his stay "at the Nile's great mouth" he philosophised with
Psenophis of Heliopolis and Sonchis of Saïs, learnèd Egyptian priests. He
began to gather information about the lost city of Atlantis and started to
write a poem about it but gave up on the task, being too old and sceptical to
proceed with the necessary intensity. Plato says he gave up because he was
too busy, but Plutarch disagrees. Modern critics sniff a forgery: Plato invented the Atlantis story for his own political argument and assigned it to
Solon to give it "factual" probity. Benjamin Jowett, introducing his translation of Plato's *Critias,* is categorical: "we may safely conclude that the entire
narrative is due to the imagination of Plato." He continues, "To the Greek
such a tale, like that of the earth-born men, would have seemed perfectly
accordant with the character of his mythology, and not more marvellous
than the wonders of the East narrated by Herodotus and others." But why
did later ages believe the myth to such an extent that they set out to discover
the lost island "in every part of the globe, America, Arabia Felix, Ceylon,
Palestine, Sardinia, Sweden"?

Plato's eponymous speaker, Critias, recounts the provenance of Solon's
story: "His manuscript was left with my grandfather Dropides, and is now
in my possession." It tells how, "in the division of the earth Poseidon obtained as his portion the island of Atlantis, and there he begat children
whose mother was a mortal. Towards the sea and in the centre of the island
there was a very fair and fertile plain, and near the centre, about fifty stadia
from the plain, there was a low mountain in which dwelt a man named
Evenor and his wife Leucippe, and their daughter Cleito, of whom Poseidon became enamoured. He to secure his love enclosed the mountain with
rings or zones varying in size, two of land and three of sea, which his divine
power readily enabled him to excavate and fashion, and, as there was no
shipping in those days, no man could get into the place. To the interior island he conveyed under the earth springs of water hot and cold, and sup-
plied the land with all things needed for the life of man. Here he begat a
family consisting of five pairs of twin male children. The eldest was Atlas,
and him he made king of the centre island, while to his twin brother, Eumelus, or Gadeirus, he assigned . . ." And so the intriguing story proceeds
until the manuscript ends abruptly just as Zeus is about to speak. Critias
says the manuscript "was carefully studied by me when I was a child." It is
fantastic and magical and belongs to the realm of childhood and of make-
believe more than to that of political fable.

Herodotus reports that, in his travels, Solon stayed with Croesus, the last king of Lydia, who wanted his guest to deem him the happiest man in the world. Solon conceded that he was fortunate, but not happy, a state which can only be finally affirmed at the conclusion, and in the conclusion, of a life. When the Athenian moved on, Croesus was not sorry to see him go. This story is almost certainly legendary because Solon's and Croesus' dates do not coincide, but Herodotus takes the opportunity to display a sage's wisdom in action. On his way back from Egypt he may have stopped off in Cyprus and stayed with Philocyprus, a tyrant whose rule he much admired. Diogenes says he died in Cyprus, aged 80, "leaving instructions to his kin-folk that his bones should be carried to Salamis and there burnt to ashes and scattered over the soil."[28]

Most agree, however, that he returned to Athens and found it in a troubled state. A good set of constitutional balances was not proof against democratic weakness: in 561 the assembly voted Pisistratus a body-guard and he was about to begin his distinguished career as tyrant. Solon rushed in, as in the Salamis intervention, but this time to the agora, not the assembly, and in full armour, not a comic hat, to urge the case against. His intervention was unsuccessful; the man whose boyhood had unsettled his heart was now in a position to destroy all that Solon had created.

There was no rancour between them, however. Solon lived to see his constitution overthrown, but then restored with some changes. He stayed on in Athens, a lonely, monitory elder who inevitably became an advisor to Pisistratus and even approved some of his actions. Solon died old. Lucian says that he, like the sages Thales and Pittacus, lived a century.[29] Eighty was a more widely accepted age. Perhaps his ashes were scattered, as Aristotle says, agreeing with Diogenes, on Salamis. Perhaps they were not.

When Solon got back to Athens, something else troubled him. Diodorus Siculus quotes a passage in which Solon likens Athenians to wily foxes trusting in shifty speeches rather than examining closely men's deeds.[30] Thespis, hardly a political figure but preying upon the fashion for public speaking, was just starting his activities. Thespis celebrated make-believe. "Yes, but if we allow ourselves to praise and honour make-believe like this, the next thing will be to find it creeping into our serious business," Solon declares, striking the ground with his stick. For him poetry is not make-believe. It is instrumental, didactic, monitory; it is a language of distilled moral truth. "Obey the archon, right or wrong."[31] Solon's attitude to Thespis and the birth of thespianism may have contributed to Plato's declared hostility to poets.

There is a change in the purpose of iambic poetry and its public performance. He uses it to defend his political programme, a use that Archilochus and Hipponax would have found odd. Solon does not satirise and scapegoat

but justifies himself, in a language the people could understand and easily remember. His verse is preserved in fragments within the texts of writers like
Aristotle and Plutarch.[32] His developments of iambic trimeter and trochaic
tetrameter may have contributed to the emergence of Attic tragedy, bringing into a popular form a higher style and more elevated content.

Solon, it is easy to forget, wrote poetry of private pleasures as well as
public responsibilities. Some of his poems would have been appropriate to
a symposium, though we visualise him more readily as a public orator. At
the beginning of the sixth century, his alone was the merit of Athenian poetry. Bowra declares, "Solon had written his political and patriotic elegiacs,
less skilful indeed than those of his friend Mimnermus but noble and undeniably moving. But after him there is hardly a trace of poetry until the patronage of the Pisistratids gradually helped into existence the majestic
forms which were to dominate the succeeding century."[33]

A humourless pithiness marks much of his writing, and because quite
substantial chunks of it survive (time preserving unjustly the political at the
expense of the lyrical—historians are to blame) we wonder whether the
firebrand of *Salamis* did not become a little like Polonius in *Hamlet,* with Pisistratus as his dear Laertes. There is wisdom in Polonius, if we do not
laugh at his resignation. Solon points out how wealth passes from hand to
hand; but nobility is non-transferable and non-negotiable. He reminds us
that "No man is happy, not one under the sun."[34] He writes a poem about
the ages of man, working not by decades but by seven-year periods, and he
dwells vividly upon the growth of teeth. At his most succinct and elegiac,
he speaks with great candour and authority.

> My heart pains me as I watch
> Ionia's oldest country
> Going down.[35]

Perhaps "poets tell many lies,"[36] but they can also learn to tell the truth.

XV

Stesichorus of Himera

> I am exhorted to sing the *palinodia*, to confess errors in regard to a paragraph of the apostle's writing, and to mimic Stesichorus, who, vacillating between discredit and praise of Helen, recovered the eyesight he had forfeited by speaking against her, by praising her.
>
> ST. JEROME, writing to St. Augustine, AD 402

 At Tivoli, outside Rome, a headless herm bears the inscription "Stesichorus, Euclides' son, Himeran." When Himera in Sicily was itself destroyed by the Carthaginians in 409 BC, the resilient Thermitani (as the people were called) regrouped and, a year later, founded a new settlement nearby, Thermae Himeraeae.[1] There they set up some of the works of art from their razed city, including, Cicero tells us, a much-prized statue of Stesichorus, "a bent old man holding a book, a masterpiece of art, so they believe."[2] This was one of the sculptures which Verres, the evil public administrator of Sicily attacked by the young Cicero, was keen to possess.[3]

Stesichorus was among the most prolific of ancient poets. The *Suda* says that, at Alexandria, twenty-six books of his works were preserved, compared with nine of Sappho, ten of Alcaeus, seven of Ibycus, five of Anacreon. With seventeen, Pindar was runner-up.

He did become the "bent old man" of the statue. Like Anacreon, he lived to be eighty-five.[4] Pythagoreans—Antipater of Thessalonica, for example, early in the first century AD—were convinced that something larger than Stesichorus lived inside him. Because in scale and theme his work was Homeric, it followed that the soul of Homer must have passed into him.

> Stesichorus, abundant unbounded mouth of the Muse,
> In Catana, under Aetna's soot, was laid to rest.
> Pythagoras said that souls pass from man to man:
> Homer's found its next home in Stesichorus' breast.[5]

If he died in the year, even on the day, of Simonides birth,[6] then his body would have released the soul of Homer for yet another poetic outing. Simonides inherited, as well as Stesichorus' venerable soul, his proclivity for survival, dying at the age of ninety.

From the moment he appeared in the world, Stesichorus was special. In his *Natural History* Pliny tells us that new-born Stesichorus was visited by a nightingale that perched on his lips and sang its richest song.[7] Christodorus, the fifth-century epic poet, describing statues at the Baths of Zeuxippus in Constantinople, evokes the scene and insists that Apollo "taught the tuning of the lyre" while the poet was still in his mother's womb.[8]

Of course, neither Pliny nor Christodorus tells us who the mother of this prodigy was. As usual, there are several candidates for paternity, but we have only one implausible nominee for mother. Tzetzes quotes Aristotle as saying that Stesichorus was the son of Hesiod by Ctimene, whom the Boeotian poet was believed to have raped. Hesiod was murdered by Ctimene's brothers because they thought he had had his will of her.[9] Stesichorus was portrayed, then, as a child of an ill-starred but poetically charged relationship.[10] Proclus gives her name as Climene.[11] The chronology does not work, however promising the gene-pool, but already Stesichorus is associated metaphysically with Homer, physically with Hesiod. That gives a measure of his ancient importance. Can we get any closer to the actual facts of the matter?

The *Suda* provides us with multiple choices for father. He was Euphorbus, Euphemus, Euclides, Euetes or Hesiod. He was born in Himera—the river and the city are mentioned in his poems. Or in Matauria (Metauron) on the north of the toe of Italy, or perhaps Locri (under the toe). Or he was born in Arcadia, at Pallantium, and was deported to Catana, where he was eventually buried in front of the eponymous Stesichorean gate. His brother was Mamertinus (or Mamercus),[12] a notable geometer; and he had another brother called Helianax, a law-giver. If these were indeed his siblings, he came of a distinguished family.

So far we have little to build on confidently, and even with this little we must go cautiously because there may actually have been three Stesichoruses at three different dates. A modern Mr. Smith may not shoe horses, but a Stesichorus probably had something to do with a chorus: the name describes a vocation rather too specific to become a common monicker. "Stesichorus" means "director of the chorus" or "stabiliser of the chorus," what Ezra Pound would have called a choral "unwobbling pivot." Our poet's original name was Tisias or Teisias, the *Suda* says: he was Stesichorus "because he first set up choruses of singing to the lyre."[13]

There are other things we know for uncertain about his life. Athenaeus claims that he composed boy-songs, though none survives. Stesichorus "was immoderately amorous,"[14] and in this as in his verse is a forerunner of Ibycus. At one point his poetry appears autobiographical. Plato quotes it in the *Phaedrus.* Stesichorus was struck blind by Helen because he slandered her in his poem *Helen,* and she restored his sight when he un-slandered her in a *Palinode.* Translated literally, *Palinode* means "back-song," recantation (re*cant* has the element of song in its etymology too). Poetry, again, made something happen. We may take the story literally, or accept the suggestion that Stesichorus wrote his *Palinode* to please a Spartan audience, because Helen was virtually divine in that city, and if he arrived with only the abusive poem *Helen* to his credit, he would not endear himself to the locals. So with a slightly archaic air, he removes the real Helen from the awful fray of Troy, replacing her with a phantom:

> That story is unfounded, never did you
> Go on the well-manned galleys, never did you
> Reach the towered city that was Troy.

Proteus snatched Helen back, away from Paris (Alexandrus), at Pharos and returned her to her rightful spouse, leaving her seducer a wooden panel with her portrait painted on it so he could aridly assuage his desire with that.

In the fourth century, stories of Stesichorus' relations with the tyrant Phalaris at Acragas (Agrigento, due south of Himera) are current. Aristotle retells the fable with which the poet cautioned his fellow-citizens.[15] The Himerans had made Phalaris their military tyrant. Now Phalaris wanted a bodyguard and they were inclined to oblige. Stesichorus spoke. A horse was alone in his field. A stag came and started grazing there. The horse asked a man's help to get rid of the trespasser. The man agreed, on condition that the horse allow himself to be bridled and ridden by the man wielding a javelin. The horse acquiesced, and the man made him a slave. The Himerans had allowed Phalaris to bridle them; if now they allowed him to mount them, they risked enslavement.

It is likely that for a time Stesichorus left Magna Graecia (the term used to describe the Greek cities on the Tarentine Gulf and those on the Tyrrhenian coast of Italy), perhaps because of his hostility to Phalaris, perhaps to earn fame and money. It seems most plausible that he went to Sparta, not only because of the care he took to revise his *oeuvre* to please a Spartan audience, but because he appears to have some first-hand knowledge of their dances and choral movements. He set his version of the story of Orestes in Sparta rather than in Mycenae and made Agamemnon a Lacedemonian, not a Mycenean, with his palace in Sparta. This effectively detaches Agamemnon from Argos, Sparta's great enemy. Stesichorus keeps out all mention of the house of Atreus, "a discreditable ancestor." This large poem may have been composed specifically as a choral song for a Spartan spring festival. A surviving snatch of verse speaks of "public song," "at the approach of spring" and swallow-time.[16]

He must have been a rich old man because, like Ibycus, he was—the *Suda* says—murdered: "it was Hicanus killed Aeschylus the piper and Stesichorus the cithara-reciter."[17] His fame was reflected in the grandeur of his tomb. It was a substantial octagonal landmark, much admired in antiquity. It had eight pillars, eight steps and eight corners,[18] and it gave rise to a figure of speech. A throw of eight was called a Stesichorus, hence the proverbial expression "eight all" (for "eight all ways").[19]

The sources of Stesichorus' verse are obscure. He emerges from a tradition which has almost entirely vanished. He is the first poet of Magna Graecia about whom we know anything much: it is the framing tradition that has vanished. Himera itself was a city rather different from other Greek colonies. It prospered early, minting its own coins before many other Greek cities, and featuring Stesichorus on one, with his lyre and walking stick. Its population was of Dorian and Chalcidian extraction, and although on the northern shore of Sicily, it was at a remove from other colonies, and exposed to Carthage. Such ports are full of storytellers. Stesichorus belongs to no chronicled Greek tradition but draws on several: he combines choral and lyric elements, for example, in ways which prefigure the drama and are remote from Alcman's choral practice.[20]

Though Stesichorus may have contained the soul of Homer, we cannot prove that he knew the Homeric poems in the forms in which the Aegean Greeks had them. He certainly knew versions of the stories. Cynaethus may first have brought the Homeric poems "west" in 504 BC. If so, Stesichorus would have encountered them only in his maturity, travelling in the Peloponnese. Homer apart, Xenocritus of Locri may have been affected by him in musical terms. He is said to have written narrative odes—dithyrambs—and Bowra comments, "it certainly looks as if Stesichorus inherited from him the main character of his art."[21] Another important and quite lost predecessor was Xanthus. He wrote an *Oresteia,* just as Stesichorus did, and Stesichorus refers to him. Xenocritus and Xanthus, both of Magna Graecia, and representing a popular strand of lyrical narrative, have almost wholly vanished.

Arion's poetry vanished, too, not having reached the Alexandrian scholars who made it their business to establish the canon as we partly know it. Was his work current and did it affect Stesichorus? Arion toured Italy and Sicily in the seventh century BC and may have left a mark on Xenocritus and Xanthus. His contribution to the dithyrambic tradition could be the element of narrative which Stesichorus, via Xenocritus and Xanthus, goes on to develop.

Another plausible influence is the local songs of Himera, Locri and other towns with which Stesichorus is associated. Bowra senses a folk-song tradition of sorts behind some of Stesichorus' narrative, especially in the bucolic, pastoral elements, early evidence of the spirit of the idyll.[22] The legend of Daphnis appears to be local, associated with bay trees and with the river Himera. The term "local" may be better than "folk": the gap between popular and high art is bridged by choral and narrative poetry, especially of the kind which has a local dimension; but "folk" implies a quite different kind of vernacular.

Nine of the fourteen long poems of which a few splinters remain would have appealed in Himera and throughout Magna Graecia. Four dealt with the adventures of Heracles, who was popular throughout Italy as the embodiment of the Greek settler and founder and patron of several colonies. The poems not composed for local consumption appear to have been devised for specific audiences in mainland Greece, and in particular a Spartan audience.

It is obvious why Stesichorus enjoyed such popularity and was read with devotion and dogged respect for over a thousand years, casting a direct, and now an indirect, influence which is ineradicable. He managed to accommodate in a language which has many of the qualities of lyric poetry much that seems by nature to belong to the epic. He scaled down the individual heroisms into compelling and dramatic narratives which were fuller, more prosaic and less allusive than Pindar's, though his work, for all its archaism, points in a Pindaric direction. "Indeed his special position is at the point where the lyric succeeds the epic as a main means of expressing what concerns a Greek audience, and starts on its task by reshaping and bringing up to date much that the epic had told in a simpler and less ingenious manner."[23] The "existence of the dactylic metres" made it easier for him to adapt epic matter without much adjustment to the language.

Yet the legacy is more complicated than that, and the new papyrus finds, especially three published in the 1960s, adjust our sense of the poet in an unexpected direction. One papyrus, writes Leslie Kurke, contained fragments of the poem about the monster Geryon. "Calculations based on the size and layout of this papyrus revealed that the poem would originally have spanned 1,300 lines at least (remarkably long for a lyric poem; indeed, analogous in length to an entire tragedy)." The extent of the poem and the apparent oddities in the prosody suggest that it would have been resistant to choral delivery. There might still have been public recitation if not incantation and one bit in particular cries out for a civic setting. New material for the rhapsode?

The words "setting" and "tragedy" suggest something of the protodramatic nature of the form of Stesichorus' extended narratives. The poet is giving not voice but voices. We hear Jocasta, Teiresias, Heracles, Geryon. Jocasta, addressing Teiresias' dire prophesies, wishes for death rather than to witness her sons slaying one another. The speech is full of a kind of raw emotion; it is repetitious and over-insistent, more an aria than part of a dialogue. Teiresias' reply is equally verbose. In 1977 the Lille papyrus, recovered from a mummy wrapping, was published with thirty-three almost complete lines of the poem, in which Jocasta speaks to her offspring Eteocles and

Polynices "on the verge of war, urging them to divide their father's property by lot and thereby spare their house and city from destruction." All but two of the lines are speech.

As with Homer before or the dramatists that follow from him, some borrowing directly from his plots, we can conclude (tentatively of course) that Stesichorus' choral poetry was pointing not only towards the obliquities of Pindar but towards the achievements of classic Greek drama. They weren't in themselves dramatic, however. He could be exhaustingly long-winded. In the Geryon poem, "the speech in which Geryon ponders his death . . . is separated by nearly 400 lines from the account of his death . . ." If "his amplitude and nobility of style could be called Homeric,"[24] his pacing could not be. The poems for the most part claim as subject-matter *damomata* ("things common to the citizenry"). Kurke takes speculation to the limit of scholarship: it is tempting to push it further.[25]

We can say that Stesichorus' work represents a transition from epic to lyric, that "he keeps much of the narrative of epic even though he presents it in a lyric form."[26] Narrative yes, un-epic yes, but lyric? Unlike lyric poets, Dionysius of Halicarnassus reminds us, "Stesichorus, Pindar and the like made their periods"—the length of their sentences, their metrical runs and larger structures—"longer and divided them into many metres and colons for sheer love of variety."[27] The length of the periods is another reason why the fragmentary nature of the surviving texts (with ends of lines, beginnings, but few extended runs) is so vexing. It is harder to imagine a long sentence than a short one from a word or two. Tzetzes insists the poems were lyric because they were accompanied on a lyre.[28] Quintilian says that, though redundant and diffuse, Stesichorus "maintains on his lyre the full weight of epic poetry."[29] By this time, however, the word "lyric" remembered its origin in the word "lyre," but no longer carried the instrument under its arm wherever it went. The texture of Stesichorus' verse is not as close as we expect from a lyric, nor the prosody as subtle in its vocalic variations. The epithets, which probably abounded, were less functional than Homer's and do not stand up to scrutiny. Quintilian found his excess a form of profligacy, vicious redundancy.[30] He lacked concentration, his was a prose mind functioning prosodically, finding the "middle way." Hermogenes loves his "abundance of epithets," the absence of a through rhythm, poetry as construction,[31] an uncomfortably modern take on the poet's vices, which are represented as virtues. Still, he had virtues or he would not have survived so long. Statius believes he rises at times to heroic utterance, what he terms "ferocity."[32]

However over-copious Stesichorus' poetry was, however far the sheer quantity of words outran their matter, he was central to sixth-century poetry and art and to subsequent centuries, though the fragments of his work hardly support the high estimation in which he was held. His impact persisted. He may have been to Virgil what Virgil was to Dante, a kind of spiritual sherpa on the long journey. Book II of Virgil's *Aeneid* may be almost as much Stesichorus' as Horace's *Dulce et decorum est* is Tyrtaeus'.

It is correct to say that little apart from fragments survives; but it is not enough. We do not have actual poems by Orpheus, yet we believe in him and his legacy. There is less magic about Stesichorus, but more history. Because of Simonides, Pindar and Virgil, we know more of Stesichorus than we do of poets whose texts have been less harshly erased by time, Archilochus, for example, or Sappho, near contemporaries to whom he owed nothing, and who owed nothing to him. But because we know less of his life, its irregularities and eccentricities, because he lived long and did not inscribe too much of himself in his verse—it was not that kind of verse that he composed—he arouses limited curiosity. He made a very good living from creating and performing. For a bourgeois age he provides something of an example, an early Grub Street model, as educator-entertainer.

The poems survive as volume titles. Scholars believe that a mythical narrative poem filled each book (with the exception of the *Oresteia,* which filled two), composed in what were regarded largely as lyric metres. Thirteen titles, with fragments or attestations, survive. The first and one of the better-known is *Geryon,* part of the Heracles cycle, recounting one of his twelve labours, the killing of a particularly revolting monster.[33] Stesichorus augments the traditional horribleness of three-bodied Geryon. But the perspective, paradoxically, appears to be that of the monster much of the time, "a strange winged red monster who lived on an island called Erytheia (which is an adjective meaning simply 'The Red Place') quietly tending a herd of magical red cattle, until one day the hero Heracles came across the sea and killed him to get the cattle."[34]

Anne Carson takes the monster's part, as she believes Stesichorus to have done. "We see his red boy's life and his little dog." We overhear his mama's appeals—Grendel and his mother are prefigured here—and the gods on Olympus foreknow his doom. Heracles' arrow slays him. "We see Heracles kill the little dog with His famous club." Carson capitalises the "h" in "his," making the hero divine. She appends the word "little" to the red dog, weighing the scales against our more conventional moral instincts and, probably, Stesichorus'. Her reading is delightfully synthetic; I am not sure that it is credible. She has joined up the dots and in order to elicit the figure she has added a few dots of her own. What there is of the poem has its moments of, among other things, baffling lyric incongruity. Geryon, wounded, "drooped his neck to one side, like a poppy which spoiling its tender beauty suddenly sheds its petals and . . ."[35] The redness is apposite, suggesting blood, but the juxtaposition of the poppy and the monster is either risible or surreal. Carson reinvents it this way, making it oddly wonderful:

> Arrow means kill It parted Geryon's skull like a comb Made
> The boy neck lean At an odd slow angle sideways as when a
> Poppy shames itself in a whip of Nude breeze

A single attestation survives to the poem called *Cycnus,* another part of the Heraclean cycle. One version of the story says that Cycnus, son of Ares, lived in a Thessalian mountain pass and offered contest to travellers, then killed them and used their skulls in the decoration of his father's temple or a temple to Panic (*Phobus*). Heracles ran into him during one of his labours, perhaps en route to the Hesperides in search of the golden apples, and did him in. Next in the Heraclean cycle was *Cerberus,* about the three-headed hound that guards Hades, and again only a single attestation survives as to the fourth poem, *Scylla.*

The Boar-Hunters, called *Suotherai,* told of Meleager's quest for the Caly-donian boar and the battle for its hide that followed. A single suggestive line of the poem survives, "and dug his snout tip beneath the earth."[36] Nothing memorable is left of *Europa,* though the poet played variations, we are told, on some traditional legends: not Cadmus but Athene sowed the dragon's teeth that turned into warriors at Thebes. The seventh poem, too, explored Theban themes: we do not know how Stesichorus developed the vexed story of *Eriphyle,* the betrayed wife, the bribed mother.

Only four small bits and a few phrases survive from *The Funeral Games of Pelias* (*Athla epi Pelia*), part of the Argonaut cycle originating in Thessaly and therefore tying in obliquely with *Cycnus* from the Heraclean cycle. Si-monides picked up on this theme and developed it on a considerable scale. It is, however, the ninth poem, *The Sack of Troy* (*Iliou Persis*), where more phrases and lines survive, that had a greater impact on later poetry. It told of the wooden horse, of Aeneas' departure from toppling Troy, and of his trip to Italy. The surviving fragments are tantalising but inconclusive. Closely re-lated to it was Stesichorus' notorious *Helen,* probably composed on main-land Greece. Theocritus, in the introduction to *Idyll* XVIII, "Helen's Epithalamium," says that "certain things have been taken from the first book of Stesichorus' *Helen.*"[37] The *Oresteia* lies behind Aeschylus' great cycle of plays. It may also underpin, Bowra suggests, Pindar's *Pythian Ode* XI. The poem, divided by Stesichorus' Alexandrian editors into two books, so vast was it, fully developed its theme.

The merest hint of Stesichorus' *Nostoi* survives.

It is clear from this brief catalogue of his vanished works that Stesicho-rus was not an epic poet. The poems were too diverse in their focus, too circumstantial and prosaic, too keen to be narrative history, to bring about the complex integration that epic must perform. They were glosses on epic, as was tragedy; they were entertainments, devised to appeal to specific audiences in Greece or Magna Graecia. Stesichorus was a performer, which meant that he must flatter his audiences, even if, in doing so, he had to adjust history. He may seem to us less a choral poet than, as M. L. West says, "a singer, performing his own songs to his cithara accompaniment." But by his own lights Stesichorus' achievement was to "establish (*stesai*) a chorus of singers to the cithara."[38] And he left an important formal grid to his successors, a structure that leads directly into the Pindaric tradition and, in another form, into the drama: *strophe,* turn; *antistrophe,* counterturn; and *epodos,* after-song. The *Suda* identifies these as "the three of Stesichorus . . . for all the poetry of Stesichorus is epodic." It conformed—though we can hardly demonstrate this from what remains—to the triadic sequence. "If someone was quite without culture and learning," the *Suda* continues, "it was said as insult that he didn't know even 'the three of Stesichorus.'"[39]

Stesichorus survived on the Himeran currency. He survives elsewhere. In Berlin there is a famous *crater* (large cup) attributed to the fifth-century BC vase painter Douris. It portrays—the earliest dated vase to do so—educational scenes from ancient Athens. Among the images of dialogue and instruction is a seated teacher holding up a scroll to a young man. On it are written two half-lines attributed to Stesichorus, "To me Muse . . . I start singing about the broad-flowing Scamander." Already in Athens this poet from the West, from Sicily, was canonical.

His poetry corresponded closely to the art of the period, and what is missing can be imagined, if not read, in other artefacts. When Pausanias describes the Chest of Cypselus and the Amyclean Throne, part of the matter is provided by Homer, but much more by Stesichorus: "it seems more likely that the artists drew on Stesichorus than that he drew on them."[40] There is, too, the famous Tabula Iliaca, a first-century AD Roman copy of an earlier piece by Theodorus based (the inscription says) on Stesichorus' poem about the fall of Troy. It was found on the Appian Way at Bovillae and can now be viewed in the Capitoline Museum, Rome. Narrative sculpture is most satisfactory when the text to which it answers survives. There are, Bowra insists, discrepancies between the carving and the missing text. All the same, not only was Stesichorus the authority the original sculptor followed; his copyist retained the attribution. If the inscription had not survived, we would be inclined to read the stone as Virgilian. The greatest Roman star borrowed its light from a lesser Greek star, which had also borrowed its light. It's how poetry works; nothing need ever be quite lost, even when it passes out of memory.

XVI

Ibycus of Rhegion (fl. 560 BC)

of Ibycus, who prayed to the birds

STATIUS, *Silvae*[1]

 Polycrates came to power on the island of Samos around 540 BC, aided and abetted by his brothers Pantagnotus and Syloson, and ruled for the next decade or more, playing both ends against the middle (the Persians against the Egyptians, the Spartans against the Persians).[2] He built up a substantial naval force and conquered several neighbouring islands. Samos established colonies, some as far away as Sicily. His combined policy of trade and piracy paid off for a time, though it earned him foes. At last Oroetes, the Persian satrap, lured him into captivity and, in 522, on the mainland opposite his magnificent island, crucified him.[3]

Still, even in ruins his palace, Suetonius reports, made the emperor Caligula jealous. Herodotus says that three of the greatest human creations in the world were down to Polycrates: the aqueduct constructed by Eupalinos to bring fresh water to the city of Samos, the mole of the harbour there, and the unfinished temple of Hera, designed by leading architects of the day. Modern travellers can view the foundations of this giant temple on the island's southern shore; it was intended to be 357 yards long and 57 yards wide. The cult of Hera was already well established on the island; his edifice was a massive acknowledgement to Zeus's often-wronged spouse. "He also established," Michael Grant says, "a brothel, based on those at Sardis in Lydia."[4]

When Polycrates' father, Aeaces, was ruler, Ibycus came to Samos, perhaps as one of the tutors for the young tyrant-to-be. Anacreon was imported to tutor the boy in music. Ibycus may have been imported for similar reasons: he had invented the *sambuke,* "a kind of three-sided *kithara*."[5]

When he assumed power from his father, Polycrates rapidly developed and improved his land and retained at his brief, spectacular court both poets. He is reputed to have had the scattered songs of Homer brought together, edited, and an authoritative copy made for recitation. He patronised the jeweller Theodorus and, Herodotus adds, the noted physician Democedes. The king of Egypt told Polycrates he was simply too lucky: he should cast away something of value to guard against bad fortune. Polycrates threw away a precious ring. A few days later, Herodotus says, a fisherman presented him with a delectable fish, and in its belly the ring was found.

A substantial papyrus fragment, attributed to Ibycus, promises to recall the sack of Troy, but ends with a passage praising the everlasting fame of Polycrates.[6] This may refer to the tyrant before he came to power, because his immortality is inferred from his dazzling beauty rather than his might and the writing is eroticised. After Polycrates' death, it is likely that Ibycus chose to leave Samos and the rule of Polycrates' embittered brother. He and Anacreon departed around 522 BC, Anacreon for Athens, Ibycus for home. He may have spent the last twenty years of his life in "the West."

He lived to be old. There was a statue of him, said to be by Praxiteles, now lost, showing him as elderly, bent and bearded.[7] Plato's Parmenides remembers a passage of Ibycus, also lost, about how, like an old horse put in the traces to run a chariot race, he trembles and shudders, knowing what it was like before: for against his will he is falling in love again.[8] There is excitement and fear, the ingredients of love, and as man grows older, fear gradually outweighs excitement. Spring comes, in Cydonia the quinces and the vines flower in the maidens' garden, growth is thick and urgent; for the poet at such times desire never sleeps but bursts upon him like a north wind alive with lightning and love, unbridled, unconsidering, driving him mad and grasping the very root of his heart.[9]

There is something real about Ibycus' passion, the way it takes a conceit and draws it deep into the body, until the poetry runs like sap in the veins of a tree. The nets of Cyprian Aphrodite are not to be eluded: young Love glances up from under downcast lids and the old heart is impaled on the gaze, helpless and hurt and grateful.[10]

Before he was adopted by Samos, Ibycus belonged to Italy. After Polycrates, he returned to the place where he had been born around 590 BC, Rhegion (modern Reggio in Calabria), a town on the very toe of Italy, on the mainland side of the Straits of Messina, with Sicily a choppy ferry crossing away. He came of a well-established family. His father was Phytius,[11] or the historian Polyzelus of Messene, or Cerdas, or Eelides.[12] Polyzelus is the least likely candidate: there was no such vocation as "historian" per se in the sixth century BC. Cerdas may have been an invention of the comic poets. Phytius has the best claim, perhaps a leader of the party and class which ruled Rhegion until Anaxilas came to power in 494 BC. Some say Ibycus *père* was a celebrated Pythagorean legislator "and received divine honours after his death."[13] This may be as much an anachronism as "historian," since Pythagoras didn't leave Samos until Polycrates came to power. But so much concern with an uncertain pedigree indicates the esteem in which Ibycus was held. The poet's sole Pythagorean statement is that the star of morning and the star of evening are one and the same. He is the first poet to make this connection.[14] He may, though it seems far-fetched, have been in line to become tyrant of Rhegion, but chose to leave instead, taking with him elements of the regional dialect, and it is because of this that the grammarians, fascinated by variation, have preserved so many of his and Stesichorus' brief phrases.

The *Suda* tells us something else about Ibycus: he was "most ardent in ephebic love," or, in a more recent translation of the same passage, "He was completely crazed with love for boys."[15] Philodemus is censorious: ". . . Ibycus, Anacreon and the like debauched young men not by their songs but by their ideas." Cicero saw Ibycus as "aflame with love," based on rather more evidence than remains to us.[16] There are moments of rapture, but it is gazing rather than embracing rapture:

> Euryalus, sprung from the grey-eyed Graces,
> Beloved of the lovely-coifed Seasons, you were
> Nursed by her of Cyprus and by
>   Persuasion among abundant rose-buds.[17]

It is not only rose-buds that abound in this Keatsian lushness: "myrtle, violet, goldenrod, apple-blossom, roses and tender bay-leaves."[18] And among the foliage and blossom, high up, "sit variegated dapple-throated wild drakes and hidden birds of purple hue and the wide-winged halcyons."[19]

Ibycus had a master, and that master was Stesichorus of Himera, who had taken the choral ode that Alcman perfected in Sparta and travelled west with it, to Himera in northern Sicily.[20] There is no conclusive evidence that Ibycus ever met his master, though they were separated only by the Straits of Messina and half of the rugged island of Sicily. One story tells that when Ibycus went to Sicily, perhaps on his way to Himera, travelling from the landing at Catana (why did he not land at Zankle?), he had a carriage accident and crushed his hand "and for a long time he gave up his music, dedicating his lyre to Apollo."[21] The story is vague, and there is no licence for asserting that he was on his way to visit Stesichorus at the time. But the authorship of one key work has been disputed between them (Simonides assigning the text to Stesichorus) and they are conveniently lumped together. Bowra seems to regard Ibycus as a kind of extension of Stesichorus, a living bit, as it were, since so much of Stesichorus is erased, and so much of what survives is inert with literature.

Ibycus as disciple probably also composed long poems on mythological themes. The poems were assembled by later editors into seven books, and he was best known in antiquity for the erotic variations he played on mythological themes. His myth-clusters, like Stesichorus', include tales associated with Heracles,[22] Meleager, the Argonauts, Troy and the returnees from Troy. Deiphobus rivals Idomeneus for the love of irresistible Helen; Menelaus, intending to slay his estranged wife, drops his sword at her feet; Achilles marries Medea—in the Elysian fields.[23] Inevitably Ibycus lingered over the

rape of Ganymede, and is said to have written on the rape of Tithonus by
the Dawn; he could not resist the beauty or the doleful death of Troilus.
Endymion's dalliance with the Moon, Talos as *erastes* of Rhadamanthus the
Just and other charged intimacies brought his Muse alive. His editor David
A. Campbell writes, "he played a part in what K. J. Dover calls 'the homo-
sexualisation of mythology.'"

The earliest epinicean poetry is ascribed to Simonides, but perhaps (recent papyruses suggest) Ibycus precedes him.

The remaining verse does not feel like choral writing. As is the case with
Alcman, the fragments of Ibycus suggest a lyric poet whose themes would
be more appropriate in the symposium than in the theatre or market-place:
his *paideioi hymnoi* ("hymns to boys"). We can assume that the objects of
erotic praise were generally young noblemen; the eroticism perhaps courtly
and conventional rather than literal. From the little that exists, we gain a
sense of much narrative activity, the production of short epyllia and maybe
even of longer epics, though not of Stesichorean proportions, literary in
character, light in texture, engaging all the senses.

Whatever his relations with Stesichorus, no fragment survives that we
can confidently assign to this first "Italian" period. He visited Syracuse and
the fleeting descriptions of the area of Ortygia have a first-hand feel about
them. The connection of Ortygia to the mainland by means of a man-made
causeway was still recent.[24] The connection of the fabled Fountain of
Arethusa on the island of Ortygia with the equally fabled river Alpheus in
Greece was earlier and strictly fabulous, but Ibycus evidently alluded to the
legend that "the cup of Olympia" was thrown into the river Alpheus at
Olympia and bobbed up to the surface in the Fountain of Arethusa, several
hundred miles away.[25]

Still, mention of those rivers inevitably puts us in mind of Orpheus, or in
any event of the far-travelling head of Orpheus, and Ibycus was the first
poet to mention the name of "famous Orpheus," either in celebration or
with satirical intent (see p. 17). What is curious is that the phrase survives
uniquely and without context in the Roman grammarian Priscian's *Grammar,* dating from the early sixth century AD, 1,200 years after Ibycus lived.

Nothing in life became Ibycus so well as the leaving of it. He is best remembered for his death. Ibycus' name may derive, the *Suda* tells us, from
the Greek word for crane, and cranes play a crucial role in the story alluded
to by Antipater of Sidon among others.[26] As an old man, Ibycus was on
his way to Corinth to a chariot race and a musical contest. Successful
poets were not poor men in those days: they had patrons, and sometimes
they received substantial awards for their performances in contests. The
awards were presented in public and the poet had to carry them about his
person. Bandits and pirates found such poets lucrative prey (we remember

the young Dionysus, kidnapped by pirates in the Homeric Hymns, and Arion thrown overboard by pirates).[27] Ibycus' fate was equally colourful and miraculous.

When he came ashore, proceeding energetically, venerable and resolute, he passed through a lonely place, the sacred grove of Neptune. A flock of cranes flew overhead and he blessed them as a good omen. He and they were both far from home and were seeking hospitality. Suddenly two robbers surprised him. He could wield a lyre but not a sword, and soon he was overpowered. Only the cranes, screaming in the sky, saw the dreadful deed that followed, the poet murdered and stripped of his wealth. He called on them to avenge him, and died. His body, despoiled and mutilated, was discovered and identified by a friend.

The festival went ahead, and in the large theatre at Corinth a huge crowd, among which the bandits were numbered, assembled to hear the recitation and music. There was grief and anger at news of the death of Ibycus, and calls for vengeance. Even as the choruses performed, the flock of cranes flew over the theatre and the bandits in terror cried out, "Look! The cranes of Ibycus!" Having given themselves away, they were apprehended and dealt the justice they deserved. It is not quite certain what that justice was, but Ibycus having been a poet, it is to be hoped that it was harsh. Having done their duty, the cranes flew on to Africa.

In the Palatine Anthology Ibycus enjoys a beautiful, anonymous epitaph:

> Of Rhegium I sing, at the toe of Italy, and its shallows,
> A city which tastes for ever the water of Sicily;
> Of Rhegium I sing because it fostered, beneath a leafy elm,
> Ibycus, lover of the lyre, of boys, after he'd
> Enjoyed sufficient pleasures. Rhegium banked
> Much ivy and laid a bed of white reeds on his tomb.[28]

XVII

Anacreon of Teos
(and His Offspring, the
Anacreontea of Alexandria)

His poems are littered with the shorn locks of Smerdies
and the bright gaze of Cleobulus and the graceful youth of
Bathyllus. But even in such verses, you can see how moderate he is.

MAXIMUS OF TYRE, *Orations*[1]

 "Anacreon is a poet whose fame and stature come from a collection of poems he did not write," says Guy Davenport.[2]
There are in fact two Anacreons, a true and a false one, a poet
who lived and an epigrammatic "Anon." whose refinements are
precious in both senses of the word. As luck would have it, the false
Anacreon, much copied in the Middle Ages and first printed in Paris in
1554,[3] is the one whose impact on European literature, right up to the nineteenth century, was decisive. A source for Ronsard, Herrick and other lyric
poets, this "pseudo-Anacreon has been one of the most persistent and rich
classical influences of them all. His tradition has been alive—is still very
much alive—since the sixteenth century."[4]

The actual Anacreon was only properly identified two hundred years ago
and, though a subtler and more complex poet than his doppelgänger, is displaced by him. Scholars at the great library in Alexandria, and the poets and
poetasters who surrounded them, started the Anacreontic fashion, which
tells us something about the poet who inspired it, just as the Homeric
Hymns tell us something about Homer and his authority: his name conferred legitimacy on the work of lesser poets. Similarly, the much more im-
itable Anacreon legitimised the charming conceits of critics and scholars
who imagined they might in their window-boxes plough the same furrow as
the master whose work they chronicled and edited. It all began as a tribute
to the poet.

We can imagine *Anacreontea* symposia. Hellenic Greeks of the diaspora
and, much later, after the world had been christened, Byzantine Greeks who
were pagan recusants may have spent the occasional evening making
Anacreontic verses, as the Japanese do haiku or the English play Consequences. In Alexandria, Athens, Constantinople and elsewhere such activity

produced the sixty or so poems of the *Anacreontea* which survive, composed
over a span of centuries and with varying degrees of skill. Thematically and
formally it is one of the most complete "collections" to have come down to
us. Modern critics find the poems insipid in comparison with the real thing,
enervated exercises rather than primary works, and the poetry that derived
its energies from them was at times diminished and artificial. Lesky is
among the critics who blame the cuckoo, pseudo-Anacreon, for tumbling
the actual chick from the nest.

The *Anacreontea* abounds not in cuckoos but in conventionalised swallows. Pseudo-Anacreon curses one babbler for waking him out of a delicious erotic dream about the boy Bathyllus.[5] Another—perfumed—swallow
he has enslaved and trained. It tells its story (many of the poems are allegorising anecdotes): it goes about doing Anacreon's errands, more Ariel
than Puck, stirring things up, carrying letters. "When he goes off to bed, I
nap on the lyre itself," the bird declares.[6] Once the poet frees him, the swallow says he will stay willingly beside him: what the master does is too interesting to leave behind. The loveliest *Anacreontea* conceit explores the nature
of the Loves or the Desires (*Erotas*) which obsess pseudo-Anacreon. The
images of the nest and the cycles of nature which Desires transcend are
cleverly exploited.

> Beloved swallow, every year
> You come, you weave a nest
> In Summer, then you're off,
> Wintering near the Nile, or Memphis.
> In my heart Eros, not regarding seasons,
> Keeps weaving a nest, where one
> Longing is fledgling, another still in egg,
> A third just hatching; and the nest is loud
> With wide-beaked chicks all crying
> For food. The larger feed the baby Longings,
> And when they are mature there in my heart
> They themselves, in Eros' nest, begin begetting.
> What am I to do, I am too weak
> To shout to silence this vast flock of Longings.[7]

As well as swallows and images of old age, pseudo-Anacreon plays with
computations: just how many lovers has the old rogue had? More than
twice as many as Don Giovanni, if we are to believe one poem.[8] Most of
the pieces are uttered by an antique voice, and this agedness is inevitably a
theme. He drinks too much, complains too much and is terribly conceited
in expression. Give him a good metaphor and he's off.

The *Anacreontea*, in the form in which we have it, begins with a dream.

The speaker concedes the fictionality of the sequence, a fact which early readers took to be a conceit in itself rather than a crucial signpost. In the dream, a man we imagine to be young and rather attractive (otherwise Anacreon's ghost would not have spared him a second glance) declares:

> Anacreon, the Teian singer, in a dream
> Saw and called to me. I ran and kissed him.
> I hugged him. He was old but still quite handsome
> And Love was working in him, the wine scented
> His lips. Since he was old, unstable on his pins,
> Eros clutched his hand and guided him.
> The poet lifted from his brows the garland
> And passed it to me, and it smelled of him.
> I was a foolish boy, I placed it on
> My own head as a crown, and ever since
> I've not lived a single moment without love.[9]

The poems are artificial but not as artful as they might be. Some are metrically irregular or incorrect. Some use refrains that give them an inappropriate balladic feel. A refrain may come at the beginning of a stanza: "When I drink wine," for example, followed by consequences.[10] One poem starts and ends with the same couplet: "Grant me Homer's lyre / Without the killing chord."[11] The wish to share Homer's skills without participating in his brutal themes is repeated elsewhere. In one of the pleasantest conceits the poet says that he set out to recount heroic tales. But he can't do it. He changes the string on his lyre. It's no good. He changes the lyre itself, but all he can ever sing about is love.[12] He asks Hephaistus to make him, rather than armour or a shield, a deep silver goblet, decorated not with gloomy galaxies and the mythology that shaped them but with grapes and vines and with Bacchantes gathering them in, a wine-press, laughing satyrs . . .[13]

The *Anacreontea* is all about seizing the day and making the most of it; and that "most" has nothing to do with fighting or competing for gain; it has to do with creature pleasures, with living the present to the full, even when—especially when—that present is approaching twilight. The real Anacreon is a man of intense pleasures, but in moderation. The fictional poet knows less restraint and longs to lose his mind in drink as the heroes had lost theirs in passion. He must do so without weapons or battles. So passions themselves become disproportionate, the microcosm of a passion for a boy displaces everything else. Against Desires, the macrocosm hasn't got a chance. This wry disproportionality reminds us less of John Donne's than of the English Anacreon Robert Herrick's verse.

> Now reigns the *Rose*, and now
> Th' Arabian Dew besmears

> My uncontrollèd brow,
> And my retorted hairs.[14]

Pseudo-Anacreon commissions paintings, first of a girl, then of his beloved Bathyllus. Bathyllus is quite detailed in what he wants depicted, including "a natural member already swelling with desire for the Paphian," namely Venus and the arts of love. But he is disappointed that the artist cannot portray the backside of his beloved. He concludes that in future the artist should model his Phoebus from Bathyllus and not vice versa.[15]

Wine, women, boys, song: many elements of Anacreon are there in pseudo-Anacreon, but in the wrong proportions, with the wrong inflections. The true poet is more various in tone and subject-matter than his shadow; his poems go deeper into language and experience than the imitations do. Gilbert Murray finds the very artificiality of the imitations at odds with the quality of the original. "The dialect, the treatment of Eros as a frivolous fat boy, the personifications, the descriptions of works of art, all are marks of a later age . . . Anacreon stands out among Greek writers for his limpid ease of rhythm, thought, and expression. A child can understand him, and he ripples into music. But the false poems are even more Anacreontic than Anacreon . . . Very likely our whole conception of the man would be higher, were it not for the incessant imitations which have fixed him as a type of the festive and amorous septuagenarian."[16]

There is something delightfully contrary about Anacreon's imagination as it emerges from the fragments that are preserved. (Pseudo-Anacreon was better served by time.) He provides a corrective to the love poetry that has preceded his. If we contrast his poetry with that of Sappho, with whom salacious legend links his name, it becomes clear that we are dealing with a poet who will not let even the deepest of feelings destroy the balance of his expression. Legend hurled poor Sappho, heart-broken when Phaon would not respond to her, off the Leukadian cliffs into the sea. Many a lover climbed the two thousand feet to bid the cruel world adieu. Sappho's leap was a trope for unhappy love, until Anacreon turned its vertigo into a positive point of departure.[17] His leap was a deliberate surrender to, not an escape from, passion, an act of affirmation rather than defeat. There are many ways to translate his famous fragment. Guy Davenport says,

> I climb the white cliff again
> To throw myself into the grey sea,
> Drunk with love again.[18]

Barbara Hughes Fowler's version is different: no "grey sea" or "white cliff" but a cliché "foaming wave" and a cliff whose name is retained to underline the Sapphic connection:

> Once again from high upon
> the Leukadian cliff I dive
> into the foaming wave,
> drunk with love.

Davenport's visual economy chips too much of the fragment, including its prosody, away. Fowler insists on linguistic context and completeness but has not quite *seen* the poem.

The ways in which Anacreon builds his poetry into the very structure of the language is illustrated by a much-translated fragment about one of his actual or would-be lovers, Cleobulus. "I love Cleobulus, I am mad about Cleobulus, I gaze at Cleobulus."[19] The lines are quoted by the second-century grammarian Herodion to illustrate a figure of speech he calls *polyptoton,* in which one word, differently declined, is used, the effect depending entirely on the inflection. Translated into an uninflected language it is hard to snare the effect. David Mulroy has:

> Yes I am Cleobulus' [Kleobulou] lover,   [genitive]
> am mad for Cleobulus [Kleobuloi],   [dative]
> ogle Cleobulus [Kleobulon]   [accusative]

Barbara Hughes Fowler successfully transposes the wit onto the prepositions:

> I'm in love with Kleoboulos.
> I'm mad for Kleoboulos.
> I'm agog at Kleoboulos.[20]

Martin West is less successful because he does not go for syntactical variation:

> Cleobulus is who I love,
> Cleobulus I'm mad about,
> Cleobulus I ogle.

In the move from Greek to English, West seems to insist rather than to vary.

Another fragment in which the actual Greek form of words *is* the poem declares, "and the room in which he didn't marry but was married."[21] A man marries (active voice), a woman is married (passive voice), and if a *man* gets married it implies that he is effeminate. We can ask, when the poet prays to Dionysus that Cleobulus reciprocate (or accept) his love, if "accept" means "allow himself to be passive." How obliquely can we read his subtleties?

Quite obliquely, in some cases. His wonderful satire of Artemon,[22] the rent-boy turned catamite, is uncharacteristically waspish. The first fragment tells of blonde Eurypyle's infatuation with "that litter-rider Artemon." The second, one of the longer fragments, is more circumstantial. Davenport's version, despite its dated diction, is the best:

> Time was, he wore a tunic from a rummage sale,
> A barbarian kind of hat, knucklebones in his ears,
> And a cloak that used to be a rawhide shieldcase,
> Artemon the pimp who got rich selling the use
> Of bakers' apprentices and teenaged nancy boys,
> Often seen in the stocks by his neck, or on the wheel,
> Or having the lash applied to his bleeding back,
> Or his beard and the hair on his head pulled out,
> And now he rides in a mule cart, wears golden earrings,
> Says he's the son of Kylê, and carries an ivory parasol
> Like the women . . .[23]

The economy here, as Bowra makes clear, is that the list of specific punishments tells the informed reader what specific crimes Artemon committed. The stocks were used to punish market fraud, the wheel for public incitement, scourging answered a multitude of sins, and the pulling out of hair was for adultery or other sexual misdemeanours.[24] Davenport is more specific in sexualising the nature of Artemon's transgressions than other translators have been.

Anacreon and sexual themes are never far apart. Few poets are so frank in expressing their desires, or so various in the objects of desire they choose, though it must be said that Anacreon's libido targets the male more readily than the female, and boys rather than men. A number of vase painters portray Anacreon: he strums his lyre while young men dance about him.[25] In one verse fragment, the poet calls for water, wine and garlands, "so I may enjoy further fisticuffs with love."[26] These words were preserved "with a portrait of Anacreon on a second-century AD mosaic at Autun."[27] His garlands consist of coriander and anise (a heady range of scents), myrtle, willow and naucratis. Also hyacinth, roses . . . Thus crowned, he would have resembled a hanging flower-basket.[28]

Asked why he celebrates young boys rather than the gods, he replies, "Because they are my gods."[29] How young were the boys? Probably adolescent, their cheeks and chins not quite on the turn, only vaguely fuzzing up with beard. What did he want from these boys? Affection? Sexual satisfaction? How culpable, morally, are the occasions of his poems, how unexceptionable? Are these symbolic encounters or more? For what is unsaid in them has its own eloquence. There is a kind of relishing which suggests initiation rather than violation; he is drawn to boys who are discovering their own beauty, their magnetism. A vivid fragment tells how a mother imagines her son is safe at home; in fact he has escaped to "the hyacinth fields" and there encountered either the goddess of Love or Love itself: "you flitted down to where the people are, and many found their hearts change pace at you . . ."[30] In another place, he evokes a fawn:

> Unweaned, almost new-born in fact, afraid,
> Abandoned in woods by its antlered
> Mother, that's how he is, be gentle . . .[31]

Love never takes him wholly by surprise because he is always on the lookout for it. Bowra calls Anacreon's and Ibycus' take on love "courtly." This medievalising is not helpful, suggesting that each encounter is merely symbolic. Some clearly are. The poem in which Anacreon falls in love with, legend has it, Sappho, is wry and amused in a way true passion cannot be. The girl with the fancy sandals fancies someone else.

> Once more love with his golden curls
> Pitches his purple ball at me
> So I'll play the age-old game with the lovely girl
>> Who sports those curious sandals . . .
>
> She harks from the island of the handsome cities,
> Lesbos, and she finds my hair too white,
> And anyway, she's gazing past me towards
>> Another girl . . .[32]

There is a beguiling theory that Eros' ball preceded Eros' arrow. Love was something unexpectedly tossed to you which you caught as a reflex and then couldn't dispose of. Later, this was replaced by the bow and arrow, the sense that love begins with an unexpected, inextricable penetration.

Sir Thomas Wyatt and Henry VIII fell in love with the same woman, Anne Boleyn. Both Athenaeus and Aelian[33] record how Anacreon and the tyrant Polycrates of Samos fell in love with the same Thracian lad, one Smerdies. Anacreon had come to Samos from Thrace, where boys wore their hair long. Did Polycrates cut off the boy's hair in a spate of jealousy or to make him more Samian in aspect? Certainly Anacreon in several fragments laments the shearing of the lad, but being politic does not blame the tyrant but Smerdies himself for thus marring his charms.[34] The contest for Smerdies' locks is hyperbolic, suggesting (not insisting on) a struggle for Thrace itself, and Smerdies' own loss of cultural identity.

Was boy-love something Polycrates promoted at Samos and was Anacreon, who until that time seems to have chosen his imagery in a more heterosexual spirit—writing about fillies, for example—conforming to his patron's proclivities in writing poems of intense desire and gentle contest?

The second-century rhetorician Maximus of Tyre saw it the other way around: ". . . Anacreon made Polycrates more gentle to the Samians by mingling love with tyranny—the hair of Smerdies and Cleobulus, the beauty of Bathyllus, and Ionian song."[35]

Though he is profligate of loves, Anacreon is not profligate with language. There is a generally direct, colloquial quality to his diction, a precise economy of image. "Love's dice, one is madness, one is frenzy."[36] "I am borne over hidden shoals."[37] "Once more bald-pate Alexis goes awooing."[38] Set beside the abundance of Apollonius, for example, where the sheer amount of language far outweighs the occasion, Anacreon's thrift is exemplary. He "has left the formulaic style of the epic far behind him and chooses his words individually for their special merits."[39] A refusal to be solemn does not make him any less serious as a poet. Love is not something to be endured: it is to be played and boxed with, to be knocked down by, to be pondered in its aftermath.

> Charioteer, who glance up like a girl,
> You, boy, I am after you,
> But you're not after me, you do not know
> You hold in your two fists the very reins of me.[40]

The charioteer metaphor comes out of nowhere and brilliantly realises the passion. The would-be tamer becomes the wild steed, and the boy he would tame, in this strange reversal, is empowered by the man's unexpressed love. Again the theme is one of control rather than loss of control. The wine must be carefully watered:

> Boy, come, bring a big bowl so that I
> May gulp and gulp and never pause for breath;
> Pour in for me ten ladlesful of water
> To temper five of wine, so that again,
> Without relinquishing my wits I can perform
> The bacchant and yet retain my self-possession.[41]

Growing older and still unable to stop loving, the poet has to change gear, even change vehicle, in pursuit of love.

> Up to Olympus on light wings I'm soaring
> Looking for Love; for the boy
> Won't condescend to share the joy of his youth with me.[42]

He resorts to prayer, first to Dionysus: *please make Cleobulus succumb to my blandishments.*[43] He even prays to the boy himself, a drink in one hand: "Come, dear boy, pledge your lean thighs to me . . ."[44] This thing called love will not stop happening. "Again, like a smith with a huge mallet, / Love struck then dunked me in his icy current."[45] He falls ill, but as soon as he is better he tunes his lyre and greets his dear loves once more in song.[46]

Plutarch declares, "Thus there's only one real Love, that's the love of boys: he does not 'glisten with desire,' as Anacreon describes the love of girls, nor doused with perfumes, 'glowing'; when you see him he will be un-embellished . . ."[47] A papyrus reflects on how delightful the old age of Anacreon and Socrates was. Old age without art is poor, but with art and language, love is available in all its variety, recurring with its ecstasies and its relaxations.

> Again I love again I do not love
> am mad again and am not mad again.[48]

Pindar and his rival Bacchylides refer to poems in Anacreon's manner as *paideioi hymnoi* ("hymns to boys"). The objects of praise were often young noblemen: the eroticism may sometimes have been conventional, without expectation of fulfilment. Whatever the case, he "strummed nightlong on his boy-loving lyre," in the words of one epitaph doubtfully attributed to Simonides, in which the later poet shades the poet's tomb with grape tendrils:

> May he forever be kept damp by your sweet dew,
> Less sweet than poems the old man breathed from tender lips.[49]

Half a century divides Sappho and Alcaeus from Anacreon. The difference in the spirit of their verse could not be more marked. For Sappho and Alcaeus, sprung as they were from ruling families, a tyrant was a foe and the system of tyranny a misfortune. For Anacreon, the tyrant was patron. He made himself at home with various powerful persons: "Polycrates in Samos, Hipparchus in Athens, and Echecrates the Aleuad in Thessaly."[50] The process that leads from aristocratic to democratic rule passes through the phase of tyranny which dispossesses hereditary privilege and interests, and the protracted moment of tyranny fosters a kind of art quite different from that which flourishes before and after. As Lesky says, "The tone of the conversation, whether at the Samian or the Athenian court, must have been very different from that in Lesbos."[51]

The tone of the poetry, even when the themes are similar, is different too. The life of the symposium was different in scale and in balance from the court of the tyrant. A host is a very different character from a king, and a friend differs in kind from a patron, no matter how benign that patron is. In a court, "respect" is a prerequisite, the whims of the tyrant must be borne, questions of politics cannot arise in any but the most oblique or attenuated form. When Michael Grant describes Anacreon's verse as intended for the symposium he archaises it. When he insists that the verse is strongly political in a conservative, Theognidean way, he most uncharacteristically misreads the context in which Anacreon wrote, from the moment he accepted the invitation of Polycrates to become a tyrant's resident poet.

> I dislike it when, stretched out beside the full
> Wine crater among friends, a drinker talks
> Conflict, battle sorrow; but the man who mixes
> Muse-gifts and Aphrodite, remembering how the feast
> Is lovely, I love him.[52]

Through Anacreon we enter a world of politeness, play, obliquity, irony. These terms are embodied in his spiritual patroness, Euphrosyne, whose name means "good cheer." It is she whom Milton invokes in "L'Allegro." "The peculiar charm of this mature Ionic art," Lesky says, "consists in a singular union of opposites. The poet who hates all excess and maintains such a careful balance between love and indifference, between drunkenness and sobriety,[53] is always master of his medium; yet the magic of his art lies in that gentle resignation which invests everything with an unconscious inevitability."[54] Athenaeus made the same point: Anacreon was sober when he wrote, an upright man feigning excess.[55]

Possibly the culture of Teos in Asia Minor, where Anacreon was born, was already less vigorous and emphatic than the culture of Lesbos had been. Bowra sees the Teian world as louche, laid back and vulnerable. There the mixed Lydian mode of poetry, indebted to the music of Polymnestus of Colophon, prefigured the kinds of poetry Plato despised, "intended more for relaxation than for public affairs and state occasions" and in love with luxury.[56] It was a poetry the church fathers loathed. Clement of Alexandria, adducing Anacreon, counsels teachers to stop boys "going along with hips swaying," a form of meretricious deportment.[57] Gregory of Corinth despises the effeminacy of the poems: the ear "is basely flattered" by erotic phrases in Anacreon and Sappho.[58] Nor was it all plain sailing in pre-Christian times. The Stoic Diogenes said that Anacreon was a corrupter of youth because of the way he touched upon his subjects, and Cicero declares, not without a trace of disgust, "All of Anacreon's poetry is erotic."[59]

Anacreon was born around 570 BC and, according to legend, lived for eighty-five years. The *Suda* says his father was Scythinus. Then, true to form, it blurs the record. Maybe his father was Eumelus, or Parthenius. Aristocritus too has a claim. And his mother? The *Suda* has no opinion on that subject.

Teos, now Sighalik, in Turkey, on the northern coast of the Gulf of Caystrus, Ionia, was dedicated to Dionysus and was famous for its wines, fish and cakes. Anacreon began composing his verse there in the Ionic form of Greek and remained, in his peripatetic career, remarkably faithful to the inflections of his childhood.

The populations of two brave cities in Asia Minor, Teos and Phocaea, migrated *en masse* to escape the threat of Persian occupation. Persia sacked Sardis around 541 and when the Teians departed were already in control of the outer walls of the city. Anacreon was by then a grown man. The exiles went to Abdera, on the Thracian border. Tradition says Heracles founded the town on the spot where Abderos was killed by the horses of Diomede. The town had been colonised over a century before, unsuccessfully, by Clazomenai. This time, around 545 BC, the settlement took. Abdera was a port city north-east of Thasos which became a key member of the Delian League, famous for its beautiful coins. Democritus, the fifth-century atomic philosopher; Protagoras, the first Sophist;[60] Anaxarchos, Alexander the Great's counsellor: all these hailed from there. Nonetheless, in ancient times Abderans had a reputation for dullness and it is no surprise that Anacreon left his second home without regret and is unlikely to have returned there to live—or die, though legend has him buried in the vicinity. Certain fictional epitaphs take him back to his first home and bury him in Teos.[61]

We can surmise that some of his early Abderan poems survive: their imagery draws from Thrace and he seems to celebrate its habits and people. Abdera and its surroundings were rich but, at least initially, hostile. The Thracians were relatively savage. The epitaph for Agathon, probably by Anacreon, is a wonderful war poem:

> Strong Agathon, dead for Abdera, mourned
> By every citizen at the giant pyre:
> In the wilderness of loathsome battle, blood-thirsty Ares
> Never killed a young man quite your peer.[62]

This is not a one-off. There is the much-translated lament for Aristocleides. Richmond Lattimore does this poem one kind of justice.[63]

> Of all my stalwart friends, Aristokleides,
> I grieve most for you, who died young
> To keep your country free.[64]

David Mulroy has "pity" for "grieve," changing the tone of the poem. He sees it as an apocryphal fragment.

> Of gallant friends, Aristocleides, I pity you the most.
> You gave up your youth to save the fatherland from slavery.[65]

Barbara Hughes Fowler is more elaborate and Wilfred Owenish: in Anacreon there is no sense of a life *wasted,* and the translator's sentiment does violence to the original.

O Aristokleides,
I pity you first
of my stouthearted friends,
for you wasted your youth
warding slavery off
from your native land.[66]

West, in turn, in his heavy couplet, gathers up the nuanced sense in prosaic fistfuls:

Aristoclides, you're the first I mourn of my brave friends:
you lost your young life to defend your land from slavery.

Out of a very short fragment four different poems, each serving a rather different reading of history, have been generated.

In Thrace, Anacreon must have encountered the "filly" who eyes him without interest. He reflects that he could be the rider, he could break her in; meanwhile, the filly can frisk and nibble grasses in the meadow.[67] Anacreon may have seen the Dionysian, bassaridic excesses,[68] which reinforced his sense of necessary moderation. Thrace may, too, have contributed to the streak of misogyny which marks the poems, though they portray a lover of women as well as boys. Some appear to exploit a female voice.[69] Some appear to solicit, but the woman solicited may be readily available: "You smile at every stranger: let me drink, I'm thirsty."[70] A prostitute is a "generous giver" a "public highway"[71] he will travel on. There is a touch of satire in his representation of gossips, and of revulsion in his description of "leg rolling women," those who wind their legs together during intercourse.[72]

No woman's name is associated with the tyrant Polycrates of Samos, patron of Ibycus as well as Anacreon. He seems to have been closer in temperament to Anacreon. Ibycus was from Magna Graecia, a world away, while Anacreon, speaking with one voice, a monodist, was from nearby Asia Minor and had suffered displacement at the hands of Polycrates' foes. Polycrates was ambitious for Samos, which is why he provided hospitality to two poets of the highest reputation. Not all his subjects were content. During his tyranny the mathematician Pythagoras, a man of the older school, left Samos to live in Croton, southern Italy, escaping the tyrant's creative megalomania.

Anacreon described Samos as the "city of the Nymphs."[73] He came to tutor the tyrant's son in music, or to teach the tyrant himself: some say that Polycrates' father imported him to teach the boy.[74] Whatever the circumstances, the two men may have become intimate. The poet was with his patron in 522 BC when a messenger arrived to lure Polycrates to his crucifixion. Herodotus reports, not without a touch of scepticism: "According to another account, less generally accepted, Oroetes sent a messenger to Samos to make some request or other . . . and on his arrival Polycrates was at table in the hall with Anacreon, the poet of Teos. It so happened that Polycrates sat facing the wall of the room with his back to the man as he came forward to say what he had to say; and—either to show his contempt for Oroetes' power, or perhaps merely by chance—he not only omitted to give an answer, but did not even bother to turn round while the messenger was speaking."[75] Polycrates was murdered in Magnesia, on the river Meander, a Greek city under Persian control.

Immediately the poet was sent for by another powerful man, Hipparchus, younger son of the greatest Athenian tyrant, Pisistratus. Hipparchus is said to have sent a fifty-oared galley, or *penteconter,* to fetch him. The vessel promised both speed and protection in a Samos already unsettled and entering a dark phase. When Hipparchus was murdered, Anacreon may have gone back to Thessaly for a time. He lived on and on, dying at last, the gossips say, from inhaling a grape pip. Valerius Maximus is more circumstantial: he "perished when a single pip obstinately stuck in his withered throat as he sustained his poor remaining strength with raisin-juice."

Bowra is of the view that much of the surviving poetry, witty, carefree, erotic, was probably written on Samos. Anacreon, in his view, then fled to Athens, revisited Thessaly, and returned to Athens to die. His friends in Athens included Xanthippus, father of Pericles, and Xanthippus' statue stood near to his own famous likeness on the Acropolis, a tribute Pericles paid his father and the poet, who lived long enough to enjoy the lyrics of Aeschylus.[76] Indeed, he survived to learn the outcome of the Battle of Marathon: it was an enormous life, and, in Michael Grant's view, he was a "new kind of lyric poet, not geographically rooted but a travelling professional" like the epic and choral poets of his and earlier times. But Anacreon also "represented the end of an epoch, being the last important composer and performer of solo song."

Around 153 BC, Aristarchus of Samothrace, one of the librarians in Alexandria, described by Athenaeus as "the absolute scholar" who was of key importance in putting Homer, Hesiod, Pindar and others in order, collated and edited the poetry of Anacreon into five (or six) books or rolls.[77] The work represented one of the climaxes of melic poetry with its personal and choral lyrics. There is little satire here and virtually no didactic content. The poems are for singing or reciting in private, or in the confines of the court, and it is important to remember their close integration with music. The legendary association of Anacreon and Sappho may be due to the fact that Lesbos was the birthplace of the most famous earlier melic poets. Among the lyric, elegiac and iambic work edited by Aristarchus were hymns, love songs, symposium or court poems, epigrams, dedications, epitaphs. If we set this *oeuvre* parallel to Ibycus', we immediately see how much more of Anacreon survives, especially the intimate and erotic. In some instances we seem to have the remains of virtually whole poems.[78]

The impact of the *Anacreontea* has already been noted. Nearer his own time, Anacreon's poetry of voice affected the next great moment of Greek literature. "His output also influenced both the metrical form and subject-matter of later Athenian tragedy," says Michael Grant.[79] Lattimore, from the vantage point of a great translator, feels on the pulse a similar connection, specifically with Aeschylus: "though there is no reason to think that Anacreon himself wrote tragedy, his metrical influence on Attic tragedy may have been very great indeed, perhaps decisive; but this feeling of mine rests on inference rather than positive statement and remains a feeling."[80]

There are no portrayals of Anacreon as a lad. Seven hundred years after his death, Athenaeus describes him as "handsome": it is about the youngest word or image associated with him. In AD 170 Pausanias saw the famous statue of the poet on the Acropolis, east of the Parthenon, Pericles' tribute to his father's friend.[81] Anacreon looked "like a man who might be singing in his cups." The statue perished but by rare good fortune a good copy of it turned up in the ruins of a Roman villa near Rieti. Paul Zanker gives a vivid account of it.[82] The lost version probably "originated in the circle of Phidias," Athens' greatest sculptor and a key player in Pericles' Acropolean construction project. Though the Roman statue is broken, Zanker sees the missing parts: Anacreon holds a barbiton. His nudity is commonplace in portrayals of male Athenian symposiasts. "My dinner: a corner of thin honey cake, but also a bowl of wine to wash it down. I strum my lovely instrument now, making a serenade to my dear one."[83]

The poet's body is strong and unwrinkled, age has not withered him. Broad of beam, almost stocky, but not Bacchic, he has not been bloated by Silenus, he is vigorous despite the length of his beard. He retains his composure, of course; that is clear from his face, however subtly his posture suggests inebriation. Anacreon's face is neutral, unemotional, not jolly and gay. He "has tied up the penis and foreskin with a string, a practice known as infibulation."[84] It may have been to express abstinence; but in the portrayal of men, and in particular older men, it was regarded as obscene and offensive to show a long penis and, in particular, the penis' head. The sense we have, from vases and from statues, that ancient Greek men were either ill-endowed or comically over-endowed like satyrs has much to do with genital aesthetics. In the statue, Anacreon's penis is artificially restrained.

This strong old age is the subject of many of Anacreon's most beguiling poems and fragments. Why does an old man still perfume his chest "that is hollower than the pipes of Pan"? Because he cannot resist love.[85]

I'm grey on the sides and white on top;
Youth that was graceful is gone, my teeth themselves
Ache old and chatter, life's span is shortening, and I
Cry more than sometimes, fearing Tartarus;
For the dark corners of Hell hold terrors for me
And the pathway drops precipitate and once
A man starts going down there's no way back.[86]

Better love, he says, than "Amalthea's horn" (she was the goat who fed Zeus and whose horns issued, respectively, nectar and honey) or even the extreme but vigorous old age that people who live in Tartessus, on the coast of Spain, enjoy.[87]

One epitaph, in the Palatine Anthology, ends with the words "for all your life, old man, was poured out as an offering to these three—the Muses, Dionysus and Eros."[88] Anacreon is the perennial old man. As the centuries passed, he was painted as more and more dissolute, but the poets always loved him, whatever the churchmen might say. In the fourteenth-century Planudean Anthology[89] his statue is evoked as an emblem of pagan revelry, seedy and stumbling but still a figure to be cherished. Actual and pseudo-Anacreon coexist in the portrait:

Observe him, old Anacreon, frayed and worn, wobbly
With wine, how he bends his shape into the stone.
    He gazes, look at him, with eyes that look
    With love, with lust, and see too how his gown
Trails right down to his heel. In a haze of wine
He's lost one sandal, but the other still conceals
    A shrivelled clutch of toes. The poet sings
    Of charming Bathyllus, full-fleshed Megistus
And he's strumming his melancholy lyre. O Dionysus,
Keep him safe, for it would be wrong indeed
    Were Bacchus' faithful servant to be felled
    By Bacchus' wine.

XVIII

Hipponax of Ephesus (c. 540 BC)

The poet Hipponax is buried here. If you're a cad, keep off;
if you're an honest man of blameless lineage, make
yourself at ease, relax and doze here if you wish.

Pliny the Elder, always entertaining and undependable, declares in his *Natural History,* "The face of Hipponax was notoriously ugly."[1] Even six centuries after his death, Hipponax was a byword for rancour; he was a monster, amusing so long as one was not caught in his line of verbal fire. At a time when poetry was becoming more mannered and polite, when the vigour of Archilochus had declined to the conceits of Semonides, it is refreshing to come upon the thoroughly urban disenchantment of Hipponax, his world of textures and smells, in which the human body at its most gross finds its laureate in the privy, on the street, or in a small dimly lit room with a woman even more lecherous than he is.

When we speak of Hipponax, are we actually speaking of a persona, a voice from which the poet has created an ironic distance? Or are we, as with Archilochus, persuaded that the voice, for all its deliberately pedestrian metrical artifice, belongs to the man who speaks? In a corner of the National Museum in Athens a grumpy second-century BC stone head which scholars suggest is Hipponax's keeps a blind eye on passing tourists. There are vestiges of a wreath around his brow—laurel, or poison ivy? Battered, like a pugilist who is being restrained, he snarls, the eyes frowning and pursed. Time has cut off his nose but the face refuses to be spited.[2] Near his grave, now vanished, wasps were said to nest: to the unworthy or dishonest passer-by they gave chase and stung. He "snarled even at his parents" and his verses still sting in Hades.[3] His grave was overgrown with bramble and thorn, and the puckering, thirst-inducing wild pear.

As with the Hesiod of *Works and Days* and Archilochus, so with Hipponax one has a sense, except in the deliberately "poetic" and the parodic poems, that this is it, the sensibility itself. The exaggerations are part of the voice, not an escape from it. The obscene diction, with half a dozen nicknames for the vagina (including "Sindian fissure"[4] and, in one fragment,[5] four untranslatable words in Lydian dialect) and the penis, and a sexual undertone to many an image and detail: such things are candid rather than artful. Even though he delivers himself of a misogynistic epigram, "In a woman's life two days stand out as most delectable: when she's wed, when she is carried out dead,"[6] it is clear that he, unlike some of his near contemporaries, enjoyed heterosexual intercourse and acknowledged women as human—in any event, as human as he was and rather more human than his foes.

Hipponax is among the first poets to defecate in verse, to reflect on the stench of faeces and the hungry, pestilential swarming of the dung-beetles, drawn to a reeking pile and to the orifice from which it dropped. M. L. West renders one of his epithets, about the gourmand who frequently retires to defecate in order to continue stuffing his gut, as "an interprandial pooper."[7] This is witty but tonally high-table, almost polite when set beside the actual, coarse and incontinent dumps that take place in the poems. Archilochus, whatever his antecedents and no matter how malcontent he was, generally strikes a warriorly, even an aristocratic, note. There is nothing aristocratic about Hipponax, except possibly his blood. If he is from a distinguished background, then his poetry systematically breaks rank.

Scholars generally agree that he did come of an established family in Ephesus.[8] It is unlikely that a poor man would have been singled out for exile as he was, unless a very early literary precocity earned him enemies. The *Suda* names his father and mother as the alliterative couple Pytheas and Protis, and adds that he was banished (in the second half of the sixth century BC) by the tyrants Athenagoras and Comas, clients of the Persian Darius I. It may not have been such a bad thing to leave Ephesus. Compared with Colophon, and even Smyrna, it was an altogether darker, less cheerful city. At least in Ionia the threats were Lydian, sunnier than those that emanated from sombre Persia.

All the same, to be poor in exile cannot have been easy, and Hipponax, if we believe the poems, was sometimes grindingly poor, and always a notable sourpuss. His poverty is reflected in his obsession with food and clothing, his refusal to rise too far above the ground of mere survival. His poetry has resolved *not* to fly. Indeed he invented an earthbound metre for the purpose, the choliambic, or limping iambic, also known as *scazon*. His iambic trimeters usually conclude in a spondee (two long syllables or stresses) rather than an iamb, and the effect is to lame the natural dynamic of the iambic line, its tendency to extend into longer cadences. He played other variations, too, mixing iamb and dactyl, for example.[9] What did such verse sound like in the sixth and fifth centuries BC? Doggerel, or something more deliberately and artfully crafted? According to Athenaeus, Hipponax was the inventor of parody.[10]

The limp of his choliambics was transposed by some later commentators onto the poet himself, condemning him, over and above his poverty, to a physical disability. Pliny says he was thought to have been of a wiry build but immensely strong. From the poems, however, we are tempted to deduce a man with a paunch or a belly. The word "stomach" appears with some frequency, and in one fragment at least, walking along the road to Smyrna and passing various landmarks, the poet concludes, "turning your belly towards the sunset."[11] Though it is "your" rather than "my" belly, it seems to belong to the speaker all the same. His most charming stomach features in another small fragment which says, "his stomach gurgled like a pot of soup"; the word for "gurgle" is the onomatopoeic *eborboruxe*.[12] A lean beggar, when he feeds and drinks copiously, may distend and gurgle.

Hipponax stayed, even if he did not settle, in Clazomenae, one of the twelve cities of Ionia, below Chytrium, not far from Smyrna. Its most famous native son was Anaxagoras (c. 500–428), the first philosopher to live in Athens, and a friend and teacher of Pericles and Euripides. Nothing much beyond what the fragments tell is known of Hipponax's life in Clazomenae. He makes no secret of the fact that he hated the sculptor brothers Bupalos and Athenis. He was repelled by the glutton Eurymedontiades. He attacks the wide- or open-arsed painter Mimnes, "a slave born of a slave." His patron saint is Hermes, in particular the infant rogue celebrated in the Homeric "Hymn to Hermes," the patron of thieves and mischief-makers.[13] He invokes him in a charmingly familiar way. He is shivering, chattering, he prays for a cloak, a tunic, sandals, felt shoes (all expressed in diminutive forms, a kind of wheedling baby-talk) and 60 gold staters "on the other side."[14] Perhaps he is asking Hermes to assist him in a burglary and "on the other side" implies that he is digging through a wall; or does it mean "on the other side of the scales," to balance them out? The felt shoes (in another version of the same passage) were to keep his chilblains from bursting.

Pliny gives a version of the tale of why Hipponax hated Bupalos and Athenis so much. Though he also says the story is false,[15] it ties in obliquely with related anecdotes and illuminates a thorough poetic revenge. Putting the accounts together, we have a story of love and a contest between two art forms. Hipponax sought the hand of Bupalos' daughter in matrimony but was turned down because of his ugliness. Bupalos and Athenis displayed portraits of the suitor to general hilarity. They may have shown busts or sculptures (caricature in sculpture "was almost the origin of Greek portraiture"),[16] but they were probably caricatures or even graffiti scratched on the plastered walls of Clazomenae. The poet, following in Archilochus' famous vendetta-footsteps, set about destroying the reputation and character of his artist assailants with his own instrument, words.

Most accounts omit Bupalos' daughter and portray two malicious sculptors attacking an easy target, an ugly man, without taking into account how ugly that man could be in deed. They survive only in his verse, their own art lost for ever. The brothers, like the sisters Archilochus ravaged in verse, committed suicide, hanging themselves. The pen was mightier than the chisel.

"Here, take my coat, I'll punch Bupalos in the eye ... I've two right hands and my punches hit their mark."[17] What is the nature of his assault? In some poems he described Bupalos as guilty of incest with his mother, who may have been called Arete. In one fragment Bupalos is quite simply a "mother-fucker" (*metrokoites*) and we witness him about to pull back his "godforsaken foreskin."[18] Elsewhere the artist has sex with a poor, blind, crippled old mother when she is asleep: he "desecrates" her "sea-urchin."[19] Scholars have conjectured that the sea-urchin may be her daughter's, and that Bupalos copulates with her while the mother sleeps. In another fragment, and as insultingly, the poet himself apparently goes to lie with Bupalos' mother or mistress (depending on who we take Arete to be); she is certainly up for it, bending obligingly towards the lamp so that he can enter her.[20] The lamp, often a feature in Greek erotic poetry, helps us to "see" the intimate revenge. In an *especially* fragmented set of fragments Hipponax goes at it with passionate lechery, tearing off clothes, biting and lusting and ("she was in a hurry") thrusting.[21] At one point he is "withdrawing the head as though drying, or skinning, a sausage." When they have finished copulating he detumesces, his penis "like a wrinkled sail."

There is a suggestion that Bupalos indulged in oral homosexual acts for eight obols. There are other terrible hints, including punishments which may have been doled out to Bupalos but may also have been visited upon Hipponax himself, the scapegoating rituals (*pharmakos*) which punished the ugly man in the interests of purifying the city. Another possibility: the "punishments" are perhaps ritual treatments for impotence, in this case the poet's.

Poetry in Hipponax's time seems to have been able to make people act. Language had a literal power, not only in recording history but also in making common ground, those shared places where voices sing together and a shared culture is evoked and evolved. As well as forging such harmonies, it could be used to generate pain and anxiety, to destroy. "Right from the outset," says Jacob Burckhardt, reflecting on Homer, "the Greeks thoroughly understood *kertomein*, the ache in the heart that words can inflict. It is particularly associated with mockery of unsuccessful attempts and actions ... In the post-Homeric age, with the iambics of Archilochus, verbal abuse (*loidoria*) became an artistic genre ..."[22] Hipponax was the ultimate master.

Iambic poetry, as we have noted before, described at first a genre as much as a metre. The genre presumed that humour would be an ingredient, but humour of a specific kind, humour at someone's expense, whether the poet's own (sending himself up as a turn-tail mercenary) or a foe's. The term "iambic" may derive from the name of the maidservant Iambe, whose tart wit, expressed perhaps in metrical form, brought laughter back to the heart of bereaved and grieving Demeter. Less mythological, more scatological, there may have been another Iambe, an old washerwoman whom Hipponax, walking by the sea, found scrubbing her wool. He touched her washing trough (with whatever nuances we wish to assign to that) and she uttered a line of verse telling him to lay off. Choeroboscus[23] offers us a choice between the two accounts. The second is of course anachronistic, because iambic metre predates Hipponax by at least a century. Perhaps the old washerwoman spoke a choliambic (Choeroboscus provides a variant), either because she was prosodically inventive or quite incompetent. In any case, the halting metre appealed to the poet, who made it his hallmark. An unfriendly critic might suggest that this encounter was Hipponax's initiation, his first transaction with a muse, but his muse, unlike those glamorous inspiriters of other poets, was a warty, snaggle-toothed, horny-handed crone.

He is more purely iambic, in the generic sense, than Archilochus, obsessed with food, sex, excretion, all the processes of a now hungry, now bloated body, a cruising lust and a lust temporarily satisfied. There is more than a touch of buffoonery. Many fragments (one is tempted to call them "splinters" in his case) involve apparently innocent acts or images which grammarians preserved as examples of usage but modern readers see as sexually charged. West identifies sour wine with vaginal secretions, for instance;[24] "he screeched like an owl in the privy" is hardly obscure in its meaning;[25] there is some highly charged keel-caulking, some siphoning of new wine ("piercing the lid") and so on. How much is actually sexual, how much is merely sexually inflected by modern scholars and readers? In the light of the longer fragments, even the most salacious readings seem tenable.

As poetry became more formalised, aureate, "civilised," its diction refined, its tonalities artful and controlled, the rougher iambic poets (Archilochus and Hipponax especially) remember that symposiasts eat and drink, and as a result digest and fart and shit. When they go home they may have sex, or furtively do so in an alley, an inn or out of doors; and beneath good manners deep resentments, rivalries and hatreds simmer. All the same, only an exceptionally ugly poet could come up with the implacable insults and vengeances of Hipponax. Had he been in Ithaca, he would have been the aggressive beggar Arnaios, nicknamed Iros, come to drive disguised Odysseus from his doorway, and he would have earned death at Odysseus' hand. Certainly Hipponax knew his *Odyssey:* he asks for a cloak in much the same way as Odysseus does;[26] there is a significant Arete, sharing her name with the Phaeacian queen who is so courteous to Telemachus, though in Hipponax she is another class of woman; when he curses an erstwhile friend he envisages a fate as cruel as Odysseus', wind-blown and battered at sea, washed ashore in Alcinous' kingdom at the end of Book V.[27]

The small fragments of Hipponax are especially suggestive. In some cases a fragment survives with what may be an error. One corrupted text speaks of the poet's "son" (a sufficiently worrying notion) where the context suggests the word intended is "pig." "May someone pluck his anus," says one of Douglas Gerber's versions, and he speculates that such "plucking" is intended to "soften it up." The actual expression seems to be not "anus" but "perineum," the zone between the scrotum and the anus, and plucking it would seem to promise pain and tension rather than relaxation.[28] Perhaps the exercise was cosmetic, to turn a late adolescent back into a hairless boy. Fragment 73 is brutally circumstantial: "he pissed blood and shat bile." Four shards of sense survive in fragment 82: a wide anus, possibly female genitalia, the moon, a cough. We can deduce that it is night and that, in the almost nonsense of the dark, some kind of intercourse is in progress.

Fragment 104 conflates material: it seems to record violence against a man and also sex, and the aftermath of defecation. Perhaps, scholars suggest, it is another "scapegoating" poem, like fragment 78.[29] It includes puns and real semantic complexity and ends in what seems to be successful masturbation. In fragment 92 a more troubling cure is in progress, involving whipping the genitals with a fig-branch, insertions in the anus, much excrement and a swarm of dung beetles. One reason such verse is troubling is that it is incomplete and unresolvable. Fragments 70 to 79 from the Oxyrhynchus papyruses are odd as well: parodic ceremonies seem to be occurring, perhaps burglaries as well, defecations from fear. Hermes is on hand.

Why spend time in such squalid, ravenous, uncompromising company? Because Hipponax reeks of the human in every sense, because his poetry includes so much of the material world, a world in which the five senses are continually aroused, repelled, *alive*. Reason sleeps, to be sure, and monsters emerge, but they are not mythical or legendary. They are the real monsters of need and desire. Introducing Hipponax's poems, Douglas Gerber declares: "Hipponax is revealed as a forceful poet whose verses contain many colourful, foreign, rare, and obscene words."[30] "Semonides had followers and influence," says C. M. Bowra. "In the sixth century, Hipponax wrote in a similar spirit, and after them both came the wide, rich world of Attic comedy, which picked up its art where they left it and applied it in a dramatic form to mock the contemporary scene."[31] One woman in Hipponax is described as a "cock-shaker";[32] another is accused, because of the mess of childbirth, of having for a vagina an "opening of filth"; another is branded a self-exposer, a clothes-lifter. These are phrases we might expect from Aristophanes, where they would have a social context, and he was a reader of Hipponax. The verse has the repulsive fascination of toilet-wall graffiti.

Callimachus and Herodas much admired Hipponax. Lesky speculates that the poet may have had an influence on Petronius (in the first century AD), whose *Satyricon* is almost as close to the ground as Hipponax's verse. In the ancient world the poet never lacked for readers.[33] He is a kind of "real-ist," not asking questions or lamenting, as Semonides does, but saying it how it is: a poet of the material and contingent world. As a result, his lan-guage is wonderfully impure, laced with foreign and loan words and using something like the dialect of his city in verse, what Lesky calls "the everyday speech of the Lydian hinterland."[34] A misfit and outcast he may be, and yet it is impossible not to—well, not to linger in his reeking company and to feel a degree of guarded affection for him. He manages to generate his own kind of squalid dignity.

XIX

Simonides of Cos (556–467 BC)

Simonides praises the man who does not willingly do what
is base.

WERNER JAEGER, *Paideia*[1]

 In a helpfully pedantic note in his *Etymologicum Magnum,* Choeroboscus, the ninth-century grammarian, says: "*Semonides:* in
connection with the iambic poet, the name is spelled with *eta*
(derived perhaps from *sema,* 'sign'); in connection with the lyric
poet, it is spelled with *iota* (maybe deriving from *simos,* 'snub-nosed')."[2] The
homonymous poets are divided by a century and several leagues of sea.

Snub-nose gained a reputation for pithy epitaph writing, celebrating first
the Athenian victims of Marathon, then a decade later those who died at
Thermopylae, Artemisium, Salamis, Plataea. He wrote the most famous of
all Greek epitaphs, translated by William Lisle Bowles:

> Go tell the Spartans, thou that passest by,
> That here, obedient to their laws,[3] we lie.

He was successful in a number of modes—elegiac, lyric, dithyrambic
(though only a single word of a dithyramb survives)[4]—and composed
epinicean odes, dirges, epigrams, paeans and, if we credit the *Suda,* even
tragedies.[5] He was reputed to be more monstrously avaricious than most
poets, and he did not scruple to mix with tyrants or pleasure any patron
with a purse. As Theocritus says, had they not purchased his talents, his patrons in Thessaly—Antiochus, Aleuas, the descendants of Scopas and
Creon—would have languished "unremembered among the miserable
dead." Thanks to him, even their horses live forever.[6] He was the first man
to make a fortune from systematically *selling* his art. Earlier poets found patrons and changed patrons but did not take themselves to market in quite
the way Simonides did. Like a barber or a wine-merchant, he had his regu-
lars, in Thessaly, south Italy and Sicily. He became a semi-official laureate of
the victories over the Persians of 480–479 BC.[7]

If there were nine Muses when he started, by the time he died there was a
tenth, a mercenary muse much courted by posterity. Callimachus found his
greed repugnant:

> . . . my Muse I'll not raise a mercenary,
> As that Cos-man did, of Hylichus' ancestry.[8]

All the same, thirst for money does not seem to have undermined the quality of his poetry, commissioned though it was; nor was he cheated of an
admiring Greek and Roman posterity. Plato and Meleager revered him,
Catullus and Horace paid him their respects, as did Plutarch (a little wryly),
Cicero and others. Peter Jay, Simonides' best modern translator, takes a
kindly view of him: "He had a great capacity for sympathy with the tastes
and ideals of different Greek cities." A more sceptical critic might say that
he knew which side his bread was buttered on. Jay continues, "the two
poems on Plataea, one written for the Athenians, the other for the Spartans,
show how subtly and tactfully he could match his poetry to its occasion."[9]
This is how Jay renders the poem he entitles "For the Spartan Dead at
Plataea (479 BC)":

> These men clothed their land with incorruptible
> Glory when they assumed death's misty cloak.
> They are not dead in death, whose memory
> Lives with us, while their courage brings them back.

The poem is in the third- not the first-person plural, while in "For the
Athenian Dead at Plataea" (479 BC) it is "we," not "they," who are not dead
in death:

> If dying well is courage's great test,
> Fate honoured us in this above the rest.
> We struggled to crown Greece with liberty:
> Buried in ageless glory now we lie.

Of all the epitaphs Peter Jay translates, the most inventive is another "collective" inscription:

> While bringing Apollo the pick of the Etruscan plunder
> One sea one night one ship sent these men under.[10]

Simonides' skill, says Jay, is in "transcending" local allegiances so that he is
Greece's "first national poet." Money liberated him from any fixed geographical or political fidelity.

So successful was he that, like Anacreon, not long after his death an anthology of "his" epigrams circulated. His name, too, became a magnet for
false attributions which were less deceits than tributes; like the tall tales that
grew out of his life, they were meant to characterise and represent him to
succeeding audiences.[11] Some were collected from (unsigned) public inscriptions, on plaques and plinths, into the so-called *Sylloge Simonidea*. Their
authorship must be a matter of conjecture in every case. A number commemorate events that occurred long after the poet's death. When Peter Jay
thinks he is translating Simonides, he may be the victim of exquisite forger-

ies. The *Sylloge* was around in the first century BC and may already have been gathering two centuries before. Indeed, fifty years after Simonides died, Philochorus assembled a collection of inscriptional verse from Attic sources. Meleager drew on the *Sylloge* for his anthology, the *Garland*.

Many of the poems possess genuinely Simonidean pathos, if we can use the term "genuine" in the context of Simonides. The epigrams are strong, patriotic little poems about sacrifices that ensure Greek freedom. Their "intact" survival, even where attribution is doubtful, give them an advantage over the fragments of longer poems: we can see a whole, clear and quite lucid intention behind each poem. In one of his own epitaphs, Simonides considers the fate of Megistus, who fell at Thermopylae. Simonides is said to have put the epitaph there "for the sake of friendship," an unusual act for him:

> This tomb is his, glorious Megistus', whom the Medes
> After fording the river Sperchius slew; a seer,
> He knew Death's ghostly agents were approaching,
> Yet could not tear himself from his Spartan lords.[12]

Simonides was in Athens at the time of Hipparchus (527–514), and shared him as patron with Lasus of Hermione and with Anacreon, rescued from Samos after the fall of Polycrates. Hipparchus left the day-to-day running of Athens to his elder brother Hippias while he, "frivolous, amorous and fond of the arts," Aristotle says, detained his poets and other artists in Athens by means of generous fees.[13] Simonides beat Lasus in a dithyramb or choral competition, a victory commemorated in a jest in Aristophanes' *Wasps*. His Simonides took it all seriously but Lasus finally declared (had he lost?), "I don't give a damn."[14] This is the same Lasus who is said to have caught out Onomacritos adding lines to Homer and inventing Orphic hymns and tattled to Hipparchus, who had him exiled.

The question of Simonides' character is an interesting one: was he posthumously caricatured and vilified or was he merely scheming and covetous? There must have been more to his personality than avarice, or he would not have commanded the respect (or the fees) that he did from wise and powerful men. Although in *The Clouds* Aristophanes has a character suggest that Simonides' poem about the shearing of a ram (a pun on the name of a well-known athlete) was a cheerful sort of song, in *Peace* he makes the poet's own name synonymous with avarice: "now that he's old and wrinkly, he'd even put to sea on a field-gate to make some money."[15] The scholiast describes him as "the first to introduce money-grubbing into his art and to compose a poem for a fee." He had two boxes, one full of money, the other empty, which he said was "full of favours."[16] Chamaeleon and Athenaeus agree, Athenaeus declaring that, "in Syracuse, when Hieron used to have him sent daily provisions, Simonides openly sold most of it and kept just a small bit for his own use. And, why? He said it was to show off Hieron's generosity and his own frugality."[17] When Hieron's wife asked him, "Which is better, to be wise or to be rich?" he replied, "Rich, for I see the wise spending their time at the rich man's gates."[18]

There is little doubt that he amassed a fortune. An admiring anonymous epigram (conceivably written by himself) celebrates his material achievements as a poet and as a trainer of choruses with information that feels like fact:

> Fifty-six, Simonides,
> Bulls and tripods you won
> Before you affixed this tablet, fifty-six
> Times after coaching the chorus, delightful, of men
> You mounted noble Nike's glittering chariot.[19]

The glitter here seems like gold rather than reflected sunlight. One does not come to Simonides looking for a consistent poetic personality or a defined voice, for probity or high principle. He was no Solon, and none of the aristocratic integrity that we find in the poets of Lesbos, for example, or Teos, or Megara, adheres to him. Poetry is what he does. He has reached an accommodation with the world. Plutarch recounts how he went to Themistocles, his friend, a man renowned as a just arbiter and at the time fulfilling the role of *strategos,* or chief magistrate, to ask him to bend the law. Themistocles replied: "You'd be a poor singer if you played out of tune, and I a poor magistrate if I did folk favours against the law."

And yet, just as Simonides always sang in tune, but was adept at changing tune, so honest Themistocles was not entirely above reproach. He knew something about beauty, and what he knew corrupted him. He became a foe of the just, even-handed and conservative Aristides because both (if we believe the philosopher Ariston of Cos, and why shouldn't we?) were in pursuit of the same lad, one Stesilaus from the island of Cos, Simonides' own birthplace. The story does not have a happy ending: Themistocles had Aristides "banished by ostracism." He also put to death, legend says, a Persian messenger demanding Athenian submission because, though a barbarian, he dared to use the Greek language to convey his message, and such appropriation of Homer's medium by a foreigner proved a capital offence.

There can be no doubt that Simonides' fame and prosperity had much to do with the protection and encouragement of Hipparchus and, by extension, of his brother Hippias. Distasteful, then, to find him writing, once democracy was his new paymaster,

> On the day Hipparchus was slain by Harmodius and Aristogiton, Athens was awash with radiance.[20]

The lines, which Bowra cannot bring himself to believe are by Simonides, were carved into the base of a monument sculpted by Critius and Nesiotes around 477 BC, to celebrate the murderers. Two further lines followed, but they have been mutilated almost beyond interpretation. Campbell speculates: did they declare that the assassins "made their native land (democratic)"? The fee for the inscription, if it is by Simonides, was sufficient to buy off his residual gratitude to his now dead patron; or perhaps it was just a measure of how far times had changed.

But there is a weight of testimony against Simonides the man. Anaxilas, tyrant of Rhegion, the winner of a mule race, Aristotle says, offered Simonides a modest fee for an epinicean poem. He declined, as if to say he couldn't versify the achievements of a mule. But when a large fee was proffered, he immediately struck up with the words, "Hail to you, daughters of thunder-shod steeds!"[21] Yet, as Aristotle comments, they were also daughters of donkeys.[22] Was Simonides an ironist? It is possible: he was closer to irony than Pindar ever came. But it is unlikely that he would have exercised irony when fulfilling even so coarse a commission.

Among the epitaphs attributed to him is one to a much-loved Thessalian hound.[23] The language used in it is similar to—undistinguishable from— what he would have used in addressing the memory of a human being, or celebrating a goddess. It does not *feel* like a parody. So strong were the conventions, so earnest the respect for verse, that irony was out of the question, though Simonides was not above sarcasm when he felt it was called for. Other conventions were less binding, for example details of myth. The editor Aristophanes of Byzantium reflects on how Simonides sometimes calls Europa's abductor a bull, but sometimes uses one or other of two words which mean sheep or goat. Europa and the goat? Something gets lost in translation.[24]

Simonides is the first poet for whom we have relatively firm dates. He was born in 556 BC on the Dodecanese island of Cos, fifteen miles south-east of the Turkish coast, the closest mainland city being Halicarnassus. Cos is twenty-eight miles long and quite narrow, severely mountainous at one end and rocky throughout. It is a place rich in grapes, watermelons, oil, cereals, vegetables, and nowadays, tobacco. It also produces the eponymous lettuce. It is singularly unflat, and horses and oxen did not thrive there, a point which Pindar and Bacchylides both make in their verse. Still, fertile and well watered, it possessed numerous healthy springs. The physician Hippocrates was born there, and there he died at the age of 104.

Cos was rather a strict, morally conservative island at the time of Simonides, lacking the brothels and pretty girls playing wind instruments that Polycrates brought to Samos to honour the goddess and perform more

conventional duties. There may have been a rather (early) Spartan atmo-
sphere, a becoming severity at a time when other cities were beginning to
discover the joys of excess, when Persian manners, scents and movements
were debasing established Greek norms. Herodotus calls the people of Cos
"an Ionian people from Attica," giving the impression that they belong to
both sides of the Aegean at once.

An important island with still significant ports, Cos is on a line between
the port of Athens and the Dardanelles. Among its towns, one set inland
out of the reach of pirates, Iulis, had more than its fair share of distinguished sons. Strabo reminds us that not only Simonides, but also his
nephew and disciple Bacchylides, Erasistratus, and Ariston the peripatetic
philosopher were all born there. He says that the law required every native,
on attaining the age of sixty, to poison himself. No wonder Simonides, who
was destined to live as much as thirty years beyond the allotted time, left
home and stayed away, eventually dying half a world away, in Sicily.[25]

Apollo was the patron of Cos and Iulis in particular, and the city kept a
hostel on Delos and sent boy-choruses to sing hymns to Apollo there. The
legendary Aristaeus, tamer of bees, would-be seducer of Eurydice,[26] was
also zealously worshipped: he saved the island from parching pestilence by
bringing the etesian winds, which still blow for about forty days a year from
the north-west, making the days bearable. And Dionysus was not neglected:
how could he have been, given the centrality of the wine industry in the island's ecology and economy. Theocritus spent time in Cos as a disciple of
the native poet Philetas, whose works have perished. His seventh *Idyll* is set
on a formalised Cos.[27] By that time it was under the aegis of the Ptolemies.

Simonides' father was Leoprepes—he is one of those rare early poets
with only one candidate for paternity. The child was nicknamed Melicertes,
the *meli* meaning "honey": honey-tongued. His career may have begun as a
composer and chorus master of Cean boys, competing at religious festivals.[28] He is also credited by the *Suda* with inventing long vowels (*eta* to
lengthen *epsilon, omega* to lengthen *omicron*) and the double consonants *xi* and
psi. He composed in the Doric dialect. In order to recite himself and to instruct his charges in recitation, he devised an "art of mnemonics" which,
according to Longinus, consisted of association and was hardly a coherent
system, though he makes much of it.[29] When he was eighty, his memory was
still phenomenal, like Sophocles'. Not everyone was keen to acquire his
skills. Themistocles, Cicero says, when Simonides promised that he would
coach him in mnemonics, replied, "I'd rather acquire a technique to forget,
since I remember what I'd prefer not to remember, and I can't forget what
I'd prefer to forget."[30]

A few Simonidean fragments may date from his formative years in Cos.[31]
Those that lack restraint in the vehemence of their hyperboles may be

apprentice-work. One, for example, compares the young boxer Glaucus to Heracles and to Polydeuces. The intention must be gently parodic; otherwise the poet displays considerable poetic *hubris,* or there has been a profound shift in religious sensibility within a very short period of time.[32] We can place little weight on authorities for dating, and even arguing from internal evidence is difficult since so few extended passages of verse survive. It is clear that he knew the poetry of Stesichorus. His first major success came in the composition of epinicean poems for the major games, the Olympian (established in 776 BC), Pythian (588 BC), Isthmian (582 BC), and Nemean (573 BC). Victories in any of those games, quite apart from providing the athlete with a personal triumph, reflected on the city, and a poet was commissioned by a leader or a city or a father or uncle to celebrate an athlete and a place in the same breath.[33]

As the form developed, it became an established feature in the athletic calendar and the poetic economy. The epinicean ode, Bowra says, grew into something "serious and stately; it assumed characteristics which had hitherto belonged to the hymn; it told instructive and illuminating stories; it contained aphorisms on man's relations with the gods. All these can be found in Pindar's Odes, and we cannot doubt that Simonides did something to prepare the way for them."[34] The twelfth-century grammarian Eustathius reports that Pindar was a pupil of Simonides and in age fitted in between the master and his nephew Bacchylides. Simonides stands in relation to Pindar rather as Gower does to Chaucer or Ben Jonson to Shakespeare, a large figure in the shadow of a giant.

Gower and Jonson survive abundantly, Simonides does not. Bowra risks a few general points. Simonides "seems to have been gayer and more lighthearted than Pindar."[35] He expresses more enthusiasm, his allusions are less far-fetched and more direct in their impact. He is less concerned with *hubris,* more with achievement. He is also sometimes vividly circumstantial rather than categorical: he will state the season and tell how the weather breaks across the poem; for Pindar what matters is the general contrast. Simonides can be *playful* in ways quite alien to Pindar. The ram-shearing poem may have been an anti-nicean ode, one deriding a loser rather than praising a winner, an equally remunerable sort of task. Pindar is not above chiding a loser (*Pythian* VIII, 86–87), but always in the context of magnifying the victor.

Among the apophthegms attributed to Simonides are two which have particular relevance in this connection: "the word is the image [*eikon*] of the thing"—a refreshingly anti-theoretical statement; and "he calls painting silent poetry and poetry painting that speaks."[36] How might such views be applied to actual composition? To begin with, in the rendering of descriptive detail. Discussing the *Iliad,* the scholiast notes: "*phrix,* 'ripple,' is the beginning of a rising wind. Simonides in an attempt to represent it said, 'the

breeze comes stippling the sea."[37] A quest for appropriate words is apparent in some of Simonides' precisions. "And from beside the wheel dust rose
high in the air."[38] The wagoner with two ill-matched horses struggles so as
not to "drop from his clenched hands the crimson thongs."[39] Theseus,
about to go after the Minotaur, promises his father a red sail if he comes
home safely: "a crimson sail dyed with the moist flower of the sturdy holm-
oak."[40] There is "The girl breathing / Words from her crimson lips."[41]

At night, "when nightingales, bubbling, green- / Necked, spring's birds"[42]
are heard, sometimes we hear too the "herald of sweet-breathed spring,"
the "blue-black swallow."[43] Another bird is the "sweet-voiced cock."[44] Another blue is the "blue-prowed" ship.[45] Precision is crucial if the poet is to
enact his meanings, as in one of his most celebrated poems:

> You're human, so never say that this,
> that or this other *will occur tomorrow,* never
> when a rich man passes say *he'll be rich until* . . .
> swifter's change than dragonfly flicks wing.[46]

This specific precision leads Dionysus of Halicarnassus to declare that Simonides surpasses Pindar in diction and in the way he combines words: "he
expresses pity not by exploiting a heightened style but by appealing to the
feelings." This is why Catullus invokes him: "send me a morsel of consolation, more sad than Simonides' tears."[47] Quintilian agrees: "his chief
merit . . . lies in the power to excite pity."

"The word is the image of the thing." For Simonides, words actually
evoke objects, conjure them in mind, and are in this sense "iconic." This is
why painting is silent poetry, poetry speaking painting: there is a level of
aesthetic equivalence between a dragonfly, its painted image and its verbal
depiction. Simonides attempts to make things alive to the senses. Colour,
sudden movement, the very things that make the image clear and defined
in the eye, have verbal equivalents. The epigrams, while more generalised,
drive home with an analogous precision.

The pithy statements in Pindar can seem trite; those in Simonides, as in
Solon, detach and "make sense out of context because of their directness
and the precision of his metaphors."[48] None of the attributed apophthegms
bears any relation to the surviving poems and fragments, "but the character
of his observations retains some sense of the character of his style."

The deep erosion of his work may have begun early. "Since stories about
Simonides were told as early as the fifth century, and relatively few citations
of his lyric verse survive, it would seem that by the fourth century the poet's
biography had become more interesting and accessible than much of his poetry."[49] That biography is more vivid than most, but no less uncertain; the
legends that grew around it are "representative," rather than merely fictional.

When he was in his late twenties and already known as a poet, Simonides was summoned to Athens by Hipparchus. His task, which he fulfilled with assiduity, included the composition of state epitaphs. The one about Hippias' daughter, on her tomb in Lampsacus, is thrifty and brilliant:[50]

> Under this dust is Archedice, Hippias' daughter;
> In his day in Greece he was chief of men.
> He, her husband, brother, her two sons were tyrants;
> She never let her heart swell with conceit.

He stayed in Athens until his patron was murdered in 514 BC and Hippias was exiled four years later. He went then to Thessaly, practising his art in various cities and securing patronage from the Aleudae, Scopadae and other rulers, though perhaps retaining close contact with Athens. He composed some of his memorable work in Thessaly. He stayed with Echecratidas, the *tagos*, or "king of kings," in Thessaly, living in Crannon, between Larissa and Pharsalus; there was a hot spring near there, and when its waters were mixed with wine, the wine retained the warmth for several days.

Echecratidas' son Antiochus died young, and Simonides dirged him. This dirge came to be regarded as a classic measure of dirges. He wrote another dirge for the Scopadae. This is the legend behind that commission.[51] During a banquet, Simonides recited a poem celebrating the Scopadae, but also speaking extensively about Castor and Polydeuces. The host declared that he would pay only half the agreed fee: the poet could secure the remainder from the Dioscuri. Suddenly the poet was summoned out of the banqueting hall by two young men, and just as he left the building the roof fell in and crushed his hosts and the rest of their guests. Only he lived to tell the tale and to identify the two young men: Castor and Polydeuces, the Dioscuri themselves, brought the house down. Simonides was called to identify the corpses. Thanks to his mnemonic system, he could remember the seating, or reclining, plan. This story is probably Hellenistic in origin.[52] Bowra believes Theocritus told it to show that the Scopades' investment in Simonides was worthwhile because without the poems he composed they, their wealth and horses, would all have been forgotten. (The fact that the victims might have survived does not seem to weigh in the balance.) Later writers reflect that, had the story been true, Simonides himself would have made much of it: what a selling point, what a justification for top fees.[53]

There is another story about transcendental payment being made on an investment of verse. One day Simonides, visiting "a certain island," found a fly-blown murdered corpse. He buried it and gave it an epitaph cursing the murderers and blessing "those who gave me burial" (namely himself).[54] On the point of sailing from the island, the blessing was delivered: the dead man's ghost visited Simonides and warned him against the journey.

Simonides stayed behind when the boat set sail. Of course, the boat went down with all hands: the poem had saved his life.

It may be that his abusive rivalry with Timocreon helped to besmirch his medium-term reputation. Timocreon made the mistake of going with the Persians to Susa, and he found it hard to come home. He was a famous athlete, and in Susa spent his time gluttonising and then challenging Persians to fight with him, which they did, though he always ended up the victor. He had thought the great Athenian statesman Themistocles to be his friend, but Themistocles did not approve his conduct and left him stranded with the foe. Timocreon came to hate Themistocles and all his friends. Timocreon stood on his dignity when he had no dignity to stand on. There is a mock-Simonidean epitaph for him:

> After abundant drinking, gorging, slandering
> Here lie I, Timocreon of Rhodes.

This was probably not Simonides' only attack. For his part, Timocreon parodied Simonides' style, which he found empty of matter, and satirised his person. Most of the fragments of Timocreon which survive are adjuncts and footnotes to the life of his hated Themistocles, who himself eventually went to work for the Persians, much to his enemy's delight.

Simonides could be haughtily dismissive of the "poetic" in writers whose work he disliked. The most famous example is his reply to Cleobolus' pious poem declaring that a work of art in stone might last longer than nature itself, immortalising its subject.

> Who with his wits about him would endorse
> Cleobolus of Lindus, who against
> Unstanchable rivers, the flowers of spring, the sun's
> Flame, or the moon's gold, or swirling
> Sea currents, set up the lastingness of a mere statue?
> The gods are above all things and even mortal hands
> Can crumble stone. He is a fool in judgement.[55]

Simonides was certainly back in Athens by 490, when he defeated Aeschylus in composing commemorative verses about Miltiades' defeat of the Persians at Marathon. His final years—ten or twenty? no one is certain—were spent in Sicily, under the benign wing of Hieron, tyrant of Syracuse, a patron too of Aeschylus. There he was joined by his nephew Bacchylides and continued what may have been a rivalry—it was certainly competition—with Pindar, another poet at Hieron's court. Pindar wrote his first three Olympian odes for Hieron and Theron; he also criticised Simonides for his excessive digressions.[56] Simonides, Plutarch declares, remarked that he often felt sorry after speaking, but never after keeping silent.[57] From Pindar's point of view, he spoke too much, and at tangents.

It is said that Simonides made peace between Theron of Acragas and Hieron of Syracuse when they were on the brink of war. Even after he died, he remained voluble. His tomb was violated and destroyed. Callimachus, in his *Aetia,* has him speak from beyond the grave against Phoenix of Acragas, who despoiled a substantial tomb "which the people of Acragas, out of respect for Zeus the Host, soon built at the entrance of their city." Phoenix went so far as to incorporate Simonides' headstone into a tower.[58] None of Simonides' own surviving poems touches directly on the experience of Sicily.

Bowra loves Simonides and wants to free him from the biographical opprobrium which dogs him. Having followed him from one court to another, he declares, "He consorted with tyrants, but there is no reason to think that he was servile to them."[59] Well, if they were paying him as a court poet, whether or not they were tyrannous tyrants, there is every reason to think that he was servile to them. There were things he would have been unlikely to say in their hearing, which he might well have said once death had put them beyond his audience.

It is sad that so little of Simonides' choral, narrative and dithyrambic poetry survives. The dithyramb was closely associated in antiquity with narrative in lyric form.[60] A lovely fragment about Danaë floating in the chest with baby Perseus and emitting her plaintive lament gives us an idea of his lightness of touch and the uninsistent nature of his prosody, even when the plot material is intense. The passage about Orpheus, possibly from a poem about the Argonauts, is almost a lyric in itself and could attach to various phases of Orpheus' life:

> Countless birds flocked
> Above his head, the fish
> Out of dark blue water leapt
> Straight into the air at his
> Beautiful song.[61]

Recent papyrus finds have helped to illuminate the nature of the mixed dithyrambic genre.[62] Volume LIX of the *Oxyrhynchus Papyri* (1992) includes a poem by Simonides about the battle of Plataea, which M. L. West has done much to reconstruct. The fragments indicate a substantial, not excessively long work, a few hundred lines in extent. It may have opened with the fanfare of a formal hymn, perhaps (West suggests) to Achilles. It was found with the remains of a roll containing symposium poems, and, not long enough to fill up a roll of papyrus, it could have been included with the *Nanno* (see pp. 144, 147).

Much of our knowledge of the choral tradition is conjectural, given the paucity of substantial surviving texts. Stesichorus and Ibycus provide shards. In the second half of the sixth century Simonides took the form further. His epinicea owe much to the choral and the dithyrambic tradition, and working back from the fragments of his poems and the substantial texts of Pindar, by means of a kind of regression we draw tentative conclusions. One thing is clear, a poet in ancient Greece had a place within the city and a serious, even a crucial, role to play composing work for religious and secular occasions, from exhortation and prayer to ode and epitaph. He was not innocent of thought, and some of the thought was original. When by a sly elision Simonides slides from "gods" to "god" (*theon* to *theos*), something important is happening in imagination as well as in argument: "no man has ever attained distinction unassisted by the gods, no city and no mortal. God knows everything, for men misery is in everything."[63] This god is a sudden table-turner, man is always at the whim of chance.[64] There is a theme in Simonides which troubled Plato, who found the poet inconsistent and morally deficient in this place.

> Here's a story:
> Arete[65] lives on unscalable
> Cliffs and near the gods tends
> A holy place. She can't be seen
> By everyone, but certainly by him
> Who strives and sweats within, the man
> Who draws near to the very peak
> Of manliness[66]

It is hard for a man to be truly good, "four-square in hands, in feet and in mind, fashioned without a flaw," because man lives in time, and time means change, so a man may achieve moments of the highest good, but they pass; even a good man's life is at best an interplay of striving and lapsing. Only the gods can *be* good, rather than pass through moments of goodness. "When his luck is good, any man is good; when it's bad he's bad (and by and large those men are best whom the gods love)." Simonides, Plato believed, was teaching that it is not worthwhile pursuing an impossible quest to *be* good; it is good enough not to be bad: "against necessity not even the gods fight." "I'm no fault-finder: I'm satisfied if a man is not bad or too shiftless, and understands the justice that helps his city, a sound man. I won't find fault with him; but the generation of fools is numberless. Everything with which baseness is not mixed is fair."[67]

There is always danger in translating poetry into the consistent categories of philosophy, because, like man in Simonides' reckoning, poetry exists in time and delivers not absolute but relative truths. Werner Jaeger shares Plato's concerns but is more forgiving because he historicises. He says that Simonides' poetry shows how "the true nature of *areté* in general was coming to be the central problem for the men of the early fifth century." Simonides evokes it and how rare it is. It lives, he says, "on difficult peaks, surrounded by the holy choir of lightfoot nymphs; few mortals can see her unless soul-torturing sweat has been wrung out of their vitals." Jaeger draws attention to the word *andreia:* "it still has the general meaning of 'manly virtue.' It is explained by the famous *skolion* which Simonides addressed to the Thessalian Scopas—a poem which reveals a conception of *areté* involving both mind and body. 'Hard it is to become a man of true *areté,* foursquare and faultless in hand and foot and mind.' The deliberate, severe, and lofty art which underlies *areté* was in these words made clear to Simonides' contemporaries . . .'"[68] What for Pindar is an unarguable moral verity for Simonides is a noble but difficult category. A world of relative truths is his. Simonides can play with ideas which, for Pindar, are truths that underpin the very mission of his verse. For Pindar seems to have mission, while Simonides has, at best, a vocation.

What makes Simonides so answerable to the "modern"? It is not just his life with its material hungers, real or imagined. It is not only his moral relativism, though that is certainly modern in a sense: "Simonides praises the man who does not willingly do what is base."[69] It is not his sense of irreversible transience, "All things thus swirl into Charybdis' terrible pool, / What is greatly good and great goods too."[70] Horace latched on to his line about the pointlessness of cowardice, a motive in itself for heroism:[71] "but Death snares too the man who flees the struggle."[72] These are elements that make Simonides familiar. His strong sense of the *eikon* and the connection between words and the things they name, the power of language to make real, his imagistic instinct, put us in mind of Pound. His arresting sense of paradox makes us rethink a cliché or a commonplace into lived language, for example, "It isn't that the soul leaves the body: the body leaves the soul."[73]

He says, "The city is the teacher of the man," and this sets him down among us.[74] I do not wish for a moment to appropriate him or to diminish his instructive otherness. But it is likely that *he* would have been more at home with Baudelaire than with Wordsworth, with Eliot than with Frost, and, like it or not, when we are not sentimental, so might most of us. The Augustans were enamoured of the Greeks because their nature was formal, more a moral than a material space, and the art of writing creates such common spaces, in which disparate elements harmonise, so that storm and calm, within and without, hold together in a single skein of words: "The city is the teacher of the man." Simonides' most hopeful poem, and we can only hope that it is by him, is an epigram celebrating the skill of two painters to make a real space. It is "real" and "space" in the sense that Wallace Stevens teaches us.

> Cimon painted the door there on the right.
> Dionysius painted the door on the right where you come back out.[75]

Corinna of Tanagra

When to her lute Corinna sings,
Her voice revives the leaden strings,
And doth in highest notes appear,
As any challeng'd echo clear;
But when she doth of mourning speak,
Ev'n with her sighs the strings do break.

And as her lute doth live or die,
Led by her passion, so must I . . .

THOMAS CAMPION, "When to Her Lute"

 In northern Boeotia are the meagre ruins of Anthedon. There the "sweet-voiced Myrtis"[1] is said to have lived, her remains even more meagre than those of her city. Plutarch claims that Myrtis taught Pindar to compose. Do we believe the *Suda*, which says that she also initiated Corinna, nicknamed "the Fly," into the art of verse? Or did Corinna, a Boeotian, too, of Tanagra, not far from Pindar's Thebes, not honour her as a foremother with such familiarity as to make us believe they were close in time rather than in spirit? Myrtis starts with confidence: the first poem in what may have been the first book of her work declares: "Terpsichore calls on me to sing pleasant tales for Tanagra's white-gowned women."[2]

Though Myrtis' poems do not survive, Plutarch summarises the narrative of one of them, a kind of epyllion about love, lying, and a heroine who betrays her unresponsive lover and then plunges from a cliff to her death. It is a more exhilarating story than those of the main fragments of Corinna that survive. Plutarch, several centuries after the events he recounts, says that Corinna, like Myrtis, counselled the young Pindar. Your poetry, she tells him, is too poor in myth and legend, too dependent on obscure diction, over-stretched meanings, periphrasis, mere prosodic virtuosity—all patterned icing, as it were, with no cake underneath. Taking her words to heart, he came back with a poem so freighted with myth that she burst out laughing.[3] A poet should "sow with the hand, not the whole sack."[4] The poem becomes, in her image, a furrow or field, and composition is part of an organic process, an approach quite at odds with the mature poetics of Pindar.

Ancient Tanagra is situated three or four miles from the modern town, on a round hill. To the north flows the river Asopos, whose daughter-bearing god is the subject of one of Corinna's poems. Gazing down from the round summit a modern traveller sees, but must be careful not to photograph, a Greek Airforce airfield and, further off, an airplane factory built on the site of an extensive necropolis. The military installations have a certain appropriateness: this is the area where Sparta famously defeated the armies of Athens and Argos in 457 BC. Further off, to the south, the brow of Mount Cithaeron, protagonist of Corinna's other surviving fragment, can sometimes be seen. In her day the crown of fir trees with which the gods garlanded the mountain's brow survived. Critics surmise that, in keeping with the regional dialect of her poems, the themes she chose were strictly local, even parochial. The people of Tanagra were civilised provincial folk, known for their good husbandry, their loyalty and their open hospitality. The land was not notably fertile: little wheat was produced, but some of Boeotia's finest wine came from the area. Tanagra was also noted for its fighting-cocks.

What remains of Corinna's world? There are covered and not very dramatically uncovered remains at Tanagra: one can make out the shape of the theatre, and partly exposed are outer fortification walls dating from around 385 BC. If one crosses the Asopos, to the east of ancient Tanagra is the Church of Saint Thomas which has built into it much ancient fabric. Tanagra pottery artists produced human figurines of terra-cotta, expressive and delicately executed, showing stately, draped matrons, but also lively figures: dancers, music makers and figures of less certain virtue.[5] In one tomb eight gilded angels were discovered, with little hanging devices: they must have been suspended above the sarcophagus, as if flying; one offers a ball, one a fan, one wears a little cape. One Eros carries a bird, and another Eros sports a Phrygian cap, both figures charred in parts as if touched by the flames of a pyre. There is a boy with ginger hair and a hat or wreath, wearing a long blue cloak, and a little girl bearing a bag of knucklebones. The figurines must all have been richly painted, suggesting in miniature what the now bleached marble statuary might have looked like. Such pieces were intended as votive offerings at temples or tombs, and the name "Tanagra" became generic for all such figures produced within and beyond the borders of Boeotia. There is a "realness" about the world they reflect: seeing them, we get close to the world from which Corinna's rather stiff legendary narratives emanate. The beautiful female figures and children in particular haunt the imagination. Lord Leighton's portrait of the poet, on display at his house in London, is altogether too formidable and forbidding.

Taking Plutarch and other classical accounts seriously, for centuries scholars assumed Corinna to be contemporary with Pindar, writing in the fifth century BC, her poems then lost until the second century BC. She was reputed to have triumphed over Pindar in a poetry contest. This is how Pausanias tells it. "The memorial [tomb?] of Corinna, the only Tanagran composer of songs, is at a conspicuous point of the city; in the training-ground [gymnasium?] there is a picture of Corinna tying her hair with a ribbon for the victory she won over Pindar at Thebes."[6] The portrait Pausanias saw, and the memorial, if they were in the spirit of the Tanagra figurines, would have touched the heart of any man or woman. Aelian, an abundant and unreliable witness in the third century AD, went one better than Pausanias and declared that Corinna triumphed over Pindar five times, which given the quality of her surviving work seems implausible, as does his allegation that Pindar, "by way of exposing [the Boeotian audience's] lack of poetic judgement," called her a "sow," presumably in his *Olympian Ode* VI, in which he alludes to the traditional rusticity of Boeotia.[7] This contradicts the poem in which Corinna reproves Myrtis of Anthedon for being so unfeminine as to compete with Pindar.

> I disapprove even of eloquent
> Myrtis; I do, for she, a woman,
> contended with Pindar.[8]

If Corinna did in fact triumph over Pindar, Pausanias has two plausible explanations, neither of them much to the credit of her verse: "I think it must have been her dialect that won, her songs not being in Doric like Pindar's, but in the language Aeolians would understand, and the fact (if this portrait is anything to go by) that she was the most beautiful woman of her time."[9] Statius refers to her as "slim Corinna" whose language is full of "mysteries."[10]

Confusions and contradictions are removed if we take Corinna's celebrity to have been a Hellenistic invention. The first surviving mention of her dates from around 50 BC and is itself "insecure"—that is, not entirely dependable. Unless she was ignored, or her work went missing, she belongs to a later age. Her editor David Campbell declares, "The *terminus ante quem* for her poems is 200 BC ± 25 years, since they are spelled in the Boeotian orthography of that date." Of course the transcription may have been modernised to conform to later Boeotian norms, but the language in which we have the poems is the given from which scholarship must take its bearings. As time passed, she became more real. Propertius knew her work; Ovid may have named his Corinna after her. The first-century elegiac poet Antipater of Thessalonica,[11] father of the dedicatees of Horace's *Ars Poetica*, includes her in his list of Mortal Muses. There are nine, and they are arranged neither chronologically nor alphabetically but, since they are listed in an epigram, to be accommodated in the metre: Praxilla, Moero, Anyte, Sappho, Erinna, Telesilla, Corinna, Nossis and, last of all, one of the first, the familiar "sweet-voiced Myrtis."

Peter Levi favours a late date for Corinna, arguing from the evidence of the poems. She writes in a period when local mythology had been systematised (fourth century) "and the personification of mountains as amiable savages which occurs only on late nymph reliefs" was accepted.[12] For Edgar Lobel, she is a Hellenistic poet affecting an archaic style. He judges this from the orthography, and the victory over Pindar he regards as fantastic and anachronistic. Had it occurred, there would surely have been accounts of it from the fifth century, yet the first surviving account dates from virtually half a millennium later.

Corinna's most famous fragments were discovered on a papyrus from the second century AD. The first, judging from the concluding passages, which are all that remain, told of a singing contest. In the Boeotian corner was the underdog, Mount Cithaeron, famous not only for separating Boeotia from Megaria and Attica, but as the place where Actaeon was hounded to death, where Pentheus perished, and where the infant Oedipus was exposed and left to die. Opposite Cithaeron is ranged the favourite, Mount Helicon, sacred to the Muses, who taught Hesiod to sing. We do not hear even a fragment of Helicon's song, but Cithaeron is delivering the closing lines of his account of how baby Zeus, concealed in a Cretan cave, survived the murderous wrath of father Cronus. Immediately the song is over, the Muses as returning officers require the gods to choose between the rival singing mountains. Hermes declares Cithaeron victor, a cry goes up, and Helicon, enraged, heaves up a huge smooth boulder and hurls it down. It bursts into pebbles, like the pebbles the gods used to cast their votes in the contest.

In two reliefs, Levi says, higher mountains peek over the rims of lower mountains and we see Helicon as a "shock-haired giant peeping over the mountain top"[13] on a third-century votive tablet. Disputes between mountains were apparently not uncommon in later Greek folk-song and verse right down to the nineteenth century. Corinna's contest, with the underdog victorious, is a paradigm for the contest between herself and Pindar: plain provincial simplicity pitted against the elaborated strains and the stilted diction of cosmopolitan convention.

The second major fragment is about a father and his nine daughters. The river Asopus, a god in the same way mountains are, by means of personification, rises in Mount Cithaeron near Plataea, passes through or near several towns and cities named after his daughters, then feeds into the long, narrow gulf of Euripus, near Oropus. All nine of his daughters have vanished. A human seer, Acraephen, reassures him. Don't fret, he says, they have been kidnapped and you are in luck, because the kidnappers are divine: Zeus has three, Apollo three, Poseidon two and Hermes one. (Hermes had Tanagra herself.) The gods, spurred on by Venus and Cupid, sneaked into your house and removed them. All will be famous: they will breed, and thanks to the divine stud farm, "a race of heroic demigods" will result, "and shall dwell in faraway places."[14] Acraephen then spends some time giving his own credentials. He is "the best of my fifty valiant / brothers," all sons of Orion. He and his progeny make an appearance in other fragments, for he was a Tanagran, and he reclaimed the land and cleared the wild beasts from it.[15]

Reflecting on the history of prophecy, Acraephen claims that he has been endowed by Apollo with skills and instincts first visited upon Euonymus, then on Poseidon's son Hyrieus. He was himself divine and is now starry Orion's most distinguished son. Corinna's seer speaks some haunting and memorable words, an Orphic echo perhaps: "Your part is to yield to the gods, / freeing your mind from grief." Asopus grasps him by the right hand and responds with a gratitude that disintegrates with the papyrus into a stutter of unconnectable phrases.

It may well be that "Corinna's style was simple, like Bacchylides."[16] But the critic who declares that she drew parallels between the world of mythology and ordinary human behaviour stretches a point. There is nothing ordinary about her gods, be they mountains or rivers; and the petulance of Mount Helicon, the easy consolation of Asopus for his nine raped daughters, suggest the great distance between the divine, mythological sphere and the human.

In total, about forty fragments survive, Asopus being the longest, with some fifty mauled lines. Even though there is so little, Corinna is second in quantity only to Sappho among women writers. Several critics wishfully insist that she "wrote for women." She declares this intention, but her writing is not exclusively for them. Some verse she composed for choral use at religious festivals; beyond that we can affirm little to support a feminist reading. She deploys local topography, plays variations on familiar legends, and develops a way of writing which can be seen either as subtly combining dialect with a "high style" or as bastardising the high style with Boeotian elements. Her work relates inevitably to Homer's, and also to Sappho's "Aeolic forms." Her effects are not, as earlier critics declared, "naturalistic" but highly artificial.

Not all women readers like her. The classicist Sarah Rudden finds the conventions in which Corinna writes risible. "I don't think she even deserves the dignified treatment she gets. She tells, for example, of two mountains having a singing contest and then a fight, with one of them heaving chunks of himself at the other . . . as in a comic animation sequence." This over-reads: Helicon's frustration is that of an angry, not an aggressive, child. Rudden continues: "it would probably be impractical to represent Corinna's grandiose bad taste with appropriate language."[17] A harsh verdict: Corinna is read only because she is female. This won't quite do.

In the first place there are unusual moments not only in the diction of

Corinna's poems but in the wider terms of expression. If there is something comical about a pair of mountains having a poetry contest judged by
the gods themselves, is it impossible that the conceit was humorous in intent? To have so large an object as Mount Helicon throwing an infantile
tantrum is a classic *reductio ad absurdum,* the "defeat" robbing that most poetic mountain of any poetic dignity, and leaving Corinna's favoured mountain to inherit all that Helicon has shed. There is a kind of psychology at
work in the poem as in Asopus' consolation, that inheres less in the characters than in the nature of the incident, which is rendered emblematic. If we
had more of the poem to consider, we might ask whether it parodied the
apocryphal contest between Hesiod and Homer, not least because Hesiod's
mountain is bested.

Though only fragments of two of her story poems survive, she seems to
have been a maker of verse narratives. Her books bore the title *Tales,* and
she may have been responsible for a *Seven Against Thebes,* of which three
words survive. ". . . I, for my part, celebrate the distinctions of heroes and
heroines," she declares elsewhere.[18] Though she comes from Hesiod's
neighbourhood, she is resolutely impersonal in her narratives. There are attributed voices, none defined as her own, none specifically female. This is,
in a sense, what makes Corinna more a disciple of Homer than of Sappho:
we come away from the thin evidence of her poems less with a sense of
having met a handsome and brilliant woman than of having read some curious, rather beguiling poems, not without folk charm in the traditional elements deployed. In an age of increasing personalisation of poetry, Corinna's
work seems in a genre of its own: self-effacement, the foregrounding of
plot, character and subject-matter, the use of dialogue and attributed
speech, are skills we associate with dramatic rather than narrative writers—
as we do the evidence of a frail psychology.

XXI

Pindar of Thebes (518–438 BC)[1]

Lift not thy spear against the Muses' bower:
The great Emathian conqueror[2] bid spare
The house of Pindarus, when temple and tower
Went to the ground: and the repeated air
Of sad Electra's Poet[3] had the power
To save th' Athenian Walls from ruin bare.

JOHN MILTON, "Captain or Colonel,
or Knight at Arms" (sonnet)

 In a letter dated July 1752 Thomas Gray told his friend Horace Walpole that he planned to send for inclusion in Dodsley's influential *Miscellany* his "The Progress of Poesy. A Pindaric Ode." He describes it as "a high Pindarick upon stilts, which one must be a better scholar than [Dodsley] is to understand a line of, and the very best scholars will understand only a little matter here and there."[4] That was one version of Pindar. Gray, like Goethe and Herder in Germany, mistook the irregular-seeming prosody of Pindar's strict triads and viewed him, as Abraham Cowley had done a century before, as inspired and free-spirited. Dryden may have been responsible for encouraging the English to misread Pindar. "Song for Saint Cecilia's Day" and "Alexander's Feast" were "Pindaric" and his Pindar was (what the Greek Pindar certainly was not) a poet of *enthusiasmos*. Pindar is the most careful architect that poetry has ever had; English poets to whom he offered emancipation from regularity, even a Romantic licence, were bending him to their own ends.

William Congreve in 1706 (prefacing his "Pindarique Ode to the Queen") described most English Pindarics as "a bundle of rambling incoherent thoughts, expressed in a like parcel of irregular stanzas, which also consist of such another complication of disproportioned, uncertain and perplexed verse and rhymes." He demonstrated the underlying regularity of Pindar's odes, the triadic principle of composition. It was Pindar's prosodic and intellectual exactness, his *politeness,* that drew him to the ode. Long before, it was the sense of his rigour that attracted Ben Jonson, the most classical poet of his age: for him Pindar was a superb verse builder, inventing complex extended forms and devising a flexible but monumental syntax to hold meaning in various kinds of poise and stillness. *Poikilia,* variety of style, the use of metaphors of all sorts, characterises Pindar: his language is an almost continuous string of metaphors. Jonson's "To the Immortal

Memory and Friendship of That Noble Pair, Sir Lucius Carey, and Sir
H. Morrison" is the first major English Pindaric poem, with "The Turne,"
"Counter-turne" and "Stand" clearly marked. His Pindarics do not lack
subjectivity, yet what interests us is not the poet's voice but the poem's thematic centredness, its air of legitimate authority. Rejecting the excesses of
the stage in its decline, Jonson says in "Ode to Himself":

> Leave things so prostitute,
> And take th'Alcaic lute;
> Or thine own Horace, or Anacreon's lyre;
> Warm thee by Pindar's fire:
> And though thy Nerves be shrunk, and blood be cold,
> Ere years have made thee old,
> Strike the disdainful heat
> Throughout, to their defeat:
> As curious fools, and envious of thy strain,
> May blushing swear, no palsy's in thy brain.[5]

The poem ends in flattery, in the way Pindar's odes do. Before that inevitable note is struck, Jonson ventures as near to the complexity and purity
of Pindarics as any English poet has done.

Only a few decades later, in 1656, Cowley published his *Pindarique Odes*
with a famous sentence in the introduction: "If a man should undertake to
translate Pindar word for word, it would be thought that one mad-man had
translated another." C. H. Sisson reflected on the unaccountable fashion for
Cowley's versions, "with their pompous preciosity and their array of notes."
For him, Pindarics "consisted in the irregular number of syllables in the
lines, producing, it may be supposed, the effect of surprise, if not astonish-
ment, and a certain wilful lunacy in the sequence of thoughts."[6]

How mad would a "word for word" translation be? Samuel Taylor
Coleridge, Pindar's best friend among the great Romantics, decided to conduct an experiment. He read the opening of Pindar's *Olympian Ode* II to a
"company of sensible and well-educated women." Next, he read Cowley's
inventive translation, and the women agreed that it was lunacy itself. Finally
Coleridge translated the poem for them word for word. He reports: "the
impression was that in the general movement of the periods, in the form of
the connections and transitions, and in the sober majesty of lofty sense, it
appeared to them to approach more nearly than any other poetry they had
heard to the style of our bible in the prophetic books." After describing
some of Pindar's strategies, he asks: "But are such rhetorical caprices con-
demnable only for their deviation from the language of real life? And are
they by no other means to be precluded, but by the rejection of all distinctions between prose and verse save that of metre?" We find in Pindar what

Coleridge, expressing himself in a dozen different ways, is always seeking in poetry: a language that achieves synthesis, "the juxtaposition and *apparent* [my italics] reconciliation of widely different and incompatible things."[7]

W. H. Auden believed that only one English poet who could be regarded as genuinely and deeply touched by Pindar was Gerard Manley Hopkins.[8] Hopkins wrote to his friend Robert Bridges in 1882 about the rhythm of "The Leaden Echo and the Golden Echo," which Bridges found redolent of Whitman. "No," declares Hopkins, "but what it *is* like is the rhythm of Greek tragic choruses or of Pindar: which is pure sprung rhythm. And that has the same changes from point to point as this piece." He insists that his poem must be read *aloud*. It is conceived for the ear and is intended, as Pindar's poems are, for delivery to the ear. The text is, in effect, a score.[9]

Most readers do not trouble themselves to consider how partial the written text of an ode by Pindar is. What of the vanished accompaniment of lyre (*phormiges, lurai*) and pipes (*auloi*), and the chorus either of singers or dancers or both, made up of men (*andres*) or youths (*neoi*) or boys (*paides*)? Pindar never in the odes alludes to their mode of delivery. Some may not have been choral: a single singer might have recited them. Some may never have been recited in fact, yet the conventions of composition presupposed actual public performance.

Music pertains to the poems not only metaphorically: they are not "musical" but instances or aspects of music in themselves, conceived in their elaboration as focal elements in a larger ceremonial. Here poetry is ritualised to an unprecedented degree. "His massive sentence-structure," says Lesky, "in which the heavy weight of ornament scarcely lets the framework be seen, his renunciation of antitheses and particles beloved of Greek authors in favour of a wilful violence in stringing together and interlacing his clauses, the weight which he places on the noun, so that the verb in contrast is little more than a colourless prop to the sentence, his wealth of images, aimed at the nature of the thing, not at its sensible properties, and mingling one with another with a headstrong recklessness—all these qualities went into Pindar's creation of that ornate style which has characterised the ode right down to modern times."[10] Misreadings of Pindar have to do with his violence to linguistic expectation: to those who could not find a "framework" under the "weight of ornament," the highly wrought language must seem wilful, subjective, extreme. But it is the extremity of art, not of personality, that makes the poems as they are.

Ezra Pound had little time for him:[11] "Pindar's characteristic style: difficult, crabbed syntax; obscure transitions; very elevated diction; and elaborate, vivid metaphors and conceits." "The prize wind-bag of all ages," he called him, irritated particularly by the subservience of the verbs, and on the strength of his judgement the Anglophone Modernists, the Imagists and poets of a naturally Pindaric bent like Marianne Moore, were absolved from any necessity of reading him for themselves.[12] The four books of epinicean odes survive "through direct manuscript tradition," and had Imagism and the Modernists taken them on board—whole Greek poems rather than the fragments from which they learned their own lessons in fragmentation—the face of early modern poetry might have been, if not less austere, in any event differently so.[13] The injustice of Pound's judgement has to do with his failure to register that the written texts were themselves only a score, a core fragment of a larger artistic whole.

The first recorded critic of Pindar is Corinna of Tanagra, who knew him, Plutarch says, in his apprentice years.[14] She commented on the poverty of myth, which was "the proper business of poetry," in his verse: he "supported his works with unusual words, strange usages, paraphrases, songs, and rhythms, which are just embellishments of the subject matter."[15] Thereupon, Pindar produced the hymn to Zeus, composed for Thebes, that begins (in Richmond Lattimore's translation):

> Shall it be Ismenos, or Melia of the golden distaff,
> or Kadmos, or the sacred generation of Sown Men,
> or Thebe of the dark blue veil,
> or the dare-all strength of Heracles,
> or the gracious cult of Dionysus,
> or the marriage of white-armed Harmonia? Which shall we sing.[16]

She laughed at his efforts.[17] By the time he came to write *Paean* XX he understood how to organise his material better. The new-born Heracles fights off the serpents sent by Hera. What makes the scene real is not how he throws off his elaborate, elaborated swaddling clothes, but how his mother, fresh from childbirth, leaps unrobed from her couch in fear, while her maids flee the chamber.[18] Pindar developed from poverty through profligacy to true economy of means.

Pausanias tells us about a lad called Lynkeus, "of whom Pindar (and one should trust Pindar) says his sight was so sharp he could see through the trunk of an oak tree."[19] Why should one trust Pindar, when it comes to establishing the truth of history or legend? What authority is vested in a poet that we should believe him, especially when what he says is so unlikely? Are we to take him literally—Lynkeus had X-ray vision—or is he telling a figurative truth? When the most precise of travel writers tells us we *must* credit Pindar even when what he says is incredible, we have come up against a formidable authority. Among Greeks, previously Homer alone had commanded by right such profound credulity, such *fundamentalism* of response.

Pindar belongs to Apollo. He sups with the gods, he has a chair in the very temple at Delphi.

Certainly much of what Pindar celebrates is factually true. In a rather special sense, he was, to use George Dillon's phrase, "the Greek sports-writer,"[20] a kind of reporter of achievements for posterity.[21] If we compare statues of Anacreon and Pindar, he emerges as crabbed, his face creased and fissured like the older Auden's, but rather leaner, and with a beard in the luxurious style we would associate with his prosperous, smooth patrons, people whose reality impinged on the poet and his epinicean or victory odes at every point, complicating his own and the reader's task.[22]

An epinicean poet's patron actually won a crown himself, or sponsored a winner in his own and his city's name, at one of the four chief pan-Hellenic games. The dates of events which Pindar incorporates allusively in his poems correspond to actual contests, where we can verify them, and the trainers and the relations evoked are literal figures. The occasion is not lost sight of. Pindar also touches gingerly on the troubled history of his time both in Greece (threatened by Persia) and in Magna Graecia (by Carthage). He "touches on" events, but his poems transcend the immediate world. "He lived through one of the most eventful periods of history," writes Bowra, "but hardly marked its salient characteristics." He was not a journalist, he took politics as a given. "He was concerned with the individuals whom he knew and with the world of gods above and around them that made them what they were."[23]

We have considerable information about the poet, and some of it may be true. The earliest account of him was "compiled by the Peripatetic Chameleon and by Callimachus' pupil Ister."[24] Four brief, contradictory lives exist to build from, as well as the account in the *Suda*. The most recently discovered life was published in 1961, a papyrus text from Oxyrhynchus dating from about AD 200. There are also the *Vitae Ambrosiana, Thomana* (attributed to Thomas Magister) and *Metrica* (31 hexameters, from the fourth or fifth century AD).[25] Much that they contain goes back to factual and legendary sources and some facts are separately attested.

He was born in Cynoscephalae ("Dog's Head"), a village near Thebes, on the road to Leuctra, which is in the heart of Hesiod country, in 518 (or, some conjecture, 522) BC. The hills of Cynoscephalae became famous a few centuries later when the Roman Flaminius defeated the Macedonians under Philip V at the eponymous battle, proving the superior power of the Roman legionary system over the conventional phalanx. Seven hundred Romans slew or captured 13,000 Macedonians. There was no Pindar to sing that extraordinary victory, no Simonides to make the collective epitaph.

Pindar was Boeotia's second major poet. He was reared in Thebes, the city of Heracles, whose life and labours are a recurrent theme in the poems. Four times he evokes Zeus and Alcmene, that hero's parents; he tells the story of baby Hercules strangling the serpents in his cot in *Nemean* I, and the Nemean lion, the golden hind, the Augean stables, the horses of Diomedes, the cattle of Geryon, the expedition against the Amazons and the wrestling with Antaeus all feature. For Pindar, Heracles' sacking of Troy was as momentous as the Trojan War itself: he alludes to it five times directly. We visit the Pillars of Heracles four times, and the founding of the Olympian Games is recounted twice. Heracles is for Pindar a spirit of human transcendence, overcoming even death; he is also a fellow townsman.

Thebes stands in the centre of Boeotia, and though the present city is disappointingly parched, provincial and prosaic, music and verse played a large part in its creation. Amphion built the original city walls not out of music precisely, but by means of it.[26] His labour was destroyed and restored a dozen times. Even in the last two centuries Thebes has twice been demolished by earthquakes and rebuilt.

Visiting in the second or first century BC. Heracleides described the city as circular in shape. In fact, it was more like a bumpy ostrich egg. It had seven gates (against which seven heroes famously marched). It claimed the invention of the Greek alphabet. Though ancient, the streets were new "because, as the histories tell us, the city has been thrice razed to the ground on account of the morose and overbearing character of the inhabitants."[27] Heracleides tells us that when the Spartan king Pausanias was knocking it down, someone wrote, in trochaic verse, on the wall of Pindar's house, "Don't fire the dwelling of the Muses' poet Pindar." Pausanias seems to have heeded this advice. The house became Thebes' hall of magistrates.

Apart from being flattened and reconstructed, what did Thebes do for a living? It bred mighty horses. At the time of Heracleides' visit, it was also a patchwork of wonderful gardens, irrigated by two rivers. The men were tough, spoiling for fights, litigious, violent, vigorous, in every respect alive. "The women are the tallest, prettiest and most graceful in all Greece." How could he know? They cover themselves, he tells us, so completely that only the eyes can be seen. But then he shows us more: "All of them dress in white and wear low purple shoes laced so as to show the bare feet. Their yellow hair is tied up in a knot on the top of the head . . . They have pleasing voices, while the voices of the men are harsh and deep."[28]

Thebes cradled some celebrated infants and was home to many famous men. Dionysus was its divine citizen, Heracles its hero, Teiresias its seer. Labdacus, a descendant of Cadmus, fathered a line of tragic kings (Oedipus was his grandson). When Pindar was born, the city was marshalling its energies to become one of the great city-states of Greece (and, for a brief period in the fourth century BC, the greatest). The powerhouse of Boeotia, its story provides Pindar with allusions, images, intensities. Some of the details are quite circumstantial and rather touching, as when he tells us his actual birth season:

> the four-yearly festival with its oxen in procession,
> During which for the first time I was laid down, a loved
> Tight-swaddled infant.[29]

Visitors looking for the afterlife of ancient Thebes today will be disappointed; apart from the good museum and the excavations of the palace, there is nothing much to see. War and earthquake have erased the heroic and the tragic city. An old sarcophagus, some juttings of Roman masonry, the parched springs and fountains . . . too much bustle, too little memory even to be called "sad."

Oedipus, a victim of faulty memory, fathered four children on his mother Jocasta. Forceful Antigone has a tragedy all of her own, and her sister, long-suffering Ismene, is her shade. Oedipus' ill-starred sons, Eteocles and Polyneices, waged a Cain and Abel rivalry that led to the ruinous war of the Seven Against Thebes, without which Greek literature would have been much the poorer. Legend places it in 1198 BC, close beside Troy's overthrow. Thebes, however, was rebuilt, not for the last time.

Pindar's Thebes distrusted and disliked Athens, and this rivalry led—during Pindar's lifetime—to one of its disastrous miscalculations: it favoured the Persians against the allied Greek states. The Medes made Thebes their centre of operations before the Battle of Plataea (479 BC). This, and the battle of Salamis a year before, touched Pindar. Sparta and Athens were merciless after the Persian defeat. When Thebes at last sided decisively with Athens against Philip of Macedon, her defeat was total. In 336, a Theban uprising against the Persians was suppressed by the "the great Emathian conqueror,"[30] the young Alexander. Pindar had celebrated Alexander's ancestor Alexander I for an athletic victory.[31] Perhaps the young leader remembered Pindar's tribute, for when he razed Thebes he too left Pindar's house standing, along with the temples. He slew 6,000 citizens and enslaved an additional 30,000. Thebes' habit of backing the wrong ally continued to cost it dear down through the Roman period. By the time Strabo and then Pausanias visited, the place had become little more than a hamlet. Vestiges of Pindar's city were still traceable in Pausanias' time, however. "If you pass down the right side of the stadium you will come to the racecourse: Pindar's memorial"—his tomb?—"is inside it."[32] Thebes flourished once again in the twelfth century as a silk-producing city, but it exported its skill and technology to Sicily: Magna Graecia once more outstripped the old country. Under the Turks, the pasha wisely made his home not in Thebes but in more temperate Levadia.

One day, when Pindar was a boy, on his way to Thespiai, he was overcome by the heat and lay down for a nap. As he slept, bees came and made their wax upon his lips. (We may be reminded of the nightingale which landed on the baby Stesichorus' lips and sang a prophetic aria.) After the visitation of the bees, Pindar began to compose songs. The story is beautiful and absurd. The bee image stays with him, his poem is like a bee that hurries from tale to tale, and there is honey in many of his poems.[33]

Another less colourful legend (sourced in the Peripatetic Chameleon) says that, as they had done with Hesiod, the Muses greeted Pindar on Mount Helicon (he was, after all, a Boeotian) and there gave him an olive branch.

Fortunately there was a serious market for songs. That market was secular and religious, though the division was not so strictly drawn then as it is today. The Pythian priestess, Apollo's voice, honoured him by telling the people of Delphi to give Pindar equal share in the tithes they paid Apollo. Money was a key part of every epinicean poet's calculation: Simonides' genius was synonymous with greed.

Pindar was more than a man of unparalleled verbal skills: he was an artist—we need to believe—whom money gratified but did not wholly govern. In his old age two strange events occurred. The god Pan was overheard by a traveller singing one of Pindar's odes. Pindar wrote a poem to Pan, thanking him for the honour. After that, the goddess Demeter grew jealous because he had not written a poem for her, so he obliged her and set up altars to both Pan and Demeter (or Rhea) outside his house. This may be an over-reading of the line "I will pray to the Mother whom girls sing to at night with Pan beside my door."[34] The story has it that he was on a mountain giving a tutorial to the *aulos*-player Olympichus when he heard a rumbling noise, saw flame and, in stone, the image of the Mother of the Gods. It was enough to occasion a spectacular effort in verse.

Another legend is a variation on the Mother of the Gods vision. In a dream Persephone (or Demeter) stood beside him and complained that she was the only deity he had never celebrated. He was mortified but he could not write a poem for her in time: he died. That was not the end of the story. An old female relation of Pindar's in Thebes had learnt how to sing his songs. He visited her, in turn, in a dream and sang a hymn to Persephone. When she awoke, Pausanias says, she *wrote down everything she had heard him sing*. We are in 438 BC and an old woman is said by Pausanias to have been able to write down a complex poem in a tradition which she understood and perhaps served herself. Pindar honoured the gods even from beyond the grave. And he did this altruistically, unless of course he was angling for ghostly benefits in Hades, where Persephone spent her winters.

Who were Pindar's parents? In one poem he calls the family of the Aigeidai "my fathers." They played a major role in founding the colony of

Thera.³⁵ If we take the speaker to be Pindar himself, he is claiming to be part of an ancient, now international clan with connections to Sparta, Thera and Cyrene. The Aigeidai are a typical "extended kinship group," and we meet such aristocracies (which is precisely what they are) elsewhere in Pindar. The extended family and the city of a victor are concerns in Pindaric poetry, which celebrates particular victories but emphasises where possible two aspects of the victor's family: its antiquity and its wide connections throughout the Greek world.

If we wish to pin him down to a particular father, we have a choice of names. Corinna, a fellow Boeotian who, the *Suda* says, won five victories against him and may have instructed him, named Scopelinus as his sire. Another source proposes Pagondas or Pagonidas.³⁶ Most poets, however, name Daiphantus; Scopelinus was his uncle, or the father of a less famous son, or Pindar's step-father. Some say he taught Pindar the *aulos,* while others claim he passed Pindar on to Lasus of Hermione for teaching. Assigning him a mother is less complicated. She was Cleodice or Cledice, according to the Ambrosian *Vita.* The name means "justly famed." We can extend his family further. The *Vita Metrica* provides him with a twin brother, Eritimus ("honoured in strife"), who distinguished himself as a boxer and wrestler, which is assumed to explain Pindar's intimate knowledge of athletic matters. Seventeen of the surviving forty-five odes, which vary in length from twenty-five to two hundred lines, are dedicated to wrestlers, boxers or winners of the *pancration,* the trial of strength which involved boxing, wrestling, kicking, strangling and twisting. Biting and gouging were forbidden, but almost everything else was allowed, including bone-breaking, wrenching limbs out of joint, neck holds and so on.

For once we can provide our poet with a wife, even a choice of wives. The first, whose name means roughly what his mother's name meant, is Megacleia, "greatly famed." Or if we prefer the *Vita Metrica* we can pair him off with Timoxeine, "honoured by strangers." And there are children. He had a son called Daiphantus for whom he wrote a *daphnephorikon,*³⁷ of which two lines survive. A son was often named after his grandfather. This lends support to Daiphantus' paternity claim.³⁸ Pindar may have had two daughters as well, Protomache and Eumetis, according to the Ambrosian *Vita.* The *Vita Metrica* also names them and says that they performed in his *parthenia.*³⁹

Athenaeus affirms that Pindar "was no moderate lover."⁴⁰ It is an odd statement on the face of it: when we think of Pindar we think of austerity, strictness, formal exercise, buttons done up. A lover? A man about town? Maybe even, David Mulroy suggests, something of a joker? "May it be mine both to make love / and to gratify another's love when appropriate," he declares. And whatever his family ties, he enjoyed a death, according to some sources, which Ibycus, Solon, Alcman and other Greek poets would have envied. He died in Argos some time after 446 (the date of his last epinicean, *Pythian* VIII), probably in 438 BC "not long after the outbreak of the Peloponnesian War, but he lived to see the liberation of Boeotia at the battle of Coroneia in 447 BC."[41]

A happy legend sets his death in the theatre, in the arms of Theoxenus of Tenedos, for whom he had written a dazzling, unambiguously erotic encomium. Lesky apologises for the surviving fragment "Pederasty is here spiritualised: the beams that dart from the eyes of Theoxenus kindle a flame in the poet's heart." Any spiritual dimension was rooted in a physical response to the boy's extraordinary beauty. Pindar was eighty, dry kindling. The flame of desire burst forth and burnt him through. Youth, not old age, is the time for love:

> But no matter who it is, whoever
> Sees those rays flash from the eyes of Theoxenus and is not
> Brimmed with desire has a heart that's black
> And founded out of adamant or steel
>
> With a heatless flame, and from bright-gazing Aphrodite
>> Earns no respect . . .

Because of love the old man melts like wax, and the image of wax ushers in the Pindaric bees, busy making sweetness and light. It also makes way for the image of Icarus, flying disastrously on wings made of feathers and meltable wax.

Between the stories of his birth and the legends of his death comes the fact of the poems. How and where did he learn to compose, who were his patrons, what genre did he write in?

Plutarch declares that he was "a pupil of Myrtis, a woman."[42] He began to learn his art in Thebes:

> glorious Thebes taught me
> to be no stranger to nor ignorant of
> the Muses.[43]

He probably went on to school in Athens to study music, poetry, choreography: "the art of the choral ode" in all its complexity.[44] His contributions to the dithyramb competitions in honour of Dionysus were noticed, though Simonides of Cos was supreme dithyrambist. Pindar was in Athens at the close of the age out of which the epinicean tradition had, rather suddenly, arisen. By the time he died, most of the tyrants had been deposed, oligarchies were more common, a kind of democracy was gathering force. Aristocratic values persisted, but the stability of that Greece had been shaken apart.[45] "Pindar spoke for the old aristocratic world which Athens opposed both in her empire and outside it."[46]

In Athens he came under the protection of the Alcmaeonid family, powerful preservers and reformers. His one Athenian epinicean ode is for Megacles, an Alcmaeonid, written shortly after he was ostracised (*Pythian* VII, 486 BC). There is evidence that he may have composed a *threnos,* or dirge, for Megacles' father. When Pindar praises Athens, it is not for its triumph over the Persians at Salamis and Plataia, but because, sponsored by the Alcmaeonids, it rebuilt with such grandeur the temple of Apollo at Delphi. Bowra claims, "As a boy he had learned his art in Athens, and for Athens he kept a certain affection until the emergence of Pericles and his treatment of Boeotia and Aegina made tolerance impossible."[47] Apollodorus and—or—Agathocles (who also taught Damon, the musical theorist) probably instructed him, and in Athens he first achieved recognition. His master left the apprentice Pindar in charge during preparations for a major festival. He trained the choruses and made a success of it.

Lasus of Hermione modernised and subtilised the dithyramb, making it possible for a once stale genre to hold its own against tragedy. Lasus was almost certainly not Pindar's teacher, despite what the *Vita Thomana* says: the dates of his presence in Athens do not stack up. Nor was Simonides his master, though legend attributed both to him as teachers. Lasus improved the dance and music and helped to establish the dithyrambic competitions in Athens. Pindar won in 497–96 BC. Simonides won no fewer than fifty-six times, but his dithyrambs have perished. Five large and one largish chunk of Pindar's dithyrambs survive.

Older scholars find in Pindar's poems the best evidence of his career. Every time he says something, they take it either as literal biographical fact or as expressing an omission, commission, oblique allusion to some fee paid or unpaid, some subtle back-handedness, some indirection. If we over-interpret, which is what Pindaric patristics were tempted to do, we can devise a complex and unsustainable life story from a series of poetic statements, largely conventional.[48] Modern scholars are more circumspect. They dismiss the *Vitae* because of their contradictions, and they do not readily credit what Pindar's poems say in the first person at all, thus going to an opposite extreme. If we can accept that a poet called Pindar wrote the four books of odes which so substantially survive, as well as at least some of the copious fragments, and that he was one person and not an atelier or a tradition, we can infer certain things about him.

His Boeotian background affected the way he acted. He rejects the bumpkin tradition that insisted that all Boeotians were crass and uneducated, by challenging someone to see "whether we truly escape that ancient reproach, 'Boeotian pig.'"[49] His Boeotian origin set him potentially at odds with Athens. It is not clear to what extent local rivalries affected such a man, who belonged to a cosmopolitan élite. Among the élite, ties of family and friendship often crossed the boundaries of the *polis*. Is it plausible, as legend has it, that Thebes fined him one thousand or ten thousand drachma for praising Athens, and Athens paid the fine? The verses from the dithyramb in question say:

> O shimmering, crowned with violet, celebrated in song,
> Hellas' fortress, famous famous Athens,
> The gods' high place . . .[50]

In later poems Athens is arrogant Bellerophon, murderous Aigisthos, the "unruly giant Porphyrion."[51] There is very little directly about Athens in the poetry. He may have been dissuaded from praising it. He admired the Athenian trainer of athletes Melesias but apologised when he included him in a poem for fear that in praising an Athenian he might be thought to be praising Athens itself.[52] Yet some say, perhaps confusing the story with the tale of the fine, that Athens gave him honorary rights and 10,000 drachmas; at Delphi he was invited annually by a special herald's cry to partake of the meal of the god's festival. Alexandrians and Romans regarded him not only as a great poet, but as the greatest lyric poet of all time.

He associated with Greek notables, had long-term relations with tyrants in Sicily and worked frequently with citizens from the small prosperous island of Aegina, a rival and eventual victim of Athens. That relationship is one of the most interesting, both biographically and poetically. Eleven odes are dedicated to Aeginetan victors, almost a quarter of Pindar's epinicean *oeuvre*.

Travellers following the coastal road from Corinth to Athens just beyond Megara look right across the gulf to Salamis, and beyond it on a clear day (less infrequent now than at one time) appears the unmissable peak of the island of Aegina. "Long-oared Aegina" Pindar calls it,[53] as though it could control its direction in a hostile sea. Once it contested Athens' control of sea trade. Pindar was attached to his Aeginetan patrons and to the place's history, for it was a nursery of heroes, including Neoptolemus and Ajax and Achilles. In an early paean he celebrates it; and its rich families commissioned epinicea. Aegina like Boeotia had a mixed Dorian and Aeolic population. Because of its enmity with Athens—it fought with the Athenian fleet at Salamis—it often found itself on the same side of the conference table as Thebes. His chief patron in Aegina was Lampon, whose son he celebrated in *Isthmian* VI.

He travelled from mainland Greece to Magna Graecia. Around 476–74 BC, he moved to Sicily and frequented the courts of two tyrants, Theron of Acragas and Hieron of Gela and Syracuse. It was for his Sicilian patrons that he wrote some of the greatest epinicean odes, in particular *Olympian* I and III. Did he enjoy his time in Sicily? Most scholars believe he spent two years on the island, directing performances of his own compositions.[14] Bowra claims that he stayed for one winter only, returning to Greece in the spring and never visiting Sicily again. "From *Pythian* II we form the impression that he was not happy in a tyrant's court and preferred to compose poems for his Sicilian patrons in the detachment of his own home."[55] Bowra's view is contestable: he is keen to imbue his poet with an anachronistic, instinctive political liberalism, evidence of how easy it is to apply to a favourite poet familiar templates, to make him a little *too* familiar.

After Sicily, Pindar found in North Africa (modern-day Libya), in the court of Telesicrates of Cyrene, another discriminating and rich patron. North Africa, like Sicily before it, opened up a range of new mythological possibilities. Arcesilas IV of Cyrene won the chariot race at Delphi in 462 and was celebrated in two poems. *Pythian* V was intended for performance in Cyrene at "the feast of the Dorian Apollo Carneius";[56] the other, *Pythian* IV, is the longest of the surviving epiniceans, and was sung at a feast in the palace.

Pindar's very mobility refreshed his poems with new material as it refreshed his purse with new patronage, and he was so restless as a formalist that every beginning is quite fresh and different from the one before. He survived into the age of Pericles, but his world view and values belong to the time before the Persian wars, and to the courts in which he did poetic service. Of an aristocratic persuasion himself, he believed as much as sour Theognis of Megara did that human excellence is blood-related and heroic or divine in origin. Poetic excellence, too, is made by and accessible to the refined, the instructed individual, who has the skill as well as the sensibility to appreciate its subject and its rooted, allusive language, the tones and images often specific to a class or clan, to a landscape or history. Quintilian says Pindar is "by far the most renowned of all the lyric poets" and stresses the scale of his undertakings, his moral teaching, his language, the wealth of matter he invests in a poem. His eloquence is a kind of mighty river. But even to the Roman poets he provided insoluble problems of comprehension.

Aristophanes of Byzantium, whom we encountered as chief librarian at Alexandria between 194 and 180 BC, and editor of Homer and Alcaeus, edited Pindar's poetry into seventeen books.[57] Our sense of the poet is seriously skewed by the accident that, of these scrolls, the contents of only four substantially survived, with fragments (some extended) from the other thirteen.

Eleven of the books were directly related to worship and can be regarded as variously liturgical in character and use. Had we all seventeen, our book list would look something like this:

1	Hymns to the Gods
2	Paeans (mainly to Apollo)[58]
3–4	Dithyrambs (mainly to Dionysus)
5–6	Prosodia (processional hymns)
7–9	*Parthenia*
10–11	Hyporchemata (dance-odes)

There would have been six non-religious books, though the division is artificial given the number of religious references, invocations and prayers in the poems.

12–15	Epinicean Odes *(Olympian, Pythian, Nemean, Isthmian)*
16	Threnoi (laments)
17	Encomia (praises, for singing at banquets)

The *Nemean* Odes originally came last, and this explains the rather odd inclusion at the end of two non-*Nemean* poems, one of which is not even epinicean but is a poem celebrating the accession of a new councillor. Probably, when the texts were copied from scrolls to codices, the two books were transposed; as a result we have also lost part of the end of the *Isthmian* Odes.

Why did the Epinicean Odes survive while the rest of the *oeuvre* was seriously damaged by the moths of time? So much of what is left of Simonides and Bacchylides is epinicean, too, that we see them as specialising in this type of poetry, as though Ted Hughes' laureate poems alone were in print and we regarded him as a generic laureate, or Whitman's Civil War poems and we regarded him solely as an elegist. Were the odes popular? Probably not in the way that lyric and epic poetry were: their expression is complex, even for an audience reared on Homer; their performance would have entailed a major production appropriate at the point of victory or on the victor's return home, but in all likelihood not often repeated afterwards. They were strictly "occasional." If tragedies in the great Athenian competitions were composed for a single performance, as scholars suggest, it seems unlikely that epinicean odes enjoyed a longer run. It is thought that after Pindar's death and the political and social changes that occurred in the Greek world, epinicean poetry lost whatever popular audience it had rather quickly, and Pindar had no very worthy successors. It was only when the Alexandrian editors at the great library got their teeth into Pindar that he was revalued, but in a different context, the poems as literary rather than as performance scores. As text, his work was relished principally by specialists who enjoyed Pindaric puzzlement and the engrossing pastime of annotation.

In the interim, in a scattered way, the poems survived. Thebes or Athens might have been proud to keep a collection of Pindar's work in its library. A noble family might have insisted that a work celebrating its antecedents and achievements and in which it had invested good money should be preserved. A city might have seen to it that a poem that praised it should survive. But the odes do not praise directly; they do not tell stories in a conventional way; their transitions are abrupt, their parallelisms so subtle that they have been known to frustrate two and a half millennia of scholars.

Could it have been a "class thing," reading and reciting Pindar, and the emergence even in a democratic society of a middle class with pretensions meant that certain older forms were preserved to signal cultural bona fides? When the comic dramatist Aristophanes portrays a standard conservative middle-aged Athenian man in the 420s BC, the man requires his son to sing him an epinicean ode composed by Simonides. Simonides died in 468. Aristophanes' caricature-Athenian asks to hear a poem about a sporting victory that took place more than forty years earlier . . .

Or was an interest in sport and its political symbolism, in particular in the great pan-Hellenic festivals, such that the actual occasions of the poems ensured their survival? The poetic celebration of sport begins with Homer and the funeral games for Patroclus, if not before, and there the heroes have the dignity of their cities weighing on them as they compete. Lesky remarks that the epinicean tradition led "to an unparalleled connection between sport and art in Greek life," a connection that reached a climax of intensity in Pindar. He argues that Simonides, in the ram-shearing poem and in the Glaucus ode, where he compares the young boxer favourably with Polydeuces and Heracles, was wry and light-hearted, "elements quite irreconcilable with the heavy seriousness of Pindar's victory odes."[9] "Heavy seriousness" is one of those phrases which push Pindar away. Serious he certainly is, but "heavy" has the wrong valency.

The odes do "affirm the common value of athletic achievement," and their function is to create continuities in various directions, to integrate the individual with the communal, the legendary and the religious. The victor is portrayed as an ideal representative member of the aristocratic class and as an ideal member of his city. His ode, commissioned at considerable expense from a professional poet by his father, his tyrant, his brother or a patron, was sung chorally by the men in the victor's home city or at the games by a chorus from his city, visiting for ceremonial purposes. The myths and legends the poems evoked were chosen for their appositeness to the victor's home city and to the location of the games, binding the one with the other. They were *par excellence* the pan-Hellenic mode, a poetry of connection which drew even the remotest cities of Magna Graecia into the heart of what was Greek and Greece. Pindar was commissioned by patrons from mainland Greece and the islands, from North Africa, Italy, Sicily. Colonists affirmed that they were Greek, the commissioned poems travelled back to Greece and reminded Greece of their remote but glorious existence.

It is possible that a tyrant or an aristocrat commissioning a poem had some say in the choice of theme, of myth and legend. Given the variety of the epinicean poems, not only in form (which we can assume was entirely the province of the poet) but in theme, we might conclude that there was an element of collaboration. At the crudest level, a patron paying 100 drachma could expect a *shorter* poem than a patron paying 500 drachma. The more a patron paid, the more solemn the piper's obligation. Some of the obscurities in the poems may have to do with requirements placed on the poet which would have gratified a patron, a victor, a community, but whose nuances are lost in history and with them the sense of a juxtaposition or allusion. Other external factors might weigh upon the poet: was the poem to be performed by amateurs or professionals, choreographed and conducted by the poet himself or by another, in the town where the victory occurred or in the victor's home town, shortly after the event or much later? How much time elapsed between a victory and the performance of an ode? How long did Pindar have in which to complete the exceptionally complex text of one of his poems? How did he write down the music, if he did, and record the choreography?

More than any other classical poetic genre, the epinicean ode is tied into a world of strict contingencies of this kind, and its task is to weave those contingencies into the timeless fabric of legend and the divine. Much of the difficulty of the poems has to do with those vanished contingencies. The obscurity of works of literature usually has less to do with the range of allusion and reference, more with the loss of informing occasions and cultures. We can usually see what a poet is attempting; often we cannot say *why* he is attempting it.

Association with Pindar brought wealthy tyrants and aristocrats an immediate prestige that money *did* in fact buy. Pindar, Bacchylides and Simonides used literary skills and reputation to inscribe their patrons in the cultural tradition of Greece. They played a role in creating a respectable, even venerable, image of their patrons in the Greek world. Pindar had much to offer the most powerful men of his time; he should not be seen as a dependent hanger-on at the courts of the great. Like Michelangelo, reproved for the idealisation of the portrait statues on the Medici tomb, Pindar knew that what mattered was what lasted, the higher truth of the achieved form: "In a hundred years who will care what they actually looked like?"

Every epinicean ode has certain givens, certain basic information it must impart, and it may fulfil this obligation directly or obliquely. Simonides outlines what is required in a snatch of dialogue which we can call an epigram:

> "Tell your name, your father's, your city, your victory."
> "Casmylus, son of Euagoras, boxing at Pythia, Rhodes."

Pindar plays variations on the formula. Obliquity is his hallmark: "bronze-shielded" indicates a race in armour; "foot" means foot race; even the location of the games can be coded in, embedded as it were, and the references to divinity may at times seem to include more than one god at a time. Certainly the gods of the place must be acknowledged and honoured, and heroic legends chosen which celebrate the place, the victor's city, his family, or which have some relevance to his achievement. The realm of myth is incorporated in a similar spirit.

Richmond Lattimore believes that Pindar is more careful and controlled in the elaborate and ceremonial openings of his poems than in their conclusions, which can seem abrupt and peremptory. He summarises the necessary epinicean elements as "invocation, occasion, victor, prayer, moral, and myth."[60] They do not necessarily follow that order. The most curiously Pindaric ingredient in the verse is the legend and myth. They are included not as story—the story is assumed already to be known to his audience and the poem simply draws upon those elements relevant to its "occasion," those narrative "moments" which share a dynamic, a light, with it.[61]

Games associated with the gods were celebrated in many parts of Greece but the four principal venues, briefly considered in our life of Simonides,[62] each possessed a distinctive purpose and history.

The games at Olympia were established in 776 BC. Heracles came to Pisa (beside Olympia) with his wealth and his followers. His very first act was to sanctify certain areas for his father Zeus and for the other gods. Having prepared the place, he inaugurated the games, which were to occur every four years. Victors were rewarded not with money or a cup but with a perishable wreath of wild olive branches. The games, part of the Festival of Zeus, were the most important of all, and the longest-lived: they were last celebrated at Olympia in AD 261, a millennium of sporting contest. The foot-race remained the main event for most of that time. At their height, the games attracted up to 50,000 visitors.

Why did they survive so long? Because Zeus survived. Because the landscape of Olympia is inspiring, literally breath-taking. It is a place that, by means of the veins of rivers and springs, connects with other parts of Greece. The sacred river Alpheus dives underground, for example, and under sea, and surfaces elsewhere, in Sicily, at the Fountain of Arethusa. The place, like the games, is a centre of *connections*. The ancient tribes of Greece assembling there, where nature manifests its most unfathomable otherness and beauty, where it is impossible *not* to believe in the gods and honour them with awe and every human gift, were reconciled. The divisions that colonisation, conflict, the alienations of time and history had made were transcended and for the duration of a games, there was a Greek nation.

After the Olympic Games, the Pythian were the most important, dedicated to the Festival of Apollo. They began at Delphi in 582 BC and at first were more concerned with poetry and music than with sport. Here the victor was rewarded with a crown of laurel, or bay leaves. Delphi is one of the holiest sites in ancient Greece. It was believed to be the very centre of the earth, the omphalos: a navel stone still exists in the museum. And if Olympia is remarkable, Delphi is no less so, a place of circles and shadows, sudden coolnesses, peculiar acoustics, a mysterious location chosen by the gods. Zeus released an eagle from the far east and another from the far west and they met at Delphos: that is how the mid-point was determined, Pindar says.[63] This was Apollo's principal sanctuary. George Chapman's Elizabethan version of the Homeric "Hymn to Apollo" describes Parnassus, the sacred rocks, the cave: the bouldery area

> through whose breast doth run
> A rocky cave, near which the King the Sun
> Cast to contrive a temple to his mind,
> And said, "Now here stands my conceit inclined
> To build a famous fane, where still shall be
> An oracle to men, that still to me
> Shall offer absolute hecatombs . . ."

To all those who come with worship and with offerings "will I / True secrets tell, by way of prophecy." Locating the scene, Chapman invents an elegant schoolboy-translation phrase: "under the with-snow-still-crowned / Parnassus." One of the original temples at Delphi was made of wax and feathers; one temple had women in it who lulled men until they wasted away, as with a drug, by the sweetness of their singing, until Zeus sent a thunderbolt and it was swallowed by the earth. Pindar alludes to them in Paean VIII, lines 70–79. They were earthbound sisters of the Sirens, a source or analogue for them, perhaps their inspiration.

Here Castalia was the Muses' spring, and a poet novice did well to drink of it. When the Christian era began and Pan was pronounced dead, the power of Delphi and of pagan truth declined. At last the oracle sent word to the emperor Julian, the benign pagan, the so-called Apostate, to say that the spell of centuries was broken:

> Go tell the king—the carven hall is felled,
> Apollo has no cell, prophetic bay
> Nor talking spring; his cadenced well is still.[64]

And as Cleopatra says in a no less tragic context, "there is nothing left re-markable / Beneath the vis'ting moon."

The other two festivals were important, but not quite so central to the unifying life of Greece. The Isthmian Games (a crown of dry parsley or pine branches) were established in 581 BC to celebrate the Festival of Posei-don at Corinth. Last, in 573 BC, come the Nemean Games (a green parsley or wild celery crown), another festival dedicated to Zeus. In Nemea, where now stands the little ancient mountain township of Phlious, Heracles slew the Nemean lion. The games were established, legend says, by members of the second expedition of the Argives against Thebes.

The poetic association of sporting competition with great battles and with actual, historical or legendary engagements is a Pindaric common-place. As in modern journalism, a similar diction is used for reporting sporting and military encounters. Competition is always and undeniably a form of controlled aggression. The fruit of competition is not only victors but losers. Some of the epinicean odes chide and scorn the losers as part of the celebration of the victor.[65] In *Pythian* VIII Pindar talks of the different homecomings of four of the defeated athletes.

At all the games, with few variations over time, a dozen sports and arts featured. Most coveted of all was the wreath for the chariot race (*tethrippon*). The chariots, drawn by four horses, had to complete twelve laps around the hippodrome. The *apene,* or mule car race (abandoned later as undignified), and the single (bareback) horse race were the other events that included quadrupeds. Pindar immortalised one horse, Pherenikos, Hieron's fleet steed, twice over; Bacchylides, too, celebrated him.

Individual and team sports were sometimes divided into three categories, one for the men, one for the boys, and one for the ripe adolescents. Thus in the footrace (*stadion*), wrestling, and boxing, there were epithalamia for vic-tors at various stages in their lives. There was also the double footrace (*diau-los*) and the long footrace (*dolichos*), and most unpleasant of all, the race in full armour (*hoplites dromos*). Among the "single sports" was *aulos*-playing, inviting the presence of a coiffed and perfumed Muse into the sweaty arena.

Two of the combined events required extraordinary stamina. The "five events," or *pentathlon,* required excellence in the *stadion,* the long jump, javelin, discus and wrestling. Most brutal and, for the bloodthirsty, most en-tertaining was the trial of strength, the *pancration*. A victor here deserved at least an ode, and a loser earned a year in traction, or a bier.

Pindar is less inscrutable than critics suggest, at least for readers accus-tomed to the poetry and prose of the Modernists. Our ancestors had prob-lems with the forms. They strike us as relatively straightforward, a series of allusions and expressive juxtapositions with an associative if not a logical progression between them. The problem for us is historical and educational: we do not any longer carry with us the points of classical reference that our ancestors, puzzled by Pindar's forms, possessed by second nature. They had no trouble recognising Proteus or Polydeuces or Teucer. What they struggled with was the way the poet moved from image cluster to image cluster, or drew pithy morals from apparently quite inappropriate classical narratives. For the modern reader, Pindar is less difficult than obscure, and we project on to the poem our distrust of a seeming obscurity (our problem rather than the poem's). Our insecurity is much diminished when we recognise without footnotes one, or two, or three allusions and can infer how and why they are connected, and infer too what the other unfamiliar allusions are doing, just as from a clear context we can deduce the meaning of a strange word. If we bear in mind that Pindar wrote not only the epinicean odes but other poems for occasions, that those occasions were public triumphs with strong political and cultural overtones, we will make, if not sense, a *sense* of sense of them.

He surprises us by the way he handles and combines elements, seldom twice in the same manner. The speed of his movement from particular to general and back again must have recommended him to Auden. His narrative is never straightforward or Homeric, though many of the stories he refers to share character and incident with the *Iliad,* the *Odyssey* and what we imagine was included in the vanished epics about the Argonauts and the *Seven Against Thebes.* It is useful that Homer's heroes have defined geographies and antecedents: a later Greek poet, seeking to glorify a present-day champion, can find geographical bearings; if the athlete is from a colony, there are ways to relate him to the founding city heroes.

Pindar assumes that his audience knows the main narrative and so he plays by brief allusion or variation, selects a narrow band from within the larger story, attempts to essentialise. There are moments of real drama, but they work only if we know the surrounding story. The poem modulates thought, feeling, a series of experiences; the ode reads us and plays us like an instrument, as Auden says a poem should do. If we are missing strings, the music fails. The enchantment depends upon us as readers; the magic works only if we can hear the spell.

One of the earliest, perhaps *the* earliest, surviving epinicean ode of Pindar is *Pythian* X, commissioned from the twenty-year-old poet by Thorax, a senior member of the Aleuad clan. He wanted to commemorate Hippocleas of Thessaly's victory in the boys' double foot-race in 498 BC. Hippocleas was from Pelinna, Thorax from nearby Larissa. These become important geographical points of reference: each has a place in Thessalian history. Though simpler than many of the subsequent odes, *Pythian* X illustrates Pindar's techniques and skills. His manner is defined, and in the poem he characterises it in a few deft images that illustrate the glancing transitions. Here the Pindaric bee moves from bloom to bloom, going briskly about its business.

An ode generally has several narrative elements with one particular strand dominant over the others, drawing the others in. Here the story of Perseus' visit to the Hyperboreans takes precedence. The Hyperboreans—"people from beyond Boreas, the north wind"—achieve more than the highest human achievement. Why this story? The Pythian Games were dedicated to Apollo. The Hyperboreans were his favourites: he spent three months of the year among them. Their easy prowess underlines human limitation, a caution against excessive pride.

The poem is seventy-two lines long and consists of four triads. A triad is a sequence of three stanzas: a strophe, an antistrophe and an epode. The strophe (turn) and antistrophe (counter-turn) are in the same stanza form (often enjambemented not only line by line but between stanzas). Their very names indicate their source in music and in dance movement. After the antistrophe has prosodically replicated the strophe, the epode (after-song, what Ben Jonson calls the "stand") brings the triadic movement to a conclusion. The epode, generally a shorter stanza, often delivers moral counsel in a highly condensed manner and is usually end-stopped. The triads, carefully designed within themselves, are juxtaposed within the larger architecture of the poem. When the poem was performed, we can imagine that the accompaniment and the choreography was repeated triad by triad, the variations between them being of pace, volume, tone. The form itself would create expectations upon which variations were played, variations which did not violate form but altered emphases within it.

An audience would respond to a series of stimuli (visual, aural, intellectual): it would follow a narrative or elements of narrative, it would await the repetitions and conclusions of the antistrophe and the rounding off of the epode, and then it would begin to hear epode against epode, a sense of aural and visual repetition, reinforcement, but as the performance proceeded what took precedence (choreographic and musical patterns established and accepted) was the specific language of the triads. An opening triad might, therefore, be expected to be subordinate to the music and movement of the reciting chorus; as the poem progresses, however, the words foreground themselves. When Lattimore declares that many of the odes open with ceremonial elaboration and then move peremptorily or end abruptly, he touches on the basic dynamic of the ode, which begins in a subordination of language and ends in its release.[66] This feature is not, as Lattimore and other critics are tempted to suggest, a loss of poetic control, a failure of integration: on the contrary.

If we briefly paraphrase *Pythian* X, we can show how the poem elides from theme to theme, key to key. It begins with a celebration of those well-governed areas of Greece, Sparta and Thessaly whose leaders are descended from Heracles. (The poem concludes, too, with an image of good government.) Having raised the figure of Heracles, Pindar leaves him there, a heroic conjuration hovering above the poem, and corrects himself, coming into the present: he is supposed to be celebrating Pytho, where the games are being celebrated, and Pelinna, Hippocleas' home town, and the Aleuad clan, because (the antistrophe begins now and the poet evokes the victor) the vale of Parnassus—a place, but also an oblique way of saying, the poem itself—proclaims him victor over all the other boys in the race. Apollo is invoked: the games are his, and so too is the poem. A man achieved what the gods willed, having inherited the skill to perform from his father. We turn then to the epode, in which Hippocleas' father is remembered for his achievements in the race in armour in the same games.[67] The epode ends by conjuring Apollo's blessing on the whole clan.

What has happened in these eighteen compact lines? First a hero is evoked, then a young athlete, then the god, then the athlete's antecedents. A moral is drawn, a prayer is made.

In the opening of the second triad, the prayer is teased out and moralised: having achieved so much, the poem implores, let the victor and his clan go on to greater and better things and suffer no setbacks from the gods. May the victor's success not pain the gods (so many human victors, in legend, call down divine retribution because they overreach the human mark). It is a blessing to be a victor oneself (the antistrophe begins, the turn, marking a movement forward in time) and then to live long enough to witness your son as victor, too. Yet there is a point beyond which a victor cannot go, a limit to human body and spirit. The Hyperboreans are beyond that limit, and the poet takes us (in the epode) thither with Perseus: having shown how high a victor can scale, he shows the much higher heights beyond human victory (a counsel against hubris).

Perseus dined among the Hyperboreans, and the epode evokes his surprise, upon arrival, at the huge sacrifices they are making, hecatombs of jackasses to Apollo. The god takes the greatest pleasure in their praises and their sacrifices (no wonder he spends three months a year among them).[68]

The third triad begins with a sharp contrast of imagery and the poem becomes more complex. There is poetry among the Hyperboreans, says Pindar, maiden choruses, lyres and wind instruments, golden laurel crowns (victors at the Pythian Games were crowned with laurel), feasting. The human body is not subject here to disease or old age, to labour or to war (antistrophe), but they have escaped vindictive justice. We are back then with Perseus (he is not named but is characterised as the son of Danaë and the Gorgon's slayer). He was subject to vindictive justice. With the Gorgon's snake-haired severed head Perseus turned his enemies to stone, making justice and freeing his captive mother from her foes. He is led by Athena herself, Apollo's sister.

All this may seem far-fetched, but the poet is not surprised, because (the epode begins), whatever the gods will is done, and nothing is beyond belief. Suddenly we encounter the poetic compression which some readers balk at. The speaker of the poem has identified himself as one able to believe in the power of the gods. He now shows obliquely how this kind of poem can work:

> Stay the oar; quick, strike anchor in seabed
> from prow, guard against jagged reef,
> for the glint of praise songs
> flits beelike from story on to story.

First a halt to stabilise us on an image: it brings the ship to a stop at the brink of danger; then the song speeds on to the next narrative.

The final triad begins. The poet imagines Hippocleas' people singing his ode beside the river and increasing by its means the victor's glory among his people, exciting too the girls. The image of the lovely girls (picking up, perhaps, an echo of the Hyperborean maidens in the previous triad) suggests desire, the various desires that affect men. In the antistrophe he reflects how whoever achieves what he most strives for will find other things falling into place. Still, we cannot foresee the future. The poem begins to come down from its grand afflatus into the present tense. The poet is content to put faith in his patron's hospitality. It is his patron who, keen to favour the poet, has harnessed four steeds to the Muses' chariot of this poem (that is, paid him a handsome fee), behaving as a friend and as a leader.

The concluding epode moralises: when tested, gold shines, and so does a good man's virtue. Not only Thorax but his brothers, Thessalian leaders, too, are worthy of celebration. On such men, and on such clans, depends the stability of cities and their continuity. We are back, as it were, with the elliptical opening lines about good government.

A paraphrase does little justice to the proportions of the poem; by marking where strophe, antistrophe and epode begin it can give a sense of the shape, but not the ways in which the audience will set parallel the elements that "rhyme," as it were, but are not connected by narrative or syntax. The echo of a cadence, of a word or epithet, makes aural connections within language which have an effect on the meanings that cannot be approached by paraphrase. A musical paraphrase is required; and if we could reconstruct the choreography, that too would be a key to meaning.

What is the unity of the epinicean ode? "The decisive answer," says Lesky, "has been given by Hermann Fränkel: the epinicean elevates the significant event of victory into the realm of values, the world from which the poet's creation flows. This world of values is displayed and exemplified in its various spheres: in the divine itself, in the tales of the heroes, in the rules of conduct and not least in the poet's own creative activity as an artistic realm in its own right."[69] That feels too much like literary criticism, which so often seeks closure. Pindar is, however, assured of certain certainties, and if we understand them (we are unlikely to share them), we can understand the poems better line by line and perhaps even triad by triad.

Each man has an inborn character, a *phuá,* a nature that nurture cannot alter. This ties in with Pindar's sense of innate nobility and is part of his aristocratic frame of mind ("best by nature is best"); the common man too has an unregenerable *phuá,* we can surmise. Men are lowly (he is impatient of "the violent crowd") but strength of will and purity of spirit can raise the exceptional man to moments of parity with the gods, as in *Nemean* VI. In *Pythian* VIII he says that man is the dream of a shadow, but it can come briefly awake in deeds and achievements: the light of the gods can shine down and illuminate and *realise* (in the sense of make real) the dream. His respect for the gods means that he invariably takes their part and asserts their right. He takes Hesiod and Homer to task for their impieties. When he comes to tell the story of Pelops in *Olympian* I, he alters it to exonerate the gods from cannibalism.

For Pindar the connection between the world of athletic achievement and that of legend, between the world of legend and the divine, seems real: they are analogous, the highest is made visible in the world in achievements. The instrument which negotiates between these realms—literal, historical and legendary, divine—is poetry. Poetry does not merely witness what happens but connects those events to the larger structure of reality, lifting them above contingencies and setting them, in a kind of equivalence, in the timeless space occupied by legend and myth. Poetry is memory but more than that. And the poet functions thanks to an Olympian grace bestowed upon him. The poet is a kind of priest whose skills and whose vision of wholeness privilege him, so that he in turn can privilege and bring into the higher realm what his language touches.

As in Simonides, there is in Pindar a curious elision towards monotheism, a speaking of the gods in the singular, as a coherent and coherence-imparting force. Theia in *Isthmian* V, for example, contains a number of forces.

When Pound calls Pindar a prize windbag, one reason is that he is impatient with the Greek poet's elusiveness, just as many modern readers are when they approach Pound's own *Cantos.* Another reason may be the subtle and nuanced regularities of Pindar's prosody. "It is impossible to reproduce Pindar's metres in English," says Bowra, "and even in Greek, where the quantitative system allows so much more variety and assurance than our own accentual system, it takes a little time to catch their lilt and movement, but once it is caught it has no rival in variety, speed, and lightness."[70] For Pound such schematic regularity and such deliberate architecture into which matter is compelled to fit, to which the voice is forced to conform, were contrary to the nature of poetry itself, where words and the world reached a natural accommodation (as in Archilochus or Sappho or Alcman), where language sought equivalences in the material world, at the same time clarifying and sharpening vision like a lens. In Pindar, language has become less a means than an end in itself: a tissue of references and cross-references, where the words point towards stories and earlier texts, and where the poem's occasion is led away from the very contingencies that shape and make it real. Once the victor is named and the poet paid to celebrate him, the poem, having bowed in the direction of its subject and its patron, takes its own course away from its moment, towards timelessness or abstraction. The architecture of the poems enforces a stability on the language which amounts to a kind of stasis, a series of balances and counter-balances which are subtle and sometimes precarious but seldom glow with a real sunlight. The bee that flits through *Pythian* X gathers no pollen.

If language and the antecedent contents of language (poetry, liturgy, legend) are a separate and sufficient realm, things will happen in the language which are themselves aesthetically sufficient. In *Olympian* VII, a poem is like wine in a golden bowl with which a father toasts a new son-in-law (1–10). Pindar delivers *Nemean* III late. He hardly apologises. He declares to the chorus that waits eagerly on Aegina for the Muse to deliver her song that he is like the eagle. He builds the fact of his tardiness into the poem itself, it becomes a chief part of its occasion. *Olympian* VI, to Hagesias of Syracuse, victor in the mule race in 472 or 468, opens with the compelling image of the poem as a palace, the beginning like a pillared porch. Language as space, language as a structurable material which can be stilled, drawn out of time. His is metaphoric language, but Pindar actually presents his craft as analogous with the material crafts of other artists.

His *hyporchemata*—poems at the same time sung and danced by the chorus, Athenaeus says—are lively and inventive. Some were encomia, others narrative, or they gave political advice, or praised the gods. Stobaeus quotes an epigrammatic couplet from one of them:

> War seems sweet until one tastes it.
> Known, it takes the heart and wastes it.[71]

While in Sicily, he wrote a *hyporchema* and indulged in characteristic wordplay, invoking his host:

> Take to heart what I am saying
> To you, holy temples is your name,
> Father, Aetna's founder.[72]

The word for "temple" is *ieron*. It is more than a pun, for a city's founder is a founder of temples. It is said that he sent this poem gratis, as a little extra to accompany *Pythian* II. If his subject in an encomium is called Alexander he binds him by name to the Alexandros of Homer, Paris, the great warrior and lover. His language is at all times *literary,* as are his poetic strategies. The two general "classes" of ode are based on his metrical choices: Doric and Aeolian. He learned his craft in Athens but its origins are Dorian and seventh century or earlier: "the Aeolian was travelling the Dorian road of hymns."[73]

In *Olympian* I (476), praising Hieron of Syracuse, he revises the story of Pelops, who was, William H. Race reminds us, the first athlete to compete at Elis. David Mulroy regards the poem as proof that Pindar is an ironist, even a rather comic poet: he cannot stomach the solemnity of most critical readings. Pindar deliberately changed the myth of Pelops ("muddy face") to let the gods off the hook. There are numerous culinary metaphors embedded in the diction. The neighbours *said* that Pelops had been stewed and served up to the gods by Tantalus ("lurching" or "most wretched"). In fact Poseidon had carried him off and taken him to Olympus. (The only thoroughly heterosexual god in the pantheon seems to have been Death, the victims of whose crushes were always girls. Zeus had Ganymede—"rejoicing in virility" or "bright penis"—and Poseidon had Pelops . . .) In relation to the games, the key part of the story is Poseidon's gift of horses to his erstwhile beloved so that Pelops could win the hand of burly Hippodamia ("horse tamer"), daughter of King Oenomaus ("impetuous with wine") of Pisa. "Pindar's purpose is entertainment, not pious edification," Mulroy insists.[74]

Although Pindar chides his irreligion, Homer remains his guiding star, different though his own techniques are from those of epic. In *Nemean* VII he declares,

> Odysseus' tale, I feel,
> Exceeds the hero's actual sufferings
> Because Homer's sweet telling made it greater.

Language can take experience to a higher register, more memorable, more seeming-real. It is Homer who made Ajax "honoured among mankind" by means of his verse.[75] Pindar prays for a similar power with words. The ancient hero is made present in the modern champion, the modern champion is made timeless in his association with the hero. The poem transfigures the living victor.[76] In *Pythian* IV he quotes Homer as supreme authority. But his approach is in no way like Homer's. Pindar's is lofty and elaborate stuff: complex word order, hyper-allusive to mythology, inventive within the realm of myth. Homer's story belongs in the past; Pindar tries to bring the ancient story alive in the present but also deliberately to distance himself from his great forebear. In Paean VII[77] he declares that he is "not following the well-trodden road of Homer / But using the horses of another . . ."

> I make my prayer to Uranus' daughter, Memory,
> And her daughter Muses, Heliconians
> To grant me skill with words
> For blind are men's imaginations if they
> Without the Muses' aid set out to seek
> The path that leads deep into wisdom.

Mikhail Bakhtin outlines the broad similarities between epic and ode. They both "tell" a story, though their methods of telling are radically different; they concentrate on heroes and exceptional deeds. In the epic we expect catalogues, epithets, full-scale characters, narrative; Thebes and Troy loom large. If they can do so in the epiniceans as well, they are differently deployed.

While the epic, remote in time, considers heroes of the past, the ode elevates those of the present and ties them in to the past. Epic is a flowing language of narration; ode a texture of cross-referencing. Like a photograph, without the deliberate continuum of epic, the epinicean ode singles out a moment of triumph. We are closer to the occasions, the athletic victories celebrated in odes, than we are to the narrative of epic, and yet Homer's poems come closer to us than Pindar's, in part at least because they occupy their time rather than propose strategies for eluding it. They tell continuous stories rather than photographing, as it were, moments of intense achievement. Pindar draws on epic as a resource, but he does not contribute to it. He *celebrates* victories but he does not *describe* them, or linger over the victors' lives or antecedents.

Nor does he contribute to tragedy, the form that was emerging from the new Athens even as the social order which sustained the epinicean tradition crumbled. Tragedy was different not only in format but also in subject. Where Pindar's poems, though specific to a victory and a city, were intended to be performed throughout the Greek world, tragedy was more locally contained. It did a tyrant from Magna Graecia no good to be celebrated only within his own realm: the epiniceans had to be performed on the mainland, the name and triumph of Syracuse or Aetna or Cyrene had to be universally acknowledged. An athlete of Rhodes, a tyrant of Sicily invested in wide publicity. Pindar's performances had to appeal to the audience that patronised the pan-Hellenic festivals and to play to other audiences as well. Tragedy, by contrast, was performed at Athens, and the citizens of Athens met each year to pass judgement on tragedies they had seen. A playwright needed to succeed at first with his local audience only: they were his patrons. It is ironic that tragedy, in origin almost a parochial Greek form, eventually gripped the imagination of the Greek and then the European world, while the lyric poetry of Pindar, aimed at a cosmopolitan audience, declined in importance with social change and was eclipsed after the poet's death. What is local is seldom *deliberately* local, and hence, although rooted in a place, it sometimes travels vigorously. An art which sets out to be "universal" and cosmopolitan in the end unanchors itself from its immediate occasions and contingencies to float, as it were, above them, out of their human range. Such art can possess the intense opacity of oracular statement: it needs to be unpacked, interpreted, translated back into the light of day. Sometimes it gets quite lost in translation.

Dionysius of Halicarnassus speaks of the "austere style": "frequent harsh and dissonant collocations," a poetry decidedly more consonantal than vocalic.[78] He uses the image of a building in which the stones are not properly squared and polished. The word "austere" for him means using big and difficult words; in some ways the verse deliberately lacks harmony, imitates nature rather than art, "reflects emotion rather than character." Pindar uses few connectives "and no articles." Just as poets speak ill of the sound qualities of Ben Jonson's poetry, so they criticise Pindar's.

He is sparing in his use of alliteration and other obvious poetic techniques. He does pun and play on homonyms, and there are numerous intentional verbal echoes that function almost like leitmotifs. C. A. M. Fennell finds in *Olympian* I over 60 words that recur once or more in 117 lines.[79] The exigencies of strict metre place a great strain on syntax, which makes the construction of the poems often very hard even for the expert reader. Hyperbatons, those awkward "stepping stones" or "oversteppings" which involve disruption of word order, abound. Two words which belong together are sometimes estranged by a run of more than twelve words. Such sentences must be carefully dismantled, understood, then fitted back together. At times there is the same heavy inertia that one experiences in the weaker Homeric Hymns, and this is due to the weak verbs and the fact that each noun walks on the crutches of at least one and often two adjectives. The passive voice, the genitive construction, and continual periphrasis are among the vices of such a style. Literal translation does brutal justice to it:

> Like a seer, I do not fail to notice the clear signs,
> when, as the chamber of the purple-robed Horai[80] is opened,
> the nectar-bearing flowers bring in the sweet-smelling spring.
> Then, then, upon the immortal earth are cast

> the lovely tresses of violets, and roses are fitted to hair
> and voices of songs echo to the accompaniment of pipes
> and choruses come to Semele of the circling headband.[81]

The rules of syntax generally hold, but they are stretched to the limit. We encounter every rhetorical trope. Among them there are *enallage* (*hypallage*), where the poet transfers an adjective or epithet that logically belongs to one noun syntactically to another (e.g., "the fearless seed of Heracles"); *zeugma*, where he uses one verb with different meanings for two subjects; *hendiadys*, where two nouns mean one thing (e.g., crowns and horses means victorious horses); *brachyology* and *ellipsis*, the suppression of relational words. He also regularly uses the rhetorical strategy known as the *priamel*, a series of superlative metaphors crowned by a "most superlative." *Olympian* I sets the tone in its opening lines:

> Best element is water; but gold gleaming like flame
> Through night outshines all noble wealth;
> But if, my heart, you wish
> To celebrate athletic games
> Don't look beyond the sun for brighter
> Star or one in daytime warmer,
>> Glowing in deserted air; nor let us name
> Games worthier than Olympia's to celebrate.

Not unrelated to the *priamel*, which usually develops in threes, is the process of "ring composition," a sequencing of events, sometimes, as in *Olympian* VII (460 BC), in a reverse chronology. We find the same structure in *Pythian* IX and *Pythian* XI, the mini-Oresteia. Pindar is also an inveterate hyperboliser: "my voice is even more sweet than honeycombs the bees made."[82] A conceit, in both senses of the word, is that his poems will make Thebes more famous not only among men but also among the gods.[83] He did not heed his own moral counsel against hubris.

Dionysus of Halicarnassus tends to be a maker of restrictive rules by which he then criticises a poet. The sigma, he declares, with its hissing sound, disgusted the ear, and poets including Lasus used it sparingly, sometimes composing a poem almost without it, a deliberate omission which, while it promoted euphony, diminished the resources of significance. In the second dithyramb Pindar protests against the unnaturalness of such omissions.[84] He deploys every possible device and technique, but the one set of rules he follows doggedly is that of prosodic correctness. He is a conservative in his art: any art which hoards meanings in strict forms, essentialises, and aspires to raise its subjects to a timeless sphere is conservative in the literal sense. The *eunomia*, or harmony, of good laws that he celebrates also entails a harmony of artistic resources. The Muses speak through the poet; if they speak well, people and events enter memory. The poet is at once a spiritual and secular means by which deeds and the names of the men who performed them survive in the teeth of time; he is a minister of sorts. In *Nemean* VII, dedicated to the boy Sogenes of Aegina, Pindar describes the process:

> . . . Sogenes, son of Thearion, is exalted in this song
> Because among pentathletes he excelled.
>
> He lives in the Aiakides' singing, spear-clashing city
> And they keenly value such an achieving spirit
>   Tempered in contest as he is.
> If a man has the skill to win, he casts a honey-sweet
> Occasion into the Muses' currents; high achievements
> Lacking their song and dance vanish into the dark.
> Only one looking glass do we have for great deeds:
> Bright-crowned Mnemosyne whose flowing grace
> Is given, the wages for all his labour
> Who labours for fame.

This ode has long been regarded as a problem and a key: "the touchstone of Pindaric interpretation."[85] How does the narrative connect with the occasion? Why was such a complex, beautiful and finally insoluble poem, asks the editor William H. Race, written for a boy athlete? Pindar may have taken particular pains because of his love for Aegina. A rich man who is also wise, says Pindar, will not hoard his wealth. Is the sense not clear? An athlete who is rich in strength and skill should achieve; a man who is materially rich should achieve. The rich man pays the poet to sing in his honour and, like the athlete, he lives for ever. No one enjoys perfect happiness, the poet concedes because, as Pound said, *Time is the evil*.

As an epinicean poet Pindar was most active in the 470s and 460s BC, and it was in Arkesilas IV, king of Cyrene, that he invested his best efforts. For him he composed *Pythian* IV, "almost epic in scale," as Bowra says, the longest of the odes. *Pythian* V was dedicated to Arkesilas as well, and both poems relate to his victory in the chariot race in 462 BC. The first was intended for performance at Delphi, or later, at the palace in Cyrene; the second was for public performance in Cyrene at "the feast of the Dorian Apollo Carneius."[86]

Pythian V is a relatively conventional and direct encomium of Arkesilas. It also celebrates his charioteer, Karrhotos, more comprehensively than other charioteers in the odes. Praise is seldom for the driver, usually for the owner, except on odd occasions when (as in *Pythian* II, for Hieron, and *Isth-*

mian I, for Herodotus of Thebes) the owner *is* the contestant. Karrhotos may have been Arkesilas' brother-in-law.

In *Pythian* IV the victory of Arkesilas' chariot is taken for granted. The poem concentrates on the foundation of the city by Battus, which leads into the story of Jason and the Argonauts and ends with political advice. Arkesilas' family claimed an Argonaut among its ancestors. Cyrene is a "doctor" city, a place full of healing. Its chief export was a plant extract known as *silphium* used in medicines. In his poem Pindar seems to be urging the claims of an exiled Cyrenian, Damophilos, who perhaps paid for the poem to be composed, a tribute and a plea.

The more conventional poem was for the wider audience; the longer, more complex poem, with its intriguing obliquities, its political nuances, was presented more directly, a mixture of flattery, entertainment and persuasion. Pindar did not write for Arkesilas again. The tyrant was murdered by his people shortly after *Pythian* IV was performed. The strict, efficient but unsustainable structures of Theron's and Hieron's tyrannies collapsed when they died. A similar collapse occurred in Cyrene. Pindar belonged to a fading courtly order: it strikes some scholars as odd that he should have felt at home with tyrants, but he did. They seemed to provide not only patronage and occasions but stability, a stability which only lasted for one man's lifetime or, at most, two.

Pythian I, from 470 BC, is the last ode dedicated to Hieron, described as "Hieron of Aetna" here rather than "Hieron of Syracuse" because he founded the new city in 476–75 BC with five thousand settlers from Syracuse and five thousand from the Peloponnese. He wanted its foundation, quite as much as his victory, celebrated. Hieron's team won the chariot race. The ode celebrates the comprehensive *eunomia* that the victory and the founding of Aetna represent. It opens with a hymn to the lyre, powerful enough to overcome divine wrath and, as Orpheus showed, to calm extremes. It can also scare Zeus' foes. The poem is decidedly civic in its themes and the counsel it gives Hieron (and his son). Pindar begins with particulars, which he then builds out from. The story is of Typhos, squashed down under Mount Aetna. After Hieron died, in 466, his son was unequal to the succession.

At the Olympic Games of 476, with the Greek victories at Salamis (480), Plataia (479) and—in Magna Graecia—Himera recently achieved, Pindar (who remained pan-Hellenic despite his Theban birth) scored the largest number of commissions.[87] The Greeks had proved that they could defend themselves and fight together. Five of the fourteen Olympian odes are for victors at that Olympiad.[88] After that, Pindar kept writing epinicean poems, the last which we can date being from 446 BC. This ode can stand as the last great poem of the "great age of Greek lyric poetry."

Pythian VIII is dedicated to Aristomenes of Aegina, victor in the wrestling. The poet is an old man, the victor a boy. The world has changed since the triumphs of 476 BC. Aegina, Athens' old foe, is in a brief ascendancy, soon to be terminated (though Pindar did not live to see his beloved island despoiled in 431 BC, its population exported en masse and its vacancy repopulated with immigrants). In 446 BC Athens had lost Boeotia at the battle of Coronea, the Spartan army was at her borders, Megara was free. Was this Aegina's moment to bolt for freedom? Pindar sees Athens, beleaguered, as the gods' enemy, like the mythical giants. The poem may celebrate a wrestling lad; it also subtly probes at the issue of freedom from the Athenian yoke. Pindar's poem is sombre as befits his age and his theme: the alternation of failure and success.

Sombre, with a poised beauty, is the brief *Olympian* XIV, to Asopichos of Orchomenos, victor in the *stadion,* maybe in 476 BC. Orchomenos was the burial-place of Hesiod, and the first city where a temple of the Graces was consecrated. According to Hazlitt, "The territory was almost undermined by moles." Be that as it may, Pindar's poem celebrates the Graces (*Charites*). This is the only ode with two strophes. In the second he names the Graces: Aglaia (Splendour), Euphrosyne (Good Cheer) and Thalia (Festivity). What is touching is the conceit whereby he asks Echo to convey news of the lad's victory to his father, who has passed into the underworld.

It is natural that fathers and sons, families, dynasties, are celebrated in epinicean poetry. In *Nemean* VI, to Alkimidas of Aegina, winner in the boys' wrestling, he remembers how Alkimidas' family has more crowns for wrestling than any other in Greece and praises not his father but his grandfather; not his great-grandfather but his great-great-grandfather. The skill leapfrogs a generation each time. *Olympian* XIII, to Xenophon of Corinth, victor in the *stadion* and *pentathlon* in 464 BC (did Pindar get twice the fee?) opens with an amazing coinage: *Trusolumpionikan,* "thrice victorious at Olympia," because Thessalos, the victor's father, had won the *stadion,* and Xenophon had a double victory in the same year. Pindar celebrates Corinth for three inventions: the dithyramb, the bridle and bit, and temple decorations. Appropriately, the central narrative concentrates on the bridle and bit of Bellerophon. He offers javelins of praise, a curious image.

Xenophon of Corinth was from an influential and prosperous family. On top of his epinicean he also wanted Pindar to write a poem glorifying his ostentatious gift to Aphrodite. "The temple of the goddess in Corinth was associated with ritual prostitution . . . and for this purpose Xenophon gave fifty female slaves. Pindar can never have had a more singular assignment."[89] Pindar obliged with a *skolion* (he uses the word within the poem) which the editors slotted in among the encomia in error. The poem directly addresses the prostitutes. "Young women, who welcome many guests, attendants / of

Persuasion in rich Corinth." It was their custom to burn incense. "Under compulsion all is fair . . ." Then he speaks to Aphrodite herself:

> O Cyprian lady, here into your temple precinct
> Xenophon has herded a hundred girls
> To pasture, in his gratitude
> That you fulfilled his prayers.[90]

There are in Pindar other sexual surprises in the detail. A fragment tells of Mendes in Egypt, where billygoats mate with women.[91]

Pindar is a poet, not a philosopher nor a consistent moral teacher. Yet there are wonderfully clear aphorisms in his writing that excited pagan and Christian minds. Clement of Alexandria quotes with approval the line *ti Theos; to pan*: "What is God? Everything."[92] In *Pythian* III (l. 81) he declares, after Homer, "for each blessing the gods give to men, they give two curses also." The moral of the poem is not generic but specific to the occasion. Hieron of Syracuse is mortally ill. His horse has won in the Pythian Games, and Pindar is celebrating the victory but also alluding indirectly to his patron's indisposition. Past victory is mentioned, and the famous horse Pherenicus is evoked. The first seventy-nine lines are philosophical, about being content with what is, and the verses are among Pindar's most famous and "theological," valued by Plato and by the Christian fathers as an exhortation to humility, to accepting mortality and the human lot and not aspiring to divinity. His real desire is to charm away Hieron's illness, but for all its power, poetry cannot make this sort of thing happen. The narrative of the ode is the story of Asklepios, the greatest of all healers. Apollo was his father. His mother, heavily pregnant, had sex with another man. Apollo had Artemis kill her in a plague and rescued his son from her dead body. Cheiron the centaur raised the boy, who became a great physician until he was corrupted by money and resurrected a patient, whereupon he was slain by a thunderbolt. Pindar wishes he could bring Hieron a great physician. Instead he prays to the Mother Goddess. This is what art can do: celebrate, pray, console. It can help shape mind and character, but it cannot affect events, except by *being* an event.

Callimachus imitated Pindar's verse and used his phrases. It is Pindar who legitimises his own manner of writing, and he says as much in the Prologue to the *Aetia*, which owes a debt to Pindar's Paean VII.[93] He begs to differ from those poets who follow Homer's "worn wagon-road." He adds that men "who do not compose poetry have 'blind hearts.'"[94] Callimachus portrays himself as following a narrow road, and as being light-winged.

Pindar's lightest and purest heir, the perennially acceptable face of Pindaric strategies, is the Latin poet Horace. He registered the Greek

ode-maker on his own pulse. When he wanted to eulogise his emperor in
Odes I, xii, he used the second line of Pindar's *Olympian* II as his base-note.

> Quem virum aut heroa lyra vel acri
> tibia sumis celebrare, Clio?
> Quem deum?

In Odes IV, ii, 25–32, he writes directly:

> Borne by strong winds, Pindar the Theban swan soars
>   high above, Antonius, through the lofty
>   realms of cloud: while I, in another fashion—
>   just like a small bee—
>   sip each sweet blossom of thyme and rove
>   the thick groves, over the slopes of Tibur
>   rich with streams—and thus, cell on cell, I labour
>   moulding my poems.[95]

The Greek bee now speaks Latin. Pindar's imitator, says Horace at the beginning of the poem, is like Icarus strapping on wings of wax and feather;
he will leave his name as a dissolving blot upon the waters of some sea. Pindar is, he says, like a deep-voiced river rising above its banks, flowing over
into the landscape, rushing down the mountain; the pell-mell song of gods,
of legend and of literal men returning home, victors, their names lauded to
the skies. The river is a wonderful image: it reflects, it contains, it flows.

XXII

Bacchylides of Cos (c. 518–452 BC)

O ye, who patiently explore
The wreck of Herculanean lore,
What rapture! could ye seize
Some Theban fragment, or unroll
One precious, tender-hearted, scroll
   Of pure Simonides.

That were, indeed, a genuine birth
Of poesy; a bursting forth
Of genius from the dust:
What Horace gloried to behold,
   What Maro[1] loved, shall we enfold?
   Can haughty Time be just!

WORDSWORTH,
"September, 1819"

 In the first half of the nineteenth century, when most readers of poetry—when most readers *tout court*—had a grounding in the classics, the steady tease of archaeology, turning up ancient papyruses in the Egyptian desert, became tedious. Who cared about tracts on dike building, lists of punishments, accounts, contracts, the débris of the Ptolomaic world? Readers craved a great lost *literary* work. Classical philologists had run through the store of existing texts. Surely beneath the lone and level sands and crumpled, sneering statuary lurked song, drama, history, oratory. Wordsworth in his 1819 poem expressed a general hunger.

The German historian Christian Matthias Theodor Mommsen—it is just to grant him his full complement of names, so neglected is the Nobel Literature laureate of 1902—Mommsen, who lived for the better part of a century (1817–1903), believed in the historical value of *material* culture. *A History of Rome* drew much of its original force from Mommsen's use of inscriptions and the "new" evidence of non-literary ancient writing. He studied Roman law in a wide cultural context. The nineteenth century, he said, had been the age of epigraphy, reading and interpreting the records held in stone; the twentieth would belong to papyrology.

Beginning in the latter half of the eighteenth century, papyruses began to find their way into the libraries and museums of Europe, and as the next century proceeded the trickle increased. A problem with papyruses is the skill required to decipher them. Early editors could be fanciful, or they were simply flummoxed by the tiny, deteriorating script. During the nineteenth century expertise developed, and by the century's end the time between accessing new papyrus acquisitions and their deciphering, transcription and publication had shortened considerably.

Wordsworth's prayer began to be answered, but too late for the poet to enjoy it. And it was not Simonides' poetry but his nephew Bacchylides' which materialised out of the duny sepulchre. Poems and other important texts came to light and were published, including six speeches of the Greek orator Hyperides, one of them complete. And then, in 1891, the *Mimes* of Herodas were dusted down, and what remains one of the most astonishing historical finds, Aristotle's, or rather the Aristotelian, text on the *Constitution of the Athenians* was published from the British Museum. The study of papyruses became an important exercise for philologists. A valuable papyrus mine was found at Tebtunis, in the Faytum, one of the chief sources being the crocodile graveyard. Sacred crocodiles were mummified and wrapped in papyrus as if parcelled up in tinfoil for the oven. In 1902 at Hibeh important manuscripts from the period of the Ptolemies were discovered, followed by other major finds at Oxyrhynchus a year later, a period of unparalleled surprise and enrichment. Then in 1908 in Abusir a large body of Alexandrian papyruses was discovered, saved from the unfriendly climate of Alexandria, in which texts readily perished, because they were regarded as rubbish and carted off into the desert.

More than 650 literary papyruses from Egypt have now been published. Roughly a third are passages of Homer, just under a third are versions of works which survive in other forms, in later copies and include philosophy, oratory, history and drama. What remains consists of fragments and longer portions of work regarded as lost forever: passages of Sappho, Alcman, chunks of Menander's comedies, of the *Iambi* of Callimachus, passages of Antiope, Euripides, Hypsipyle, the *Paeans* of Pindar and (for our purposes here) most important of all, the odes of Pindar's rival, or competitor, Bacchylides.

The papyrus with the odes was found in Egypt by local diggers. It arrived at the British Museum in 1896, in the autumn. What had been a roll was now a jigsaw of about 200 friable pieces. The skilful and patient scholarship of F. G. Kenyon bore fruit, and in 1897 he published the *editio princeps,* the "first edition," of the poems, increasing the amount of Bacchylides from around a hundred disconnected lines and phrases to more than a thousand lines of relatively continuous verse. In Kenyon's painstaking reconstruction, the papyrus is in three parts. The first includes twenty-two columns of writing and ends abruptly just after the start of Ode XII. Column 23 has more or less vanished: the second section of the papyrus runs from the ves-

tiges of column 23 to column 29 and contains what is left of Odes XIII and
XIV. The last section includes nine further columns, the first again damaged, and includes Dithyramb XV, breaking off suddenly. Each column has
between thirty-two and thirty-six lines.

Fourteen or thirteen epinicean odes[2] and six dithyrambs survive in this
one papyrus. The odes were arranged like Simonides', by the type of athletic event celebrated, rather than like Pindar's, by the place in which the
games occurred. To this material were added further fragments, in 1956,
from the Oxyrhynchus trove.[3] Like Simonides and Pindar, Bacchylides had
received commissions from all over the Greek world, from Aegina, Athens,
Cos, Macedonia, Metapontion, Philus, Sparta, Syracuse and Thessaly, and
these are the remains of his labours. Albin Lesky values Bacchylides principally for the light his poems cast, given the substantial nature of the remains, on Pindar; also because in a quite unique way Bacchylides is "ours,"
almost a twentieth-century ancient Greek.[4]

Readers of the new Bacchylides were initially disappointed: Simonides'
nephew was not Pindar. Once this fact was accepted, readers began to puzzle
out who he *was,* a writer whose narratives were less allusive, more continuous than Pindar's, who was on occasion a brilliant describer and evoker of
specific details and specific emotional moments; who was, in short, a
dramatist *avant la lettre,* a lucid teller of stories. In the underworld Meleager
recalls the moment of his death, and Heracles responds; Croesus, despairing, is saved from his pyre; best of all is the confrontation of Minos and
Theseus, and Theseus' plunge into his father's, Poseidon's, churning realm.
In the eighteenth ode, Aegeus and a chorus conduct a dramatic dialogue.
Or take this brief passage from Ode X, in Campbell's prose translation:
"For when he had come to a halt at the finishing-line of the sprint, panting
out a hot storm of breath, and again when he had wet with his oil the cloaks
of the spectators as he tumbled into the packed crowd after rounding the
course with its four turns . . ."[5] We could hardly get closer to the action.

In Ode XIII, by contrast, his inadequacy is clear: the truisms and truths
he tells are morally and poetically undistinguished. They lack focus and
pith; they ramble, they are merely ceremonious. "Nowhere," says Lesky,
"do we find the profundity of Pindar's perception of values."[6] His morals
are very like his uncle's: Ode XIV might have been written by Simonides:
". . . To be granted a good lot by God [singular] is best for men; but if luck
comes with a burden of suffering, she wrecks an admirable man, while even
a low-born fellow, set on a happy highroad, can shine."[7]

The myth story in each ode attaches to the victor celebrated, to his city or
to his sport, and its purpose is to connect his mortal deeds with the timeless
deeds of the gods and heroes, as it were to deposit his achievement in a
timeless realm. In his first epinicean ode, for Argeius of Cos, Bacchylides

distinguished between mere "lightweight" ambition, which wins honour only for a lifetime, and true excellence, which is hard-won, yet when concluded correctly leads to a man's fame becoming part of a durable glory. It is as if there is a kind of entity called "glory*ness*" into which true excellence, at its demise, spills its qualities, the way a soul might rise to merge into an oversoul.

Pindar and Bacchylides both set out to make such connections, but Bacchylides is more limpid, less complex and hermetic. This difference between them was noted by a first- (or third-) century critic, possibly Cassius Longinus, or whoever was the author of *On the Sublime,* which is generally attributed to him.[8] He wonders whether faulty greatness in writing is preferable to the smooth and undisrupted work of the great technician. He concludes that greatness is to be preferred. In the area of poetry, we prefer Pindar to Bacchylides even though in the latter we find elegance and polish (the style is *glaphuros*): he may produce unblemished verse, but he falls short of the higher beauty. In the end, Bacchylides' art is simpler in conception and easier in execution than Pindar's. You can imagine buying Bacchylides by the yard: he is, after all, his uncle's nephew. Pindar delivers his verse in less standard measures.

Bacchylides is not Pindar, and yet critics and readers keep wanting him to be. Even the textual scholars approach him with Pindaric expectations, and their editorial work—especially in proposing emendations on bridge-passages where text is missing—can be coloured by this predisposition. It is as though we were to edit Christopher Marlowe entirely in the light of Shakespeare's practice. We distort the structure and the language of both poets in the process.

Meleager spoke of the "ripe ears from the harvest of Bacchylides."[9] In old age Simonides left Athens and went to Sicily, to the court of Hiero of Syracuse, and seeing there was work to be had, summoned his nephew Bacchylides of Cos, who was then living in Athens or Thessaly or perhaps was exiled[10] in the Peloponnese.[11] Poetry was a family business and, in the absence of a son, a nephew would have to do. There was demand for epinicean odes. Pindar was making a good living, and so was Simonides. Some traditions say that Pindar and Simonides were in competition; the latter, being old, needed reinforcements and Bacchylides, already well known, came to the rescue. Other (late) traditions suggest that Pindar studied under Simonides. In any event, Bacchylides may have settled in Syracuse for a serious spell (478–467 BC).

Bacchylides' mother was Simonides' sister, probably a younger one. His father was Meidon, the name deriving, the ninth-century *Etymologicum Genuinum* tells us, from *meidin,* "smile." His grandfather was "Bacchylides the athlete," so from boyhood he knew about the great sporting fixtures and may have heard some of the poems composed to celebrate the victors, his grandfather included.[12]

He was probably some forty-nine years younger than his uncle, and perhaps fifteen years younger than Pindar, though Campbell believes they were more or less exact contemporaries. His first surviving poem may be a drinking song for Alexander, son of Amyntas, king of Macedonia, composed before 490 BC.[13] The poet takes up his lyre and plays loudly, "with its seven notes silencing your clear voice." He longs to send a gift of value and beauty. Drink leads on to amorous thoughts, and then to thoughts of bravery and opulence. He imagines the company of Alexander. The poem celebrates imagination (lubricated and stimulated) and the power of poetry to bring into the open what is imagined, in order to share it.

The earliest datable epinicean ode is XIV, from 485–83 BC, and the last is from 452 BC, which Campbell believes was the year of his death. Severyns divides his work, and his life, into three phases and geographies, the first concentrated in the east (498–486, Thessaly, Macedonia, Aegina), the second in mainland Greece and points west in Magna Graecia (486–466, Athens, Syracuse), and the last in the Peloponnese and back to points east, including a return to Cos (466–452 BC, Cos, Sparta, Phlius, Asine). At Alexandria his work was edited into nine books, Campbell says, the divisions apparently generic: the epinicean odes, for which he was best known and best paid; paeans; dithyrambs; hymns; *prosodia,* or processional poems; maiden songs; *hyporchemata,* or dance songs; erotica; and encomia. There were a few epigrams, of which two survive, and yet Bacchylides is mentioned in the first poem in Meleager's *Garland.*[14]

On the face of it, there would seem to be no expressed animosity between Pindar and Bacchylides. Pindar celebrated the island of Cos as a provider of poets, and he must have been referring to Simonides and his nephew. But the scholiast, considering Pindar's *Olympian* II,[15] declares that it targets the garrulity of uncle and nephew, comparing them to crows "stuttering out pointless words against Zeus' holy bird," the eagle, namely himself.[16] Carrying forward the bird analogy, elsewhere he appears to refer to Bacchylides as a jackdaw, to himself again as the eagle.[17] And is Bacchylides the monkey, entertaining to children but ridiculous to a man of mature judgement like Hiero? Perhaps. Some say that Bacchylides, in his turn, slandered Pindar privately to Hiero, stressing his obscurity, his bookishness, the cold artifice of his compositions.[18]

The rivalry, if it existed, was probably due to the fact that both poets were trying to beguile a single patron, their customer and tyrant. Tradition says that Hiero preferred Bacchylides, the easy-going Ionian, to the severe, courtly manner of the Boeotian who kept reminding his listeners of ancestry and seemed to praise his patrons for their wisdom in associating with *him*.[19] He could understand Bacchylides' poems more easily, and Bacchylides was less prone than the sometimes arrogant Pindar to insert himself into the poem as a dominant "I." It may not be mere chance that, whereas in 476 and 470 BC both Pindar and Bacchylides wrote Hiero epinicean odes, in 468, the most important of Hiero's victories, only Bacchylides would appear to have been asked, though Pindar composed an ode for another victor from Syracuse (*Olympian* VI).

Bacchylides' three odes celebrating Hiero's victories can be dated with some certainty. Ode V commemorates Hiero's single-horse-race victory—the most augustly sung of Greek horses, Pherenicus, is stabled here—at Olympia in 476, as does Pindar's *Olympian* I. The brief Ode IV celebrates the 470 Pythian chariot race, and Pindar's *Pythian* I does the same. In 468 BC Hiero won the Olympic four-horse chariot race, and Bacchylides composed Ode III.[20] Here he pays the highest praise to Hiero's taste and judgement in poetry.

Marking Hiero's Olympic victory, the poet invokes Clio, the Muse of history. He goes on to celebrate the tyrant's wealth, power and open-handedness. The myth he explores is that of Croesus and his dreadful plight when the Persians were over-running his city, Sardis. He built his pyre and mounted it, lamenting, his dear wife and daughter with him. It is a brilliant evocation, with something like a Homeric pathos about it. "The death that can be seen advancing from far off is most dreaded by mortals." At the last moment Zeus quenches the pyre with a downpour and Apollo bears the old king, his wife and daughter off to the Hyperboreans, where he settles them, in recompense for their pieties (Croesus' people, meanwhile, fall under the dreadful yoke). What point could such a story have in the Olympic context? Is it that Hiero has sent even *more* gold to Delphi than Croesus did? Or is the poet aware that Hiero is dying, and is this a delicate acknowledgement and consolation? If so, the connection is less tenuous; the story moves us. Bacchylides then adds the myth of Apollo, compelled by Zeus to be servant to Admetus because Admetus killed the Cyclops. Apollo speaks to Admetus, but as we listen, the voice modulates into the voice of Bacchylides himself, counselling Hiero and including himself, Pindarically as it were, in the kite-tail of the offered praise. Here is how it goes:

> "You are mortal, Admetus, remember,
> And hold these two opposing thoughts in mind:
> Tomorrow is your final day of sunlight;
> You'll live for fifty years in utter wealth.
> Do right things and be glad at heart, that's best."
> I speak the words that a wise man will hear:
> The deep skies are stainless, the ocean depths

Do not decay, gold pleases, but no man
No matter who he is, can cast aside
Ashen age and get back budding boyhood.
The flame of good deeds does not flicker with
The body, but the Muse will fan and fuel it.
You, Hiero, have shown to men wealth's fairest blossoms.
When a man has prospered, silence does not grace him:
As well as celebrating what you've done, for ever men
Will speak too of the honey-tongued, the Cean nightingale.

In Ode IV he refers to himself as lyre-mastering Urania's "sweet-crowing cock." No wonder Pindar likened his foes to coarse-voiced, rough-plumed birds: he found the birds in their own poems. And then, in his Ode X, Bacchylides becomes "the clear-voiced island bee."

What is cloying about Bacchylides' verse, and what puts us in mind of the weaker of the Homeric Hymns, which they sometimes resemble, is the profusion of adjectives, praised by some ancient critics as "epithets." Clearly their intention is Homeric and conventional, but in Ode IV, when Heracles goes into Hades to bring back Cerberus, for example, not a single noun escapes without having to carry an adjective or two on its shoulders. These words are not "uniquely chosen." Copious ornament stiffens the work. Many of the epithets are compound words used nowhere else in Greek poetry, perhaps Bacchylides' own effusive coinings.

His similes, too, while sometimes effective, can be over-elaborate: too much gold in the brocade, so that the poem cannot dance, can hardly move. He is paying a tribute to Homer, but his similes work to quite different ends, not (as Homer's do) to produce sudden clarification, but rather to add a frill, a decoration, to what is already clear. His satisfaction as a poet would have derived from the sense that he had produced something expected and acceptable to his patron or his audience, rather than something that touched deeply upon his subject. At times the flash of metaphor does illuminate in both directions, the audience and the subject, as when he sees the afterlives of men lining the river Cocytus like wind-shuddered leaves on "Ida's shimmering promontories."[21]

What redeems the over-wrought passage in Ode IV is not a suddenly successful simile but the power of narrative realisation. Heracles meets the afterlife of Meleager and seeks to re-slay him. Instead they have a conversation. Meleager tells of his father's failure to appease Artemis, and how the goddess sent the Calydonian boar to hunt him down. Meleager's speech is wonderful, recounting pell-mell what the boar hunt and battle were like, the victims, the blind rage and the sad consequences. Heracles weeps only once in his life, and this is the occasion.

One can imagine how the object of the epinicean ode, the patron who commissioned it, would hearken as the poet and the chorus recited, waiting to see how the long mythical narrative might relate to his life and achievement. It is not easy to say exactly how the exchange between Heracles and Meleager relates to Hiero's achievement. It may have to do with the ephemerality of even the greatest heroic achievements, which survive as narrative alone. The poem ends with Heracles asking Meleager if he left any suitable maiden sisters in the mortal world, and Meleager saying, yes. His sister was in fact Deianira, who, an audience would have realised, was to be Heracles' wife and, when he proved unfaithful to her, was inadvertently to cause his death, having presented him with a shirt impregnated with the blood of Nessus, his centaur victim. What interests the poet is not the later, but the present story, so he leaves the future unspoken. This narrowing of narrative focus can be highly effective.

Whatever the connection of the poem with the occasion of victory, Ode IV is dramatic. Dithyramb XV is also a play of voices. The sons of Antenor request the return of Helen. Odysseus and Menelaus attend the court of Priam, arguing the toss for giving Helen back on the grounds of justice. Very near at hand, the forces of the drama are gathering. Indeed, Aeschylus is less than ten years Bacchylides' junior and will predecease him. Dithyramb XVI, with the (poetically postponed, as it were) cloak of Nessus and the death of Heracles, also verges on dramatic form.

The most beguiling Bacchylidean poem is Dithyramb XVII, which had a direct impact on Virgil.[22] A ship is conveying the seven young boys and the seven young girls to Crete, the annual tribute of protein for the Minotaur (the story of whose mother Pasiphae, Minos' wife, with her bestial appetites, Bacchylides tells).[23] Minos, who is accompanying the sacrificial victims along with Theseus, finds one of the seven girls, Eriboia, sexually irresistible. Theseus tells him to behave, a chivalry dictated as much by necessity (the fourteen victims were supposed to be virgin) as out of humane concern. Then both Minos, son of Zeus, and Theseus, son of Poseidon, boast of their parentage. Minos asks Zeus to send a thunderbolt to prove his lineage, and Zeus obliges. Then Minos throws a jewel into the sea and challenges Theseus to retrieve it with Poseidon's help. Theseus dives off the stern and Minos maliciously orders that the ship keep course and speed on. The Athenian crew are worried and weepy. But the dolphins do their trick, carrying Theseus to his father's deep mansion, which is evoked in sumptuous and erotic images. He returns "unwet" from the sea depths to great rejoicing; Minos is compelled to control his lust.

Dithyramb XVIII is stageably dramatic. Aegeus and a chorus of Athenians conduct a dialogue which may have been composed for an ephebic festival.[24] The chorus questions Aegeus: What's happening? Why is there this terrifying trumpeting? Aegeus replies: a herald has come from the Isthmus bringing news that a stranger (Theseus, Aegeus' son, though Aegeus does not yet know it) is on his way along the (widely familiar) road from Epidaurus to Athens. He has destroyed a sequence of legendary malefactors:

a) Sinis, who tied victims to bent pine-trees and let the trees go;
b) The man-killing sow "in the vales of Cremmyon";
c) Sciron, the robber who threw his victims over the Scironian cliffs;
d) Cercyon, who forced passers-by to wrestle with him and killed the losers; and
e) Procoptes, the Cutter, also known as Procrustes.

The herald, Aegeus says, reports that the stranger is accompanied by two lesser men, that his eyes are fiery, his sword heroic . . . Bacchylides creates dramatic tension of a real if rather dogged kind.

There are other Bacchylidean fragments, two—reported by Clement of Alexandria—with the force of Simonides' apophthegms. "One gets his skill from another, now as in days of old," the poet says, in a definition of tradition which few pre-Modernists would gainsay. He adds that it is hard "to discover the gates of verse unspoken before."[25] The quest for originality, within the strict confines of conventions of form and diction, is a serious challenge for a poet, and Bacchylides does not consistently rise to that challenge. Yet sometimes he does, occasionally in a long run, occasionally in brief:

> . . . Fate that metes out all things moves
> A cloud; it hangs now here above this
> Country, then there hanging above that.[26]

He is certainly impersonal, sharing with his uncle a degree of reticence, including himself in the frame of a poem only when convention would seem to dictate it.

The Alexandrian critics set Bacchylides ungrudgingly among the nine canonical lyric poets.[27] Didymus, the Alexandrian grammarian, composed a commentary on the Odes. Horace studied and imitated him, Virgil took bearings from him, and the historians and anthologists went to him as a dependable and authoritative source. The benign and maligned emperor Julian the Apostate, a lover of Greek culture who was compelled to serve an empire against his will, loved Bacchylides.[28] And then, between the fourth and twentieth centuries, the poet virtually disappeared.

XXIII

Callimachus of Cyrene (310–240 BC)

Shades of Callimachus, Coan ghosts of Philetas
It is in your grove I would walk,
I who come first from the clear fount
Bringing the Grecian orgies into Italy,
and the dance into Italy.

EZRA POUND, "Homage to Sextus Propertius"

Oral cultures value what is old, attested, *legitimate*. There is little room for what is novel or goes against the grain of legend or custom. No copyright inhibits the transmission of oral poems: everyone, from bard to ploughboy, can store them in the retrieval system of memory and repeat them at will. But if you add lines and passages you run the political risks of that great forger-editor Onomacritos. The word "original" has a pejorative sense.

Accuracy of fact in such verse is secondary to fidelity of transmission. Facts are local, poetry universal. Historical fact can give way, in epic narrative and hymn, to the demands of poetic pattern. A singer of tales is after characteristic rather than specific truth. In epic, things are too far in the past to be verified. It is another country peopled by larger men. Hyperbole, unlikely connections between disparate narratives, anachronism, all have a place there. A synthesis of elements, even of dialects, in a single, specifically poetic idiom occurs. Oral tradition is an arresting amber: words, images and forms survive beyond extinction. Oral traditions develop at a glacial pace.

Then comes writing, and, gradually at first, the thaw commences.

A millennium before the Trojan War, a boy called Pepy was being taken up the Nile to be placed in a writing school. Khety, Pepy's father, declared, "I shall make you love writing more than you love your own mother; and thus I shall make beauty enter before your face." The main thing, Khety insists, is that a scribe will always have work.[1] Egyptians valued writing because it was a source of control and therefore of power. The Greeks in due course came to love it for itself.

It is time to turn to Egypt, where the closing chapters of *The First Poets* are set. "As Mesopotamia may be considered the cradle of writing, so may Egypt be considered the cradle of 'the book,'" says David Diringer. "From the earliest ages the Egyptians had the greatest veneration for books, writing and learning."[2] Greek literature could hardly have found a more hospitable long-term home: without the climate of Egypt, papyrus, and a religion which involved mummification, we would have only a fragment of the fragment of Greek poetry that survives.

Writing borrows energy from the oral tradition and at first seeks to replicate its means and serve its ends. But the reciting bard and the individual writer engage their subjects—place, character, legend, myth—rather differently. A writer composes away from the undifferentiated audience; perhaps he has scrolls of other texts around him which he can draw upon. He has in mind as his reader or fellow symposiast a crowd different from Homer's or Hesiod's, different from those who frequented the theatre. It consists of almost-individuals, better washed, fed and informed than common men. A written tradition as it evolves encourages variation, individuality, even originality in handling forms, metres and subject-matter itself. What was sacred or legendary becomes "textual"; what is "textual" can be a specifically *literary* resource.

By the end of the classical period, the written tradition, still grounded in Homer and Hesiod, had become a theatre of originality and variety. Theatre itself took hold of the tradition, and from 450 BC onwards—after Pindar, pending Alexandria—verse thrived primarily in the drama. Before 450, prose literature was limited: we see into earlier ages through poems—there we hear voices, view landscapes, hear the sounds of the street and the worlds of love and conflict. Aristotle and Plutarch depend upon the poets for a sense of place and moral reflection: they read Tyrtaeus to learn about Sparta, Solon to learn about Athens. There is a special kind of truth in such poetic traditions, but they pass. The arts of prose develop alongside the drama.

Already in Pindar there is the baroque elaboration that an unkind critic calls "merely literary," as though that heavily political and earnest author was a pince-nezed *art pour l'artiste*. His poems are certainly not spontaneous (but then not even the freshest-seeming, the archaic Greek poetry, is off the cuff as modern readers would like it to be). Greater elaboration, in Pindar, appeals to a specialised audience; if an audience loves puzzles, a poet will be a riddler; if a patron delights in obliquity and allusion the poet will be obligingly oblique and allusive. The more a poet tunes in to a particular audience, genre and approach, the fewer (and fitter) his readers and hearers will be. But with Pindar, however local the victor he celebrates, we know that the poem is intended for transmission to the entire Greek world, or those audiences within that world primed to the epinicean tradition.

Cultural accompanied the political changes of the ancient world. In 404 BC, Athens was decisively defeated: the Old Comedy and much else went out of fashion. The century after 360 BC saw transformation and a reformation of the Greek world; the centre of gravity moved from Athens, south and west. Philip II of Macedon defeated the Greeks at Chaeronea in Boeotia in 338 BC, sealing "classical Greece" as such in its tomb. Between 334 and 323 BC, Alexander conquered the Near East and Egypt, then went on as far as Pakistan, perhaps crossing the Indus. But the *polis* system of agora, gymnasium, theatre and other accoutrements, along with Greek-style administrative structures, he imposed in facsimile over a huge area. There were many Alexandrias, especially to the east. The *koine,* the Athens dialect, was a sort of *lingua franca.* Ancient Greek texts have been found as far east as Afghanistan. Hellenism, the version of Greek culture that Alexander spread so successfully with his conquests, survived under later patronage, set apart from the cultures of cities whose first language was not Greek. Greek common folk had provided the nurturing context for epic, drama and their familiar, familial geographies. The literary culture of the non-Greek cities was Hellenistic, and in many places a "native" tradition was displaced by this pious imposition, an imposition taken further and deeper still by the Romans in their imperial travels.

Born of Alexander's devotion to every aspect of Greek culture, the greatest Alexandria—founded in 331 BC—was no less Egyptian. Under the Ptolemies, it grew to more than half a million souls. In this world, literature became specifically *writing.* The classical Greek diaspora was one thing, ethnic and even tribal in character; the Hellenic dispensation was something else. Now Greek culture was available to non-Greeks (it had been spread, after all, by the greatest Macedonian of all time), to the previously despised *barbaroi.* What had been an instrument of national identity for Greeks from all over the Mediterranean world, a prophylactic against the barbarians, was now open to all.

Those Greeks who lived for the culture felt defensive, separated, aloof. To retain possession, they needed to devise protective strategies. "I hate everything public" or "common," says Callimachus,[3] perhaps because the Alexandrian public expressed a value system at odds with the culture he had acquired through the Greek language and in his studies in Athens. Poetry had to move indoors, out of the literal sun: it lived in libraries. What had been language responding to nature, history, the social world began to become language responding to prior language. The epigram came into its elegant own, honed and admirable and polite. "Great art overshadowed and checked new growth, as it is wont to do."[4] Now no great art overshadowed.

Thus the code and the traditions that had bound the scattered Greeks into a sense of nation became an acquirable culture. The classical period ended with a *Geist* of Greek culture haunting Greek cities around the Mediterranean and further afield, each with its Homer, Hesiod and heritage, part of a Greece of mind and spirit and sport; by the time that Rome, with its dogged respect for Greek culture and precedent, ruled the world, Greek was a language of stale learning, a class and cultural token. An oral tradition is conservative, a developing written tradition radical; but the Hellenising and Romanising of the Greek legacy meant that poetry, which had blazed in different ways, could now flicker here and there, formal and polite.

There was leisure, in any case, for scholars to work on the ancient texts, to put them in order and edit them. After Niniveh, Ugarit and Jerusalem, in Athens, Ephesus, Pergamum, Antioch, Damascus and Rome there were great libraries, but none so great as the Alexandrian library. It began with a collection of some 200,000 scrolls. By the time Mark Antony was courting Cleopatra, there was something in excess of 700,000 works, and the greatest gift he made her was the contents of the Pergamum library, 200,000 scrolls to be added. It is also likely that elements in his army were responsible for the fires that destroyed a substantial portion of the collection, primarily in warehouses along the river, awaiting cataloguing, though the library in a diminished form survived for a further millennium. When the Arabs took Alexandria, the library's days were already over.

It is uncertain in what year the Alexandrina, or the Alexandrian Museum and Library, was founded. Many scholars attribute it to the reign of Ptolemy II (Philadelphus) (283–247 BC); a few name his predecessor Ptolemy I (Soter) (from 323 BC). There is a long-standing tradition that Demetrius Phalereus (c. 354–283, 2 BC) was the actual founder. Aristotle had created a large personal library in Athens, which, as Strabo says, could "teach the kings in Egypt how to arrange a library." The dates are not wholly convincing, but Demetrius, Theophrastus' pupil, may have known Aristotle, and in his exile from Athens, where he had been viceroy, he was a friend of the first Ptolemy. Perhaps he was a conduit and that great library grew out of Aristotle's personal collection.

The museum had a central hall where scholars congregated and feasted together. Around the hall ran a handsome arcade, with recesses and seats for study. Scroll rooms were beyond, and as the library expanded, an annex was built a few streets away. At least some of the scholars who came were given bursaries and looked after by the institution.

For its first century and a half, we can construct a rough table of director-librarians, several of whom we have encountered as compilers and editors of the work of the Greek poets. Zenodotus of Ephesus, head of the library during part of Ptolemy II's time, published Homeric and Hesiodic texts and glossaries. His successor may have been Callimachus, who we know worked at the library, though there is no textual confirmation that he was librarian-in-chief. The father of bibliography, he devised and executed a system of cataloguing, the celebrated *Pinakes*, "Tables of Persons Eminent in Every Branch of Learning Together with a List of their Writings," which, Casson

tells us, filled "no less than 120 books, five times as many as Homer's *Iliad*."[5]
He divided the library's holdings into eight categories, including drama and
poetry. His listings gave author, a brief biographical note, titles of books,
first line(s) on each scroll, and a line-count to indicate extent. The authenticity of texts had to be verified as well, a substantial editorial task, given the
variety of scribal sources and the diversity of scrolls.

Having assembled the works of a writer, established the texts, purged
them of interpolations and tidied them up, scribes got to work on making
new, authoritative editions and preparing separate treatises on them. The
major authors were organised into lists according to type, class and genre,
and the lists or *canones* became the tyrannical canonical texts of the legitimate and authorised. Thus a great literature was preserved and stabilised or,
as one critic says, "petrified"; there were inevitable errors and omissions.
Voltaire in *Temple du goût* (1732) invented "God's Library," a kind of hell for
the Muses in which they must spend the rest of their days like Didymuses
revising and condensing the recognised classics: there is no room on the
shelves for anything new.[6]

After Callimachus came his one-time pupil Eratosthenes of Cyrene, an
intellectual pentathlete. He calculated with astonishing accuracy, some declare to within 200 miles, the circumference of the earth. He drew the first
lines of latitude and longitude on the imagined globe. As well as being a
mathematician and geographer, he wrote poems and treatises on literature,
theatre, actors and costumes, travel, history and much else. He was followed
by the legendary editor and scholar Aristophanes of Byzantium (195–180),
who published an edition of Aristophanes the dramatist and drew up a list
of the best Greek writers. The *Canon Alexandrinus* comprises work by about
180 poets, fifty philosophers, fifty historians, and thirty-five orators.

Aristarchus of Samothrace came into his own in the middle of the second century BC, the last recorded director of the Alexandrina with standing
as a major scholar. The greatest critic among the Alexandrian scholars, he
was perhaps the best scholar in antiquity.[7] He wrote commentaries on
Homer and was alive to the topography and archaeology of the poems. He
is remembered primarily from the *Epitome* of Didymus, another substantial
grammarian and critic who flourished around 30 BC.

The Alexandrina was an irresistible magnet to writers and scholars.
Every significant intellectual was likely to have studied or taught there, or
both: Euclid, Archimedes, Theocritus . . . Athens remained famous, but its
cultural authority had removed to Egypt.

When Hellenic poetry began to appear, no tradition was discarded but new
impulses were at work. With Antimachus of Colophon and Philetas of Cos
(teacher of Theocritus, of the librarian Zenodotus, and of Ptolemy II)

things began to take a new direction. A grammarian and poet, Philetas composed poems of carnal love to his lady Battis (or Bittis) which appealed to Propertius, who preferred his poems to those of Callimachus, and to Ovid before him. He was so thin, it is said, that he had to ballast himself with leaden weights in his footwear so as not to be blown over by the wind. Callimachus called for a "lean" poetry; here was a perilously lean *poet*. He studied the dialect of Megara and worked on a vocabulary explaining the sense of hard and unusual words with such assiduity that he wore out his frail life prematurely. Time has winnowed away most of his work.

Time has dealt less terminally, but still cruelly, with Antimachus. Some two hundred fragments and attestations to him survive, nothing very long or memorable. He may have been the opposite of Philetas, profligate and expansive. Quintilian in *Principles of Oratory* declared that we must praise his strength, his seriousness, and "a style remote from the commonplace." Scholars agreed that "he lacks feeling, sweetness, structuring, artfulness, and so displays the difference between a second and a *good* second."[8] His name came to be synonymous with long-windedness. After his wife, Lydè, died, he wrote a famous elegy, retailing the tragedies of mythological and legendary figures and consoling himself with their larger miseries and discomforts. This exercise he pursued over leagues of language. His recent editors believe this was not a portmanteau poem able to accommodate a variety of tragical narratives but a continuous dirge.

Proclus declared that when we find in a poet's work ostentatious perfection of technique we can be sure that the verse will bristle with "calculated effect and bombast, deploying metaphorical language all over the place, like Antimachus." This ostentatious technical accomplishment is one of the less fortunate elements in the new Hellenic tradition. Callimachus himself is not entirely innocent of it, though he despised its excess in others: over-ornamentation and metrical harshness were the chief transgressions that a poet could commit against the Muses. Still, Antimachus had his place in the transformation of elegy and of mythological poetry on an epic scale, especially his *Thebaid*. Little else survives of Alexandrian elegy. We have no shards of Alexandrian drama either, though the names of more than sixty dramatists survive.

The work of three poets of the period does exist in substantial quantity. They come close upon one another's heels and together they describe a diverse tradition. Callimachus of Cyrene, Apollonius of Rhodes and Theocritus of Syracuse could hardly be more different. The first, a charming enigma, is the most compelling for those readers who love Modernism. Ironically, several of his major works survived the Dark Ages substantially whole: it was only in the Middle Ages, around 1204, that they were damaged and erased.[9]

A big book, Callimachus declared famously, is a big evil: *méga biblíon, méga kakón*. For a long time critics took this to be the opening salvo in Callimachus' putative battle with his onetime student Apollonius, whose life as a poet was given over to composing vast, mercilessly detailed poems, of which the *Argonautica* is the single more or less intact survivor. Big book, big evil. Or big mess? Whether or not Callimachus was the *chief* librarian, he was *a* librarian at the museum. One task that fell to librarians or their minions was re-shelving scrolls. This entailed, first, making sure that the scrolls were rewound: thoughtless scholars returned some halfway or completely un-rewound, or twisted on their reels.

Papyrus rolls could be seriously long—five yards verged on the unmanageable; sixteen, twenty-one, twenty-four and others over thirty yards in length existed: *méga kakón* indeed. At the British Museum the Great Harris Papyrus, the longest known, runs to over forty yards. The scribe worked in horizontal columns against the width of the papyrus. The scholiasts speak of Thucydides and of Homer being written on one long roll, Thucydides in 378 columns, nearly 100 yards long. A role of over 110 yards, longer than a football pitch, was said to exist in Constantinople. A roll of 140 feet would accommodate the *Iliad*, a rather shorter one the *Odyssey*.[10] Losing one's place or wanting to refer back doesn't bear thinking about. A modern poet-librarian, Philip Larkin, echoing Callimachus, declared, "Books are a load of crap," and he didn't even have the labour of re-winding them.

Most Greek rolls did not exceed thirty-five feet, and when rolled tight their circumference was about 2.5 inches, their width about ten inches. They could easily be held in one hand, though they were often too large to fit even in a capacious pocket. The weight must have meant that it was easier to spread them out on a surface than hold them long on the knee or up before the eyes, though readers portrayed on Greek pottery or in statuary generally hold the scroll effortlessly before them.

Callimachus came to the library by indirection. He was from Cyrene in what is today Libya. This independent Greek city had been conquered in 322 BC and added to the satrapy of Egypt under Ptolemy I. Three years before Callimachus was born, in 313 BC, it revolted against Egypt. By the time the poet was two years old, it had been forcibly re-annexed. Thereafter there were revolts, but these were settled by marriages rather than by protracted wars. There were thus close, well-established connections between Cyrene and Greece, but also newer links between Cyrene and Egypt, its big neighbour to the east.

Most of what we know of Callimachus' life is found in the *Suda*. "Callimachus, son of Battus and Mesatma, of Cyrene, grammarian, pupil of Hermocrates of Iasos, the grammarian,[11] married the daughter of Euphrates of Syracuse." This is the real Callimachus. Beware of imitations and relations. The *Suda* continues, "His sister's son was Callimachus the Younger, who wrote an epic, *On Islands*."[12] Why would his nephew have become an epic poet if he was himself hostile to epic? Sure there was bad blood in that family.

The *Suda* records that our Callimachus was prolific in every verse form and also in prose, author of "eight hundred books." If he lived to be seventy, and started when he was twenty, this averages out at thirty books a year or just under three per month. It all depends on what is meant by a book and how much life he enjoyed outside the library.

He spent his maturity, and received preferment, under Ptolemy Philadelphus. Before that, he taught grammar at Eleusis, a suburb of Alexandria, which suggests he had come from Cyrene to seek, rather than lose, his fortune. Not that his family was necessarily poor. He claimed that he was descended from the Battus who was Cyrene's founder; his grandfather was an active military man; and the boy was sent to Athens to study, alongside Aratus, his near contemporary, under the tutelage of Praxiphanes of Mytilene, a peripatetic philosopher who wrote essays on history, poetry and much else. Callimachus may later have written directly against Praxiphanes, though none of that work survives, only an attestation that in it he praised Aratus as a learned man and a good poet. If he had trouble with *his* teacher, it was perhaps to be expected that Apollonius would have trouble with him.

From Athens, he could not resist the pull of Alexandria and was willing to start as a meagre grammarian. He was introduced into the court of Ptolemy and enjoyed royal patronage until he died, between 240 and 235 BC.

The *Suda* lists his works in detail. First come poems which do not survive. They may in fact have been assimilated into, or existed as subsections of, his major sequence, the *Aetia* (*Aitia*). They include "The Coming of Io," "Semele," "Glaucus" and so on. The missing plays follow—satiric, tragic, comic; the lyrics, "Ibis," prose works including the *Pinakes,* and more general works: a "Table of Glosses and Compositions of Democritus," "Foundations of Islands and Cities and Changes of Name," "On Strange and Marvellous Things in the Peloponnese and Italy," "On the Rivers of the World" and so on. The *Suda* fails to name what is of most urgent interest to us, the poems that in one form or another have passed through the sieve of time: *Aetia, Hecale,* "On Games," "Galatea," the *Iambi,* epigrams, hymns, the *Locks of Berenice* and much else. Most of them (apart from six hymns and sixty epigrams) exist in fragments only.

Several times in the poems the poet-speaker or singer presents himself as embattled. Apollo has instructed him: keep your Muses lean and avoid the common way. He follows his divine master's injunctions, preferring to un-scroll an intense, focussed little poem rather than roll out an endless carpet. Pound's Propertius declares, "There is no high road to the Muses."

He chides Plato for praising Antimachus' elegy *Lydè*, calling it "fat writing, unthrilling" in an epigram.[13] Posidippus and Asclepiades had produced epi-grams praising *Lydè*. They became the enemy. The scholia names others: two Dionysiuses, Asclepiades, Posidippus, Praxiphanes and a couple of syllables, the orator "yrippus," who survives as a mere half-name, like a severed worm. Yet among all the enemies, Apollonius is not listed. All the same, an epigram doubtfully attributed to Apollonius calls Callimachus "rubbish, laughable, a head of wood," adding that his first sin was composing the *Aetia*.[14]

Mary Lefkowitz, shrewd and cautious, reminds us that much ancient bi-ography is fiction, the kind which senses a conflict *may* have existed and then seeks parties (even if the dates don't work) and stages a battle. When a poet depicts a conflict and a triumph, it may be a device for asserting superi-ority or victory in a contest, intellectual or artistic, a kind of self-referential epinicean poem, but such victories can be figurative as well. There is a gap between factual and didactic biography, between literal and characteristic truth. In Callimachus' "Hymn to Apollo," Apollo answers Envy that a poet who is a river carries rubbish; the bee-poet brings purest water or nectar to Demeter (lines 105–113). Lefkowitz objects that the scholia seek to attach a human identity to the figure of Envy. Callimachus, in Apollo's company, as-sumes the stance of a victor snapped at by losers. His burning argument seems to be that Homer is Homer, and that those who imitate Homer sell him short and at the same time drown in his waters, while a poet who flows like a pure spring (Homer being the source of all rivers and springs)[15] is truer to the great original and to himself. The small hymn, Callimachus' poem seems to say, gets closer to the source, the flow of Homeric Hymns (no one doubted that they were by Homer), than the Euphrates effluent of other (unnamed) poets.

Apollonius was assumed to have come into conflict with Callimachus, but apart from the doubtful epigram only a biographical tradition sustains the story. Apollonius was a student, or *mathetes,* of Callimachus and the teacher may have been party to the rejection of the *Argonautica* when Apol-lonius tried to read or publish it in Alexandria, and therefore in part respon-sible for Apollonius' subsequent self-imposed exile at Rhodes (if that is indeed what it was). In his later years he revised the poem, or started again from scratch, returned to Alexandria, and was welcomed. He was found worthy of inclusion in the museum and library, a reference not to the acceptance of the work but of the man as a chief librarian—that sort of inclusion—and (no end of restitution) he was finally buried beside Calli-machus. How they are spending eternity together is not recorded.

Callimachus affected the Romans: Virgil, Ovid (whose *Metamorphoses* are indebted directly to the *Aetia*), Propertius, and Catullus adapted his account of the Lock of Berenice.[16] The 7,000-line *Aetia* (only portions remain), translated as *The Causes*,[17] is an elegy in four books. It recounts Greek legends to do with custom, history and ritual, and we have no idea how many *Causes,* or aetiologies, were included. Each *Cause* can be taken as a single, separate and separable poem. The text of the overall elegy is so tattered that it is impossible to determine whether it had a more organic form.

The prologue, clearly written after the *Aetia* and other poems had been in circulation and had received some bad reviews, strikes a defensive note: "Responding to the Telchines," rebutting his critics. In legend the Telchines were the earliest inhabitants of Rhodes, Cyprus, Cos and Crete: magicians, workers in metal, wise men, reluctant to share knowledge. They were slain by the gods on Cos as a result of their hubris. Callimachus' Telchines are backstabbers of the Muse, ignorant, and they do not like his poems. Their case against him, which he summarises, is that he never wrote a continuous poem "of thousands and thousands of lines" on some epic theme but, like a child, even though he is advanced in years, he "spools out a short tale." He proceeds to defend the short poem, probably making a case for the superiority of Philetas' and Mimnermus' shorter poems to their long ones, and proceedes by stages to himself.

> From now on, assess poetry not by the chain the Persians use
> To measure distances but by the rules of the art.

As a lad, propping his writing tablet on his knee, he had heard Apollo's command "Feed up the victim, make him really fat," but "keep the Muse quite trim." He also urged the boy not to take the wagons' road, to avoid the highway and choose "the road less travelled by," even if the going got hard. Zeus makes the thunder; a human poet makes a different noise. His own would be the voice of the cicada, considered sweet by the Hellenic Greeks. That persistent, maddening creature was believed to live on air and mist, to sing ceaselessly, and to slough old age seasonally as a snake does, with its shell. Cicada's song, not the heehaw of donkeys: he rests his case and his hopes upon the Muses, his friends in youth and therefore now in age.

It is a thrifty defence, embodying the case in the economy and clarity both of argument and metaphor. The *Aetia* proper begins in a dream. The poet, borne away from Cyrene, finds himself on Mount Helicon. There the Muses provide him (as they had Hesiod and Pindar) with tutorials about all sorts of things, and much of the magic of the fragments is his first-person, or first-persona, response. Books I and II were connected by the conceit of instruction, while what is left of Books III and IV suggests that Callimachus let the later stories stand unframed. The narratives are characterised by a variety of approaches and forms. Almost immediately a maxim swims clear of the broken text: "harming another, man harms his own heart." Succeeding poem-shards are disappointingly brief, though the occasional run of lines gives an impression of a precise, witty poet, alive to the world of the senses, the implications of legend and the possibilities of language.

> That elder ages with a cheerfuller heart
> Whom young boys love and lead up to his door,
> Taking his hand as if he was their father . . .

The fragment that may have opened Book II, concerning the cities of Sicily, appears to describe sea-sickness, making the crossing all the more credible, and the cities of that island and their history are briskly evoked. About some of the conceits there is a freshness, as when he invokes the nymphs of the Argive springs, and the water of the springs is itself the flowing nymphs, not so much embodiment as identity.[18] When Acontius is about to court Cydippe, she is conjured with economy and paradox:

> No one stepped down to the slow-welling spring of hairy old
> Silenus with a face more full of dawn than she . . .

This is one of the fullest surviving *Aetia,* and it makes the reader hope the Egyptian sands will prove generous and give back more. The snatches of Epilogue deliver us back to Helicon, the Muses conclude their narrative instruction, the poet sets off for prose pastures.

The *Iambi* were thirteen poems, about a thousand lines all told, distinguished by their iambic or choliambic metre. In the first poem that sour, disfigured Hipponax of Colophon rises from the dead, convokes the scholars of the world and urges them to stop arguing with one another, telling them a tale about the Seven Sages. Next, an Aesopian animal fable is used to ridicule the disagreeable voices of men and what they say. (Aesop, who criticised the people of Delphos for devouring too much of the sacrificial meat, was stoned and pursued over a cliff.) The third poem chastises the age that prefers wealth to virtue, in particular the self-touting, tarty Euthydemos, who put himself up for sale. Then comes the quarrel of the laurel (a prophetic tree) and the olive. When the bramble bush tries to broker a peace, the laurel tree stands upon its tenuous dignity and calls on Zeus, with the voice of a wild bull, to dispose of the riff-raff bramble.

The quite fragmentary Iambus V speaks as a friend urging a teacher not to abuse his pupils again, using imagery of fire and of chariot racing. We read through the images to the central theme. It is an accusation masquerading as a poem of counsel. The sixth iambus consists of scraps of a dull description of the Olympian Zeus at Elis, written to a friend travelling thither and containing so much specific detail that it is inert. Little survives of the seventh, spoken by a Thracian Hermes through the lips of an iconic horse. One lovely line survives of the eighth iambus, an epinicean poem in a simple metre: "Once the Argo, a soft southerly in its sails . . ."

We know more about the *Iambi* than the scraps of text. For example, of IX we have only two lines:

> Hermes, with long beard, say why your penis points
> Up at your beard not down to your feet . . . ?

We would infer from such a fragment that someone was addressing an ithy-phallic image of Hermes: they were not uncommon, standing outside many houses. What else could we deduce? There were learned commentaries on Callimachus dating from the time of Augustus. Three *Diegeseis* from a much later date survive and they tell us the plots of poems which exist only as tat-ters. The *Diegesis* explains that the admirer of a lad called Philetadas—it may be Callimachus sending himself up, or attacking a rival—saw the statue "in a small palestra" and asked it if Philetadas was not the cause of its arousal. Hermes replied in the negative: there was a mystical source for his condi-tion. The poem told the mystical story and then Hermes accused his inter-locutor of desiring Philetadas in an inappropriate way. The theme of the fifth iambus is not far away.

A large part of Iambus XII survives, a poem Callimachus wrote for the seventh-day celebration of the daughter of a friend of his. It is a prayer and a blessing, and it claims that Apollo's gift—the poem—was better than all the other gifts the child received. Again the theme is competition, the rival-ries of the gods over whose gift is the best. The poem survives while all ma-terial gifts fade, break or perish. In this case, the poem tells a truth.

The last iambus addresses literary issues. Though mutilated, we can see in it the verve and assurance of a poet who knew what he was about and was keen to make himself understood. First, he insists that it is good, not bad, to write in a variety of genres. His example is Ion of Chios, a master of all genres and a jack of none. He also weaves in a handsome tribute to Mim-nermus of Colophon. If we could wish for the full restoration of only one poem in antiquity, this would be a candidate, characterising the new litera-ture and the reaction to it in a vivid fashion.

The lyric poems hardly exist at all. The first of them appears to be about the fate of the men of Lemnos. Aphrodite, whose rites they had neglected, inflicted on the women of Lemnos a disgusting smell. The men, as a result, took either concubines or handsome lads from Thrace as lovers. The women killed the men and boys. The Argonauts stopped at the island, coupled with the Lemnian women, and the place was repopulated. Apollonius recounts the story at greater length.[19] Of Callimachus' poem only the first line survives. Another lyric deifies Queen Arsinoë, wife of Ptolemy II, who died in 270 BC. "Wherever you look, the cities of the earth are decked in mourning . . ."

There is, next, the *Hecale,* once a thousand-line mini-epic evoking not so much Theseus' victory over the bull of Marathon as his stay with old Hecale, a crone who gave him unstinting hospitality and who, when he returned to repay her kindness after his triumph, he found dead. As a result he established a *deme,* or sector, of Attica ("Once upon a time, on an Erechthean hill, lived an Attic woman . . .") and called it by her name, and a sanctuary to Zeus Hecaleios at her hut. While staying with her, Theseus appears to have told her his life story, with its magic and charms; in any case the fragments are full of known details of the legendary life. Hecale too tells her life: she was not poor always, she is of a good family but has fallen on hard times.

The narrative must have been brisk and strong. In particular, the capture of the bull, and Theseus parading it alive through his father's city before sacrificing it at the temple, are vividly contained. There are obscuring digressions: a crow speaks, for example, and an old woman who may be Hecale, or another bird of some description. There are noble lines of dedication to Hecale at the end, spoken, I imagine, by Theseus himself.

The little epics, elegies and elegiac epinicean poems are not accompanied by *Diegesis* and it is hard to reconstruct their narrative, and what Callimachus was doing with legend and history to give it that turn of novelty, the new perspectives, that are believed to characterise his work. There are other fragments, and what they say, what can be interpreted and inferred from them, make it clear that what he wrote was always *full* of sense and information, aiming not at classical closure but at a kind of balancing of meanings. Here is lean poetry, every sinew functioning and not the merest gram of fat. No wonder he dismisses the *Lydè* as "a fat" (that word again) "graceless book."

There are over 300 fragments of uncertain provenance, all belonging to Callimachus, who was, after Homer, the most widely attested authority on correct usage. His correctness was not dryly proper but precise and full, like the best English eighteenth-century writing. Some fragments hang in the air like aphorisms: "Always the gods grant little graces to little men," "Troilus lamented less than Priam," "I am not niggardly of my poems," "Anxieties oppress a man less, and one thirtieth of the weight is removed, when he spills his troubles to a friend, a stranger going down the same road, or to the unlistening puffs of a breeze." "I sing nothing without evidence"—a strictly scholarly aesthetic. When he says, "The good-looking will sell everything for coin," we can set this beside some of his epigrams and conclude that he was a less-than-successful lover and perhaps not the best looker in Alexandria.

There are more than sixty complete epigrams, some merely conventional, some strange and replete with philosophical, linguistic and emotional surprises. The most famously translated is Epigram II, which William (Johnson) Cory included in *Ionica* in 1858, and which subsequent British composers turned into a song lyric:

> They told me, Heraclitus, they told me you were dead,
> They brought me bitter news to hear and bitter tears to shed.
> I wept, as I remembered, how often you and I
> Had tired the sun with talking and sent him down the sky.
>
> And now that thou art lying, my dear old Carian guest,
> A handful of grey ashes, long long ago at rest,
> Still are thy pleasant voices, thy nightingales, awake;
> For Death, he taketh all away, but them he cannot take.

Such nightingales are like Yeats's Byzantine birds, artificial yet beautiful and timeless. Indeed, in reading Callimachus, and in following some of his subtler translations, we are not far from the imaginative world of the Yeats of the *Byzantium* poems.

Some of the epigrams dispense social advice with measured elegance (do not marry above your station;[20] beware of stepmothers even when they're dead;[21] no one knows what tomorrow will bring;[22] be thrifty[23]). But these are not the most arresting. The ones that stay with us are *formally* surprising. The use of dialogue can be pointed and dramatic. In this poem a tombstone is addressed:

> "Does Charidas lie beneath you?" "If you mean
> The son of Cyrenean Arimmas, beneath me."
> "Ho, Charidas, what of the underworld?"
> "A lot of darkness." "What of the way back?"
> "A lie." "And Pluto?" "An invention." "We are doomed."
> "What I am telling you is true; if you prefer
> A pleasant tale, just think: in Hell
> A great ox costs no more than a penny."[24]

What seem like personal declarations have the purity of rage about them, and poetry is always hand in glove with love.

> I loathe poem cycles, I do not take delight
> In crowded highways. I hate too the lover
> Wandering from love to love. I do not drink
> At every spring. I despise all that's common.
> You are fair, Lysanias, fair, but before Echo
> Repeats, a voice declares, "He's someone else's."[25]

There is much of this kind of desire and recognition in the epigrams. They seldom get beyond the frisson, wry disappointment, or deferral. "This is the way my love works: it pursues what flees it, but lets go what lies to hand."[26]

The most ambitious of Callimachus' poems were the most potentially conventional, his six hymns, where he set himself in what was regarded as a Homeric tradition, the most sacred line of Greek poetry. All surviving manuscripts of the hymns derive from a Byzantine source collection that combined the Homeric with hymns attributed to Orpheus, Proclus and Callimachus, an amalgamation of work composed and revised over many centuries.

Changes in the Greek world and in the poetic tradition meant that the "modern" Alexandrian hymn, inevitably conscious of precedent and there-fore self-conscious in its voice as a Modernist poem might be, was touched by the epinicean fashion: a god was celebrated in his origins and in his tri-umphs, and the poems register larger and smaller triumphs, the elements that constitute divine legitimacy. Hymn and epinicean are, short of the drama, the most public forms of poetry and, combined, harmonise the sa-cred and the civic. "Civic" implies city, it suggests less the places of the gods than the places of men, less *their* than *our* places, including those that we build with our hands (or with our words) in their honour. Some of Calli-machus' hymns seem to me—as I think they will to anyone who has stumbled around the fascinating palimpsest of ruins in modern Libya—to have a specific geography and to be conceived for a cityscape not unlike that of Ptolemaic Cyrene, the poet's birthplace, when the enormous temple of Zeus was restored. In the end it is not so much the god that is Callimachus' subject as the god *manifest in,* present and presented in, a certain set of cir-cumstances in history and legend, and in certain physical locations on earth. Presence, if you like, rather than essence.

This supposition is not scholarly, in part because scholars and critics who are happy to tie Archilochus, Theognis or Solon to specific places are reluc-tant to do so when the poet is cosmopolitan, and when the poetry is so very *literary*. Discussing Callimachus' epigrams, Doris Meyer shows how many pretend to be inscriptions on roadside tombs: a fictional speaker is created, speaking through his stone. This imposes on the reader a role in the poem as well, that of passer-by. The speaker behind the stone and the stroller are within the text, whereas in fact we and the poet are outside this fiction and watch ourselves performing within it.[27] In her persuasive essays, she does not dwell on the possibility that these epigrams may indeed have been in-tended to be carved, or were in reality carved, on actual tombstones, some of them at least: that they were what they purport to be.

For those less literal-minded than I am, however, her argument might apply to the hymns: the imagined geography of the ceremony they enact may be Cyrene, but the enactment itself can be imagined. As with the epigrams, we stand by a specific (remembered) roadside as a procession goes by, and our relation as living readers with the poet who made the poem is separate from our place within his projected "ceremonial." Too subtle? Perhaps: my sense of the hymns is that despite their complexity, some were intended for use, and that they were actually used in a specific city. This is especially true of Hymns V and VI.

There are hymns to Zeus, Apollo and Artemis, to Delos, and then to Pallas and Demeter. In the Homeric canon there are precedents to all except the "Hymn to Delos." Callimachus, gratifying future intertextual critics, relates this hymn to the Homeric "Hymn to Delian Apollo." With respect *and* irony, he weaves threads from the Homeric poems into his own textures. The more general question of Callimachean intertextuality is hard to address, given that many of the texts on which his poems may have drawn no longer exist and any conclusions we draw from perceived echoes will be partial at best. The hymns are the safest place to look because we have Homeric and other hymns, and substantial epinicean texts for comparison as well.

Cyrene and its territory, Cyrenaica, was originally a kind of fertile island with a sea of sand behind and a sea of water before, linked to Greece by maritime routes, the usual line being via Crete. Settlers had landed in a fertile area belonging to a North African tribe. The tribe agreed that their territory was lovely but proposed to take the colonists to an even lovelier spot where there were "holes in the sky" (signifying generous rainfall). They sherpaed the Greeks by night through (unseen) lush lands to the place that would be Cyrenaica, and that happened to belong to a rival tribe. Having transferred the colonists off their land, the sherpas withdrew. The tribe on whom the Greeks were deposited did not mind too much. Indeed, they picked up Greek habits and worked with the colonists. It was only later that division came.

The city of Cyrene was established a little way inland, at the edge of a plateau known today as Jebel Akdar, the Green Mountain. It was around 630 BC. A port was built fifteen kilometres away, and it became in time the city of Apollonia. Cyrenaica remained closely integrated into the Greek and then the Hellenic world, its people, culture and religion part and parcel of them. The layout of the city of Cyrene imitated the actual layout of Thera (now Santorini), the founding city which sent Battus and his people out because Thera's population had outgrown its environment. The temples and the divine images of the new city imitated the great temples of mainland Greece. With the rise of the Ptolemies, Cyrene looked east and acknowledged the finally irresistible presence of Egypt. It defied, now successfully, now tragically, until it became part of Africa.

Callimachus, even when he was in Alexandria, remained aware of his native city. During the expansion of the agora, when the old *prytaneum,* or public hall, was demolished, the new one was described by Callimachus. It was built on the south side of the ceremonial way, the Skyrotà, a building with a handsome portico and peristyle. In the last two hymns the movement of the celebrants seems to follow closely ceremonial ways which we can trace (without Roman anachronism) on the archaeological maps of the site.

The Temple of Zeus in Cyrene was restored during the Ptolemaic period, and the portrait of Ptolemy III, raised in the "area of the heads,"[28] possibly relates to this event. Later restorations during the Roman ascendancy are irrelevant here, as is the fact that the temple was totally destroyed in an earthquake in AD 365. The Temple of Apollo had a more organic development, extended in the sixth century BC with a rectangular peristyle, six columns by eleven, with further modifications in the fourth century BC. The unfluted columns we see today are much later, part of the restoration after the Jewish uprising. There is a handsome fourth-century BC door through which we can step into the sacred space, as perhaps the poet did.

This temple casts a curious spell, even though there is such a confusion of elements exposed by earthquake, quarrying and erosion. Inside it, though Apollo's name is "over the door," there are temples to other gods, just as saints have chapels inside a church dedicated to another saint. Thus Artemis (significantly), Latona, Isis and Hecate had their "chapels," as well as other, more obscure deities, some perhaps local to the area. The Temple of Artemis inside the Temple of Apollo was substantially increased and emphasised in the fourth-century BC reconstruction and would have been familiar to the poet.

Early in the morning or towards evening, it is not too hard to get to the Sanctuary of Demeter, on the opposite side of the site of Cyrene from Apollo's temples and outside the city walls, where Wadi Ben Gadir shelves to the south. Looking back one has a clear view of the agora. This is a very ancient part of the site. In the second century the place was monumentalised, but in the poet's time it retained the darker mystery and magic of its deity.

The "Hymn to Zeus" was composed between 280 and 275 BC. It begins with rather a dramatic aetiology: the origins of Zeus. But the poem serves multiple purposes: Zeus's birth ties in with other origins. Arcadia, a desert when Zeus's mother, Rhea, delivers the baby, gives birth (at her behest) to great rivers, so that she can wash away the gore of afterbirth and bathe the infant god. When Callimachus deals with origins, he also, always, deals with *connections:* the divine and transcendent always find expression in the realm of the literal; consequences are never merely heavenly and apart. As the poem progresses, other aetiologies are adduced, for example, the place where the baby Zeus's navel-cord drops away becomes (unsurprisingly) the

Plain of the Navel. The bees arrive because of Zeus's birth and are graced by him with their gold stripes.

Callimachus favours Arcadia's claim over Crete's when it comes to specifying Zeus's birthplace, but he reconciles the legends: born in Arcadia, Zeus was spirited away to a Cretan cave to be out of father Cronus' vindictive range, and there he was cradled by Adrasteia, looked after by Meliae of Dicte, fed with honey by the Panacrian bees and suckled by Amalthea the she-goat. The Curetes danced and kept Cronus away. Zeus got the top job on Olympus by agreement with his brothers: he was manifestly supreme among them. Callimachus rejects the legend that the realms of earth, sea and underworld were distributed by lots. His reading takes legend more seriously, less cynically. The old poets told untruths: when he dispenses fiction (poets lie to tell a truth), it should persuade the listener.[29] This Callimachean calculation was part of his legacy to the Roman poets, not only to the playful ones but to Virgil himself.

All kings derive power and legitimacy from Zeus. This includes as much the kings of the birds as the kings of men. But power and legitimacy are not distributed in equal measure. Some kings are more favoured, and one is most favoured: Ptolemy Philadelphus. The poem's "all hail" to the god is, at the same time, due to the way in which Callimachus has dovetailed the human and the divine, an "all hail" to his Egyptian and Cyrenean king; the hymn would have been performed in the royal presence.

The "Hymn to Apollo" was written perhaps for the Carnean Festival. The Carnean Festival, dedicated to Apollo as protector of flocks, originated in Sparta. It may also have been celebrated in Cyrene. The poem was written between 258 and 247 BC, when Cyrene and Egypt were on good terms.[30] Callimachus creates a series of balances. By alluding to Apollo's two major ceremonial centres he also alludes to the two Homeric Hymns to Apollo, the Delian and Pythian. His is a hymn to Apollo *and* a celebration of the god's lion-slaying human lover Cyrene, her city and its foundation: thus the divine quite naturally counterbalances (having previously embraced) the human, both individual and collective. Callimachus makes it clear through personal reference that he associates himself with the city and the god. The poem's narratives run from primitive rural to sophisticated metropolitan.

There are other complementarities. They lead to the celebrated conclusion: the battle at Delphi between Python, the dragon who guards the archaic place, and Apollo, who wrests possession from the monster to make it his own city (as Cyrene slew the lion and made her city). Callimachus translates the contest into a literary confrontation between Apollo and Envy, affirming his own place beside the god. The Homeric "Hymn to Delian Apollo" ends with the poet enjoining his hearers to admit that he, a blind

old man, is poet of poets. Thucydides calls that hymn a *prooimion*, a prologue or overture, to something longer. Some critics regard Callimachus'
poem, which also ends (more contentiously than the hymn) on the theme
of poetry, as "leading into" something else, a prelude.

The "Hymn to Artemis" may have been composed around 260 BC. It is
one of the most literary of the poems: according to Michael Haslam, a
structure of contrasting language registers, now high, now colloquial, dis-
orient reader—and audience?—and the divine and the human are also in-
terleaved. This makes it of a piece with the first and second hymns not only
in narrative but in diction, a deliberate juxtaposition of the demotic and the
formulaic. Artemis' earliest act in the poem (she is portrayed as a little girl)
is to pray to Zeus for eternal virginity and for a variety of identities so she
can get the better of competitive Apollo. It is as though she addresses Santa
Claus, not Zeus: her childish shopping list includes a fetching costume, a
virgin choir, and much else. The goddess is infantilised by Callimachus in a
curiously ironic-seeming manner. The poem is frisky, full of amusement,
leading us off at various tangents. All the hymns are unusual, but this one in
especially peculiar ways.[31] The theatricality of the "Hymn to Delos," composed around 271 BC, puts it in the same category of linguistic play and subtlety with Artemis. Haslam draws attention to the intertextual exchange
between this poem and the Homeric "Hymn to Delian Apollo," a deliberate
counterpointing with a text familiar to every Greek.

The last two hymns, "The Bath of Pallas" and "To Demeter" respectively, cannot be dated, though "To Demeter" may be the earliest of the six.
Both are in Doric dialect and "The Bath of Pallas" is alone in being in elegiac rather than heroic measure. Both tie in to specific ceremonies and answer uncannily in their "procession" and movement to the actual
disposition of the temples in Cyrene. Hymn V accompanies the annual
bathing of the holy figure of Athena, and we can follow a kind of imaginative map as the poem progresses, the goddess speaking. It was wholly a female occasion, and a nymph's son who gazes on the goddess has his sight
snatched away, a horrible moment which the goddess justifies in a highly
rhetorical way. This awful, irreversible incident is woven in with several
other legends of Artemis, but since the deed has happened, as it were, in
this world and during the women's ceremony, it brings home the awful
peremptoriness of the gods.

Fortunately, the sequence of hymns ends on a different note with Demeter, a hymn accompanying the Procession of the Basket. Again the occasion is female, and the poet begins by greeting the basket as it arrives, full of
the bounty of harvest. The hymn dwells briefly on Demeter's bereavement
and suffering, but soon turns to the gifts she has made to men in terms of
the aetiology of agriculture and the fruition of fields and orchards. There is,

however, a harsh story to tell. Some of her devotees built her a garden with which she was passionately pleased. She favoured them, but their foes came to destroy the garden, starting with the tall poplar tree at the heart of the place, where her nymphs danced and played. The poplar cried out and Demeter, disguised as the tutelary spirit of the garden, urged the vandals to desist. They scorned her, and in a rage she took divine form: her feet were on the ground, but her head was Olympus-high. They fled, leaving their bronze axes in the wounded trunks of the trees. The chief of the thugs she imbued with a relentless hunger and an awful illness: the more he ate, the more he hungered. His mother wept, trying to conceal his illness as he wasted away, feasting on the mules, the racehorse, even the cat before whom the mouse had trembled. He ate his father literally out of house and home, and sat at the crossroads begging for crusts. He was the type for the bad neighbour.

The hymn returns to good cheer, to celebration, having instanced first the goddess's willingness to be merciful and next her severity in justice. It actually charts the procession: to the new city chambers, and then the uninitiated must stay behind and only the initiates proceed with the grateful burden of the basket to the sacred place. The prayer is for plenty: may the livestock be fed, may the harvests prosper, may peace prevail. Human and divine could not be more closely connected; the connection, too, between the Greek city and the rural order was traditionally intimate and sacred. This must indeed be the earliest of the hymns: it is clearly functional, of a piece with the Homeric Hymns, from which, more innocently, with less irony and artifice than the later hymns, it draws its energy, form and purpose.

XXIV

Apollonius of Rhodes (305–290 BC–c. 230 BC)

> What could be more straightforward? Everybody has the
> same vision, all feel the same dismay, all help build the
> same altar. But what happens if there are no Argonauts, all
> sharing the same experience? What if no one knows how
> to build an altar? What if no one dares make an offering?
>
> ROBERTO CALASSO, *Literature and the Gods*[1]

 Ancient scholars sometimes imposed on literary lives conflict-
ual symmetries which passed for literary history. The conflict
between Callimachus and Apollonius is generally seen from Callimachus' point of view. He was the older poet and the teacher;
passages in his writings appear to answer specific critics and criticisms, justifying his own practice and attacking theirs. Callimachus does not stipulate
Apollonius, but Apollonius' *Argonautica* is a poem vulnerable to Callimachean strictures. It is expansive, elaborate and undramatic. The narrative
does not have a single focus, it shifts and blurs, its tone is unstable. Apollonius owes poetic and narrative debts to Callimachus, but his work is different
in kind: "the first romantic" according to one Callimachean,[2] and the *Argonautica* "the first Romantic epic" according to another.[3] In the poem itself
the king of Colchis, from whom Jason wrests the Fleece, has the poet's number when he declares, "Stranger, no need to bore us with endless details . . ."[4]

It is that very endlessness—admittedly, the *Argo* had a long way to go in
leagues and legends—that makes the *Argonautica* an inexhaustible resource
for later poets, most notably (two centuries later) Virgil, and a poem which
general readers remember if at all for one relationship in particular, that of
Jason and the handsome young sorceress Medea. Most readers know the
story of Book III and half of Book IV of the *Argonautica* and by-pass the
journey to Colchis and the journey home. Apollonius is a poet of set pieces
and protracted longueurs. He is also something else, something unusual,
even unique, in classical and Hellenistic poetry: a writer who understands,
honours and even privileges the female perspective. Had feminism walked
the streets of ancient Alexandria, it would have saluted Apollonius.

Who was this man? There are two divergent versions of his life, both
peremptory, prefacing the manuscript of the *Argonautica*.[5] His father was
called Silleus or Illeus, his mother Rhode. He was born after 305 BC and before 290 BC in Alexandria or the suburb of Naucratis, the only major Greek
poet to have been born in Egypt itself. He is sometimes called "Naucarites,"

an allusion to his lost poem on the founding of the place, "long the sole trading mart of the Greeks in Egypt,"[6] or a hostile allusion to his Egyptian origins. Or was he not born in Africa at all? Mary Lefkowitz suggests that he may have been a native of, rather than an exile in, Rhodes.[7] Her evidence is his name and the fact that there is no firm factual source for his birth in Egypt. Her speculation has not persuaded many, though occasionally a guidebook assumes the poet was one of the island's "most famous sons."[8]

One thing is certain, however: while he was in bright Rhodes, a maritime republic whose harbour was during his time bestridden by a wonder of the world, the giant Colossus representing the sun god (built in 304 BC, it fell in an earthquake after six decades), he acquainted himself in detail with sea lore. He understood how ships work, how sailors behave, how masts and sails are raised and lowered, how to navigate by landmarks and by the skies, and the routes real men took to real as well as to imagined places. He may have embarked on long literal sea journeys. When he describes the launch of the *Argo,* he does so with meticulous particularity. As the Argonauts set sail, the gods and nymphs view them from different vantage-points, creating a kind of mountain and sky theatre. Cheiron comes down to the shore with his wife, and they watch and wave the ship off. Cheiron's wife holds in her arms the baby Achilles: the hero of Troy, in infancy, witnesses the departure of the Argonauts.[9]

The technical and detailed account of sailing is either loving or pedantic, depending on the reader's interest in boats and the sea. The fish, big and little, follow the ship in which Orpheus serenades, as (a Homeric simile) sheep follow the shepherd home at evening.[10] Apollonius, a scholar and a learned poet, was also a man with more than a literary understanding of the world. No matter how fanciful the plot, the contingent world he depicts is credible to the senses. The sea is real, though the metaphorical sheep may have more Theocritus than wool about them.

There are few attestations to his other poetry. He is thought to have written hexameters about Alexandria's foundation, and after commemorating the origins of Naucratis, celebrating those of Cnidos, Rhodes and Caunus as well. In choliambics he wrote about Canopus. He composed scholarly works on Homer, Hesiod, Archilochus and Antimachus. In youth he published—that is, performed—what is thought to have been an early version of his *Argonautica* and it was not a success in Alexandria.[11] Humiliated, he exiled himself in Rhodes. He returned, also voluntarily, to Alexandria with the scroll of his revised poem tucked under his arm. This time he was applauded. He was "found worthy" of the library.[12] He died around 230 BC and was buried beside Callimachus.

The last detail has given rise to much speculation, some of it touching on romantic themes: how close were the two men in the first place, during the teacher-pupil period, for Callimachus had a pederastic reputation; why did they fall out, and were they ever truly reconciled (assuming they had actually become estranged)? Or is the reference to burial merely a way of saying that Apollonius merited burial in a cemetery reserved for those who, like Callimachus, had served the library and *musaion*? It is startling once again to see how much scholarship is generated by an absence of facts. We do not *know* anything for certain, and into this ignorance flows a veritable torrent of opinionation, much of it intemperate.

We do know that Apollonius was not the sole writer of epics in a post-epic age. His immediate predecessor was Antimachus of Colophon, about whom he wrote, and whose *Thebaid* and elegiac anthology of stories *Lydè* (so despised by Callimachus) may have been of use to him in composing his narrative poems. The hexameter which Homer and Hesiod had deployed continued to be used for major narratives. But every poet walking in the shadow of the two founders of the tradition was burdened with an awareness of what had been and what could be done in the medium. Apollonius exists at a vast imaginative distance from Homer, and only slightly less far from Hesiod, yet would he have existed without them?

The *Argonautica* is the only major poem which substantially survives from the period between the writing-down of Homer and the time of Nonnus, the fourth-century AD poet and author of an epic based on Dionysian myths.[13] Many conclusions are based narrowly on Apollonius' poem, as though it somehow represented all those vanished epics that provided its context. It is safe to say that in a few respects the *Argonautica* is typical. It never loses sight of Homer as source and legitimator, for example, and every time it stages a simile, it does so imitatively, seeking not so much what is apposite as what will be perceived to be correct. That correctness is seldom formulaic: the language is Homeric in strategy, but tricked out with non-Homeric elements in diction and elsewhere. The tradition being literary rather than oral, formulae have no necessary place.

This leads to a movement towards particularity of detail, place, time and emotion, away from characteristic (or formulaic) to specific detail, from classical to romantic perspectives. An epic poem was now to be of use, like the epinicean ode: it could focus on particular cities, peoples and persons.[14] Hellenistic epic had been transformed by the drama, too, Euripides' in particular: "The effective portrayal of an individual emotion is more important than a completely drawn picture of a character."[15] This does not mean that the poet writes dramatically: he focuses on the same kinds of moment, the same occasions, which arrested the dramatic writer, but his work is different in kind. Some descriptions are poised and poetic in ways unthinkable in the old poetry but also unavailable to the drama. Oliver Taplin translates a scrap of an epic by Choirilos of Samos about the Persians. Nothing is new, the poet says: What can he do?

> Ah, happy he who in that era was expert in poetry,
> a servant of the Muses, when the meadow was still unscythed.
> But now when everything has been apportioned out,
> and the crafts all have their own spheres, we are left behind,
> like the last off the starting-grid. And though
> I glance all round, I cannot light on any new chariot to harness.

The poet seeking the new, or to make the familiar new, could have recourse to allegory, taking the old stories and finding in them indicative rather than literal truth, and then unpacking them as though they were a Christmas hamper of double meanings. Peter Green, Apollonius' most inventive modern translator, insists that in the *Argonautica* the poet writes virtually without allegory, believing in the story as history. He stresses how, at the time, the growth of knowledge (*logos*) was taking place at the expense of story (*mythos*). The poet was on the side of *mythos:* it was his end and his means, a way of seeing and of showing the world. It had to absorb *logos* to justify itself. Allegory bowdlerises myth, depriving it of its actuality in the interests of oblique moral instruction. Rationalism, on the other hand, historicises it, which is equally reductive because it cuts away the elements of legend and myth which reason cannot abide. The *Argonautica,* says Green, is free of allegory and historicism.[16] It does draw a large quantity of *logos* into the net of *mythos,* however.

It shares with Callimachus' poetry a fascination with origins, aetiologies, the births of cities, customs, traditions. The "and then . . . and then . . . and then" travelogue puts us in mind of Callimachus' fragmentary Iambus VI, but here stretched out, it can seem, to the edge of doom. Indeed it shares specific aetiologies with Callimachus' writings and occasionally, in phrase and form, echoes the master rather closely, though the general texture of Apollonius' poem is loose and un-Callimachean. The age of the heroes, Apollonius' poem seems to argue, is an "age of origins." Exploring origins is a way of exploring identities, histories and through them the present.[17] No less than the *Aetia,* the *Argonautica* is a "systematic aetiological enquiry."[18] Aetiologies are a core element in Hellenistic writing, perhaps because the further the Greek language and Greek men and women got from Greece itself, the more they needed to understand and affirm their roots.

By the time Apollonius composed the *Argonautica,* the imagined geography of earlier poets had been explored and charted. Invention gave way to uneasy description; there was still hyperbole, there were blank zones on the maps, but the borders of the known had been rolled far back into the Black

Sea. Many a monster and many unusual peoples had either been tamed by colonists or erased by explorers. In part, this knowledge is what the poem is about, reconciling legend and fact, explaining or adding to the explanations of origins. The gods have become bourgeois, their interventions infrequent, calculated and more selfish than ever. Lesky sees them almost as ornamental. But then the heroes, too, have by Homeric standards become singularly unheroic. The imaginative world is different, even if the scene Apollonius is trying to paint pre-dates the Trojan War by a score of years. Language is used in a different way and to different ends. It is no longer transparent, a lens, but opaque, an element in itself, so much so that it is in a sense the subject of the poem. There is no longer a feeling of necessity in the connection between divine and human, Lesky says; in fact, the connection between the heroic, as conceived by Homer, and the human is no longer tenable. The heroic must be reconceived in a scaled-down version.

The structure of Apollonius' poem is simple: plot and story are hardly differentiated. Compared with Homer's subtle scheme for unifying the action of the *Iliad,* Apollonius is crude, his merely linear narrative at odds with the elaborated surface and texture of the poem. He achieves wonderful local scenes and effects but lacks the larger, integrating formal sense of a less self-conscious epic writer.

Jason sets out to take back the throne of which he has been unjustly deprived. He arrives at Iolcus having lost a sandal fording a river, and the omen identifies him to the usurping King Pelias, who promises to give him back the throne if Jason will first undertake a heroic, and Pelias hopes an impossible, challenge. A stiff politeness prevails between pretender and usurper. Jason accepts Pelias' challenge and sets out for Colchis to bring back the Golden Fleece. Two long books trace, settlement by settlement, headland by headland, the trip of the *Argo* to Colchis. Book III comes alive because it belongs to Medea and borrows some of her magic and charm. Then in Book IV the Fleece is taken, and the heroes flee back by seaways still belonging to myth. They return via a series of hardships to their point of departure, Iolcus, aided by and finally dependent upon Medea's subtle sorcery.

The pace of the poem is uneven. What makes it readable is the oddity and definition of the detail and the occasional blinding beauty of some passages. Apollonius is fascinated by certain details, peculiarities, exoticisms; then he seems bored by a series of possible stops and possible epiphanies, until again his eye is arrested by something which demands to be described and explained. This verse is a kind of stuttering catalogue, in which some items are passed over and many lovingly defined.

If we list the things that do detain him, we can detect a kind of pattern. It may well be that Apollonius lingers instinctively rather than by deliberate design, but we can, I believe, see into the artist through the kinds of windows he shapes in his poem. Starting with the gods, it is not Apollo, his namesake, whom the poet invokes at the outset, or Zeus, who intervenes briefly and grumpily, but Hera who governs the action, seconded by Athena. Hera is the schemer whose scheming goes largely unopposed. She likes Jason because once, when she was disguised as an old woman, he carried her across a raging torrent.[19] This passage—and in Book I the presentation of frail Iphias, the priestess of Artemis who wishes to speak to and bless Jason, but only manages to kiss his hand—puts us in mind of Callimachus' *Hecale,* not because of the imagery of crones but because of what those crones do and what they will to happen.

Hera is Jason's and Apollonius' tutelary spirit and the first of many feminising elements, some structural, some metaphorical, that make the poem unique. At the level of plot and character, it is Hera and not Zeus, Medea and not Jason who cause things to happen. Athena and Aphrodite (with her hair down) play major parts too. Goddesses and women, and the feelings and concerns of women, are privileged, and the masculine is ironised and reduced, the *traditional* heroic scaled right back.

The good ship *Argo* itself had nominally been designed by Argos, but his hand was guided at every stage by Athena. The ship is virtually her own invention, a fact repeated by the poet.[20]

When Jason is about to go down to the *Argo* and depart on his journey, his mother, Alkimede, clings to him. Apollonius likens her to a girl persecuted by an evil stepmother, clinging on to her nanny for comfort. Where does this elaborate simile come from? How apposite is it? How proper is it to see Jason, ostensibly the hero and subject of the poem, pressed to his mother's bosom, without any indication of his feelings, but a total concentration on hers? She never makes a second appearance. Jason tells her not to inflict pain on him, she is pressing him too hard. His consolation is cold, conventional: *you stay here and wait; that's the lot of women.*

Then comes an extended episode with the women of Lemnos. Their conduct is not judged, and the stud-farm morality of the Argonauts goes morally unquestioned as well. We will remember, from Callimachus' telling of the story,[21] how the Lemnian women, having failed in their duties to Aphrodite, began to stink. Their husbands turned to the girls of nearby Thrace. The Lemnian women killed the menfolk and their lovers and set up a matriarchy, more or less democratic in structure and successful except that, without men, they began to die out. Cue the *Argo* bound for Colchis and crewed by handsome gene-rich heroes. After initial Lemnian misgivings, there is universal copulation until Heracles, whose affections are bound up with the boy Hylas and who with a few companions has stayed on the ship, calls everyone to order and the heroes depart, having sowed their seed to repopulate Lemnos.

Jason's robe, when he visits the Lemnian leader Hipsypile, is described in detail, like Achilles' shield in the *Iliad*. It is covered with legends, not least (self-referentially) the ram whose Golden Fleece he is on his way to steal. He walks into town not like Apollo, with whom he has previously been compared, but like the bright star that brides-to-be observe and pray to. Hipsypile, whose feelings, like those of her people, are identified, asks him to accept the Lemnian crown, but he declines.

Later in Book I there are serious storms. Rhea, the mother god, requires propitiation. Argos, master craftsman and ship-builder, sculpts her image and Orpheus choreographs a mollifying ritual. The task is undertaken more seriously, one is tempted to say more *sincerely,* than the propitiatory ceremonies dedicated to Apollo before the heroes set sail. Indeed, a literal Apollo passes through the poem at one point. He is colossally striding home to Olympus at dawn, returning from his annual vacation among the Hyperboreans. The Argonauts avert their terrified gazes, Orpheus sings, an altar is built and they name the place for the dawn Apollo, but he has very little impact on events.

Apollonius is a sort of ur-Levi-Strauss, registering odd customs. When he gets to Colchis, he tells us an interesting fact which has no bearing at all on the plot: the people of Colchis have the custom of "burying" dead men in the trees, wrapped in untanned ox hides, a kind of Zoroastrian rite. Women are buried in the ground. Briefly puzzled, he soon returns to his story. Long before Colchis, back in Book II, the *Argo* sights the land of the Tibareni of Pontus. Among them, the men "do" childbirth. That is to say, when a woman goes into labour, her husband takes to his bed and moans and groans while the woman applies poultices to his head and cooks him a meal and heats up a *post partum* bath. The man thus draws off the pain from the woman. Again, the female experience focuses his attention, as it does elsewhere in the catalogue of curious customs that accompanies the catalogue of places sighted as the ship makes its way towards the Fleece. It is a relief when the navigator declares at the end of Book II, "We have reached the land of Colchis and the river Phasis."[22] The human drama can begin.

Apollonius invokes the Muse Erato, conventionally associated less with epic poetry than with the lyre and lyric. It is dawn, and the tone of the poem changes from the dogged and scholarly. There is a sudden focussed brightness about the narrative, as we enter boldly for the first time into the world of the gods—or rather, into the world of goddesses, because the conversation is between Athena and Hera, who then visit Aphrodite, a single parent with an unruly child in the form of Eros, whom she must bribe and beguile to get him to do her bidding. Much of the impact of the scene is that, after the stuttering itinerary of Books I and II, which at times give the impression of being mere decorated lists, we linger, characters grow from dialogue, rooms fill with voices and movement. There is leisure, hair is being brushed, a day—albeit a divine one—is being prepared for. Goddesses have preserved the *Argo* and will now preserve the heroes in their quest. They will use wiles, of course: the irresistible magic of love secretly administered as an arrow by Eros, and administered to a powerful young woman with deep magical skills of her own. There is tension and jealousy between the goddesses, but their common interests override their bitchiness.

Eros shoots his arrow into the already predisposed Medea. The moment when is recounted exhaustively. Apollonius, with his insistence on detail (which here descends unarguably into pedantry) takes us through every stage of the act of erotic archery. When at last the missile is discharged, love laboriously blazes up in Medea's heart. She witnesses Jason accepting Aeetes' challenge: the hero looks so handsome that her stimulated love bubbles dangerously and threatens to dislodge the lid of decorum.

One of the heroes is a good old-fashioned Homeric sort who objects to the Argonauts depending on women. What has happened to traditional male heroism? Idas demands:

> "What, is it with women that we've voyaged hither,
> the way we're begging Kypris to be our saviour?
> No longer do you look at the war god's might . . .
> Begone with you, take no thought for deeds of warfare,
> but plan to cajole weak girls with supplication . . ."[23]

Idas realises, as we cannot fail to do, that we are so many miles from the world of Homer that the word "epic" is a ghost of itself, the word "romance" is nearly on our lips. Idas signals the generic transformation. In this post-heroic world, which still uses the rhetoric of heroism and Homer, he is naturally overruled.

Close upon the heels of the Idas passage we come upon Medea in an agony of love and confusion. She is likened to a widow, deserted and miserable, falling passionately, helplessly on her bed. Just then sister Chalciope arrives: the Argonauts beg Medea's assistance. Here begin her recovery and transformation. Oppressed with guilt and doubt at her intended treachery, she nonetheless resolves to act, the way a Homeric hero might, but Medea is a woman: something fundamental has changed.

Dawn comes. She puts on her make-up and preparation for the first trial commences. She meets Jason in a flurry of similes: he is an ascending bright star (as before, with Hipsypile); they stand silently facing one another like oaks. Jason at no point responds to her beauty: it is his beauty that the poem celebrates. Jason at no point shows sexual desire: it is her desire that the poem emphasises. Medea's perspective is our perspective. Jason's lack of interest, or vision, is part of his neutrality as the central "heroic" figure. He does not have the energy, intelligence or passion to hold the poem together. Medea does. The poet alludes to another enabling woman, Ariadne, a sinister precedent from Medea's point of view.

Decisively Medea instructs the blank-faced, blank-hearted hero what to do with the bulls and the dragon teeth. The magic she prescribes (including an unguent to make him invulnerable) has elements of other legends mixed in with it, not least an echo of the instructions to Orpheus when attempting to rescue his Eurydice. Jason will follow instructions. That much we can depend on. He thanks Medea by proposing to her. He declares that he is— grateful. There is no declaration of love, but then Eros has not struck him under the left pap. He says that *if* he gets back to Iolcus (that means, he will need a lot more magic, not just this first instalment), he will make an honest sorceress of her. She weeps and is passionate, he receives her thanks with guile. Now she is silent, he is voluble.

When the trials begin, Aeetes arrives like Poseidon in his chariot, and Jason stamps the ground like a war horse. Then, as he strips to the waist for battle, he resembles first Ares, then Apollo. The male gods are presented in the postures and movements of the protagonists, but they are not there as presences. Apollonius recounts the taming of the fiery-breathed bulls and the sowing of the dragon teeth that grow into hostile warriors with a continuing abundance of metaphor. The account is exciting in the way that a great tapestry is exciting, entertaining the eye but not speeding the pulse.

For the fourth book Apollonius invokes the aid of Athena as his Muse. He describes Jason's theft of the Fleece and the Argonauts' much-interrupted return, and the book belongs to Medea in more ways than one. The Colchians wanted to retrieve the Golden Fleece, but they would not have pursued so hotly had Medea not fled with the heroes. They intended to capture and punish her.

When Medea fled, driven by Hera, she left a long lock of her hair behind for her mother as a memento that she is still a virgin, an important point to remember: her sexual virtue is intact, there was no Lemnian looseness about her. Apollonius goes out of his way to clear Medea of the various charges usually laid at her door. Her love was divinely caused, not chosen, and her actions throughout are marked by an instinct to virtue, a habit of probity.

Her magic remains potent. She makes the dragon guarding the Fleece fall asleep, and Jason performs the theft. The simile Apollonius uses is at once powerful in itself and strange in context, feminising the hero who has, in any case, sold out to the female:

> As a full moon climbs the sky, and its risen brightness
> shimmers down on the garret bedroom of some young creature
> who catches it on her fine dress, and the heart within her

lifts at the sight of that pure radiance, so now Jason
was filled with joy as he hefted the great Fleece in his hands,
and over his fair cheeks and brow the bright glint of its texture
cast a ruddy blush like a flame.²⁴

The Argonauts flee, followed by a flotilla of Colchians. After the eventful
escape, aided time after time by Medea's magic rather than heroic prowess,
Idas must have been really out of sorts. The Argonauts were intended to be
heroes, but apart from a few vivid battles *en route* to Colchis and some narrow escapes on the way home, heroism is precisely what they lack. They are
even tempted to abandon Medea on the way home so as to curb the pursuit
of the Colchians. It is not Jason who saves her. She saves herself, threatening revenge if she is abandoned, and the men are cowed and compliant.

It is Jason who plots the death of Medea's brother. Apollonius lets
Medea off that hook as well. They murder him and his crew; the other pursuing Colchians are furious but Hera keeps them at bay. Zeus takes their
part angrily and at last makes a brief intervention, condemning the Argonauts to a series of serious setbacks before they get home, but get home
they will. Circe, Aeetes' sister, absolves but does not welcome Jason or
Medea. This Circe has none of the passionate charm and seduction of the
one who snares Odysseus.

Hera eases the way so that the *Argo* can get through the mysterious geography of the western passages. We meet Thetis attempting to make Achilles
invulnerable; we meet the sirens and hear Orpheus' counter-melody.

The preservation of Medea's virginity continues well into Book IV
(l. 1024). In Phaiakia, where they land a generation before Odysseus (storm-
tossed, he finds lovely young Nausicaa playing on the beach), they are well
received. Queen Arete pleads Medea's cause to her husband, Alcinous, hug-
ging him in wifely arms in bed, a woman arguing the case for another and
using not only words but loving persuasion. He judges that Medea, to be
saved from the pursuing Colchians, must wed Jason. The ceremony is conducted, Jason obedient as usual, and they consummate their union bedded
on the Golden Fleece itself.

It is a goddess who rouses the heroes later, during the parched Libyan interlude when they expect to perish under the sun's unremitting disc. This
touch of geography would have brought the poem home to Apollonius'
Egyptian audiences. There were further obstacles, some serious but none
dramatic. They meet with the sea god Triton, who is suptuously described,
especially his tail. When the heroes get home, the poem is over. They step
ashore and Apollonius abandons them and us on the beach. The usurper is
not overthrown, Jason's mother is not allowed her moment of relief and
joy. The trip is finished, and that's that.

Medea is a character: she has motives, she acts, her actions have consequences, she changes. In this, she is alone in a poem that consists largely of
cardboard figures. Only Heracles is a proper hero, and he is removed from
the poem early on. His beloved Hylas is drawn by a lusty nymph into a pool
and drowned. The heroes set sail without noticing that Heracles is missing,
even though his seat was at the very heart of the ship.

> As soon as the morning star rose clear above the topmost
> peaks, the wind gusted down, and Tiphys quickly
> urged them aboard, to make good use of the land breeze;
> then straight away they embarked with a will, and raised the
> ship's anchor stones, and hauled hard on the sheet-lines,
> the sail bellied out in the wind, and they, rejoicing,
> were borne away from shore, past Poseidon's headland.
> At the hour when dawn's grey half-light first shines in the heavens,
> rising from the horizon, and paths become visible,
> and dew-pointed meadows glitter brightly, then they
> perceived that, all unknowing, they'd left those two ashore.[25]

With so unobservant a captain and crew, the success of the enterprise is
little short of miraculous.

At times Jason reminds us of Telemachus, at times of Agamemnon at his
most trying, when he is testing his comrades to see if they want to go home
(and suddenly they do). He never calls to mind the serious heroes. At the
conclave before the *Argo* sets sail in Book I, Jason speaks like a company director. It is time to elect a chairman. Heracles? He declines, and the task
falls to Jason, whose quest in any case it is.

He broods. Old-fashioned, hot-blooded Idas confronts him, asking if he
is afraid. Idmon remonstrates with Idas for taking this tack with the
thoughtful young leader and an argument ensues which Orpheus calms
with a song. He sings a creation myth, theogonies, aetiologies. But the question, "Is Jason scared?" is never answered. When the ship departs, Jason
weeps to be leaving home. Another argument blows up and Jason, still de-
pressed, says nothing. Attacked for his silence, he does not explain himself.
It is Glaucus the sea spirit who comes up out of the depths and with a little
emollient prophecy brings things back to calm.

In Book II Jason and the heroes are actually described as afraid and
weak-willed.[26] Jason suffers from overwhelming fear and in an Agamem-
nonish spirit suggests retreat. "So he / spoke, making trial of the heroes,
but they shouted / bold words of encouragement."[27]

Reciting his poem a second time in Alexandria, if we are to believe the
lives and legends, Apollonius was greeted with "bold words of encouragement" and stayed, to become librarian and to be honoured, esteemed and

buried with pomp. His surviving work is a storehouse of stories and similes. It may be rather more radical in outlook than it is in form. To call it an epic poem because it is written in hexameters and belongs to a Homeric tradition is to sell the idea of epic short. It has elements of epic, deliberately cultivated. It has something else that anachronistic critics call romance. Certainly from Book III through the first two thirds of Book IV an amazing and coherent narrative unfolds and, as in some of the drama, the character of a woman in love and in danger is presented with, as a larger context, more about woman and women, their circumstances and perspectives, than we expect from non-dramatic Greek poetry. It would be fanciful to suggest that it was to this that Callimachus objected. What he didn't like, if he didn't like it, was the sheer volubility of Apollonius, the degree to which the language exceeded its occasions, the degree to which the poem fell short of Homer.

XXV

Theocritus of Syracuse (c. 308–240 BC)[1]

Wordsworth on Nature is like Virgil on boxing; I prefer
Theocritus, who had obviously been a bit of a bruiser himself, as his account of the Amycus-Pollux match shows.

ROBERT GRAVES, "The Road to Rydal Mount"[2]

 An Athenian poet of the sixth century BC enjoyed an abundance of givens. He knew his fellow-citizens shared his dialect,
landscape, history, and traditions, and when it came to poetry
itself, expectations having to do with music, genre, and diction.
A poet writing in Syracuse in the third century BC couldn't bank on such a
commonality. Syracuse was big, with Alexandria the largest Greek city at the
time. It had had a turbulent history, and, despite political vagaries, the messy
interregna between tyrants, there was the tenuous memory of a mother culture, the Corinthian source. Unsettling and enriching elements derived
from its relations with the rest of Sicily, with Italy and the north of Africa.
The population had diversified well beyond the Greek core. A poet writing
there could not take much for granted.

In Alexandria, nothing at all could be taken for granted. In the first century of its existence, few Alexandrians felt like natives. In the busy port,
with its wide avenues and narrow alleys, a mess of languages and dialects
was spoken. The city was Greek, but the racial mix was unlike that in any
previous Greek city. Here religious observances and superstitions were a
tangle. At the great library writers and intellectuals from the entire known
world—not only Greeks—were at work, many of them supported, scholars
suggest, by the Ptolemies themselves. In a few decades Alexandria had
grown from a literal backwater into an imperial capital, a spectacular colonial imposition upon Egypt, with dazzling façades, the architectural weight,
the colonial determination of a phenomenon intended to last.

Theocritus' Idyll XV, "The Festival of Adonis," evokes the city at his
time through the eyes of two immigrant gossips, Gorgo and Praxinoa, who,
as he did, came from Syracuse. Arsinoe, Ptolemy Philadelphus' queen, has
organised an exhibition and concert at the royal palace in honour of Adonis. The general public is to be admitted. These gossips, though bumptious
and coarse, are independent-minded and agreeably awed by the scale and
opulence of festive Alexandria. The little drama of the idyll begins with
Gorgo knocking on Praxinoa's door and urging her to come out into the
festive streets. Praxinoa leaves her two-year-old with a maid and the women

(they are prosperous) accompanied by two servants set out, chatting about husbands and other brittle subjects. Scene two is set in the street: they struggle through the crowd, exchanging words. In the third scene they reach the palace, banter with other exhibition-goers, defend the dignity of their dialect, and listen to a famous singer who ends her song by conjuring Adonis. Gorgo adds a little coda, praying that next year will bring around the same plenty and celebration.

The poem gives Theocritus occasion to note some of the benefits that Ptolemy Philadelphus has effected. There is a sense of popular access to the king, improvements in street safety, a widening prosperity, a general tolerance. The poem also celebrates the resilient virtues of Syracuse in the immigrant women. As they chatter, an Alexandrian tries to silence them:

> Quiet, women! Chattering like two barn-door fowls.
> You set my teeth on edge with your flattened vowels.

To this, unhesitatingly, remembering that Corinth was the mother city of Syracuse, and that Bellerophon was one of Corinth's most famous sons, albeit equine, Praxinoa retorts,

> What bird might you be? The crested ignoramus?
> We come from good Corinthian stock, the same as
> Bellerophon.

C. M. Bowra insists that, for poetry, the move in time and space from Athens to Alexandria entailed a narrowing of imagination and expressive freedom: the "openness" of democratic Greece is attenuated into poetic servility in Ptolemaic Alexandria.[3] About these Syracusan women there is nothing servile, nor does the city they inhabit seem restrictive. Bowra forgets how centuries of poets served tyrants with praise: Pindar, his favourite, is hardly a democratic spirit. Poets' lives themselves were, he declares, "narrower," as though political integration and the acceleration of history it entails, the freedom to travel, the amazing resource of the libraries in Alexandria and elsewhere, the diversity of cultures on show, impoverished imagination. Bowra's is an odd take on the growth of cosmopolitan culture, nostalgic for the brief stabilities of tyranny and democracy, with their very different dynamics and their fragmented poetry.

By destiny and design, Alexandria was cosmopolitan. The sustaining countryside, the fields and olive orchards, the pastures and enclosures close at hand and familiar to the citizen of most Greek cities through to the third century, were unfamiliar in North Africa. Apollonius in *Argonautica,* Book IV portrayed its climate as mercilessly hot, dry and unredeemed. The steamy Nile delta sustained flora and fauna quite unlike those to which the Greek immigrant was accustomed. Apart from Apollonius, Alexandrian poets came from older Greek cities and brought in their luggage more co-herent cultures. They unpacked them gingerly in the shimmering strange-ness of a new kind of world. Here diverse Greek traditions come together in a complex flowering of verse, before it atrophies under the devoted care of Rome.

Idyll II, the magical "Pharmaceutria," like Idyll XV develops a female character. As with Apollonius' Medea and Callimachus in the *Hecale,* an Alexandrian poet creates and explores a feminine sensibility, and here, also, female sexuality. Elsewhere his verse emerges from paedophile and homo-sexual enthusiasms, but here a woman finds a convincing voice.[4] Simaetha, his protagonist, is desperate to draw her lover back. He has gone off with another, male or female, she is not sure which. Simaetha proves to be a sor-ceress and witch, an apprentice Medea. Her confusion, skittering between emotions, contributes to the clarity of a poem which understands how hate and love, desire and resentment inhabit a single mind, torture and extend without dividing it.

In the first section Simaetha is desperate for her man Delphis, and not vice versa: a poetic innovation. Delphis has failed to visit her for twelve whole days (and nights). She plans to confront him with his neglect tomor-row at the wrestling school where he spends most of his spare time. Obvi-ously he is a young man of leisure, and she a girl with time to stand and stare—one who owns a slave. Pending tomorrow, she exercises magic to lure him back, calling on the mysterious moon and on Hecate. In the sec-ond section she begins to chant. Delphis is from Myndus, a town on the coast of Asia Minor, not far from Cos. He is self-obsessed and has stolen her happiness. Her magic involves melting images, burning bits of his clothes and chanting awful imprecations, all of which end demanding not his death but his desperate and needy return, a fantasy that plainly images her own desire for him.

In the concluding section, having spun a magic wheel, she evokes the Lady Moon and tells her the story of her love. She went to watch a parade and spotted Delphis and a mate coming from the gym with their shining brown-curled beards and their handsome naked chests. Her heart "burst into flame" and she went into a decline. She sent her slave girl to summon him from the wrestling school. He came, she was paralysed with fear and desire. Her careful stanza-and-refrain account continues until, overcome by the memory of desire, her verse turns to straightforward narrative of what she did, drawing him into her bed, and what he did. They loved. But now his eye has wandered. One detail electrifies the poem. Delphis used to leave his oil-flask, for greasing his body at the wrestling school, at her house. It gave him an excuse to come there three or four times a day. This particular stays in the mind, a token of trust and intimacy—betrayed. The fact that he has left his precious oil-flask indicates the intensity of his supplanting passion. Simaetha ties her story in with Ariadne's and Medea's. She bids farewell to the Moon, who has listened patiently and silently to her tale and her lament.

More characteristically, Theocritus is an elegist; he incorporates into his verse elements from the drama, mime, epic, epinicean poetry and the "new poetics" of Callimachus. There is remarkable wholeness in his artificial poetic world, and integrity of purpose, too: it is a paradox that thematic artificiality and poetic integrity—at odds in earlier phases of Greek culture—go together in Alexandria.

Theocritus wrote idylls. The term, unrelated to the term "idyllic" in modern English, was first used by Pliny the Younger as a way of describing poems which were *not long*.[5] An "idyll" was originally a small picture or portrait (stressing not only the scale but the human content—an idyll is not merely descriptive but follows a character or set of characters). Tennyson loved the open genre and the term and used it to describe widely divergent kinds of poem in his own *oeuvre*. In the case of Theocritus, whose surviving poems apart from the epigrams are lumped together under the head, the idyll can include bucolic work, town mimes, panegyrics, hymns, lyrics and brief epics.

Theocritus' little epics are among his most compelling work, concentrating on a brief episode in a larger legend or myth. His "scaling down" of narrative tends to foreground characters and their state of mind, or their moral significance. The poems arrest the familiar flow of larger tales—Homer's, Apollonius'—to distil and define. In Idyll XI, "The Cyclops," the poet addresses his friend Nicias. Love is incurable. Only the Muses—by way of therapeutic love-song—can alleviate its discomforts. Nicias as a physician and poet should know this. The story of Polyphemus and Galatea takes on a new pathos. Polyphemus is a young Cyclops, his chin only just fuzzing with beard. He may not be handsome, he concedes, but he is rich. He sits above the sea longing and calling to the sea nymph Galatea. He wants to learn to swim so he can dive into the sea and find and kiss her. In this beauty-and-beast fable the beast, sincere and touching, and irredeemably ugly, loses.

Idyll XIII, "Hylas," Tennyson's favourite idyll, retells a tale Apollonius includes in the *Argonautica,* but here with a thrift that endeared him to Callimachus. Again, the poet addresses Nicias. Heracles, being in love, took lovely young Hylas with him when he joined the quest for the Fleece. This passion of Heracles proved that boy-love was not effeminate or weak. Hylas' death is rendered with piercing precision, a star falling out of the sky. Heracles survived his loss and, the poet adds consolingly, Nicias will survive his lover's passing on to other pleasures. This poem is the pure water which, in his "Hymn to Apollo," Callimachus says a poet must raise to Demeter's lips.

Impure but powerful, Idyll XXII, "The Dioscuri," is the most discussed and interpreted of the idylls in recent times. It begins by announcing the two parts to follow, the boxing match and the armour and spear contest. The aetiology of Castor and Polydeuces, sons of Leda and Zeus, is established. Polydeuces' part combines epic narrative and dialogue, a mixed genre appropriate to an event in which the god is sweetly reasonable and the ensuing conflict not his fault. Castor's part of the poem is rendered wholly in epic terms and recalls the cruelly wasteful combats in the *Iliad*.

The brothers are by vocation rescuers of men in trouble, whether they are storm-tossed, threatened, betrayed.

> You, the twin-helpers of men on earth, excellers
> In words and music, on horseback, at the games . . .

Theocritus enters Apollonius' narrative territory again, but with a light knapsack. The *Argo,* passing the turbulent rocks, lands at Bebrycia. "Out went the ladders, down the vessel's side" suggests how high the ship was, how vast its hull. The twins find a lovely unspoiled spring surrounded with trees and prepare to drink. What appears to be a steroid-addicted body-builder with thick ears and iridescent muscle confronts them: King Amycus. He challenges Polydeuces: the loser will become the victor's slave. Amycus blows through a stentorian conch and summons the Bebrycians out of the woods to watch. The threat to Polydeuces is Amycus' sheer bulk: like a New Zealand All-Black, he strolls down the pitch and scores a try; opponents simply bounce off him. But Amycus has met his match: he is pummelled and dented; he sweats until he seems to melt and at last concedes defeat. Polydeuces makes him swear not to attack future travellers, a gentle fate for one who fights as dirtily as Amycus does. Compared with Apollonius' circumstantial narrative, Theocritus' version is more vivid and thematically purposeful.

The complementary half of the poem concerns Lynceus and Idas, Aphareus' sons. They were betrothed to the daughters of Leucippus by an old family pact. Castor and Polydeuces stole the girls away. The brothers ambushed the divine rapists at Aphareus' tomb. In this instance Lynceus and Idas were sweet reason, the Dioscuri the aggressors. Castor chopped off Lynceus' fingers and when Lynceus turned away he was hacked upward "from flank to navel," spilling out his guts. This story does little credit to Castor. Idas in rage wrenched a column from his father's tomb and attacked Castor. Zeus deflected the attack and himself killed Idas with a lightning flash. The moral is that the sons of Tyndareus are invincible, whether their cause is just or not. Theocritus concludes with a paean to poets, blessed by the Dioscuri and by Helen and all the heroes who went to Troy.

> They owe their glory to a poet, the man of Chios
> Who took for theme Priam's city, the Achaean ships,
> The battles round Troy, and Achilles, tower of the field.
> I, too, offer tokens of the clear-voiced Muses . . .

This idyll relates to the Homeric and later hymns, that unbroken tradition which flowers again in Callimachus' six poems. In recovering the legendary and archaic, the Alexandrian poets turned to the hymn tradition as an unalloyed source not only of materials but of forms. Such formal appropriation and allusion is integral to their sense of shaping and authenticating matter and tone. "Poems which reconstruct and adapt the past are, in two senses, a kind of historical writing," says Richard Hunter. "The past, here represented by an earlier text, is seen through the new text, so that both ends of a historical process are displayed."[6] Joining the past poem with the new one is part of structuring, he adds. It is "to some extent their very purpose."

The connection between Homeric Hymn XXXIII, "To the Dioscuri," and the opening of Idyll XXII, is instructive. The earlier poem is a prayer, the later adds narrative, aetiology, and a set of contrasts, or *agons*, not only in narrative but in narrative style, contrasts which underline the paradox of the poem's "moral," that whatever the gods do is right, even when it is wrong. Men and gods have become hard to distinguish: the Dioscuri, the Ptolemies. Comparable moral cruelty marks the end of Idyll XXVI, "The Bacchae," which tells the same story as Euripides' play. Pentheus spies on the Bacchantes' ritual. They catch him and dismember him: his mother wrenches off his head, his aunts his arms; he is torn asunder. Rejecting emotion, rejecting "natural feeling," the poem declares: Pentheus transgressed, his doom was just.[7]

Most of the poems are composed in hexameters, but the hexameter had changed in balance, volume, suppleness, allusiveness. Not only the classical narratives but the new bucolic note that Theocritus strikes, and for which over many centuries he was most celebrated, was original. What would the poetic beginnings have made of these ends: moon-faced Hesiod, peering over the wall into a Theocritean pasture? Theocritus' rustic world, like that of his imitators Moschus, also of Syracuse, and Bion of Smyrna, and of other urban and urbane shepherds of later ages in Rome and in Europe, was scented with something other than sweat and manure. Here the reader experiences not the awful daily boredom and discomfort of real shepherds, but cultured leisure, subtly metered, with pretty, kempt shepherdesses, fluffy livestock, rich harvests which seem to tumble of their own accord into the barns. And winter? Not this year. Death happens and provides the pretext for a delicious, protracted plangency. And no matter how many pipes and flutes are mentioned, the poetry is not accompanied by literal music. The music is as much a fiction as the pastures, goats and sheep are.

Hesiod, who spoke plainly to his ne'er-do-well brother Perses, to the Muses and the gods, would have been similarly forthright with Theocritus, though the Syracusan was a type of man remote from any he had ever met. Is this, he might have asked, the last chapter of my once hard-bitten tradition? In early times poets were accosted by the Muses, who filled them with grace by making use of them: poets were vehicles through which the Muses spoke. Now the Muses are at best an archaising trope to serve the poet, the gods have receded along with the actual stones and dust of the fields and the panting, scrawny reality of *real* midsummer sheep. This is not the end of the Hesiodic tradition but the beginning of something else. Or else agriculture and landscape have evolved beyond recognition in a short five centuries. Theocritus' idyll is a fantasy of rural life, a travesty of the rural world. The poet is no longer a preceptor, delivering practical and moral wisdom in memorable language, disclosing the mysteries of the origin of the world and the hierarchies of the gods. Now lambing and shearing and milking and herding, sowing and tending and harvesting, binding the vines, pruning the olives, and all the drab, brutish dailiness and nightliness of rural life have been refined away. This is not unlike Paradise, or Eden retrieved.

Bowra insists that Theocritus loved "the country," unlike, he says, Callimachus.[8] If he loved the country, why is there not more weather? The very expression "he loved the country" is a sentimental anachronism. In the bucolic idylls, the duties of men to one another and to the gods are more or less forgotten. The skies are blue, the grass green. Such conflicts as exist are staged and resolved. What starts with Theocritus, not with the didactic literalist Hesiod, is a pastoral tradition, and we tend to look back at his bucolic poems and distort them through lenses he ground in the first place. "Bucolic" is a term Theocritus introduces in Idyll I to describe the kind of poem he is writing. It derives from the word for cowherd. The sense came to include sheep herds and goatherds as well. In Idyll VII, the most complex and rewarding of the bucolic poems, Simichidas, whom critics take to be the voice of Theocritus himself, invents a verb: to *bucolicate,* or make herdsmen's songs.[9]

The emergence of bucolic poetry as a distinct genre marks a "dissociation of sensibility," the break between a fundamentally urban and a rural, or rurally informed, imagination. Once a city reached a certain size, a break was inevitable and transactions between city and countryside necessarily and fundamentally changed. The bumpkin, the rural innocent, the melodious and romantic herdsman all come of age in a poetry which is more escapist than nostalgic, since it reflects not a lost order but an idealised one. Theocritus' best modern translator, Robert Wells, insists too much on the poet's "realism," as though acknowledging invention would somehow devalue the verse. He repeats the seventeenth-century view that Theocritus "keeps too close to the clown."[10] Is it realism to portray rural people as hicks? Only from a resolutely urban perspective. How much banter, wit and verbal humour occurred in actual meetings between shepherds?

Proximity to the clown is a negative aspect of Theocritean idealisation. We do not pretend that caricature is *realistic* when it emphasises a nose, moles and beetling brows, displacing the natural balance of a face. Idealisation can lead to sentimentalism and, as the urban sensibility takes hold, to the intolerable condescension from which Wordsworth decisively delivers the countryman and the tradition two millennia later. What Wells calls the "paradox of graceful clumsiness" is part of the problem of pastoral: the grace belongs inevitably to the language and is attributable to the poet; the clumsiness belongs to the subject he is describing—or whose stereotype he is invoking. It is less a paradox than a natural divorce, as in all parodic forms, between the delivery and the thing said. A decorative anguish can be great poetry, but it is not to be confused with actual anguish. Daphnis in Idyll I is no more grieved for than Milton's Lycidas: elegy is a pretext, the *text* is something else. "Even when Theocritus takes up an ancient legend about Daphnis, who must have been a kind of year-god"—why *must?*—"he scales it down to a touching and not too disturbing pathos."[11] There is an aloof unkindness in making death a pretext, or the pained lover risible, however "scaled down" the tragedy or the passion, however genteel and forgiving the laughter. In the end bucolic poetry and its pastoral legacy patronise intimate feeling because they are inherently parodic. They contribute to the sceptic's and the stoic's cause: disbelieve it, or control it.

Idyll I, of all Theocritus' poems, has the clearest legacy in Greek, Latin and European poetry. It stands behind Bion's "Adonis" and Moschus's "Bion," it marks the poetry of Virgil and Catullus, it prefigures "Lycidas," Shelley's "Adonais" and Arnold's "Thyrsis." The theme is less Daphnis' death than elegy itself: Theocritus' conceit is that one shepherd begs another to recite a favourite song. The poem proposes a kind of hierarchy: at the bottom a nameless Coan *goat*-herd, suppliant and willing to pay for the performance; and above him the talented *sheep*-herd Thyrsis, from far-off Aetna in Sicily (he may be another stand-in for Sicilian Theocritus). The dialogue between goatherd and shepherd frames the elegy. Each enjoins the other to perform and the goatherd prevails, inducing Thyrsis to sing the old favourite the "Passion of Daphnis." He has offered Thyrsis a very good fee: a nanny goat producing copious milk and a wooden cup richly sculpted.

The cup itself is an interesting artefact. Carved ivy runs around the rim, and below it three panels are arrayed: a woman courted by two lovers, her "kindly indifference" to both; an aged fisherman with a heavy net; beyond him, a vineyard in which a boy stands guard and two foxes circle, one to steal his quarter-loaf, while unaware he fashions a cricket cage. The cup is brightly coloured. Poets may not receive payment from tyrants and rich patrons, but here in the pasture a simple goatherd is willing to part with his all for a few minutes' exquisite song. Wells compares the descriptions of the cup, with its discrete panels, to the structuring of the sequence idyll by idyll: each a separate sections, yet relating to the poems before and after.

If the poem is taken as a whole and compared with other idylls, the Pindaric strophe, antistrophe and epode structure of the epinicean odes comes to mind. Many of the idylls divide into three or six natural sections, and the form, though attenuated and subtilised, seems to integrate the poems. In the second part of this idyll, Thyrsis performs his "Lament for Daphnis," a song which feels familiar to English readers because of "Lycidas" and other elegies. Daphnis dies of unrequited love. Hermes comes, then Aphrodite. She teases Daphnis and he taunts her in return with Anchises, Adonis, her mortal loves. He bids farewell to Aetna (because, like Thyrsis, he too is a Sicilian shepherd) and urges Pan to leave Greece for Sicily. He envisages a nature turned topsy-turvy with his death, and then he dies, and even Aphrodite cannot rouse him. The lament is lovely and light, with a charmed refrain.

After dialogue and lament, the third part of the idyll, the epode as it were, consists of Thyrsis peremptorily demanding his fee. The plangent notes have hardly died down before he declares, "Now give me the goat and the carved cup." And the goatherd gratefully and promptly obliges. We have been party to a simple, graceful, unclumsy poetic transaction.

Theocritus' bucolic poems—just under half of his surviving corpus—inhabit a world designed by sentiment on a kind of Platonic template. Inevitably, for all their elegance of expression, even the vivid recollection of open-air buggery in Idyll V, "Goatherd and Shepherd," has a designer feel. The poem is set in the south of Italy, in the instep. Comatas looks after the goats and Lacon the sheep. They start arguing, then gamble a kid against a lamb in a singing competition. It is dialogue-cum-debate, like the famous contest of Hesiod and Homer, with an equally dubious outcome. Comatas, the elder, claims to have taught Lacon to sing. What kind of singing? How did he teach him?

> When I buggered you I taught you to moan and groan
> Like a nanny bleating when the billy shoves it in.

After more insults or home truths are exchanged, Morson, on his way from town, turns up and both contestants accept him as judge. Now that they have an audience, the second section begins. Lacon clearly inclines to lad-love (Cratidas being his particular favourite) while Comatas likes girls. But Comatas recalls, a second time, buggering Lacon.

> Remember the time I bent you over that tree,
> How you wriggled, grimaced and pushed back hard on me?

In the third section, the time for prizes arrives and Morson rewards Comatas, requesting a slice of lamb when the time of sacrifice arrives. Morson all along has had his mind more on the eventual feast than on the actual contest. The judge has been pre-emptively corrupted.

Such writing beguiles and persuades, but what it contains of rusticity, real in context, is not realistic. Critics who love Theocritus but are uncertain of his legacy insist on the actuality of his geography and try to tease out an answerable, literal world. Conditioned by a poetic tradition in which— hitherto—word has answered deed and object, even though in increasingly attenuated ways, they are reluctant to accept that in Theocritus, who suffers less acutely the formal strains and stresses of Callimachus or Apollonius, a crucial shift has occurred: the poetry exists in and for the illusions it creates in a language no longer necessarily earthed in contingencies.

Behind the deliberately coarse Doric diction and forms Theocritus devised from his native dialect for the bucolic poems there are, some critics affirm, echoes of actual "folk" material, rural song, traditional rhymes.[12] Such elements are detected at the root of Stesichorus' Sicilian verses, too. In Theocritus, "The effect is perfectly calculated, and derives not least from a three-way incongruity between the speaker and subject-matter, linguistic register, and literary form."[13] If indeed a long battle between *mythos* and *logos* was in progress, however, bucolic poets removed themselves from the battlefield into a buzzy, breezy parallel universe.[14] Sir Kenneth Dover tells us that Theocritus delighted in building "a sophisticated construction on a popular foundation."[15] Would his poems have appealed to a shepherd or a common seaman? No, they are intended for readers rather than for popular recital. Would peasant or sailor have recognised *their* contribution to the "sophisticated construction"? If so, they might have resented the implicit condescension.

It seems unlikely that, in anything other than an allusive way, the bucolic idylls drew upon a rustic rural or oral tradition. They are poems based upon earlier poems, in a language deliberated not on a hillside but among the twists and coils of books in a library or on a terrace among professional men—doctors, lawyers, public officials—with a view of pastures and fields, livestock and herdsmen, about whom the poems purport to be. The transposition of polite dialogue from terrace or library on to these common figures was a pleasant task: what was particular became characteristic, the occasion moved from a contingent to a universal world. The point of bucolic poetry is that it is fiction, and as in all fiction the aim is to make it credible rather than literal. What might be realistic is the "courtesies of speech" which occur in the dialogue poems,[16] but such courtesies belong to the "polite" classes. "The truth in his poems," says Wells "lies between the speakers rather than with any single voice."[17] The use of proverbs grounds the poems in seeming folk wisdom, but the proverbs occur in a context which translates, and a dialect which refines them, assuming they were proverbs in the first place. It is possible that they are Theocritus' invention or are sourced not in the fields but in preceding poems, including Hesiod's.

Much is made of the actuality of Theocritus' paths and landmarks. The long walk the shepherds take in Idyll VII is as readily traceable on Cos, pedestrian critics declare, as Leopold Bloom's way through Dublin. The shepherds' voices are credible, they add, even though the Doric dialect is synthetic and no one ever spoke it. There are no texts of folk-songs to corroborate the critics' argument. Would folk metres have resembled the metres of the idylls (do popular Scottish and English ballad metres resemble blank verse?), would the spoken or sung diction relate in any way to the refined diction of the poems? Theocritus has left us *writing,* not song. Verse and music had been moving apart: the greater the weight of "meaning"—in the theatre, in the victory ode—the more the volume of the music had to be turned down, until it survived only in the patterning of verbal sounds, in metre, in repetitions and the formal rounds of the language itself. The divorce from music in written poems is complete, though they remember and acknowledge one another by fond allusion. A deliberate, walker's reading of an idyll, following the very route the poem follows, hardly makes voices and incidents more actual. Even the pipes are, in a literal sense, silent: readers must conjure from the language another music, another world.

Such conjuring is pleasurable, nowhere more so than in Idyll VII, "The Harvest Festival." Richard Hunter compares its form to Plato's *Lysis* and *Phaedrus,* notes that the meeting with Lycidas is modelled on Homeric meetings, and draws attention to echoes of the proeme of Hesiod's *Theogony.*[18] It is a poem made of earlier poetry, and no less valid for that. Simichidas declares that his words have got through even to Zeus, who might be taken to be the divine Ptolemy Philadelphus addressed in Idyll XVII. If Zeus is Ptolemy and Simichidas is Theocritus, identities may be sought for other characters in this leisurely idyll. Some scholars argue that it provides evidence for a Coan school of poets.

The narrator Simichidas and two friends are walking to Haleis, where other rural friends are to offer first fruits at the festival of Demeter. *En route* they meet with rustic Lycidas. Simichidas in the nicest of terms challenges Lycidas to a singing contest. Lycidas declares his settled dislike for overreaching poets and for those who feel they must compete with Homer. He agrees to the contest and delivers his poem first. It is about wishing an absent friend well and it is also about Daphnis' hopeless love for Xenea. And about Comatas, locked in a box and fed by bees for a whole season because of the sweetness of his musical lips.

Simichidas declares that he too has been a shepherd and begins his song. He chooses Myrto, trots after her, but his friend Aratus is in love with the lad Philenus; and just as Lycidas has prayed for his friend's deliverance from the box, so Simichidas prays that Philenus may lie unresisting beside Aratus. Should Pan fail to answer his prayer, Simichidas will invoke terrible punishments on the god and on the disobliging lad. It is a heated poem, and Simichidas wins the contest. Lycidas gives him his crook and exits, cheerful in defeat. The others continue on to Demeter's feast and find a lush and relaxing scene, hardly ceremonial, strewn about in the grass, with fruit at every hand. They join in. The wine is especially rewarding. The poem ends with a prayer for next year's ceremony, just as Idyll XV does.

These bucolic herdsmen are a means and a disguise: the poet speaks through them and hides behind them, their refined rusticity, their arch archaism. The herdsmen stand in for irony: they provide the necessary distance between the poem and the poet, the reader and the poem. Hesiod's shepherding is credible, the advice he gives homely and even valid. Theocritus' is stylised, the advice he gives in elegant aphorism has more to do with mannerly entertainment than with herding, germination and harvest. In an age like the Alexandrian, in love with aetiologies, at first the bucolic may seem like a return, in imagination, to beginnings; in fact, it is a parodic strategy, in some instances sending up, as the mimes can do, the search for "origins" itself, in others fulfilling a satirical function.

Theocritus' bucolic poetry is leavened by his poetic personality, his gently penetrating imagination, his guilelessness. Later bucolic poetry is less generously, less virtuosically practised. Bucolic Theocritus is the poet our parents and grandparents encountered, hoary and venerable, a figure quite different from the poet we meet today. For them what mattered was the pastoral he gave rise to, an emphasis due to the impact of the idylls on later Roman and European poetry. F. T. Griffiths in *Theocritus at Court* was one of the first English-language scholars to attend closely to the non-bucolic poems. Many have followed him into this area.

Theocritus of Syracuse: a poet from a busy city. The scholia to Idyll VII say that his mother was Philina and his father Simichus.[19] He was raised in relatively prosperous circumstances, receiving a good education and developing a strong attachment to the place. One particular literary form, the mime, was developed in Syracuse by Sophron (c. 470–400 BC), whom Plato read with pleasure and approval. Indeed mime may have left a mark on the form of Plato's dialogues. Mime had its place in the growth of Attic comedy and certainly marked the idylls. Idyll XV is deeply indebted to it: the two women embody in their manner, speech and action the tradition initiated by Sophron: in them and other idylls mime itself adjusts to a changing world.[20]

In Alexandria Herodas, roughly a contemporary of the Alexandrian poets, developed the form, and eight of his mimes survive. He wrote of lower to low life in satirical iambs which could be made closely to resemble vulgar speech. His subjects too are vulgar: illicit forms of love, truculence, the charms of low life. Idyll XV is about as coarse as Theocritus gets, and even there the formality of the language provides a certain distancing. He does not resort to the iambic. The satire is less in incident and character than in the language, the distances it creates between how and what it says. Had Theocritus aspired to realism, he would have descended to the iambic. The mime tradition ensures, in Lesky's view, that he does not become over-fanciful. In Idyll II, the magic wheel and spells, the whole drama of a woman trying to charm her lover back, is based on Sophron's witch mime, a papyrus fragment of which survives. The kinds of magic are "low" and "popular"; there is corroboration for the techniques and spells in some surviving papyruses. Yet it does seem wilful to describe such vignettes as realistic, despite the exquisite and convincing detail.

The poet, it is generally thought, left Syracuse relatively early in his adult life. During the anarchic aftermath of the death of Agathocles, he may have made himself a refugee.[21] Wanting to return later, when the political situation stabilised, around 275 BC he invited Hiero II of Syracuse to be his patron.[22] Put another way, he wrote a magnificent begging letter with epinicean elements, Idyll XVI, commonly called "The Graces" or "The Charities," to which Hiero appears to have remained insensible. Poets and artists, Theocritus says, bring graces, and tyrants, as well as other potential patrons, for the most part turn them away from their doors. In this case the graces who go out begging are the poems themselves, poor waifs; unvalued, they return at evening, dejected. It is a plangent and wry conceit.

> Now the cry is, "Give me the money, keep the praise,"
> And each man cradles silver under his shirt,
> Jealous even of its tarnish, with greed in his eyes
> And a smug rebuff on his lips: "It's all in Homer";
> "The gods will look after poets—that's their job";
> "Charity begins at home"—and goes no further;
> "The poet I like is the one who costs me nothing."

The case for supporting poets is straightforward: material need (on their part) and transcendent need (on the patron's). "We remember even their horses" when they—the rich and powerful—commission wisely. As witness he calls Homer's poems into the box, proving by demonstration how they have memorialised men, and deftly evoking in a small space Homer's vast narratives. It is a strategy of miniaturisation which Callimachus would have praised, as he would the closing prayer for Hiero himself and for Syracuse. The poem was, sadly for Theocritus, its own reward: Hiero II got a free advertisement. When Theocritus delivers the much-quoted line "Homer is enough for everybody,"[23] his intention is ironic: the sufficiency of Homer is a tactic that those who do not wish to patronise a new poet, a new poem, deploy. It lets them off the hook.

From Syracuse the young poet went to southern Italy and then to Cos, to which he is deeply indebted. There he may have become a disciple of the native poet Philetas, whose works perished. Perhaps he knew and studied under Asclepiades of Samos, the epigrammatist. The *Vita* says, "he listened to Philetas and Asclepiades, whom he mentions."[24] The fact that he mentions them may be why the *Suda* suggests he studies with them. Did he also pursue medical studies under Praxagoras on Cos?[25] He certainly met Nicias of Miletus—poet and physician—who became a friend and earned three warm mentions in the poems. Indeed, Idyll XXVIII, called "The Distaff," talks about the journey from Syracuse[26] to Miletus, the poet carrying a Sicilian distaff as a gift for his friend's wife, Theugenis. He addresses the distaff as though it were a person, female, his travelling companion. The poem owes much to Sappho and Alcaeus.

The bucolic poems, judging from the plants Theocritus mentions, were composed on Cos, not in Alexandria or back in Sicily. Theocritus, Wells suggests, has two aspects: the Syracusan, which is bucolic, and the Alexandrian, which explores myth and legend. One revels in relative freedom; the other, while not cowering, feels the weight of asserted authority as a burden. Cos is the pivot, as it were. "Dorian in culture yet a part of Ptolemy's empire, Cos enabled him to hold the contradictory elements in his life more fully in play."[27] It is a persuasive, though a schematic, account.

Cos, just off the coast of Asia Minor, a whole archipelago north of Rhodes and two away from Egypt, was important to the Ptolemies. Ptolemy Philadelphus was born on the island; Cleopatra, a generation later, may have parked some of her treasures there. The island was "in the family," as it were, and to live on Cos was to be subject to Ptolemaic rule, though authority was attenuated by remoteness. When his poem to Hiero went unanswered, Theocritus wrote another kind of begging letter to Ptolemy Philadelphus, Idyll XVII, an encomium to the king and to his deified mother and father. Starched with respect, it is a kind of epinicean grovel. Addressing a patron who regards himself as divine and with whom, unlike Hiero II, the poet can share little in common, Theocritus does not make him*self* heard.

Where Hiero II remained silent, Ptolemy Philadelphus responded; or, in any event, Theocritus arrived in Alexandria and remained there long enough to become identified, with Callimachus and Apollonius, as one of the great Alexandrian poets. Lesky insists there was contact between Theocritus and Callimachus, and a close aesthetic understanding. It is reckoned that his verse was composed on Cos and in Alexandria, but the Doric dialect was a form of the speech of Syracuse, the idiom of all but Idyll XXII, which is in Ionic, and Idylls XXVIII, XXIX and XXX, which are in Aeolic. The issue of dialect arises with Callimachus as well: he was, after all, a scholar of dialects. Each dialect has different literary associations: a poet might signal generic or thematic elements, affiliations or shifts by choosing one dialect over another. Among the epinicean poets, the choice of dialect often relates to the provenance of the patron, but by the time of the Alexandrian poets, practical had given way to poetical considerations. The choice of dialect was part of the artifice of a poem. Dialect becomes an important element in a poem's *technique*.[28]

Theocritus' poems survive in relative abundance. "The most complete representative of our manuscript tradition," Lesky says, "the Ambrosianus 104 (15th/–16th c.), contains thirty *Idylls* and the *Epigrams*."[29] Papyrus fragments of a thirty-first idyll have been found, and a *Syrinx*, which, as a technopaignia, uses a variable prosody to imitate objects. Not all the idylls and epigrams that survive under his name were by Theocritus.[30] If we divide the attributable poems into categories, thirteen are bucolic (including in this category poems of a personal nature), three are mimes, four poems are based on legend and two are addresses to kings.[31] Athenaeus in *Scholars at Dinner* preserves a fragment of a *Berenice,* probably a tribute to Ptolemy Philadelphus' mother,[32] but the passage that detains Athenaeus is not about Berenice or her locks but about the sacred white-fish:

> And the fisherman prays, prays for a fortunate catch,
> For full nets, since from the sea's fields he draws his living,
> His trailing nets are ploughs, at evening he pays the goddess
> A sacrifice, the sacred white mullet, most sacred of all,
> So his nets will be bursting when, straining, he reclaims them
> Rich with the sea's abundance.

At his most original, Theocritus is a poet of love in a similar spirit to Alcaeus or Sappho, but in a different key. His Idyll XXIX, "Drinking Song," is written in Aeolic dialect as a kind of tribute to them. It envisages a traditional man-boy love, the kind that is usually sudden, passionate and brief, which might—the poem reflects—become a friendship and endure, without losing the ingredient of love. The foe to such relationships is inequality in love between the partners, and time. Theocritus starts with Alcaeus' words "Wine, my dear young fellow, and the truth."[33] The poet counsels a young man to find a single nest and stay in it rather than play around.

> No satisfaction? But it's there to find
> Where it went missing. Has pride made you blind?
> Keep faith with me.

The original lover, referred to as a slight acquaintance while the young man cruises from mate to mate, from bough to bough, calls him back. Youth briskly passes, a man grows old apace. In Idyll XXX, "The Fever," the poet is seriously overwhelmed by desire for a young man. He reminds himself that his hair is turning white, he counsels his very soul, and the soul replies: you cannot control love any more than an astronomer can count the stars. After all, even Zeus and Aphrodite succumbed to passion. The last three idylls are a suite for middle to old age.

Theocritus' poems reconcile by example the positions that Callimachus and Apollonius are assumed to hold. They integrate epic narrative with the particularity of focus that Callimachus advocates. The introduction of mime elements multiplies the poet's resources for irony, obliquity and indirection, without (as sometimes happens in Callimachus) obscuring the surface of the poem. The kinds of wholeness Theocritus achieves in his "little pictures" are satisfactory in ways that Callimachean aetiologies or protracted Apollonian narratives are not. They are tonally consistent in themselves, often wry or humorous, and when they have a satirical sub-text it is generally patent and unobscured. In prosody, narrative and allusive structure they have the strictly *poetic* wholeness we look for in vain in the other Alexandrians. And they are dramatic in cast, so that each poem balances voices, or makes consistent voices speak. Though we infer things about the poet from the poems, what matters at every stage is the staging, the poem itself.

The scale of such poetry is appealing; it also suggests that poets no longer dared—or this poet no longer dared—to tackle larger forms. He flatters and praises, wheedles and complains, but he will not climb Olympus or dive into the underworld; he will not wrestle with power but remains gentle; he will linger in imagined fields rather than throw up barricades and fight tyranny, or democracy, in the streets. When the people of Syracuse rose up in the aftermath of Agathocles' populist tyranny, Theocritus was sailing as fast as he could to Italy. He is not a conservative spirit but a poet bent on survival. His heart may belong to Syracuse, but the rest of him belongs somewhere more prosperous and stable. For poets in the third century BC, the committed political "belonging" of Theognis and Solon is over; a poet goes where there is demand for writing, where there are patrons, or libraries, or simply peace in which to write. He gains in personal freedom but loses the authority to speak on certain themes. To write—which is what the Alexandrian poet does—can seem an indulgence, given the Homeric precedent.

Theocritus has no time for the cock that crows in competition with Homer.[34] There is no rivalling, no emulation. Times have changed and poetry with them. It sings unaccompanied, it is written down on a sheet of papyrus or parchment, it addresses a creature who hardly existed in Homer's day, the reader. Knowing, as the Alexandrian poets did, what had come before, they knew too their limitations, how far they could and could not go. For Homer anything in the world was possible. The world having been traced, all future poems were transactions which included the first poems and poets. For a poet, understanding history entails understanding literary history, or the parts of it that survive. Late in a tradition, transactions with that history, unstable as it now appears, are half the labour of the writer and half the pleasure of the reader.

Notes

PREFACE

1. George Seferis (1900–1971), *Collected Poems* (London, 1982), p. 7.

INTRODUCTION

1. Seneca, *Letters to Lucilius,* discussing Sappho, testimonium 22.
2. *chalkanteros.*
3. *bibliolathas.*
4. *Deipnosophistae* dates from around AD 200.
5. Theodor Mommsen.
6. David Diringer, *The Book Before Printing: Ancient, Medieval and Oriental* (New York, 1982); facsimile of the book originally titled *The Hand-Produced Book* (London, 1952), p. 151.
7. Herodotus, *The Histories of Herodotus,* trans. George Rawlinson (London, 1942).
8. Oliver Taplin (ed.), *Literature in the Greek and Roman Worlds: A New Perspective* (Oxford, 2000), p. 6.
9. Later it was removed as spoils of war to Syria. The tradition of the upright inscribed black stone survives in the Muslim faith.
10. Translated by L. W. King (1910).
11. Diringer, op. cit., pp. 80, 109f.
12. *Charta* (Greek *khártes*) is another word for the pith of the papyrus plant, source of *chart, carta* and so on.
13. *kylindros.*
14. XIII, 69.
15. *Iliad* VI, 168f.
16. IX, ll. 522–5.
      dextra tenet ferrum, vacuam tenet altera ceram.
      incipit et dubitat, scribit damnatque tabellas,
      et notat et delet, mutat culpatque probatque
      inque vicem sumptas ponit positasque resumit.
17. Quintilian, *Institutio Oratoria* x, chapter 3.
18. Lionel Casson, *Libraries in the Ancient World* (Yale, 2001), p. 26.
19. See p. 307.
20. Albin Lesky, *A History of Greek Literature* (Methuen, 1966; Duckworth, 1996), chapter I: "The Transmission of Greek Literature."
21. c. 446–411 BC.

22. Diringer, op. cit., p. 233.

23. Casson, op. cit., pp. 22f.

24. Ibid., p. 29.

25. Ibid., p. 3.

26. Leslie Kurke, "The Strangeness of 'Song Culture': Archaic Greek Poetry," in Taplin, *Literature in the Greek and Roman Worlds: A New Perspective* (Oxford, 2000), p. 59.

27. Ibid., p. 60.

28. Ibid., p. 60.

29. Ibid., pp. 64–7.

30. *catalectic:* of verse, wanting a syllable in the last foot.

31. Barbara Hughes Fowler, *Archaic Greek Poetry: An Anthology* (Madison, Wisconsin, 1992).

32. Michael Grant, *The Rise of the Greeks* (London, 1997), p. 335 (notes 38, 40).

33. Robert Bridges (ed.), *The Spirit of Man* (London, 1916), item 421 and note 421 (pages unnumbered).

34. W. H. Auden, *The Portable Greek Reader* (New York, 1948), p. 4.

35. Grant, op. cit., pp. 14–16.

36. Ibid., p. 335.

37. Ibid., footnote.

38. Friedrich Nietzsche, "Homer's Contest" (1872), in *The Portable Nietzsche* (Harmondsworth, 1976), pp. 32ff.

39. Jacob Burckhardt, *The Greeks and Greek Civilization,* trans. Sheila Stern, ed. Oswyn Murray (London, 1998), p. xxiii.

40. Donald Davie (ed.), *The Psalms in English* (Harmondsworth, 1996), p. xxvi.

41. Roberto Calasso, *Literature and the Gods,* trans. Tim Parks (London, 2001), p. 3.

I ORPHEUS OF THRACE

1. Paul Cartledge, *Times Literary Supplement,* 31 December 1993, p. 9.

2. Diodorus Siculus, 3.67.2.

3. Pausanias, *Guide to Greece,* Volume I, *Central Greece,* translated by Peter Levi (Harmondsworth, 1971). Page 421 tells of the singing contests at Delphi. There were various winners. "But Orpheus they say gave himself such an air of grandeur over the mysteries and was so generally conceited that he and Musaeus who imitated him in everything refused to be tested by musical competition."

4. Guillaume Apollinaire, *Le Bestiaire ou Cortège d'Orphée,* illustrated with woodcuts by Raoul Dufy (Paris, 1911).

5. In 1463, Marsilio Ficino, commanded by Cosimo de' Medici, translated into Latin the rediscovered *Corpus Hermeticum.* This consisted of fourteen "books." He called them *Pimander* (Greek: "shepherd of men"?). *Pimander* lies behind the Renaissance revival of Neoplatonism.

6. Hermes Trismegistus and Thoth, the Egyptian god of knowledge, curing and divine will, are one and the same.

7. Samuel Butler's prose translation of the *Iliad* appeared in 1898, of the *Odyssey* in 1900.

8. W. K. C. Guthrie, *Orpheus and Greek Religion* (Princeton, 1993 edition), p. 30.

9. . . . and was unfaithful to him as he was to her, bearing other children to another god.

10. Virgil, *The Georgics,* trans. Robert Wells (Manchester, 1982), ll. 453–527.

11. Robert Graves, *The Greek Myths* (Manchester, 2001), § 82.

12. Guthrie, op. cit., p. 31.

13. Dante.

14. Virgil, op. cit., p. 93.

15. Ibid.

16. *Metamorphoses* X.

17. Calliope.

18. John Milton, "Lycidas," ll. 58–63.

19. Thomas Taylor (1768–1835), *A Dissertation on the Life and Theology of Orpheus:* "The former part of this fable is thus excellently explained by Proclus in his commentaries (or rather fragments of commentaries) on Plato's *Republic*."

20. Herus Pamphilius, in Plato, says the soul of Orpheus, which was due to transmigrate into another body at his death, chose to be a swan rather than a man so as not to have to be born of a woman, hating the whole sex as a result of their fatal attentions.

21. Pausanias suggests that when Eurydice died, having failed to revive her, he took his own life, and that nightingales nested on his tomb, raising their young whose melody surpassed that of every other creature.

22. Taylor, op. cit. Diogenes was of this opinion and composed an epitaph for his master: "Here, by the Muses placed, with golden lyre, / Great Orpheus rests; destroy'd by heavenly fire."

23. Pausanias, Volume I, op. cit., pp. 373–4.

24. Apollonius of Rhodes (Apollonios Rhodios), *Argonautika*, trans. Peter Green (Berkeley, 1997), Book I, ll. 22ff.

25. Ibid., ll. 496–518.

26. Ibid., ll. 540f.

27. Apollonius, op. cit., Book II, ll. 674ff.

28. Ibid., ll. 705ff.

29. Grant, op. cit., p. 303.

30. Pausanias, Volume I, op. cit., pp. 373–4.

31. Guthrie, op. cit., p. 11. Alexis, c. 372–c. 270 BC, from southern Italy, lived in Athens. He is said to have written 245 plays and crossed the bridge from Middle to New Comedy. He deployed mythological and contemporary plots and influenced the Roman playwright Plautus.

32. At the end of the list Alexis introduces, after the epic poets, tragedians and writers of religious explications, a comic writer almost his contemporary, a satirist and a representative of the lower orders of literature; the reductive irony of his inclusion was clear to any play-goer of the time.

33. Guthrie, op. cit., p. xxiv.

34. "wooden image or idol."

35. Herodotus, op. cit.

36. Grant, op. cit., p. 229.

37. Onomacritos later regained favour, when Athens had need again of his skills in deception and persuasion.

38. A mythical religious poet, Olen developed a cult. Delian hymns are attributed to him. Pausanias, Volume I (op. cit., p. 416), tells how he was celebrated. To Phemonoe, "the greatest and most universal glory belongs": "she was the god's first

prophetess and the first to sing the hexameter. But a woman of the district called Boio wrote a hymn for Delphi saying Olen and the remote northerners came and founded the oracle of the god, and it was Olen who first prophesied and first sang the hexameter." Finally she names Olen: "Phoibos' first interpreter, / first singing carpenter of ancient verse." Peter Levi comments, "Boio is a very obscure lady. If she was later than the earliest forgeries or attributions to Olen, she was Hellenistic. Clement of Alexandria says the prophetic women were called Boio, Hippo, and Manto."

39. Pamphos is perhaps the first of the hymn writers, a legendary figure like the others, and a magnet for forgeries. Pausanias claims he was the first to write a hymn to the Graces.

40. Pausanias, Volume I, op. cit., p. 72: "When Demetrios had freed Athens from dictatorship, immediately after the flight of Lachares he kept control of Piraeus, and later after some military success he brought a garrison into the city itself, and fortified what they call the Museum."

41. Charles Boer, *The Homeric Hymns* (Athens, Ohio, 1970).

42. Ibid., p. 181.

43. Taylor, op. cit.

44. Ibid.: "the Orphic method of instruction consists in signifying divine concerns by symbols alone."

45. The crossing where three roads meet.

46. Guthrie, op. cit., p. xxxvii.

47. Roy MacLeod (ed.), *The Library of Alexandria* (London, 2000): Ficino, "De Immort. Anim., XVII.i.386," quoted by Patricia Cannon Johnson in "The Neoplatonists and the Mystery Schools of the Mediterranean," p. 145.

48. From Apollinaire's own notes on the *Bestiaire*.

II THE LEGEND POETS

1. He is not to be confused with his contemporary the lyric poet Poseidippus of Pella, a contributor to the Greek Anthology.

2. Paul Zanker, *The Mask of Socrates,* trans. Alan Shapiro (Berkeley, 1995), p. 137f.

3. Pausanias, Volume I, op. cit., p. 184, note 135.

4. Terpander was a musician of Lesbos who probably flourished in the first half of the seventh century BC. He was probably adopted by Sparta, founded the Spartan school of music, replacing the four- with the seven-string lyre. He may have invented (or popularised) Aeolian and Boeotian modes. He composed *nomes* and wrote lyrical songs.

5. Elaine Feinstein (ed.), *After Pushkin* (Manchester, 1999), p. 83.

6. Grant, op. cit., p. 87.

7. C. M. Bowra, *Greek Lyric Poetry: From Alcman to Simonides* (Oxford, 1961), p. 82.

8. The Greek choral lyric was originally connected with Dionysus worship, sung by *kuklios choros,* or a circular choir, of about fifty singers. The chorus may have been dressed as satyrs. The etymology is uncertain: probably a revel song started by a leader (*exarcos*) of a band of revellers using traditional or improvised language, answered by refrain. It probably started in Phrygia and came to Greece with Dionysus worship. Arion made it a literary form.

9. Grant, op. cit., adduces Herodotus (note 22, p. 341) and says, "*Sudas,* s.v., dubiously ascribes the introduction of spoken verses to Arion. There was also a legend that he invented the *paean* (in honour of Apollo); and a statement that he presented the first tragic drama was ascribed to Solon (Johannes Diaconus, *Commentary on Hermogenes*)."

10. Graves, op. cit.

11. Ezra Pound, *Selected Poems* (London, 1975), p. 80.

12. Pausanias, Volume I, op. cit., p. 43.

13. Peter Levi, op. cit., notes (see page 63): "Onomacritos collected in Athens the oracles attributed to Musaeus and Orpheus, some of which he wrote himself. He was exiled for this by the dictator Hipparchos and ran away to Persia."

14. Pausanias, Volume I, op. cit., p. 429.

15. Ibid., p. 63.

16. Ibid., p. 72.

17. Ibid., p. 421.

18. Ibid., p. 415.

19. Herodotus, op. cit.

20. See *Iliad* II, ll. 590–600.

III HOMER

1. Lewis Carroll, *Alice in Wonderland.*

2. Ford Madox Ford, *The March of Literature* (London, 1947), p. 108. The seven birthplaces were Smyrna, Rhodes, Colophon, Salamis, Chios, Argos and Athens.

3. Hugh G. Evelyn-White, *Hesiod, Homeric Hymns, Epic Cycle, Homerica* (London, 1914), p. 533: *Amphiarau Exelasis* (pseudo-Herodotus "Life of Homer").

4. See this volume, chapter XXV, note 23.

5. Oliver Taplin, "Homer," in John Boardman, Jasper Griffin and Oswyn Murray (eds.), *The Oxford History of Greece and the Hellenistic World* (Oxford, 1986).

6. See also Charles Boer, *The Homeric Hymns* (Athens, Ohio, 1970), for a modern version, dedicated to Charles Olson:

> Remember me later on,
> whenever someone of the men of earth
> finds himself here, a stranger
> who has suffered a lot,
> and he says to you, "O girls, who is the sweetest man
> that comes here
> with his songs for you
> who is it
> that pleases you most?"
> Then, all together, answer him: "A blind man,
> he lives in rocky Chios,
> and all his songs will still be the best
> at the end of time."

7. Italo Calvino, "The Odysseys Within the *Odyssey,*" *Why Read the Classics* (London, 1999), has the following monitory aside: "(It is worth registering here, since it will recur, that the word for 'lord' is *basileus,* often mistranslated as 'king,' which is what

it meant in later Greek.)" Liddell and Scott (*Greek-English Lexicon,* Oxford, 1889) do not reflect this evolution in meaning very clearly, and an anachronistic sense of the word's meaning produces a distorted image in the reader's mind.

8. Burckhardt, op. cit., p. 51. See also *Iliad* XI, l. 807, and *Odyssey* VIII, l. 4.

9. Burckhardt, op. cit., p. 51.

10. The name "Demodocus" might be translated "he who is loved by the people."

11. Aristotle, *Poetics.*

12. See pp. 114–16, this volume, for an account.

13. Lesky, op. cit., pp. 15, 40.

14. Also called Leucas, where Sappho would later commit suicide, according to legend, throwing herself from a now eponymous promontory.

15. Evelyn-Williams, op. cit., p. 597.

16. Pausanias, Volume I, op. cit., p. 467.

17. Zanker, op. cit., p. 16.

18. Ibid., p. 164.

19. On Eratosthenes, see page 306, this volume.

20. Lesky, op. cit., p. 74.

21. Samuel Butler, *Notebooks* (London, 1902), p. 196.

22. Zanker, op. cit., p. 161.

23. Richard Bentley, 1662–1742, keeper of the King's Library (1694), controversial master of Trinity College, Cambridge.

24. On the west coast of Asia Minor, Ionians pushed north, overrunning Aeolic areas such as Smyrna. In the nineteenth century a theory that the poems were composed in Ionic, then revised into Aeolic, made the scholar August Fick translate the poem "back into" Ionic. This revealed that there were places where equivalences could be found, others where Ionic had elements unavailable in Aeolic. We lack knowledge of the dialects at the time(s) of composition: conclusions are tentative. Often in close proximity elements from different dialects and different "periods" are used, without a sense of relative geographical or temporal sources. Thus the new flowed into the old, enhancing and preserving it.

25. Oliver Taplin (ed.), *Literature in the Greek and Roman Worlds: A New Perspective* (Oxford, 2000).

26. Ibid., p. 31.

27. Samuel Johnson, *Lives of the English Poets* (London, 1975), pp. 223f.

28. J. V. Luce, *Celebrating Homer's Landscapes: Troy and Ithaca Revisited* (New Haven, 1998), p. 176.

29. Lesky, op. cit., p. 58.

30. Johnson, op. cit., p. 250, "Dryden."

31. Gregory Nagy, "Reading Bakhtin Reading the Classics: Ten Quotes from Bakhtin's 'Epic and Novel,'" in R. Bracht Branham, *Bakhtin and the Classics* (Northwestern, 2002), pp. 80–2.

32. The "planet" may draw, commentators say, on "the vivid description of Herschel's discovery of the planet Uranus in John Bonnycastle's *Introduction to Astronomy* given to Keats as a school prize in 1811." This was five or six years before he wrote "On First Looking into Chapman's Homer."

33. Auden, op. cit., p. 20.

34. *Shame and Necessity* (University of California Press, Berkeley; *Times Literary Supplement,* 23 April 1993).

35. *Iliad* VI, l. 208, and XI, l. 784.

36. Ford, op. cit., p. 107, expresses a conventional, anachronistic view of the poem that reflects academic and critical orthodoxies of his day: "the work of Homer is at once a religion, a code of ethics, a map of chivalry, of health, domestic pursuits and of metaphysics."

37. Luce, op. cit., p. 65.

38. Lesky, op. cit., p. 19.

39. Luce, op. cit., pp. 70f.

40. Taplin, *Literature in the Greek and Roman Worlds,* p. 74.

41. Luce, op. cit., 2.

42. Luce, op. cit., p. 3.

43. Ibid., p. 9.

44. Ibid., p. 38: Alexander the Great is said to have had the *Iliad* always at hand during his campaigns, to read for instruction or consolation.

45. Casson, op. cit., p. 17.

46. Burckhardt, op. cit., 65.

47. Taplin, op. cit., p. 65.

48. George Steiner, "From Caxton to Omeros," *Times Literary Supplement,* 27 August 1993, text of the *TLS* Lecture delivered in May of that year at the Hay-on-Wye festival. Steiner does not acknowlege here the fact that the manufacture of papyrus was a major industry in Egypt long before the Greeks sought to stabilise the text of Homer, and that there was no material bar to the setting down of the poems even two, three or more centuries before they are thought to have been set down.

49. Gregory Nagy, *The Best of the Achaeans: Concepts of the Hero in Archaic Greek Poetry* (Johns Hopkins, 1979, 1999), §3.

50. Ibid., §§5–7: "These theoretical underpinnings have fostered a general attitude of literal mindedness in my approach to the concept of the hero in archaic Greek poetry . . . I will as a policy assume that the application of an epithet—whether it be fixed or particularised—is thematically appropriate as well as traditional. Moreover, my working assumption extends from the usage of epithets in particular to the usage of words in general: the entire formula, to repeat, is an accurate response to the requirements of traditional theme. I stress this point now in order to prepare the reader for the oncoming plethora of transliterated Greek words that I will be continually citing in my discussion of central poetic themes. My reliance on key words in context cannot be dismissed as a reductive and oversimplified method of delving into the thematic complexities of archaic Greek poetry, if indeed the words themselves are functioning elements of an integral formulaic system inherited precisely for the purpose of actively expressing these complexities. The words should not be viewed merely as random vocabulary that passively reflects the themes sought by the poet. The semantic range of a key word in context can be expected to be as subtle and complex as the poetry in which it is encased."

51. Plato, *Ion,* translated by Benjamin Jowett.

52. *Iliad* II, l. 558.

53. Herodotus, op. cit., VII, 6.

54. The epithet is familiar from the Homeric Hymns.

55. Herodotus, op. cit., V, 58.

56. Casson, op. cit., p. 19.

57. Ibid., pp. 22f.

58. Taplin, "Homer."
59. Lesky, op. cit., p. 77.

IV THE HOMERIC APOCRYPHA

 1. Lesky, op. cit., p. 84.
 2. I follow the order of Hugh G. Evelyn-White, op. cit.
 3. Cronus' only daughter. He ate her first and vomited her up last.
 4. Thus, a withering sacred tree means a dying nymph.
 5. Oar locks.
 6. *Epigrams;* see Evelyn-White, op. cit., p. xxxix.
 7. Op cit., fr 2.
 8. Lesky, op. cit., p. 89.
 9. See *Iliad* VII, l. 213a, editorially disputed.
10. Thomas Parnell (1679–1718), "Homer's Battle of the Frogs and Mice with the Remarks of Zoilus" (1917).

V THE *ILIAD* AND THE *ODYSSEY*

 1. Quoted by Matthew Arnold in "On Translating Homer," *Selected Criticism,* edited by Christopher Ricks (New York, 1972), p. 200.
 2. Every reader is struck by the amount of physical observation in Homer's poems and how nuanced each speech is. The poems must have been heard many times; each time (as when we see a play by Shakespeare) new elements emerge, unnoticed before, in tone, setting, action or inaction. This is language fully charged. There are two approaches to its translation: the first straightforward, to render the sense as directly as possible, in workmanlike verse or in prose; the other to try to find English equivalents for the poetic effects, to choreograph by means of metre, rhyme or enjambement, to *poeticise*. With longer poems, the less poetic the translation, the better. If a reader dips in, reading a scene here, a description there, a deliberately poetic translation tells more about the texture of language than a prose version whose responsibility is to the whole poem. "Poetic" translations are tedious *in extenso*: read aloud, they wear out patience. Butler's prose version is dependably adequate. It may not fly, but it never limps.
 3. In the *Sack of Troy* it is Odysseus who slays her son, Astyanax.
 4. Samuel Butler, *Iliad* (London, 1898): "As he held the scales by the middle, the doom of Hector fell down deep into the house of Hades—and then Phoebus Apollo left him" (xxii).
 5. Ford, op. cit., p. 106.
 6. Taplin, *Literature in the Greek and Roman Worlds*, pp. 78–9.
 7. Taplin, "Homer."
 8. Oliver Taplin, "The Spring of the Muses: Homer and Related Poetry," in Taplin (ed.), *Literature in the Greek and Roman Worlds*, p. 23.
 9. Butler *Iliad*.
10. Ibid.
11. *Iliad* VIII, ll. 73–4.

12. *Iliad* VIII, l. 261.

13. Burckhardt, op. cit.

14. Taplin, *Literature in the Greek and Roman Worlds,* p. 49.

15. Burckhardt, op. cit., p. 137.

16. Lesky, op. cit., p. 37.

17. Butler, *Notebooks,* p. 198.

18. Lesky, op. cit., p. 1.

19. The *coronis* could be given an illustrative shape—a bird for example.

20. Taplin, "Homer," p. 74.

21. Lesky, op. cit., pp. 79ff.

22. Ibid., p. 43.

23. See *Iliad* IX.

24. Evelyn-White, op. cit.

25. S. H. Butcher translation (Aristotle, *Poetics,* New York, 1955).

26. They are assumed to be eighth century.

27. Evelyn-White, fr 22.

28. Taplin, *Literature in the Greek and Roman Worlds,* p. 51, cites Walter Burkert.

29. Collection in the Ruhr-Universität, Bochum.

30. Lillian E. Doherty, *Siren Songs: Gender, Audience, and Narrators in the Odyssey* (1995).

31. Lesky, op. cit., p. 77.

32. Taplin, op. cit., p. 53.

33. Elements in the *Iliad* are extraneous and contradictory. It is the ninth year of the Trojan War. The famous Catalogue of Ships may have been imported from another poem in the cycle. Certainly, so late in the day, Helen telling Priam the names of the Greek warriors is useful to us as auditors but in terms of plausible realism it does not score very high. There are other odd elements, some structural, some lapses of memory, where a character is dead and then appears alive and fighting, or lamenting, later on.

34. Jacqueline de Romilly, *A Short History of Greek Literature* (Chicago, 1985).

35. Lesky, op. cit. details some awkwardness and inconsistencies in the *Odyssey*. There is a problem of the "Telemachiad" itself, the strange repetition—what Romilly calls "Doublets"—of the council of the gods in I and IV, Poseidon's intermittent, inconsistent rage. There are many smaller and larger problems in narrative structure, inconsistencies: one thing promised, another delivered. The *nekyia* (visit to the dead) probably includes archaic material, interpolation, etc. These problems were clear to some ancient editors, e.g., Aristarchus, Aristophanes of Byzantium.

36. Ibid., p. 52.

37. Taplin, "Homer," p. 72.

38. Ibid., p. 73.

39. Ibid., p. 73.

40. He insists kings and noble *basilees* are generally shown in a bad light, and the lay people, the *laos* or *demos,* are always present and not despised (though they are not individuated either).

41. Luce, op. cit., p. 22.

42. Ibid., p. 49.

43. Lesky, op. cit., p. 70.

44. James Morrison, *Homeric Misdirection: False Predictions in the* Iliad (Michigan, 1994).

45. Lesky, op. cit., p. 32.

46. Burckhardt, op. cit., p. 145, insists on comic effects in *Iliad* III, l. 437, for example. Humour, directness, guilelessness in *Odyssey* IV, ll. 100–3, 190–5, 212–7.

47. See John Peradotto's "Bakhtin, Milman Parry, and the Problem of Homeric Originality," in R. Bracht Banham (ed.), *Bakhtin and the Classics* (Evanston, 2002), where he considers Weber, Durkheim, Lévy-Bruhl and the syntheses effected by Bakhtin with his notions of heteroglossia, centripetal and centrifugal language, and the multiple dialogue each text represents: a character speaking in a poem, to whom, how many, about what; and the poem speaking to reader/auditor, where, why. Language is conducting a number of negotiations at any one time. He refers us to Peter Rose's historicist-Marxist reading, *Sons of God, Children of Earth: Ideology and Literary Form in Ancient Greece* (Ithaca, 1992), which sees the *Iliad* as torn between a centripetal linguistic ideology, endorsing forms of kingship, and social relation and centrifugal ideology, critical of them.

48. Lesky, op. cit., p. 39.

49. Taplin, "Homer."

50. Calvino, op. cit.

51. Luce, op. cit., p. 37.

VI HESIOD

1. Evelyn-White, op. cit., test (testimonium) 47 (j), Simonides' apophthegms.

2. *aoidos* is "poet-singer" (used by Hesiod and Homer).

3. Pausanias, Volume I, op. cit., IX, l. 29, "In my time one tower and nothing more was left of Askre to remember it by."

4. Hesiod, *Works and Days* and *Theogony,* translated by Stanley Lombardo, introduction by Robert Lamberton (Indianapolis, 1993), p. 2.

5. Mary R. Lefkowitz, *The Lives of the Greek Poets* (London, 1981), p. 6, p. 64.

6. I say "firmly," but Pausanias, Volume I, p. 365, says, ". . . I know Hesiod or the forger of Hesiod's *Theogony* writes that Chaos was born first, then Earth and Hell and Love."

7. Evelyn-White, op. cit., p. 48, ll. 636f.

8. Legend, keen to make divine associations, gives him an exalted mother. "Now some say that he [Homer] was earlier than Hesiod, others that he was younger and akin to him. They give his descent thus: Apollo and Arethusa, daughter of Poseidon, had a son Linus, to whom was born Pierus. From Pierus and the nymph Methone sprang Oeager; and from Oeager and Calliope, Orpheus; from Orpheus, Dres; and from him, Eucles. The descent is continued through Iadmonides, Philoterpes, Euphemus, Epiphrades and Melanopus, who had sons Dius and Apelles. Dius by Pycimede, the daughter of Apollo had two sons, Hesiod and Perses; while Apelles begot Maeon, who was the father of Homer by a daughter of the River Meles" (Evelyn-White, op. cit., "The Contest of Homer and Hesiod ").

9. Hesiod makes a joke about Chalcis, Robert Lamberton in *Hesiod* (New Haven, 1988), points out: he says in *Works and Days* (ll. 648–59) that his one experience of the sea is crossing the straits between Aulis and Chalcis (about a hundred metres, the closest point between the Boeotian mainland and Euboea), hardly a maritime achievement.

10. Hesiod, op. cit., p. 43, ll. 726ff.

11. Evelyn-White, op. cit., *Theogony,* ll. 31–4.

12. T. F. Higham and C. M. Bowra (eds.), *The Oxford Book of Greek Verse in Translation* (Oxford, 1938), Jack Lindsay's translation.

13. Pausanias, Volume I, op. cit., p. 375.

14. Hesiod, op. cit., p. 23, ll. 21–24.

15. Friedrich Nietzsche, "Homer on Competition," *The Portable Nietzsche* (Harmondsworth, 1976).

16. Hesiod, op. cit., p. 146, ll. 806–811.

17. Ibid., p. 46, ll. 812f.

18. Ibid., p. 32, ll. 324–335.

19. Pausanias, IX (30).

20. Lamberton, op. cit., p. 16.

21. Hesiod, op. cit., p. 63, ll. 66ff.

22. Ibid., p. 64, 81ff.

23. *Odyssey* XI, l. 631.

24. Hesiod, op. cit., 97–103: l. 100.

25. Taplin, *Literature in the Greek and Roman Worlds,* p. 31.

26. Hesiod, op. cit., p. 77.

27. Hesiod, op. cit., p. 68, ll. 243f.

28. Pausanias, Volume I, op. cit., p. 368,: "Hesiod being a country-mannered man who disliked moving about."

29. Lines 126–133, 339–344.

30. Evelyn-White, op. cit., pp. 586–7.

31. Tzetzes, in his *Life of Hesiod,* suggest that Phegeus' daughter was Ctimene, and that Hesiod begot upon her (possibly by rape) the poet Stesichorus.

32. In his notes to Pausanias, Volume I, op. cit., p. 327.

33. Pausanias, IX, 31, p. 376.

VII ARCHILOCHUS OF PAROS

1. fragment 247, in Gay Davenport, *Archilochus Sappho Alkman* (Los Angeles, 1980), p. 216.

2. fr 98.

3. fr 116.

4. Herodotus, op. cit, p. 378.

5. fr 102.

6. Shrine or chapel dedicated to a demigod or exalted mortal.

7. Pausanias, *Description of Greece,* translated by W. H. S. Jones, and H. A. Ormerod (London, 1918): "The other part of the picture, the one on the left, shows Odysseus, who has descended into what is called Hades to inquire of the soul of Teiresias about his safe return home. The objects depicted are as follow. There is water like a river, clearly intended for Acheron, with reeds growing in it; the forms of the fishes appear so dim that you will take them to be shadows rather than fish. On the river is a boat, with the ferryman at the oars. Polygnotus followed, I think, the poem called the *Minyad.* For in this poem occur lines referring to Theseus and Peirithous ... Then the boat on which embark the dead, that the old Ferryman,

Charon, used to steer, they found not within its moorings. For this reason then Polygnotus too painted Charon as a man well stricken in years. Those on board the boat are not altogether distinguished. Tellis appears as a youth in years, and Cleoboea as still a maiden, holding on her knees a chest such as they are wont to make for Demeter. All I heard about Tellis was that Archilochus the poet was his grandson, while as for Cleoboea, they say that she was the first to bring the orgies of Demeter to Thasos from Paros (p. 185).

8. Herodotus, op. cit., p. 382.
9. Employed in looking after livestock, from bullocks to cows and heifers.
10. *Historia Ecclesiastica Gentis Anglorum.*
11. test 3, the Inscription of Mnesiepes.
12. fr 48.
13. fr 197.
14. fr 196.
15. fr 41.
16. Herodotus, op. cit., calls the Thracians "barbarians"; he also suggests that the Thracians had a custom that wives were held in common, so that men would not fall out. "The Agathyrsi are a race of men, very luxurious, and very fond of wearing gold on their persons. They have wives in common, that so they may be all brothers, and, as members of one family, may neither envy nor hate one another. In other respects their customs approach nearly to those of the Thracians."
17. fr 42. West adds that she was "engaged too from behind," though the Greek does not quite say this.
18. fr 45.
19. Book XI, ll. 596 ff.
20. *Therapon*: implies free service rather than enslavement or employment, but also subordination; in Homer it means "companion in arms": Patroclus is the *companion in arms* or *esquire* of Achilles. Later the word came to mean, simply, servant.
21. fr 201.
22. Davenport made two versions, 183 in his numbering.
23. fr 114.
24. fr 196a (Davenport: 18).
25. Aristotle, *Poetics* (translation by S. H. Butcher).
26. Douglas E. Gerber, *Greek Iambic Poetry* (Cambridge, Massachusetts, 1999), p. 1; also p. 151, fr 111.
27. *Pythian* II, ll. 54–6.
28. C. M. Bowra, *Landmarks in Greek Literature* (London, 1970). Bowra's translation.

VIII ALCMAN OF SARDIS

1. David A. Campbell, *Greek Lyric Poetry II* (Cambridge, Massachusetts, 1988), fr 26: "Male halcyons are called ceryli. When they become weak from old age and are no longer able to fly, the females carry them, taking them on their wings. What Alcman says is connected with this: weak from old age and unable to whirl about with the choirs and the girls . . ." From Antigonus of Carystus (sculptor, writer on art, biographer, fl. 240 BC), *Marvels*.
2. L. H. Jeffrey, *Archaic Greece: The City-States* (London, 1976), pp. 120f.

3. Ibid., pp. 120f.

4. Richmond Lattimore, *Greek Lyrics* (Chicago, 1960), p. 36. Fr 41 (Loeb translation) reads, "for when weighed against the steel fine lyre-playing tips the scales."

5. Athenaeus 15. 678b: "According to Sosibios in *On Sacrifices,* there is a kind of garland at Sparta, made of palm leaves, and known nowadays as *psilinos.* These garlands, he says, are worn in memory of the victory at Thyrea by the leaders of the choruses which dance on the festival of that victory, which coincides with the *Gymnopaideiai,* or 'Feast of Naked Youths.' These choruses are three in number, the youths in front, the old men on the right, and the men on the left; and they dance naked, singing songs by Thaletas and Alcman and the paeans of the Laconian Dionysodotos."

6. test 22.

7. Guy Davenport, *Seven Greeks* (New York, 1995), p. 14.

8. Bowra, *Greek Lyric Poetry,* p. 12.

9. fr 1.

10. Bowra, op. cit., p. 13.

11. Kurke, op. cit., pp. 79ff.

12. Kurke, op. cit., p. 81.

13. "Hymns to boys"; see also p. 214, this volume.

14. Kurke, op. cit., p. 83.

15. Ibid.

16. fr 59.

17. Bowra, op. cit., pp. 31–3.

18. Ibid., p. 64.

19. Grant, op. cit.

20. Plutarch, *On Sparta,* trans. Richard J. A. Talbert (Harmondsworth, 1988), p. 71.

21. Ibid., p. 152.

22. Horace, *Odes,* iii ii 13, "It is sweet and proper to die for the fatherland."

23. From Wilfred Owen's "Dulce Et Decorum Est."

> . . . If in some smothering dreams you too could pace
> Behind the wagon that we flung him in,
> And watch the white eyes writhing in his face . . .
> If you could hear, at every jolt, the blood
> Come gargling from the froth-corrupted lungs . . .
> My friend, you would not tell with such high zest
> To children ardent for some desperate glory,
> The old lie: *Dulce et decorum est*
> *Pro patria mori.*

24. David Mulroy, *Early Greek Lyric Poetry* (Ann Arbor, 1992).

25. Bowra, *Greek Lyric Poetry,* p. 5.

26. Bowra, op. cit., p. 11.

27. Mulroy, op. cit., p. 55.

28. Bowra, op. cit., p. 17, fr 12.

29. Ibid., p. 72.

30. fr 3.

31. fr 56, from Athenaeus, *Scholars at Dinner.*

32. fr 92.

33. fr 94.
34. fr 19.
35. fr 99.
36. fr 17.
37. fr 19.
38. test 1.
39. fr 67.
40. Bowra, op. cit., p. 2.
41. Alcman, fr 89.
42. fr 39.
43. fr 1: "Choir-leader—if I may speak—I am myself only a girl screeching pointlessly, an owl from a rafter; but even so I long to please Aotis most of all, for she proved the healer of our sufferings."
44. fr 40.
45. fr 89.
46. fr 82.
47. fr 76 (*Iliad* XIX, ll. 404ff.).
48. fr 90.
49. The poet Hilda Doolittle (1886–1961).
50. Pausanias, Volume II, op. cit., p. 51.
51. fr 3.

IX   MIMNERMUS OF COLOPHON

1. Mulroy, op. cit., p. 18.
2. Lesky, op. cit., p. 855.
3. M. L. West on fr 20 comments on the total solar eclipse ("more likely that of 6 April 648 than that of 28 May 585"). Probably floruit 632–629.
4. Hipponax 153.
5. Bowra, op. cit., p. 90; lines 5–10, West and Mulroy translate "vessel" as "couch."
6. *Plus in amore valet Mimnermi versus Homero* (Propertius 1.9.11).
7. fr 1.
8. Archibald Allen, *The Fragments of Mimnermus: Text and Commentary*. Palingenesia 44 (Stuttgart, 1993), p. 60.
9. Mulroy, op. cit., p. 45.
10. Most of the longer passages (frs 1–5, 8, 14 [24–25]).
11. Allen, op. cit., p. 18.
12. Kurke, op. cit., p. 72.
13. Bowra, op. cit., p. 161.
14. C. M. Bowra, *Landmarks in Greek Literature,* p. 76.
15. M. L. West, *Greek Lyric Poetry* (Oxford, 1993), p. 30, fr 14.

X   SEMONIDES OF AMORGOS

1. Peter Jay (ed.), *The Greek Anthology* (Harmondsworth, 1973); Jay's translation, p. 37.
2. Bowra, *Landmarks in Greek Literature,* p. 70.
3. Douglas E. Gerber, *Greek Iambic Poetry* (Cambridge, Mass., 1999), p. 323, fr 17.

4. Ibid., p. 327, fr 20.

5. Some regard the poem as a fragment, with a lost continuation of indeterminate length, but given the completeness of the argument, if elements are missing, they may be minor.

6. B. C. Hubbard, "Elemental Psychology and the Date of Semonides of Amorgos," *American Journal of Philology* 115, 2 (1994), pp. 175–97: Hubbard and others insist that Semonides is in fact sixth century.

7. West, op. cit., fr 7; Hesiod, *Theogony,* 535–616, *Works and Days,* 42–105.

8. Some attribute the poem to Simonides of Cos.

9. Gerber, op. cit., p. 341, fr 43. The passage may refer to Simonides and is much disputed.

10. Bowra, *Landmarks in Greek Literature,* p. 70.

11. Gerber, op. cit., p. 299.

12. Bowra, op. cit., p. 70.

13. Lesky, op. cit., p. 154.

14. Bowra, *Greek Lyric Poetry,* p. 14.

15. See pages 143–44.

16. fr (11D) See West, op. cit., 13.

17. His conclusion is beautifully condescending: "I have already apologised for this author's want of delicacy, and must further premise, that the following satire affects only some of the lower part of the sex, and not those who have been refined by a polite education, which was not so common in the age of this poet."

18. West, op. cit.

19. Diane Arnson Svarlien writes: "This is a problematic line. The Greek of lines 41–42 seems to mean, 'Such a woman is most of all like that [the sea] in temperament (*orgē*); but the sea has a different appearance (*phyē*).' So West, in his 1993 verse translation: 'That's what this kind of woman's like—in mood, / I mean; there's no resemblance in her looks!' *Orgēn* stands at the beginning of line 42, prominently, in enjambement, followed immediately by *phyēn de;* it certainly looks as if the poet is drawing a contrast between inward disposition and outward form. But for the poet to cap his description of the sea-woman with, 'But a large body of salt water is unlike a woman in physical appearance!' seems bizarrely inept."

20. Gerber, op. cit., p. 329, fr 23.

21. Ibid., p. 331, fr 25.

XI ALCAEUS OF MYTILENE

1. Tantalus.

2. E. Lobel and D. L. Page, *Poetarum Lesbiorum Fragmenta* (Oxford, 1995).

3. Graves, op. cit.: "mighty one," the original name of Heracles.

4. "fragments where it is uncertain which is the author."

5. Denis Ferry, *Times Literary Supplement,* 28 April 2000.

6. test 15.

7. Sons of Zeus, brothers of Helen, the so-called Dioscuri.

8. fr 50.

9. Strabo: test 1.

10. *Sic.*

11. fr 350.

12. fr 426.

13. Herodotus, op. cit., "War accordingly continued, with many and various incidents, whereof the following was one. In a battle which was gained by the Athenians, the poet Alcaeus took to flight, and saved himself, but lost his arms, which fell into the hands of the conquerors. They hung them up in the temple of Minerva at Sigeum; and Alcaeus made a poem, describing his misadventure to his friend Melanippus, and sent it to him at Mytilene. The Mytileneans and Athenians were reconciled by Periander, the son of Cypselus, who was chosen by both parties as arbiter—he decided that they should each retain that of which they were at the time possessed; and Sigeum passed in this way under the dominion of Athens."

14. fr 208.

15. test 4.

16. See Betty Radice, "The Sayings of the Seven Sages of Greece," in *The Translator's Art* (Harmondsworth, 1987).

17. fr 432.

18. fr 348.

19. fr 429.

20. test 20.

21. test 21.

22. test 23.

23. test 7.

24. sense uncertain.

25. fr 38a.

26. fr 45.

27. fr 50.

28. fr 129.

29. Peleus, who married Thetis and fathered Achilles.

30. fr 42.

31. fr 130b.

32. fr 140.

33. fr 283.

34. fr 298.

35. fr 332.

36. fr 335.

37. fr 330.

38. fr 346.

39. fr 338.

40. fr 347a.

41. fr 358.

42. fr 406.

43. fr 366.

44. fr 333.

45. fr 341.

46. fr 360.

47. fr 364.

48. fr 434.

49. Alexandrian scholar, c. 257–180 BC.
50. fr 10b.
51. test 11.
52. fr 347b.
53. fr 307c.
54. Cf. *Odyssey* XI, ll. 238ff.

XII SAPPHO OF ERESSUS

1. Administrator.
2. "Some say there are nine Muses: how careless! Look—Sappho of Lesbos is the tenth!" test 60.
3. Zanker, op. cit., p. 26.
4. test fr 1.
5. Athenaeus, *Scholars at Dinner,* test 38, attributes the statement to Menaechmus: the *pectis,* Menaechmus says, is the same as the *magadis,* an instrument with twenty strings; David A. Campbell, the editor, tells us it was Lydian or Thracian in origin.
6. David A. Campbell, *Greek Lyric Poetry I: Sappho and Alcaeus* (Cambridge, Massachusetts, 1982), p. x.
7. fr 176.
8. Campbell, op. cit., test 37.
9. fr 31.
10. fr 165.
11. fr 48.
12. fr 47.
13. fr 44a.
14. The Aeolic dactylic tetrameter acatalectic.
15. fr 130.
16. J. M. Edmonds, *Elegy and Iambus II* (London, 1931), p. 109.
17. Aelian, quoted in Stobaeus, Anthology, in Campbell, op. cit., p. 13.
18. François Lissarrague, *Greek Vases: The Athenians and Their Images* (New York, 1999, 2001).
19. See p. 58, this volume, on Hermes' lyre.
20. fr 54.
21. fr 100.
22. fr 101.
23. fr 177.
24. fr 179.
25. fr 53.
26. fr 123.
27. fr 44.
28. fr 55.
29. fr 155.
30. fr 104a.
31. fr 105a.
32. fr 128.
33. fr 156.

34. fr 146.
35. test 42.
36. Swinburne, "Anactoria," ll. 11–16.
37. Kurke, op. cit., pp. 75 ff.
38. Some accounts make her slightly older than he.
39. fr 98, preserved on the very earliest papyrus, from the third century BC.
40. fr 132.
41. fr 210.
42. fr 203.
43. In several poems, cf. 213, series of fragments.
44. See Herodotus, op. cit., II 135. He confuses Doricha with Rhodopis. "Rhodopis really arrived in Egypt under the conduct of Xantheus the Samian; she was brought there to exercise her trade, but was redeemed for a vast sum by Charaxus, a Mytilenaean, the son of Scamandronymus, and brother of Sappho the poetess. After thus obtaining her freedom, she remained in Egypt, and, as she was very beautiful, amassed great wealth, for a person in her condition; not, however, enough to enable her to erect such a work as this pyramid. Anyone who likes may go and see to what the tenth part of her wealth amounted, and he will thereby learn that her riches must not be imagined to have been very wonderfully great. Wishing to leave a memorial of herself in Greece, she determined to have something made the like of which was not to be found in any temple, and to offer it at the shrine at Delphi. So she set apart a tenth of her possessions, and purchased with the money a quantity of iron spits, such as are fit for roasting oxen whole, whereof she made a present to the oracle. They are still to be seen there, lying of a heap, behind the altar which the Chians dedicated, opposite the sanctuary. Naucratis seems somehow to be the place where such women are most attractive. First there was this Rhodopis of whom we have been speaking, so celebrated a person that her name came to be familiar to all the Greeks; and, afterwards, there was another, called Archidice, notorious throughout Greece, though not so much talked of as her predecessor. Charaxus, after ransoming Rhodopis, returned to Mytilene, and was often lashed by Sappho in her poetry. But enough has been said on the subject of this courtesan."
45. Photius; see fr 202.
46. See pp. 191–2.
47. frs 71, 98b, 213.
48. Campbell, op. cit., fr 2, p. 7.
49. test 21.
50. fr 28.
51. fr 16.
52. test 34: "Boyish Sappho modifies Archilochus' muse by her choice of metre..." (Horace, *Epistles*).
53. Campbell, op. cit., p. 20.
54. fr 168b.
55. Campbell, op. cit., p. xii, referring to Himerus: test 50.
56. test 7.
57. test 4.
58. fr 211b.

59. test 20, fr 155.
60. test fr 2.
61. fr 140.
62. Kurke, op. cit., p. 75.
63. test 51.
64. Alcaeus, fr 384.

XIII THEOGNIS OF MEGARA

1. "Good, brave."
2. Pausanias, Volume I, op. cit., p. 120.
3. Edmonds I, op. cit., "The Elegiac Poems of Theognis," ll. 11–14.
4. Pausanias, Volume I, op. cit., p. 115.
5. Kurke, op. cit., pp. 72–3.
6. Eva Cantarella and Cormac Ocuilleanain, *Bisexuality in the Ancient World* (New Haven, 1994), pp. 13f.
7. Edmonds I, op. cit., "The Elegiac Poems of Theognis," ll. 19–26.
8. Ibid., ll. 1219–1220.
9. Ibid., ll. 248–254.
10. Bowra, *Greek Lyric Poetry,* p. 291.
11. *kakoi.*
12. *agathoi.*
13. Edmonds I, op. cit., ll. 31–37.
14. *agathoi.*
15. *kakoi.*
16. Edmonds I, op. cit., ll. 53–60.
17. Ibid., ll. 129–130.
18. It is November.
19. Edmonds I, op. cit., ll. 1197–1202. The reading of the fragmented last line is uncertain, so I have left it blank.

XIV SOLON OF ATHENS

1. Jowett translation.
2. Thucydides does not mention him at all.
3. From fr 13.
4. fr 13.
5. *Lexicon,* p. 105.
6. Edmonds I, op. cit., p. 137, fr 22.
7. Cantarella, op. cit.
8. fr 25.
9. Burckhardt, op. cit., p. 82.
10. frs 13 and 23.
11. fr 31.
12. fr 1.
13. Lefkowitz, op. cit., pp. 40–48.
14. Taplin, *Literature in the Greek and Roman Worlds,* p. 159.

15. Ibid., p. 160.
16. See p. 239.
17. Betty Radice, "The Sayings of the Seven Sages of Greece," *The Translator's Art* (Harmondsworth, 1987).
18. frs 83–4, in Lefkowitz, op. cit., p. 46f.
19. OED: *archon* was the chief magistrate or, after Solon's time, one of the nine chief magistrates of Athens. Liddell and Scott say *archon* is "ruler, commander, chief, captain."
20. Lefkowitz, op. cit., p. 43.
21. From fr 36.
22. Ibid.
23. Edmonds I, op. cit., fr 5, p. 121.
24. Lefkowitz, op. cit., pp. 40–8.
25. Edmonds I, op. cit., fr 7, p. 123.
26. fr 30.
27. Herodotus, op. cit.
28. Lefkowitz, op. cit., pp. 43–8, Edmonds I, op. cit., p. 111.
29. *Longevity,* p. 109.
30. fr 10, Edmonds I, op. cit., p. 125.
31. fr 41.
32. Kurke, op. cit., p. 71.
33. Bowra, *Greek Lyric Poetry.*
34. Edmonds I, op. cit., fr 14.
35. fr 28a.
36. fr 29.

XV STESICHORUS OF HIMERA

1. David A. Campbell, *Greek Lyric Poetry III* (Cambridge, Massachusetts, 1991), Stesichorus, fr 270, note.
2. test 23.
3. See p. 170.
4. test 1.
5. test 24, from the Palatine Anthology, attributed to Antipater of Thessalonica.
6. test 1.
7. test 40.
8. test 44. His verses are quoted in the Palatine Anthology.
9. See p. 117.
10. test 10.
11. test 11.
12. test 15.
13. Lefkowitz, op. cit., p. 31ff.
14. fr 276.
15. test 16.
16. fr 212.
17. test 20.
18. test 22.
19. test 21.

20. Bowra, *Greek Lyric Poetry,* pp. 76ff.
21. Bowra, op. cit., p. 82.
22. Ibid., pp. 84–5.
23. Ibid., p. 87.
24. Campbell, op. cit., p. 4.
25. Kurke, op. cit., p. 80.
26. Bowra, op. cit., p. 127.
27. test 28.
28. test 29.
29. test 41.
30. test 41.
31. test 42.
32. *ferox.*
33. Kurke, op. cit., p. 80.
34. Anne Carson, *Autobiography of Red* (London, 1999), p. 5.
35. fr S15(ii).
36. fr 221.
37. fr 189.
38. test 1.
39. test 30.
40. Bowra, op. cit., p. 120.

XVI IBYCUS OF RHEGION

1. David A. Campbell, *Greek Lyric Poetry III: From Alcman to Simonides* (Cambridge, Massachusetts, 1991), test 14.
2. "At the outset he divided the state into three parts, and shared the kingdom with his brothers, Pantagnotus and Syloson; but later, having killed the former and banished the latter, who was the younger of the two, he held the whole island." Herodotus, op. cit., Book III.
3. Ibid.
4. Grant, op. cit., pp. 154–5.
5. test 1.
6. fr 282.
7. test 8.
8. fr 287.
9. fr 286.
10. fr 287.
11. test 7.
12. Eelides: test 2.
13. Bowra, op. cit., p. 241.
14. fr 331 (the reference dates from more than nine hundred years after the poet's death).
15. test 1.
16. test 12.
17. fr 288.
18. fr 315.
19. fr 317.

20. Bowra, op. cit., p. 241.

21. fr 343.

22. fr 285. Heracles kills the conjoined twins, children of Molione (here two heads on one body, as in Hesiod, not in Homer, where they are twins but not joined; "... and I killed those white-horsed youths, the children of Molione, like-aged, equal-headed, single-bodied, both born in a silver egg."

23. fr 291.

24. fr 321.

25. fr 323.

26. test 9.

27. test 5.

28. test 6.

XVII ANACREON OF TEOS

1. fr 402.

2. Davenport, *Seven Greeks,* p. 15.

3. Ibid.

4. Ibid.

5. *Anacreontea* 10.

6. *Anacreontea* 15.

7. *Anacreontea* 25.

8. *Anacreontea* 14.

9. *Anacreontea* 1.

10. *Anacreontea* 50.

11. *Anacreontea* 2. *chord:* string.

12. *Anacreontea* 23.

13. *Anacreontea* 4.

14. Robert Herrick, "To Live Merrily, and to Trust to Good Verses."

15. *Anacreontea* 16 and 17.

16. Gilbert Murray, *A History of Greek Literature* (New York, 1897), pp. 90–95.

17. fr 376.

18. Davenport, op. cit., p. 142.

19. fr 359.

20. Fowler, op. cit., p. 180.

21. fr 424.

22. frs 372, 388.

23. Davenport, op. cit., p. 143.

24. Bowra, op. cit., pp. 298–9.

25. Bowra, op. cit., p. 303.

26. fr 396.

27. Campbell, *Greek Lyric II,* p. 81.

28. fr 496.

29. test 7.

30. fr 346.

31. fr 408.

32. fr 358.

33. fr 414.

34. fr 347.
35. Bowra, op. cit., p. 277.
36. fr 398.
37. fr 403.
38. 394b.
39. Bowra, op. cit., p. 296.
40. fr 360.
41. fr 356.
42. fr 378.
43. fr 357.
44. fr 407.
45. fr 413.
46. fr 494.
47. fr 444, extract from Plutarch, *Dialogue on Love*.
48. fr 428.
49. fr 500, Lucian, also Campbell, *Greek Lyric III,* Simonides Epitaph LXVI, p. 577.
50. Murray, *Early Greece,* pp. 90–95.
51. Lesky, op. cit., p. 176.
52. elegiac frs, elegiac 2 (p. 147).
53. fr 79.
54. Lesky, op. cit., p. 176.
55. test 18.
56. Bowra, op. cit., p. 269.
57. fr 458.
58. fr 488.
59. test 20.
60. Hazlitt assigns Protagoras' birth to Teos.
61. Lesky, op. cit., pp. 174ff.
62. Epigrams, fr 100D.
63. fr 419.
64. Davenport, op. cit., 80, p. 148.
65. Mulroy, op. cit., p. 133.
66. Fowler, op. cit., p. 188.
67. fr 417.
68. fr 411b.
69. e.g., frs 385, 432.
70. fr 389.
71. fr 446.
72. fr 439.
73. fr 448.
74. fr 491, Himerius.
75. Herodotus, op. cit., Book III, *Histories.*
76. Bowra, op. cit., p. 307.
77. The five volumes of Anacreon's verse were probably presented to Antonia, daughter of Mark Antony and Octavia, mother of Germanicus and the emperor Claudius. The *oeuvre* must have contained edifying as well as delighting verse; it is worth noting that the delighting verse has survived while the edifying has perished.
78. Kurke, op. cit., pp. 78f.

79. Grant, op. cit., pp. 154–5.
80. Lattimore, op. cit., p. 45.
81. Pausanias, Volume I, op. cit., p. 70.
82. Zanker, op. cit., pp. 22–31.
83. fr 373.
84. Zanker, op. cit., p. 28.
85. fr 363.
86. fr 395.
87. fr 361.
88. test 12.
89. test 11.

XVIII HIPPONAX OF EPHESUS

 1. Gerber, op. cit., p. 345.
 2. Zanker, op. cit.
 3. Gerber, op. cit., p. 349, test 9.
 4. fr 2.
 5. fr 174.
 6. fr 88.
 7. fr 114c.
 8. Lesky, op. cit., p. 115.
 9. fr 35.
10. Athenaeus, *Scholars at Dinner.*
11. fr 42.
12. fr 29a (Gerber's translation).
13. See page 58.
14. fr 32.
15. After Hipponax's invective was said to have killed them, statues by them appeared in Delos and elsewhere.
16. Burckhardt, op. cit., p. 73.
17. frs 120–121.
18. fr 12.
19. fr 70.
20. fr 17.
21. fr 84.
22. Burckhardt, op. cit., p. 72.
23. fr 183.
24. fr 57.
25. fr 61.
26. frs 32 and 34.
27. fr 116.
28. fr 114a.
29. fr 78 may include parody of a rite to cure impotence.
30. Gerber, op. cit., p. 8.
31. Bowra, *Landmarks in Greek Literature,* p. 70.
32. fr 135.

33. Lesky, op. cit., p. 115.
34. See fragment 92.

XIX SIMONIDES OF COS

1. Werner Jaeger, *Paideia: The Ideal of Greek Culture,* Volume I, trans. Gilbert Highet, (Oxford, 1986), p. 213.
2. Gerber, op. cit., pp. 296, 298.
3. The Greek word *rhemata* should be rendered "orders," as in "military orders," not "laws."
4. Bowra, *Greek Lyric Poetry,* p. 319.
5. test 1. Bowra suggests that Simonides' dithyrambs may have been, like Bacchylides' Ode XVIII, though choral in structure, a transitional form towards the tragic.
6. test 13.
7. Taplin, op. cit., p. 8.
8. test 3. Simonides was of the *deme* (township, in ancient Greece, or "division") called Hylichidai (Bowra, op. cit., p. 309).
9. Jay, op. cit., p. 40.
10. Epigram LXXV (a) and (b).
11. Lefkowitz, op. cit., p. 56.
12. Epigram VI, p. 524.
13. test 10.
14. Campbell, *Greek Lyric III*, p. 299, fr 3.
15. test 22 (Lefkowitz, op. cit., p. 52).
16. test 22.
17. test 23.
18. Apothegms, test 47(d).
19. test 11 (Tzetzes), Epigram XXVII (from the Palatine Anthology).
20. Epigram I, from Hephaestion, *Handbook on Metres,* Campbell, *Greek Lyric III,* p. 521. Mulroy op. cit., p. 143. This is quoted by Hephaestion, criticising the way Simonides ends the line with half a word, following on with the rest, an odd enjambement.
21. Mulroy, op. cit., p. 139.
22. fr 515.
23. Epigram LXIX, p. 581.
24. fr 562.
25. test 2.
26. See p. 225, this volume.
27. See p. 347, this volume.
28. Mulroy, op. cit., p. 135.
29. test 26.
30. test 25.
31. Bowra, *Greek Lyric Poetry,* p. 309.
32. fr 509.
33. See pp. 272–83, this volume, for a fuller account of the epinicean tradition.
34. Bowra, op. cit., p. 311.
35. Ibid., p. 324.
36. 47(a) and 47(b).

37. fr 600 (Campbell translation).
38. fr 516.
39. fr 517.
40. fr 550.
41. fr 585.
42. fr 586.
43. fr 597.
44. fr 583.
45. fr 625.
46. fr 521.
47. test 40.
48. Lefkowitz, op. cit., p. 50.
49. Ibid., p. 56.
50. Epigram XXVIa, p. 545.
51. Callimachus, p. 47, in Campbell fr 510, and quoted from Cicero, *On the Orator,* and Quintilian's *Principles of Oratory.*
52. Lefkowitz, op. cit., p. 55.
53. Bowra, op. cit., pp. 325 f.
54. Epigram LXXXIV, p. 589.
55. fr 581.
56. Lefkowitz, op. cit., p. 55.
57. test 47 (h).
58. Callimachus, fr 64.
59. Bowra, op. cit., p. 323.
60. Ibid., p. 320.
61. fr 567.
62. Kurke, op. cit., pp. 74–81.
63. fr 526.
64. fr 527.
65. "Virtue, excellence of body and mind."
66. fr 579.
67. frs 541, 542.
68. Jaeger, op. cit., p. 213.
69. Ibid.
70. fr 522.
71. Carm 3.2.14.
72. fr 524.
73. fr 641.
74. Mulroy, op. cit., p. 142, eleg 15, p. 517.
75. Epigram XXXIII(b).

XX CORINNA OF TANAGRA

1. Campbell, *Greek Lyric* IV, p. 15, fr 4, by Antipater of Thessalonica.
2. Ibid., p. 37, fr 655.
3. See p. 262 for Richmond Lattimore's translation of the offending verses.
4. Campbell, *Greek Lyric IV,* p. 15, test 2.

5. The British Museum has a quite wonderful collection.

6. Pausanias, Volume I, op. cit., p. 354.

7. Lines 89f.

8. Lattimore, op. cit., p. 53.

9. Pausanias, Volume I, op. cit., 354.

10. Campbell takes these "mysteries" to be the "result of the Boeotian orthography."

11. A poet whose work is so similar to that of Antipater of Sidon as to be virtually undistinguishable.

12. Pausanias, Volume I, op. cit., p. 354.

13. Ibid.

14. Mulroy, op. cit.

15. fr 673.

16. Mulroy, op. cit., p. 168.

17. *Bryn Mawr Classical Review* 97.3.4: Sarah Ruden, review of Andrew M. Miller (trans.), *Greek Lyric: An Anthology in Translation* (Indianapolis, 1996), p. 184.

18. Campbell, *Greek Lyric IV*, p. 45, fr 664b.

XXI PINDAR OF THEBES

1. 522–446 BC Perseus.

2. Alexander the Great.

3. Euripides. Lysander spared Athens from destruction, moved by the beauty of the chorus in *Electra*.

4. Roger Lonsdale (ed.), *The Poems of Gray, Collins and Goldsmith* (Longman, 1969), p. 156.

5. 1640, published posthumously.

6. C. H. Sisson (ed.), *Johnathan Swift: Selected Poems* (Manchester, 1977), pp. 11–12.

7. Samuel Taylor Coleridge, *Biographia Literaria* (London, 1956), Chapter 3.

8. Auden, op. cit., p. 5.

9. John Pick (ed.), *A Hopkins Reader* (Oxford, 1953), letter to Robert Bridges, 18 October 1882, p. 112.

10. Lesky, op. cit., p. 202.

11. He did actually quote the second line of *Olympian* II in "Hugh Selwyn Mauberley," but the intention was ironic.

12. Ezra Pound, *Selected Letters 1907–1941*, p. 87.

13. Kurke, op. cit.

14. See page 286.

15. Commentary to fr 29.

16. fr 29.

17. See page 286.

18. William H. Race (ed.), *Pindar: Nemean Odes, Isthmian Odes, Fragments* (Cambridge, Massachusetts, 1997), p. 293.

19. Pausanias, Volume II, op. cit., p. 108.

20. Quoted in Richmond Lattimore, *The Odes of Pindar* (Chicago, 1947), pp. v–xii.

21. Many later and some near-contemporary writers despised the games as useless, the residue of a discredited age, and the poems of victory as pointless exercises.

22. Zanker, op. cit., figs 7 and 8, pp. 28f.

23. C. M. Bowra, *The Odes of Pindar* (Harmondsworth, 1969), p. xii.
24. Lesky, op. cit., p. 191.
25. Ibid.
26. See p. 25.
27. J. G. Frazer (trans.), *Pausanias and Other Greek Sketches* (London, 1900).
28. Ibid.
29. fr 193.
30. Milton, sonnet VIII.
31. fr 120.
32. Pausanias, Volume I, op. cit.
33. *Pythian* X.
34. Lefkowitz, op. cit., p. 61.
35. *Pythian* V, 76.
36. Lesky, op. cit., p. 191n.
37. Lesky, op. cit., p. 197, says *daphnephorica* were "sung at Thebes where a staff wreathed in laurel, flowers and ribbons (the *koto*) was carried in procession to Apollo Ismenius."
38. Lefkowitz, op. cit.
39. fr 94c.
40. fr 127, Vol. II, p. 359.
41. Bowra, op. cit.
42. Campbell, op. cit., p. 15.
43. fr 198a.
44. Bowra, op. cit.
45. Lesky, op. cit., p. 191.
46. C. M. Bowra, *Periclean Athens* (London, 1971), p. 136.
47. Bowra, op. cit., p. 133.
48. Lefkowitz, op. cit., pp. 57–9, ridicules over-interpreters and biographical subtilists.
49. *Olympian* VI, ll. 89–90.
50. Bowra, op. cit., p. 133, Dithyramb fr 76, "For the Athenians," Loeb II p. 313.
51. C. M. Bowra, *The Odes of Pindar* (Harmondsworth, 1969), p. xi.
52. *Olympian* VIII, ll. 54–5. Bowra, *Periclean Athens.*
53. *Olympian* VIII, l. 22.
54. Lesky, op. cit., p. 193.
55. Bowra, *Odes of Pindar,* p. x.
56. Lesky, op. cit., p. 195.
57. Ibid., p. 196, "he divided the lyrical text into cola" (i.e., marked line and stanza breaks, hence strophe, antistrophe, epode) "and edited all that then survived into seventeen books."
58. Fragments of ten survive, from Oxyrhynchus, first published 1908; more fragments added in 1961.
59. Lesky, op. cit., p. 186.
60. Lattimore, *Odes of Pindar,* p. xi.
61. Ibid.
62. See p. 245.
63. fr 54.
64. Jay, op. cit., p. 298.

65. Michael Grant, "Pindar: The Old Values," *The Classical Greeks* (New York, 1997), pp. 34–9.
66. Lattimore, *Odes of Pindar,* p. xi.
67. A character called Phrikias is named, either the boy's father or, some conjecture, his horse, in which case his triumph was in a horse-, not a foot-race.
68. Apollo delights to see the "braying insolence" of the quadrupeds. Scholars nowadays say that he laughs at their erect phalluses.
69. Lesky, op. cit., pp. 190f.
70. Bowra, *Odes of Pindar,* p. xiii.
71. fr 110.
72. fr 105a, Vol. II, p. 337.
73. fr 191.
74. Mulroy, op. cit., p. 159.
75. *Isthmian* IV, 37ff.
76. Lattimore, op. cit., p. viii.
77. fr 52h.
78. *De Compositione* 22.
79. C. A. M. Fennell, *Pindar: The Olympian and Pythian Odes* (Cambridge, 1893).
80. Goddesses of the seasons.
81. Race, op. cit., fr 75.
82. fr 152.
83. fr 194.
84. frs, p. 301.
85. B. L. Gildersleeve, *Pindar: The Olympian and Pythian Odes* (New York, 1890).
86. Lesky, op. cit., p. 195.
87. In 480 Gelen of Syracuse, elder brother of Hieron, joined with Theron of Acragas to defeat a huge Carthaginian force numbering 100,000 at the battle of Himera.
88. I, II, III, X, XI and perhaps XIV.
89. Lesky, op. cit., pp. 194f.
90. fr 122, 17–20.
91. fr 201.
92. fr 140d.
93. Lefkowitz, op. cit., p. 65 (fr 52b).
94. Lefkowitz, op. cit., p. 66.
95. Gilbert Highet, *Poets in a Landscape* (London, 1999), translation, p. 125.

XXII BACCHYLIDES OF COS

1. Virgil (Publius Vergilius Maro).
2. Blass believes that Odes VI and VII, as numbered by Kenyon, are parts of a single ode.
3. Lesky, op. cit., p. 202.
4. Ibid.
5. Campbell, *Greek Lyric Poetry IV,* p. 173.
6. Lesky, op. cit., p. 203.
7. fr XXX.
8. *On the Sources of Elevation in Style* would be a more appropriate translation.

9. test 13.
10. Plutarch (test 6) says Bacchylides was exiled from Cos, and reflects that exile is a collaborator with many writers. Bacchylides went to the Peloponnese. We are not sure why he was exiled.
11. As Lesky, op. cit., points out, there is no evidence that Bacchylides actually went to Syracuse; on the other hand, there is no evidence that he did not. In the circumstances we do well to give the benefit of the doubt to tradition.
12. test 1, 2, 3.
13. fr 20b.
14. fr 13.
15. Lines 86ff.
16. test 8. The passage, in Mulroy's prose translation, reads: "A true poet knows many things by nature; learners chatter in vain, furious in their verbosity, like a pair of crows cawing at the godlike bird of Zeus" (op. cit., p. 148).
17. test 10.
18. test 9.
19. For example, in *Olympian* I.
20. Pindar's *Pythian* II, too, may possibly belong to the same occasion, and if so the tradition of Pindar's having fallen out with Hiero as patron may be contradicted, but its dating remains controversial.
21. Ode V, ll. 65f.
22. *Aeneid* VI, 21.
23. XXVI.
24. Ephebes were youths of eighteen to twenty years who spent their time on garrison duty.
25. fr 5.
26. fr 24.
27. The others, we recall, were Alcman, Sappho, Alcaeus, Stesichorus, Ibycus, Anacreon, Simonides and Pindar.
28. Ammianus Marcellinus, xxv, 4.

XXIII CALLIMACHUS OF CYRENE

1. Diringer, op. cit., p. 115.
2. Ibid.
3. sikcaíno pánta tà dehmósia.
4. Constantine A. Trypanis, *Callimachus: Aetia, Iambi, Hecale, and Other Fragments* (Cambridge, Massachusetts, 1958), introduction.
5. Casson, op. cit., p. 39.
6. Cited by Gregory Nagy, *Pindar's Homer: The Lyric Possesion of an Epic Past* (Johns Hopkins, 1980, 1997), §3.
7. Diringer, op. cit., p. 155.
8. Edmonds, op. cit., p. 500.
9. Lesky, op. cit., p. 717.
10. Diringer, op. cit., pp. 129–30.
11. Said to have been an expert on accents.
12. A. W. Mair (ed.), *Callimachus and Lycophron* (London, 1922).

13. fr 398.
14. Apollonius, op. cit., p. 13.
15. Lefkowitz, op. cit., p. 122.
16. fr 110; see Catullus, lxvi.
17. Or as *The Changes*.
18. fr 66.
19. See p. 365.
20. Mair, op. cit., Epigram I.
21. Ibid., Epigram VIII.
22. Ibid., Epigram XVI, passim.
23. Ibid., Epigram XLVIII.
24. Ibid., Epigram XV.
25. Ibid., Epigram XXX.
26. Ibid., Epigram XXXIII.
27. M. A. Harder, R. F. Regtuit and G. C. Wakker (eds.), "Die Einbeziehung des Lesers in den Epigrammen des Kallimachos," *Callimachus: Hellenistica Groningana* I (Groningen, 1993).
28. The area before the pedestal upon which the statue of the god would have been placed.
29. "Hymn to Zeus," l. 64.
30. Mair (op. cit.) favours 247 BC.
31. Harder et al., op. cit.

XXIV APOLLONIUS OF RHODES

1. Calasso, op. cit., p. 44.
2. Mair, op. cit., p. 4.
3. Trypanis, op. cit., introduction.
4. Apollonius, op. cit., Book III, 401.
5. Lefkowitz, op. cit., pp. 128ff.
6. Hazlitt.
7. Lefkowitz, op. cit., pp. 128ff.
8. Richard Stoneman (ed.), *A Literary Companion to Travel in Greece* (Malibu, 1994), p. 275.
9. Apollonius, op. cit., ll. 556–558.
10. Ibid., Book I, ll. 574f.
11. One *Vita* says that he published the original *Argonautica* via an "epideixis" (display), or reading, but it failed.
12. See p. 310, this volume. He was found worthy as a librarian, not as an author—a common misreading of the passage.
13. Nonnus' poem is poetically uninteresting but prosodically it shows a stage on the transition from quantitative to accentual versification.
14. Taplin, *Literature in the Greek and Roman Worlds*, p. 57.
15. Lesky, op. cit., p. 735.
16. Apollonius, op. cit., p. 16.
17. Ibid., p. xi.
18. Ibid., p. 17.

19. Ibid., Book III, ll. 66f.
20. Ibid., Book I, ll. 18–19, 111–113, for example.
21. See p. 313, this volume.
22. Ibid., Book II, ll. 1277f.
23. Ibid., Book III, 558ff.
24. Ibid., Book IV, ll. 167f.
25. Ibid., Book I, ll. 1273–1283.
26. Ibid., Book II, ll. 408, 410.
27. Ibid., Book II, ll. 627ff.

XXV THEOCRITUS OF SYRACUSE

1. Some sources say *c.* 300–*c.* 260 BC or 316–260 BC.
2. Graves, op. cit., pp. 170f.
3. Bowra, *Landmarks in Greek Literature,* pp. 262f.
4. Idyll XII, "The Touchstones," is, for example, about boy love and its attendant ceremonial, incorporating a prayer for real amorous reciprocity. Wells sees Idyll XII as "a medley," a mind "confused by gladness," rushing from thought to thought.
5. 4.14.9, see Lesky, op. cit., p. 720.
6. Richard Hunter, *Theocritus and the Archaeology of Greek Poetry* (Cambridge, 1996).
7. Simpler, lighter, and with debts to the Homeric Hymns (Hymn XVIII, "To Hermes" in particular), is Idyll XXIV, "The Childhood of Heracles." The hero is ten months old. It is bed time and he and his younger twin are about to drift off. Hera, who implacably hates the infants, sends serpents to slay them, but Heracles turns the tables and strangles them. Alcmene, the twins' mother, calls Teiresias to interpret the event. He tells the future and gives instructions on how to exorcise the bad spirits and purify the house. There follows an account of the education and training of Heracles. Thirty lines are missing at the end, the text dies in mid-flow. Those lines, Wells says, may have been a prayer for victory: Was the poem an entry in a competition celebrating Heracles, Ptolemy's "ancestor"? (See Wells, op. cit., p. 154.)
8. Bowra, op. cit., p. 263.
9. Wells, op. cit., p. 23.
10. Ibid., p. 28.
11. Bowra, op. cit., p. 263.
12. Wells; Bowra.
13. Jane L. Lightfoot, "Sophisticates and Solecisms: Greek Literature After the Classical Period," pp. 231–3, in Taplin, op. cit.
14. See p. 206, this volume.
15. Sir Kenneth J. Dover, *Theocritus* (London, 1971).
16. Wells, op. cit., p. 47.
17. Ibid., p. 49.
18. Richard Hunter, *Theocritus: A Selection* (Cambridge, 1999).
19. Lefkowitz, op. cit. The *Vita* proposes Praxagoras and Simichidas as candidates for the poet's paternity (citing Idyll VII, 28, the second name a fiction).
20. Hunter, op. cit.

21. Agathocles, the son of a potter of Himera, after time in the army, marriage to his patron's widow, and much battle in Italy and Africa (he nearly took Carthage at one point), settled down as king and ruled in peace, but the aftermath was anarchic.

22. Hiero II was elected to lead the expedition against Carthage (275–4); maybe Theocritus was in Syracuse at the time, says Lesky, op. cit., pp. 718ff.

23. See Idyll XVI, ll. 18ff.

24. Lefkowitz, op. cit., p. 131.

25. The *Vita* calls him "his father's namesake."

26. Or Cos: The distaff is from Sicily, but there is no reason to imagine that the journey is from Sicily. As a Sicilian, the poet would have had in his possession objects from his native land.

27. Wells, op. cit., p. 46.

28. Hunter, op. cit., "The Languages of Theocritus."

29. Lesky, op. cit., p. 721.

30. Idylls XIX, XX, XI, XXIII, XXV and XXVII are probably by other hands. Of the twenty-four surviving epigrams, two or three are probably spurious.

31. Robert Wells, op. cit., divides them as follows, with some inevitable overlapping:.

    A. Bucolic: 1, 3, 4, 5, 6, 7, 10, 11, 12, 16, 28, 29, 30

    B. Mimes: 2, 14, 15

    C. Mythological: 13, 22, 26, 24

    D. Personal Poems: 12, 28, 29, 30

    E. Addresses to kings: 16, 17 ("The Graces" and "Encomium")

    F. Epigrams

32. See Athenaeus, vii.284.a.

33. fr 366; see translated verse on p. 167.

34. VII, 47–8.

Glossary

AGLAIA one of the Graces, who "graces" success with its magnificence

AIDOS sense of shame, or moral restraint; in peacetime it entails reverence for the laws and respect for fellow citizens; in war it entails courage

AINOS a story, a tale, a proverb (tending towards praise), praise poetry

AKMAZON nicer way of saying **ANER**: someone in the prime of his life

ANER (**PAIS**: young boy; **MEIRAKION**: young person; **NEANISKOS**: youth; **ANER**: man; **PRESBYTES**: older man; **GERON**: old man)

ANTISTROPHE in the ode, the counter-turn following the **STROPHE** (turn) and followed by the **EPODOS** (after-song)

AOIDOS poet-singer (used by Hesiod and Homer)

APENE mule-car race

APOIKIAI colonies

ARCHON one of the nine magistrates of Athens

ARETÉ (ARETA) "the realisation of human excellence in achievements"

AULOS a musical instrument, generally taken to mean "flute" but actually denoting an oboe-like instrument

BARBARIAN someone who is not Greek. In its original use the word was not negative in implication, though eventually a sense of Greek cultural superiority coloured it.

BARBITOS a many-stringed musical instrument, lute- or lyre-like

BASILEUS noble proprietor, master, lord, leader of the people, king

BASSARID female worshipper of Dionysus

CHORIZONTES those who maintain that the *Iliad* and the *Odyssey* were composed by different poets

CITHARIS rudimentary lyre

DEME an Attic village

DIASCEUAST reviser, interpolator

DIAULOS double foot-race

DIKE justice

DITHYRAMB a Greek choral lyric, usually with a narrative, originally connected with Dionysus' worship, sung by a *kuklios coros,* or circular chorus, of about fifty singers, sometimes dressed as satyrs. The etymology is uncertain: probably a revel song started by the leader (*exarcos*) of a band of revellers using traditional or improvised language, answered by a refrain. Its origins may have been in Phrygia; it came to Greece with Dionysus. Arion in Corinth made it a literary form.

DOLICHOS long foot-race; Lattimore renders it "distance run"

EIKEI "taking it as it comes"

ELEGIA   from **ELEGOS**, a lament; a funeral lamentation or ode written in elegiacs and, by extension, any poem written in elegiac verse

ENARGES   divine epiphany

ENCOMIA   eulogies, poems of formal and high-flown praise

EPHOR   one of the five annually appointed Spartan magistrates who was responsible for seeing to the management of the city

EPIDEIXASTHAI   publish

EPINICEA   after-victory odes

EPODOS   after-song, after-ode, following the **STROPHE** (turn) and **ANTISTROPHE** (counter-turn)

EUNOMIA   the order of good laws which harmonise the lives of citizens

GERON   (**PAIS:** young boy; **MEIRAKION:** young person; **NEANISKOS:** youth; **ANER:** man; **PRESBYTES:** older man; **GERON:** old man)

HELOT   a slave of Sparta

HOPLITE   an armed Spartan warrior. The term derives from the *hoplon,* the round shield he held in his left hand.

HUBRIS or **HYBRIS:**   tragic pride, overweening self-confidence which requires punishment

HYPORCHEMA (pl. **HYPORCHEMATA**)   dance ode

IAMBOPOIOS   writers of iambics

KARIS   one of the Graces; poetry's enchantment, the pleasure of celebration

KARITES   the Graces

KELES   single-horse race

KERTOMEIN   sneer, mock

KITHARA   an ancient stringed instrument, triangular in shape, with from seven to eleven strings ("cithern" and "guitar" derive from this word)

KLEOS   glory and fame, which dignify worked-for success

KREOS   the obligation a poet has to praise

LEMMA   a rubric preceding a poem describing its theme or form or providing it with a title (a *lemmatist* is one who adds such lemma, as in the *Anacreontea*)

LOIDORIA   verbal abuse

MAGADIS   an instrument with twenty strings, their arrangement in octaves: Athenaeus conjectures that the magadis might have been strings or pipes, and he quotes Anacreon: "Holding the magadis I strike its twenty strings, while you, Leucaspis, enjoy the fun of youth." He goes on to quote another authority who makes the strings into pipes.

MEIRAKION   (**PAIS:** young boy; **MEIRAKION:** young person; **NEANISKOS:** youth; **ANER:** man; **PRESBYTES:** older man; **GERON:** old man)

MELOS   music

MOIRA   destiny, fate

NEANISKOS   (**PAIS:** young boy; **MEIRAKION:** young person; **NEANISKOS:** youth; **ANER:** man; **PRESBYTES:** older man; **GERON:** old man)

NOSTOI   tales of the returns of heroes, homecomings

NOSTOS   heart-ache for homecoming, *saudade* (cf. Luce, p. 165: root of "nostalgia")

OBELOS   "a horizontal stroke as a critical sign" used by Aristarchus to mark lines in poems which he thought might be spurious

OLBOS, OLBIOS   one with cherished male offspring, stables and hounds, and a friend to offer hospitality. Herodotus contrasts *olbios* and *eutuches,* enjoyer of superficial good fortune.

OSTRACISM   an Athenian custom which led to the exiling of a citizen for ten years, the purpose being to limit the influence a single man could have within the city, to (as it were) make the city proof against tyranny. Voting was conducted by writing the name of the candidate for ostracism on a potsherd, an *ostrakon.*

PAIS   young boy (followed by **MEIRAKION:** young person; **NEANISKOS:** youth; **ANER:** man; **PRESBYTES:** older man; **GERON:** old man)

PALIMPSEST   a papyrus or parchment which has been erased and reused one or more times, the original writing still perceptible beneath the later texts

PANCRATION   trial of strength involving boxing, wrestling, kicking, strangling, twisting (biting and gouging were forbidden, but almost everything else was allowed: bone-breaking, wrenching limbs out of joint, neck holds, etc.)

PARAGRAPHOS   a horizontal dash used in the drama to indicate a change of speaker. Diringer: "a short stroke called *parágraphos* (hence our word 'paragraph') which is placed under [the] last line of a clause, below the first letter of this line."

PENTATHLON   five-sports competition: running, long-jump, discus, javelin, wrestling

PERIODONIKES   winner in all four major Games

PERIOECI   "dwellers in the neighbourhood," free men living in Sparta, not full citizens, unenfranchised, providing certain services

PHILIA   the affectionate bond between men of good character and will

PHORMINX   an early simple lyre

PHUA   innate character

POIKILIA   variety

POLIS (pl. **POLEIS**)   city, city-state

PONEIN   to toil, imposed on men by Zeus

PRESBYTES   (**PAIS:** young boy; **MEIRAKION:** young person; **NEANISKOS:** youth; **ANER:** man; **PRESBYTES:** older man; **GERON:** old man)

PRIAMEL   creating a foil for the subject, as at the opening of Pindar's *Olympic* I: water and gold, the best in their realms, are foils for the Olympic Games, the best of games.

PROOIMION, PROEME   a prologue or overture

PROSODION   a processional song

PSYCHE   appears when a man dies, a spirit residue: breath-soul or shadow-soul; while he lives, a man's psyche is the source of thoughts and desires. Can be seen as dividing into *thumos* (concerned with emotions), *thren* (Lesky, p. 71: "the midriff as the seat of intellectual activity, hence intellectual activity itself") and *nous* ("imagination, conception"). We cannot systematise these terms.

SAMBUCA, SAMBUKE   an ancient stringed instrument, triangular like the *kithara*, with a shrill sound

SCHOLIA   interpretative notes or bodies of notes

SKOLION   a poem that made the rounds at banquets, sung accompanied by a lyre, often derogatory, satirical (cf. Timocreon). It comes from the zig-zag course of the song: a myrtle branch was passed back and forth from singer to singer as the poem went its rounds.

SKOLIOS (pl. **SKOLIA**)   "tortuous," the name for an early form of drinking song

SKOPTIKA hate epigrams

SKYPHOS a drinking bowl with small handles at the rim

SOMA body or, in Homer, corpse

SOPHIA wisdom, moral understanding, a poet's wisdom and the skills and crafts that go with its expression

SPARTIATES full citizens of Sparta

STADION a footrace that, in Olympia, was an eponymous *stade* long (an eighth of a Roman mile, rendered in the Bible as a *furlong*); Lattimore renders it "dash"

STROPHE the opening movement of the ode, the turn, followed by *antistrophe* (counter-turn) and *epodos* (after-song)

TETHRIPOÖN four-horse chariot race

THEMIS the power given by Zeus to kings; what is obligatory on man through the bonds of nature or usage; the power commerce between the sexes; the goddess who carries through Zeus's commands

THEOS god, the element of the divine in human deeds

THRENOS (pl. **THRENOI**) lament, laments for the dead

TIMÉ love of honour

TYRANT derives from "a language of Asia Minor" and means, in essence, "sole ruler," generally distinguished from a king or other hereditary or elected leader

XENIA the cordiality and courtesy due to a guest

Bibliography

PRIMARY TEXTS, TRANSLATIONS AND STUDIES

Alcaeus of Mytilene
Campbell, David A., *Greek Lyric Poetry I: Sappho, Alcaeus* (Cambridge, Massachusetts, 1982)
Page, D. L., *Sappho and Alcaeus* (Oxford, 1979)
Burnett, Anne Pippin, *Three Archaic Poets: Archilochus, Alcaeus, Sappho* (London, 1983)

Alcman of Sardis
Campbell, David A., *Greek Lyric Poetry II: Anacreon, Anacreontea, Choral Lyric from Olympus to Alcman* (Cambridge, Massachusetts, 1988)
Page, D. L., *Alcman: the Partheneion* (Oxford, 1951)

Anacreon of Teos and the Anacreontea
Campbell, David A., *Greek Lyric Poetry II: Anacreon, Anacreontea, Choral Lyric from Olympus to Alcman* (Cambridge, Massachusetts, 1988)
Gentili, B., *Anacreon* (Rome, 1958)

Apollonius of Rhodes
Green, Peter, translator, *Argonautika* (Berkeley, 1997)
Hunter, R. L., *The Argonautica of Apollonius: Library Studies* (Cambridge, 1993)
————., translator, *Jason and the Golden Fleece* (Oxford, 1998)
Rieu, E. V., translator, *The Voyage of the Argo* (Harmondsworth, 1959)

Archilochus of Paros
Burnett, Anne Pippin, *Three Archaic Poets: Archilochus, Alcaeus, Sappho* (London, 1983)
Edmonds, J. M., *Elegy and Iambus II* (London, 1931)
Gerber, Douglas E., *Greek Iambic Poetry* (Cambridge, Massachusetts, 1999)

Bacchylides of Cos
Bowra, C. M., *Early Greek Elegists* (Cambridge, Massachusetts, 1935)
————, *Greek Lyric Poetry: From Alcman to Simonides* (second edition, Oxford, 1961)
Burnett, Anne Pippin, *The Art of Bacchylides* (Cambridge, Massachusetts, 1985)

Campbell, David A., *Greek Lyric Poetry IV: Bacchylides, Corinna, and Others* (Cambridge, Massachusetts, 1992)

Fagles, R., and A. Parry, *Bacchylides: Complete Poems* (New Haven, 1961)

Slavitt, David R., *Epinician Odes and Dithyrambs of Bacchylides* (Philadelphia, 1998)

Callimachus of Cyrene

Cameron, A., *Callimachus and His Critics* (Princeton, 1995)

Harder, M. A., R. F. Regtuit, and G. C. Walker, editors, "Die Einbeziehung des Lesers in den Epigrammen des Kallimachos," *Callimachus: Hellenistica Groningana* I (Groningen, 1993)

Hollis, A. S., *Callimachus' Hecale* (Oxford, 1990)

Hutchinson, C. O., *Hellenistic Poetry* (Oxford, 1990)

Lombardo, S., and D. Rayor, translators, *Callimachus: Hymns, Epigrams, Select Fragments* (Baltimore, 1988)

Mair, A. W., ed., *Callimachus and Lycophron* (London, 1921)

Pfeiffer, R., *Kallimachos*, two volumes (Oxford, 1949, 1953 [1998])

Trypanis, Constantine A., *Callimachus: Aetia, Iambi, Hecale and Other Fragments* (Cambridge, Massachusetts, 1958)

Webster, T. B. L., *Hellenistic Poetry and Art* (London, 1964)

Young, G. M., *The Epigrams of Callimachus* (Oxford, 1934)

Corinna of Tanagra

Balmer, Josephine, translator, *Classical Women Poets* (Newcastle-upon-Tyne, 1996)

Campbell, David A., *Greek Lyric Poetry IV: Bacchylides, Corinna, and Others* (Cambridge, Massachusetts, 1992)

Page, D. L., *Corinna* (London, 1963)

Hesiod

Burn, A. R., *The World of Hesiod* (London, 1936)

Evelyn-White, Hugh C., *Hesiod, Homeric Hymns, Epic Cycle, Homerica* (London, 1914)

Janko, R. C. M., *Homer, Hesiod and the Hymns* (Cambridge, 1982)

Lamberton, Robert, *Hesiod* (New Haven, 1988)

Lattimore, Richmond, trans., *The Works and Days, Theogony, The Shield of Achilles* (Ann Arbor, 1959)

Lombardo, Stanley, trans., *Works and Days* and *Theogony,* Introduction by Robert Lamberton (Indianapolis, 1993)

West, M. L., ed., *Theogony* (Oxford, 1966)

————, ed., *Works and Days* (Oxford, 1978)

————, trans., *Hesiod and the Homeric Hymns* (Oxford, 1988)

Hipponax of Ephesus

Gerber, Douglas E., *Greek Iambic Poetry* (Cambridge, Massachusetts, 1999)

West, M. L., *Studies in Greek Elegy and Iambus* (New York/Berlin, 1974)

Homer

Boer, Charles, *The Homeric Hymns* (Athens, Ohio, 1970)

Butler, Samuel, *Iliad* (London, 1898), prose translation

——, *Odyssey* (London, 1900), prose translation

Evelyn-White, Hugh G., *Hesiod, Homeric Hymns, Epic Cycle, Homerica* (London, 1914)

Fagles, R., *Iliad* (New York, 1990), verse translation

——, *Odyssey* (Harmondsworth, 1996), verse translation

Fitzgerald, Robert, *Iliad* (New York, 1974), verse translation

——, *Odyssey* (New York, 1961), verse translation

Foley, H., *Hymn to Demeter* (Princeton, 1993)

Hammond, J. M., *Iliad* (Harmondsworth, 1987), prose translation

Lattimore, Richmond, *Iliad* (Chicago, 1951), verse translation

——, *Odyssey* (New York, 1965), verse translation

Logue, Christopher, *War Music: An Account of Books 1–4 and 16–19 of Homer's Iliad* (London, 2001)

Murray, A. T., editor and translator, *Iliad: Books 1–12*, revised by William F. Wyatt (Cambridge, Massachusetts, 1999)

——, *Iliad: Books 13–24*, revised by William F. Wyatt (Cambridge, Massachusetts, 1999)

——, *The Odyssey: Books 1–12*, revised by George E. Dimmock (Cambridge, Massachusetts, 1995)

——, *The Odyssey: Books 13–24*, revised by George E. Dimmock (Cambridge, Massachusetts, 1995)

Rieu, E. V., *Odyssey* (Harmondsworth, 1991), prose translation

Sargeant, T., *Homeric Hymns* (New York, 1973)

Sherwing, Walter, *Odyssey* (Oxford, 1980), prose translation

Steiner, George, ed., *Homer in English* (Harmondsworth, 1996)

West, M. L., trans., *Hesiod and the Homeric Hymns* (Oxford, 1988)

References for Homeric Texts

Autenrieth, Georg, *Homeric Dictionary* (London, 1984)

Athanasakis, A., *The Homeric Hymns* (Baltimore, 1976)

Clay, J. S., *The Politics of Olympus: Form and Meaning in the Major Homeric Hymns* (Princeton, 1989)

Doherty, Lillian E., *Siren Songs: Gender, Audience, and Narrators in the Odyssey* (Ann Arbor, Michigan, 1995)

Edwards, M. W., *Homer, Poet of the Iliad* (Baltimore, 1987)

Finley, M. I., *The World of Odysseus* (New York, 1954)

Griffin, Jasper, *Homer* (Oxford, 1980)

——, *Homer on Life and Death* (Oxford, 1983)

Janko, R. C. M., *Homer, Hesiod and the Hymns* (Cambridge, 1982)

de Jong, I., ed., *Homer: Critical Assessments* (New York, 1998)

Kirk, G. S., *The Songs of Homer* (Cambridge, 1962)

Latacz, J., *Homer, His Art and His World* (1985; translation, Ann Arbor, 1996)

Luce, J. V., *Celebrating Homer's Landscapes: Troy and Ithaca Revisited* (New Haven, 1998)

Morrison, James, *Homeric Misdirection: False Predictions in the* Iliad (Michigan, 1994)

Murray, Oswyn, *Early Greece* (London, 1980)

Nagy, Gregory, *Poetry as Performance: Homer and Beyond* (Cambridge, 1996)

————, *Homeric Questions* (Texas, 1996)

Page, D. L., *History and the Homeric Iliad* (1959, Berkeley)

Parry, Milman, *The Making of Homeric Verse: The Collected Papers of Milman Parry* (Oxford, 1970)

Schein, S., *The Mortal Hero* (Berkeley, 1984)

————, ed., *Reading the Odyssey* (Princeton, 1996)

Silk, Michael, *The Iliad* (Cambridge, 1987)

Stanford, W. B., *The Ulysses Theme* (second edition, Oxford, 1958)

Thalmann, W. M., *Conventions of Form and Thought in Early Greek Epic Poetry* (Baltimore, 1984)

Wace, A. J. B., and F. H. Stubbings, eds., *A Companion to Homer* (London, 1962)

Ibycus of Rhegion

Bowra, C. M., *Greek Lyric Poetry: From Alcman to Simonides* (Oxford, 1961)

Campbell, David A., *Greek Lyric Poetry III: Stesichorus, Ibycus, Simonides, and Others* (Cambridge, Massachusetts, 1991)

Mimnermus of Colophon

Allen, Archibald, *The Fragments of Mimnermus: Text and Commentary*, Palingenesia 44 (Stuttgart, 1993)

Edmonds, J. M., *Elegy and Iambus I* (London, 1931)

West, M. L., *Studies in Greek Elegy and Iambus* (New York/Berlin, 1974)

Pindar of Thebes

Bowra, C. M., *Pindar* (Oxford, 1964)

————, *The Odes of Pindar* (Harmondsworth, 1969)

Bundy, E. L., *Studia Pindarica* (Berkeley, 1962)

Carey, C., *A Commentary on Five Odes of Pindar* (New York, 1981)

Carne-Ross, D. S., *Pindar* (New Haven, 1985)

Crotty, Kevin, *Song and Action: The Victory Odes of Pindar* (Baltimore, 1982)

Fennell, C. A. M., *Pindar: The Olympian and Pythian Odes* (Cambridge, 1893)

Gildersleeve, B. L., *Pindar: The Olympian and Pythian Odes* (New York, 1890)

Kurke, Leslie, *The Traffic in Praise: Pindar and the Poetics of Social Economy* (Ithaca, 1991)

Lattimore, Richmond, *The Odes of Pindar* (Chicago, 1947)

Lefkowitz, Mary, *The Victory Ode: An Introduction* (Park Ridge, New Jersey, 1976)

Mullen, W., *Pindar and the Dance* (Princeton, 1982)

Nagy, Gregory, *Pindar's Homer: The Lyric Possession of an Epic Past* (Baltimore, 1990)

Nisetich, Frank J., *Pindar and Homer* (Baltimore, 1989)

————, translator, *Pindar's Victory Songs* (Baltimore, 1980)

Norwood, C., *Pindar* (Berkeley, 1945)

Race, William H., ed., *Pindar: Olympian Odes, Pythian Odes* (Cambridge, Massachusetts, 1997)

Race, William H., editor, *Pindar: Nemean Odes, Isthmian Odes, Fragments* (Cambridge, Massachusetts, 1997)

Steiner, Deborah, *The Crown of Song: Metaphor in Pindar* (New York, 1986)

Sappho of Eressus

Balmer, Josephine, *Classical Women Poets* (Newcastle-upon-Tyne, 1996)

Barnestone, W., *Sappho and the Greek Lyric Poets* (New York, 1988)

Burnett, Anne Pippin, *Three Archaic Poets: Archilochus, Alcaeus, Sappho* (London, 1983)

Campbell, David A., *Greek Lyric Poetry I: Sappho and Alcaeus* (Cambridge, Massachusetts, 1982)

Chandler, Robert, ed., *Sappho* (London, 1998)

Lombardo, Stanley, trans., *Sappho: Poems and Fragments* (Indianapolis, 2002)

Page, D. L., *Sappho and Alcaeus* (Oxford, 1979)

Reynolds, Margaret, ed., *The Sappho Companion* (London, 2000)

Semonides of Amorgos

Barnstone, Willis, *Sappho and the Greek Lyric Poets* (New York, 1988)

Edmonds, J. M., *Elegy and Iambus II* (London, 1931)

Gerber, Douglas E., *Greek Iambic Poetry* (Cambridge, Massachusetts, 1999)

Lloyd-Jones, Hugh, ed., trans. & comm., *Females of the Species: Semonides on Women* (Park Ridge, New Jersey, 1975)

Page, D. L., *Further Greek Epigrams* (Cambridge, 1981)

Simonides of Cos

Campbell, David A., *Greek Lyric Poetry III: Stesichorus, Ibycus, Simonides, and Others* (Cambridge, Massachusetts, 1991)

Molyneux, J. H., *Simonides: A Historical Study* (Wauconda, Illinois, 1992)

Page, D. L., *Further Greek Epigrams* (Cambridge, 1981)

Solon of Athens

Edmonds, J. M., *Elegy and Iambus I* (London, 1931)

Linforth, I. M., *Solon the Athenian* (Berkeley, 1919)

Murray, Oswyn, *Early Greece* (London, 1980)

Stesichorus of Himera

Campbell, David A., *Greek Lyric Poetry III: Stesichorus, Ibycus, Simonides, and Others* (Cambridge, Massachusetts, 1991)

Theocritus of Syracuse

Dover, Sir Kenneth J., *Theocritus* (London, 1971)

Edmonds, J. M., *The Greek Bucolic Poets* (London, 1912)

Gow, A. S. F., *Theocritus* (Cambridge, 1950)

———, *The Greek Bucolic Poets* (Cambridge, 1953)

Hubbard, Thomas K., *The Pipes of Pan: Intertextuality and Literary Filiation in the Pastoral Tradition from Theocritus to Milton* (Ann Arbor, 1998)

Hunter, Richard, *Theocritus: A Selection* (Cambridge, 1999) (includes Idylls 1, 3, 4, 6, 7, 10, 11, 13)

———, *Theocritus and the Archaeology of Greek Poetry* (Cambridge, 1996)

Hutchinson, G. O., *Hellenistic Poetry* (Oxford, 1990)

Sens, Alexander, *Theocritus: Dioscuri (Idyll 22); Introduction, Text, and Commentary, Hypomnemata 114* (Göttingen, 1997)

Wells, Robert, *Theocritus: The Idylls* (Manchester, 1988)

Theognis of Megara

Edmonds, J. M., *Elegy and Iambus I* (London, 1931)

Figueira, T. J., and Gregory Nagy, editors, *Theognis of Megara: Poetry and the Polis* (Ann Arbor, 1997)

West, M. L., *Studies in Greek Elegy and Iambus* (New York/Berlin, 1974)

Other Texts

McKeon, Richard, ed., introduction by C. D. C. Reeve, *The Basic Works of Aristotle* (Oxford, 1992)

Herodotus, *The Histories of Herodotus*, translated by George Rawlinson (London, 1942)

Pausanias, *Description of Greece*, translated by W. H. S. Jones and H. A. Ormerod (London, 1918)

Pausanias, *Guide to Greece: Volume I, Central Greece*, translated by Peter Levi (Harmondsworth, 1971)

Pausanias, *Guide to Greece: Volume II, Southern Greece*, translated by Peter Levi (Harmondsworth, 1971)

Plato, *Ion*, translated by Benjamin Jowett (London, 1871)

Plutarch, *On Sparta*, translated by Richard J. A. Talbert (Harmondsworth, 1988)

ANTHOLOGIES

Auden, W. H., *The Portable Greek Reader* (Viking, New York, 1948)

Balmer, Josephine, *Classical Women Poets* (Newcastle-upon-Tyne, 1996)

Bowra, C. M., *Oxford Book of Greek Verse* (Oxford, 1930)

Davenport, Guy, *Archilochos Sappho Alkman* (Los Angeles, 1980)

———, *Seven Greeks* (New York, 1995)

Fowler, Barbara Hughes, *Archaic Greek Poetry: An Anthology* (Madison, Wisconsin, 1992)

Gow, A. S. F., and D. L. Page, *The Greek Anthology: Hellenistic Epigrams* (Cambridge, 1965)

Grant, Michael, ed., *Greek Literature: An Anthology* (Harmondsworth, 1973)

Higham, T. F., and C. M. Bowra, eds., *The Oxford Book of Greek Verse in Translation* (Oxford, 1938)

Holden, Anthony, *Greek Pastoral Poetry* (Harmondsworth, 1974)
Jay, Peter, ed., *The Greek Anthology* (Harmondsworth, 1973)
Lattimore, Richmond, *Greek Lyrics* (Chicago, 1960)
Lobel, E., and D. L. Page, *Poetarum Lesbiorum Fragmenta* (Oxford, 1955)
Miller, Andrew M., trans., *Greek Lyric: An Anthology in Translation* (Indianapolis, 1996)
Mulroy, David, *Early Greek Lyric Poetry* (Ann Arbor, 1992)
Paton, W. R., *The Greek Anthology, Books I–VI* (London, 1916–18)
Snyder, Jane McIntosh, *The Women and the Lyre* (Carbondale, 1991)
Stoneman, Richard, *Daphne into Laurel* (London, 1982)
Trypanis, Constantine A., *The Penguin Book of Greek Verse* (Harmondsworth, 1971)
West, M. L., *Iambi et Elegi Graeci,* Volumes I and II (Oxford, 1972, 1992)
———, *Greek Lyric Poetry: The Poems and Fragments of the Greek Iambic, Elegiac, and Melic Poets* (Oxford, 1992)

A SELECTION OF SCHOLARLY, HISTORICAL
AND GENERAL CRITICAL TEXTS

The Cambridge History of Classical Literature I: Greek Literature (Cambridge, 1985)
The Oxford History of the Classical World (Oxford, 1986)
Adkins, A. W. H., *Poetic Craft in the Early Greek Elegists* (Chicago, 1985)
Boardman, John, Jasper Griffin, and Oswyn Murray, eds., *The Oxford History of Greece and the Hellenistic World* (Oxford, 1986)
Bowra, C. M., *Early Greek Elegists* (Cambridge, Massachusetts, 1938)
———, *Greek Lyric Poetry: From Alcman to Simonides* (second edition, Oxford, 1961)
———, *Landmarks in Greek Literature* (London, 1970)
Burckhardt, Jacob, *The Greeks and Greek Civilization,* translated by Sheila Stern, edited by Oswyn Murray (London, 1998)
Burn, A. R., *The Lyric Age of Greece* (London, 1960)
Calame, Claude, *Choruses of Young Women in Ancient Greece* (trans. London, 1997)
———, *The Poetics of Eros in Ancient Greece* (trans. Princeton, 1992)
Cameron, A., *The Greek Anthology: From Meleager to Planudes* (Oxford, 1993)
Campbell, D. A., *The Golden Lyre: The Themes of the Greek Lyric Poets* (London, 1983)
———, *Greek Lyric Poetry* (Bristol, 1982)
Cantarella, Eva, and Cormac Ocuilleanain, *Bisexuality in the Ancient World* (New Haven, 1994)
Carson, Anne, *Eros the Bittersweet* (Princeton, 1986)
Doody, Margaret Anne, *The True Story of the Novel* (London, 1996)
Dover, K. J., *Greek and the Greeks: Collected Papers I* (Oxford, 1987)
Easterling, P. E., and B. M. W. Knox, eds., *Cambridge History of Classical Literature I: Greek Literature* (Cambridge, 1985)
Fränkel, H., *Early Greek Poetry and Philosophy* (New York, 1975)
Gentili, B., *Poetry and Its Public in Ancient Greece from Homer to the Fifth Century* (Baltimore, 1988)

Grant, Michael, *The Rise of the Greeks* (London, 1997)

———, *The Classical Greeks* (New York, 1997)

———, *Greek and Roman Historians: Information and Misinformation* (London, 1997)

Graves, Robert, *The Greek Myths* (Manchester, 2001)

Green, Peter, *Classical Bearings: Interpreting Ancient History and Culture* (Berkeley, 1989)

Guthrie, W. K. C., *Orpheus and Greek Religion* (Princeton, 1993 edition)

Hazlitt, William, *The Classical Gazetteer: A Dictionary of Ancient Sites* (London, 1851, 1995)

Jaeger, Werner, *Paideia: The Ideal of Greek Culture, Volume I,* trans. Gilbert Highet (Oxford, 1986)

Jeffery, L. H., *Archaic Greece: The City-States c. 700–500 BC* (London, 1976)

Jenkyns, R. H. A., *Three Classical Poets* (London, 1982)

Kirkwood, G. M., *Early Greek Monody* (Ithica, 1974)

Kitto, H. D. F., *The Greeks* (London, 1951)

Lefkowitz, Mary R., *The Victory Ode: An Introduction* (Park Ridge, New Jersey, 1976)

———, *Heroines and Hysterics* (London, 1981)

———, *The Lives of the Greek Poets* (London, 1981)

Lesky, Albin, *A History of Greek Literature* (Methuen, 1966; Duckworth, 1996)

Lissarague, F., *The Aesthetics of the Greek Banquet: Images of Wine and Ritual* (trans. Princeton, 1990)

Lord, Albert B., *The Singer of Tales,* second edition, edited by Stephen Mitchell and Gregory Nagy (Cambridge, Massachusetts, 2000)

Meier, C. A., *Healing Dream and Ritual: Ancient Incubation and Modern Psychotherapy* (Einsiedeln, Switzerland, 1989)

Murray, Gilbert, *A History of Greek Literature* (New York, 1897)

Murray, Oswyn, ed., *Sympotica: A Symposium on the Symposion* (Oxford, 1990)

———, *Early Greece* (London, 1980)

Nagy, Gregory, *The Best of the Achaeans: Concepts of the Hero in Archaic Greek Poetry* (Baltimore, 1979)

Osborne, R., *Greece in the Making 1200–479 BC* (London, 1996)

Podlecki, A. J., *The Early Greek Poets and Their Times* (Vancouver, 1984)

de Romilly, Jacqueline, *A Short History of Greek Literature* (Chicago, 1985)

Rose, Peter, *Sons of God, Children of Earth: Ideology and Literary Form in Ancient Greece* (Ithaca, 1992)

Seaford, R., *Reciprocity and Ritual: Homer and Tragedy in the Developing City-State* (Oxford, 1994)

Snodgrass, A., *Archaic Greece* (London, 1980)

Snyder, Jane, *The Woman and the Lyre: Women Writers in Classical Greece and Rome* (Carbondale, 1989)

Stehle, Eva, *Performance and Gender in Ancient Greece: Nondramatic Poetry in Its Setting* (Princeton, 1997)

Taplin, Oliver, ed., *Literature in the Greek and Roman Worlds: A New Perspective* (Oxford, 2000)

Thalmann, W. M., *Conventions of Form and Thought in Early Greek Epic Poetry* (Baltimore, 1984)

Veyne, Paul, *Did the Greeks Believe Their Myths? An Essay on the Constitutive Imagination*, translated by Paula Wissing (Chicago, 1988)

West, M. L., *Studies in Greek Elegy and Iambus* (Berlin, 1974)

———, *Greek Metre* (Oxford, 1982)

———, *Ancient Greek Music* (Oxford, 1992)

Whigham, Peter, translator, *The Poems of Meleager* (London, 1975)

Zanker, Paul, *The Mask of Socrates*, translated by Alan Shapiro (Berkeley, 1995)

ON BOOKS AND LIBRARIES

Casson, Lionel, *Libraries in the Ancient World* (Yale, 2001)

Diringer, David, *The Book Before Printing: Ancient, Medieval and Oriental* (New York, 1982)

Fraser, P., *Ptolemaic Alexandria* (Oxford, 1972)

MacLeod, Roy, ed., *The Library of Alexandria* (London, 2000)

Turner, E., *Greek Papyri: An Introduction* (Oxford, 1980)

MISCELLANEOUS

Apollinaire, Guillaume, *Le Bestiaire ou Cortège d'Orphée*, illustrated with woodcuts by Raoul Dufy (Paris, 1911)

Arnold, Matthew, "On Translating Homer," *Selected Criticism*, edited by Christopher Ricks (New York, 1972)

Branham, R. Bracht, ed., *Bakhtin and the Classics* (Evanston, Illinois, 2002)

Bridges, Robert, ed., *The Spirit of Man* (London, 1916)

Butler, Samuel, *Notebooks* (London, 1902)

Calasso, Roberto, *Literature and the Gods*, translated by Tim Parks (London, 2001)

Calvino, Italo, *Why Read the Classics?* (London, 1999)

Carson, Anne, *Autobiography of Red* (London, 1999)

Curtius, E. R., *Essays on European Literature,* translation (Princeton, 1973)

Davie, Donald, ed., *The Pslams in English* (Harmondsworth, 1996)

Ford, Ford Madox, *The March of Literature* (London, 1947)

Frazer, J. G., *Pausanias and Other Greek Sketches* (London, 1900)

Highet, Gilbert, *Poets in a Landscape* (London, 1999)

Johnson, Samuel, *Lives of the English Poets* (London, 1975)

Lissarrague, François, *Greek Vases: The Athenians and Their Images* (Riverside, 1999, 2001)

Mitchell, Carroll, *Greek Women* (Philadelphia, 1908)

Nietzsche, Friedrich, "Homer's Contest" (1872), *The Portable Nietzsche* (Harmondsworth, 1976)

Radice, Betty, *The Translator's Art* (Harmondsworth, 1987)

Seferis, George, *Collected Poems* (London, 1982)

Stoneman, Richard, ed., *A Literary Companion to Travel in Greece* (Malibu, 1994)

Tomlinson, Charles, *The Oxford Book of Verse in English Translation* (Oxford, 1980)

Virgil, *The Georgics*, translated by Robert Wells (Manchester, 1982)

Index

Acknowledgments

The editor and publisher gratefully acknowledge permission to reprint the following poems and extracts in this book:

David Mulroy, *Early Greek Lyric Poetry* (University of Michigan Press, 1992), by permission of the publisher; Apollonios Rhodios, *The Argonautika: The Story of Jason and the Quest for the Golden Fleece*, edited and translated by Peter Green (University of California Press, 1997), by permission of the publisher; Virgil, *The Georgics,* edited and translated by Robert Wells (Carcanet Press Ltd, 1982), by permission of the publisher; Elaine Feinstein, editor, *After Pushkin* (Carcanet Press Ltd., 1999), by permission of the publisher; Guy Davenport, *Thasos and Ohio* (Carcanet Press Ltd., 1985), by permission of the publisher; William Carlos Williams, *Complete Poems I* and *II* (Carcanet Press Ltd., 1987, 1988), by permission of the publisher; Richmond Lattimore, *Greek Lyrics*, second edition (University of Chicago Press, 1949, 1955 and 1960), by permission of the publisher; Pindar, *The Odes,* translated by Richmond Lattimore (University of Chicago Press, 1947), by permission of the publisher; Wallace Stevens, "Two Illustrations That the World Is What You Make of It" II, from *Collected Poems* (Faber & Faber, 1955), by permission of the publisher; Ezra Pound, "Lustra" and "Homage to Sextus Propertius," *Collected Shorter Poems* (Faber & Faber, 1968), by permission of the publisher; David Campbell, editor and translator, *Greek Lyric I: Sappho and Alcaeus,* testimonia 22 (Harvard University Press, 1982), by permission of the publisher; Hesiod, *Works and Days* and *Theogony*, translated by Stanley Lombardo, introduction by Robert Lamerton (Hackett Publishing Company, 1993), by permission of the publisher; Barbara Hughes Fowler, *Archaic Greek Poetry* (University of Wisconsin Press, 1992), by permission of the publisher; Guy Davenport, *Seven Greeks* (New Directions, 1976, 1978, 1979, 1981, 1991, 1995), by permission of the publisher; Martin Litchfield West, *Greek Lyric Poetry: The Poems and Fragments of the Greek Iambic, Elegiac, and Melic Poets* (Oxford University Press, 1999), by permission of the publisher; Pausanias, *Guide to Greece,* Volume 1: *Central Greece*, translated by Peter Levi (Penguin Classics, 1971), by permission of the Penguin Group (UK); Peter Jay, *The Greek Anthology and Other Ancient Greek Epigrams: A Selection of Modern Verse Translations* (Allen Lane, 1973, Penguin Classics, 1981), by permission of the Penguin Group (UK); Friedrich Nietzsche, *The Portable Nietzsche,* edited and translated by Walter Kaufmann (Viking Press, 1954, Viking Penguin Inc., 1982), by permission of the Penguin Group (USA) Inc.

Every effort has been made to contact holders of material quoted and reproduced in this book, but any omissions will be restituted at the earliest opportunity.

ALSO BY MICHAEL SCHMIDT

*"Exceedingly pleasurable. . . . If you care about poetry,
you must read this book."* —The Boston Book Review

LIVES OF THE POETS

In this stunning volume of epic breadth, Michael Schmidt
connects the lives and works of over three hundred English-
language poets of the last seven hundred years from Scotland
to Australia to the Caribbean. *Lives of the Poets* traverses
the landscapes of biography, form, cultural pressures, and
important historical moments to reveal how each poet has
transformed "a common language of poetry" into the rustic
rhythms and elegiac ballads, love sonnets, and experimental postmodern verse that make up our lyrical canon. A
prominent British publisher and reviewer of verse, Schmidt
travels the inroads of inspiration and experience to provide
the seasoned reader and newcomer alike with a context in
which to explore the poems themselves. A comprehensive
guided tour that is lively and always accessible, *Lives of the
Poets* illuminates our most transcendent literary tradition.

Biography/Poetry/0-375-70604-6